the bars are ours

LUCAS HILDERBRAND

the bars

are   ours

Histories and Cultures of
Gay Bars in America, 1960 and After

DUKE UNIVERSITY PRESS
Durham and London
2023

© 2023 DUKE UNIVERSITY PRESS
All rights reserved
Printed in the United States of America on acid-free paper ∞
Project Editor: Lisa Lawley
Designed by A. Mattson Gallagher
Typeset in Warnock Pro, Degular, and Comma Base
by Westchester Publishing Services

Library of Congress Cataloging-in-Publication Data
Names: Hilderbrand, Lucas, [date] author.
Title: The bars are ours : histories and cultures of gay bars in America, 1960 and after / Lucas Hilderbrand.
Other titles: Histories and cultures of gay bars in America, 1960 and after
Description: Durham : Duke University Press, 2023. | Includes bibliographical references and index.
Identifiers: LCCN 2022056737 (print)
LCCN 2022056738 (ebook)
ISBN 9781478024958 (paperback)
ISBN 9781478020301 (hardcover)
ISBN 9781478027287 (ebook)
Subjects: LCSH: Gay bars—United States—History. | Nineteen sixties. | United States—History—1961–1969. | BISAC: SOCIAL SCIENCE / LGBTQ Studies / Gay Studies
Classification: LCC HQ76.965.B395 H553 2023 (print) | LCC HQ76.965.B395 (ebook) | DDC 647.95086/640973—dc23/eng/20230518
LC record available at https://lccn.loc.gov/2022056737
LC ebook record available at https://lccn.loc.gov/2022056738

Cover art: Snowflake (Glenn Zehrbaugh, 1928–1992), *Cocktail Hour* (detail), 1982. Painting of the Ambush in San Francisco, permanently on view at the Omaha Mining Company bar, Omaha, Nebraska. Photo by Kameron Bayne, by permission of Robert Roberts and Joseph Allen/Omaha Mining Company.

A toast

to the homophiles

to the liberationists

to the trans sisters who fought harder for these spaces than anyone else

to the butches, femmes, they, them, and hims

to the fairies, the Marys, and *maricas*

to the gal pals that escorted gay boys to the clubs

to the drag queens who lead our culture

to the leatherfolk who invented theirs

to the DJs who made music sound better than we knew it could

to everyone who has given all of themselves on the dance floor

to those who showed up and turned it out

to the bartenders with heavy pours

to the gregarious drunks

to the wallflowers

to the elders who are still going out

to those who have found love, even if only for a night

to those who've gone home alone

to the former drinking buddies

to the friends we reunite with

to those we've lost

This is for all of us and the histories we've lived

The bars are ours

[handwritten margin notes: "▓▓▓ the dear, dear friend who gave me this book, is one of them. ♥" and "(stuff's gotten scarier. I don't wanna out him. or me. hopefully it changed for the better, soon.)"]

"Inspire me, till I lisp an' wink"

— Robert Burns, "Scotch Drink"

"The people are thirsty."

— Kansas City Mayor Thomas J. Pendergast, flouting Prohibition

"If I can't dance,
 I don't want your revolution."

— Emma Goldman (paraphrased)

"Beauty's where you find it"

— Madonna, "Vogue"

"We're not equal.
 But love is here."

— Restroom mural, SinFin Cantina, Guadalajara, Mexico

Contents

Preface
Drunk History, or I Just Wanna Hear a Good Beat
xiii

Acknowledgments
I Feel Love/Can't Get You Out of My Head
xxi

Introduction
We Were Never Being Boring
1

PART I. CULTURES

1. Nights in Black Leather
Inventing a Bar Culture in Chicago
37

Interlude 1
Triangle Lounge in Denver
62

2. Show Me Love
Female Impersonation and Drag in Kansas City
68

Interlude 2
Safe Spaces in Detroit
94

PART II. POLITICS

3. Somewhere There's a Place for Us
Urban Renewal, Gentrification, and Class Conflicts in Boston
101

Interlude 3
Seattle Counseling Service
124

4. Midtown Goddam
Discrimination, Coalition, and Community in Atlanta
127

Interlude 4
Gay Switchboard in Philadelphia
151

PART III. INSTITUTIONS

5. Welcome to the Pleasuredome
Legends of Sex and Dancing in New York
157

Interlude 5
The Saloon in Minneapolis
192

6. Proud Mary's
An Institution in Houston
193

Interlude 6
The Main Club in Superior, WI
220

PART IV. REINVENTIONS

7. Further Tales of the City
Queer Parties in Post-disco
San Francisco
227

Interlude 7
The Casa Nova in Somerset County, PA
255

8. Donde Todo es Diferente
Queer Latinx Nightlife in
Los Angeles
RESEARCHED AND WRITTEN WITH
DAN BUSTILLO
260

Interlude 8
Mable Peabody's Beauty Parlor and Chainsaw Repair in Denton, TX
289

Epilogue: After Hours
Pulse in Orlando
294

Appendix 1
Selected Bars and Clubs
303

Appendix 2
LGBTQ+ Periodical Sources
313

Notes
317
Bibliography
395
Index
425

Preface

Drunk History, or I Just Wanna Hear a Good Beat

This preface addresses my academic readers. If you don't have a stake in scholarly questions or methods, feel free to skip ahead to the introduction. But before you do, you'll likely want to take a gander at figure P.1 on page xvi.

Despite the omnipresence of gay bars and nightclubs, until recently we have had little published work that offers a panoramic historical analysis of them. Around 2008, I realized that no academic book had synthesized the cultures and politics of gay bars during the era when they have been most visible, so I set out to write one before they disappeared. A more personal impetus was that I felt starved for nightlife, which previously had been ingrained in my life rhythms, after moving into faculty housing for a new job; research became my peculiar way to manifest a connection to the broader queer world. This book presents fifteen years of researching, writing, and rethinking. My original goal was to complete this book before the fiftieth anniversary of the Stonewall riots in 2019, but these things—as well as school commitments, doom-scrolling, and life itself—take time. In this interval, many gay bars have closed and a few new ones have opened. As it turns out, this book is not an elegy. The gay bar as an institution has not died, nor have its cultures ended.

 When I began working on this project and talking to other people, I quickly recognized that everyone had a different personal take on bar history, on what about it matters, and on which bars define those pasts. Bar histories are inevitably subjective: what was reported, what was collected, what caught one's attention, where one went, who one talked to, if one had fun, and if one got lucky. One's understanding of the past depends on what one's looking for and what structures one's perspective, including taste, politics, generation, and location. Like a disco ball, which is "not made of a single mirror, but numerous tiny mirrors [that] each reflects and refracts light at different angles," historical interpretation and personal experience evoke the "generative flashes of nows in which pasts are present."[1] My title gestures toward plural histories and cultures because no singular experience of the past exists.

Scholars have produced historical work that recovers local pasts, social science studies that chart contemporary shifts, and performance theories that open up queer affects, liveness, mediation, and ephemera.[2] Significantly, much of the essential scholarship thinking with queer communities of color takes up the capacious framework of *queer nightlife* rather than focusing on bars per se, at least in part because bars have histories of exclusion, as I detail in chapter 3.[3] I have worked to negotiate between and beyond these methods. Three intersecting books were published as I was completing this project: Jeremy Atherton Lin's *Gay Bar*, a memoir-driven set of reflections aimed at a popular audience; *Queer Nightlife*, a performance studies anthology on nightlife practices, capaciously conceived; and Greggor Mattson's *Who Needs Gay Bars?*, an ambitious nationwide sociological study of gay bars and their diversity in the present, based upon interviews with bar owners. Two more books have been in the pipeline concurrently with mine: Luis Manuel Garcia-Mispireta's *Together, Somehow*, which examines intimate collectivities on the queer dance floor, and Amin Ghaziani's forthcoming *Long Live Queer Nightlife*, which responds to a proliferation of queer happenings in the wake of gay bars' widespread closures. Each makes a significant contribution, and each has its own orientation that differs from my archival account of gay bar modes and meanings. This wave of scholarship suggests a belated critical mass of attention to gay bars and clubs. As I have argued previously, technologies capture our attention most intensely at moments of ballyhooed newness and apparent obsolescence; the same logic extends to bars and nightlife.[4]

My home discipline of cinema and media studies prepared me to think through the significance of the popular, the pervasive, even the pornographic; I'm drawn to texts, technologies, and infrastructures that achieve cultural saturation but that have been so obvious as to become overlooked. As a media scholar, I have in some senses invented my methods for this project, but I effectively approach gay bars as a *medium*: a form that gives structure to social actions and worldviews, that poses expressive conventions, and that constrains what's possible given its inherent properties. Analyzing bars as a medium allows us to grapple with their affordances, limitations, and contradictions for cultivating queer sensibilities and for articulating community politics. Bars function as *queer forms*, as Ramzi Fawaz theorizes the concept: "*enabling structures*" that give shape to queer identities, experiences, and politics. Such forms "establish the conditions for something new to appear in the world, including previously unfathomable expressions and interpretations of gender and sexual being."[5] Bars constitute physical venues and cultural expressions—forms in both senses of the word.

Thinking about and with gay bars demands negotiating between bars' material conditions (such as their status as businesses, their built environments, and the various transactions that happen between men inside them) and their ideological functions (expressed in advertisements, the gay press, and activism) as representations of and even *as* the LGBTQ+ community. I understand my access to bygone gay bars as mediated by representations and texts—from gay press reporting, ads, and party flyers to songs that I streamed to simulate how the past might have sounded and felt. I am present throughout this book to situate my interpretations and historiographic vantage point.

In many cases, advertisements are what remain of bars that have closed and buildings that have been razed. Such ads have always been *texts* that construct enchanting images of bars for their prospective clienteles rather than indexically record their actuality. Early on in this research, I became fascinated by an ad featuring a perverse sketch of a lion mounting a macho clone from behind (see figure P.1). This ad, for the Lion Pub in San Francisco, was part of a series that traded in problematic safari and conquest imagery; the campaign ran in the *Advocate* and the *Bay Area Reporter* over the course of a year and was so popular that the bar produced posters and T-shirts from it. As in most bar ads, the space and the people who go there remain out of sight. This ad expressed a *sensibility* rather than documented a place; the slogan "midnight thinking" suggests a logic—even a form of knowledge—unique to the gay bar milieu. Like the ad's scene of bestiality, its come-on, "animals love maneaters," was confounding, titillating, and evocative; the artist lovingly sketched the image so that the lion's curled tongue appears both affectionate and primal. The viewers' identification likely shifted between wanting to be the lion and

FIGURE P.1 "Animals Love Maneaters" was the most popular in a series of mid-1970s safari- and conquest-themed fantasy advertisements for the Lion Pub in San Francisco. This image appeared in the local and national gay press and was available on posters and T-shirts (see the order form at the bottom of the image). *Bay Area Reporter*, November 26, 1975. Courtesy of ONE Archives at the USC Libraries.

desiring to be the man. This ad constructed a dreamworld that radically transgressed sexual taboos and fostered versatile subject positions. More people would have seen this ad than ever crossed the bar's threshold, so the bar remained in many readers' imaginations a place where men hunt for and submit to whatever pleasures may come. I have been attracted by the ad's audacity and sense of fabulation; it queerly refused plausibility or convention in favor of envisioning wild possibilities.[6]

    I have sought to be a rigorous queen in my research without losing sight that people go to bars to have *fun*. Following the philosophy usually attributed to Mae West and Liberace, I believe that too much of a good thing can be wonderful. One might claim that indulgence has been my primary method for conveying bars' vivacity. For more than a decade, I spent days working through materials in community archives and nights exploring unfamiliar cities to try to map the past on to the present landscape. I have relied on the kindness of strangers and near-strangers as gateways to their cities: archivists who welcomed me, colleagues I cold-contacted, people I met on apps, and men with whom I danced to Rihanna at Twist in Miami Beach and to Britney Spears at the Max in Omaha.[7] Most of the bars I write about closed long before I began my research, so I can only infer what they were like by listening to others' accounts. Throughout this book, I draw on anecdotes as evidence of gay bars' meanings. Recounted bar stories tend to be 80 proof, spiked with innuendo and embellishment, but it may be these excesses that precisely reveal the thirsts that bars sought to satiate.[8]

My primary sources for this project come from the archives. Queer archives and collections are usually local, subjective, partial, and idiosyncratic. What makes these archives *queer* is not only the sexuality of their caretakers but also what they *value* as significant expressions of our cultural heritage and what erotic, campy, or glittering forms they may take.[9] Only in queer collections was I likely to encounter newspaper clippings pasted to letterhead for the movie *Beaches* or rhinestoned disco shoes lovingly preserved in tissue paper.[10] When I came across an ad for the Copa Disco in Fort Lauderdale announcing appearances by both Madonna and Divine during the same weekend in 1983, I squeed as I imagined having been there.[11] Other times, when I flipped through photo albums, I found myself looking at pictures of unidentified men from another time in bars that had closed long ago. Such photos showed someone else's memories, like intimacy without familiarity or context; they communicated what I couldn't know for sure yet stimulated something like recognition for me.

Outcomes, rather than intentions, remain speculative in the queer archive.[12] I have encountered numerous fragmentary documents of bar activism in process: flyers soliciting participants for protests, anticipatory reporting in the gay press, proposals for organizations and for policy reform, and handwritten notes and edits on drafts. What I have found far less often are follow-up accounts or any kind of closure that confirmed what actually happened, who showed up, or what changed. Likewise, numerous collections contain matchbooks and trick cards from bars, which include blank lines for information such as name, phone number, type, fetish, or sexual position. Hula's in Waikiki produced matchbooks with a line for designating "island." Others, such as a matchbook from Tiffany's in Detroit, offer space to collect multiple numbers, thereby promoting a culture of promiscuity.[13] These objects point to the *potential* for social and sexual contacts in bars, but they do not document whether the men ever actually called, how the sex was, or whose heart was broken. As Lin suggests, "Gay history is a palimpsest of *what ifs*," and "gay bars are about potentiality, not resolution."[14]

Queer theory has for decades embraced ephemera over permanence and exploded the concept of the archive to suggest that any text, object, or even affect might operate as an "archive." Archives, including queer archives, have been critiqued for excluding marginalized perspectives as unworthy of documenting and for reinforcing definitions of "evidence" that serve to delegitimate queer, women's, trans, and BIPOC scholarship and lives.[15] Still, I insist that both actually existing queer archives and the gay press provide essential access to how queer life and culture were represented *by* LGBTQ+ people *for* LGBTQ+ people. The gay press (now typically housed in queer archives) remains a largely untapped resource for historians and one of the few sites where the LGBTQ+ past was narrated in its present. In the archives I have found, again and again, that so many of our current critiques, frictions, and activisms among and between queer people were previously incisively debated decades ago; we have much to learn from this well-documented record that has become neglected. We must engage and learn from these collections, even as we remain cognizant of the ideologies that shape and buttress them.

As a study of US gay bars, this book inevitably examines many predominantly white male venues that effectively defined or reflected public gay cultures and histories. In my research, I have found that gay bars by and large really were *that white* and *that male*. To suggest otherwise would be misrepresentative and ahistorical; this book's emphasis on predominantly white male venues derives from my attempt to accurately reflect my research findings. The overwhelming whiteness of this book's exemplary bars—and its images that reflect what bars looked like and who they sought to attract—demonstrate the necessity for the protests and alternative venues in chapters 4 and 8. I attempt, however imperfectly, to study these venues in their full complexity: to recognize their potentials for personal and social transformation while also holding them accountable for their past and present wrongs. Rather than reductively position bars as good or bad, however, I look to them to understand how they made gay subcultures intelligible and inspired political debate.

This book takes an admittedly urban framework, both because what we think of as gay bars have primarily existed in cities and because the gay press and community-based archives that have documented gay bars are likewise usually products of urban densities. Challenging the logics of the urban-rural dichotomy, my generation of scholars argues for the significance of suburban and small-city "micropolitan" formations.[16] Today, outpost gay bars, which serve as the only gay bar in their town or region, have become one of the most pervasive kinds of gay bars; there are more towns with one gay bar than cities with multiples.[17] The documentary *Small Town Gay Bar* demonstrates that such places can also be wilder than what one finds in cities.[18] There are also remote regions of the country where gay public spaces simply do not exist, so patrons must drive hours to access a bar—if they can find one at all.[19] I grew up on the northern plains in a small town without a gay bar; as an adult I have chosen to live in New York City, Minneapolis, and Los Angeles (and have moved back and forth between them). I recognize that queers exist beyond cities, but my own story nonetheless resembles those of many others who looked to urban beacons to imagine and make new lives.

This is but one necessarily partial chronicle of the more complex histories and cultures of gay bars in the United States after 1960. I allowed the serendipity and the *punctum* of the archive to reveal which stories I could tell and in which cities they would be set.[20] Half the chapters developed out of local archival collections (in the cases of Chicago, Kansas City, Atlanta, and Houston) and others out of flurries of articles in the local gay press that I paged through at the ONE National Gay & Lesbian Archives in Los Angeles (in the cases of Boston, New York, and San Francisco). The Los Angeles chapter came out of living there and collaboration, which afforded a hybrid methodology and voice. Some of the bars that I write about wouldn't have been my own choice of scene, but they nonetheless exemplified their cultures, their cities, and their times.

I conducted research in more cities than I could include, and this book does not pretend to be encyclopedic. I do not discuss resort areas such as Provincetown and Palm Springs, nor do I emphasize the most iconic gay ghettos, including the Castro, the West Village, or West Hollywood. Likewise, various genres of bars do not get their own chapters, including lesbian, country-western, piano, hotel, hustler, hipster, video, sports, stripper, wrinkle room, and chicken bars.[21] (However, I do note that my boyfriend, Ernesto, fondly recalls singing "Part of Your World" atop the piano as a pretty young thing at the Townhouse of New York piano bar, which attracted older midtown gentlemen; he was proud that he rarely had to buy his own drinks there.)[22] Throughout, I prioritize attention to the spaces that gay men have created and the community debates that

PREFACE xix

they raised rather than to external forces that have constrained them. This means that I reference liquor laws, zoning, police payoffs and raids, and organized-crime ownership of bars as context rather than centering these issues. Not everything I learned could be included; for instance, in San Antonio I was told that after World War II, military police raids and inclusion on "off-limits" lists simultaneously prohibited and publicized gay bars near military bases for servicepeople in an era before they could be openly gay.[23] Gay bar history also includes an alarming prevalence of fires from electrical malfunctions and arson—by homophobes, aggrieved patrons, competing entrepreneurs, and bar owners themselves. In New Orleans I conducted research on the June 1973 Up Stairs Lounge fire, which killed thirty-two patrons, but this tragedy has been thoroughly documented elsewhere.[24] Finally, although I have experienced the invasion of gay male bars by straight bachelorette parties, I do not dwell on this or other tensions caused by the dilution of queer spaces in recent decades.[25]

My own bar years span the mid-1990s to the present. My formative exploration of gay bars happened in the company of (then) female-identified queer friends. These outings just predated the transformative effects of both the internet and highly active antiretroviral treatments for HIV/AIDS. What I've found in the archives has often felt familiar, insofar as virtually everything I know of gay bars has had precedents. It appears that gay bars of the recent past and present are ingrained cultural institutions that adapt to current tastes and trends rather than creating wholly new paradigms. For instance, now-ubiquitous karaoke nights—which arguably replaced the old-school piano bars—incorporate the attraction into preexisting spaces.[26] Nonetheless, gay bars can still feel essential and ingenious (see the Denton interlude). I've recognized that my students perennially experience going out with a euphoric sense of discovery. I have tried not to kill their joy but have tried to train them to think critically about these spaces and to recognize that they have histories. I hope I have done the same here for you, my readers.

Acknowledgments
I Feel Love/Can't Get You Out of My Head

Forever's gonna start tonight: this book was possible only because of the labors and commitment of numerous archivists, so I begin by expressing my gratitude to them: Loni Shibuyama, Bud Thomas, Michael Oliveira, Kyle Morgan, Pat Allen, Rick Mechtly, and Joseph Hawkins at ONE National Gay & Lesbian Archives at USC Libraries in Los Angeles. Rick Storer and Mel Leverich at the Leather Archives & Museum and Will Brandt at the Gerber/Hart Library and Archives in Chicago. Laura Ruttum Senturia at History Colorado Center and Brian Trembath, Abby Hoverstock, and Alex Hernandez at the Denver Public Library. Stuart Hinds at the Gay and Lesbian Archives of Mid-America at the University of Missouri–Kansas City Libraries. Libby Bouvier and Joan Ilacqua at the History Project in Boston. James Stack at the University of Washington Libraries Special Collections in Seattle (and to Charna Klein for permission to access her collection there). Felicia Render at the Atlanta History Center, Morna Gerrard at Georgia State University Library special collections, Kelly Cornwell at Fulton County Library System, and Derek T. Mosely at Auburn Avenue Research Library in Atlanta. John Anderies and Bob Skiba at the John J. Wilcox Archives of the William Way LGBT Community Center in Philadelphia. Thomas Lannon at the New York Public Library Manuscripts and Archives Division, Barrye Brown at the Schomburg Center for Research in Black Culture, and the staff at the LGBT Community Center National History Archive in New York City. Arvid Nelson at the Jean-Nickolaus Tretter Collection in GLBT Studies at the University of

Minnesota Libraries in Minneapolis and Larry Watson at the Quatrefoil Library in St. Paul. JD Doyle of the JD Doyle Archives, Larry Criscone of the Charles Botts Collection of LGBT History, and Judy Reeves, Ty Burns, and Craig Farrell of the Gulf Coast Archive and Museum in Houston. Rebekah Kim and Isaac Fellman at the GLBT Historical Society and Tim Wilson at the San Francisco Public Library. Jennifer Needham at the University of Pittsburgh Libraries Special Collections and Tim Haggerty and Harrison Apple of the Pittsburgh Queer History Project. Courtney Jacobs and Morgan Gieringer at the University of North Texas Libraries Special Collections in Denton. Julie Herrada at the University of Michigan Libraries in Ann Arbor. Shawn C. Wilson at the Kinsey Institute for Sex Research at Indiana University in Bloomington. Vicki Catozza and Margaret Roulett at the Western Reserve Historical Society in Cleveland. William LeFevre at the Reuther Library Special Collections at Wayne State University in Detroit. The staff of the Stonewall National Museum and Archives in Fort Lauderdale. Brenda Marston at the Human Sexuality Archives at Cornell University in Ithaca. Su Kim at the UNLV Libraries Special Collections in Las Vegas. Rebecca Smith and Jennifer Williams at the Historic New Orleans Collection, Sean Benjamin at the Louisiana Research Collection, and Christopher Harter at the Amistad Research Center in New Orleans. Geoff Wexler at the Oregon Historical Society in Portland. Nikki Thomas at the University of Texas–San Antonio Special Collections and Gene Elder at the Happy Foundation in San Antonio. Daniela Hudson at the Lambda Archives in San Diego. Alan Miller at the Canadian Lesbian and Gay Archives in Toronto. Harrison Apple and Jamie Lee at the Arizona Queer Archives in Tucson. Anne McDonough at the Historical Society of Washington, DC, and Bonnie Morris, Vincent Slatt, and Jose Gutierrez of the Rainbow History Project in Washington, DC. In addition, Victor Ultra Omni, Kat Brewster, Kristen Galvin, and Jess Ziegenfuss contributed archival research assistance.

Closer to fine: My understandings of local gay bar histories have been deeply enriched by conversations with people who generously shared their insights and memories of their communities, including Dave Hayward, Young Hughley, Hillery Rink, Charles Stephens, Freddie Styles, Phillip Boone, and Reverend Duncan Teague in Atlanta. Michael Bronski in Boston. David Boyer in Chicago. Chris Bingston, Donnie Wayne Brown, Michael Doughman, Patti Fink, Rodd Gray, Larone Landis, Chuck Marcelo, and David Taffett in Dallas. Karen Wisely in Denton. David Duffield and

Arthur Gilkison in Denver. Larry Bagneris, John Broadhurst, Ty Burns, Mark DeLange, JD Doyle, Craig Farrell, Ray Hill, Judy Reeves, and Brian Reidel in Houston. Jessica Dressler, Kirk Nelson, and Bruce Winter in Kansas City. Enrique Castrejon, Dino Dinco, Ramón García, Sergio Hernandez, Agustín Garcia Meza, and Carlos Samaniego in Los Angeles. Skylar Fein, Otis Fennell, and Frank Perez in New Orleans. Bill Bahlman and Brian Howard in New York City. Kyle Mason Hollingsworth and Brian M. Wood in Orlando. David Kohl, Steve Suss, and Robin Will in Portland. M. Apparition, Robert Barrett, Drew Daniel, Page Hodel, Tom Jennings, and S. Topiary Landberg in San Francisco. And especially Bob Jansen in Superior.

I'll take you there: Numerous people hosted me, helped me navigate their cities, or connected me with local contacts: Kadji Amin, Harrison Apple, Larry Biddle, James Carviou, Dean Daderko, Rajiv Desai, Alexander Doty, Jane Feuer, Johnny Flex, Michael David Franklin, Elena Gorfinkel, Raquel Gutierrez, Joseph Hallman, Christina Hanhardt, Scott Herring, Jeff Hnilincka, Kwame Holmes, Abbas Hyderi, David Johnson, Aaron Lacayo, Greggor Mattson, Allison McCracken, Rostom Mesli, Frederic Moffet, KJ Mohr, Jonathan Molina-Garcia, Ricardo Montez, Candace Moore, Roy Pérez, Angelo Restivo, Scott Richmond, Charles Rosenberg, Nick Salvato, Keegan Shepard, Felix Solano, Lauren Steimer, Chris Vargas, Shane Vogel, Thomas Waugh, Craig Willse, Kelly Wolf, Greg Youmans, and Agustin Zarzosa. I also wish to thank the various people in bars, on apps, or otherwise who contributed to this project. It's been a long journey, and I apologize to anyone I've failed to mention. My parents took in my dog, Bowie, during my more extended research gallivants; Bowie has not been particularly helpful in this endeavor, but I love him anyway. I am especially grateful to Dean Otto in Minneapolis and to Oliver Link in New York, who generously hosted me in their homes, where I lived for months while doing research.

La vie en rose: In addition to the above, I must also thank the following people for their assistance with or permissions for book images: Joseph Allen at the Omaha Mining Company, Bill Barbanes, Scott Swoveland, Nerve Macaspac, Nan Goldin, Catherine Belloy at the Marian Goodman Gallery, Tina Paul, Melissa Hawkins, Martin Sorrondeguy, Gayle Rubin, David Evans Frantz, Diana Bachman at the Bentley Historical Library at the University of Michigan, Gabrielle M. Dudley and Kathy Shoemaker at the Rose Library at Emory University, Stephen Pevner and Robert

Zash at the Saint Foundation, Michael Robinson at the Contemporary Art Museum Houston, Lisa Vecoli and Aiden Bettine at the Tretter Collection, and Paulina Lara.

When I think of you: This project was conceivable only because of José Esteban Muñoz's life and work. Darius Bost, Marie Cartier, James M. Estrella, Finley Freibert, Luis Manuel Garcia-Mispireta, Marshall Green, Theo Greene, Greggor Mattson, Brian Reidel, and Karen Wisely each graciously shared their research. Dan Bustillo was a true collaborator for the Los Angeles chapter.

Put the thing down, flip it, and reverse it: I have workshopped each part of this book by sending portions of the manuscript to friends and colleagues for their feedback. Thanks to all of you, this is a much better book: Michael Bronski, Dan Bustillo, Andy Campbell, JD Doyle, Ramzi Fawaz, Ramón García, Jack Gieseking, Elena Gorfinkel, Joshua Javier Guzman, Kristen Hatch, Harris Kornstein, Nerve Macaspac, Greggor Mattson, Rostom Mesli, Frederic Moffet, Candace Moore, Allison Perlman, Ricky Rodriguez, Marc Seigel, Whit Strub, Martabel Wasserman, and Joe Wlodarz. In addition, I thank my two anonymous reviewers. At Duke University Press, I thank my editor Ken Wissoker for his years of enthusiasm for this project and Ryan Kendall, Lisa Lawley, Donald Pharr, A. Mattson Gallagher, Chad Royal, and Laura Sell for their expertise and support through the editing, design, production, and marketing processes.

You better work: I have been supported by colleagues at UC Irvine, including Kristen Hatch, Allison Perlman, Fatimah Tobing Rony, Bliss Lim, and Keiji Kunigami; department chairs Victoria E. Johnson, Peter Krapp, Catherine Liu, and Fatimah Toing Rony; heroic department staff members Elizabeth Pace, Caroline McGuire, Eva Yonas, and especially Amy Fujitani; and School of Humanities leadership, including Dean Tyrus Miller, Associate Deans Julia Lupton and Judy Tzu-Chun Wu, and Humanities Center executive director Amanda Swain. Publication of this book was supported in part by two grants from the UC Irvine Humanities Center as well as travel funding from the School of Humanities and the Council on Research, Computing, and Libraries.

I've got friends in low places: I want to bring these acknowledgments full circle by raising an Absolut soda with lime to my dancing and drinking buddies throughout the years, including Mao, Chantilly, Brian, Francis, Christina, Karl, Marci, Walter, Brad, Dean, Oliver, Guto, Agustin, Elena, Carla, Joe, Bhaskar, Bishnu, Marc, Juan, Hoang, Candace, Tom, Greg, Jose, Liza, KJ, Jeff, Jen, Kristen, Julia, Angela, David, Karen, Ali, David, Ryan, Michael,

Craig, Christina, Dean, Rostom, Brian, Chris, Chris, Hentyle, Ivan, Liz, Nerve, Mazdak, Frederic, Enrique, Josh, Albert, Lori, and Bobby, among many others. We'll always have the Tunnel, First Avenue, the Saloon, Club Metro, Touchez, Wonderbar, the Cock, Fat Cock, Marie's Crisis, Luxx, the Metropolitan, the 19 Bar, Pi, Julius', Big Chicks, Side Track, the Second Story, the Granville Anvil, the Jackhammer, the Drinkery, This Is It, the Woodward, the Brit, Ripples, MJ's, the Eagle, the Faultline, Casita del Campo, Tee Gee, Taix, Gold Coast, Charlie's (Denver and Phoenix), Pony, Pilsner Inn, Twin Peaks, and venues that haven't opened yet. (To be clear, I love my sober friends, too.) Sara Meilke was my first fag hag—or *fag mag*, as she prefers. Karl Surkan opened up the worlds of lesbian culture and trans life to me; I didn't recognize how much he influenced my way of being queer until he died unexpectedly while I was finishing copy edits for this book.

 I want to take you far from the cynics in this town and kiss you on the mouth: Ernesto Lopez came into my life in early 2020, by which time I was a spinster (not a daddy). We immediately found love, survived loss, and became partners. A Virgo to my Libra, he saw this book through completion and the multiple times I said that I had finished it. Let's get a drink at Akbar after this.

Introduction

We Were Never Being Boring

Gay bars are known for their heavy pours and their life-changing possibilities. For generations of LGBTQ+ people, going to the gay bar has served as a rite of passage: we came out by going out. Whether patrons imbibed rotgut or top-shelf vodka, gay bars have been where queer people have gone to affirm their identities and to seek camaraderie among sympathetic strangers.[1] Our clubs provide the stages for queer world making, and they play better music, too.[2] These have been the preconditions for livable gay lives, communities, and political consciousness. In this book, I contend that bars have functioned as *the medium* for the historical emergence of gay public life in the United States.

Gay bars have operated as the most visible institution of LGBTQ+ public life for the better part of a century, from before gay liberation until after gay bars' reported obsolescence. Gay bars have been essential to many queer people because only here could patrons let down their proverbial hair and be *gay*. In the chapters that follow, I focus on bars that cater to gay men, although their clienteles are often fluid.[3] Bars were where gay male cultures could be imagined and expressed, and where gay male identities became recognizable in ways that were generative, normative, emulatable, constraining, and exclusionary.[4] As I demonstrate, these venues have fostered distinct subcultures and new sexual practices; they have provoked intracommunity critiques and activist organizing; they have created temples of dancing, fucking, and fellowship; and they have inspired alternative cultural expressions. Bars in general (i.e., not just gay ones) have been conceptualized as informal public "third places" distinct from the home and the workplace that provide "both the basis for community and the celebration of it."[5] They may also be understood as public spheres or even counterpublics for producing debate and dissent.[6] As the primary institution of gay public life, bars have performed each of these roles. I argue that most gay political and cultural formations of the recent past developed out of or in reaction to the bars. Today, LGBTQ+ people still gather at bars to toast political gains and to mourn community losses.

What we call "gay bars" are actually many things, and that capacious term encompasses numerous venues. Historically, some bars attracted congregations of queer people but were not avowedly gay venues. Some bohemian clubs cultivated a nonconformist vibe that attracted artists, queers, and other free thinkers. Some straight bars became ephemerally queer at certain hours or in specific pockets of the space, and some reached a tipping point and *turned* gay when patrons kept showing up and effectively took over the place (as with the early leather bars discussed in chapter 1). This book focuses primarily on bars, but the continuities in cultures and practices among bars, private clubs, speakeasies, cabarets, dance clubs, parties, and sex clubs render precise legal distinctions between genres of venues to be of limited importance in lived experience. Queer nightlife also extends beyond these venues as patrons spill outside to parking lots, to transit stops, to bathhouses, and to nearby greasy spoons, pizzerias, taco stands, and bodegas. Coffee shops and all-night diners have long operated as symbiotic spaces by offering late-night refuges for those too young to attend bars and social spaces to continue conversations and stave off hangovers after bars close.[7] Although rarely explicitly gay venues, these were often places where queer convergences claimed the right to public assembly.[8]

The potential for same-sex sex is what makes gay bars *gay*. Yet whereas historically common cruising venues such as bus stations, parks, and department-store restrooms all afford anonymous sex, bars offer *social* contact as well. Bars rely on a mix of familiar faces and new connections. Indeed, the presence of strangers is as important as the company of friends.

A bar needs to be dynamic, familiar, and availing of new experiences, exchanges, and acquaintances characteristic of urban social contact more generally. Some bars may seem to exemplify particular neighborhoods, demographics, fetishes, fashions, or historical moments, but to be vital businesses they must either attract a diversity of clients or manifest a very specific scene. Most bars change character across the week, some over the course of the evening. Gay bars are part of the fabric of their locations by serving clienteles that travel from across an entire city or region and by occupying older buildings rather than newly constructed ones, thereby weaving themselves into preexisting urban landscapes.[9] Gay bars in different cities often resemble one another, even as each individual bar is inevitably subject to the competition and whims of its local market.

Gay bars are both constituted by and refuse their historical conditions. A long-standing function of the bar has been to offer escape from the tedium of daily life or the oppression of and isolation from the broader homophobic society. Gay bars even serve a purpose for those who rarely go to them: it's important to know that they exist and are available. One historian movingly recounts the story of a married woman who would call her local gay bar just to hear the ambient sounds of a parallel queer life.[10] As long-running bars introduce new theme nights, new features, and new ways to stay relevant, they nonetheless sustain attachments to ideas of shared identity and of continuity with local and national gay pasts.[11]

Every element inside these venues mediates social and sexual connections: the layout of the space, the libations, the lighting, the musical choices, the cigarette smoke, the color-coded hankies, and the dance-floor sweat that evaporates and then recondenses.[12] Nights out linger in such temporary residues as tinnitus at bedtime and glitter that adheres the morning after. Going out involves multiple temporalities while also posing unique vulnerabilities. There are the hours of getting ready, including the disco nap, the evening shower, the snack to sustain energy, and perhaps the pregame cocktail to save money or to relax into the right headspace. Going to a gay bar or club means submitting to assessments of fashion, desirability, double entendre–laced repartee, gender performance, and class. Deciding what to wear becomes a strategy: to dress to impress, to conform, to pass, to get sweaty while dancing, to self-express, or to armor. Gay men can be haughty, and judging other men is a cherished bar activity. For some, the codes of self-presentation can be learned and adopted; for others, they may be self-consciously refused. Femme, gender-nonconforming, and trans people—particularly of color—are the most vulnerable both to the sneers and stigma of catty gay men and to verbal harassment and assault getting to and from the venue. Calculations of self-fashioning must also take into account the risks inherent in encounters with a taxi driver, at the bus stop, or amid straight people on the street.[13] Stopping by the convenience store to buy cigarettes further exposes queers to the trap of hypervisibility, stares, and potential attack. (On public safety in and near gay bars, see chapter 3; interludes 2 and 7 on Detroit and Somerset, PA; and the epilogue "After Hours.") Youths often carpool with friends, piling into a car with a designated driver who drinks slightly less than everyone else. Younger men also often first navigate gay clubs with fag hags and baby dykes (both are terms of endearment) as social buffers until they have established a gay male social circle of their own; some of us continue in this preference for socializing and dancing with women in primarily male spaces.

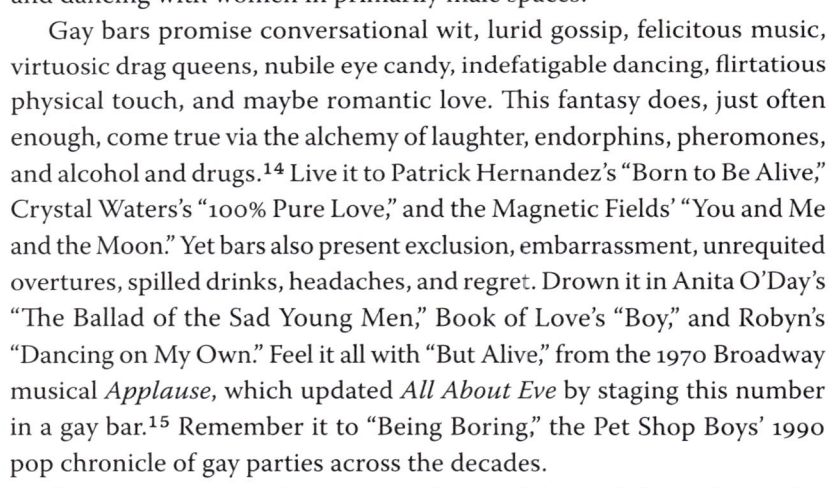

Gay bars promise conversational wit, lurid gossip, felicitous music, virtuosic drag queens, nubile eye candy, indefatigable dancing, flirtatious physical touch, and maybe romantic love. This fantasy does, just often enough, come true via the alchemy of laughter, endorphins, pheromones, and alcohol and drugs.[14] Live it to Patrick Hernandez's "Born to Be Alive," Crystal Waters's "100% Pure Love," and the Magnetic Fields' "You and Me and the Moon." Yet bars also present exclusion, embarrassment, unrequited overtures, spilled drinks, headaches, and regret. Drown it in Anita O'Day's "The Ballad of the Sad Young Men," Book of Love's "Boy," and Robyn's "Dancing on My Own." Feel it all with "But Alive," from the 1970 Broadway musical *Applause*, which updated *All About Eve* by staging this number in a gay bar.[15] Remember it to "Being Boring," the Pet Shop Boys' 1990 pop chronicle of gay parties across the decades.

For young queers, going out to gay bars and dance clubs can be revelatory, even giving them the feeling that they are inventing queer nightlife itself when they are actually inventing themselves. For aging queens, bars' familiarity can feel tedious, comforting, or just novel enough to be reinvigorating. As an introvert, I have rarely found gay bars to be as genial as safe spaces purport to be, and I am laughably inept at cruising; I'm also usually ready to depart as soon as my happy buzz fades into drowsiness. Even so, almost every time I go out, there's a peculiar moment, detail, song, or encounter that makes me feel like gay bars are where queerness flowers. A good night at a gay bar can be very persuasive, and I keep going back out of that sense of potential.

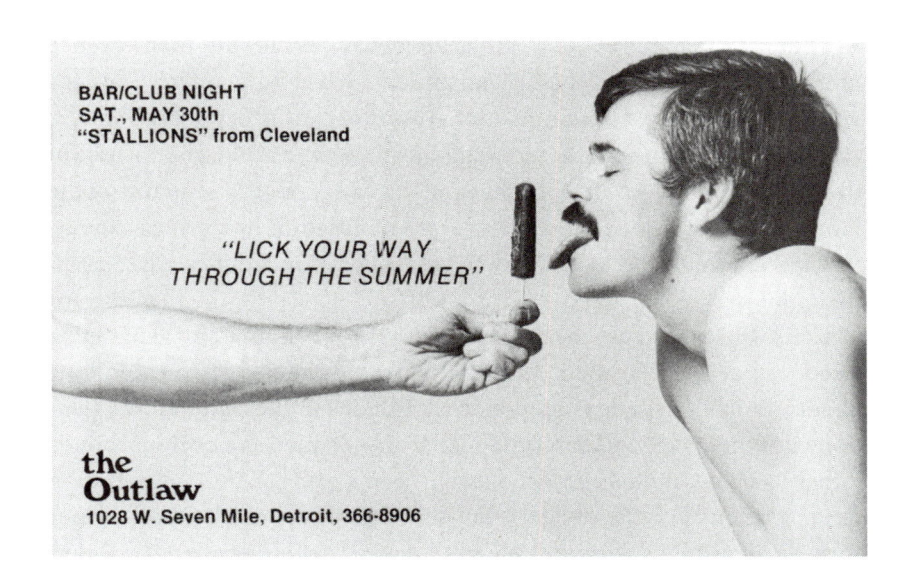

BAR/CLUB NIGHT
SAT., MAY 30th
"STALLIONS" from Cleveland

"LICK YOUR WAY
THROUGH THE SUMMER"

the
Outlaw
1028 W. Seven Mile, Detroit, 366-8906

FIGURE I.1 Gay bar ads, such as this one for the Outlaw, drip with double entendres as they promise to refresh their patrons' thirsts and satiate their desires. Operating in the register of fantasy, bar advertisements often shamelessly trade in phallic imagery but rarely visualize the venue itself (see also figure I.9). *Cruise Weekly,* May 29, 1981. Courtesy of Bentley Historical Library at the University of Michigan.

Is That All There Is? Gay Bar History

Gay bars are effectively an American development of the twentieth century.[16] In the 1970s the Villa Fontana in Dallas advertised itself as "America's Oldest Gay Bar."[17] Today the White Horse Inn in Oakland and Café Lafitte in Exile in New Orleans each claim to be the longest continuously operating gay bar in the United States; each has been running since at least 1933, the date of Prohibition's repeal. Despite these legacy claims, it would be impossible to definitively identify the first or the oldest US gay bar. Records for gay bars are unreliable because venues were often illicit, unlicensed, local, and short-lived, and, as stated above, their orientations were often more fluid than fixed. Consequently, this book does not emphasize a chronology of firsts. Instead, I look to exemplary instances that help explain the ways that bars have conditioned the invention of gay public life.

Scholars argue that the developments of gay identity and spaces as they exist in the United States have been uniquely the products of the private market, from bars and bathhouses to newsstands, movie theaters, and mail-order catalogues.[18] Gay liberation developed as "the coemergence of the gay consumer and the gay constituent," which was conceived of as a whole new lifestyle.[19] In a foundational essay of gay history, John D'Emilio makes an even bigger claim: that capitalism, urbanization, and the rise of the wage-labor system changed the fundamental economic structure of the family unit and created the structural possibilities for modern gay identities and communities to emerge. Whereas agrarian families relied upon their children's labor to operate as a self-sufficient unit, the turn toward workers who earned paychecks allowed for new economic and geographic freedoms, at least for men. This had two major effects: men could now choose to live as singles independent of their families, and family relationships (marriage and parenthood) became defined as emotional bonds rather than as economic arrangements. The migration to and concentration of populations in cities fostered the development of commercial venues such as taverns; in these places, men could forge new affectional and sexual relationships. My graduate students challenged D'Emilio's model as unreflective of family patterns in communities of color. I had never previously questioned his argument; upon reflection, I determined that D'Emilio's premise was not invalid but was specific and partial: his account historicizes a predominantly white male formation.[20] Such distinctions in kinship, community structures, and economic access also, in part, explain how gay bars primarily developed as *white* gay male institutions. We must also recognize that all the spaces that LGBTQ+ people claimed that appear in this book have been located on stolen Indigenous lands.

There have been numerous historical studies that trace early gay life and nightlife (the two often intertwine) to the 1920s or to World War II. These offer invaluable, usually local recovery narratives of previously repressed public life.[21] The seminal tome in this genre remains George Chauncey's magisterial history of the "gay world" in New York during the early twentieth century; he argues that queer public life was more visible and integrated into the city during that period than it would be during the next few decades. In this account, Prohibition was *good* for queer nightlife insofar as it meant that venues serving "fairies," "pansies," and other nonnormative clientele were no more vulnerable than straight joints; they all operated beyond the law and through the protection of payoffs. Rather, the *repeal* of Prohibition had a number of significant effects that created the conditions for gay bars to develop as a distinct phenomenon. In the mid-twentieth century, liquor-control boards became the primary force regulating venues serving alcohol, at times explicitly forbidding venues from catering to so-called

FIGURE I.2 This advertisement for the Speakeasy in Charlotte, North Carolina, evokes a clandestine era of queer nightlife with its image of a door with peek slot to screen admission. The graphic design—with its simple line art and text—is reflective of many gay bar ads in the 1960s and early 1970s. References to the venue's liquor permit and the fact that patrons must bring their own booze ("B.Y.O.L.") reflect the peculiarities of local alcohol regulations. *David*, May 1971. Collection of the author.

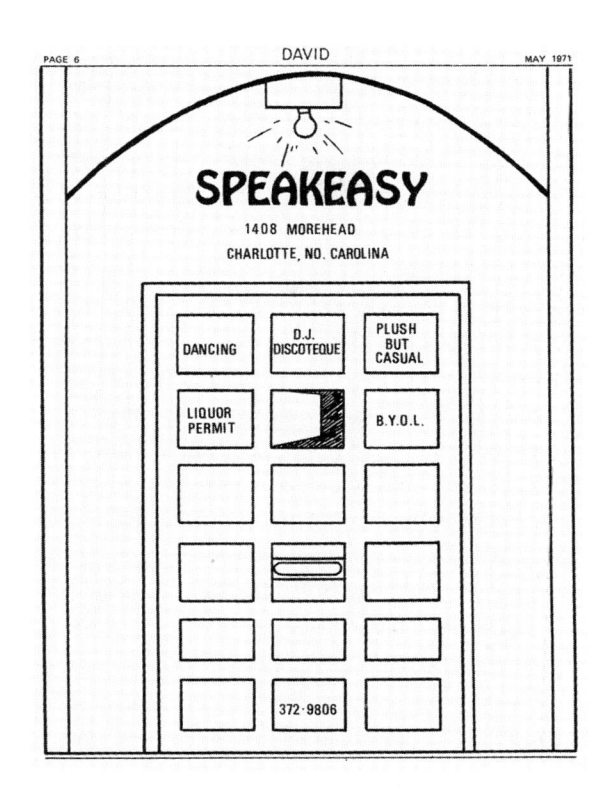

sexual deviants. The legal precarity of these businesses in turn made them ripe for mafia control, which lasted in many cities for decades. Significantly, the pressures on bars to disallow *any* perceptible queer clientele created a segregated nightlife scene. Whereas queer gatherings previously could be integrated into anything-goes venues, post-Prohibition homophobic regulations motivated *exclusively* gay venues to coalesce.[22] These venues operated separately from straight bars and often discreetly out of view from the so-called general public.

Historians have argued that World War II significantly remapped US gay life and positioned the gay bar as its primary locus. Gay bars in red-light districts and tenderloins were the most immediate way for servicepeople on temporary leave to access queer scenes in unfamiliar cities.[23] When the war ended, many of these veterans resettled in the cities where they had first found others like themselves. For many queers who grew up feeling isolated in rural areas, small towns, and suburbs, there was a "great gay migration" to major cities in search of the possibility of a gay life.[24] This built upon preexisting patterns of queer urban migration, further centralizing bars as the primary sites of gay public life and laying a foundation for gay political organizing in the postwar period—a more virulently homophobic time than the prewar era. As D'Emilio asserts, "Alone among the expressions of gay life [of the time], the bar fostered an identity that was both public and collective."[25]

In the postwar period, a relatively stable infrastructure of bars developed despite pervasive societal homophobia. The law and law enforcement viewed "any assembly of homosexuals in one place" as "a virtual conspiracy."[26] Yet, even when licensing agencies or the police shut down specific bars amid politically motivated clean-up campaigns, new venues would soon replace them. Many bar patrons did not disclose their names or carry identification because of the risks of arrest, shakedown, or blackmail. Gay bars offered outlets for closeted people in heterosexual marriages as well as those who had resisted such social conventions. People who ventured to bars were vulnerable to potential loss of employment, housing, family, and social standing when bar raids were publicized; other men did not dare to go to gay bars at all.[27] As demonstrated by the 1957 book *Gay Bar*, written by a staunch but sympathetic heterosexual female gay bar owner, these venues also enforced strict codes of conduct and gender presentation for the men who went there.[28] Patrons comported themselves within the norms of the venue or risked getting themselves eighty-sixed from the one safe-ish place they had.

During the 1950s the differential legal status of bars serving known or suspected homosexuals became a matter for legal challenges and political organizing. In California the State Supreme Court ruled in 1951 that the presence of homosexuals in a bar did not, in and of itself, constitute a violation of the law as long as no other "illegal or immoral acts" could be proven. This ruling "made California the only state in the nation to provide a modicum of legal legitimacy to gay and lesbian bars."[29] (Virginia was the last state to repeal its law prohibiting the operation of gay bars, in late 1991.)[30] However, by the decade's end, another ruling mitigated these legal protections by suggesting that "any activity (not just sexual activity) that could be construed as homosexual" might be considered immoral and thus the basis for fines, license revocation, or closure.[31] San Francisco gay bar owners responded by joining forces. First, they orchestrated a campaign to expose and fight extortion from the police—dubbed "gayola" for gay payola—in 1960. The effects of this effort were mixed; exposing such shakedowns alleviated harassment by precinct beat cops, but this move made bars more vulnerable to top-down antivice campaigns from the mayor's office or police department leadership. Next, in 1961 gay bar owners formed a tavern guild, a professional organization to share information and legal strategies that would be emulated in other cities soon thereafter. Then, in 1964, the San Francisco–based homophile group Society for Individual Rights distributed a "Pocket Lawyer," a small booklet with information about citizens' legal rights in the event of an arrest during a bar raid or entrapment.[32]

Refuting a progress narrative, two mass-market books by homosexual-identified sociologist Donald Webster Cory (a pseudonym for Edward Sagarin) suggest that gay bars became *less* reputable between the early 1950s and the early 1960s. In 1951 Cory wrote that "one wanders into the bar in the hope of finding the convivial spirit that comes from being with one's own [kind] . . . for here is a gaiety, a vivacity, that is seldom seen in the other comparable taverns, nightclubs, bars, and inns." A dozen years later, he and his coauthor offered a more severe assessment: "The conditions under which gay bars can operate and function are often similar to those under which homosexuals themselves function; namely, insecurity, fear, suspicion, and uncertainty. . . . People may go to bars and enjoy them, but nobody respects them because the things they symbolize are considered vices: liquor, sex, and escapism."[33]

When a 1958 issue of the early homophile magazine *One* featured a story on gay bars, its ambivalence was marked by phrasing them as a question: "What about Gay Bars?" In the cover photo, a patron of color has swiveled to return the camera's gaze with lacquered lips, one arm akimbo, and the other holding a cigarette aloft; other people's faces remain obscured, possibly out of discretion or possibly because they were engaged in other goings-on (see figure I.3). The article's author refers to gay bars as both an "institution" and a "medium," and he narrates an overview of the social dynamics in these spaces.[34]

> Anyone who has "made the rounds," as they say, is readily acquainted with the milieu—the hustlers, the screaming faggots, the queers, the nice ivy-leaguers—sometimes all in easy exchange with one another, while at other times each isolated into groups maintaining their own classification within the bars that reflect their specific personalities. . . . If [patrons of color] feel a little uncertain of their welcome, they will usually monopolize one corner of the bar, and emerge only if invited. . . . the

FIGURE I.3 An unidentified but self-assured gay bar patron returns the camera's gaze on the cover of early homophile magazine *One*, February 1958. Courtesy of ONE Archives at the USC Libraries.

> Gay Bar is exceptionally important to many homosexuals, as the one institution where they can be sure of finding some measure of kinship with others.[35]

This account of gay bars makes clear how varied the clienteles of specific bars could be, which manifested in spatialized convergences and dispersals along the lines of class, race, gender, and decorum. Some midcentury bars—described as "piss elegant" by their detractors—aspired to upper-class refinement, as with hotel bars, sweater-queen bars, and piano bars.[36] (The Tavern on Camac piano bar in Philadelphia is the only gay bar where I've felt underdressed without a dinner jacket; this made it feel like a wonderful anachronism as I sipped a martini.) Other rough-and-tumble dives drew straight rough trade and hustlers, and leather bars still occasionally simulate this titillating patina of danger. *One*'s report also exposes racial tensions in the gay scene that reflected American society at large. Significantly, the author foregrounds this portrait by suggesting that the dynamics in these spaces are *already known* by his readership.

In the 1960s and beyond, journalists wrote about bars in exposés of gay life; psychologists and social scientists likewise went to bars looking for evidence to explain the "pathology" and "social problem" of homosexuality.[37] (See also interlude 3 on Seattle.) Gay bars were often perceived as dens of maladjustment and social deviance; their marginality also made them ripe for developing political dissent and organizing. Before and after gay liberation, bars knowingly satirized their status as dens of ill repute by referencing poor personal choices, sleaze, and shame with such names as the Mistake, Club Hangover, Marie's Crisis, the Toilet, Sewers of Paris, the City Dump, Rumors, and even the Closet. Other bar names brazenly made innocuous terms sound prurient, such as the Sweet Gum Head, the White Swallow, and the Goat Roper. These bars' owners subverted their venues' low cultural status with humor, and their patrons were in on the joke.

This book's chapters begin in 1960 because by this time gay bars were established as the core sites for queer public life. By then, gay bars had developed as unambiguously gay with gay clienteles, owners, and managers and with the symbiotic gay press to publicize them.[38] At this moment, unique subcultures were beginning to coalesce within and through gay bars; the Gold Coast leather bar in Chicago (chapter 1) and the Colony Bar and the Jewel Box Lounge in Kansas City (chapter 2) each debuted between 1959 and 1960. Starting in the early 1960s, gay travel guides, such as Guy Strait's *The Lavender Baedeker* (from 1963) and Bob Damron's *The Address Book* (from 1965), compiled listings of gay bars in cities across the country in ways that not only affirmed their primacy but also made distinctions between genres of bars. These publications not only helped men find particular watering holes but also demonstrated for their readers that a greater public gay world existed, with multiple ways of being gay.[39] In 1963 John Rechy's *City of Night* became a literary cause célèbre for his unapologetic chronicle of hustling in the homosexual underworld of bars and parks across the country. By 1980, one could imagine a visible "gay America," and Edmund White traveled to see it in his droll *States of Desire*. What changed between those two books was an epochal shift in gay consciousness and public life that could be witnessed at gay bars.

We Found Love in a Hopeless Place: The Stonewall Riots

History, for LGTBQ+ communities, is often periodized as before and after Stonewall: the riots that erupted at the New York City gay bar in late June 1969. By beginning in 1960, this book deliberately moves away from Stonewall as the pivot of *bar* history; that venue did not so much invent a culture—its scene is strikingly similar to accounts of the Colony Bar in Kansas City before it (see chapter 2) and to Jacque's and the Other Side in Boston after it (see chapter 3)—nor was it the first or last gay bar to be raided and to inspire protests in response. Yet the name *Stonewall* has become so iconic that it now references *any* moment that catalyzed gay political activity regardless of chronology; for instance, Los Angeles' Stonewall—organized protests following a 1967 raid on the Black Cat and New Faces bars—*preceded* New York's (see figure I.4).[40] Still, the *legacy* of the events at Stonewall loom so large that any history of gay bars must reckon with it. The riot has been commemorated with annual pride celebrations in June in cities around the world, and milestone anniversaries have been marked by a tenth-anniversary march on Washington (in 1979) and a wave of exhibitions and publications for the twenty-fifth and fiftieth anniversaries (1994 and 2019, respectively).[41]

The Stonewall Inn opened on Christopher Street in the West Village proximate to other gay bars in 1967. The venue kept the name of the previous business that had been in the space, with a story-and-half vertical sign that flanked the front of the building and made the Stonewall flagrantly visible (see figure I.5). The venue purported, in legal terms, to be a "bottle club," where patrons were supposed to bring their own liquor to be served by the staff rather than buy it from the bar. This loophole bypassed legitimate licensing. Serving known homosexuals had been illegal in New York for years, as publicized when the Mattachine Society enlisted a reporter to go on a "sip-in" (a spin on the Black civil rights movement's sit-ins) at Julius', located around the corner from the Stonewall, in 1966.[42] In 1968 a New York judge ruled that gay bars were not illegal per se, nearly two decades after the California precedent. Yet the state liquor authority persisted in refusing licenses to acknowledged gay bars, which perpetuated mafia control of the market with unlicensed joints. The Stonewall was widely recognized as a syndicate operation, and its more affluent patrons were reportedly extorted to keep their sexuality secret.[43] Conditions inside the Stonewall were famously unhygienic, and its poorly washed glassware was blamed for hepatitis outbreaks. Drinks

FIGURE I.4 On February 11, 1967, PRIDE (Personal Rights in Defense and Education) led protests against a New Year's Eve police raid of the Black Cat and New Faces bars in Los Angeles, where officers beat patrons and a bartender. Courtesy of ONE Archives at the USC Libraries.

were watered down and overpriced, there was little ventilation, and the air-conditioning didn't work. Nonetheless, it was the largest and "most popular gay bar in Greenwich Village."[44]

Accounts of the bar indicate that it welcomed a cross section of white, Black, and Puerto Rican patrons. It was especially a sanctuary for people on the trans spectrum, for sex workers, and for street kids. Indigent youths would panhandle for the cover charge to seek refuge from the weather or from vagrancy charges.[45] As one patron recounted, "All you had to do was find an empty beer can, so the waiter would think you'd bought a drink, and the night was yours."[46] These patrons were often refused by or were "too much" for other gay venues.[47] As Dick Leitsch of the Mattachine Society reflected, "The Stonewall became 'home' to these kids. When it was raided, they fought for it. That, and the fact that they had nothing to lose other than the most tolerant and broadminded gay place in town, explains why the Stonewall riots were begun, led, and spearheaded by the 'queens.'"[48]

"WE WERE NEVER BEING BORING" 13

FIGURE I.5 Exterior of the Stonewall Inn, site of the June 1969 raid and riots, photographed in September 1969 by Diana Davies. With a massive sign, the Stonewall was the most visible gay venue in the city at the time; the remnants of an activist message to the community remain visible on the boarded-up window. The bar closed a month later. © New York Public Library.

The 1969 raid on the Stonewall was part of a wave of harassment, including an earlier raid there that same week. The bar had been raided "at least ten times" since opening, but this time around it "looked to many like part of an effort to close all gay bars and clubs in the Village."[49] The first night of the riots, it was hot, there was a full moon, and Judy Garland had just been buried. Garland was a gay icon beloved by an older and whiter audience than the Stonewall's core crowd, but the coincidence of her death became one of the riots' apocryphal causes. Police arrived at peak time; they checked IDs, detaining trans and underage people inside while releasing others one by one. The crowd on the curb grew as people waited for their friends or loitered to watch, and customers leaving the bar started to catwalk for their audience. A few trans patrons and bar staff were taken away in the first police van without altercation. The situation escalated when the police became more violent in forcing a woman into a police car after she made repeated escape attempts. The crowd started to throw pennies at the police, shouting, "Dirty coppers." Soon, the projectiles included beer cans and bottles. There has been much debate about who "threw the first brick" or "first punch" at Stonewall, with Black butch lesbian Stormé DeLarverie and Puerto Rican trans activist Sylvia Rivera as the most nominated candidates.[50] As the crowd got riled up, the police took refuge inside the bar. Someone uprooted a parking meter and used it as a battering ram on the boarded-up front window; then someone tossed a firebomb through the opening, which was greeted with shouts of "cook the pigs."[51] The police were trapped inside, and the bar—like many gay dives—did not have fire exits. The queens stomped on both civilian and police cars. The ruckus attracted onlookers and joiners-in who converged via the West Village's angled streets, avenues, and subways.[52] Estimates of the crowd the first night vary between two hundred and a thousand. Chants of "gay power" articulated the incident as a political rebellion in the spirit of black power and the pervasive urban uprisings of the preceding years. After the first night, activists wrote in chalk on buildings along Christopher Street instructing people to assemble again at the Stonewall, where there were speeches as well as continued protests. The energy and antics of the uprising continued for days.[53]

The Stonewall riots indisputably signaled a turning point in gay politics. But this was possible only because a public culture of gay bars and political consciousness about their stakes *already existed* when the insurgency erupted. Leitsch observed that whereas Mayor Robert F. Wagner Jr.'s administration (1954–65) had persecuted queer people and spaces to the point that they internalized the expectation of such treatment, Mayor John Lindsay's administration (starting in 1966) had taken a much more tolerant approach that gave the LGBTQ+ community a new enfranchisement.[54] The uprising occurred because the queer community had developed a sense of relative security that was newly threatened. Following the riots, the Stonewall itself became the target of an anti-mafia boycott and closed in October 1969; it reopened decades later as a new business venture that capitalized on the location's fame.

The longer-term effects of the uprising were that it *felt* like something transformative and that it made new liberated queer consciousness, activisms, and publicities possible. As one account proclaimed, "WE WANT

THE WORLD AND WE WANT IT NOW!"[55] The riots at the Stonewall sparked the formation of the Gay Liberation Front and the Gay Activists' Alliance political groups.[56] The GLF took up a revolutionary ethos and organized in solidarity with other leftist movements, whereas the GAA focused more narrowly on gay rights specifically.[57] The GLF began hosting popular dances in August 1969; the GAA likewise had a "pleasure committee" and began hosting dances in June 1970 as the first Stonewall anniversary pride event. The GAA moved operations to a converted firehouse in 1971 and continued dances there until 1974, when the firehouse was destroyed, ironically, by arson.[58] Together, the GLF and GAA dances strategically shifted dance music from jukeboxes to live DJs in order to outfox the mafia (which controlled jukeboxes and other bar concessions, such as cigarette machines) and ultimately popularized the disco phenomenon among gay men.[59] Yet one account suggests that gay bars became even more profitable for the mafia *after* gay liberation expanded their numbers. At times, crime syndicates owned bars directly, at times they invested in bars with a gay owner as a front, and at times they used them for money laundering or drug running; they also relied on them for their various vending, distribution, and supply businesses. Such business arrangements lasted into the 1990s and possibly even later.[60]

Nonetheless, raids persisted. When the police raided the Snake Pit bar following a GAA action in spring 1970, an undocumented arrestee named Diego Viñales jumped out of a police station window because he feared deportation. He impaled himself on an iron fence and moaned in agony; miraculously, he lived. The GAA published a pamphlet in response to the incident: "Any way you look at it, Diego Viñales was pushed. We are all being pushed."[61] The following year, the city witnessed its largest bar raids yet.[62] A decade later, in 1982, police conducted one of the most brutal raids in the city's history on the Times Square bar Blue's, which drew a predominantly Black and Latinx gay and trans patronage.[63] Whereas a similar clientele had fought back at the Stonewall, the version of gay liberation that followed from the riots primarily benefited white gay men. Queer and trans people of color remained politically and socially marginalized in the community.

Even though the Stonewall was closed before the riots were commemorated by what would be known as pride parades, the relation between bars and these annual events has been long-standing. The first few Christopher Street Liberation Day marches started in the Village and made their way to Central Park. In other words, the liberationists deliberately left the gay ghetto and its bars to occupy more visible public spaces. However, in 1973 the parade reversed direction to *end up* at the bars, thus guaranteeing major revenues; a decade later, this would become the standard route.[64]

A Little Respect: Gay Liberation and After

Gay bars became ubiquitous during the liberation era, and they remained the most pervasive and visible institution of the gay community through the end of the millennium and beyond. During the 1970s, the number of gay bars across the country swelled as more businesses opened to cash in on a growing market. (At this time, researchers estimated that a city population of fifty thousand was generally necessary to sustain a gay bar, although in some regions the minimum threshold could be as high as a combined urban and outlying rural population of two hundred thousand.)[65] But in the wake of Stonewall, bars' roles in gay politics evolved. Gay bar activism expanded from protesting external forces, such as alcohol-control agencies, the mafia, and the police, to critiquing bars themselves and their outsized role in gay life.

Early 1970s bar activism called attention to financial exploitation and other oppressive conditions at bars. As a 1970 commentary in the Philadelphia's leftist newspaper *Gay Dealer* espoused, "the 'gay bar' is the tool by which the oppressor and his underworld cohorts perpetuate their hatred of us as an oppressed people and the lifestyle in which we desire to express ourselves."[66] In 1970 the Berkeley GLF chapter staged pickets, guerrilla theater, and a sit-in at the White Horse Inn to protest straight exploitation of gay people in bars. The GLF's demands included the right to touch and dance, an end to verbal and physical abuse from owners and staff, the freedom to distribute gay-liberation newspapers, nondiscrimination based on dress, a space for minors, and lowered prices on drinks.[67] The cover of the October 1970 issue of *Gay Sunshine* showcased a photo of the protesters reclaiming the bar on their own terms, flanked by the headline "The Bars Are Ours" (see figure 1.6).[68]

That same year the Los Angeles GLF produced a poster encouraging bar patrons to "touch one another" as a civil right. In a homophobic society, same-sex physical contact constituted gay bars' primary threat to dominant cultural values and was often the basis upon which they were policed. Vice officers arrested men who hugged or danced together on charges of public indecency as routinely as they targeted bar owners and

FIGURE I.6 Front-page coverage of the Berkeley Gay Liberation Front's protest of the White Horse Inn in Oakland. *Gay Sunshine*, October 1970. Courtesy of ONE Archives at the USC Libraries.

staff for liquor-license violations. Stories abound that well into the 1960s, when police raided mixed-gender bars, the management would turn on a special light to alert dancers to switch partners; gay men and lesbians then quickly moved to slow dancing with each other. Liberationists sought to move beyond such subterfuge. The LA GLF advised its constituents, "You may hold hands, keep your arm around a friend's shoulder or waist, give a friendly kiss," but "groping, caressing below 'the belt,' soul kissing or sexually carrying-on is not tolerated in either straight or gay bars—*it is illegal*" (see figure I.7).[69] These forms of activism were inspired by and intersected with other social movements, including the civil rights movement and black power, second-wave feminism, and the antiwar and student movements. Records of this time, however, expose the lack of consensus among gay bar patrons. Significantly, bar-goers and activists

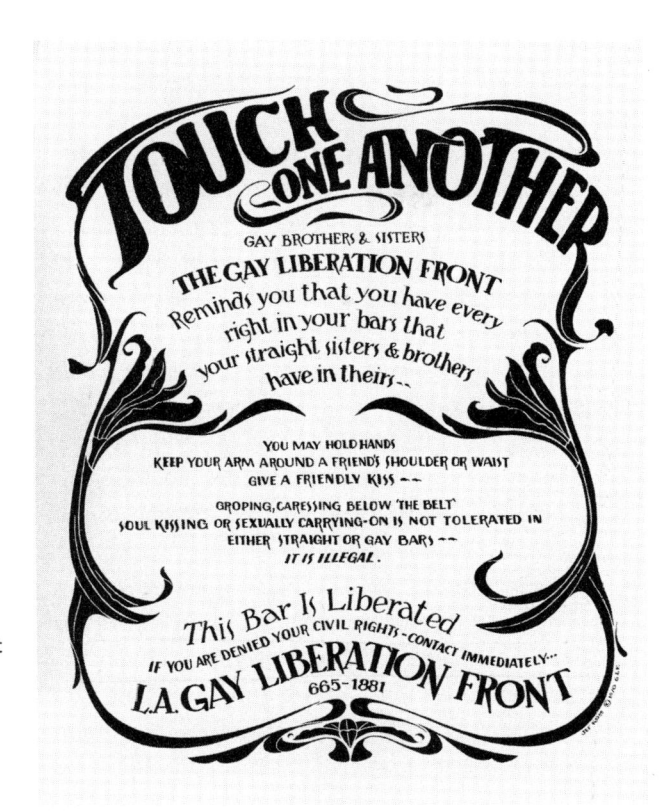

FIGURE I.7 The Los Angeles Gay Liberation Front produced this flyer in 1970 to advise bar patrons of their right to public displays of affection. Courtesy of ONE Archives at the USC Libraries.

often operated at cross-purposes. A 1974 *Pittsburgh Gay News* editorial titled "Is 'Gay Lib' Hurting 'Gay Life?'" acknowledged tensions between activists who were critical of gay bars and "the vast majority of gay women and men [who] are still enjoying the old 'gay life,' with all of the sometimes negative connotations."[70] (See also interlude 3 about Seattle.)

Bars were critiqued for their dominance in gay socializing and the corollary effects of pervasive alcoholism among their patrons.[71] Oftentimes, consuming alcohol became a precondition for access to queer public venues, and this fact exacerbated self-medicating tendencies among LGBTQ+ people to alleviate feelings of shame. The management at some bars aggressively hassled patrons to keep buying rounds; others more subtly drove patrons to drink with poor ventilation that irritated customers' throats or with music so loud that patrons strained their voices to talk.[72] In many cities, gay bars frequently used to open at 6 a.m.—the earliest allowed by local liquor regulations—and had crowds of regulars at that hour. Set entirely in a gay bar, the 1971 film *Some of My Best Friends Are . . .* portrays gay binge drinking as sloppy and self-destructive, and it suggests that this behavior was representative of the gay lifestyle at the time.[73] Some bars even mocked emergent efforts to problematize alcohol consumption. Contemporaneous with early publicity for gay addiction-treatment programs, the EndUp in San Francisco ran an ad querying, "Got a drinking problem? We do too! Join us."[74] The practices and meanings of drinking have changed over the decades. As a longtime bar owner in Portland succinctly remarked to me, "Gay people don't drink like they used to."[75]

During the 1970s, as more men came out, the connotations of bars began to shift from being sites of stigma to sites of exuberance. No phenomenon better reflected this new gay world than the emergence of "super-bars," which combined dance floors, drag lounges, leather bars, piano bars, patios, boutiques, and the like into massive complexes where men could fluidly circulate and cruise between spaces.[76] The Farmhouse super-bar in Houston boasted a swimming pool, and the Copa in Fort Lauderdale claimed "a cast of thousands" across multiple venues within a single compound (see figure I.8).[77] These clubs offered an embodied sense of new political power in sheer numbers and the heady lure of infinite potential hookups; they also promised to bring everyone together for a full menu of amusements.

In contrast to the super-bars, as the number of gay bars grew in each local market, other individual bars increasingly specialized in particular subcultures, aesthetics, attractions, or demographics; this, in turn, produced trends toward homogenization within specific venues' clienteles. Many bars cultivated milieus that fetishized masculinity and denied entry to women, including trans women; some bars also deliberately excluded men of color in order to attract white men only. Live-and-let-live working-class and rural bars have tended to serve inclusive crowds that are representative of their regional demographics; in contrast, larger city bars have been *less* likely to reflect diverse urban demographics as they compete for discrete—usually affluent white male—segments of the urban market.[78] As lesbian feminist Felice Newman pointedly argued, "The bars are not a gay community, but a substitute for a gay community."[79] The *ours* who could claim enfranchisement at the *bars* in this book were often historically contested.

Dissonant lived realities mark gay bar histories. Bars at times created a false consciousness for their clienteles about who constitutes the LGBTQ+ community—what Ramzi Fawaz has described as "a relic of gay white liberalism's racist claim to universality."[80] White gay men have understood bars primarily as spaces for empowering self-expression; sometimes creating

FIGURE I.8 Double-page advertisement for the Copa super-bar and disco in Fort Lauderdale listing its multiple distinct venues (left) and coaxing dancers to "act out your fantasies and be a star every night." *Knight Life* magazine, November 23, 1978. Collection of the author.

these sanctuaries was predicated on deliberate practices of exclusion—for example, protecting all-male spaces for sexual play. In contrast, queers of color, women, and trans patrons have too often found gay bars to be locations of structural and interpersonal hostility. Bars reflected shifting sexual mores, sexisms, and racisms among white gay men—as well as provided the sites for protesting them.

Gay liberation emerged in tandem with the sexual revolution. As such, all-male gay venues often fostered a new ethos of communal permissiveness and celebrated sexual expression (see chapters 1 and 5 and interlude 1 on Denver). For gay men, entering into these bars and nightclubs communicated tacit consent to participate in—or at least witness—erotic scenes and possibilities. This happened at *bars* in part because alcohol and drugs lessen inhibitions. People often went to these spaces deliberately in search of new erotic experiences, even to transgress their personal limits. Anonymous public sex became a staple of men's nightlife and effectively brought long-standing practices such as tearoom (public restroom) cruising into the open as the main attraction. Even though venues often staged these activities in dimly lit back rooms, these scenes legitimated same-sex desire and unleashed years of repression. In the 1980s, the AIDS epidemic began changing these cultures of public eroticism; it spurred external regulation from cities that closed down many venues and divided gay men over these sites' implications for fueling and fighting the spread of HIV (see chapter 5).

Public sexual cultures often manifested in playful ways, as demonstrated by a mid-1980s account of the famed jockstrap contest at the EndUp. When a member of the crowd asked a contestant, "Are you a natural blonde?," the emcee commanded the contestant to "bend over and let me look at your roots." The contestant complied, "spreading his asshole for all of the world to see." Then, when the audience quizzed another contestant about his favorite masturbation fantasy, "someone in the crowd shout[ed] out, 'Ann Miller tap-dancing!'"[81] In the context of the mid-1980s, when this night happened, voyeurism ranked among the safest forms of sex amid the escalating AIDS epidemic. This event has had parallels that date back decades at bars across the country, most often billed as underwear contests offering a cash prize. These contests attract cocky twinks basking in validation, ballsy butch women seeking attention, and even unhoused men looking to feed themselves. Such exhibitionist stunts reveal the complex erotic and monetary economies of the gay bar scene.

In recent years, public discourses about the necessity of affirmative sexual consent may recast some of the historical practices at gay bars as no longer tenable to some members of the LGBTQ+ community. After decades of being pathologized and criminalized, gay men reclaimed the idea of being sexual outlaws in the 1970s. Lascivious physical contact between strangers was so commonplace as to be expected, even normalized as part of being in gay bars and clubs. For instance, the Manhandler Saloon in Los Angeles effectively *promised* such action with its name and with a logo that included a hand jerking off the stem of its "h" (see figure I.9). My friend Brad campily invoked this pervasive gay bar connotation of lechery whenever he referred to Touchez in Sioux Falls, South Dakota, as "Touches"—despite the fact that it was not a cruisy bar. Of course, unsolicited and unwanted groping has always occurred in these spaces, too; that has never made such advances okay, but typically these incidents have been treated as relatively unfraught by simply brushing aside stray hands and moving on. Today, go-go boys and drag queens are

FIGURE I.9 This logo for the Manhandler Saloon in Los Angeles appeared on matchbooks and marketed lewd touching between strangers. A Chicago bar with the same name operated for forty years, which suggests the enduring promise of public sex for gay men. Collection of the author.

far more consistently subject to being pawed than patrons in gay venues; depending on the context, such touch may be invited as carnivalesque behavior or may be experienced as assault. No universal norm exists. We are now several years into a transitional period with conflicting, somewhat generational paradigms among queer-identified people that alternately advance ideologies of sexual liberation (freedom to explore and express sexuality) and of sexual protection (freedom from sexual harm and trauma).[82] New practices to protect bargoers from being violated—such as offering consent beads for patrons to opt-in or opt-out—have been introduced at some venues, while others seek to reference, if not quite replicate, public sexual cultures of a seedy past.[83] The bars I examine in this book almost all reflect the liberation ideology, in keeping with the dominant gay political philosophy of their times.

The cultures of public sex and masculinity in the gay scene operated in alternately affirming and exclusionary ways. Masculinity became hegemonic, nearly compulsory, in much of the gay male scene during the 1970s and beyond—and in many ways remains entrenched. This often manifested in misogynist and transphobic ways as men distanced themselves from associations with women, trans people, and even drag queens. For some gay men, coming out and coming into one's own entailed embodying a validating masculinity from which they had previously felt estranged; for many gay men, it also meant conforming to the new norms of the gay scene, often derided as "clone" culture (see interlude 1 on Denver). Others critiqued and refused such performances of machismo as effemiphobic, coercive, and toxic.

Lesbians frequented both mixed-gender and women's bars. (Plenty of lesbians engaged in restroom sex at bars, too, but they did not build a culture or infrastructure of backroom bars and sex clubs comparable to gay men's.) Yet, even when men and women attended the same venues, they often occupied different spaces within the same place. As the bar scenes expanded in the 1970s, they also became ever-more gender segregated. Given disparities in women's incomes, lesbians were less often able to support their own exclusive bars, and the number of women's bars never achieved parity with men's. Women's house parties have provided another important, more economical but less public form of nightlife. In addition, lesbians were far more likely than gay men to seek out affordable housing with more space to accommodate families; this meant living in neighborhoods beyond boystowns rather than prioritizing proximity to bars. With the rise of second-wave feminism, lesbians often found or made their places within new feminist groups and sites—from coffee shops and bookstores to women's centers—that offered alternatives to bars. Inspired by their feminist sisters, some gay male activists called for similar alternatives to the gay bar, but this rhetoric nevertheless reiterated the bars' continued primacy for gay men.[84] Lesbian bars and mixed venues continued to be *parts* of lesbian culture and socializing (and in many cases may still have drawn larger crowds), but—and this is key—after the 1960s, bars no longer retained the symbolic centrality for lesbians that they continued to have in shaping gay male culture and politics.[85]

Discrimination and segregation were common realities of the gay bar scene across the country. Some bars were overt in their bias, such as when staff denied entry to would-be patrons; this was comparatively easy for community organizers to document and protest (see chapter 4). More venues, however, fostered and reproduced their maleness and whiteness in more subtle ways that were nonetheless still palpable to anyone made to feel unwelcome. Bars thus became the medium through which pervasive white gay male sexism and racism were made visible and combated.

Many cities have sustained majority Black and Latinx gay bars, respectively, as well.[86] Black gay bars operate as alternatives to the overt discrimination and microaggressions at white gay bars, and they offer self-determined community spaces unbothered by what is happening in white venues (see chapter 4). In Washington, DC, for instance, many of these black gay spaces operated as private social clubs.[87] Likewise, Spanish-language Latinx gay bars reinvent the gay bar in hybrid and culturally specific ways (see chapter 8). Yet queer-of-color bars have never operated in numbers proportionate to white bars. Rather, queer-of-color communities come together and make space well beyond, not just in relation to, gay bars.[88]

Circa the late 1980s to early 1990s, some DJs and club promoters deliberately worked to advance co-gender and racially mixed queer parties (see chapter 7). These were radical propositions at the time and have still never become the dominant model. Inclusive political organizing and the gay bar converged perhaps most spectacularly in 1993 when the nightclub Tracks hosted the 72 Hour Party on Washington to coincide with the March on Washington for Lesbian, Gay, and Bi Equal Rights and Liberation. The march featured a diverse roster of platform speakers and advanced demands for nondiscrimination protections, increased AIDS research and treatment funding, reproductive rights, and an end to all forms of racism. In promoting its party, Tracks proclaimed, "With nights that cater to women and minorities, TRACKS is Washington's most politically correct dance club." This rhetorical move suggested an embrace of multiculturalism and simultaneously signaled that its parties were demographically segmented. A series of full-page advertisements in the *Washington Blade* promised that the club would double its usual 25,000 square feet, yet despite such scaling up, it planned different parties for predominantly white gay men (which stood in as an event for the LGBTQ+ community in general), for Black men, for women, and for march volunteers, respectively (see figures I.10 and I.11).[89] These events demonstrate the contradictory logic that continues to structure much of LGBTQ+ nightlife: in order to serve diverse communities, many venues divide the week among demographically separate nightly parties.

Sociologist Greggor Mattson's research suggests that gender-integrated bars became the biggest growth segment starting in the 1990s and that, as the overall number of LGBTQ+ bars diminished from the 2010s onward, venues increasingly self-defined as queer bars, everybody bars, or even straight-friendly bars.[90] Yet my research has confirmed, again and again, that the primary strategy to correct for the whiteness and maleness of gay bars in major cities has been the creation of differentiated nights or alternative venues—that is, separatism—for women, Black, Latinx, Asian, and/or other underserved segments of the larger LGBTQ+ community (see chapters 4 and 8, and "After Hours").

FIGURES I.10 & I.11 Two of five consecutive pages of ads for Tracks nightclub's 72 Hour Party on Washington, programmed to coincide with the March on Washington for Lesbian, Gay, and Bi Equal Rights and Liberation in 1993. The club boasted about its inclusive politics yet scheduled separate nightly parties marketed to different demographics, such as a white gay male party that stands in as an event for the LGBTQ community in general, its weekly Sunday night house party marketed to Black men, and its weekly women's party, which was not part of the 72-hour party. Strikingly, in the ad on the left, white gay men appear clothed and immersed in social and erotic collectives, whereas, in the ad on the right, a Black man appears almost nude and isolated as he solicits the attention of the reader. *Washington Blade*, April 23, 1993. Courtesy of the Jean-Nickolaus Tretter Collection in GLBT Studies, University of Minnesota Libraries.

The social dynamics in gay bars have always reflected and informed how gay men interact when they come together. As early as the 1970s, bars were critiqued for creating alienating meat markets among gay men.[91] In the 1980s, video bars were similarly viewed skeptically by critics for constructing spaces that discouraged social interaction due to their video-jockey mixes and broadcasts of *Dynasty* and *The Golden Girls* (see figure I.12). These venues redirected men's gazes from scoping out one another to collectively staring at mounted screens decades before smartphones would do the same in more individualized ways.[92] Yet history repeats itself. Forty years after the first gay commentaries on bars' dehumanizing tendencies, I would find myself outside the Green Lantern bar in Washington, DC,

FIGURE I.12 "Before they put in video, we had to stand around and look at gorgeous guys. Now we stand around and look at *Golden Girls*." Bill Barbanes's comic comments on the 1980s rise of video bars, contemporaneous with the first decade of the AIDS epidemic. *New York Native*, May 12, 1986. Courtesy of ONE Archives at the USC Libraries. Reprinted by permission of the artist.

having an unusually intense conversation with a charming stranger about gay loneliness and intimacy.[93] He made fun of me for giving guarded responses to his questions and avoiding eye contact, yet this interaction has imprinted on my thinking about social dynamics in gay bars. In the 2010s men also flocked back to gay bars to laugh and gasp in unison at communal viewings of *RuPaul's Drag Race*; these bar screenings, in turn, grew the series' fan base and entrenched references to the show as the new gay male lingua franca (see figure I.13).

The past and recent present seemed to converge one evening in Chicago in 2017, when my friend Frederic took me to an old-school neighborhood bar called the Granville Anvil. We sat at the bar, which is constructed in a loop so that each person seated at the countertop can make eye contact with everyone else. (I first experienced this layout at the Drinkery in Baltimore.) We noticed that most of the patrons were looking at their phones instead. Belatedly, we realized that people were queuing songs for the digital jukebox from their devices—a new technology I hadn't en-

FIGURE I.13 Season 2 promotional image of *RuPaul's Drag Race*. Communal viewings became one of the most popular staples of gay bar culture in the 2010s and beyond. Courtesy of World of Wonder Productions.

countered before. As a new song came on, a thirtysomething South Asian American queen acidly exclaimed, "I do not object to Barbra Streisand. However, I do object to *shitty* Barbra Streisand!" This policing of the gay canon signaled intergenerational fighting words flung at one of the undetermined older white men at the bar whose diva worship he considered undiscerning. However, the tension diffused a few songs later when the Bee Gees' "How Deep Is Your Love" came on.[94] Looking around, it appeared that everyone had closed their eyes as they sang along in a moment of communal reverie to sounds of decades prior.

Perhaps the most radical change during my own bar-going years has been among the most ephemeral: the air itself. As a lesbian acquaintance once quipped, before New York implemented its indoor smoking ban in the early 2000s, at the East Village's crammed Wonderbar "you had to light up a Marlboro for a breath of fresh air." It's difficult to convey how intensely clothes used to reek of permeated smoke after a night out before governments implemented smoking regulations or how assaultive it felt to enter a bar in a city where indoor smoking was still allowed. (Full disclosure: I used to be a social smoker, which meant I rarely drank without smoking but usually bummed my cigarettes like a leech.) Smoking regulations also shifted the social geographies of bars to front sidewalks and to back patios, creating parallel universes where friends might disappear for long periods and, in the usual absence of music, find spaces more conducive to conversation (see interlude 2 on Detroit).

I Will Survive: The Demise and Endurance of Gay Bars

Although I claim a specific historical starting point of 1960 for this book, its endpoint remains purposely open-ended because gay bars have not ceased to exist, despite the pervasive refrain that they have become passé. When I started researching this book, people kept telling me that the gay bar as a cultural institution was dying. June Thomas soon wrote a series of articles for *Slate* effectively eulogizing bars.[95] A decade later, Jeremy Atherton Lin's book *Gay Bar* garnered significant attention for offering a tribute to bars at a moment when it seemed like we might lose them; the book's subtitle, *Why We Went Out*, felt pointedly past tense.[96] Yet the gay bar's death has been prematurely declared before (see plate 1).

The gay bar economy has always seen turnover, from fly-by-night mafia operations to faddish spots that shutter as soon as the next new thing comes along. In the 1970s, the heyday of the gay bar boom, many people without a lick of business experience opened bars that quickly folded amid an oversaturated market. During the 1980s, gay bars endured the existential threats of the AIDS epidemic and changes in drinking behaviors (see chapter 6) as well as the first post-liberation generational rift in the community (see chapter 7). As Mattson avers, "Gay bars are not dying, they're evolving."[97] I agree and have resisted framing this book as a declension narrative.

The culture and sites of drinking in the United States changed profoundly after World War II. Whereas in the late 1940s Americans consumed "about ninety percent" of their alcoholic beverages at public venues, by the early 1980s that figure had plummeted to "about thirty percent." The number of drinking establishments correspondingly shrank during this period.[98] The general turn away from public drinking toward domesticity in mainstream society was likely a product of reorientations toward the nuclear family, the single-family home, and suburban sprawl—life choices that were unavailable or untenable to many queer people. These trends continued between the 1970s and 1990s: the frequency with which people went to bars and nightclubs further declined by approximately half, as did the total number of such venues. These figures correspond to numerous data sets indicating pervasive societal disengagement from civic participation in the second half of the twentieth century.[99]

Strikingly, as bars in general declined, the number of gay bars grew exponentially. Given that gay bars would have figured in the overall tally of bars, the drop in straight bars was even more precipitous than the statistics initially imply. The stark divergence in these parallel bar scenes indicates that bars served a different and essential purpose for LGBTQ+ people—even if the majority of LGBTQ+ people never actually frequented bars.[100] Statistically, the number of gay venues crested in the later part of the twentieth century, followed by a precipitous decrease in recent decades. Mattson's research has found that half of all gay bars closed between 2012 and 2021. Sixteen percent closed between 2019 and 2021, most due to the COVID-19 pandemic. This recent statistic is strikingly consistent with the peak years of bar closures during the AIDS crisis (14 percent from 1987–92) and with trends in the years preceding 2019.[101] That fifty percent have closed is not nothing, but it's not *everything*, either. Significantly, the latter-day perceptual and numerical decline of gay bars belatedly aligns with decades-old patterns in straight society.[102]

Gay bar cultures necessarily adapt to their political and social contexts. Looking back, the HIV/AIDS epidemic had a transformative and traumatizing impact on LGBTQ+ public life, politics, cultures, sexuality, and sociality.[103] Bars saw their patronage dwindle during the early years of the epidemic as some of their core patronage died and as a larger share felt unsafe socializing in public because the disease's transmission and epidemiology were not yet understood. From the mid-1980s onward, bar activism increasingly entailed sponsoring charity fundraisers for HIV/AIDS service organizations or other causes; some bars also hosted safer-sex demonstrations and distributed condoms. This gave gay bars a new role to play in the gay community and helped redefine what they meant. Certainly not all venues were benevolent, but many were. In addition, bars and clubs resumed their escapist role, whether to allow men to pretend for a moment that the HIV/AIDS crisis wasn't happening or to release the emotional weight of it all by dancing (see chapters 5, 6, and 7).

I've encountered multiple explanations for the more recent diminishment of gay bars, including competition from the internet and hookup apps, gentrification and the straightening of gayborhoods, mainstream acceptance and assimilation of LTBTQ+ people, and younger generations' disinterest in the scene. I've seen evidence affirming and countering each of these theories, and I believe there is a confluence of each. The internet, social media, and hook-up/dating apps have changed social norms, when and how people come out, and how people access community and sexual partners. Repeated cycles of gentrification and redevelopment have made urban areas more difficult for small businesses and residents alike to afford. Significantly, the mass adoption of cruising apps coincided with the mortgage crisis and Great Recession of the late 2000s, signaling that social and economic forces converged. Broader social acceptance of LGBTQ+ people has opened up more life choices for gay people, including getting married, having children, living in suburbs or small towns, and going to chain restaurants. This might be called progress or assimilation, depending on one's ideological perspective. Gay bars have long featured drag performances and movie nights, but nightly programming increasingly has become a business necessity for venues to coax patrons off their couches.[104] Speaking of couches' gravitational pull, the developing legalization of marijuana poses as much recreational competition to bars as any other factor. Even younger queer scholars have turned to staying in and domesticity.[105]

Importantly, bar closures have happened in uneven patterns, demographically and geographically. Closures have disproportionately impacted bars catering to lesbians and queers of color, both of which have historically served clienteles with lower disposable income. Strikingly, however, the highest closure rate has been among cruise bars that cultivate cultures of public sex; these venues have faced stiff competition from hookup apps.[106] The map of closures does not show the same picture everywhere, nor are the reasons all the same. In Cleveland, for instance, bar closures have followed decades of disinvestment, not gentrification.[107] In contrast, in Dallas I encountered a thriving bar district, where I marveled at the two-story lesbian club Sue Ellen's (which featured hard hip-hop on the dance floor and live bluegrass upstairs the night I visited) and the bustling western bar Round Up Saloon (where urban cowboys twirl elegantly while men watch from surrounding viewing platforms), among other venues. There in Big D, I was told that the Cedar Springs Merchants Association had studied the effects of gentrification on other cities' gayborhoods and organized to prevent overdevelopment via chain stores and condos in order to protect the Oak Lawn bar strip.[108]

Although the absolute number of gay bars has waned, gay bars' roles have not been directly replaced by other institutions. I also maintain that virtual platforms cannot replace the experience of dancing in a crowd of sweaty, sexy, intoxicated people or of getting lost in kissing while the rest of the bar fades from consciousness.[109] What's more, men routinely use apps such as Grindr and Scruff *inside* bars like an augmented reality game to find out who's available and what they're into. Queer people may feel more comfortable than ever in mixed and straight venues, but neither same-sex dancing nor blow jobs abound in these spaces.[110] Some gay bars carry on in crisis, and others remain popular enterprises that define specific cities, scenes, and subcultures. Some bars may seem like holdovers from an earlier era but continue to serve a clientele of regulars who may not be valued by other venues. Newer ventures have opportunities to reconceive what queer spaces might be.

At the zenith of the gay liberation era, Liza Minnelli bellowed, "What good is sitting alone in your room?"[111] In 2020 we had no other choice. Much of the writing and revision of this book took place as gay bars faced their greatest challenge yet: the COVID-19 pandemic. Cities instituted stay-at-home orders, business revenues halted, and epidemiological uncertainty created widespread anxiety about public socializing. Numerous bars rank among the business casualties of the pandemic, but others were saved when they drew donations via crowd-sourcing campaigns. The pandemic's longer-term effects on nightlife practices may not be fully recognizable for years to come. I don't want to overdetermine this history with a presentist perspective, but this context inevitably colors my analysis. Personally, I found that pandemic-era attempts to simulate nightlife—with Zoom virtual happy hours and dance parties—exacerbated lockdown alienation rather than alleviated it; such practices instantly demonstrated the irreplaceability of mutuality, shared physical presence, and spontaneous social contact. As this period extended, I was often alarmed by Instagram posts showing gay clubs crowded with unmasked men; it felt too soon and too risky even though I wanted bars to recover. The pandemic produced a widespread longing to return to bars, at times acted upon as a matter of personal liberty. My own initial return visits to bars were an affective jumble of trepidation, then relief, and then unease again when the crowd thickened. Curiously, this moment also yielded a wave of new club bangers by Dua Lipa, Agnes, and Beyoncé with the releases of their poignantly titled albums *Future Nostalgia, Magic Still Exists,* and *Renaissance,* respectively.[112] More broadly, I observed a commonly voiced desire to return to normal and to resume what was familiar rather than to rethink or reimagine something new. The gay bar as an institution carries on, as contradictorily as ever.

Yo, D.J., Pump This Party: This Book

The Bars Are Ours explores what has been productive and world making about gay bars and clubs, how they produced structures of exclusion, and how they have figured as mediums to work through these contradictions. The chapters that follow are roughly chronological and focus on specific case-study cities, although each strives to scale between past and present, local and national. Local contexts uniquely matter because, unlike other twentieth-century minority equal rights movements, the lesbian and gay movement during its first decades primarily focused on achieving local change rather than federal protections.[113] The formation of gay communities has often been lived and understood at the local and even neighborhood level. (On the bars' role in local political debate and organizing, see chapters 3, 4, and 6 and interlude 1 on Denver.) Yet each local gay community would have understood itself in relation to an emergent national gay culture and political organizing. For most of the period covered in this book, men in the bars would have had access to a national gay press as well as local gay publications.

Many of the cities in this book have long been recognized as gay capitals, such as New York City and San Francisco, or were boomtowns in the late twentieth century, such as Atlanta and Houston. Gay men moved to these cities to be gay, in search of work opportunities, or both. By the 1970s, there was also a recognizable gay tourism market, which means that men often traveled between these cities, and bars were typically how travelers accessed local gay scenes. Bars were often the first attractions listed in gay travel guides, and local gay newspapers included directories of local bars for newcomers.[114] Bars also sustained the early gay press through advertising and inspired much of its early reportage. In recent decades, gay bars have pivoted to rely primarily on social media for marketing rather than on the gay print press, a fact that has mirrored and accelerated the decline of print culture. Although Gotham and Frisco loom large in the queer cultural imaginary and have set many historical precedents, I deliberately start this book's case-study chapters in the heartland to insist that queer cultures did not flourish only on the coasts. Interludes 6 and 7, which look to Superior, Wisconsin, and Somerset County, Pennsylvania, offer representation of small-city and rural bars as well.

Schematically, the chapters proceed two-by-two in pairs that address cultures (leather in Chicago and drag in Kansas City, chapters 1 and 2), politics (gentrification in Boston and racism in Atlanta, chapters 3 and 4), institutions (iconic gay clubs in New York City and Houston, chapters 5 and 6), and reinventions (queer parties in San Francisco and Latinx spaces in Los Angeles, chapters 7 and 8). I focus on leather and drag in chapters 1 and 2 as the two most iconic cultural formations specific to gay bars. They may seem dichotomous in their celebrations of masculinity and femininity, yet both reveal gender as performed, and both revel in queer practices of community building. Leather bars today often reference a particular heritage of 1970s sleaze, whereas drag may appear to be timelessly gay; in fact, both leather and drag became codified as gay bar cultures in the 1960s. As I demonstrate in chapters 3 and 4, in Boston and Atlanta gay bars functioned as the mediums to make class tensions and racial bias visible within these gay communities, respectively; stakeholders protested the bars' clientele or door policies and sought government intervention, but these specific, local instances were understood to be indicative of nationwide concerns about gentrification and discrimination. Yet these chapters also document that particular venues became sanctuaries serving otherwise marginalized segments of the LGBTQ+ rainbow. Chapters 5 and 6 examine the sex clubs, discos, and bars in New York City and Houston that effectively defined gay public life, provided models that other clubs aspired to, and exemplified what a gay bar could be. The last two chapters look to San Francisco and Los Angeles for Generation X queer parties and Latinx venues, respectively, that created alternatives to the hegemony of white gay male bars and clubs as they had developed in the liberation era. Other artifacts, documents, news stories, and nights out that compelled me to write about them became the basis of the book's interludes, and each one models different knowledges and experiences of gay bars. I close this book with an epilogue about Pulse in Orlando, where a mass shooting on Latin Night produced international grief and, amid the mourning, testimonies about the continued importance of queer clubs. These histories indicate that bars may have never been utopias, but they have been ours.

Part I

Cultures

1

Nights in Black Leather

Inventing a Bar Culture in Chicago

In the later part of the twentieth century, the term *gay bar* most often connoted three things: leather men, drag queens, and disco dancing. We'll get to drag and disco in later chapters, but here leather comes first (and returns in chapters 5 and 6). The leather bar was seminal in differentiating between gay male identities and in claiming space. Because of laws forbidding same-sex contact or dancing, leather bars predate gay dance clubs in many cities, and they generally continued to refuse the trappings of other kinds of gay bars later on. As an ad for the Stud in Southern California promised, "No dancing, no entertainment, no nothing. Just cruising the way you like it!"[1] Such venues purported to distill the gay bar down to its essence.

Leather bars coalesced between the 1950s and 1960s as new queer phenomena and exploded in popularity during the 1970s. Virtually every city that has sustained more than one gay bar has hosted at least one leather bar. Leather bars attracted men who sought to radically redefine gay male sexuality, to reclaim their masculinity, and to constitute a community, a tribe even.[2] These bars emerged as one of the first truly distinct subgenres of gay bars, and they developed bars' most elaborated subcultural norms

FIGURE 1.1 Chuck Arnett's 1962 mural for an interior wall of the Tool Box leather bar in San Francisco's South of Market neighborhood was prominently featured in *Life* magazine. When the building was demolished a decade later, the exposed mural remained standing and publicly visible for a time. Photo by R. Michael Kelley. Courtesy of Gayle S. Rubin.

and specific imagery, so much so that they often figure as gay bars' most iconic form. Already in 1964, *Life* magazine featured a two-page spread with a photo taken inside the Tool Box bar in San Francisco to introduce its infamous profile on "Homosexuality in America." In an image that would become emblematic of gay male culture, leather men stood in silhouette in front of the bar's massive mural by Chuck Arnett (see figure 1.1).[3] Two decades later, the first representation of a gay bar that I ever encountered was also of a leather bar: the Blue Oyster in *Police Academy*.[4] That fictional bar functioned as a homophobic punch line to make straight audiences laugh in discomfort, yet it also vividly imprinted on my juvenile mind with its instantly decipherable codes.

Bars gave the leather scene coherence and provided it sites for assembly. As leather commentator Guy Baldwin reflected, "My introduction to leather life was really my introduction to leather *bar* life.... [In the mid-1960s,] they were one and the same."[5] Bars contributed to the emergence of the leather lifestyle in two senses: first, they gathered a community that shared an erotic ethos and allowed others to discover leather and BDSM as a way of life; second, they turned leather into a consumable aesthetic and identity, one that gay men could put on at will without having to commit to the scene exclusively. Some bars tried to maintain a clientele that was serious about leather, and some were membership based. But as public commercial spaces, it was not always possible to police whether patrons were rigorously leather oriented in their sexual practices.

Although leather, BDSM practice, public sex, and motorcycle clubs were not necessarily always intertwined, they came together in the leather bar. The leather bar and its visual environment set the stage for new desires and played a central role in defining the gay male fetish for masculinity. Cultural critic Michael Bronski has suggested that the turn away from previous conflations of male homosexuality and effeminacy toward leather marked a paradigm shift: "Gay men of my generation and experience were beginning to understand that *we* could become the men we wanted and felt we could never have: the men of our dreams."[6] The performance of masculinity and the promise of sexual transgression have long been central to the pleasures of the leather bar. Such venues began as primarily social clubs, but by the 1970s, they often had back rooms, dark corners, or basements that allowed for erotic contact (see also interlude 1 on Denver and chapter 5). Hard-core gay pornography continues to be shown on screens in leather bars even in the absence of onsite sex—and in some cases surely standing in for it. Club affiliations, sexual practices, and fashion have shifted over time, but leather bars remain among the most ubiquitous and prototypical genres of gay bars.

With a focus on the Gold Coast in Chicago, this chapter looks at leather bars as sites of invention. Though not the first leather bar, the Gold Coast became one of the most legendary and was probably the first to be gay owned and operated when Chuck Renslow took over its reins in 1960. The Gold Coast was nothing less than a landmark that developed its own local culture and demonstrated the ways in which bars intertwine with other nodes in the gay community. Circa 1979, the gay travel magazine *Ciao!* asserted that it was "surely the most famous bar of its kind in the country."[7]

Whaddaya Got? Inventing a Sexual Subculture

Accounts of leather's history—written from within the community for its members—indicate that the culture emerged in the wake of World War II, was constituted by military veterans, and intersected with motorcycle clubs. Participants made do with the leather gear they could find or craft, and local scenes developed prior to a national network with coordinated norms. Leather bars first came about when groups of men took residence in an existing bar and effectively transitioned its scene. Leather elder Thom Magister has recounted that the biker culture—where straight and gay men mixed—developed among veterans who had been traumatized by their experiences in battle and who couldn't reassimilate into their preservice hometowns and lives. Some had done time in a military prison ("the brig") for homosexuality, others had been tortured by enemies, and some had been physically disfigured. "The brig" would later recirculate as a popular name for leather bars or dungeon-style rooms within them. Magister's own master had been castrated as a prisoner of war.[8] But the affirmative same-sex culture of the military likewise informed the emergent biker/leather culture. In Los Angeles the leather scene comprised two camps: men who maintained military comportment and those who embraced biker rebellion.[9] Magister suggests that the homosociality of 1950s biker bars reflected the general culture of the era: "In 1950, most bars were for men only, so it was not unusual to see one crowded with guys drinking and enjoying one another's company. It was almost impossible to tell the difference between a straight biker bar and a gay one."[10] Although motorcycle-club culture has diminished in visibility in recent decades, many leather bars still operate as the home bars for motorcycle clubs and continue to have glass display cases for club regalia.

Alienated from the existing cultural models, postwar leathermen invented their own tribes, codes, and customs and donned second skins in the form of black leather. The gay leather style was to a large extent modeled on Marlon Brando's costume in the 1953 film *The Wild One* (see figure 1.2). Although the film created a mainstream sensation, it had particular impact on gay men and helped to codify *black* leather as the preferred look.[11] As Magister recalls, "The only new leather clothing available in the U.S. back then were the basic BLMJ (black leather motorcycle jacket) and western riding gear, including buckskin jackets and chaps. Both styles became iconic and fired up many a sexual fantasy."[12] However, for purists there were distinct fantasies that must not be mixed.[13] The gay leather scene developed guidelines for how dress communicated sexual roles. In *The Leatherman's Handbook*, Larry Townsend indicates that sadists "should never wear any leather that isn't black." In contrast, for masochists, "A masculine outlook is really the only firm essential. Many younger Ms find

FIGURE 1.2 Marlon Brando's black motorcycle jacket in *The Wild One* (dir. Lásló Benedek, 1953) inspired many homoerotic fantasies and provided the template for the gay leather look that emerged the following decade. Publicity still. Collection of the author.

themselves successful in Levi's, white T-shirt, belt and boots.... As to the limits, I would certainly not recommend your wearing tennis shoes or a sweater of any sort."[14] Along similar lines, Magister reflects, "In the early years it was not considered 'correct' for a bottom man to wear leather, so a guy in a leather jacket was usually presumed to be a top."[15] He states that once dedicated leather shops began to open in the mid-1960s, bottoms could also start to don dyed cowhide.

In the absence of an established market, early gay leather men had to be innovative and resourceful: "Since there were no popular leather magazines, porn videos, or even books to inform the novice, everything was passed on by legend and word-of-mouth tradition.... In those days there were no ready-made leather shops with on-the-rack and off-the-rack kinky items." Magister continues: "If you wanted a dildo you carved it. A harness was created by visiting the local saddle shop and improvising. Leather pants and jackets came from Harley-Davidson. Chaps came from

LEATHER IN CHICAGO   41

western shops as did boots and vests. Each item was made with care and imagination."[16] In tandem with this sense of improvisation, core values in the culture included training and discipline. According to Magister, "One glaring difference between leathermen in the 1950s and [later] leathermen" was that "What s/m men now call *play* we called *work*."[17]

The earliest documented bars frequented by the gay leather crowd were in New York City: a cluster of venues called the "bird circuit" at 50th Street and 3rd Avenue, including the Golden Pheasant, the Blue Parrot, and the Swan. Shaw's, the Lodge, and the Big Dollar soon followed as a series of favored watering holes. Shaw's was an Irish pub that transitioned to a gay crowd after 6 p.m.[18] One man recalled visiting Shaw's: "The men ... dressed up as city cowboys, in Levi's and boots and as much leather ... as they could pack onto one body." He continues: "I was intrigued by the thought of men who took such extreme measures to avoid effeminacy."[19] The New York police routinely closed these leather bars, but when one shut down, patrons would find another venue with slow business to colonize.[20] When gay man Jock Modica acquired an old longshoreman's pub called the Eagle Open Kitchen in 1970, the Eagle's Nest was "rumored to be" the first gay-owned bar in New York City—a full decade after the Gold Coast came under Renslow's ownership.[21] It was also the first gay leather bar called the Eagle, which evoked the prior connection between types of fowl and gay bars but in fact simply reworked the location's existing name. Though a product of the 1960s, gay leather bars would become pervasive by the mid-1970s, moving from the margins to the center of gay public life and aesthetics. At that time, the Eagle in Washington, DC, was believed to be the largest leather bar in the world; its tagline tested its patrons: "If you're man enough" (see figure 1.3).[22] The numerous Eagles that now exist across the United States and internationally remain formally independent of one another but are aligned by connotation.

John Preston offers one of the most powerful statements on the significance of leather bars: "The original leather bars were places where men could gather and ... say: *In your face!* Leather was gay sexuality stripped of being nice. It offended. It confronted. It took sex as its own ultimate value. It was a reaffirmation of the revolution, not a dilution of it." Preston continues: "The whole point of the liberation of our sexuality in past decades was to allow this to exist—so long as no real damage was done—without all the trappings of love, romance, and other controlling devices."[23] What Preston suggests as leather liberation predates the Stonewall riots and the gay lib movement, and bars played a central role in this emergent radical turn.

FIGURE 1.3 By the mid-1970s, the DC Eagle was reputedly the largest leather bar in the country at the peak of leather bars' popularity. As early as 1972, its advertising tested potential patrons: "If you're man enough." In late 1976 a second location called the Eagle in Exile opened as a leather disco. *Advocate*, August 27, 1975. Collection of the author.

Leader of the Pack: The Gold Coast

Before cross-country travel became routinized via the interstate freeway system and commercial air travel, gay leather and BDSM scenes were more localized than standardized. New York City and Los Angeles were the avant-garde in this culture; these cities were home to the first leather bars and gay motorcycle clubs, respectively, "with nothing in between" during the 1950s. Even the term S/M had different meanings in different places: in New York the letters indicated "sadist" and "masochist," whereas in Los Angeles they served to denote "slave" and "master."[24] San Francisco and Chicago would rise to prominence in the 1960s.[25]

In the late 1950s, Renslow and a small circle of friends in Chicago "established a network between New York and California" because leather scenes had not yet coalesced between the coasts.[26] Renslow had already

LEATHER IN CHICAGO 43

established his relationship with lover Dom Orejudos (pronounced "Or-Judas") and started some of his businesses when his kink awakening came via an improvisatory group scene with the scholar, tattoo artist, and writer Samuel Steward (alternately known as Sam Sparrow and as Phil Andros) and professor Hal Stevens. Steward biographer Justin Spring vividly details the formative encounter, "which involved heavy bondage, a mock kidnapping, various forms of whipping, and then, to cap it all off, terrorizing the blindfolded Stevens by dragging Orejudos's pet rat across Stevens's naked back. Renslow enjoyed the encounter so much that he later described it as the beginning of his life as a sexual dominant."[27] Renslow also credited Steward with telling him to start wearing a leather jacket—in black, naturally.[28]

Like nomads, Renslow and his crew started an itinerant search for a home bar in Chicago. In 1957 they began by frequenting a downtown bar with minimal business called Omar's; simply by showing up in leather on weekends, they changed its scene. Their get-togethers grew from a handful to a dozen regulars. After a couple of months, the owner drove them away, complaining, "All you guys in motorcycle jackets and caps are scaring the shit out of our patrons! Get the hell out." Then they tested out the bar at the Lane Hotel before finding a more receptive venue at the Hi-Ho, where the owners, a straight couple, appreciated their business. Their clique expanded to a couple dozen men, and Orejudos designed a new leather/biker logo for the bar (see figure 1.4). Soon one of the Hi-Ho owners died, and the bar closed. In turn, the men started frequenting Jamie's, a mafia-owned hustler bar, but were kicked out after a few weeks. Finally, in 1959 the men started hanging out at the Gold Coast Show Lounge across the street. At the Gold Coast, the owner asked Renslow's group to assume operations to save him the hassle. Within months the owner died, and his son suggested that the leathermen buy the business. They did, and the Gold Coast became the first official leather bar in Chicago in March 1960.[29]

The Gold Coast extended and anchored Renslow's numerous enterprises, including the Kris physique photography studio that preceded it and Man's Country bathhouse and the *Gay Life* newspaper later. Renslow and Orejudos were polyamorous, and Renslow's lovers often took various roles in his businesses or as staff. Because of a raid on the Kris studio in 1958, Renslow was ineligible for a liquor license in his own name, so he and co-owners Herbie Schmidt and Art Marotta bought the bar in his then-lover Cliff Ingram's name.[30] In 1972 Renslow married the bar's upstairs neighbor, lesbian Agnes Hassett, in order to renew his liquor

FIGURE 1.4 Dom Orejudos's first logo for a leather bar, the Hi-Ho Club, circa the late 1950s. He signed this image Stephen rather than Etienne, the pseudonym he later used for his Gold Coast artwork. Chuck Renslow Collection. Courtesy of the Leather Archives & Museum.

license and continue legally operating his "spouse's" business. Later, Ron Ehemann became Renslow's life and business partner of thirty-five years, surviving Renslow in death. In 1976, signaling his phenomenal commercial success, Renslow was the first person referenced in a long-form *Advocate* article about the ascendance of gay bars and baths as a $100 million business nationwide.[31]

As the proprietor of the Gold Coast, Renslow had to pay off both the police *and* the mafia. This was just the cost of doing business in Chicago. From Prohibition through the postwar period, the mafia controlled the gay bar scene in many cities, including Chicago. Police payoffs and raids were common at gay bars of all stripes across the country, and a number

LEATHER IN CHICAGO   45

of police bribery and mafia extortion cases went to trial in Chicago in the 1970s and 1980s.[32] Renslow's payoff connections and later his political clout protected him to the point that his multiple businesses and home were raided "only" four times between the 1950s and the 1980s.[33] As Renslow recounted, "We were making regular payoffs to the Police Department. We were raided and they took everybody in. I called up the watch commander. . . . He said, 'Oh, my God, they went to the wrong place, they were supposed to go next door.' So they brought everybody back." The Chicago police were "more expensive" to bribe than the mafia, which "made most of its money through suppliers for bars" and therefore demanded lower cash payments. If the mafia extorted too heavily off the top, bars would go out of business, and the syndicates would lose an important revenue stream for their supply companies.[34] Wryly suggesting that gays had achieved equality, a 1978 *Advocate* profile of the community's political clout in Chicago remarked, "The fact that police now hit up gay businesses for the same pay-offs expected of non-gay businesses also indicates the pragmatic nature of the new Chicago egalitarianism."[35]

In all, the Gold Coast (often called the GC) had five locations. Renslow and his associates had purchased only the business, not the building. When the landlord decided to hike up the rent at the end of the preexisting lease in their first location, they sneakily moved the business to a storefront a few doors down. The longest-lasting location was, appropriately, at 501 N. Clark; Levi's 501s would soon become the defining garment of gay men's performance of working-class masculinity.[36] (See interlude 1 about Denver.)

In keeping with the motorcycle clubhouse feel, the goal for the Gold Coast was primarily to create a familiar social environment. In taking up a biker gang aesthetic, leather bars gave the initial impression of an intimidating den of rebels, but once someone broke into the social circle, these spaces were primarily sites for beer-guzzling camaraderie. Sex, although it would come to be synonymous with leather bars, was secondary. As Renslow told *Cruise* magazine in 1980, "I have interviewed many people going into the Gold Coast. On certain nights, I have interviewed every single person that's gone in and invariably the people are going there for social reasons. I'm not saying they'd turn down a trick, because they probably wouldn't, but that's not their primary reason for going."[37] Nonetheless, the Gold Coast was the original home bar for the Chicago Hellfire Club, which started in 1971 as the first unapologetically outré gay S/M club modeled on the biker clubs—but without the pretense of riding motorcycles.[38]

Further reinforcing connections between the leather tribe and the bar, Renslow began hosting the annual Mr. Gold Coast leather pageant in 1972. By 1979, the event was attracting crowds too large to fit in the bar. Expanding as it moved off-site, the event was rebranded Mr. International Leather (and soon thereafter renamed International Mr. Leather, or IML).[39] The "International" in the event's name was initially accomplished by mailing posters to leather bars in Germany. Of the numerous photos documenting pageant proceedings from the 1970s, my favorite shows a sinewy man with a thick mustache and a toothy grin posing for the camera as a disembodied arm in a leather jacket (possibly Renslow's) reaches to judge his package. Moments later that beaming contestant, Dan Lansing, won the 1977 Mr. Gold Coast title (see figure 1.5).[40] In turn, IML would solidify Chicago's place on the map as a leather capital, drawing crowds of tourists to events, parties, and vendor exhibits. For some, this event signaled a commercialization of leather rather than a true congregation of the BDSM tribe. Like the leather bar scene out of which it developed, the relationship between leather as a look and as a lifestyle at IML was at times ambiguous and debated. Pageant contests continue on multiple scales and circuits; in my travels, I watched the outgoing Mr. Cleveland Bear title holder sing "My Way" in his sash and leather kilt to uproarious applause at the Leather Stallion bar.

Paint It Black: Etienne's Artwork

Significantly, leather bars were the first subgenre of gay bars to develop a strong visual aesthetic, forging relationships between specific bars and artists to create interior murals and drawings for ads, posters, and T-shirts.[41] These consistently featured musclemen with embellished physiognomies in tableaux of cruising, kink scenarios, and workers brandishing suggestive tools. (Pipes alluringly connote both the phallus and the hole, as does the *shaft* in Mineshaft.) By the time Renslow took over the Gold Coast, he was already an entrepreneur with multiple businesses, including the Kris physique photography studio and mail-order business, *Mars* physique magazine, and Triumph Gym, which was a significant source of models.[42] His partner and submissive Orejudos was a physique artist known as Etienne, who created illustrations and murals for all of Renslow's venues (see figure 1.6).[43] In other words, the two came to the bar business from

FIGURE 1.5 Mr. Gold Coast 1977 Dan Lansing gleefully submitting to a judging hand. Photo by Tom Coughlin. Chuck Renslow Collection. Courtesy of the Leather Archives & Museum.

careers in erotic visual culture and understood the importance of setting the scene visually to stimulate their clientele's desires.

Whereas photography and film-based pornography's appeal is rooted in its documentary exposure of real bodies performing veritable sex acts, handmade erotic graphics operate in the realm of *fantasy*. As Etienne, Orejudos's drawings and paintings embellished reality as they aspired to provoke real-world sexual gratification. Orejudos was a ballet dancer and choreographer as well as a foot fetishist. Because of the conservatism of ballet culture, his career in dance was compartmentalized from his lives as a visual artist and leatherman, but his training nonetheless gave him an expert understanding of physique, musculature, and movement. His figures tend to have larger cocks and bulges—not to mention feet and boots—than all but the most supernaturally endowed men, as well as a

FIGURE 1.6 Gold Coast owner Chuck Renslow, Dom Orejudos (aka Etienne), and Touko Valio Laasksonen (aka Tom of Finland), *left to right*, at the Mr. Gold Coast 1977 pageant. Chuck Renslow Collection. Courtesy of the Leather Archives & Museum.

gravity-defying range of motion. Yet Orejudos reflected, "As for the models in my drawing being 'well-endowed,' I try to keep the measurements within the realm of possibility. I mean, the entire figure is, to an extent, exaggerated, glorified ... proportionally 'enhanced.' But never, I hope, enlarged to the point of being unbelievable or grotesque."[44] A local gay press profile remarked on the massive scale of his work: "His paintings are larger because he enjoys 'getting sloppy.'"[45] More precisely, Orejudo created carefully crafted imagery meant to inspire other men to get messy.

The first Gold Coast location's exterior was painted black without any signage beyond the street number: "You had to know where you were going and why."[46] Inside, however, Orejudos painted a mural directly onto the walls that depicted a brick back alley; he also included female figures to give the gay bar the subterfuge of a straight biker bar. When Renslow and company moved locations, Orejudos painted over this mural to ensure that the landlord would not try to open his own competing leather bar.

Unfortunately, he did not have the foresight to document his work in photographs. From then on, Orejudos always painted his murals on plywood or Masonite so that they could move to new locations with the bar.

Orejudos's art direction extended to constructing the illusion of decay to match the bar's connotations of depravity. At the 501 location, city inspectors responded to complaints because Orejudos "had painted it to look like plaster was falling.... It had been purposely chipped and other paint put on top of it to make it look grungy." In addition, "The bar top really looked rough. We sandblasted it to give it that effect and then sealed it in varnish." The city inspectors "ended up writing us up because we didn't have a contractual agreement with a company for extermination" even though they did not have any roaches.[47] Further shaping the scene of the venue, the 501 location had a center island bar that allowed patrons to circulate, socialize, and cruise. Sonically, Tom Lehrer's 1959 novelty recording "The Masochism Tango" provided the bar's theme as one of the most-played records on the jukebox.[48]

Although other Renslow enterprises also consistently featured Etienne artwork, the Gold Coast was the preeminent venue for these painted altars to leather masculinity. One of the most famous, dating from 1966, features a blond mustachioed man with a sculpted torso and meaty legs who reclines on his left side, propping his head with his left arm and covering his genitalia with a suggestive boot; he appears nude aside from his black leather regalia and his white (but one imagines fragrant) tube socks (see plate 2). The man's hat features the name insignia "Dom" as references both to a sexual top ("dominant") and the artist's real first name.[49] This image was reproduced in popular four-color posters that "were hung on walls of homes, bars, and dungeons around the world."[50] (A framed reproduction currently adorns my bedroom as a research souvenir.) This image was also repurposed for advertisements, including for the International Mr. Leather contest. The mural would hang in four different Gold Coast locations. Upon the final location's closure in 1988, Renslow sold the painting to raise money for Orejudos's AIDS-related medical expenses. (Orejudos died in 1991.) Since 2007 the painting has appeared on permanent loan alongside several others in the Etienne Auditorium of the Leather Archives and Museum, another Renslow initiative.

Leather bars without an artist in residence now tend to default to Tom of Finland prints for decor. But in the 1960s and 1970s, symbiotic relationships between artists and leather venues defined the most influential scenes, including Chuck Arnett's work for the Tool Box (see figure 1.1), the Stud,

FIGURE 1.7 In 1966 Fe-Be's bar in San Francisco commissioned Mike Caffee to carve a statue of a gay leatherman based on Michelangelo's *David*. Caffee's original sculpture was destroyed when a mold was made to produce multiple plaster-cast copies. LGBT Business Ephemera collection. Courtesy of GLBT Historical Society.

and the Ambush in San Francisco, and Rex's work for the Mineshaft in New York (see figure 5.5).[51] Kink could also bend toward kitsch, as when Fe-Be's, the first leather bar to open on San Francisco's Folsom Street, commissioned sculptor Mike Caffee to create a replica of Michelangelo's *David* in biker gear in 1966 (see figure 1.7). In a more exuberant fauvist style, Snowflake (Glenn Zehrbaugh) made a series of paintings of the Ambush in the 1970s and '80s, such as *Cocktail Hour* (see plate 3). Other delightful embellishments include a custom-made leather-themed pinball machine called Studz at the Fun Hog Ranch in Las Vegas and a multipart hot-pink and white neon installation at the Faultline in Los Angeles that simulated the motions of a rising cock shooting ejaculate.[52] Across these instances, leather bars produced a mise-en-scène that was at once titillating and witty, signaling multiple registers of meaning.

LEATHER IN CHICAGO   51

Ladies with an Attitude, Fellas That Were in the Mood: Movie Nights

One of the most popular nights at the Gold Coast was Sunday, when the venue hosted movie nights with screenings at 5 p.m. and 10 p.m. The bar rented prints from the local film warehouse and set up a projector on the bar and a screen on the pool table. Orejudos's film selections alternated between a camp canon of old Hollywood women's pictures starring gay icons and new representations reflecting the sexual revolution; such choices signaled a shared history of gay cinephilia, cultural pedagogy for men coming into the gay vernacular, and the fluidity of gendered identifications.[53] As one patron recalled, "I had never heard of *All about Eve* until one movie Sunday when I went there—all these leather guys I had found so intimidating knew it line for line. The veneer cracked. I found out they were nice, they were fun, they knew movies, and they knew opera.... What I discovered was a wonderful brotherhood."[54] Communal viewing at bars forged "a sense of camaraderie and group consciousness" for postwar gay men.[55] Such programming extended to Man's Country, too; one ad promoted a "Have-a-Bawl film festival" of mid-century Hollywood melodramas starring Joan Crawford, Bette Davis, and Lana Turner. The ad featured an Etienne illustration of a crying man in a skimpy towel with the text "How long's it been since you've had a really good cry?" (see figure 1.8). The titular "bawling" contrasts with the "balling" that was more commonly associated with the venue; its come-on of "free hankies for all!" maintains the tear-jerker motif while simultaneously evoking the hanky code. As an intracommunity code, gay men hung colored bandanas from their rear pockets to signal their sexual preferences and positions; although the hanky code remains a legendary reference, I have never been able to determine how widely it was employed in actuality (see table 1.1).[56]

Although macho embodiment predominated by the 1970s, leathermen's capacity to indulge in shared camp references was less contradictory than it might appear. In contrast to Magister's previously referenced emphasis on discipline, Orejudos was prone to playfulness and irony (as was the gang at Mary's—see chapter 6).[57] Women's films in leather bars not only demonstrated such incongruity but also accentuated the performativity of gender and provided dialogue for so many of the quips that were the lingua franca of the gay scene. As Vito Russo suggested at the time, camp operates as both a "secret code" for gay men and produces bonds between them with a spirit of generosity, its frequent embrace of bitchi-

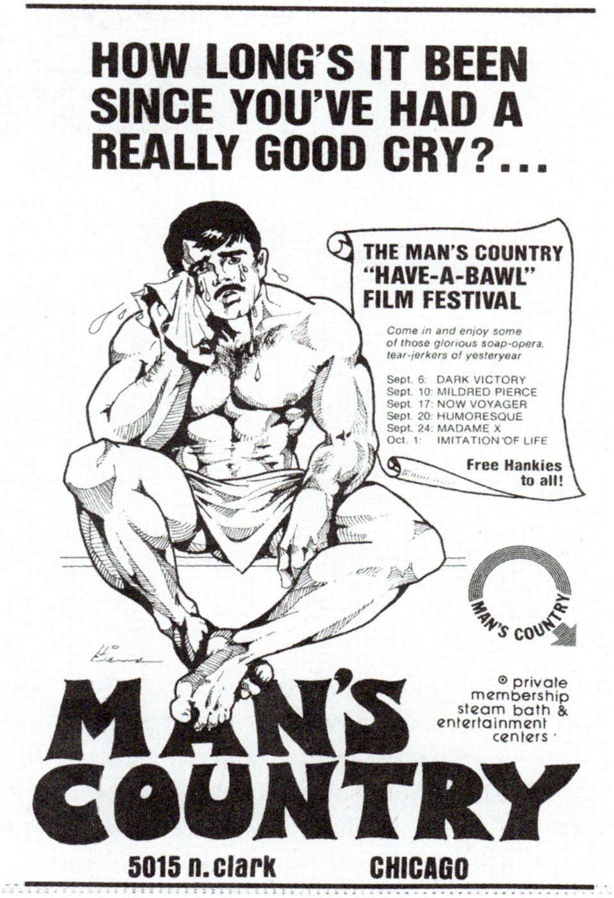

FIGURE 1.8 The Have-a-Bawl Film Festival featured mid-century women's melodramas at the Man's Country macho bathhouse. The advertisement promises "Free Hankies to all!"—a tear-jerker double entendre at the peak of the gay hanky code. Artwork by Dom Orejudos as Etienne. *Gay Life*, August 25, 1978. Courtesy of ONE Archives at the USC Libraries.

ness notwithstanding.[58] (On camp, see chapter 2.) Leather bar patrons continue to embrace diva appreciation and incongruous juxtapositions in these hypermasculine settings. The most vivid example in my experience comes from Tom's Leather Bar in Mexico City, where the video screens occasionally disrupted hard-core gay pornography by interjecting clips of Maria Callas performing an aria.[59]

The Gold Coast would get so packed on movie nights that dozens of men would be turned away. The primary draw for many was the body-to-body men in the dark. One patron recalled that "people didn't pay much attention to the screen. It was packed in there, nothing but cocksucking and fucking going on during the movie. I have vivid memories of one sevenway that I

LEATHER IN CHICAGO 53

TABLE 1.1 The Hanky Code: Classic Colors

Rear left pocket	Color	Rear right pocket
S&M top	Black	S&M bottom
Fisting top	Red	Fisting bottom
Anal top	Navy	Anal bottom
Fellatio recipient	Light blue	Fellatio giver
Piss top	Yellow	Piss bottom
Scat top	Brown	Scat bottom
Hustler (wants payment)	Green	John (wants to pay)
Anything goes top	Orange	Anything goes bottom
Piercing top	Purple	Piercing bottom
Bondage top	Grey	Bondage bottom

Adapted from Larry Townsend, *The Leatherman's Handbook II*, 26.

had that lasted between the movies. They actually had to ask us to leave." Another concurred: "You couldn't move with all the fucking and whatnot going on.... On those nights, if you wanted sex it was upstairs, and if you wanted to drink you went to The Pit," which was where the heavy action happened on other nights. Renslow remarked that "the place was packed with everything going on—guys groping, playing with each other, going down, and more.... Some guys used to go in there with their Levi's slit up the back so they could turn around and back into somebody and get fucked."[60] As Bette Davis's Margo Channing would surmise, "It's going to be a bumpy night." One account of the New York bar scene suggests that gay bars' infamous dark back rooms for anonymous sex actually started as spaces for movie screenings but that bar owners stopped bothering with showing films because the men were otherwise engaged.[61]

Pits and Perverts: Creating Sexual Spaces

Perhaps the single most significant difference between gay bars and straight ones is the culture of public sex in gay bars. Historian Allan Bérubé's recuperative work on bathhouses speaks as well to leather bars: "Because *all* sex acts between men were... illegal... gay men were forced to become sexual outlaws... experts at stealing moments of privacy and at finding the cracks in society where they could meet and not get caught."[62] Spaces for public sex—typically in a back room or basement, often with minimal lighting for anonymity and privacy—have been pervasive in gay bars across the country and internationally. In some cities these spaces continue to operate into the present, contingent on local zoning and degrees of policing.[63] The Gold Coast and its kin created what Jason Orne, in a recent autoethnographic study of Chicago gay scenes, has called "sexy community": the erotic/affective formations that can happen in queer public venues that produce "collective effervescence."[64]

The downstairs of 501 N. Clark became the Pit, which made use of dark recesses underneath the sidewalks that had been left behind when the city raised the street level (see plate 4). First-timers and out-of-towners—lured by its reputation—were reportedly easy to spot because the Pit was so dimly lit that they would trip at a turn in the stairs.[65] The bar stools were fashioned from saddles, and an actual prison cell that Renslow had purchased at a police auction housed the Leather Cell shop inside the Pit starting in 1969. (The boutique later expanded into the stand-alone Male Hide leather shop next door.)[66] Renslow often deflected questions of whether sex was allowed at the Gold Coast, although he was adamant that patrons were not walking around naked at the bar: "The rule [for the staff]... was that if you could see, stop it.... Now, I admit,... [in the Pit] we were just taking advantage of the old city catacombs that were down there. There were an awful lot of dark corners."[67] One of the bartenders was less circumspect about what went on. Frank Kellas recalled tending bar downstairs during a party when "Renslow came downstairs [as] I had my arm up somebody's ass and somebody [else] was giving me head. He said, 'What the fuck is going on here?' and I said, 'I can still work this bar.' I was reaching in and pulling beers and still serving. He was not amused."[68] In 1983 the Pit was raided; bartender Frank Burrage was charged with keeping a disorderly house, and seven patrons were arrested for public indecency. The *Chicago Tribune* listed the names and home addresses of each arrestee. But because the Pit was licensed separately from the Gold Coast, only the basement had its license temporarily suspended.[69]

Back rooms and underground spaces often purposely kept the action in the dark. Tom's Bar in Berlin stands as the exemplar of lightless subterranean caverns for public sex. On the one hand, this lowered inhibitions for some and heightened the likelihood of chance anonymous encounters. But this effect also heightened the acuity of other senses, such as touch, which becomes necessary to literally feel one's away around, and scent. The *smell* of leather bars and sex clubs elicits occasional mention in written accounts, and the pungent odor of such hyper-carnal spaces would have embellished the experience for some men and scared off others. I can only imagine the odoriferous effect of bygone venues, but their sensory impact surely mattered. Most venues would have had windows that were covered over and sealed shut, if there were windows at all. New or freshly oiled leather gives off a distinctively pleasurable musk, which would have fused with an ambience of ripe body odor; many leather venues famously banned colognes, aftershaves, and deodorants to maximize the manly stench (see chapter 5). In venues where water sports were popular, there would have been the lingering scent of a latrine, and other sex acts would have added to the pungent mix. Poppers often wafted and dissipated in the air, as would the liquefying oils of Crisco or Vaseline. Poppers—amyl nitrate, an inhalant cardiovascular drug typically sniffed in liquid form from small vials—gave their users a headrush and unclenched muscles (including the sphincter); they were popular in backrooms, bathhouses, and discos (see chapter 5). Some poppers were marketed as "room odorizers" in the 1970s (see figure 1.9). And to top it off, indoor smoking was still pervasive, which likely would have muddied the funk or dulled smokers' own senses of smell. In the Pit, the olfactory cocktail of stale beer, smoke, funk, sweat, cum, poppers, and leather would have clashed with the smell of basement mildew and bleach or industrial-grade astringent cleaning products. Nearly a year into the COVID-19 pandemic stay-at-home orders, I nostalgically bought my boyfriend, Ernesto, a vial of leather-bar–themed beard oil for our anniversary; I should have anticipated that neither of us would be able to stand the smell.

Leather bars generally fostered a cult of masculinity and often had dress codes, but back rooms and sex clubs were even more inaccessible to women. Gayle Rubin, a leather historian, anthropologist, and practitioner who had access to some but not all of the BDSM/leather spaces in San Francisco, reflects that "one might argue that one major activity of this sexual subculture was and is the establishment of boundaries that then create and contain a ritualized, sexualized, 'taboo' space. In such spaces, the restrictions that kept out women or unsuitable men were an aspect of the process that rendered them safe, private, and erotically

FIGURE 1.9 Liquid amyl nitrate—known as poppers—was a popular inhalant at gay bars and dance clubs. It produces a head rush, quickens the heart, and relaxes muscles. In the 1970s, poppers were synonymous with public sex and were at times branded as "room odorizers," as in this ad for Cum, marketed by S&M Products. *Advocate*, December 28, 1977. Collection of the author.

charged. Although some leathermen do not like women and some are misogynistic, simply attributing such exclusions of women to misogyny would fail to grasp the complexity of their functions."[70] Greggor Mattson effectively expresses his ambivalence that cruise, leather, and bear bars "have often denigrated femininity and women in their celebration of macho masculine bonding. But, on the other [hand], they celebrate larger and hairier bodies, older men, and the kinks and affectionate eroticism that often get sidelined or belittled in conventional gay bars."[71] Anecdotally, my lesbian friends have remarked to me over the years that they believed that leather bars were typically *more* welcoming to women than other gay male bars, despite their predilection for public sex. Even in these spaces, one can encounter unexpected gender performances. I once observed a gorgeous man who accessorized his jockstrap with pink lace-up ballet slippers in the basement of the Bike Stop in Philadelphia on underwear night. Leather bars remain sites of playful and original self-expression.

LEATHER IN CHICAGO 57

Fun City: Chicago's Gay Geography

The Gold Coast at 501 N. Clark anchored Chicago's early gay ghetto, located in a warehouse district north of the Loop. Without much residential use, the area was wide open after working hours, and parking was ample at night.[72] Renslow opened a number of gay-serving businesses that opened in the vicinity, including the local Club Baths franchise. In addition, the area was home to the Baton (the first gay bar in the Near North, also featuring drag shows and go-go boys), P.J.'s (the first disco in town), Dugan's Bistro[73] (the city's most popular disco), Redoubt (a bar "to take care of the Gold Coast overflow"), Jamie's (the mafia bar, which Renslow later took over), the Ritz (a black gay disco), and Male Hide Leathers (a leather gear shop). As early as the mid-1970s, developers began flipping the North Loop into what would be rebranded River North.[74] (On urban renewal and gentrification, see chapter 3.) This cluster preceded the migration of gay venues to North Halsted, aka Boystown.

The Boystown strip of bars is situated five miles north of the historic Gold Coast. The latter-day gayborhood's development was inaugurated in 1975 with the opening of Little Jim's and blossomed in the 1980s, 1990s, and 2000s.[75] There have been leather and leather-adjacent bars in Boystown, including the Bushes, which opened in 1976 and simulated park sex with seasonal landscaping by a display designer from one of the local department stores.[76] Its marketing pièce de résistance appeared in a 1980 ad in *Drummer*, offering an obscene list of sexual gerunds (see figure 1.10).[77] The Loading Dock, later sold and renamed the Cell Block, has subsequently operated for decades. But for the most part, the leather scene—and Renslow's enterprises in particular—have maintained their distance, separating the men from the boys.

Man's Country bathhouse, Renslow's most prominent other venue, opened in 1972 as Chicago's answer to the Continental Baths in New York (see chapter 5). Located in Uptown, it boasted standard bathhouse water features, public sex spaces, private rooms, workout equipment, a disco, film screenings, and live performances. It was part of what was called "the K-Y circuit" of gay bathhouses and discos that featured touring acts. Early on in the developing AIDS epidemic, Renslow consulted with city public health officials and the Howard Brown gay clinic; he shut down the orgy rooms and glory holes and dispensed condoms. These early proactive efforts likely saved Man's Country from the fate of being closed, as happened to such venues in New York and San Francisco.

58 CHAPTER 1

```
happy
hog tieing
toe sucking
pig piling
face fucking
piss drinking
fist eating
mud wallowing
slave swatting
ass stuffing
snot swapping
wax dripping
cheese cleaning
shit sharing
welt raising
armpit licking
butt plugging
spit slinging
dog collaring
master worshiping
name calling
drool lapping
crotch begging
tit torturing
belly eating
face sitting
nuts twisting
enema forcing
foreskin pulling
cum swallowing
from the pigs in the bushes meeting bar
3720 north halsted, chicago.
```

FIGURE 1.10 The Bushes, located in Chicago's Boystown neighborhood, promised a capacious range of perverse acts on site in this advertisement. *Drummer*, December 1980. Courtesy of ONE Archives at the USC Libraries.

Along an eight-mile route from the Gold Coast to Man's Country to Touché in Rogers Park, Clark Avenue has endured as the primary street address for the leather scene; this major thoroughfare bypasses the Boystown bars. When Renslow moved the Gold Coast at the end of his lease at 501 N. Clark, he relocated the bar into a building on the same block as Man's Country. The Uptown Gold Coast never performed as well as its preceding location, nor did it include an equivalent of the Pit. But the major problem was a transfer of ownership. Renslow sold the bar to bartender Kellas in exchange for stock in *Gay Life* newspaper (which Renslow already owned). As Renslow reflected, "He fired all the bartenders, worked the bar himself, [and] he was not a leatherman. That's where I made my mistake. And his idea of leather people was just very wrong. He equated leather with dirt, so he never cleaned the bar. He let it get filthy.... The city ended up revoking his license because of various violations."[78] The bar closed when Renslow refused to renew Kellas's lease in February 1988.[79]

Although Renslow created institutions that defined the leather culture, he nonetheless continued to adapt them to changing times. With fewer men using the bathhouse, Renslow converted part of the Man's Country space into the Bistro Too dance club in 1987. (The name referenced the bygone disco Dugan's Bistro.) Five years later, Renslow closed the dance club and converted part of the space back into Man's Country and part of it into the newly formed Eagle, which in effect attempted to reincarnate the Gold Coast. The space featured posters, murals, and artifacts from the Gold Coast to the point that it seemed like a museum. It even featured a back room evocative of the Pit.[80] The Eagle continued to operate until 2006. Man's Country later closed with a final New Year's Eve party ushering in 2018, six months after Renslow had passed away at age eighty-seven.

As Renslow biographers Tracy Baim and Owen Keehnen argue, the Gold Coast was "emblematic of a new gay identity." Historian Timothy Stewart-Winter suggests that Renslow "was rightly seen as a pioneer in the political incorporation of gay people into urban machine politics."[81] Renslow was inducted in the Chicago LGBT Hall of Fame in 1991; his leadership and legacy exemplify the ways that bars anchored gay sexual, social, and political community building, as well as the fluidity between the bars and bathhouses.

Yet Chicago leather carries on. Touché (not a Renslow venture) opened in 1976 as a neighborhood bar and was rebranded as a leather bar in 1977. Touché's programming has been imaginative at finding ways to integrate public drinking with its kink communities. Monthly flyers from the 1980s announced nightly themed drink specials and parties, such as Cheap Drunk with Grease ("Don't lean against the walls; you'll slide to the floor."), Handballer's Night ("You don't have to be experienced, you just have to be willing."), Sleazy Sunday ("Bring your unfulfilled fantasies and a fistful of quarters. Something can be arranged."), and Water Sports Fetish Night and Enemas ("A yellow bandana is sufficient for 50 cent drinks, but a rubber hose will get attention.").[82] As *Drummer* magazine advised, "If you come to Touché, douche first! This is Chicago's *action* leather bar."[83] Touché has hosted the Chicago Hellfire Club since the Gold Coast's closure and has been the home bar for the Midwest chapter of Onyx, the national leather fraternity for men of color, since 2004.[84] The Leather Archives & Museum is within walking distance.

Leather bars provided spaces for a new community to coalesce and invent a subculture in the 1960s. Although these venues distinguished themselves from other watering holes early on, in the 1970s their influence on the broader gay nightlife culture became pervasive, even legendary (see chapter 5). Gay men now often look back on the leather bars and sexual spaces of the pre-AIDS gay liberation era with nostalgia and fascination, whether they were part of these scenes or these bars predated their experience. Part of this allure certainly comes from the fantasy of unlimited sexual intensities without consequences, but for me the attraction is primarily the euphoric feeling of innovation and exploration that pervades the accounts of past gay bars. I have visited my share of leather bars, but I've seen relatively few men arrive dressed in black leather or engage in BDSM play in them. Rather, these bars seem to operate primarily as themed environments for socializing, cruising, and imagining what used to happen there. Leather bars exemplify our vision of what gay bars used to look like, and they continue to demonstrate what gay bars could be.

INTERLUDE 1

Triangle Lounge in Denver

An advertisement for the Triangle Lounge in Denver dating from 1976 distills the bar's image down to the garment synonymous with gay male self-fashioning of the era: Levi's 501 jeans (see figure I1.1). This seemingly simple ad was reproduced repeatedly in the local and national gay press, as well as on posters. Teasingly, there are telltale signs that the jeans were photographed with a man inside them; the denim alternates between taut and gaping along the button fly, a detail that marks the jeans as 501s. But the focal point is just to the left, where the crotch's faded and tensed denim catches the light to signal a phallic bulge; here the high-contrast lighting accentuates the model's natural curves. The photo appears to have been carefully cropped to strip the Levi's from their wearer so that potential patrons could envision their own ideal man filling them up. Popping the buttons on a pair of 501's fly was the gay male equivalent of bodice ripping in women's erotica, so this image invites its viewer to imagine unfurling the engorged cock straining against the fabric. The ad also, quite efficiently, informs gay men about what to wear to the bar.

FIGURE I1.1 Levi's 501s figure iconically in this advertisement for Denver's Triangle Lounge. This garment exemplified 1970s gay masculinity, and this image taught readers what to wear to the bar. Note the way the bulging, strained denim to the left of the button fly catches the light and directs the eye. *Out Front*, May 6, 1977. Western History Collection. Courtesy of Denver Public Library.

At the time, gay male masculinity was, more than anything else, about dressing the part. And the part usually involved denim. The macho clone look, which developed in the 1970s, appropriated the accoutrements of the working class: work boots, jeans, flannel shirts, and facial hair, usually a mustache. Think of the Village People's costumes, except the "Indian." Levi's connoted men who worked with their hands, as did Wranglers, Dickies, and Dungarees. Therefore, the gay male preference for Levi's 501s was based on the style of their cut and the weave of their denim.[1] Marketed as "shrink to fit," 501s were believed to cup the wearer's basket and buttocks most flatteringly, thus drawing the eye to a man's most important assets. For maximum effect, some men prepared for a night out by washing and machine drying their jeans so that the cotton would shrink to fit as tightly as possible; they would then avoiding sitting down to prevent the 501s from stretching out again. Longer-term strategies included spraying the crotch area with water and scrubbing the denim with a firm brush or sandpaper to distress the fabric for better transparency; some men also used bleach. Given that many men wore their jeans without underwear (and sometimes with a cock ring), 501s also eliminated the risk of getting pubic hair or skin caught in a zipper. The preference for 501s grew exponentially, and they became a canonical gay cultural reference.[2]

So many bars were called "Levi/leather bars" that they became their own variation on the leather bar. Although jeans were staple attire at leather bars, they were versatile enough that they were *also* standard fare in country-western gay bars, another emergent genre of bar that prized performances of masculinity. At the Triangle Lounge, 501s skillfully straddled these leather and western fetishes. In fact, the Triangle's precursor Don's Alley ran an ad intermixing these styles with a drawing of a man wearing a cowboy hat *and* a black leather jacket accessorizing his jeans.[3] Seventy percent of the Triangle's patrons donned Levi's. There, women were effectively shunned, and in conversation men policed each other's comportment by addressing anyone who seemed too effeminate as "Miss Thing" or "Mary."[4] Such blatant misogyny operated in service of reclaiming gay men's masculinity and in constructing an all-male world for public sex.

Back rooms and basements—spaces dedicated to and effectively sanctioning public sex—became pervasive and part of the everyday of gay male urban life (see also chapters 1 and 5). Not every bar had a back room, nor did every gay man engage in these activities. But both became core to the emergent culture and imaginary of gay male life. In many cities, on-site sexual activities enacted a liberation politics; although the activities may not have been strictly permitted under the law, men claimed the right to do so as vice raids abated. In my experience, public sex practices and prohibitions vary by city, depending on degrees of local policing. Yet public sex practices have also evolved under the influence of other cultural factors, including public health crises, competition from hook-up apps, increased gender integration (and variance) in venues, and changing norms about consent and touch between strangers.

In Denver specifically, a culture of public sex followed the first significant local gay-rights activism, which mobilized in direct response to the criminalization of sex. In 1972 Colorado became one of only five US states to decriminalize sodomy. Or so it seemed. More accurately, the legislature changed the archaic language "crimes against nature" to "deviate sexual intercourse."[5] The state law revision prompted the city council to update its ordinances and coincided with city police's escalating practices of entrapment. The existing city code considered any sex act outside of heterosexual marriage as equivalent to prostitution and criminalized public verbal consent to sex, even if the sex acts would happen in private.[6] This portion of the law was regularly used to entrap men seeking sex with other men without need for physical contact. The state capitol grounds were a popular cruising spot known as "sodomy circle" and were outside local jurisdiction; vice cops would lure and arrest men when they stepped onto city turf. In December 1972 a Denver judge dismissed thirty-two cases against entrapped men, claimed that the city's law was unconstitutional, and "advised Denver police not to make any more arrests under it." Nonetheless, "arrests of homosexuals soared . . . [as a] police backlash against the court ruling."[7]

In 1973 the Gay Coalition of Denver (GCOD) organized to influence the mayor and the city council on both the law and police practices; it drew a crowd of nearly three hundred citizens to a public hearing and submitted comments on new ordinance drafts. (The city law that went into effect in 1974 reflected limited success for the gay lobby.)[8] Concurrently in 1973, the GCOD filed a lawsuit against the city and county of Denver and various local officials as a "class action" against vice-officer practices.[9] The GCOD and the city reached an agreement in fall 1974, to be reviewed after one year. As the *Advocate* reported, "By a written legal agreement, unprecedented for any municipality in the U.S., the Denver Police Department has agreed to end harassment against Gays."[10] The agreement stipulated nondiscrimination in policing and prosecuting local sex laws, and it determined "that conduct such as kissing, hugging, dancing, holding hands between members of the same sex shall not be deemed the basis for an arrest under the provisions of any public indecency law." In addition, it created a position for the city's first liaison between the police department and the gay community.[11] In Denver as elsewhere, legal enforcement—rather than laws per se—seemed to condition what bars and clubs allow to happen on site.

In 1978 the Triangle opened a basement space that became the city's most infamous venue for gay public sex. When a reporter for *Drummer* traveled to Denver to offer one of magazine's signature hot-blooded travelogues, he made the Triangle his primary stop. If you'll indulge me a lengthy excerpt, you won't regret it:

> One tall, slim guy in front of me caught my eye just as I was working on the fantasy [of a real cowboy]. He had on a Stetson hat and rugged, worn jeans. I could barely make out the cowboy boots on his feet [because the basement was so dark].... Thinking about the ass that for sure rode on saddles during the week. I was nearly drooling over him, waiting for him to turn and catch my eye when I felt a hand rest on my butt.
> ... I could feel the well-known presence of leather on the arms and legs of the figure as it moved in closer behind me. A hard cock pushed through his crotch against my mounds, his hands went to my waist and pulled me in further.
> Just then the Cowboy began to notice me.... The cowboy didn't waste any time. He moved backwards and got into position to place a hand right on my crotch....
> They hadn't noticed each other yet. I could tell neither was aware that another man had been working on me. I almost laughed at that part of their cruising—being so cool and making believe that there was nothing special going on that they couldn't really see one another.
> I used all of my manual dexterity, and used both hands to open each of the button-fly jeans at once. Their hot flesh popped out of their openings at the same time, and I stood there stroking on two of the most beautiful poles I had ever felt. Carefully, and slowly, so they wouldn't get suspicious, I pulled each one by his cock until I had them in position and then I dove down and swallowed the two pricks at once, pushing the limits of my mouth's expansion to accommodate both of them. The sweat [sic] taste of two men inside my mouth sent me into orbits of sexual pleasure. I barely noticed the two of them stiffen their bodies as they realized what was going on. I lifted my eyes just in time to see them staring at one another: the cowboy and the leatherman, each of their cocks in the same mouth. They hesitated for a moment while I stared up. And then a small smile came across the leatherman's face as he reached over and dragged the cowboy into a tight, clutching embrace.[12] *this was hot as fuck, omg*

This gonzo journalist acknowledges that make-believe mediates the experiences of the gay bar, yet he has an eye for details that make the fantasy seem tangible: both the cowboy and the leatherman were clad in button-fly jeans. The magazine's stories were often illustrated by photos of the shenanigans inside bars, but this one was accompanied instead by a reproduction of the Triangle's iconic ad.

Despite—or perhaps reacting to—scenes like this one from *Drummer*, "incidents of police and vice-squad abuse reached epidemic proportions" in 1979. Indeed, although the city was gaining national attention as a gay mecca, vice-cop harassment and entrapment escalated once again.[13] A gay community task force formed to meet with the city's commission on community relations. The task force's recommendations effectively asked for renewal of the 1974 agreement between the city and the gay community, in addition to recruiting gays to apply for the police force, among other issues.[14]

The Triangle Lounge carried on until 2007. A 1999 compendium of Colorado's (mostly straight) bar history included the bar, remarking a bit skittishly, "Beware: This place is not for the squeamish."[15] A decade after the original Triangle shuttered, new proprietors opened a restaurant and bar on the site, reclaiming its name but reflecting a significantly gentrified scene with craft cocktails, locally sourced "farm to bar food," and an "elevated experience."[16] When I passed through the Mile High City again in 2020, I made a special pilgrimage to the new Triangle, but its basement was inaccessible except through the stories I had previously found in the archive.

May there be other spaces like it again soon (if there are not already ;)).

2

Show Me Love

Female Impersonation and Drag in Kansas City

When Esther Newton traveled to the Show-Me State (Missouri) to conduct research in the mid-1960s for what would become her field-making study *Mother Camp: Female Impersonators in America*, there were two nightclub venues in town featuring female impersonators and drag queens, respectively: the Jewel Box Lounge and the Colony Bar. These two venues were located only one block apart, were owned by the same people, and even featured some of the same performers, yet they were understood to cater to different audiences.[1] The Jewel Box marketed to straight tourists and slummers (see figure 2.1), whereas the Colony Bar billed itself as the oldest gay bar in the city. These two sites' proximity and contrast help to articulate the boundaries of what was then recognized as a gay venue and what was *not*. Whereas a few decades earlier gender play flourished in ambiguously mixed clubs (see the introduction), by the 1960s, gay bars operated as distinctly gay milieu and produced their own specific subcultural forms, such as leather and drag.

Drag, in distinction to female impersonation, became a gay bar staple in the 1960s as a shared audience expression of gay sensibility; the relationship

JEWEL BOX LOUNGE
3219 TROOST LO. 1—2905

K. C.'S MOST UNUSUAL
SHOWS 8:45 • 10:20 • 11:55
SATURDAY 8:45•10:00•11:15•12:20

CLOSE COVER BEFORE STRIKING

AMERICAN MATCH CO. KANSAS CITY, MO.

FIGURE 2.1 Matchbook for the Jewel Box Lounge featuring headshots of its femme mimic cast, including Skip Arnold (*second from right*). The marketing euphemistically bills it "K.C.'s most unusual." In contrast, the Colony Bar's matchbooks proclaim it "the GAYEST spot in town." Courtesy of the Gay and Lesbian Archive of Mid-America, University of Missouri–Kansas City.

between the performers and their fans marked these bars as *gay*. The terms *female impersonation* and *drag* have historically been used interchangeably, but in this chapter I use them differentially to distinguish between acts performed for predominantly straight audiences (for which I use *female impersonation*) and those for predominantly gay ones (for which I use *drag*). Female impersonation comes out of a vaudeville tradition, whereas drag has historically been a gay male cultural practice in the contexts of private parties and bars. Female impersonators, sometimes called female illusionists or femme mimics, worked by testing the credulity of the straight audience with a skillful masquerade of gender verisimilitude; in contrast, drag has by and large foregrounded the incongruity of a man in a dress—which makes it camp.[2] (The term *drag queen* has been used to reference any gay man who dressed up like a woman in public, regardless of whether they were performers.)[3] This bifurcation was long-standing, although these distinctions were porous in practice.

Female impersonation appears to have waned in popularity with straight audiences contemporaneously with the rise of gay liberation, which redefined the public image of homosexuality on its own terms. Drag performances were then newly assumed to be the exclusive province of the gay community, which harbored ambivalent feelings about drag yet felt protective of it when straight audiences continued to show up to see performances. Complicating this historical bifurcation, drag pageants developed concurrently with but separately from drag in gay bars, yet largely maintained

DRAG IN KANSAS CITY   69

female impersonation's emphases on femininity, glamour, and talent. In turn, earning pageant titles helps performers gain bookings and higher appearance fees in gay clubs.[4]

Both female impersonation and drag typically presumed a cis-male–identified person donning female-coded attire, but cross-dressing, female impersonation, and drag have also long offered ways for performers to explore gender and have provided pathways to transitioning. Performing has also long presented a viable way for trans performers to earn a living. Thus, though often performed and understood within binary frameworks—male/female, straight/gay—these forms and performers are often more fluid in lived reality and open to a range of identities and identifications. Ironically, when they read others, drag queens and trans women can also at times be especially rigid in defining who measures up in terms of femininity or womanhood.

What emerges in this history of drag is the idea that the audience and its context as much as the performers or the show's content determined what counted as straight and gay. Newton was inspired to conduct her research after she first saw drag queen Skip Arnold perform at a gay bar in Chicago; as she recalls in her memoir, "My head raced around with the power of what I had seen: Skip looking down from the stage at his rapt audience, who were giving back an energy that ricocheted around the performance space and through our bodies."[5] The beauty of drag exists not only in the opulence of a dress or the elegance of a gesture but also in the enlivening affects it manifests in a crowd. As Kareem Khubchandani theorizes, "A drag queen doesn't just perform, she incites performance" from the participating audience.[6]

Drag operated then and now to constitute a queer public with a shared sensibility—typically doing so through the vernacular of camp—that differed from the long history of female impersonation in straight contexts. Whereas camp teased the limits of leather masculinity in the previous chapter, in this chapter it provides the core of drag culture. Gay male drag has been critiqued by some second-wave feminists as misogynist, yet, as Jeremy Atherton Lin has averred, "A drag queen—a good drag queen—is not there to mock women, but to transcend the limitations of masculinity."[7] Drag performers and audiences cherish feminine excess with adoration, not derision. Although the theory of sexual inversion and its colloquial phrasing as "a woman trapped in a man's body" now seem archaic, drag queens nonetheless routinely express that drag reveals their inner selves.

In Oscar Wildean logic, it's a drag queen's masquerade that allows her to express an incisive truth that resonates with her faithful fans.

My research for this chapter revealed that the integration of drag queens into the gay bar developed out of an intersecting set of factors and practices of differentiation, including a shift from impersonation to drag, the emergence of an imagined and politicized gay audience, and an insider's camp mode of address. Drag queens regularly appeared at a few gay bars in San Francisco, Chicago, and Kansas City by the time of Newton's study, but the key point here is that they were not yet as ubiquitous in nor as exclusive to gay venues as they would soon become. In part, the increasing number, differentiation, and scale of gay bars and nightclubs helped to accommodate drag performances, particularly with the rise of super-bars and discos with sufficient space and sound systems in the 1970s. The proliferation of gay venues happened concurrently with the waning popularity of female-impersonator revues and show lounges marketed to straight audiences. Belated changes in local enforcement or repeal of cross-dressing laws likewise made drag shows a more viable endeavor across the country. Finally, a paradigm shift emerged in the craft itself between the 1960s and '70s, with a transition from female impersonators and impressionists who sang live to a new generation of queens who lip-synched to records, a change that made drag much more accessible as a performance form and logistically easier to integrate into gay bars and dance clubs.

Although there were precursors and occasional examples of drag queens in gay bars before the 1960s, drag did not become common in gay bars and nightclubs until the 1960s and became increasingly prevalent in subsequent decades. Rather than a singular historical turning point, however, there appear to be multiple local time lines for drag's development in gay bars. For instance, Atlanta's emergence as a drag capital during the 1970s was contemporaneous with the form's waning popularity in Kansas City.[8]

Drag's popularity has been cyclical, but it has never disappeared completely from gay bars. As drag evolved to include genderfuck and other liberation-era variations alongside more traditional modes, it thrived during much of the 1970s, only to fall out of favor by the decade's end.[9] A generation later, a new queer political sensibility embraced drag as hip in the early 1990s (see chapter 7 on this new generational sensibility).[10] Stalwart drag queens also volunteered their labor for endless charity benefits for AIDS service organizations and other causes in the 1980s, 1990s, and 2000s throughout the ups and downs of the form's popularity. Then

DRAG IN KANSAS CITY   71

drag brought men *back* to bars in the 2010s with *RuPaul's Drag Race*. The gay bar and nightclub now seem unimaginable without drag as integral to their cultures, but one of the epiphanies for me while researching this project was that this wasn't always the case.

False Eyelashes: Histories of Female Impersonation and Drag

Not until the 1960s did female impersonation shift to what we now recognize as drag: gay-identified men lip-synching in predominantly gay bars and nightclubs.[11] Although this appears to be true to a large extent, the history of drag and its relationship to queerness are more complex than this, and female-impersonation revues playing to predominantly straight audiences continued for decades. Kansas City demonstrates the coexistence of this female impersonation/drag dichotomy. Furthermore, anxieties about female impersonation and claims that the venues for it were *not gay* helped to define self-proclaimed gay bars in the 1960s in contradistinction.

Numerous histories of female (and male) impersonation position drag as part of a centuries-old typology of theatrical performance.[12] The term *drag* has apocryphally been cited as a Shakespearean-era acronym for performers "dressed resembling a girl." Two centuries after the tradition of men playing women's roles in Anglo stage dramas ended, female impersonation rose to popularity in the mid-nineteenth century in the contexts of the American minstrel show and vaudeville and the British music hall.[13] In these contexts the biggest stars were avowedly heterosexual— as exemplified by Julian Eltinge in the early twentieth century—and the marvel of the attraction was that a man could enact a femininity that in no way reflected upon his own gender or sexuality.[14] Vocal performance in vaudeville worked much the same way, with singers performing a range of gendered, classed, and racialized vocal styles that were understood *not* to reflect their identities; rather than an authentic reflection of interior life, these performances were understood to be "in character" and evidence of the vocalists' dexterity.[15]

From the mid-nineteenth century through the mid-twentieth, dozens of cities had laws forbidding cross-dressing. Such laws typically stipulated that people had to wear at least three articles of clothing corresponding to their sex assigned at birth; the laws became pretexts to criminalize butch women, effeminate men, and trans and nonbinary people in vice arrests on the streets and in bars.[16] Ironically, these laws were enforced contemporaneously with the massive popularity of female impersonation. In many localities female impersonation was permitted onstage as an amusement but not in the audience, in the barroom, or on the street. A performer could even be arrested for stepping off the stage and mixing with the audience.[17] In some cities performances were tolerated in theaters but not in cabarets where alcohol was served. In Los Angeles belated enforcement signaled reactionary shifts in policing gender normativity starting in the 1930s and escalating in the 1940s; even former toast of the town Eltinge had to alter his comeback act by performing next to mannequins modeling his gowns rather than wearing them himself.[18] One effect of these laws was that performers typically asserted normative gender and sexuality offstage, which worked to deflect queer connotations from the art form or its stars. Female-impersonation acts and their promotional materials often worked to entrench and police normative genders and sexualities more than they parodied them.[19] In effect, onstage performances of gender illusion did not signal transgender or homosexual identities, whereas offstage cross-dressing did.

Well into the postwar period, publicity for performers routinely—perhaps even more vociferously—espoused homophobic and effemiphobic attitudes to dispel speculation about their offstage identities and behaviors, which indicates that audiences began to conflate performers and their characters. Nonetheless, by the mid to late 1960s, more performers openly identified as gay, and some began transitioning gender medically.[20] At this time, more-established performers, who tended to maintain conventional gender presentations offstage, derided "street fairies" and "street impersonators" (the in-community terms of the time, the latter referenced people who would likely identify as trans today). Street fairies and impersonators were also reputedly more likely to hustle and to take "pills"; stage performers, as a sign of professionalism, preferred the legitimacy of alcohol (and alcoholism).[21] Gigs were typically undercompensated and inconsistent, and often required moving around. Female impersonation was among the few career paths available to trans women, yet jobs were precarious if performers transitioned precisely because the genre's marketing insisted upon the premise that the performers were *men* playing women.[22] At the Jewel Box Lounge as at other such clubs, performers were expected to enter and exit the venue as men, and they were expected to embody a convincing *illusion* of gender.[23] As many as five hundred professional full-time female impersonators worked in the United States around 1966.²⁴

Contrasting this history of onstage female impersonation, two popular public forms of gender transgression intersect with its history. First, drag balls, dating from the 1890s and booming in the 1920s and 1930s, offered massive public events that appropriated the masquerade balls and cotillions of the straight world and made them fully queer. These functions effectively democratized drag: the *crowd* cross-dressed, not just the entertainers. Second, the Prohibition-era pansy craze, contemporaneous with the drag balls' peak, brought androgynous drag-adjacent queer performance into the speakeasy, with men dolled up with makeup and effeminate mannerisms but masculine evening wear. Pansy performers ranged between exploitative straight men who would "mimic and ridicule gay men" for slumming audiences and "fairies" who performed dandified versions of themselves for more integrated bohemian ones. The legendary queer pansy performer Jean Malin would step off the stage to engage the audience directly; he would savage straight audience members with his cutting wit, a prototypical use of reading (a queer art of insult) that drag queens have employed ever after.²⁵ As the legendary "male actress" and female celebrity impressionist Charles Pierce recounted, "Until the night club came along in the '30s, 'homo' was not inevitably attached to female impersonation. The female impersonation image was shattered when impersonators were forced to fraternize with customers."²⁶

After the waning of vaudeville and the shorter-lived pansy craze, ensemble female impersonator revues developed in the late 1930s and boomed in popularity again by the 1950s. Across these contexts, female impersonation was often promoted and received like an exotic freakshow attraction, and its resurgent popularity during the Cold War seems to have reflected a fascination with gender and sexual deviance at a time of normativity and repression. The number of venues featuring female impersonators doubled between 1950 and 1954, and by 1962, "several dozen" female impersonation companies were touring the United States and "playing to record crowds."²⁷ By comparison, there were but a handful of dedicated female-impersonator show lounges across the country, most notably Finocchio's in San Francisco, the My-O-My in New Orleans, the 82 Club in New York, and the Jewel Box Lounge in Kansas City.

The Jewel Box Lounge was a product of the 1960s. It was neither the first nor the most famous female-impersonator theater or revue. Finocchio's and the Jewel Box Revue touring company (no relation to the

Lounge in Kansas City), based in Miami and later New York City, both claimed more longevity and national notoriety. Finocchio's was initially a speakeasy; after a move to a larger venue in 1936, it expanded its cast of female impersonators and the lavishness of its costumes and sets.[28] In the process it transitioned from an intimate cabaret to a theatrical spectacle. Over the decades, Finocchio's performed for up to three hundred thousand audience members per year, half of whom arrived via Gray Line bus tours.[29]

Danny Brown and Doc Benner established the Jewel Box Revue in Miami in 1939; the company performed in residence there for the winter season and toured in summers to nightclubs, fairs, and carnivals. As the troupe's popularity grew, it expanded the revue to two touring companies and moved the booking office to New York by the late 1950s.[30] By the 1960s, the revue tour began performing exclusively in theaters rather than nightclubs, which allowed for larger audiences, avoided potential legal skirmishes, and disassociated the show with gay bars; this transition was also driven by the fact that nightclubs as live performance venues were succumbing to competition from television.[31] The Jewel Box Revue boasted more than 2.5 million audience members during its engagements at seven different New York metropolitan-area venues in 1959 alone. By the mid-1960s, its touring company played more than eighty venues across North America, performing thirteen shows per week.[32]

Female-impersonation revues varied in cast size but generally featured a range of different kinds of solo acts, bookended by opening and closing group production numbers. In some revues the opening number presented the ensemble getting into drag to prove that the performers were men. Newton identified four types of female impersonation: glamour (beauty and femininity), singing (vocal talent and impressions), dancing (ballet toe dancers or burlesque), and comedy (stand-up or slapstick).[33] Typically, each ensemble cast member performed a specific type of impersonation so that the show became a revue of different kinds of acts. These revues also sometimes included male dancers, who were billed as "boy-lesque" performers. The touring Jewel Box Revue regularly billed itself as "25 boys and 1 girl"; the girl was a male impersonator, master of ceremonies Stormé DeLarverie, who may have ignited the Stonewall riots. In addition to these different styles of female impersonation, the revues were often multiracial. The effect of this inclusive casting was contradictory: on the one hand, such revues made queer men of color more visible than probably any other public venue and presented a relatively integrated worldview; on the other hand, they were tokenized, and production numbers often traded in Orientalism. Further complicating questions of representation, white Jewel Box Revue headliner Lynn Carter performed celebrated vocal impressions of Pearl Bailey and Josephine Baker that showed off both his virtuosity and the constructedness of how voices are racialized and gendered.[34] In the case of the touring Jewel Box Revue, its multicultural cast also allowed the troupe to play in both racially unmarked theaters and historically black venues known as "the chitlin' circuit."[35] By the Jewel Box Revue's later days, an African American female-impersonator quartet called the Pearl Box Revue (featuring Dorian Corey) also toured and released a record titled *Call Me MISSter*.[36]

Although the basic conception for the onstage shows appears to have been comparable between touring acts and fixed show lounges, there were significant distinctions between the two. For theatrical tours such as the Jewel Box Revue, the show itself was the primary attraction with minor merchandising tie-ins, such as extensively illustrated souvenir programs. In contrast, cabaret venues featured live entertainment to sell as many high-priced cocktails as possible. Performers in show lounges engaged more directly with audiences and were often required to hustle customers into buying drinks between acts; they earned much of their income as commissions on the bar tabs.[37] In addition to differing business models, the tenor differed between the relatively staid theater venues and the comparatively more risqué acts and tipsy audiences in nightclubs.

Here I focus at some length on the touring Jewel Box Revue because it not only created the most influential template for female-impersonator shows in the twentieth century; it also informed public discourses about its audiences. The revue's content was typically deemed unobjectionable, but the tour did stoke anxieties about the queer people it attracted, such as during its popular but curtailed runs in Minneapolis in 1949 and again in 1955. Acknowledging that "there are no legal grounds on which the show could be closed," the Minneapolis police nonetheless asked the show to leave town at the end of its contract in early 1950.[38] This intervention, in the absence of any obscenity or relevant ordinances, effectively sought to preempt the development of a gay scene. Minneapolis then implemented a ban on female-impersonation shows, which it lifted five years later to allow for the revue to return. Newspaper ads for the show's return engagement hailed it as "the GAYest Show in Town." During its second short run, two men were arrested in separate incidents in downtown Minneapolis for cross-dressing; the Revue was blamed for inducing these gender outlaws.[39]

By the end of the decade, trade press reviews of the show repeatedly referenced gay life offstage. In 1958 *Variety* remarked that the "soprano-hipped kids just walking around being themselves" in Greenwich Village, where "AC-DCers aren't confined by a script," provided a better show than the Jewel Box Revue.[40] In successive reviews the same critic made clear that he perceived the show and its crowd as queer, with remarks such as "it's evident that the kids create a gay atmosphere," "it is so gay, all of it," and "it's an even better show in the audience."[41] By the 1960s, female impersonation was connotatively queer even if its audiences were still predominantly heterosexual, or at least female. One account suggested that the audience was 90 percent women. The revue ceased performing in 1975.[42]

For the most part, both tours and show lounges deflected gay identities. Nonetheless, historians have recovered a few notable exceptions. In a loving account of the Garden of Allah in Seattle, the authors affirm that it was the first gay-owned cabaret in the city. Its 1946 opening night featured the touring Jewel Box Revue; from the start, the venue sought to negotiate its appeal to both straight slummers and queer audiences.[43] The venue closed in 1956: these shows were already losing their appeal with local gay patrons. Around this time, bars across the country were becoming more codified as exclusively gay by, in part, *excluding* both drag performances and so-called drags (trans patrons). Yet, in San Francisco during the 1950s, the Black Cat was the queerer counterpoint to Finocchio's and became gay through José Sarria's drag performances. Although straight allies and gawkers attended, the Black Cat was *culturally* gay in that "Sarria addressed everyone, without discrimination, as if they were gay."[44] (See plate 5.) By the mid-1950s, drag personality Michelle likewise began a decades-long career as hostess at other Frisco gay bars and events.[45]

Decades later, the sexuality of the venues where female impersonators and drag queens perform continues to be ambiguous and contested. A millennial study of drag queens at Key West's 801 Cabaret found different interpretations of the space, with the most accurate likely being that patrons entered and passed through a gay bar to get to the second-story cabaret; the cabaret was not defined as a gay bar itself but as a mixed venue that insisted its patrons at least be gay-friendly.[46] This account mirrors my own early experience and contemporaneous debates about the LaFemme Lounge and drag show (previously named the Casablanca Show Lounge) on the second floor of the Gay 90's super-bar complex in Minneapolis in the mid to late 1990s. Inside Dallas's S4, the Rose Room—the nation's largest purpose-built drag theater inside a gay club—operates much the same way today. These venues often attract straight "tourists" and especially bachelorette parties, provoking tensions about the invasion and de-gaying of queer spaces. These shows replicate the prior history of female audiences for impersonation revues and relying upon their financial patronage.

[handwritten annotation: Yeah, I think it's tricky. I get wanting to have queer-only spaces. But 1) sometimes queer-only isn't enough to keep a business running 2) many straight, cis people are very supportive and respectful.]

Walk on the Wild Side: The Jewel Box Lounge and the Colony Bar

Kansas City, like most US cities, had seen female impersonators—though documentation is limited—dating back to the nineteenth-century vaudeville stage. In the early twentieth century, "Kansas City became nationally known as a 'Wide Open Town'—a place that skirted Prohibition laws and let its nightlife extend well into the day."[47] The city had hosted a jazz-age nightclub called Dante's Inferno, which opened the day that Prohibition ended in 1933 and featured impersonators.[48] Female impersonation had effectively disappeared from Kansas City nightlife by World War II, but the Jewel Box Lounge revived its popularity in the 1960s.[49]

Kansas City revised the local law that had made cross-dressing a misdemeanor in 1946 by changing the law to forbid "indecent" dress and leaving the offense open to interpretation. Yet it remained illegal to employ or serve alcohol to homosexuals in the city until 1976.[50] In contrast to cities where local gay political activism started in response to police harassment and mafia ownership of bars, in Kansas City the *vitality* of bars attracted early gay-rights organizers despite the bars' technical illegality. Coincidentally, the same year that Newton conducted her research, the Phoenix Society for Individual Freedom formed as the first homophile organization in Kansas City after hosting the National Planning Conference of Homophile Organizations.[51] This literally made Kansas City the center of national gay political organizing, circa 1966. San Francisco Mattachine leader Hal Call, who had previously lived in Kansas City, suggested it as the location for the conference specifically because its gay bar and drag scene "made the city a safer place to visit" than St. Louis (the alternate location considered) and "rivaled the nation's coastal metropolises."[52] Seeming to concur, the following year another California organizer called the city "wild" and said, "I expected Kansas City to be a small Midwestern town, but found that I was from a much more backward 'midwestern' town—Los Angeles."[53]

The Jewel Box Lounge originally opened in 1945 as a straight neighborhood bar. Reportedly inspired by some prankster drunks in wigs who stormed the stage one night and brought down the house, the owner transitioned the venue into a femme-mimic show bar in 1960. As providence would have it, the joint already shared the name of the most famous touring female-impersonator troupe in America; the revue does not appear to have ever played Kansas City. The Jewel Box Lounge promised the glamour and sophistication of nightclubs on the cosmopolitan coasts and evoked a heritage of stage performance. The production was a staged affair, and audiences were seated at tables. Audiences could purchase souvenir programs and even expandable cardboard fan postcards with images of the cast.[54] (See plate 6.)

Retrospective accounts offer a sense of the scene at the Jewel Box, inside and out. The venue "resembled a high school auditorium. Upon entering, the doorway was draped with curtains and plants, and adorned with two huge white columns and a white, headless Adonis statue, holding the head of a man with one hand and the head of a woman with the other." The account continues: "The stage floor was elevated five and a half feet off the floor . . . with curtains drawn around it. The shows consisted of female impersonators who sang live (no lip synching) and . . . in true Queen form, The Jewel Box had a genuine aura of theatre."[55] At its peak, the lounge hosted three shows nightly and four on Saturdays; it was closed on Mondays. This audience-churning repeat-performance schedule was typical of such venues. Even with so many shows, "It was not unusual on a Friday or Saturday night to have to stand for two hours at the tail end of a line that stretched around the corner for over three or more blocks, if you forgot to make your reservations."[56]

The Jewel Box Lounge hailed different headlining stars during its run. Skip Arnold debuted in Kansas City at the Colony Bar in 1959 before being hired as the first performer for the Jewel Box Lounge (see figure 2.2); Arnold also became one of the primary informants for Newton's *Mother Camp*.[57] Therefore, Arnold was a crossover figure in a transitional period for the meaning of drag. He came to Kansas City after previously performing in San Francisco and would later have extended engagements in Chicago and Fort Lauderdale. Arnold always performed with his own voice rather than lip-synching and performed under his own name rather than a feminine alter ego. He was a comedy queen, launching spontaneous audience insults; his masterful ability to read audiences worked as a strategy to win over gay audiences and to neutralize straight ones. Arnold was arguably

FIGURE 2.2 Skip Arnold (*seated*) with the Jewel Box Lounge cast decked out in synthetic and metallic fabrics, circa 1972–74. Tommy Temple appears on the right; other performers are unidentified. Olene Crowley Collection. Courtesy of the Gay and Lesbian Archive of Mid-America, University of Missouri–Kansas City.

the most visible gay figure on the Kansas City scene during the 1960s and characterized Kansas City's gays as "a 'closety' group."[58]

Perhaps the most infamous headliner at the Jewel Box Lounge was Mexican American vaudeville veteran Rae Bourbon, who was already in his seventies by the time of his residency. (He had first performed in the city in 1934.) Bourbon performed at Finocchio's in the 1930s and toured with Mae West in the 1940s, then claimed to have had a "sex-change" operation in Mexico as a publicity stunt in the mid-1950s. His biography is fascinatingly contradictory and ultimately tragic, and his self-fabulation confounds the traditional categories of sex, gender, sexuality, and nationality.[59] Bourbon's act featured bawdy humor and double entendres, as documented in his 1964 live album *A Trick Ain't Always a Treat*, which he recorded at the Jewel Box Lounge and released as a novelty record. At the end of the show, Bourbon would come out dressed as a haggard cleaning lady named Mavis and make derisive commentary about the previous performers—in effect offering a classed critique of the previous acts' aspirational pageantry. Bourbon's career transcended different eras of female impersonation and to some extent satirized its norms.

Female impersonation and drag not only perform gender but also race (including whiteness) and class (from elegance to white trash, regal to ratchet).[60] In the photographs and ephemera I've seen in the archive, the Jewel Box Lounge troupe was predominantly white, in contrast with the casting of the touring Jewel Box Revue. Newton remarks that Kansas City was more segregated and its female impersonators and gay scene more exclusively white than in Chicago.[61] I have found accounts of three African American performers between the 1960s and early '70s—Ronnie Winter, Godiva, and Mr. Gerri—each of whom expressed that they endured hostility there. Perhaps signaling a shift, performer Edye Gregory was prominently featured in the publicity for the venue in the mid-1970s.[62] I have not found evidence of alternative local venues for drag of color contemporaneous with the Jewel Box; earlier, however, there had been venues in the Black entertainment district at 18th and Vine that featured performers in the 1920s and '30s.[63]

In its early days the Jewel Box Lounge *did* operate as a de facto gay bar for a brief time before it began attracting a suburban audience. It also solicited talent nationwide by taking out ads in gay periodicals that searched for "unusual" nightclub acts alongside female impersonators, singers, comics, and dancers.[64] In 1965 *Citizen News*, based in San Francisco, not only listed it first among Kansas City venues but also compared it favorably to Finocchio's; the writer also observed that the art form was waning, calling the venue "one of the last of the first class establishments offering a complete drag revue."[65] The phrasing here is telling, noting a transition in the form and the embrace of "drag" in gay vernacular. In the mid-1960s the lounge was adjoined by two venues featuring cis-female entertainers: the Cat Balleu burlesque club and later the Yum-Yum strip club (which *Citizen News* called "artfully directed"). The three venues were advertised both individually and collectively as "Mid-America's Greatest Fun Complex" and as an "Internationally Famous Slumming Spot" in the local press and on matchbooks (see figure 2.3).[66] The opening of the Yum-Yum effectively eroded much of the Jewel Box's respectability and began transitioning the club's audience away from middle-class couples toward traveling businessmen looking for a thrill.[67] The Colony Bar was located on the next block and shared the same owner, yet it was not included in this marketing because it was understood to serve a gay clientele, in contrast to the Jewel Box Lounge.

FIGURE 2.3 The Jewel Box Lounge marketed, alongside the adjoining Cat Balleu burlesque club and Yum-Yum strip club, as "Mid-America's Greatest Fun Complex" for straight slummers. *Kansas City Times*, December 31, 1965. Courtesy of the Gay and Lesbian Archive of Mid-America, University of Missouri–Kansas City.

In the early 1970s the owners moved the Jewel Box Lounge from Troost Avenue to Main Street in reaction to shifting racial politics in the city as well as anxieties about urban decay. Troost was long understood as a racial dividing line in the city. In April 1968, Kansas City was among dozens of cities to erupt in civil unrest in the wake of the assassination of Martin Luther King Jr. The neighborhood surrounding the original Jewel Box Lounge subsequently experienced white flight, and its core audience of straight white patrons perceived the area as unsafe. In contrast to the first location's elegance, the latter-day location was smaller and exemplified 1970s tackiness. At the second location, the owners also opened an adjoining straight strip club—this time called the Pink Garter Strip-O-Rama—and painted the complex hot pink.[68] Despite the move and continued press coverage, business at the Jewel Box never fully recovered. Nightclubs with live entertainment were struggling across the city, and owners pinned their hopes on a new convention center reviving the market.[69] The show dwindled to half its heyday cast—from eight to four performers—and finally transitioned from live singing to lip-synching (see figure 2.4). When the Jewel Box Lounge closed,

FIGURE 2.4 Jewel Box Lounge cast onstage at the club's second location in 1976. Edye Gregory appears on the left; other performers are unidentified. Olene Crowley Collection. Courtesy of the Gay and Lesbian Archive of Mid-America, University of Missouri–Kansas City.

in 1982, the local newspaper described the venue as "a decaying Kansas City landmark."[70] A Wendy's restaurant replaced the second location.

Although the original Jewel Box Lounge was part of a "sin" strip of clubs by the time Newton came to the city, it was nonetheless a much grander venue in scale and had a higher cultural status than the Colony Bar. Newton described the Colony as "a low hustling bar, where street fairies, other gay people, dating couples, and working-class men rub elbows. This club is small but has a stage and sometimes a drag queen." Bob Damron's travel guide concurred that the Colony crowd featured "'raunchy types,' often commercial" (sex workers).[71] These descriptions suggest the Colony produced a scene similar to Jacque's and the Other Side in Boston (see chapter 3). As Newton's account indicates, the crowd at the Colony Bar was more inclusive of patrons who would now likely identify as transgender, gender nonconforming, or nonbinary than most gay male bars would be in subsequent decades. This likely correlated both to live-and-let-live working-class mores and to the fact that there were few alternative venues for these patrons; such historical inclusion might

DRAG IN KANSAS CITY   83

more accurately be described as coexistence. As the number of venues expanded and as effemiphobic codes of masculinity rigidified in the gay scene, trans and gender-nonconforming patrons often became more marginalized from and within these spaces.

The Kansas City gay press touted the Colony Bar as a local institution where "drag shows got their start in Kansas City." It also euphemistically described the bar as "patronized by a most varied, interesting clientele."[72] Other gay bars operated nearby, but "the Colony broke the norm by openly advertising—with emphatic typography—in the phone book as 'the GAYest bar in town.'"[73] Similar design appears on its matchbooks. The Colony Bar attracted a circle of regulars and routinely closed on Saturdays for private afternoon tea dances, which allowed underage queer youths to dance and flout other legal constraints.[74] The owner also occasionally treated younger men—chickens—to drinks as bait for the older patrons.[75] The Colony Bar likely closed in 1973, and the building was later razed. When I walked down the block to see its former site, a woman standing on the sidewalk addressed me. "If you're going to buy up the neighborhood," she said, "you should at least say, 'Hi.'" She was right to call me out for not acknowledging her. Significantly, her remark attested that decades of disinvestment have made the area ripe for exploitative redevelopment (see chapter 3).

Ironically, the Jewel Box Lounge now looms larger in local queer memory, whereas retrospective accounts of the Colony Bar, once proclaimed as a center of gay life, are scarce. A columnist for the gay press began a series of articles on local queer history by focusing on the Jewel Box Lounge. Likewise, a bounty of materials from the Jewel Box are now housed at the fabulously named GLAMA (Gay and Lesbian Archives of Mid-America), including the personal papers of cocktail waitress Olene Crowley.[76] Because of the Jewel Box's crossover success, the owners produced more ephemera, such as souvenir fans, matchbooks, and ads; in contrast, the owners didn't reinvest money into the Colony Bar or spend nearly as much money promoting it. Thus, it has left behind less of a trace.

People Who Need People: Social Dynamics at the Clubs

Newton's study of female impersonators and drag queens was also a study of their venues, including gay bars. Although a work of anthropology, it now stands as an invaluable historical document of the social and spatial dynamics that distinguished straight and gay venues.[77] Drag queens occupy a complex status in Newton's study; they embody the stigma of homosexuality yet also, by performing glamour and wit that seemed to push back against their marginalization, came to be lionized within the gay scene—but almost exclusively within the space of the gay bar.[78]

Newton offers contrasting accounts of the same performer's reception. At the Jewel Box Lounge, the straight audience perceived headliner Skip Arnold as monstrous: "In Kansas City, I saw the... performer come down into the straight audience, and the people at the tables as he walked among them visibly shrank back. At one point he accidentally touched a seated woman, and she actually screamed out, 'Get it away from me!'" Yet when Newton saw Arnold in a gay bar in Chicago, he "came down off the stage as part of his act and held out his hands to the gay audience sitting along the bar. The people in the audience virtually climbed all over each other to touch him." Newton suggests that drag performances in gay bars, in contrast to straight venues, offer "*affirmation* of gay values" and "solidarity, familiarity, and competition between audience and performer."[79] Arnold was similarly beloved in the context of the Colony Bar.[80]

As in many accounts of mid-twentieth-century female-impersonation shows, Newton makes distinctions between the Jewel Box Lounge as a heterosexual tourist club and the Colony Bar as a gay bar. Insightfully, the distinctions between the two, as she saw them, were about cultures and customs within the venues. One of Newton's informants asserted that "a clear division can always be maintained between homosexual and 'straight' taste." The price of admission and drinks marked the Jewel Box Lounge as a destination for special occasions; patrons were seated at tables, which discouraged conversation between strangers, and the talent performed well-rehearsed and routinized shows on a stage at a remove from the audience. Newton observes of the audience that "their sitting posture emphasizes that they are spectators, not participants."[81] As late as 1975, a gay travel profile indicated that the Jewel Box operated as a freak show for much of its audience: "Many of the straights go to laugh at the gays, but if you ignore them and some of their asides, you will have a pleasant time."[82] So although a night out at the Jewel Box might have felt slightly outré to its straight audience, it also reinforced an ultimately conservative understanding of gender and sexuality.

In contrast, gay bars were *social* venues with repeat business. Significantly, the Colony Bar lacked tables and chairs, which forced patrons to stand and prompted milling around or making conversation. Although

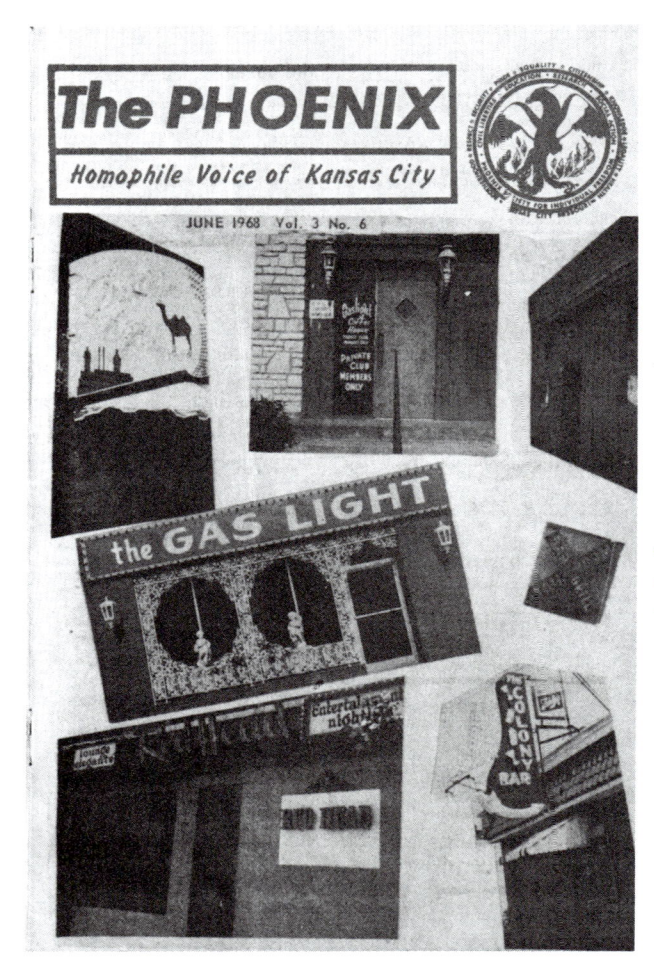

FIGURE 2.5 Kansas City gay bar facades on the cover of *Phoenix News*, June 1968. The Colony Bar appears in the bottom right corner, but the Jewel Box Lounge was excluded: it was not considered a gay venue in its time. Courtesy of the Gay and Lesbian Archive of Mid-America, University of Missouri–Kansas City.

the drinks might have been more expensive than at straight dives, the bar maintained a working-class accessibility.[83] The social norms—as well as the spatial and economic ones—likewise differed. As Newton writes, "In straight clubs, straight rules of behavior must be observed by gay people in the audience. This is enforced by the management." In gay bars, conversely, straight tourists were subject to the social customs of gay spaces. Newton further explains that "adventurous straight people do come to gay bars to see [drag shows], and they are always tolerated by the management, but sometimes meet with open hostility from the rest of the audience, especially if they are making an open issue of their straightness by holding hands or kissing. They are definitely outsiders and they are made to feel it. The performers often strengthen their solidarity with gay audiences by openly denigrating straights from the stage, thus publicly expressing the general, but sometimes unspoken, hostility."[84]

Solidarity with audiences notwithstanding, the talent generally preferred working in the tourist clubs to gay bars. The Jewel Box Lounge offered higher and more stable salaries, provided costumes, and involved far more rote labor because the shows typically changed only seasonally or annually. In addition, the tourist clubs were far less likely to be raided by police or to go out of business. By contrast, performing in gay bars paid less and often *cost* the performers more time and money. Because of repeat business in gay bars, performers could not simply recycle the same material; rather, they had to constantly devise fresh numbers, pay for new costumes, and develop improvisation skills. In addition, gay bar patrons both demanded more of performers as seasoned drag audiences yet were fickle with their attention if they were in the midst of conversations. Newton makes clear the pressures on performers in gay bars, yet at times "a powerful catharsis is effected. The atmosphere in a gay bar during a good drag performance is electric and consuming."[85] This forging of community via vicious wit and catharsis can best be explained through the concept of camp.

She's So Swishy in Her Satin and Tat: Thinking Through Camp

Drag as a gay bar form hails audiences into a feeling of communal belonging through shared space and through a shared sensibility or vernacular called *camp*. Mary, indulge your auntie, won't you, in an exegesis of camp? Camp, like beauty, is in the eye of the beholder.[86] The concept famously eludes prescriptive definition but operates via knowingness, perspective, and recognition for an insider community. Camp has influentially been called "*the* gay sensibility," with irony, aestheticism, theatricality, and humor as its basic features.[87] In a more theoretical vein, a Hollywood historian defines camp as "the ensemble of strategies used to enact a queer recognition of the incongruities arising from the cultural regulation of gender and sexuality." These "strategies for achieving ironic distance from the normative" manifest as "flamboyance ... inflected as style, taste, wit, parody, or drag."[88] Camp is intuitive and idiosyncratic, although it can also be cultivated and capacious. The active form of socially camping or "having a camp" can be "a way of being human, witty and vital, without conforming to the drabness and rigidity of the hetero male role." In its lightest form, camping simply means being amusing or queeny or over the top.[89] Camp can also work as a noun—as in a person who *is* a camp, such as virtually any drag queen worth her padding. Indicating that camp is self-evidently queer, Kansas City's local LGBTQ+ publication from 2004 to 2016 was titled *Camp*.

Although camp has been called "'our' aesthetic category,"[90] few texts can be claimed to be innately camp. Conversations about camp refute what other people construe as camp as often as they anoint what seems axiomatically so for oneself.[91] Shared adoration for old Hollywood cinema and its divas became an archive through which gay men articulated their own aspirations and sadness, discovered commonality, and honed wit as their weapon of choice. Drag performers at times perform impersonations of particular divas and gay icons: what has been called "archival drag."[92] For instance, I once saw vocal impressionist Jimmy James sing as Bette Davis in the basement cabaret of the hot-pink Casita del Campo restaurant in Los Angeles; his act exemplified camp when he performed Davis with a chain-smoker's wheeze between each phrase. (I also once saw a Dame Edna impersonator in Puerto Vallarta, which was the only time I've seen a female impersonator *impersonator*.) But more often queens construct either a generalized femininity or individual drag personas.[93] Drag and camp cultures can delight in transgressing good taste; for instance, to celebrate the release of the film of *Mommie Dearest*, a gay bar advertised—both problematically and hilariously—that "anyone dressing as Joan Crawford or as a battered child will be admitted free."[94]

Camp often has a barbed, critical quality and valorizes bitchiness. As mentioned above, drag queens use reading to discipline straight audiences and to affectionately roast queer ones. At times, it can be difficult to differentiate when drag, camp, and shade are coming from a place of love, resentment, or both.[95] Nonetheless, queens take their camp texts seriously, with both emotional attachment and humor: as "passion with irony," as Richard Dyer described gay male fandom for Judy Garland.[96] Seeming to illustrate just this point, when a gay piano bar named Camp opened in St. Paul in the 2000s, it featured an absolutely divine large-scale Madonna-and-child portrait with Garland as Mary and a baby Liza Minnelli in her *Cabaret* costume as the Christ child.[97] Camp sensibility and references sometimes transcend cultures, languages, and borders; for instance, I saw a fabulous drag queen in Guadalajara, Mexico, who called herself Ariana Grindr.

Drag remains the camp site par excellence. As an insider's vernacular, camp references may not be legible across generations or cultures, as I've learned in trying to explain camp to students. Perhaps the most accessible recent examples of camp can be found on *RuPaul's Drag Race* (2009–present), which works to educate its audience in the ways of camp and to vet its contestants' facility with it. (Some contestants clearly fail at it.) This becomes most pronounced during the recurring *Snatch Game* challenge, wherein drag and impersonation converge when the queens invoke classic gay cult personalities (such as Alaska as Mae West, Jujubee as Eartha Kitt, and Jinx Monsoon as Little Edie and Garland), play with incongruity (such as Bob the Drag Queen as *both* Carol Channing and Uzo Aduba), or transgress the political norms of what can be satirized (such as Symone as Harriet Tubman). The series' longevity has meant that whereas virtually all the queens used to hone their craft by working in gay bars or on the pageant circuit, in later seasons some queens developed via social media platforms. Some drag queens are critical of the series' influence on drag culture, from standardizing drag to creating aspiring stars whose egos have prematurely swelled before they have truly put in the work. But *Drag Race*'s impact on both drag and on gay bars is irrefutable. Across the country (including in Kansas City), viewings of *RuPaul's Drag Race*, often hosted by local talent or featuring appearances by touring *Drag Race* alumni, beckoned crowds of patrons back to gay bars at a time when these venues were otherwise deemed obsolete. The audience's communal laughter and gasps heightened the pleasures of the show and maintained a claim on drag as *ours* despite the show's crossover success.

Falling in Love Again: Kansas City Drag after the Colony Bar

After the Colony Bar closed and the Jewel Box Lounge waned, drag became less central to gay life in Kansas City during the 1970s. The Ivanhoe Cabaret, located north of downtown, effectively replaced the Colony Bar in the 1970s when it expanded into a super-bar complex with a piano bar called Brassie's, a dance club called Cabaret, and a small lesbian bar called Sapphos. The venue was marketed as "The Bar for Everyone" as a statement of intracommunity inclusion, although action would be taken against the bar for its racist door policy by 1980 (for other examples of this history, see chapter 4).[98] After several years without drag performances at gay venues, in the mid to late 1970s Bruce Winter began performing as Melinda Ryder for sporadic shows at the Ivanhoe, where he also bartended out of drag.[99] Winter initially staged these acts in the complex's smaller lesbian space until audience demand promoted them to the main room; these performances also became more frequent because of their popularity. The club relocated near the Plaza in the early 1980s, was renamed Pegasus ("Peggy Sue's"), and then later resumed the name Cabaret. Tuesdays and Wednesdays would eventually become the show nights to draw crowds on what were otherwise slow nights; each week, there would be a guest appearance by a porn star one night and a headlining drag queen visiting from out of town the other night.[100] In contrast to coastal and larger cities, the 1980s remained a party era for the gay scene in Kansas City; although sexual behaviors changed in the age of AIDS, social behaviors did not necessarily change.[101] Cabaret remained the stalwart party bar through the 1990s and beyond.

From the mid-1990s into the 2000s, drag experienced another resurgence at the Cabaret, this time via Sunday AIDS benefit beer busts featuring the Flo & Friends shows hosted by John Koop.[102] The shows, all-volunteer and all-charity, attracted weekly crowds of five hundred patrons and regularly ran for four hours. By 2000, the Cabaret had raised half a million dollars for AmFAR (American Foundation for AIDS Research)—more money than any other single venue in the country.[103] It's also during this millennial period that there was an explosion of gay clubs locally, although these venues simultaneously became more integrated, gay and straight.[104] As many as a half-dozen Kansas City venues hosted drag performances in the 2000s.

As fabulous as my findings in the GLAMA collection were, KC won me over when I went to the Dirty Dorothy show, which ran at Missie B's from 2008 to 2020 (when it ended because of the COVID-19 pandemic).[105] The titular Dorothy is a gleefully foul-mouthed lesbian from Kansas who wears a wig, a gingham dress, and red sequined shoes (Uggs, the first time I saw her) and performs in a breathy Judy Garland voice (see figure 2.6).[106] Jessica Dressler, who plays Dorothy, began the character as a party trick "because it's much funnier when you put naughty things in [Dorothy's] mouth." As Dressler remarked, before her shows, drag in Kansas City was "old-school pristine." *Her* shows featured ensembles who punked each other and their audiences, and came out of the ethos that "there's more to queer culture than just gay men in dresses as drag." Indeed, the Dirty Dorothy show offered an expansive reimagination of drag, with a commit-

FIGURE 2.6 Queering her home-state connection to Kansas, Jessica Dressler appears as Dirty Dorothy in this publicity still. As a cis female lesbian, Dressler advanced an expansive notion of who could perform as a drag queen. Missie B's, where her show ran, sits just blocks from the Missouri/Kansas state line. Photo by Ann K. Brown. Courtesy of Jessica Dressler.

ment to humor and rotating casts that included a cis female host and a cis male clown. The show combined a range of sensibilities and acts, ranging from live singing to lip-synching to performance art, and often dared the audience to participate in goofy drinking games. Dressler embraced shock and liked for things to get messy.[107]

When I saw the act for the first time—a "hangover show" on the night of January 1, 2012—it surprised me as the most fun and unexpected drag show I'd ever seen. The show began with the cast passed out onstage in front of a large papier-mâché volcano referencing the Mayans' prediction of an apocalypse in 2012. The Whore of '84 sang the opening number, "Last New Year's Eve," as a parody of Katy Perry's "Last Friday Night."[108] One of the advantages of singing live has always been that the performer could change the lyrics to include more risqué content and in-jokes. When Astro the Clown belatedly roused himself, he performed to the J. Geils Band's "Love Stinks"[109] with a chocolate pudding stain on the seat of his underwear—and eventually all over his hands. The lineup that night also

DRAG IN KANSAS CITY 91

included a powerhouse diva and a walk-of-shame comedy queen covered in condoms. Finally, Sandy Kaye, billed as "the oldest living drag queen," bridged generations and conceptions of drag. Kaye hailed from the Jewel Box Lounge, where she had performed stripteases to reveal her male chest; she even appeared in the final show there.[110] Each act embodied a distinct typology of drag, and Dressler managed up to thirty-six different performers per month for her show and other venues.[111]

On the night I first attended the Dirty Dorothy Show, the appreciative audience amplified the performers' energy. The crowd was nearly evenly mixed between lesbians and gay men, and the scene had a homecoming feel: numerous former regulars were back in town for the holidays. The crowd was predominantly white when the night began but became progressively more diverse as it grew later. Dorothy, for her part, cajoled the viewers to get as drunk as possible and ensured that there were multiple rounds of free fruity shots awarded to audience members who went onstage for various contests. When I returned to Kansas City for research at GLAMA in August 2016, I caught the midweek "chat show," loosely modeled on *The View* and featuring a scaled-down cast. Nonetheless, Dorothy remained in high spirits and congratulated the audience for being so committed to drinking that it would "fist your Thursday" by going out on a Wednesday night.

I have been struck that whereas the Dirty Dorothy Show carried on the legacy of the Colony Bar, Hamburger Mary's, a local franchise of the national drag diner/bar chain, effectively serves much the same role that the Jewel Box Lounge did in its heyday. Hamburger Mary's here, as in many cities, serves a largely straight clientele who come out for its drag bingo, brunch, and diva drag shows. As with other locations, the bingo nights are fund-raisers for various charities and continue the tradition of drag at philanthropic events. The restaurant is the most visible and accessible drag venue for audiences beyond the LGBTQ+ community and thus opens out beyond it. Because it's an all-ages venue, I suspect that it also provides many young queers with a gateway into somewhere over the rainbow.[112]

Hamburger Mary's curates a festive and slightly transgressive atmosphere (winning bingo board shapes include "hard on" and "4 hookers headed to the free clinic"), and the show's address works to include allies and tourists. The crowd typically includes groups of friends, family, or coworkers who've gathered for special occasions, such as birthday parties, bridal showers, bachelorette parties, and send-offs. The shows here conform to and affirm the audience's expectations of drag. With a full food-and-drink menu, it is effectively dinner theater. I've also learned that, as with the Jewel Box Lounge before it, the pay, the tips, and the reliability of the gig are much better than at the gay clubs.[113] When I returned to town in 2021, I took my mom to drag bingo and had the pleasure of taking a picture of her with host Ryder, a forty-five-year drag veteran in the city who identifies as a female impersonator. I would not have taken my mom to the Dirty Dorothy Show, which feels more exclusively for *us queers*.

Nonetheless, the key difference between Hamburger Mary's and the Jewel Box Lounge before it is that Hamburger Mary's is *culturally gay* by addressing everyone as though they are part of the community (much like Serria's performances at the Black Cat) and by affirming gay identities (much like Newton's account of drag in gay bars). The effect is to cross over and to welcome the straight audience *in* rather than to perform an estranging freak show or startling gender illusion. Hamburger Mary's is where impersonation and drag—as I have differentiated them—seem to converge. I have often thought dismissively of the chain as a gay bar for straight people, although it's not *not* a gay bar. Rather, it's something more ambiguous and more generous—like drag itself.

Though now largely culturally conflated, female impersonation and drag once had distinct histories, audiences, and meanings. Female impersonation was typically a mainstream form in a theatrical tradition, reaching its peak popularity in vaudeville and later in cabaret nightclubs and touring ensembles; these shows typically addressed a straight audience and even worked to *dispel* queer associations. In contrast, drag was a popular subcultural gay practice of playful transgression that typically appeared in private at parties and only belatedly became a staple feature of gay bars in the 1960s. At that moment of emergence, female impersonation and drag, respectively, differentiated straight clubs from gay ones.

INTERLUDE 2

Safe Spaces in Detroit

Whereas most of the chapters in this book attempt to illustrate broad patterns with examples from specific cities, Detroit feels distinctly unlike anyplace else. When I visited the Motor City for research in 2011, it had a reputation as a city in crisis, yet it seemed ripe for grassroots renaissance. In contrast to most cities I've visited, the urban gay bars are far-flung and isolated from one another—an extreme example of dispersal zoning—whereas the region's middle-class gayborhoods nest in suburban Ferndale and Royal Oak. Many white gay men avoid Detroit proper, but its reputation for danger perhaps exceeds the actual crime rate. It seems that the people who think the worst of Detroit are those who live just beyond its city limits. There, I was struck by the city's dichotomy of security practices and congeniality.

Simultaneously literalizing the notion of gay bars as safe spaces and foregrounding the outside world's risks, Detroit is the only city where I recall having to be buzzed through a locked security door in order to enter a gay venue. I encountered such arrangements often enough—at Club Gold Coast, the R&R Saloon, and the Woodward Bar—that they seem to operate as the norm there; it also evoked an earlier era, when access to gay spaces often involved speaking to a guard through a slot in a locked door and hoping to be let in. I noticed that Yelp reviews for local bars made sensationalized references to violence on the premises or in the adjoining street gutters, and bar entrances tended to orient toward rear parking lots rather than their street addresses.[1] Such configurations reflect and exacerbate the perception that the city is unsafe by effectively depopulating it of street life.

    The Woodward opened north of the city's center in 1954; it was already commemorated as the oldest gay bar in the city by 1979 and transitioned to serving a primarily Black gay clientele at an undetermined date. When trying to find the Woodward, my friend Candace and I overshot the block, made a U-turn, and crept to the address to find no signage announcing the bar. The front door was locked, but a bulb lit the door, and bass could be heard throbbing from inside. The absence of car or pedestrian traffic along the major thoroughfare—Woodward Avenue, aka Michigan Highway 1, the first paved highway in the nation—was unsettling. Only after circling the block one-and-a-half times and then venturing down an unmarked alley did we find a manned parking lot and the bar entrance. This inadvertently re-created the historical experience of trying to locate discreet bars. (I didn't yet use my phone for GPS.) Inside, Candace and I were greeted by the friendliest bouncer either of us had ever encountered. Elsewhere, the professional affect for this position typically varies from indifferent to surly.

    The social dynamics inside the Woodward felt welcoming, in contrast to the street beyond it. In the side room with a dance floor, groups of friends moved back and forth between dancing and watching from high-top tables. A woman danced with her reflection in the mirror and worked a doorway. Some of the dancers performed incredible kicks, spins, and splits. The spirit of the dancing, though at times about showing off, was friendly rather than competitive; two voguers hugged after egging each other on with their moves. The rest of the crowd applauded appreciatively. One house song, about releasing the tension, seemed particularly appropriate given my friend's and my ongoing conversation that evening about work stress. I cannot claim to know anything about the other patrons' lives beyond the bar, but being in community together felt like a collective exhale. We felt ebullient. On our way out, we decided to check out the back patio, which was an enormous fenced-in area of the alley with more patrons than we had seen inside. Looking up, we realized that this area appropriated space behind adjoining storefronts that were boarded up and appeared to have been destroyed by fires. Out of catastrophe came reclamation, then devastation again. A fire destroyed the bar in 2022.

From the Woodward, we ventured further north to Menjo's nightclub in Highland Park, where Madonna reputedly danced in her youth. It was a Thursday, which was college night at Menjo's. The members of the young crowd—many arriving as groups of friends—were collectively exploring the city and auditioning their identities by night. At the bar, three bartenders eagerly offered to serve us, two of them successively asking if we'd been helped while the first mixed our drinks. The club had a festive vibe, and it felt *social* in a way I have rarely experienced. The mixed-gender line for the restroom was also more chatty than usual. Candace and I each remarked that we hadn't been dancing in a long time, and the club's energy made us feel young again. Maybe it was the vodka talking, but throughout the night I found myself proclaiming, "I love Detroit!"

Two nights later, I ventured out solo to Gigi's, located on the southwestern edge of the city. I had heard that in its early pre-gay days, the place had been a military bar named G.I.-G.I.'s (as in general infantry). Out-of-town friends had talked this bar up to me on account of its drag shows and its working-class trans clientele. Not so long ago, a trans slur was commonly used to describe this genre of bar; although some people used the word as a term of endearment, it has fallen out of favor. Gigi's entrance was through a back parking lot, and again, I was cheerfully greeted on arrival. I received purple and green wristbands upon paying a cover to access both the club's floors. Drag shows are staged downstairs in the Cabaret Room; the main bar and dance floor occupy the ground floor. Although people moved between these spaces, they felt like distinct scenes. Downstairs, mixed groups of friends and white straight people watched the show, which featured a diverse cast. Upstairs, a racially diverse (Black, white, Latinx, and Arab American) crowd of people danced, socialized, and looked for connections; the clientele ranged in age and in gender presentation, reflecting a spectrum of trans feminine expression. I inferred that patrons would have claimed various preferred identity terms, some of which might seem dated now; some likely self-presented as femme only in the relative safety of this club. Generationally, younger patrons likely had more and earlier access to the possibility of transitioning than their elders. Yet a friendly recognition seemed to bond all the trans women here. Gigi's belonged to them.

When I went back downstairs to catch the second drag show, a gregarious woman in a form-fitting red dress and librarian glasses chatted me up while "interviewing" an older, presumably straight-identifying male date seated next to her. We were a queer threesome. Almost immediately, she said that when people see her, they assume she can be bought. "And I *can* be bought," she said, taking the punch line in a different direction than I expected from the setup. She informed me that she was a showgirl, had won pageant titles, and would be performing at Gigi's again soon. She was always the first to tip the performers, often shouting out to them over the songs and engaging in conversation with other people she knew on the way back to her seat. She was the unofficial mayor of Gigi's and an unabashed flirt. When I said that I live in Los Angeles, she responded, "I can commute!" Eventually, she pointedly asked me, "Don't you like black girls?" I defensively froze for a second before I blurted, "I like boys." Without missing a beat, she said she was just fucking with me and expected me to laugh. I read her question as a test, but it was something more layered than that. She clocked what she knew were likely to be my erotic biases—a familiar lived experience in interpersonal attractions and in LGBTQ+ politics at large. But it was also an invitation, as she signaled that Gigi's exists precisely to facilitate queer social and sexual connections, including surprising affinities across race and gender that most other gay venues do not foster. She later suggested that if I pointed out a couple of men I liked, she would let them know I was interested—but only if they were "decent" guys. I didn't take her up on this offer, but I appreciated her good humor and generosity, even protectiveness. This bar was a place of care.[2]

Like the Colony Bar in Kansas City and Jacque's and the Other Side in Boston (see chapters 2 and 3), Gigi's models the ways that what we call a "gay bar" can provide a social home to a queer array of genders and sexualities beyond gay identities and orientations. *Gay bar* operates as a capacious term because we may not yet have the language for all the things these spaces are. Detroit may be marked by abandonment, and its queer venues may be geographically atomized fortresses, but it also feels like anything is possible there.

Part II

Politics

3

Somewhere There's a Place for Us
Urban Renewal, Gentrification, and Class Conflicts in Boston

"It's happening in Boston." So begins a 1980 cover story on gay gentrification in the *Advocate*, the most prominent mainstream national gay news periodical. "The South End slums are taking on a new look, as . . . 19th century townhouses are bought and restored, often by gay couples."[1] The reporter continues to articulate an already familiar narrative of white gay urban pioneers who encountered tensions with implicitly straight residents of color at risk of displacement in cities across the country. In Boston there was already a discourse interrogating urban economics in transition and the literal place for queer people. Reflecting on the complexity of these issues at the end of the 1970s, a writer for Boston's radical gay periodical *Fag Rag* expressed his ambivalence in unapologetic language: "I find myself agreeing with the accusation that rich white faggots are forcing poor third world people out of their neighborhoods. On the other hand, I find myself praising the valuable gay contribution to urban renewal, and expressing anger at homophobic white Marxists and third world 'leaders' who are scapegoating gay men because they themselves are incapable of offering any solutions to the twin problems of housing and urban decay." The author surmises that gentrification "is probably one of the most important social issues of our time, and gay men are often in the middle of it."[2]

In the contexts of urban renewal and gay gentrification, conflicts between bars and neighborhood residents revealed classed divisions within the LGBTQ+ community over the right to assemble and claim access to public space. Cities in the 1970s were subject to changes in urban-planning policies and to new concentrations of gay residency; the emergence of what were then called gay ghettos and are now more commonly called gayborhoods or gay villages during the 1970s and 1980s occurred in relation to both forces.[3] Then as now, gay bars served as these neighborhoods' anchors and beacons. Macroeconomic shifts were felt on the local level and raised tense questions about who constituted the gay community, who could claim the right to occupy urban space, and who was excluded from both. Gay neighborhoods as they emerged in the 1970s and after have typically been understood as white gay male cultural phenomena that expose fundamental racisms, sexisms, and classisms.[4] Critiques of gay gentrification in more recent decades have continued to focus on affluent same-sex home ownership raising property values and displacing lower-income residents of color *or*, conversely, on super-gentrification, wherein queer enclaves lose both gay businesses and residents when property values rise and straight families move in.[5] Waves of gentrification in gay enclaves from the 1980s onward were also, in part, enabled by real estate vacancies when people with AIDS died.[6] By the turn of the millennium, local gay periodicals across the country rarely questioned capitalism but, instead, were filled with advertisements for realtors and condominium developments.[7]

Until fairly recently, gay businesses were disreputable institutions that didn't have the political or economic clout to fight city hall or developers; they were commonly casualties rather than drivers of urban change. In Boston, Jacque's (with a maddeningly misplaced apostrophe) and the Other Side resembled what Elizabeth Lapovsky Kennedy and Madeline D. Davis have called "street bars," which in the mid-twentieth century "were a meeting ground for diverse elements of the sexual fringe," with a mixed clientele of working-class gay men, lesbians, straights, and trans and gender-nonconforming people, as well as sex workers and pimps, across races and ethnicities. These rough-and-tumble venues maintained an unapologetic visibility rather than aiming for respectability or discretion.[8] This was what many historical gay bars were like, including the Stonewall Inn in

New York City and the Colony Bar in Kansas City (see the introduction and chapter 2, respectively).

Queer urban nightlife existed because of and at the peril of macroeconomic shifts in the postwar period. The 1970s development of ever-expanding gay venues—such as multifloor bathhouses, super-bars, and discos—coincided with broader deindustrialization, population migration from central cities to suburbs, and urban-renewal efforts. Because queer people found anonymity, independence, and social ties in cities, they were far less likely to move to the suburbs than their straight peers. Gay venues reclaimed the abandoned territories of cities, such as downtowns, red-light districts, skid rows, and warehouse districts that offered cheap real estate far from residential tracts where people might complain about noise and public cruising. These spaces could be queered because zoning there tended to be lax and they were off the radar of the so-called general public. But such zones were also viewed as undesirable—disposable, even—by city planners, developers, entrepreneurs, politicians, and other citizens.

Urban-renewal and development projects of the 1960s and 1970s frequently allowed cities to eradicate gay bars, bathhouses, and other venues that were located in the only districts available to them.[9] Particularly in northern metropoles, deindustrialization had a devastating financial impact on cities in tandem with white flight to suburbs. Real estate speculation—and the drive to bring an affluent tax base back within city limits—bolstered urban economies in the wake of runaway manufacturing jobs that were moving to suburbs, to southern states, and across borders. Urban renewal relied upon direct intervention on the part of city governments, often using eminent domain to buy and raze blocks of land for what was called "slum clearance" in low-income, minority, or maligned areas and for attempts to revitalize declining downtowns. These projects used bonds, tax rebates, or public-private partnerships to construct large-scale projects, such as convention centers, arts centers, urban malls, stadiums, government offices, and mixed-use complexes. In some cases the interim goal was merely disappearing "undesirable" people and places.

Gentrification, in contrast to urban renewal, was and is primarily a market phenomenon driven by banks and realtors that happens more gradually as housing values rise through in-migration, renovation, and reselling. City governments often encourage gentrification through home-improvement grants, tax incentives, and zoning, thereby producing what has been termed the "Real Estate State."[10] New residents are drawn to gay entertainment zones because of their walkability, unique storefronts, and vibrant nightlife, yet they in turn often complain about noise, traffic, parking, and other "quality-of-life" issues. Scholars argue that nightlife operates "with and against" gentrification and that the 1970s were "the years in which militant gay liberalism began to assume hegemonic form and that at its center were issues of violence, safety, and neighborhood."[11] Urban renewal served to relocate congregations of sexual outlaws, whereas gentrification splinters queer communities into assimilable and nonassimilable consumer demographics.[12]

The logics of gay neighborhoods—as dual residential and business districts—reflect the dichotomy of settling down and going out. Scholars argue that we need to understand sex districts and gay neighborhoods not only in terms of who lives and/or owns property in them but also in terms of who patronizes their businesses, claims an identification with them, and, in Theodore Greene's terms, experiences "vicarious citizenship" in them.[13] Neighborhoods become gay when they are *perceived* to be gay, via queer street life, venues that serve LGBTQ+ clientele, and a modicum of gay residency. Virtually no gay neighborhood has ever had a statistical majority of gay residents, property owners, or businesses. But these areas nonetheless attract a critical mass of visibly queer people who make use of the neighborhood bars, restaurants, shops, services, and public spaces, which then act as magnets for other LGBTQ+ people. Although all of these spaces and venues contribute to the area's vitality, *bars* have been the most regulated and policed, which has also made them the most politicized.[14]

Significantly, *perceptions* of such transitions are often contingent on the whiteness of new residents and business patrons. Queer-of-color residents and uses of space often precede the in-migration of white gay men, so attention to burgeoning gay neighborhoods operates to occlude already existing queer lives.[15] The populations of gentrified neighborhoods likewise exceed a reductive black/white binary; in the case of Boston's South End, there were concentrations of African American, Armenian, Syrian, and Latinx residents, whereas the racial and ethnic populations in Bay Village go without specification in most of the coverage I have found.

To be clear, this chapter examines tensions about gay complicity in the processes and effects of gentrification but does not allege that gay home owners are the dominant force behind them. Studies have found that queer residents of gay neighborhoods are more likely to be *renters* than property owners and often at exploitative rates; heterosexuals have generally owned the majority of real estate in these areas, although white gay men may be more conspicuous when they move to a neighborhood because they are marked as different. Furthermore, unless all private property is to be abolished, it would be untenable to suggest that LGBTQ+ people must *not* own homes. The unanswerable question then arises: where *should* white gay men live?[16] My focus here is less on the empirical economics of gay participation in gentrification than on the ideologies that conflicts about this issue make visible.

In the early 1970s, Boston witnessed not only identifiable gay contributions to gentrification but also classed divisions *within* the LGBTQ+ community between gay home owners and queer patrons of gay bars (and their straight owners). Although parallels can be seen in numerous cities, Boston provides one of the earliest and best-documented case studies to examine this history. Bay Village was one of the earliest neighborhoods in the country to gentrify through conspicuous white gay male in-migration and home renovations. By the early 1970s, a prolonged dispute erupted between the Bay Village Neighborhood Association (with prominent but not exclusively gay members) and the nightclubs Jacque's, which predated the new residents, and the Other Side, the first gay disco in the city. Jacque's and the Other Side served diverse racially mixed and working-class clienteles that included gay men, lesbians, straights, transgender women, and drag queens, as well as sex workers and johns. These venues faced debate about their right to exist and their clientele's place in the city. The Other Side closed in the mid-1970s as a casualty of neighbors' lobbying, although residue of its signage remained visible for decades.[17] Jacque's has persisted despite confrontations with residents that continued for decades during ongoing cycles of gentrification.

The Winner Takes It All: Urban Renewal and Containment Zoning

In the 1970s Boston was a city in transition and crisis.[18] Between the late 1950s and the 1970s, Boston underwent major urban-renewal projects and gentrification in multiple neighborhoods. During the 1970s the city was also the site of charged political controversies, such as busing to desegregate schools (starting in 1974 after several years of organizing), and scandals, such as the late-1970s child "sex-ring" scandal (which led to the formation of the Boston-Boise committee and debates about man-boy love).[19] Economically, the city had already faced financial ruin from downturns

GENTRIFICATION IN BOSTON 105

in its textile, fishing, and banking industries during the postwar period.[20] Physically, its architecture was aging, and some city planners sought to remake the city as a modern, forward-looking city rather than to invest in its historical charm.

The first federal programs to fund the rebuilding of blighted inner cities date from 1949 and 1955, and these created an almost immediate sense of emergency to destroy and rebuild.[21] One of the earliest targets of this federal program was Boston's West End neighborhood, a low-rent district that was home to a working-class Italian population. The area was overzealously declared a slum in 1955 and razed completely by the decade's end; in its place, upscale high-rises with thousands fewer units were built adjacent to Mass General Hospital. Publicity for the project persuaded most Bostonians that slum clearance was necessary "for the good of the residents." However, the project disregarded residents' own experiences, needs, and desires. The West End clearance project did not improve residents' standard of living; rather, it dispersed and isolated former tenants while also generally forcing them to pay higher rents elsewhere. It also reduced the overall number of affordable housing units.[22] Such early urban-renewal projects effectively ruptured communities and made poor people's lives more impoverished through mass displacement. Boston provided a cautionary tale for urban planning.

History repeated itself in Scollay Square, which for decades had functioned as Boston's unofficial but infamous adult-entertainment zone. Shortly on the heels of the West End clearance program, the Boston Redevelopment Agency (BRA) took control of every building in Scollay Square and razed the area in 1962. By the end of the decade, the city erected a brutalist complex with a new city hall and government center that symbolized a break with the past and its built environment. Although most of the adult businesses and venues in Scollay Square closed with the transformation of the neighborhood, some moved southward to a short stretch of lower Washington Street, where they and a number of new businesses congregated to form a new vice district. Once called "Gay Times Square" ("gay" connoting libertine frivolity), the area came to be officially known as the Combat Zone—a term that reportedly came from the recurrent fights that would erupt among youths and servicemen.[23] Playland, located in this area, was for decades the city's longest-running gay bar; it took all comers and was nicknamed "the upholstered sewer." Well into the disco era, Playland's jukebox continued to spin old records by Judy Garland, Marlene Dietrich, and Dionne Warwick.[24] Its decor seemed equally old

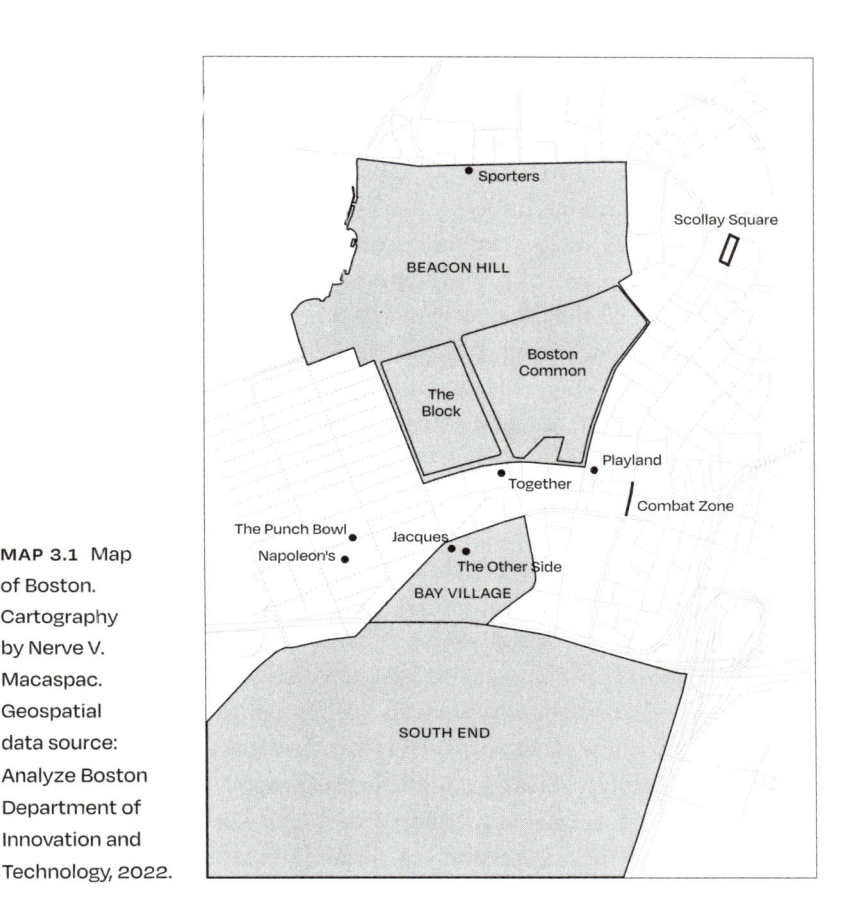

MAP 3.1 Map of Boston. Cartography by Nerve V. Macaspac. Geospatial data source: Analyze Boston Department of Innovation and Technology, 2022.

school, with flocked red wallpaper and soda-fountain–style red vinyl stools at the bar; the venue was also known for its elaborate decorations marking different holidays.[25]

Amid a national trend toward ever-more-explicit sexual expressions, the city of Boston enacted new zoning regulations in 1974 to circumscribe the Combat Zone as the place where adult entertainment would be tolerated. (Sex work remained illegal there as elsewhere.) Boston's Combat Zone became the exemplar of the containment approach to municipal regulation of sex businesses as city officials sought to prevent creep into other parts of the city. This contrasted with Detroit's strategy of dispersal, which effectively used zoning to prohibit the clustering of adult businesses in any single neighborhood; Detroit's model would ultimately become the dominant one for other cities.[26] (See interlude 2 on Detroit.)

GENTRIFICATION IN BOSTON 107

The Combat Zone was predominantly a straight vice district, although its permissiveness was gay-inclusive. In an early-1970s gay travel guide to Boston, the author remarked, "Tenderloins are disappearing from the metropolitan scene as cities step up their Urban Renewal programs, but... God knows Boston's Combat Zone is still kicking (I didn't say 'alive & well')."[27] As this throwaway assessment indicates, surveyors of the gay scene were cognizant of city planning projects and their impact on gay spaces. Some politicians derided the Combat Zone as "a notorious gathering place for homosexuals." Concurring, a journalist pointed to the existence of gay spaces and intimacies as evidence of the neighborhood's moral decrepitude, describing a scene in one bar: "Two homosexuals kissed, embraced and whispered terms of endearment."[28] This latter scene, intended to disgust, sounds positively sweet to me.

Despite statistics that major crimes were "much lower than in other parts of Boston," the taint of vice contributed to wide perceptions that the Combat Zone was a failure of urban policy and safety. During the twenty-five-year period between 1977 and 2002, the number of adult businesses in the Combat Zone shrank from thirty-eight to five, yet the neighborhood continued to elicit moralizing discourse into the new millennium.[29] City planners understood that it would be impossible to eradicate adult businesses altogether, but when containment did not succeed in public opinion, they supported private market gentrification of the business district. A reappraisal of the Combat Zone argued that its "downfall... was real estate.... In the emerging economic boom, the city suddenly realized that some of its most valuable land was occupied by its least valued citizens."[30]

During the 1970s, Boston began to change its strategy of urban renaissance from dehumanizing demolition to restoring its heritage architecture. In 1976, the same year that a moral panic about the Combat Zone hit its frenzied peak, the refurbished Quincy Market–Faneuil Hall complex opened with food stands and boutique stalls and "succeeded beyond all expectations."[31] The endeavor was such a phenomenon that it was replicated in city centers elsewhere. In Boston, however, the market quickly transitioned from serving locals to catering to more lucrative tourists. So although the project became emblematic of a new old-fashioned Boston, it raised questions about whose interests it served. In effect, Faneuil Hall presented a commercial version of gentrification that was simultaneously happening across the city via residential restoration of brick row houses in Bay Village, Beacon Hill, Back Bay, and especially the South End.

Do You Know Where You're Going To: Gentrification and Gay Urban Spaces in the 1970s

Though often elided in accounts of Boston's gay neighborhoods, Bay Village—sometimes called "a poor man's Beacon Hill"—began its transition from a low-rent district to a bastion of gay property renovation as early as the late 1950s. This process of gentrification started concurrently with the seizure and clearance of the West End but via a different process. Bay Village is a small, central, mostly commercial neighborhood; by the 1970s, the residential options largely comprised rooming houses. The area is nestled between the Boston Common to the north and the Massachusetts Turnpike to the south, east of Back Bay and across the freeway from the South End. When the Mass Pike opened in 1957, it cut the neighborhood off from the adjoining area to the south but made the neighborhood more accessible to visitors. Some independent gay men renovated their homes and then strategically bought up other blighted houses to effectively claim the area. Gay renters also made improvements at their own expense and sweat equity with their landlords' permission. These early gay residents, who typically had "limited incomes..., 'simply want[ed] a place to live'... where they would not encounter an atmosphere of social alienation."[32] During the 1960s, realtors began to promote the neighborhood, recognizing and building upon gay men's renovations. The Bay Village Neighborhood Association formed to prevent the city from destroying the neighborhood as it had done to the West End and Scollay Square. The BVNA would later lead the charge against area bars.

Bay Village was home to a number of gay bars that dated back decades and that preceded the in-migration of gay home owners; these included the Punch Bowl, Jacque's, and later the Other Side, all owned by Henry Vara.[33] The Punch Bowl opened in 1946 as Vara's first gay venture and was known for its prominent neon marquee; it was razed to become a parking lot in 1969 as part of the South Cove Urban Renewal Plan.[34] Jacque's opened as a small corner bar in the mid-1930s, went gay in the mid-1940s, and remains open as of this writing. The Other Side, located across Broadway from Jacque's, opened in 1965 and was first gay disco in Boston; it won the legal right for same-sex dancing in 1968 and hosted famous drag shows starring the irascible Sylvia Sidney, among other queens (see figure 3.1). Mixed-class bars such as these and Playland in the Combat Zone were often characterized as more friendly and inclusive than other gay bars.[35] Playland, in particular, drew a mixed clientele of downtown professionals,

FIGURE 3.1 Nan Goldin, *Marlene as a showgirl on stage with Sylvia Sidney, The Other Side, Boston*, 1973. This photo was taken during the weekly Beauty Parade; ironically, host Sylvia Sidney was known as a "scare queen" for forgoing conventional drag glamour. Silver gelatin print. 16 in. × 16 in. (40.6 cm × 40.6 cm). © Nan Goldin. Courtesy of the artist and Marian Goodman Gallery.

working-class patrons, and sex workers.[36] Thus, business owners became the unlikely champions of the economically and socially marginalized.

A few affectionate firsthand accounts vividly capture the scene. A 1972 national gay bar guide described Jacque's this way: "You'll find a colorful, wild mixture, genitally speaking, young and old, sleek and sleazy."[37] *Fag Rag* characterized the Other Side as "loud, active, quite a mixture. Straights come here to 'slum.'"[38] Although the two clubs are often referenced in tandem, acclaimed photographer Nan Goldin conveys the Other Side's singularity. Her roommate and friends performed at the Other Side in the

FIGURE 3.2 Nan Goldin, *Naomi in the audience, The Other Side, Boston*, 1973. Note the side-eye coming from the woman in a floral print dress. Silver gelatin print 16 in. × 20 in. (40.6 cm × 50.8 cm). © Nan Goldin. Courtesy of the artist and Marian Goodman Gallery.

early 1970s; she went there six nights a week in 1972–73, including for the weekly Beauty Parade modeling contests on Mondays and the bologna buffets on Thursdays. Police harassment in Boston made public spaces dangerous for gender non-conforming people during the daytime, so her friends and roommates mostly stayed home or went out at night to the club. Goldin developed her art practice by photographing this scene; these photos now stand as vital documentation of this period and anchor her intimate photo series of drag queens and transwomen titled for the club, *The Other Side* (see figure 3.2).[39] In the documentary *All the Beauty and the Bloodshed*, Goldin recalls that she and her friends were "running away from America" and lived the lives they needed to live. For them, "survival was an art." The film's end-credit in memoriam includes "all the girls of The Other Side," indicating their untimely passing.[40]

The late teenage runaway, DJ, and photographer Bobby Busnach described the nook where Jacque's and the Other Side were situated as "gay heaven." These clubs attracted "scare queens," "really hot guys," fag hags with "eyebrows shaved and drawn on like Jean Harlow," working girls and

GENTRIFICATION IN BOSTON   111

their johns, and others. As Busnach recalled, "I felt like I was home. And I was. Along with other 14, 15, 16 year olds that were runaways or were thrown out of the house for being gay. The people I met there became my family." The doormen at the Other Side "decided if you were cute enough and gay enough to [be] let in." The walls were black, and "dim, fake Tiffany lamps" hung over the booths. Altogether, "it was dangerous, but it was wonderful."[41] The Other Side was renovated in 1973 to add a second-story see-through dance floor, and the straight crowd began to invade by 1974, changing the scene.

In a later *Boston Magazine* profile of Jacque's, the reporter recounts that the city council and the BRA had attempted to eradicate gay bars through urban-renewal projects: "'We will be better off without these incubators of homosexuality and indecency,' one city councilor fumed publicly in 1965. 'We must uproot these joints so innocent kids won't be contaminated.' About a dozen bars were bulldozed in the ensuing 'revitalization.' Somehow, Jacque's survived, and even expanded."[42] In the mid-1970s, a writer for *Gay Community News* remarked that "the bars, Jacque's and The Other Side, are victims of change. Five years ago . . . they were located in an entertainment district and not a residential neighborhood." The commentary continues: "During this time the bars' clientele also changed. Gays were attracted to new bars. Jacque's and The Other Side became mixed: gay, straight, and bisexual, mostly from the working class. The bars adapted, the neighborhood did not. . . . Lost in this struggle, however, are the gay people that work in and attend these bars. If the bars close there will be nowhere else for these people to go. No other gay bar outside the Combat Zone welcomes transvestites and transsexuals, legitimate sexual minority members of our community."[43] Critics of the neighborhood and city efforts to close the bars down warned of the kind of displacement and community ruptures that Boston had already seen in the West End and Scollay Square.

As the bar owners contended, the BRA created the conditions that led to the tensions between residents and the bars. At the turn of the 1960s and into the 1970s, the Varas attempted to buy a tract of land from the city that would have allowed traffic to flow away from Bay Village.[44] Instead, the city approved a development known as the 57 Complex, which interrupted ("vivisected" in one account) Broadway—a short and narrow street contrary to its name—between Park Square and the bars. The development was planted with its back to the bars and created an awkward ninety-degree intersection on Broadway that forced drivers leaving the

FIGURE 3.3 Panoramic view of Jacque's Cabaret's exterior on Broadway, circa 2020. The urban planning creates awkward traffic flows: Broadway ends just outside the frame at the 57 Complex on the right, and both side streets along the bar end at Broadway. Residences face Jacque's across Broadway.

bars back along residential streets (see figure 3.3).[45] This created congestion, noise, and parking nuisances for residents, as well as street crime, vandalism, loitering, and cross-class conflicts.

The neighborhood fight against Jacque's, the Other Side, and their clientele erupted concurrently with attention to the Combat Zone, the very existence of which raised the idea that all such businesses should be moved and contained within it. But cities are porous, and people navigate and make use of urban space in ways that defy zoning. Jacque's and the Other Side were within walking distance of the Club Baths in the Combat Zone and a short drive from the cruising area known as "the Block" (the streets surrounding the Public Garden), which drew men from outside the city center in their cars. Bay Village's proximity to highways effectively opened the area to nonresidents looking for a good time or some trouble.[46]

As a precursor to the conflicts in Bay Village, residents in the South End contested straight bars' liquor licenses as a central tactic of neighborhood gentrification from the late 1960s onward. In 1975 South End neighborhood organizers pushed the city to form the Bars Task Force, which shut down twenty-eight bars. Although bars were targeted as a public nuisance, this was a classed effort; once watering holes serving lower-income clients were forced out of business, they were often replaced by upscale restaurants and bars. As the economic demographics of these business's clientele changed, mafia ownership of local businesses likewise diminished. For early LGBTQ+ migrants to the neighborhood (many of whom were still relatively closeted), middle-class identification rather than sexuality was the basis of solidarity. At least as late as 1983, the neighborhood association in the South End was still contesting a local gay bar.[47]

What we see in Boston were not only aggressive urban-renewal projects but also an itinerant gay population, both of which contributed to new residential patterns and worked in tandem with gentrification. The mayor's office in Boston conducted a survey of the gay and lesbian community in 1983, collecting 1,340 responses. The data revealed that 69 percent of respondents were renters and that 73 percent had lived in their neighborhood five years or less; the most common neighborhoods where respondents lived were South End (29 percent), Back Bay (15 percent), and Jamaica Plain (a lesbian enclave, 10 percent). This indicates that a sizable majority had relocated into new neighborhoods relatively recently, that no one gay neighborhood predominated, and that most respondents could not afford to buy property. But the demographics were also as telling as the economic and geographic data collected: 78 percent of respondents identified as gay men, and 93 percent of all respondents identified as white. From this survey, the LGBTQ+ community, as far as the mayor's office could tell, was white and male.[48]

Another factor complicates these findings: Boston is a college town where students and recent graduates sustain the bars and contribute significantly to the churn of its rental market. This chapter's period coincides with the swell of baby boomers who came to the city for higher education between the late 1960s and early 1980s. Whereas the military had facilitated the migration of numerous gays and lesbians away from home and into urban meccas during and after World War II, colleges would provide much the same function for generations in the postwar era and beyond, but with far more freedom of choice about where to go and potential for upward mobility.[49]

Gentrification has largely been understood as an economic process that in turn drives cultural changes in a neighborhood. In his influential 1979 economic theory of gentrification, Neil Smith argued for what he termed the "rent gap." Effectively, he suggests that real estate markets are cyclical. Postwar suburban areas were built up because they maximized return on investment for developers; by the 1970s, with proximate suburbs completed, deindustrialized and depreciated inner-city neighborhoods were more profitable to redevelop. The neighborhoods that gentrified were those that had the most significant return on investment after renovations and rebuilding.[50] Smith's theory has been critiqued as economically determinist, and other scholars have argued for the importance of cultural factors, particularly for gay male populations, in these processes.[51]

Gentrification changes the basic structure of neighborhood housing markets primarily by replacing rental properties with owned ones and by introducing a new residential population that patronizes different local businesses than prior tenants do. In part, this distinguishes traditional gentrification from in-migration of LGBTQ+ renters to gayborhoods. Scholars have indicated that moving into gay neighborhoods can be economically *dis*advantageous, motivated by social drives rather than financial ones. In a San Francisco study during this period, gays were *less* likely to own their homes.[52] Other analyses suggest that, historically, gay men have been willing to pay higher rents to live in urban areas with proximity to queer-friendly amenities and away from overtly homophobic cultures and policies. Scholars suggest that "gay involvement in the 'urban renaissance' constitutes part of a spatial response to a historically specific form of oppression."[53] Research on gentrification has argued that in contrast to urban-renewal projects and contrary to nearly all the public commentary on the topic, it has not necessarily always had an effect of mass displacement; in fact, one controversial study found that low-income residents are actually *less* likely to relocate from gentrifying neighborhoods—presumably as long as they are not evicted and probably because their existing housing is more affordable than options anywhere else.[54] However, the juxtaposition of residual and new residents in transitioning neighborhoods "makes inequality more visible." Nationally, the demographic groups most frequently affected by gentrification pivoted in 1973 from working-class and ethnic whites to African Americans and other minorities.[55] This date also holds true for Boston's South End as well as to the Bay Village clubs Jacque's and the Other Side.[56]

Asserting the importance of nuance, Christina B. Hanhardt argues that gay gentrification is not a homogenous force but one that selectively constructs and exploits the desirability of a *certain type* of gay resident—white, affluent, normative, and discreet: "By the start of the 1970s, popular acceptance of homosexuality had grown, and realtors began marketing gay people as the ideal *tenants* of changing neighborhoods, focusing especially on middle-class white gay men as high-earning, risk-taking, and family-free. But, in an important distinction, the celebration of renters and owners did not include those whose displays of *queerness* primarily took the form of public intimacy, gender non-conformity, or participation in street-based economies."[57] These latter forms of queer public life are precisely what the attacks on Jacque's were attempting to police. Whatever the drivers of in-migration, gentrification manifests in complex ways that erode prior community norms and contacts and that make new tensions visible.[58]

Importantly, the nightclubs in this chapter not only navigated changing urban landscapes but also reconceptualizations of the queer community. Jacque's and the Other Side demonstrate the duality of bars as community sanctuaries and as hunting grounds for homophobes, and raise questions about bar owners' responsibilities to their patrons and neighbors. But most of all, they expose and reinforce intracommunity divisions about who is enfranchised and who is marginalized.

Saturday Night's Alright for Fighting: Bay Village Venues versus Residents

What makes Boston such a rich case study is that the battle over Jacque's and other venues produced extraordinary and ongoing debates about the place of gay bars in the community and whose interests the bars served. I learned of these bars and the discussions surrounding them because they were extensively reported and commented upon in *Gay Community News*, a collectively run newspaper with a leftist orientation; its journalistic quality distinguished it as one of the most indispensable gay publications to emerge in the 1970s. In her witty memoir of her time at *GCN* (which was after the peak of the bar battles), Amy Hoffman reflects on the newspaper's complex relationships to gay bars: "*GCN* had been founded in part as a protest *against* gay bars, whose straight, possibly Mafia owners profited from our oppression. Gay bars were dark, expensive, and unhealthy. They encouraged alcoholism, shame, and the life of the closet. They were secret, romantic, and fun. You never knew what would happen or who you would meet. We criticized them, but at night we patronized them every chance we got."[59]

Neighborhood complaints against Jacque's and the Other Side apparently started in 1971, although *GCN* did not began publication until 1973. From its first year in print, the bars made front-page news for complaints about late-night noise, violence, and corruption, and the Boston Licensing Board's shifting regulations for the bars' hours of service.[60] Even the flagship daily newspaper *Boston Globe* covered the brouhaha surrounding Jacque's and the Other Side, along with their co-owners Henry and Carmine Vara and manager Frank Cashman, far beyond what I've seen for gay bars in any other city.[61] Henry Vara, in particular, became a lightning rod for press attention, especially by *Globe* political columnist David Farrell, who seemed fixated on him as a public enemy.[62] Rumors also circulated that Vara had Chester Wolfe, the owner of rival gay bar Sporters, murdered and that Vara's mother was thrown out of a window to her death in retribution.[63]

Jacque's and the Other Side effectively appeared as symbols of a class struggle in the pages of *GCN*, for little coverage spoke from the perspectives of the actual people who frequented these clubs. The *GCN* embraced these bars' patrons as the lumpen proletariat of the gay community, whereas the *Globe* characterized them as "the undesirables of the gay community,"[64] effectively saying the same thing from different ideological vantage points. In 1971 a woman writing to the local Daughters of Bilitis journal complained that Jacque's was one of the few venues frequented by women but that these women were "freaks" and the club was "a long-lasting, depressing, demoralizing, degrading side show."[65] The chairman of the Massachusetts Alcoholic Beverages Control Commission remarked to the *Globe* in 1975 that the bars were "designed to cater to homosexuals, male and female prostitutes, transvestites, exhibitionists, and other 'exotics,' who, in turn, attract thieves, drug users, pushers, ruffians, rowdies, and voyeurs to their social nether world."[66] What emerges from the gay press reporting is that transgender and sex-worker clientele, in particular, were being targeted under the guise of noise and violence complaints. Public debate about these venues and reporting from the time often used the term *drag queen* to interchangeably reference show performers, cross-dressers (another term common at the time), and trans female sex workers.

As the controversy, including allegations of classism within the gay community, escalated, *GCN* published a center-spread debate with long commentaries on the bars. Taking the "pro" position, Charley Shively contextualized the predicament within a longer process of gentrification in the neighborhood, indeed the whole city: "Since World War II there has been a campaign against *all* poor people in Boston." He observed that Bay Village had been a nightlife district with gay venues dating back to the 1920s and '30s, as well as having a now decades-long history of bulldozing these sites. Shively argued that the banks were the real benefactors of gentrification: property values in the neighborhood had increased tenfold. He then alleged that the uptick in violence in the area, dating from 1971, was actually a police and private-interest campaign against queer, trans, and poor people: "They say (gay *leaders*, Village Association, Barney Frank and the police even) that they only oppose the 'criminal' elements in the gay community—that is, the poor elements such as hustlers or street transvestites or noisy faggots and dykes who don't have big-paying jobs, forcing them to be closety. They would divide us into good gays and trashy gays.... No wonder most people in the bars don't trust anything too connected with gay liberation."[67]

David Brill, taking the "con" position, argued that the bars were corrupt and made gays into sitting ducks: "What have the bars done for gay people? With the unasked-for assistance of the straight media, they have afforded the opportunity for every homophobe and fag-roller in the city to have a field day." Brill likewise painted a vivid scene for neighborhood residents: "As citizens of Boston, they have the right to live wherever they please, and should not have to put up with passed-out bodies in their doorways reeking of beer and seeping in urine, with flying bullets and blood-stained sidewalks, or with police, prostitutes, and pieces of glass at their front doors at all hours."[68] The bars' owners would refute much of the coverage and allegations against the bar in a letter to the editor of *GCN*, pointing out that sex work and crime rates near their bars were lower than in other areas of the city. They also pointed out that their adjoining neighbors had not complained about noise except for voices during the nightly closing-time exodus; most nuisance complaints, they alleged, came from residents three or more blocks away.[69] Complicating any clear determination of these venues' culpability, most of the incidents that drew neighbors' ire did not happen on the clubs' premises but in their general vicinity; thus, bars were accused of being magnets for undesirables.

Whereas *GCN* focused on community bias against the bars' clientele, the *Boston Globe*'s coverage sensationalized the bars' role in street violence. Gay bars, gay cruising areas, and gay neighborhoods everywhere serve simultaneously as sites for community formation and as places where the visibility of queer people exposes them to potential violence—the classic trap of visibility.[70] Police superintendent Joseph Jordan suggested that the bars should be shut down because they attracted youths from South Boston who traveled to the bars to assault patrons and people in the surrounding area.[71] Jacque's and the Other Side did hire security in the form of off-duty police, and the Tactical Police Force made nightly visits to the venues. The bars were criticized as both excessive drains on police resources and as using their influence to minimize police report filings on incidents in the area.[72] (On street safety, hate crimes, and violence, see also interludes 2 and 7 about Detroit and Somerset County, PA, and "After Hours.")

Community complaints and charges against the bars ranged from double-parking, vandalism, and late-night noise after closing time to multiple counts of assault and battery with a weapon, "assault with intent to murder a police officer," and "shooting of a bystander while police attempted to break up a brawl." A particularly gruesome homicide of a young Latino man was "spawned by a brawl in one of the bars, which ended when a group of white toughs slashed the victim's throat before crushing his head with a rock."[73] This murder, in turn, prompted more than 150 local residents to protest for the closure of the Varas' bars.[74] Although the BVNA was the most organized voice representing home owners' grievances against the bars, a competing neighborhood group, the Bay Village Neighborhood Association, Inc., sponsored a rally with 100 participants in *support* of the bars a week later. Perhaps creating deliberate confusion, two opposing groups' names were distinguished only by the word *Inc.* One reporter cheekily differentiated the two by adding "Unincorporated" to the name of the former.[75]

Such discourses of public safety reflect critiques of these issues by Hanhardt and Laam Hae. Hanhardt demonstrates that in the 1970s, "new residents would demand policing" in transitioning neighborhoods, which signaled a new claim over space, a new sense of certain neighborhoods as sites of precarity and protection, and new rationalizations about who belonged in these spaces and who did not.[76] Conversely, Hae argues that "nightlife *should* be noisy and disorderly in order to provide the kind of socialization that is unique to it, and which is required to nurture creative, transgressive and counter-cultural subcultures." However, she finds that "during the 'quality of life' era [in the 1990s], and in the midst of gentrification, these ordinary features of nightlife were not only decried as nuisances, but also came to be punished as *crimes*."[77]

In spring 1975 more than fifteen hearings extended over the course of four weeks to determine the legal fate of Jacque's and the Other Side. The hearings responded to twenty-seven complaints against the bars, including serving minors, on-site drug violations, overcrowding, patrons leaving with alcoholic beverages, firearms violations, and disorderly persons. The bars were also under separate police investigation for three months for alleged criminal activities.[78] Upping the drama, during this time Jacque's experienced an electrical fire, manager Frank Cashman was alleged to have extorted the mayor for $50,000, the venues were revealed to owe $80,000 in taxes, and Vara filed for bankruptcy.[79] All of this provided fodder for muckraking and political commentary.

In the wake of the hearings, Jacque's and the Other Side were ordered to relocate (which they did not) and to curtail their hours of operation, closing earlier than other establishments with liquor licenses (which they did). Residents claimed that the early closing time significantly reduced area noise, traffic, crime, and sex work. It also drastically reduced the bars' revenues. But even these attempts at controlling the clubs became ineffectual as the local Boston Licensing Board and the state Alcoholic Beverages Control Commission disputed which had jurisdiction to regulate them.[80] The *GCN* reported that the state agency "cleared the bars of all legal barriers to remain open, and strongly suggested that the city has no authority to limit their hours." Perhaps most significantly, commissioners argued that "the location of the bars—'in a single, unified entertainment area'—had a long history of providing 'adult entertainment'" and that "'people who moved into this area . . . certainly were aware of the existence of these two nightclubs.'"[81] Thus, the state authorities ruled 2–1 that the bars were grandfathered by operating within a de facto combat zone and by preceding the new residents.

For white gay men, who had felt themselves oppressed, it may have been difficult to recognize that they had economic and social capital and that they contributed to a form of class warfare. As with discussions of racism in the gay community, gentrification raised uncomfortable truths about their complicity with broader structures of power and bias (see also chapter 4). Histories of gay neighborhoods and nightlife districts expose tensions between affluent white gay men and economically marginalized queer and trans people. Questions arise about what rights property ownership entitles, who has the right to use and congregate in public spaces, and where commercial venues fit in this private/public binary. We must also recognize, as recent research does, that "most LGBTQ people do not live" in gay neighborhoods and that queer communities and spaces coalesce in multiple sites and manifestations beyond a singular, predominantly white and male gayborhood.[82] Scholars have posed conceptual shifts to thinking in terms of archipelagos or constellations rather than fixed neighborhoods in order to understand how LGBTQ+ people navigate and manifest alternative, often-personal urban spaces.[83]

As *GCN* commentators saw it, Jacque's and the Other Side provided a community service that would need to be otherwise addressed if the bars were to close: "There remains a need which will not go away with the destruction of the bars or the destruction of their neighborhood.... If the bars do not, cannot, or ought not fulfill those needs, someone must. And if these needs are important to gay people, the gay community must accept that challenge."[84] Again, the gay bar became the site for political debate, policy, and recognizing who constitutes—or is excluded from—the gay community. In the absence of any other infrastructures, gay bars became social services.

The intracommunity rifts documented in this chapter anticipated Gayle S. Rubin's argument that the acceptance of some sexualities (such as middle-class gay males) typically operates via the demonization of others (such as trans people, queers of color, working-class people, and sex workers).[85] Leftist queers have critiqued what they view as assimilationist gay-rights agendas for selling out and marginalizing radical sexual practices, queers of color, and trans people. Economic gentrification, in turn, breeds social and political assimilation: what Sarah Schulman has called "gentrification of the mind."[86]

In contrast to Jacque's, the popular cruise bar Sporters, located across the Boston Common in Beacon Hill, provided the model of a "good" gay bar in Boston. The bar "brag[ged] about the good relations" with neighborhoods, and a former manager even acknowledged that the lack of signage outside Sporters "was a concession to the Beacon Hill Civic Association, which asked Sporters not to flaunt it on Cambridge Street."[87] Sporters started operating as a gay bar in 1957 and functioned as a beloved institution. The *Advocate* called it the city's "grand poo-bah of gay bars" in 1976.[88] It was also hailed for welcoming a cross section of gay men, who roved around the venue: "White and black men, older men, younger men, the hairy and the shaven, the large and the small, hippies and realtors, Republicans and Trotskyites, the unemployed and the shopkeepers, college students and their professors, longtime residents of Beacon Hill and kids from the suburbs, smokers and non-smokers, drinkers and non-drinkers, the bold and the shy. No type dominates. That is the point."[89] Another gay review of the place assessed the venue's cross-class contact: "Scions of Back Bay families mingle here with button-down educators and boozey [*sic*] barflies of every conceivable description. Sporter's needs no bally-hoo on home ground. It is super-popular, roomy and randy enough for anybody's taste."[90] In a 1985 account, Michael Bronski positioned Sporters in relation to redevelopment in Scollay Square and gentrification in Beacon Hill and the South End, hypothesizing that the bar's endurance must be understood in relation to the geography of the city. It was, as he suggested, the entire city's neighborhood gay bar.[91] In significant contrast to Jacque's and the Other Side, however, Sporters' version of inclusion was exclusively male; the bar had effectively pushed women out by removing seating at a time when local laws prohibited women from being served while standing in bars.[92] The Fort Hill Faggots playfully protested Sporter's gender policies by crashing the bar in drag.[93] They likely embraced the Bay Village bars.

After a decade as the city's leading gay disco and drag venue, the Other Side was ultimately forced to close in 1976 because of ongoing noise complaints.[94] The drag shows moved to Jacque's. Meanwhile, Vara started new operations in the former Sugar Shack venue, rebranding it as Together, another gay nightclub.[95] The Other Side reopened in 1978 as an all-night juice bar (thereby bypassing liquor regulators) and was immediately the focus of renewed neighborhood claims of a correlation between the venue and street harassment, litter, and violence.[96]

I'm Still Here: Jacque's Carries On

Jacque's has survived with uncommon tenacity despite repeatedly being targeted by neighborhood residents and the city over subsequent decades: "People have been trying to close down Jacque's for as long as it has existed."[97] In coverage of the bars, these efforts were explicitly connected to gentrification and issues of "quality of life" for residents.[98] In 1984 Jacque's was charged with unlawfully permitting dancing *after forty-six years of allowing dancing* and despite having an entertainment license.[99] Henry Vara reportedly left the bar business in 1989.[100] Yet in 2010 the *Boston Herald* reported that "Henry Vara is baaaaack. Ah, but then he never went away. Boston's legendary czar of multiple gin mills and fleshpots has popped up before the licensing board once again, to further torment the residents of Bay Village." This time the neighborhood residents complained that "women who flock to Jacque's for the bachelorette shows Friday and Saturday nights have been barfing up a storm" on the streets and in flowerpots.[101]

Regulars defended the venue on the basis that it had been "one of the few bars in Boston where Blacks, Hispanics, and whites mix easily, and where there are both men and women.'"[102] The local chapter of Black and White Men Together concurred when it released a study of racial discrimination at gay bars; although several bars were cited for racism, Jacque's was not.¹⁰³ (See chapter 4 for more on BWMT and efforts to document and ameliorate racial discrimination at gay bars.) In the mid-2000s a *Boston Magazine* writer affirmed that Jacque's was still a "cherished oddity that sticks out in largely segregated Boston—a place where gay, straight, black, Asian, white, old, lesbian, transgendered, Hispanic, transsexual, and anyone and everyone who denies or defies a label can come together for a drink." The reporter then proceeds to portray the venue as seedy, describing scenes of cruising, hustling, and solicitation. Pointing to decades-long tensions between the venue and its neighbors, the article continues: "This is the tale of two neighborhoods, which just happen to both occupy the same physical space. Following the South End's lead, Bay Village has become increasingly attractive to professionals priced out of Beacon Hill and the Back Bay. Some of them are gay themselves, and even moved here for its reputation for tolerance." Once again, the BVNA claimed that because some of its members were gay men, it could not be biased against the bar. Going further, a representative argued that "if there's any discrimination ... it's the attitude of the licensing board that the whores have to be somewhere, and it might as well be the fags that have to deal with it. That's the reality I perceive."¹⁰⁴

Bay Village's heritage as a hub for nightlife—and home-owner opposition to it—extends beyond Jacque's to straight clubs as well. The neighborhood was also home to the Cocoanut Grove nightclub, the Boston It spot of the 1930s and early '40s. In 1942 a fire destroyed the venue and killed a crowd of 492 people inside. A commemorative bronze plaque marked the spot of the incident until 2016, when owners in a luxury condominium building newly constructed on that site enlisted the BVNA to have the marker moved so they would not have to be reminded of the tragedy or encounter tourists at the site. The *Boston Globe* remarked that "they complained that all that history was intruding on their privacy."¹⁰⁵

Bars acted as beacons and anchors for the development of gay entertainment districts, which often evolved into residential neighborhoods. Boston was unique both in its containment approach to zoning adult businesses and in how early and vociferously class tensions erupted between gay home owners and queer bar patrons over who could claim rights to their neighborhood. Similar processes have triggered cycles of gentrification in cities across the country, and later in-migrants, in turn, contest the nightlife that founded their neighborhoods' culture.

INTERLUDE 3

Seattle Counseling Service

In 1971 the Seattle Counseling Service, the first gay-oriented practice in the country, conducted a survey of gay bar patrons to understand their uses of bars.[1] The survey was conducted at Spags Tavern, the Golden Horseshoe, and the 611 bar in Pioneer Square, the city's longtime postwar gay nightlife and vice district.[2] Encountering documents from this survey in the archive, I gleaned that the SCS staff developed it as outreach to funnel respondents into therapy; the questions and standardized responses suggest that the counselors expected to encounter barflies who were chronically lonely, self-loathing, and alcoholic. Instead, a majority of respondents said that they were "almost completely satisfied" with their lives.[3]

Survey results document bars and bar-goers who defied the two dominant paradigms of the early 1970s.[4] The Pioneer Square bars were not as dire and oppressive as gay bars of the recent past were imagined to be, nor did they embrace the new liberation ideologies. Instead, these bars are better understood as residual places where homosexual public life carried on for working-class and underclass queer outsiders who remained unincorporated in visions of the new gay man. In the SCS survey, most respondents reported being closeted in some contexts ("leading a double life," as the survey phrased it), and the majority had never attended a meeting for a gay organization. These were not old men who were just behind the times; most respondents were between the ages of twenty-one and thirty. Nonetheless, the cultures, economies, and geographies of the city were changing around them.

Clocking in with ninety-five questions, the SCS survey was extensive. Its questions reveal as much about the counselors' preconceived notions as the response data illuminated about bar patrons. Tellingly, questions that fished for patrons' complaints about gay bars were posed with multiple-choice answers, as if the *problems* with bars were predictable. In contrast, questions about why patrons go to bars and what they *liked* about them were asked without standardized answers, as though SCS staff could not imagine why. For example:

What do you dislike about it [the bar scene or bar life]?
a) Don't like to drink
b) Noise level too high to visit
c) Superficiality of relationships
d) Sex market or meat rack environment
e) Other...

What positive aspects of the bar scene do you enjoy?
[no suggested answers]

Nonetheless, when the staff collated and coded survey responses, clear enough patterns emerged. The most popular reasons that respondents gave for going to gay bars were to "drink and relax," "meet/socialize with friends," and "dance."

A number of survey questions indicated salacious interest in men's sexual practices, asking "How many of the people here now would you particularly like to have sex with...?"[5] and "How many of the people here now have you had sex with at one time or another?"[6] Several other questions offered the response option "c) Possible trick or acquaintance with whom you may have sex." That such questions and answers were so pervasive reflects common stereotypes about gay male promiscuity and, to my eyes, the counseling staff's assumptions that bars exist for finding meaningless sex when what gay men "should" want were committed relationships and social alternatives. A majority responded that they found 80–100 percent of their sexual partners at bars, yet most also said they had not come to the bar intending to cruise on the night they were interviewed. Responses indicate that gay social networks fostered fluid relationships wherein people occasionally have sex with friends or acquaintances but that such engagements did not necessarily lead to romantic coupling or redefine the prior social ties. Sometimes friends slept with friends and then continued hanging out; then again, sometimes there was surely drama. Some survey respondents also identified as "homosexually married." Sexual activity thus figured as part of gay bar culture but not necessarily as its driving force.

Based upon the records that survive in the archive, it is unclear how many—if any—of the surveyed men sought out counseling or other kinds of treatment. Annotations on incomplete surveys indicate that some respondents were too drunk or distracted to finish the questionnaire. What the survey shows, instead, is how *sustaining* these bars were for their patrons at the time. Twenty-five years later, gay bars remained an alternative to therapy: in 1996 a bar in the Detroit suburbs advertised itself as "the place gay people go in Ferndale if they *don't* need a support group."[7]

This survey teaches us that bar regulars often experienced these venues differently than activists, social workers, and researchers imagined. SCS found happy-enough drunks and queers who resisted so-called gay liberation. These poor and working-class homosexual and gender-nonconforming people found community at bars and didn't view their sanctuaries as social problems or as urban blight. Still, gentrification and heterosexual incursion threatened to take these spaces away. By the mid-1970s, the confluence of the sexual revolution and urban renewal triggered crossover popularity for the Pioneer Square venue Shelly's Leg, the city's first gay disco. The influx of straight people became so charged that the club posted a massive sign proclaiming "Shelly's Leg is a GAY BAR provided for Seattle's gay community and their guests" to protect it as a gay space.[8] Nonetheless, about a decade later the Capitol Hill neighborhood would replace Pioneer Square as the center of Seattle's gay nightlife scene. Pioneer Square's last gay bar, the Double Header, closed in 2015.[9]

4

Midtown Goddam

Discrimination, Coalition, and Community in Atlanta

In spring 1982 the *Advocate* featured an article titled "Racism from a Black Perspective," with a cover image of a young Black man holding an ID card as he faces a white man barring entrance to a doorway (see figure 4.1). The word *racism* appears in all-caps orange over the scene.[1] This illustration reenacts familiar discriminatory admission practices that had been reported and protested at gay bars and dance clubs across the country for more than a decade. Activists understood bars and dance clubs as the mediums that institutionalized and made visible the racism and sexism that were pervasive in the white gay male community at large, and changing entry practices became activists' primary strategy to desegregate the community. This strategic focus on bars afforded concrete evidence of bias, framed practices as systematic rather than merely personal, and understood that access to shared spaces was essential to participation in the gay community. In the archives I have found activist handbills and gay press coverage for protests of bars in Houston, Washington, Atlanta, St. Paul, Tucson, Philadelphia, Los Angeles, San Francisco, Boston, New Haven, Chicago, Baltimore, Seattle, Providence, Kansas City, Denver, and

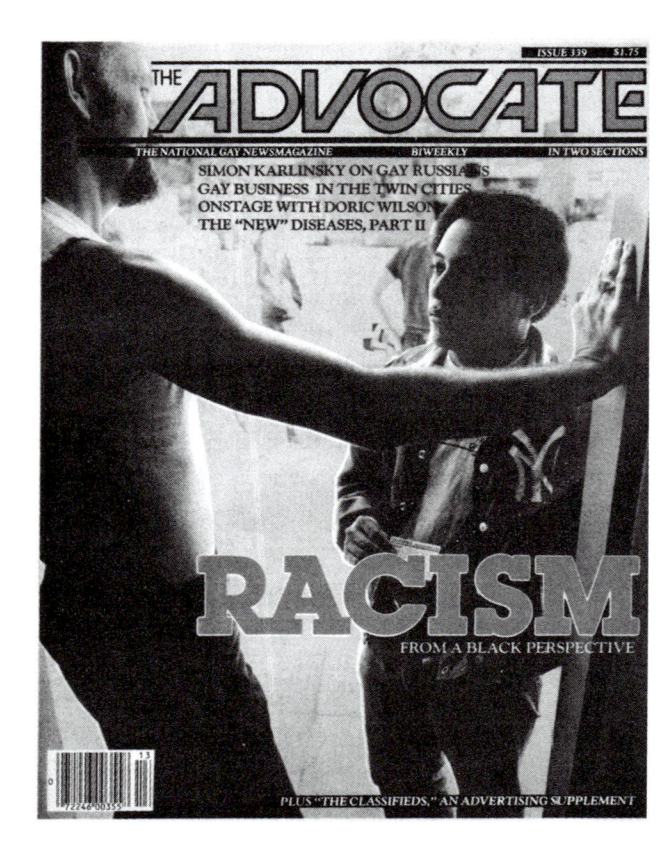

FIGURE 4.1 Photo dramatizing a discriminatory gay bar ID check for a cover story on racism in the gay community in the *Advocate*, April 1, 1982. Courtesy of ONE Archives at the USC Libraries.

Memphis between 1971 and 1981. Parallel efforts surely happened in other cities as well. Despite how widespread such gay bar bias and antidiscrimination efforts were, these issues and actions have not received sustained attention from historians of racially defined civil rights movements or of gay and lesbian politics.[2]

In account after account, institutionalized racism at gay bars in the 1970s and 1980s most commonly happened at the door when a bouncer demanded three—even up to *five*—forms of ID (referred to as *carding*) or refused entry, charged arbitrarily inflated covers, and enforced implicitly racialized dress codes.[3] Some bars instituted quotas to limit the number of men of color admitted or admitted men of color only if they were accompanied by white men. At membership clubs, men of color experienced delays or denials for their applications. Such patterns were conspicuous for the disparities in how men of color were treated compared to the white men next to them in line, and each of these practices operated to humiliate patrons of color and discourage them from returning. Men of color have been further subjected to invisibility when majority-Black gay venues are omitted in gay bar listings in the local gay press—the publications that, in effect, define the gay scene for readers.[4]

Racial animus continued inside bars, where hostile service or lack of service altogether from bartenders deliberately made patrons of color feel unwelcome. Staff hiring practices further privileged and reinforced a preference for whiteness in stark disproportion to local demographics. Such exclusionary practices deliberately operated to prevent venues from *losing* their whiteness—a whiteness often unacknowledged yet intentional and evident enough to be protected—and to preempt these spaces from reaching a tipping point where they would turn "too" Black.[5] Queer-of-color bar-goers also experienced hostility, rejection, fetishization, feelings of invisibility, and micro-aggressions in their interactions with white patrons. In an essay that presents varied personal accounts by Black gay men in Philadelphia in the early 1980s, multiple sources describe the anxiety that white bars trigger. Refusing to internalize pervasive antiblackness, however, one man asserted that "I've learned that racism is a White problem, not mine. So I go into bars and clubs with that attitude. If they don't respond to me, that's their problem." Another man responded that he "feels strongly that 'there are more important places to fight for civil rights.'"[6]

Although the efforts I revisit in this chapter created awareness of bias and effected some policy changes, they fell short of ending racism, integrating the community, or nurturing queer-of-color alternative spaces. These movements often appear to have been initiated by white activists acting as allies rather than starting from and centering queer-of-color perspectives. The LGBTQ+ community—as with any community—is constituted as much by who gets excluded from its constituency as by who gets counted.[7] Queer activist organizing has repeatedly produced internal divisions about equitable gender, racial, and class inclusion, as well as debates about advancing single-issue platforms versus expansive coalitional and intersectional ones.[8] This chapter looks at community groups that were focused on reforming existing institutions through legal protections and prioritized desegregating white male spaces. Whereas early activist efforts often responded to both gender and racial discrimination, by the 1980s such actions primarily focused on racism alone.[9] This may be because by that time gay venues had become more gender bifurcated than they were when the gay-liberation movement started, not necessarily because misogyny and transphobia had diminished. Despite ongoing diversity and inclusion efforts, the issue of racism within the white gay community has continued, although bars became less central to these discussions after the 1980s.[10] Activists made initial political progress on racism in the predominantly white gay male scene, but across the country LGBTQ+ activists and the news media soon pivoted their attention to the urgent AIDS epidemic, which effectively eclipsed a decade-plus of antidiscrimination organizing. This epidemic, in turn, continues to disproportionately affect communities of color.

In this chapter I focus on Atlanta because a coalition of community groups there was highly effective at addressing discrimination in bars and at working within the system to enact a new city antidiscrimination act in 1983. Issues of racism at bars were not limited to Atlanta or the South in general—nor to the past; in contrast, the city of Atlanta was unusually responsive to this issue. Atlanta held a unique status as both the Black and the gay mecca of the South, and organizing efforts there reflected the city's self-perception as the locus of the civil rights movement. Although the municipal government passed new protections and community groups worked to enforce them, these bureaucratic remedies did not fundamentally integrate gay spaces. Thus, this example demonstrates the contradictions of the *potential* for activists to drive liberal policy reform as well as the *limitations* of its efficacy in transforming racist cultures.[11]

Numerous majority-Black LGBTQ+ venues developed chronologically before and after this chapter's documented efforts to redress racism in the white gay male scene. The existence of distinctly Black gay venues indicates the desire—even necessity—of manifesting scenes by and for queer people of color. Activist efforts to fight racism focused on equal access under the law with the goal of integrating venues. Although well intentioned, this strategy has not necessarily produced integration nor corrected racist dynamics between patrons within these spaces; furthermore, the integration cause can have the inadvertent but harmful effect of keeping marginalized members of a community always marginalized in every space. To be clear, I am not arguing against integration; equal access must be a fundamental right. But it is not enough in and of itself. An alternate strategy has focused on building and sustaining a *diversity of venues* that serve as safe spaces for multiple, at-times intersecting clienteles. Such diversity of venues is only sustainable, in market terms, in urban areas that can sustain multiple businesses; as I have remarked elsewhere in this book, outpost bars serving small towns and large rural regions are typically more integrated across class, gender, racial, and ethnic differences (see the introduction), as are working-class urban bars (see chapter 3). My research has revealed that white gay publications and archives and Black gay publications and archives reflect different frameworks: whereas the former offer abundant evidence of racism and activist efforts to integrate gay venues, the latter present little evidence of gay bars at all—and when they do, they feature Black queer venues as self-determined and wholly independent of the hegemonic white gay scene. This chapter reproduces this bifurcation because it is what I found.

Don't Need No Hateration, Holleration in This Dancery: Discrimination in Atlanta

Atlanta has claimed a noble history of peaceful legal desegregation in contrast to the rest of the US South.[12] Likewise, Mayor William B. Hartsfield famously called Atlanta "the city too busy to hate" as it entered a postwar economic and population boom. Historians have both hailed the city's "biracial coalition" between white business leaders and Black politicians and contested such interpretations by arguing that white flight to perimeter suburbs reproduced de facto segregation.[13] The conventional wisdom in Atlanta advises people of color and queers to never go "outside the perimeter"—beltway Interstate 285—which serves as a political and demographic dividing line. According to 1980 and 1990 census data, residential racial segregation in Atlanta surpassed that of any other southern city, and concurrently income and property-value disparities widened between white and Black Atlantans.[14] By the early 1990s, the city and the region were demographic inverses of each other: the city of Atlanta was 65 percent Black, whereas the metropolitan region was 35 percent Black.[15] Reflecting the city's pro-business orientation, however, community organizer Reverend Duncan Teague told me, "Atlanta's favorite color isn't black or white. It's green."[16]

Gay bars and nightclubs exist as commercial entities, and owners and managers effectively differentiated between which clients they considered valuable and which they deemed bad for business. As in other cities, the local chapter of Gay Liberation Front (GLF) was the first to organize protests of area gay bars, critiquing the primary institution of gay life as oppressive (see the introduction). Atlanta's gay venues came into their own when entrepreneur Frank Powell moved to town from the relatively liberated scene in Kansas City. In 1968 his club the Cove became the first venue in town to allow same-sex dancing; not long after, his Sweet Gum Head (named after his birthplace in Florida) became the legendary "Showplace of the South" for drag in the 1970s.[17] When the GLF organized Atlanta's first gay pride event in 1971, Powell's bars kicked out GLF members for promoting the events. The GLF responded by publishing an article in the local alternative newspaper that read, "Frank Powell... wants to stifle Gay Liberation, to keep gay people from being free and undiscriminated against because he fears that they will no longer need to go to a secluded bar and pay to commune with their brothers."[18] Powell maintained his opposition to gay activism to the press fifteen years later: "'Reputable gay people don't carry signs in the streets,' sniffs bar owner Frank Powell. '... I've opened 13 bars here and every one has been gay as a goose. But I don't have to flaunt it.'"[19] Circa 1972, the GLF argued that "bars help to perpetuate sexism more than any other institution in gay life."[20] However, it would be nearly a decade before significant publicity and action addressed *racism* in local gay bars.

In the interim, Midtown evolved as the center of the city's white gay male scene, and Peachtree Street became the major artery for gay bar and dance club discrimination (although no venue's entrance faced the street until the 1980s).[21] Like the Montrose in Houston (see chapter 6), Midtown initially transitioned into a countercultural haven of hippies and sex businesses that in turn attracted a gay scene. As local drag legend Diamond Lil told it, during the late 1960s Midtown Atlanta was invaded by hippies so rapidly that it was like being in Alfred Hitchcock's *The Birds*: you'd see a couple of hippies congregated, look away, and turn back to suddenly find a whole flock of them.[22] Anchoring the Peachtree strip for decades, Backstreet opened in the mid-1970s as the city's legendary super-bar and disco; it boasted three flours and seven bars and expanded to twenty-four-hour operations in 1987. Backstreet was owned by members of the Vara family, which ran the Punch Bowl, Jacque's, and Other Side nightclubs in Boston (see chapter 3). In its early days, it instituted discriminatory door policies to cultivate an aura of exclusivity; these practices shifted when the younger Vara generation took over managing the bar.[23] In 2004 Backstreet closed and was razed for a condominium high-rise development. Ironically, given local history, the last remaining gay bar on Peachtree Street in Midtown is Bulldogs, which predominantly serves Black men.

When Midtown was burgeoning during the 1970s and 1980s, its white population contrasted with the racial demographics of the city. Racial separatism in gay male venues both mirrored the city's residential patterns and extended long-standing histories of same-sex spaces themselves; the most prominent postwar public spaces in Atlanta for men who had sex with men had been whites-only spaces, which entrenched and normalized racial segregation in the decades leading up to gay liberation.[24] Atlanta city planners repeatedly intervened to redevelop Midtown for office towers, condominiums, and arts facilities to shift it from connotations of vice toward more "respectable" purposes. These plans excluded input from gay businesses or community representatives and led to the razing or closing of numerous venues. Planners invoked the discourse of "diversity"—implicitly influenced by Jane Jacobs's work—but did so to rationalize the need for a diversity of building uses and densities, not of racial and sexual communities.[25] Whereas city planners sought to dilute the gay presence in Midtown, local activists sought to make gay venues there more inclusive.

Local antidiscrimination activism against gay bars developed out of a coalition of Black and interracial gay male, lesbian feminist, civil liberties, and Democratic Party organizations in the early 1980s. These groups exposed, protested, and documented discrimination at gay bars, and they influenced the city council to take action. The late 1970s and 1980s witnessed a proliferation of gay organizations in Atlanta, including the Gay Atlanta Minorities Association (GAMA, formed in 1979), National Coalition of Black Gays (NCBG, local chapter formed in 1980), and Black and White Men Together (BWMT, local chapter formed in 1981). By the mid-1980s, BWMT became the city's largest gay organization. The drive for these community groups was motivated in large part by discrimination at gay bars and the need for alternatives to them. Explaining the inspiration to form GAMA, Greg Worthy recalled his experience after a march protesting Anita Bryant's appearance at the Southern Baptist Convention Pastors' Conference following her homophobic "Save Our Children" campaign the year before: "I was walking down the street holding the hands of blacks, whites, and lesbians. I thought at long last gay unity. Then I was invited to a party after the march, and everyone at the party went to Backstreet when it broke up. I was not able to get in. It then hit me that gay unity was not real."[26] GAMA appears to have organized the earliest protests against racially discriminatory bars in 1981, but it disbanded soon thereafter.

The gay caucus of the local ACLU chapter—known colloquially as the GayCLU—took up the cause in collaboration with the Atlanta Lesbian Feminist Association (ALFA, as in *alpha* women) and the First Tuesday gay

Democratic club. The local BWMT chapter joined the crusade immediately after forming and soon became the most visible participant group. Atlanta Friends of Lesbian/Gay Organizations (AFLGO) also participated in the Atlanta Anti-Discrimination Project.[27] Collaboration between groups grew to the point that in the mid-1980s an alphabet soup of twenty-six organizations were coordinated by the Metro Council of Lesbian and Gay Organizations (MACGLO). These coalitions were importantly bigender as well as biracial, and they built upon a local history of coalition and civil rights discourses. Yet by 1986, "There [were] no active organizations for gay blacks"—as opposed to biracial ones such as BWMT—in Atlanta despite its large Black gay population.[28]

U.N.I.T.Y.: Black and White Men Together

Before proceeding, I want to offer some history and contextualization for BWMT, which was both important and controversial nationally. It started in San Francisco in 1980 when Michael J. Smith, a white man, placed an ad in the *Advocate* seeking other men interested in forming an interracial group. After initial personal correspondence, Smith started a newsletter, and local groups formed in San Francisco, Chicago, Boston, and New York. By the end of 1981, there were thirty local BWMT groups, including in Atlanta.[29] Smith conceived the organization as a social outlet and as an alternative to the bar scene, but multiple chapters also became visible for activism documenting and challenging gay-venue discrimination. By the mid-1980s, questions of inclusion and a move beyond a binary understanding of race divided the organization again, with various local chapters changing their name to Men of All Colors Together (MACT) and pushing for the national organization to follow suit.

Divergent priorities and perceptions date from the group's beginning. Within months of its founding, the more politicized BWMT/New York group wrote an open letter to Smith, critiquing his "national" newsletter (scare quotes appear in the original) for being unrepresentative of the local chapters, for deleting "all significant references to racism," and for including personal ads "which feature the kind of racist sexual bartering we in New York are questioning." The New Yorkers also expressed serious concern about the founding San Francisco chapter's predominantly social orientation, in which "no serious attempt is made to explore the racist bedrock on which much of black/white relating is founded."[30]

BWMT has been divisive among Black gay men, and strong views on the organization persist. For some, the group is inextricable from the perception that it existed to encourage interracial sex and that it eroticized long-standing racialized power dynamics.[31] Fetishism and objectification of men of color are common manifestations of white gay male racism and surely motivated some men's participation in BWMT; fetishism, like racialized sexual rejection, can corrode men of color's self-esteem.[32] Joseph Beam's proclamation—"Black men loving black men is the revolutionary act"—has been proclaimed as an ideal and a curative for internalized racism among Black gay men.[33] Affectional bonds between Black men should be nurtured and celebrated. In actuality, however, interracial relationships have existed even among those who amplify Beam's slogan.[34] Many of the members and leaders of BWMT across the country were in interracial relationships; thus, the group's integrationist politics were rooted in personal attractions and attachments. We must also recognize that the Black men who participated in BWMT had their own agency to join and chose to do so. I find it untenable for queer people to shame or stigmatize other queer people about whom they love and desire. The messy truth is that erotic attraction and community organizing are often coconstitutive rather than mutually exclusive.

Both the umbrella organization and local chapters of BWMT maintained biracial leadership with Black and white cochairs, and the organization's focus, as suggested by its name, was on racial integration rather than cultivating a distinct Black gay community. This focus also became a basis for critique. L. Lloyd Jordon offered an incisive account of the limitations and achievements of BWMT in *BLK* magazine in 1990:

> BWMT has not, in fact, concentrated its efforts within the black community. Its middle class *en route* black members have not generally supported outreach to gays of lower socioeconomic status or neighborhoods. The organization's political activism is largely confined to the white gay community, an easier target than either white heterosexual or black gay institutions. The BWMT's successful campaigns to ban discriminatory gay bar practices are of little benefit to *black gays* [who primarily socialize in and identify with the predominantly straight black community] uninterested in patronizing white bars. Ditto its integration of white gay organizations.
>
> For *gay blacks* [who primarily socialize in and identify with the predominantly white gay community], however, BWMT has served well.[35]

Jordan makes valid distinctions about whose interests the group served. Integrating white gay spaces and fostering Black gay ones are different projects that come out of different priorities.

Although the group's name and image foreground interracial interactions, the group brought together Black gay men who in turn built support systems specifically for Black gay men—in other words, *Black men loving Black men*. Teague told me that he joined BWMT/Atlanta—and dressed to make an entrance—in 1985 because he was looking for a safe space to meet friends; he couldn't find any Black gay groups listed in the gay press. The group proved life changing for him because he found community with other Black gay men, and together they became leaders in local and national organizing.[36] Teague would later be involved in developing the local organizations African American Lesbian/Gay Alliance and the gay Coalition of African Descent.

Multiple local BWMT chapters, including in Atlanta, San Francisco, Boston, New York, Chicago, and Philadelphia, as well as the umbrella organization, systematically documented discrimination in white gay bars. They gathered information from bar owners about admission policies and employee demographics, and they conducted community surveys and covert observation studies.[37] These local studies were often undertaken in collaboration with other local groups. In addition to its work to combat bar discrimination, BWMT became important in community-based outreach to men of color during the first decade of the AIDS crisis and, in Atlanta, with gay prisoner outreach.[38] No social group or movement is above critique, and BWMT earned its share. But what BWMT manifested—in social and caring networks, in political discourse and action, and maybe even in healing—outweighs its problems.

Don't Leave Me This Way: Organizing in Atlanta

By 1981, an economic recession was eroding bar and club attendance, and a number of predominantly Black gay venues closed in 1981 and 1982.[39] When clientele from these defunct venues tried to patronize predominantly white gay bars and clubs, racist door policies became more concerted. In 1982 the local chapter of BWMT asserted that "Atlanta is now more racist than it has been in many years."[40] That summer, BWMT fielded complaints against the Midtown dance club the Armory, which ramped up exclusionary practices after the nearby Black gay dance club Jocks closed.[41] As a member of BWMT recounted, "The gay community had, for years, acquiesced in the fact that certain bars would not admit blacks or women," but "the admission problem became acute... when one of the oldest and most racially mixed bars [the Armory] decided to go 'private' and issue membership cards to its patrons."[42] In a call to action against the Armory, the BWMT newsletter referenced prior complaints against a number of other venues, including Backstreet, Weekends, and Sportspage, thereby recognizing the issue as pervasive rather than isolated to the Armory. The group also flagged the participation of the police in these practices.[43] Leaders of BWMT met with Armory management and, perhaps naively, were satisfied that its change to a membership club was just to prevent their longtime patrons from having to wait in long lines.[44] However, representatives of BWMT later recounted that "several [Armory] employees were quite explicit in stating that the change in policy was an effort to reduce the number of blacks in the bar."[45] Despite complaints, the Armory was the unofficial BWMT bar, with a specific wall inside where an interracial crowd convened.[46] This may, in fact, be what motivated BWMT to take action.

Different stakeholders had already begun strategizing how to document bar practices before the complaints against the Armory. Archival records demonstrate that First Tuesday and ALFA initiated efforts to collect evidence; ALFA's participation indicates a coalitional feminist investment in remedying discrimination in any form, even at overwhelmingly male venues.[47] Meanwhile, the GayCLU set about collecting data in the form of a survey for bar owners that would effectively serve as legal discovery about admission policies as well as employee and patron demographics.[48] Perhaps more illuminating than the survey questions is an internal memo that debated its tactics—such as a concern that it "smacks of quotas"—and expressed skepticism that it would yield honest answers or any responses at all. Signaling that the focus on bars was ultimately about the bigger picture, the memo remarks that "if the [bar] owners' concerns of lost business [in the event of integration] are correct, then it's the general faggot that needs an education, not necessarily the bar owner."[49]

Members of the GayCLU also deliberated on how to best ingratiate themselves with bar owners to generate survey responses, as indicated by two draft cover letters in the archive with different pitches. The longer version repeatedly affirms gay bars' centrality to the community (thereby flattering the bar owners) and somewhat optimistically invites bar owners to be allies: "We also hope that you will consider working with us to ensure that racism, or the perceptions of racism, will not continue to plague our community. Our cooperative efforts can help to provide the basis for a new political coalition in Atlanta—a political coalition that recognizes, at once, the contributions gay bars have made up to the present and the necessary changes inherent in the promise of a positive future."[50] The alternate draft directed critique away from the gay community and toward the broader society: "Our community is struggling to establish lesbian and gay lifestyles as valid alternatives in a predominantly heterosexual, family-centered society." This letter suggests that racism hinders such efforts at broader legitimacy: "We've got to show that we deserve the serious attention being paid us by so many within the political establishment. If we are to preserve our gains and maintain our credibility as a political movement, we must broaden our base of support to include *all* of Atlanta's lesbians and gay men." The alternate draft then reaffirms the bars' unique role: "Here is where you can play a deciding role in our future equal to, if not surpassing, your historical function of providing a focus for community activities. The gay bar, critical as it is to the social fabric of the lesbian/gay community, can lead the way to broadening its political base as well."[51] Curiously, the longer draft suggests the possibility that "the perceptions of racism" may be false, whereas the alternate draft implies that the gay community might not deserve its rights yet.

Whether positioning hostility as coming from within the community or external to it, these drafts reflect that devising and revising rhetorical frames are part of activist work. In both iterations, though, the GayCLU centers bars in gay public life. I attend to the GayCLU's paratexts for their insights into the strategies and the incremental dead ends of political organizing. From the archival file, it remains unclear if either GayCLU cover letter was ever sent out; later materials in the archives indicate that no bars responded to the survey. Although BWMT was one of the leaders in the effort to document and remediate discrimination at bars, I have primarily encountered BWMT's press releases, bulletins, and newsletters announcing progress already made rather than documents that reveal the group's process.

Following complaints against the Armory, AFLGO drafted another survey—a nearly verbatim copy of the GayCLU's from the year before—for gay bar owners and managers in fall 1982. This survey changed only one question, asking bar owners to more specifically quantify minorities in various positions: management, bartender, disc jockey, waiter/waitress, maintenance, food preparer, other (specify).[52] This revision mirrors one of the key distinctions made in critiques of gay bar employment practices: that in the rare cases where bars hire nonwhite, nonmale staff members, they tend to be placed in lower-paid and lower-visibility positions such as cooks and janitors rather than in more lucrative and visible roles such as bartenders (who earn tips) and managers.[53] The AFLGO also drafted a survey for community members at large, collecting information about their race, sex, neighborhood residency, frequency of visits to gay venues, and whether they have experienced or witnessed discrimination at gay venues.[54] The community survey appears to have been sent to the mailing lists of various local gay, lesbian, and feminist organizations, although I have not found completed surveys or aggregated data from them.[55]

Hiring practices in Atlanta's gay bars gained national attention in summer 1983, when San Francisco–based BWMT founder Smith circulated a poster reproducing a staff photo from the Saint that originally appeared in a local Atlanta gay publication (see figure 4.2). The poster stated the following:

> This is a phenomenal photo.... Two thirds of Atlanta's residents are black, but... they ain't at The Saint. What are the odds, all thirty-eight jobs to Whites, zero to Blacks? Less than one in a trillion.... But that's not what's phenomenal. WHAT'S PHENOMENAL... is nearly every Gay bar in the country is just like The Saint.... End RACISM now.[56]

The poster used this photo to illustrate and publicize similar findings in San Francisco. BWMT/SF conducted its own gay bar employment report and found that in a city that was 48 percent white, 91 percent of employees across 99 bars were white. In the bar-observation studies and as shown in this poster, BWMT members often presumed that racial Blackness could be determined at a glance. As the report stated, "While acknowledging that most White people abhor racism, we learned that they nonetheless support a society which institutionalizes racism."[57] (In San Francisco, the Box party would be seen as novel, even radical, for drawing a diverse crowd several years after this study—see chapter 7.) This campaign advanced the logic that bar hiring practices should proportionately reflect their local racial demographics and that failure to do amounts to employment discrimination; by extension, such staffing models the patrons whom the bar wants to attract. BWMT/Atlanta, responding to the publicity that the poster generated, picketed the Saint for its hiring practices; this action was reported as part of a wave of protests nationwide.[58] However, what was perhaps more critical was the poster's claim that "nearly every

FIGURE 4.2 This 1983 poster, created by Black and White Men Together/San Francisco and featuring a staff photo from the Saint bar in Atlanta, publicized biased hiring practices at gay bars across the country. The word *racism* appears in red at the bottom ("END RACISM NOW"). LGBTQ collection, 1969–2019. Courtesy of the Stuart A. Rose Manuscript, Archives, and Rare Book Library, Emory University.

Gay bar in the country is just like The Saint." The third national BWMT convention, held that August, featured a workshop titled "Why Are There No Black Bartenders?"[59]

In fall 1983 the coalition of local organizations pressed the Atlanta City Council to respond to gay bar discrimination as a civil rights issue.[60] After two years of collecting information, coordinating protests, and the national embarrassment of BWMT/SF's Saint poster, the city council acted with remarkable expedience. Councilmember Mary Davis, who represented part of the Midtown gayborhood, introduced the Alcoholic Beverage Antidiscrimination Act of 1983; civil rights icon John Lewis was among the cosponsors. The city council unanimously approved it at the following meeting.[61] Its passage was understood to continue the legacy and self-image of Atlanta as the forefront of the civil rights movement, an enlightened beacon in a still conservative American South.[62] The new law focused specifically on venues licensed to serve alcohol but anticipated the city's adoption of a more comprehensive antidiscrimination law in 1986. Atlanta was the first major southern city to pass such broad protections (after the smaller Austin, Texas, in 1975) and did so a full seven years before New York City.[63]

The Alcoholic Beverage Antidiscrimination Act contained three significant provisions: nondiscrimination in admission or service, nondiscrimination in cover charges or membership fees, and limitation of proof of age to one government-issued photo ID. The latter provision sought to remedy pervasive practices of discriminatory carding. The act specifically prohibited discrimination based on sex, race, and national origin.[64] It did not differentiate between gay and straight venues, but it was understood to address a problem specific to gay ones. I have found no indication from this period suggesting parallel or connected claims related to racial discrimination in straight bars or a sense of alliance between gay and straight activisms. This coalitional work articulated racism as a *gay* problem, one specifically sited at bars and nightclubs. It remains ambiguous whether this indicates that gay male venues were in fact more overtly racist than straight ones or that there was more will within the LGBTQ+ community to address such discrimination. In addition, the act clarified that clubs would be classified as "private" following IRS guidelines. As BWMT later revealed, "None of the bars that called themselves 'private' qualified as a private club under the regulations."[65]

The bar antidiscrimination ordinance was a major victory for the coalition of groups in the city and for BWMT in particular. Nonetheless, enforcement and amelioration necessitated continued work. Following the passage of the new law, BWMT and ALFA together initiated the Discrimination Response System (DRS), with a hotline for reporting incidents modeled upon one created by the Washington, DC, chapter of BWMT (see figure 4.3). BWMT/DC even supplied a grant to the Atlanta effort, paid for with award monies that the DC Human Rights Commission earned through bar-discrimination cases there.[66] The Atlanta Anti-Discrimination Project (AADP) was the name given to the coalition overseeing the DRS system. When the city's Alcoholic Beverage Antidiscrimination Act took effect, AADP sent letters to bars informing them of the new law and began to conduct follow-up visits to bars to check on compliance. The AADP also developed an official discrimination report form to collect information on specific complaints.[67] In addition, a police advisory committee was formed with representatives of community organizations and city council members.

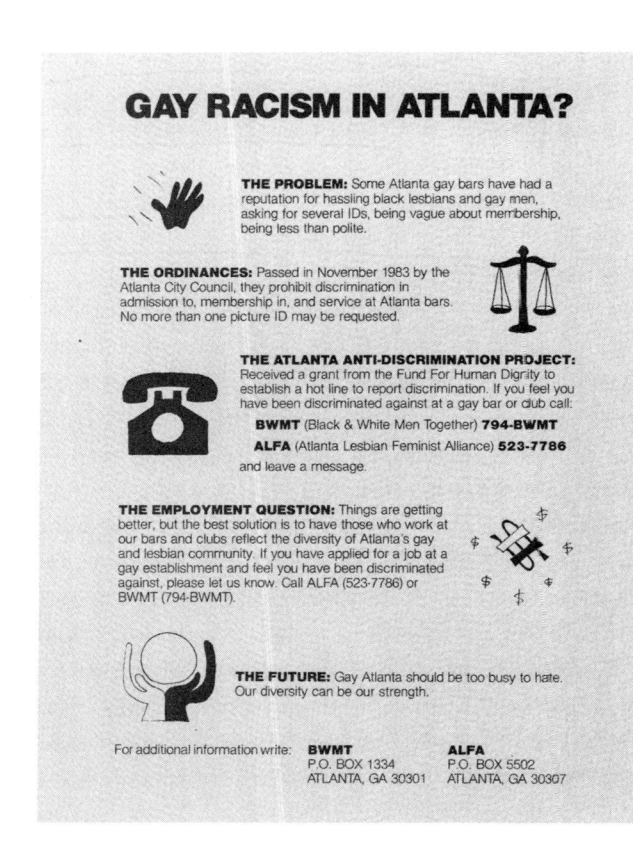

FIGURE 4.3 Flyer for the Atlanta Anti-Discrimination Project hotline, cosponsored by Black and White Men Together and Atlanta Lesbian Feminist Alliance. Courtesy of the Kenan Research Center at the Atlanta History Center.

Coalitional activism proved highly effective in publicizing discrimination in the gay community at bars and in driving liberal bureaucratic responses. However, this organizing was less efficacious at changing social racism in the community or supporting queer-of-color–specific spaces. The efforts I revisit here prioritized legal protections after the model of prior civil rights movements, which had proven important but only partially effective—the dual successes and limitations of which would have been especially evident in Atlanta. In affirming protections, antidiscrimination laws typically function to formalize legal recourse for those who are wronged and may prove bureaucratically inaccessible or ineffectual. Such laws do not have the power to prevent or dismantle racist ideologies and behaviors. Trans legal scholar Dean Spade argues that antidiscrimination law "misunderstands how power works" by focusing on individuals' rights and individuals' acts instead of on structural biases and subjections. Furthermore, the passage of such laws can give the "false impression" that equality has been achieved and can instead expand the very institutions that perpetuate the most violence.⁶⁸ In this case study, the Atlanta City Council affirmed an inclusive liberal position, but the immediate necessity for a subsequent community-based DRS demonstrates that bias was expected to and did continue to persist in the gay community. Discriminatory carding practices may have diminished at bars across the country thanks to coalitional efforts such as these in Atlanta, yet Black ownership and proportionate hiring practices have generally remained more difficult to achieve.⁶⁹

The 1984 convention of the International Association of BWMT was held in Atlanta to celebrate the political victory and was scheduled to coincide with local gay pride festivities.⁷⁰ A Canadian reporter in town for the events observed the stark racial divisions in the city, effectively demonstrating how limited the integrationist progress had been so far despite the new law: "Most of the [gay] bars are predominantly white male, the 'mixed' bars cater to an 85-percent-white clientele, and there's a small minority of exclusively black establishments for gay men."⁷¹ Teague, who moved to the city in 1984, told me that although segregation persisted and racial hostility was still palpable, the new law did ensure that customers would be asked for only one ID and would be charged the same cover. Most bars remained racially homogenous, and people knew where to go to feel welcome and where to avoid. In addition, he told me, there was always one or two other bars where men who dated across the color line were admitted. Nevertheless, even venues that were friendly toward interracial socializing maintained "a five percent rule": no more than 5 percent of the crowd could be Black.⁷²

Activists recognized that protesting gay bars was never just about particular venues but more importantly about their centrality in gay culture. As a member of BWMT aptly remarked, "Bars function as community social centers. They're more than just drinking establishments, they're institutions. By barring admission, you are barring access to a primary institution for many members of the gay community."⁷³ Not all bars participated in or condoned conspicuously racist measures, but enough of them did that the gay bar scene as a whole could take on a connotation of racism for many gay men of color.⁷⁴ Activist efforts thus sought to enfranchise gay men of color within the community and to combat antiblack racism among white gay men by focusing on integrating nightlife venues. Although this is laudatory, it operates on the presumption that welcoming Black men into white spaces should be the goal and defaults back to the primacy of *white* spaces as where the queer community converges. This risks simply absorbing and eliding Blackness. Attention to gay bars was often framed as a lens to understand racism more broadly, yet focusing on anti*discrimination* policies, one could convincingly argue, fell short of anti*racist* transformation; in other words, activists focused on achieving equitable access under the law rather than changing the societal foundations for such policies. In effect, this history affirms Audre Lorde's contemporaneous adage that "the master's tools will never dismantle the master's house," as well as Cathy J. Cohen's later critique that the gay and lesbian movement has reproduced racisms and, in focusing on existing paradigms of sexuality and civil rights, has fallen short of queer politics' potential to imagine more radical alternative formations.[75]

In 1991 a BWMT/Atlanta bar study found that out of twenty-four gay bars and clubs in Atlanta, five were predominantly Black. At the nineteen non-Black bars, only 8 percent of the patrons and less than 2 percent of the staff were observed to be Black in a city with a majority-black population.[76] These findings indicate at least two things: progress toward integrated venues had been limited and there was an emergent plurality of Black gay venues in Atlanta.

You're Alright with Me: Black Gay Clubs

Bars and nightclubs have occupied a less central role—socially, culturally, and politically—for Black gay men than they have for white gay men. I do not know of any city where the number of queer-of-color venues or fully integrated ones has reached population-proportionate parity with majority-white ones. The reasons for this are both entrenched and ongoing, ranging from discrimination at white venues to social and housing segregation, economic disparities, distinct community and familial norms, and sometimes different sexual identifications.[77] Some men of color choose to go out to predominantly white gay venues, but many more do not. In Atlanta, Black gay men have historically often gathered for house or hotel room parties, balls, and holiday socials organized by the Atlanta Committee; these events have been promoted through word of mouth rather than through a symbiotic gay press.[78] In Washington, DC—the most comparable peer to Atlanta's scene—a number of private clubs, such as Nob Hill and the Clubhouse, have served as important venues for community.[79] As a profile of DC remarked, "Most local black gays refuse to risk the indignity of a quota system" in white gay venues and instead have built a market of Black gay clubs or go to straight Black ones.[80] Southern Black men also socialize in more quotidian ways through churches.[81] Nonetheless, Black gay bars have histories and foster diverse ways of living Black queerness within and between them.

Creating Black queer venues—rather than integrating white ones—became the dominant local outcome in the years following the early 1980s coalitional organizing against discrimination. Craig Washington's history of Black gay Atlanta nightlife affirms that the 1980s marked a transition when white gay bars began concertedly implementing discriminatory door policies and, correspondingly, when a number of Black gay clubs opened.[82] Reflecting the emergence of Black gay community institutions in the decade following the antidiscrimination efforts, Atlanta has also hosted annual Black pride events since 1995.[83] In 1999 a two-part article on race relations in gay Atlanta in the local gay newspaper *Southern Voice* observed that "as Atlanta's black gay community has grown in strength and unity, it has developed its own institutions—black gay bars, churches, support groups, HIV/AIDS organizations and youth outreach—prompting cries of self-segregation from some white gays." The reporter remarks that some white gays characterize Black gay organizations as "separatist," whereas a Black gay community leader characterizes them as "self-determined."[84] *Southern Voice* revisited these debates in 2006 with the subheading "Separate bars, churches sign of segregation or just different cultures?" In this follow-up, various sources affirmed that gay spaces in the city are segregated but in a way that is "benign" and that "comes from different cultural styles."[85]

The Marquette has carried on since the mid-1960s as Atlanta's most enduring Black LGBTQ+ brick-and-mortar venue. It has been gay for at least as long as Midtown has, but it has fostered its own scene far away from that gayborhood. It was already considered the oldest gay venue in Atlanta by the mid-1980s.[86] Sometimes called the "Sleazy Queezy," the Marquette has always drawn a cross section of people—working people, students, self-styled bad boys and bad girls—and has been a tolerant space where everyone could do their own thing.[87] The patrons invented a dance at the Marquette called "hitting the wall," where they would line the club's perimeter and high-five the wall.[88] Importantly, the Marquette also served a large student clientele in its original location, which was in walking distance from the Morehouse College, Spelman College, and Clark Atlanta University campuses. This functionally made it an adjunct Black queer student center. (Conversely, when Midtown gay bars closed during the historically black colleges and universities' street festival Freaknik in the 1990s, they effectively prevented Black student patronage.)[89] Because the club reputedly did not check patrons' IDs—whether in rejection of carding practices in Midtown or not—young people congregated there to explore gay life.[90]

In most written accounts I've found, the Marquette has been portrayed in classed terms as a rough club that refused assimilationist respectability politics. One community member I spoke with told me that a date once took him to the Marquette to "test" his Blackness; although he enjoyed the "down and dirty" drag performances there, he ended their courtship afterward.[91] A review published in the local Black gay press compared the clientele to talk-show guests who "spend most of their time cursing and fighting each other for no apparent reason" and suggested that "with better screening of their patrons," the venue could be a "Class A Club."[92] The venue has often been excluded from listings in the gay press, even in some Black gay publications; perhaps relatedly, I do not recall ever seeing print ads for the venue. The earliest published Atlanta Black gay nightlife overview that I have found appeared in *Blacklight* in 1981 and viewed the scene with a touch of dismay: "That Black Gay life is centered in the home comes as no surprise when one learns there are no Black Gay bars in Atlanta. Well, there is one, 'The Marquette,' but patrons are frisked before entering to remove any knives or guns."[93] Offering an acerbic—yet comical—articulation of the Los Angeles Black queer scene, a bar guide in *BLK* magazine, circa 1989, developed a rating system to assess different venues' Blackness. The scale ranged from one star for "Slightly Black" to four stars for "Whites are shot on sight." No club earned four stars, and subsequent issues softened the highest score as "Whites don't get a warm and cozy reception" and later, "All black."[94] These guides imagined the possibility of an all-Black queer space but found that no place in Los Angeles had yet achieved it.[95] If *BLK* had surveyed the Marquette, I imagine it would have earned a perfect score.

The venue's location of more than three decades was razed in 2000 for a retail development anchored by a Walmart. *Southern Voice* columnist Lisa Henderson penned a "requiem" for the venue: "My world is divided into two kinds of people—those who loved the Marquette, and those who would not step a toe into her red vinyl interior. I, unabashedly, am among the former." She recalled that many people considered the bar an unsafe, "lowdown" spot, yet it maintained an open-door policy: "I don't recall once being asked for ID. If you made the trek, you got in." The men came, she imagined, "from some of the most hellish corners of greater Atlanta.... I often wonder, what feats of inner strength or nerves of steel were called upon" to get there. Women "comprised a surprising majority" there and were either "ultra-femme" or "stone stud."[96] *Venus* magazine estimated a 50–50 gender split at the Marquette, making it one of the only places where gay men and lesbians held equal presence.[97]

The club soon relocated a mile north, where it continues as of this writing and bills itself as "The Legendary Marquette." The club still serves a mixed-gender clientele, and most of its current social media publicity images include both a man and a woman; the club also features drag shows, go-go dancers, and Black pride events. The venue hosts a large dance floor bathed in purple light, and social media posts demonstrate that it packs in crowds. Although the venue clearly markets its orientation toward partying, benefit events demonstrate support for community members who are trans, underresourced, domestic abuse survivors, and/or unhoused.[98]

Beyond the Marquette, a couple of Black queer clubs would become legendary dance palaces in the late 1980s. In part, the blossoming of this scene reflected and reinforced the development of an emergent new Black gay culture and consciousness at the time.[99] Loretta's, called "Lo-Lo's," opened in 1987 and was a beloved dance club. Loretta's was owned by a Black woman named Loretta Young who held the liquor license and bartended at her boyfriend's bar, Foster's on Peachtree, which catered to Black men.[100] When that venue closed, Young opened this namesake dance venue. She was a strong community supporter, and the venue was class diverse. It was accessibly located two blocks from a MARTA transit station, and one night a week—known as "welfare night"—there was no cover. The expansive dance floor accommodated different crowds in different zones.[101] The AIDS crisis devastated its community, and the club closed in the 1990s. Club 708 took residence in the space as a long-running party that drew a young Black gay crowd. Loretta's has been described as the "African-American community's answer to Backstreet," a designation that might more accurately pertain to its competitor Traxx.[102]

In 1989 Traxx (later known as the Legendary Traxx) started in the former Phoenix dance club building as the largest gay Black venue in the South; it spanned three stories and two dance floors with balconies overlooking the dancers. Founding owners David Hampton and Philip Boone, cousins and Detroit natives, were taken aback by the racist door policies at white gay venues when they came to Atlanta. Hampton moved to Atlanta to attend Morehouse College, and Boone soon followed in 1982, just as attention to carding practices in Midtown was rising. Together, they began hosting rent parties at their apartment in 1983. Because they worked in hospitality at the Ritz Carlton hotel, they assumed the name the Ritz Boyz as promoters of upscale Black gay events in 1985. Hampton later worked as the first general manager at Loretta's before opening Traxx. With Traxx, they sought to provide an *experience*. "We wanted to ooh and ahh the girl," Boone told me with a laugh. Traxx attracted a more middle-class and more male clientele than Loretta's or the Marquette.[103]

The building housing the club was called the Warehouse Traxx. The Warehouse was a straight club named after DJ Frankie Knuckle's venue in Chicago (see chapter 5), and Traxx was a gay club named after Tracks in Washington, DC (see the introduction). Slyly, the building had separate entrances with different street addresses so that straight patrons wouldn't think they were going to a gay club; straights entered on Marietta Street, and on Saturdays gays entered on Luckie Street. The Warehouse proved to be as important in the local straight hip-hop culture as the Legendary Traxx was in the gay scene.[104]

Traxx provided transcendence, even spiritual catharsis for its faithful, including scholars E. Patrick Johnson and Jafari S. Allen. In his essay "Feeling the Spirit in the Dark," Johnson recalls that dancing at Traxx was life changing and theorizes about the convergence of the gay club and the Black church.[105] Despite the club's large scale, "There [was] barely enough room to breathe, let alone move. Every inch of the space [was] filled with a body ... every body imaginable." The fashions ranged from fitted designer clothes to baggy hip-hop fashions to drag, and the atmosphere was filled with a sensorium of colognes. With "sweat drenching our shirts," Johnson reflected, "the holy sexual spirit that presides works us into a shamanistic state of euphoria."[106] Dancing there, Allen felt "if not ... 'community,' certainly *congregation*." Allen testifies that "my Black queer people are sensual, abstract hieroglyphs in motion, seen best in blacklight—disco balls mirroring and refracting their complex facets."[107]

A critical mass of Black LGBTQ+ venues coalesced in Atlanta by the millennium; up to a dozen local bars and weekly dance parties catered to Black LGBTQ+ patrons at the time, although these remained outnumbered by full-time white gay venues.[108] For Black pride 2004, Traxx ran an ad for a party named Integration; in contrast to the historical meanings of the term, this party was marketed as an all-Black event alongside others called Merge, All of Us, Blend, and Mix under the banner of "Bringing Men

FIGURE 4.4 Traxx nightclub's Black pride 2004 lineup of events included parties with the themes Merge, Intergration, All of Us, Blend, and Mix. *Clikque*, August 2004. African American Lesbian and Gay Print Culture Collection. Courtesy of Auburn Avenue Research Library on African American Culture and History, Atlanta-Fulton Public Library System.

from across the Nation Together" (see figure 4.4).[109] In advance of the following year's Black pride event, Traxx ran an ad asserting that "we have trained vigorously to provide you with the most intense, invigorating and dramatic event of all time. Remember we have remained the PIONEERS of this industry and the original source of Atlanta's Nightlife Entertainment . . . catering to every facet of the gay community and we will continue to do so."[110] Although some of these claims are overstated, they nonetheless indicate that a vibrant, even highly competitive Black gay club scene had come into its own—one that now claimed its own history.[111] Traxx later moved locations and scaled up, taking up residence in Decatur in a fifty-thousand-square-foot venue that could host six thousand patrons; its parties continued until 2012.

As this study of Atlanta demonstrates, white gay bars became the venues to make visible and respond to racism in the gay community at

RACISM AND BLACK GAY ATLANTA   149

large. Coalitions of activist groups gathered evidence of discrimination in bar admission practices (most commonly via biased carding) and lobbied for remedies to these problems. Although these efforts importantly raised awareness of structural discrimination at gay venues and new legal protections, they did not effect equitable integration of the scene or transformation of gay male bar cultures. Instead, a parallel scene of venues catering to and sustaining Black queer people developed on its own terms to serve its own communities.

INTERLUDE 4

Gay Switchboard in Philadelphia

In late 1972 the Gay Activists Alliance of Philadelphia endeavored to start a local gay switchboard, a telephone hotline for callers to access information about gay events and organizations, seek counseling, or just talk to someone gay to not feel so alone: "Not knowing quite what to expect, they had meetings, Consciousness Raising sessions, and lectures by experts in counseling, suicide, law, and Venereal Disease." The phone line was up and running in February 1973, staffed by "less than a dozen volunteers and a card file with about twenty cards."[1] The Gay Switchboard soon became part of the Gay Health Consortium (later renamed the Eromin Center) and then, in 1976, became independent but housed within the Gay Community Center. The Gay Switchboard initiative was part of a movement that sought to provide an alternative community infrastructure to the bars. "And Lesbian" became part of the switchboard's name sometime later.

As its background indicates, the Gay Switchboard was the product of gay-liberation political organizing, attention to sexual and mental health, and a drive to create community-based resources.[2] Operators performed care work—listening to callers in crisis or providing a sense of connection—and acted as information references.³ The switchboard developed alongside similar efforts locally and nationally to create gay-affirming social services, inspired by the emergent women's health movement. (See the Seattle interlude for a parallel example with the Seattle Counseling Service.) Volunteers staffed the phone lines most evenings from 6 or 7 p.m. until 11 p.m. or midnight, thus coinciding with prime bar hours.

For years the Gay Switchboard volunteers relied on information collected in a bifold leather-bound index card organizer, and cards for individual bars take up the majority of its left side (see figure 14.1).⁴ This fascinating object materially demonstrates that there were more bars than any other kind of community resource, and the cards' placement suggests that they were the most frequently consulted information. The Gay Switchboard thus functioned as a medium for callers who didn't know where to find gay bars. In an earlier era, men might ask a taxi driver to take them to a gay bar; drivers often knew where these venues were, even if their passengers didn't. Lesbians were advised to find bars by hanging out at ball fields and then following softball players to see where they went drinking after games.⁵ The very existence of the Gay Switchboard attested to a new era, but the question remained for callers about how to navigate the new gay world. In effect, the switchboard replicated the gay bar directories that were routinely included in national gay travel guides and local gay newspapers. Such listings often used a key to taxonomize different genres of bars and clienteles; annotations on the switchboard's reference cards did much the same. Therefore, operators could offer information about each bar and, in the process, signal that there were different kinds of gay bars for different kinds of gay people.

The switchboard's bar cards also document that the bar scene was marked by frequent turnover; venues changed names, moved, or closed, and the scene at particular venues would evolve over time. Cards feature comments in different handwriting and were updated by crossing out dated information. (The latest edits on the cards date from 1984, although the switchboard continued until 1998.) For instance, the card for the Post features layers of altered information and strike-throughs by multiple hands; some of the details may be a matter of perspective. On the line for "clientele," the card originally designated, "Pred. Male, 20's–30's." Later someone scratched out "30's" and scrawled "60's" above it; it is unclear if the revision signaled a change in the clientele, an inclusive effort to make older gay men seen, or an ageist perspective on the bar. The card for another venue, the three-story Odyssey II, maps the segmenting of spaces and demographics on to a single

FIGURE 14.1 Philadelphia Gay Switchboard's card file. Courtesy of the John J. Wilcox Jr. Archives at the William Way LGBT Community Center.

site. The original information on the card indicated that the first floor was a bar, the second floor a dance floor, and the third floor a women's space. However, the women's area was crossed out and new distinctions written in: the first floor was "popular with 40–50 age group," the dance floor "popular with "20–30 age group," and the third floor goes unspecified. A final comment remarks, "mostly male but females welcome."

Among the notations on cards for other Philadelphia-area bars:

The Bikestop: "levi leather ... predominantly white"

Bravo's Lounge: "caters to Spanish speaking"

Cell Block: "BACK ROOM" ... "very popular after 1 a.m."

DCA: "Probably the most popular of the after hours private clubs, somewhat cliquish"

El Bravo (a duplicate listing for Bravo's Lounge, reflecting uncertainty about its name and how to alphabetize it): "caters to Hispanics"

JP's: "some hustlers and quasi-hustlers (lower class gays without jobs)... working class... the bar is safe but be careful whom you take home"

Smart Place: "caters to blacks"

The Swan: "Predominantly black; some mix..."

Venture Inn: "many 'regulars' at bar"

Lark Bar (in Bridgeport): "*Very* local neighborhood bar.... Attracts main liners as well as working class folks. People seem to know one another and are fairly friendly to a new face.... Clientele: suburban...."

The remarked upon specificities of each bar signal differentiation along lines of gender, race, class, and language, as well as uses of the space, peak hours, and social dynamics—signaling which bar is unfriendly, has a core group of regulars, or welcomes strangers. "TOO MUCH" appears handwritten in all caps across the bottom of the card for the Swan. At first I thought that this was an effusive comment about the predominantly Black venue, but I later realized that it meant the site had changed names. A separate card for the Much (as it was listed) identifies the same address. These cards make clear which information was deemed relevant for people to find the places and people they sought out—and which they likely wanted to avoid. As a repository of gay knowledge, the Philadelphia switchboard card file documents the differences that marked the local gay bar scene and that recurred elsewhere.[6]

Although the operators were likely advised to give information referrals rather than recommendations, taste and bias surely figured in what they communicated. Some distinctions would have been matters of preference (such as a leather bar versus a dance club), but the segmentation of the gay bar scene could also produce segregation, even discrimination. Such discrimination at gay venues was understood as structural and as an index of broader biases in the gay community at large; activists picketed and boycotted racist bars, documented discriminatory door policies, and worked to change public consciousness and even city policy (see chapter 4). In Philadelphia a coalition of community groups conducted a two-year study of discrimination at gay bars, which they completed in 1986.[7] Unfortunately, these issues recur without resolution; when I visited Philly for research, its gayborhood was yet again reeling from newly stoked attention to racism at gay bars.[8]

Part III

Institutions

5

Welcome to the Pleasuredome

Legends of Sex and Dancing in New York

"Flamingo could assemble all the necessary ingredients—the beauties and jesters, the intellectuals and artists, the social climbers and power brokers. It showed that there could in fact *be* a gay society, that one could in fact *make* this society and make one's way in it." So states a tribute to the Flamingo gay disco upon its closing in spring 1981. This writer positions the Flamingo as gay disco's "classic" phase, which manifested the promise of gay liberation for white men during the 1970s; however, the Saint disco quickly usurped the Flamingo's status when it opened in 1980. "To have been [at the Flamingo] at the height of its glory was to have imagined oneself, for a night or a moment, at the center of the world."[1] I take this last statement as emblematic of how gay New York saw itself then—and still does.

In the liberation era, gay men built new institutions that advanced the politics of pleasure in sex and dancing; in New York City, these influential clubs suggested that a new gay world was possible, if not sustainable. New York's nightclubs often take center stage in popular histories and the cultural imaginary of queer nightlife. Gotham is perhaps the only place where venues have achieved such name recognition beyond the city that they stand in for the very ideas of gay liberation, bacchanalia, and disco with the likes of the Stonewall Inn, the Continental Baths, and Studio 54. For gay men living in the city, the Anvil, the Mineshaft, the Paradise Garage, and the Saint likewise defined their times. During the first decade of the AIDS crisis, New York was the city most affected in terms of cases and the best-documented site for activism and media coverage. Each major city had its own versions of gay political awakenings, of bathhouses and sex clubs, of discos, and of the AIDS crisis, and San Francisco offered the other most prominent vision for what gay life could be like and its nearest actualization. Yet whereas San Francisco seemed a gay mecca unto itself, New York sought to lead the rest of the world.

Rather than turn away from the city's outsized influence or what might be called the city's pompous self-aggrandizement, in this chapter I look to it, for the city's myth-making status, its sense of invention, its ambition, its overstimulation, its hype, and its lure all contribute to its cultural power. This chapter is something of a greatest-hits compilation, referencing the clubs that made the biggest splash in their moment and that continue to be the most replayed. The specific conditions in New York as a city on the brink in the 1970s—which offered cheap real estate and anything-goes nihilism—and as a media capital positioned it to be where new sexual formations could be both explored and publicized. The city fosters a bar culture and operates on a twenty-four-hour schedule, including its subway, which is virtually unmatched anywhere else in the world. The city's competitive streak likewise pushed these experiments in public sex and queer venues to be the *most* and the *best* the world had ever seen.

In this chapter I look to New York in the 1970s and 1980s to revisit the gay venues that came to be paradigmatic of their genres or seen as the pinnacles of nightlife genealogies: the Continental Baths, the Anvil and the Mineshaft sex clubs, and the Paradise Garage and the Saint discos. These were the new institutions that the gay-lib generation, largely comprising baby boomers, built as an expression of a new world and in their own image. Here I understand bathhouses, sex clubs, and discos as collectively constituting the cultures of the gay sexual revolution, such that parsing which clubs were bars—and which technically weren't—would negate understanding their imbrication. These venues opened in succession and were understood in relation to and rivalry with one another.

The clubs I reference in this chapter not only drew memberships in the thousands but also elicited heady accounts of their decadence that entrenched their fabulous status. Accounts of these venues "tend toward awe."[2] The word *ritual* appears across tales of these places, and for their faithful, it sometimes felt that only inside these pleasure palaces was one really living. These clubs promised to transform one's sense of time and transcended one's own physical limits via sex or dancing or both. Going to them often inverted the traditional prioritization of day over night and constituted parallel nocturnal lifeworlds all their own, often sustained by a cocktail of drugs and the allure of total carnal satiation.[3] One Saint employee compared working at the disco to a weekly flight to Tokyo for the ways it disoriented his biorhythms.[4]

Licensed bars had to stop serving liquor at 4 a.m., but many of these venues operated as private clubs without temporal constraints. Often, men did not enter these venues until midnight at the earliest, and they typically peaked after 4 a.m. (in the case of sex clubs or baths) or even 6 or 7 a.m. (in discos) and continued until noon or even for days on end. The DJs would spin sets for ten hours or more as dancers would push beyond exhaustion to a kind of euphoric state; off the floor, friends would massage each other to keep their muscles primed to continue.[5] Men might spend entire weekends inside the baths. This lifestyle was unsustainable for most and almost immediately inspired such cautionary novels as Andrew Holleran's *Dancer from the Dance* and Larry Kramer's *Faggots* (both 1978). This culture was threatening because it obliterated long-naturalized social and sexual norms and promoted alternative ways of living. But in focusing on pleasure, gay men had done little to change conditions in the society at large. As a reader's column in the *Village Voice* remarked in 1977, gay men embraced public sexuality in the gay ghetto but "have traded off job protection, economic guarantees, and a social atmosphere of understanding.... Without political or economic base, the gay community has no power. What is called progress, then, is in fact paving the way for a gay backlash that could surpass anything this city has known."[6] I understand the political critique but also unabashedly romanticize this history for the thrill of remaking the world.

As much as these clubs symbolized the exemplary expressions of gay life, the Mineshaft and the Saint, in particular, would also become synonymous with AIDS when the epidemic ravaged their memberships. The disease was not only a cluster of medical, political, and symbolic crises, but it also threatened these new public cultures of gay male urban life.[7] The first cases were reported in 1981, but the historical rupture was less clean than we might imagine retrospectively; the cultures of the 1970s carried on and overlapped for years with evolving new practices and developing knowledges.[8] The clubs' closings in the mid to late 1980s symbolized the end of the liberation era and the disappearance of a culture, concurrent with a broader reactionary political pivot to the right and changing economics. To be clear, the Mineshaft and the Saint were not closed by AIDS; they were closed by public policies and the real estate market, both of which virtually assured that their likenesses could never exist again. This was even before Mayor Rudy Giuliani's 1990s "quality of life" campaign against adult businesses and nightlife transformed the city even more. In their own moment the Continental Baths, the Anvil, the Mineshaft, the Paradise Garage, and the Saint were recognized as embodiments of the gay zeitgeist, and their legacies now constitute the sites of a golden-age history.

It's Raining Men: Gay Bathhouses

Gay bathhouses emerged as a parallel and sometimes symbiotic phenomenon with gay bars and gay liberation. Some men preferred the baths to the bars; others used the baths after the bars if they hadn't picked someone up. Some baths—or "tubs" as they were often called—even featured bars, although most did not; local liquor-licensing regulations dictated which could. Importantly, the baths were much more accessible to all comers than exclusive membership discos. Although they were hailed for equalizing class differences when men disrobed, other hierarchies—of endowment and body type—came into play. Nonetheless, they promised unlimited sexual contacts, from momentary coupling to orgiastic congregations, as well as ample opportunities for both exhibitionists and voyeurs.

Bathhouses date back centuries, providing hygiene and homosociality across cultures. As indoor plumbing became more standard, these venues largely lost their original purpose, although they continued as recreation centers for ethnic communities and increasingly for same-sex encounters by the mid to late twentieth century. Although sexual activity surely took place very early on in bathhouses, historian Allan Bérubé dates the emergence of modern gay bathhouses to the 1890s: first incidentally in "ordinary" bathhouses, then at venues that gained a reputation for action (at certain hours or in certain rooms, with a permissive manager or transgressive masseur), and later at places that explicitly permitted or even marketed themselves as dens for same-sex play. Gyms and hostels, such as the YMCA, likewise developed associations with gay cruising.[9]

Explicitly gay baths date from the mid-1960s and exploded in scale and number in the early 1970s; major cities typically boasted multiple baths by mid-decade. Gay bathhouses typically featured spa facilities, such as locker rooms and showers, steam rooms and saunas, hot tubs and pools, and sometimes workout equipment, as well as private rooms for more intimate hookups and public spaces for group sex. As these facilities expanded, they often included TV lounges, sunbathing decks, refreshment stands, and in the larger venues dance floors and live entertainment. The range of entertainment options and the more vanilla sex acts distinguished these venues from sex clubs, which tended to focus more on kink and forgo many of these amenities.

Manhattan had ten gay baths by 1977 (and ten times as many gay bars).[10] As their memberships climbed into the thousands, these venues became central to gay male public sexual culture in the 1970s, although even at this scale, it appears that only a minority of gay men frequented them. In New York a series of venues successively marked the advances of the gay male scene: the Continental Baths, the Club Baths, and the New St. Marks Baths. In many bathhouses the interactions were nonverbal, but in others they provided an alternative social milieu.[11] Yet despite their popularity and occasional raids, baths did not mobilize the same kinds of political activism that bars did until they became a flashpoint in the AIDS-era debates over sexual freedom and public health regulations.

Steve Ostrow opened the Continental Baths in 1968 in the basement of the Ansonia Hotel on the Upper West Side (see figure 5.1). By the mid-1970s, the Continental would boast the "largest dormitory in the world," with 250 private rooms and 500 lockers.[12] Ostrow, who identified as bisexual and had a wife and children, told a reporter for *Rolling Stone* in 1973 that "it started out as a commercial venture, then it became a mission, and now it is a lifestyle, my life."[13] When it opened, the Continental was unlike any other offering in the city in both amenities and, initially, cleanliness. It invented a kind of gay male utopia of cruising and other diversions. A report in *Gay Power* quoted a patron: "The bars are too uptight and the streets too degrading. The simple fact is that everyone wants to go to an orgy and this is the nicest possible way."[14]

In 1970 the Continental began offering live entertainment and that summer began hosting performances by Bette Midler and her pianist Barry Manilow by the pool, where they would be surrounded by men in towels. (Some accounts specify that Manilow was in a towel, too.) Midler's initial, extended gig soon made the Continental chic, revived cabaret culture, and launched

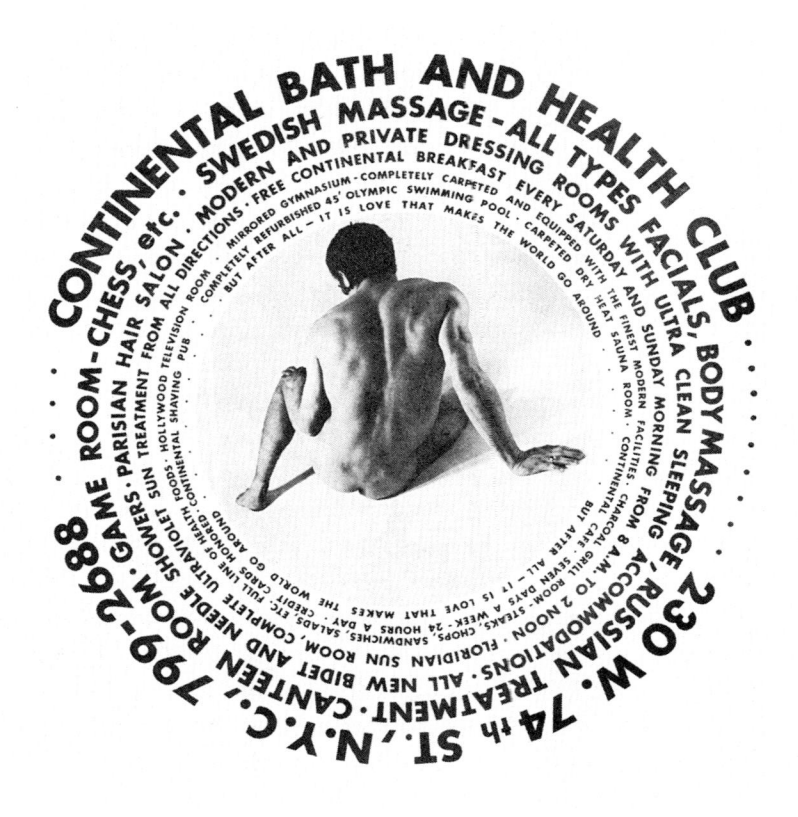

FIGURE 5.1 The legendary Continental Baths in New York City elevated and expanded bathhouse offerings into a total gay entertainment emporium. Advertisement in *Queen's Quarterly*, Spring 1970. Courtesy of ONE Archives at the USC Libraries.

the Divine Miss M's and Manilow's careers. By the time of Midler's return engagement, the Continental began opening to women and straight couples for the performances. The Continental also introduced a licensed cocktail bar called the Top of the Pits and a dance floor. The DJs Larry Levan, who would soon define the sound of the Paradise Garage, and Frankie Knuckles, who would do the same for the Warehouse in Chicago, were best friends who first developed their skills at the Continental in 1973–74. One history of disco alleges that "when he finally set foot" in the Continental, Knuckles "didn't leave for three weeks."[15] Knuckles would go on to invent house music, which he called "disco's revenge."[16]

162   CHAPTER 5

Flush with capital, Ostrow hired interior decorator Richard Orbach, who had worked for Halston and Liza Minnelli, to remake the venue in 1970s Lucite chic; the decorator hoped to buy "several" peacocks for the baths "and have them walking around freely 'nibbling everybody's toes.'"[17] Ostrow even merchandized branded towels at Bloomingdale's. Yet gay critics would paint a dire portrait of the Continental's latter days, claiming it was a den of thieves and rapists, rats and roaches, broken lockers and overflowing toilets when the venue had fallen into disrepair and disrepute amid competition. It closed in 1976, and the space reopened as the heterosexual swinger's club Plato's Retreat.[18]

The Continental Baths would be the most famous and influential early gay bathhouse, but other cities developed their own versions, including Man's Country in Chicago (see figure 1.8), the Locker Room in Atlanta (which adjoined the Hollywood Hot drag lounge and allowed patrons to cross over and view shows in their towels), and the "half-acre" Hollywood Spa in Los Angeles (see figure 5.2). (Los Angeles has consistently had the most bathhouses and sex clubs of any city in North America.)[19] Unlike older, more traditional bathhouses, each of these blurred the lines between a health club, sex club, and nightclub and operated as total gay entertainment emporia. Nearly every city also had a Club Bath (see figure 5.3). The first Club Bath opened in Cleveland when Jack Campbell purchased a small local sauna in 1965; within a year he opened a second location in Cleveland and one in Toledo. The business quickly expanded into an empire of franchises with locations in more than forty US cities, plus some in Canada, by the late 1970s. The New York location opened in 1970 as the first openly gay-owned (as opposed to bisexual-owned) bathhouse in the city and by mid-decade would effectively displace the Continental's position as the nicest gay bath.[20]

Then in 1978 Bruce Mailman unveiled the New St. Marks Baths. The old venue had long attracted men who have sex with men but had become decrepit; Mailman renovated and turned it into a palace for gay clone masculinity, socializing, and sex.[21] The New St. Marks Baths opened with marketing that explicitly mythologized itself by featuring a muscular barbarian in shredded clothing riding a monoclonius dinosaur (see figure 5.4). With the disco phenomenon in full swing, the New St. Marks Baths narrowed focus back to the sex—although it did this in tandem with the nearby Saint disco, which Mailman opened a couple years later. Like the Continental and the Club Baths before it, the New St. Marks claimed to be the cleanest and grandest bathhouse in the city when it opened; it

FIGURE 5.2 Advertisement for the Hollywood Spa visualizing the range of facilities and the men who cruise throughout them inside the massive bathhouse complex. *Advocate*, August 24, 1977. Collection of the author.

was even outfitted with an enema room, which affirmed both points.[22] As the AIDS crisis developed, safe-sex posters dotted the entry kiosk, and the attendant distributed condoms; in order to enter, patrons had to sign a pledge that they would abide by safe-sex guidelines endorsed by the Gay Men's Health Crisis (GMHC).[23] Nonetheless, the city shut down the New St. Marks Baths in 1985 (more on these new policies below). At the time, the employees had to go out and buy a padlock because they had no way to lock the front doors; once opened, it had never closed.[24]

Fuck the Pain Away: The Anvil and the Mineshaft

Whereas bathhouses by their very definition promised clean fun, sex clubs staged themselves as theaters of sleaze. The Anvil and the Mineshaft (sometimes written as Mine Shaft) became the legendary bastions for men

FIGURE 5.3 The Club Baths was the largest chain of gay male bathhouses, with at least forty locations in the US and Canada. *Advocate,* April 19, 1978. Courtesy of ONE Archives at the USC Libraries.

to test their own erotic limits and engage in role playing, fisting, piss play, and occasionally scat. These venues not only provided a space to reinvent sexual practices but also advanced a new model of gay hypermasculinity that recoded bottoming as taking it like a man. In effect, they expanded the meanings of sex acts and gender norms. But just as importantly, for the more casual visitor or even the reader at home, the Mineshaft's significance was to demonstrate that such intense visceral experiences and such a place were even *possible.*[25] Novelist Edmund White suggested that "people have seen things in the Mine Shaft they would not dream of performing themselves, but the spectacle of such varied sexual scenarios can awaken their imaginations."[26] Fisting—also called fist fucking or handballing—came to exemplify new intensities and pleasures that redefined sexual practice for gay men of this era and was claimed to be the only sexual practice invented in the twentieth century (at least until

FIGURE 5.4 Mythical promotional image for Bruce Mailman's New St. Marks Baths, billed as the largest bathhouse in the US when it opened in 1978. Courtesy of The Saint Foundation Archives.

sex via phone or computer came along).[27] Of course, not all men in the 1970s engaged in fisting, but many were piqued by the practice. Sexual fantasies need not align with what one wants to experience in actuality, but in these clubs fantasy and flesh converged to fuel further fantasies.

Although both venues featured bars, they claimed to be private membership clubs and operated well beyond conventional bar hours. The Anvil operated with "no licenses of any kind."[28] The Mineshaft likewise operated without a liquor license but did have nonprofit status; nonetheless, it was investigated for not paying sales, payroll, or corporate taxes.[29] Both had mafia connections. Thus, these were not only dens for sexual outlaws but literally existed outside the law as well. Located in the meatpacking district, they were perched on the far northwest edge of the West Village gay ghetto and proximate to cruising areas such as the West Side piers and trucks, as well as macho bars such as the Ramrod, the Spike, the Toilet, the International Stud, and, in Chelsea, the Eagle's Nest. By day, laborers still processed meat in industrial buildings fronted by lines of hooks suspended from the awnings. By night, the neighborhood was even more animalistic.

The Anvil opened in 1974 and featured a bar, a dance floor, a "burlesque runway" for both go-go boys and drag performances, a trapeze swing used for sex, a setup for porn screenings, a back room, and catacombs underneath the dance floor for cruising and whatever else men were willing to try.[30] The downstairs bar "had manacles so a slave could be chained up and forced to suck cock or be pissed on."[31] The club opened around midnight and would continue until about noon, although its peak hours were after bar closing time, when patrons would come from other venues already buzzed. During its first year, the club hosted a 234th birthday party for its unofficial patron saint, the Marquis de Sade.[32] Felipe Rose, one of the club's go-go dancers, was discovered there and would become the "Indian" in the Village People. However, the bar's legacy was sealed for popularizing fisting in New York after it was performed during a "floorshow."[33]

The experience of the Anvil engaged the entire body's faculties, as well as fantasies of the queer past and possible futures. As Tony DeBlase recounted, "I stood in the Anvil, allowing all my senses to be multiply stimulated at once and realized how [Christopher] Isherwood must have felt in pre-WWII Berlin. Life was indeed a CABARET!"[34] An account from 1978 suggests that the venue "nearly lived up to its fame" but that "tourists from the uptown discos" had effectively spoiled the practice of early-morning "fistfucking demonstrations."[35] A 1984 account in the *New York Native* signaled a qualitative shift in the scene: "The abandonment I wanted to experience now, that I had experienced in the past, was robbed, here, as in other sexual circumstances, by the specter of AIDS. Yes Dorothy, sex still happens at the Anvil, but for most it occurs with a restraint not seen on the dance floor.... It has been, and will continue to be, a badly needed gay enclave of real or imagined nocturnal emissions." Although the club may not have been as outrageous as it had been a decade earlier, an early 1985 bar guide still maintained, "Dress: clothes that can be machine washed in hot water."[36]

Exemplary of the interplays of sex and dancing, the Anvil featured a small but popular dance floor and, at the turn of the decade, drew crowds with its packed Tuesday night new-wave dance parties started by

Bill Bahlman, who was also a resident DJ at Hurrah's disco and later at Danceteria. Bahlman considered playing progressive music at the Anvil to be an extension of gay activism, and he insisted that Tuesdays, like Sundays, be open to women even if the back rooms remained active. (Women were not admitted on other nights.) Live performances at 4:30 a.m. cross-pollinated West Side Black and Latinx drag queens with East Village genderfuck performance artists, cultivating a midweek alternative queer scene.[37] British New Romantics band Visage even released an album and song titled after the club in 1982.[38] This turn toward new wave maintained the club's orientation toward cutting-edge fun.

Whereas the Anvil was known to attract a broad range of types, the Mineshaft was more precise in targeting a leather demographic and more storied as a sex club. Owner Wally Wallace wrote a manifesto for the venue in 1976 stating that "the Mineshaft is basically a unique playground conceived by and dedicated to the fun-loving raunchy gay male minority who exist in the underworld of gay society.... As a social club, the Mineshaft provides the opportunity for guys to meet and to play with men of a like persuasion or with men so rare and so different that they inspire new ways to play, or might even change their entire life."[39] Early on, Wallace hired men "to set the tone of the place" and to train novices. For some regulars, it also functioned like a neighborhood bar, a community center.[40]

The Mineshaft had no signage except for "Members Only" and the street number stenciled on the exterior, "for knowing the correct address was part of being one of the initiates."[41] The venue would grow to be the largest nondisco gay bar in New York and loom even larger in legend. Rex's artwork for the Mineshaft Man contests helped construct its aura (see figure 5.5). During the club's first year, it was smaller and more outré in its bodily explorations. It featured a scat room ("soon abandoned as too intense even for the Mineshaft patrons") and did not initially provide bathtubs for the piss play that was already happening.[42] The Mineshaft's second-floor location was previously a fledgling disco with the same name; the club grew and took over a straight bar and a carpentry shop that were on the ground floor of the same building.[43] From the street, patrons would climb a steep staircase, "the first of many procenia," to the second-floor entryway, where they were met by a doorman for inspection and the cover charge, as well as a clothing check.[44] It opened in the late evening most nights and closed at 6 a.m. most mornings during its first year; it expanded operations so that, starting in 1977, it didn't close at all between Saturday night and Monday morning.[45] When a tourist recounted that he had

FIGURE 5.5 Promotional poster with original artwork by Rex produced for the first Mineshaft Man contest at the legendary private club, circa the early 1980s. This manual laborer's hairy (and probably ripe) armpit is central to the image; note, as well, his pert nipples. Wally Wallace Collection. Courtesy of the Leather Archives & Museum.

come to the club a little after midnight, a "startled habitué" responded, "I didn't know it opened that early."[46] Thanks to low domestic airfares and favorable exchange rates for Europeans, tourists flocked to the Mineshaft to see if it lived up to the stories people told about it.[47]

The front-room bar was the most social and brightly lit area in the venue. The first playroom was located through an archway with a leather curtain and a sign announcing "Mine Shaft," as though this was the true threshold to the club. Into the beyond, the bulbs cast a red light, and occasional spotlights elevated sexual implements to staged productions. The main-floor backroom featured a small bar serving Crisco, the preferred lubricant for fisting because, as the can proclaimed, "It's digestible." Reportedly, "a bartender wielded a grease gun filled with actual motor grease that prepared those about to be fisted" during the club's early days.[48] This back room had wooden booths and an elevated sling for fisting. A latter-day profile described this space as "a Mr. Pac-Man-type computer game that beeps and gurgles as you walk by ... [with] sounds of slurping mouths, bodies shuffling, and the occasional cry of ecstasy and/or pain."[49] The downstairs Playground was through a heavy metal trapdoor in the floor. When the staff flung it open and let it slam to the floor, members would eagerly descend to street level into a maze-like series of spaces: in the first room, one navigated by touch in the absence of lighting; in the second were three tubs installed for water sports (inspired by the Barracks in San Francisco); and in the deepest recesses was the Den, where one's imagination could go wild.[50] One regular described getting to the final room as running the gauntlet. An early review of the venue in *Drummer* magazine described the sonic environment: "The music is truly weird, but played low enough not to cover the slurps, moans, whippings, and piss scenes."[51] As others would recount, the music played included works by Vangelis, Steve Reich, and Philip Glass: "The most conventional the music ever got was Laurie Anderson." The sonic environment reverberated the club's commitment to polymorphous experimentation. One account even lists "electronic synthesizer music" among the fetishes the club popularized.[52]

Moving through the spaces took patrons on a metaphorical journey.[53] A night at the Mineshaft often entailed transitioning between spaces and states: gossiping at the front bar, waiting for one's eyes to adjust while moving to the back room or downstairs, feeling one's way around, navigating one's own and others' unease, making contact and kissing, participating in an assemblage of bodies and then pulling away, refueling at the front bar, and then going back for another experience.[54] Waxing semiotic, a writer gushed that "there is no mode for writing about such things which will alert readers to the loveliness of it, there is no code."[55]

At its height, 500–600 men visited the Mineshaft on weekend nights.[56] However, it was not inclusive. The venue barred women from entry[57] and posted an infamous dress code that enforced masculinity, including natural male musk:

> Approved dress includes the following: cycle leather & western gear, Levi's, jocks, action ready wear, uniforms, T shirts, plaid shirts, just plain shirts, club overlays, patches, & sweat.
> NO COLOGNES or PERFUMES
> NO SUITS, TIES, DRESS PANTS
> NO RUGBY SHIRTS, DESIGNER SWEATERS, or TUXEDOS
> NO DISCO DRAG OR DRESSES
> Also NO heavy outer wear is to be worn in the Playground.[58]

The dress code was not just about enforcing a particular aesthetic, but it was also—perhaps even primarily—about rejecting the trappings of "respectable" society. The dress code was introduced a couple of months after the club began because members wanted their space to be protected from becoming "infiltrated by people who didn't belong."[59]

The Mineshaft also disciplined its members with a strict code of conduct. One flyer instructed members, "Keep Your Damn Mouth Shut When Playing in the Playground! The MINESHAFT playrooms are for one purpose and it surely is not the place to gossip, discuss your European trip, or how well Joan Sutherland sang 'Carmen' at the Met. This you do in the Main Bar which is a social area. Please remember this simple rule when visiting the Shaft."[60] A 1981 newsletter likewise addressed squandered resources: "CRISCO IS WASTED ON PEOPLE WHO NEVER PUT IT TO THE USE INTENDED: It is a fact that only about 25% of the Crisco dispensed ever reached its intended destination. Beginning in November there will be a small fee of 25 cents to help cut down on waste."[61] The Mineshaft's kink play intersected with leather but also signaled a generational evolution; as Pat Califia observed, some of the old guard were "not about to get Crisco on their leather."[62]

Sex acts at the Mineshaft were at once liberating and highly codified; the idea there was that every taboo could be performatively broken. Many men embraced the opportunity to test their thresholds for submission. Other men ensured rigor, gathering to witness a fisting session, "anxious to see the act performed, wanting to make sure it was done correctly, to ensure veracity."[63] Wallace enlisted DeBlase among the "faculty" of the School for Lower Education, where he "demonstrated what one friend call[ed] a 'filet of scrotum'" involving a butterfly spreading board, electroshock, and piercing needles.[64] For other commentators, the Mineshaft represented sexual fashions that would soon become passé in the modish New York gay scene: "The truth has always been a deal more sanguine [than the club's reputation]. Sadomasochism, fistfucking, and scat are elements that, in this town, serve as histrionic props in camp theatre, and they've become as tired as drag shows.... It will bore or delight you, depending not on your morals but on your mood."[65]

The Mineshaft would be vividly simulated for the 1980 film *Cruising*, a thriller starring Al Pacino as an undercover detective exploring the gay leather scene in pursuit of a serial killer (see figure 5.6).[66] The exteriors were shot on location, but Wallace claimed that his bar was raided and shut down by police in cahoots with the producers; he alleged that while he and

FIGURE 5.6 The controversial film *Cruising* (dir. William Friedkin, 1980), starring Al Pacino (*center*), re-created the Mineshaft. Members of the gay leather community participated as extras, but the film's production and release were protested by gay activists who objected to its representation of gay men as pathologically violent. *Cruising* was later the first film screened at the Mineshaft. Publicity still. Collection of the author.

his staff were in jail, the production team photographed the interior of the Mineshaft to reconstruct it on a soundstage. The production and release of the film were protested by gay activists—as many as eight thousand at one event—but also featured at least five hundred extras from the gay community who contributed to its claims of verisimilitude. Opposition to *Cruising* from within the gay community varied from those who felt the film was exploitative and misrepresentative of gay S&M culture to those who thought that any portrayal of the leather scene and gay promiscuity would be bad publicity for the gay movement as a whole.[67] Although Wallace took issue with the harassment of his venue during production, he did not object to the film itself and dismissed protesters as vanilla gays. When the Mineshaft started screening films inside, *Cruising* was the first.[68]

With the rise of the AIDS crisis in the 1980s, the Mineshaft would become the primary target for policing gay sex in the city. The club was made an example as the first to be padlocked in November 1985—conspicuously, the day after Mayor Ed Koch's reelection—under new city guidelines forbidding any oral or anal sex in public venues. The law did not distinguish between safe and unsafe acts; the legal finding against the club stated that "it is impossible, as a practical matter, to ascertain whether . . . preventative action is being taken." Although the law addressed *acts*, it was primarily enforced against *venues*. The complaint against the club charged that it "knowingly and recklessly created a condition" for prohibited sex acts.[69] The law, like the epidemic itself, seemed to target the very cultures that gay men had constructed in the 1970s.

This regulation sought to stem the spread of HIV by attempting to foreclose promiscuity, which it equated with sex outside the bedroom. Although it was critiqued at the time as well as after, I understand the logic of this approach and the sense of urgency for some kind of governmental intervention in the face of an escalating and uncertain epidemiological catastrophe. The core problem with the law was that it focused on public sex rather than unsafe sex, whereas research and much anecdotal evidence have ultimately demonstrated that people are *less* vigilant about safer-sex protocols at home and within relationships.[70] Counter to the assumptions undergirding the law, as Douglas Crimp famously asserted, "*It is our promiscuity that will save us*"—both in terms of taking more precautions with unfamiliar partners and in terms of imagining safe erotic alternatives.[71] Activists argued that safer-sex education and enforcement could best be done in public venues such as the Mineshaft.[72]

Already in 1981, Mineshaft regular Arnie Kantrowitz felt "ennui" about going to the club and presciently remarked, after recounting the venereal diseases he'd caught and treated over the years, "There's more chance of meeting up with an epidemic than a lover in the bars and baths." A couple pages later, he remarked, "One clear lesson from history is that freedom is a temporary state of affairs."[73] In a 1983 article titled "Policing the Libido," Darrell Yates Rist observed that safer-sex notices hung throughout Mineshaft but that "few clients paid these precautions—or encouragements—much mind. Not out of carelessness, but because in the gay male world, anal intercourse has long been out of vogue" in response to the epidemic. Contemporaneous data on other sexually transmitted infection rates demonstrate that most gay men *did* change their sexual behaviors. The cultures of gay sex were shifting, and attendance was also in decline.[74] Accounts indicate dozens rather than hundreds of men visited the Mineshaft each night by the mid-1980s. A profile published a few months before the club's closure remarked that attendance had slumped for a couple of years but had grown back after 1983. As Wallace told *Stallion*, "I think people are back to basics. I think there's more s&m, because a lot of people say s&m is probably the safest of anything as far as health concerns."[75]

Ultimately, the city—not waning membership—closed the venue in November 1985. On the eve of the closing, an anonymous letter (signed Deep Throat) to Wallace offered an elaborate list of nineteen strategies (many of which involved collecting used condoms from members) to help the club stay open by promoting safe sex and aiding in questionable epidemiological research. The letter makes clear that the club was well informed of best practices as well as key players in the Gay Men's Health Crisis and the city's health department. But it was too late.[76] In this political moment, it was unlikely that enhancing safe-sex protocols at the Mineshaft could have saved it. The Anvil shuttered voluntarily around the same time, and the city's closing of the St. Marks Baths soon followed in December. City officials may have misunderstood the actual best practices in terms of public health, but they did recognize the Mineshaft's symbolic power. An open letter by a group of s/m women called the closure "an attack on all sexual non-conformists."[77]

Total sexual liberation, invention, and public expression had been world making for many gay men, and many were understandably resistant to any politics that would constrain these advances. In principle, I too oppose any legal constraints on one's sexual freedom or self-expression as long as no one else is harmed by one's choices and actions. (I acknowledge that what constitutes "harm" is open to interpretation and shifts historically.) The early government response to the emergent epidemic was unconscionably delayed, insufficient, and misdirected at local and national levels. Complicating matters, researchers, doctors, and policy makers were responding to partial, developing knowledge of the spread and prognosis of HIV/AIDS and could not offer definitive best practices; this also allowed skeptics to reject advice and rationalize behaviors that were generally believed unsafe. Part of the problem at the time was that much of the public rhetoric positioned gay men—and other early identified at-risk populations, such as injecting drug users—as expendable, and policy makers seemed to care only about preventing transmission to the "general population." Of course, gay men found such rhetoric and policies homophobic and rejected them as politically untenable. But gay men were divided about what the policies *should* be.[78] Looking back at this period from after the COVID-19 pandemic, it is also clear that many people—gay men included—were and are willing to ignore reliable epidemiological knowledge and to put others at risk in the name of their own personal liberty. For some, the Mineshaft's role in expanding sexual practices was retrospectively controversial, even among people who went there. Commenting upon the epochal shift that the Mineshaft's closure marked, one commentator wrote, "How fitting, how bitter that our history should be identified with two bars: from the Age of Stonewall to the Age of the Mine Shaft!"[79] (On the Stonewall, see the introduction.)

More, More, More: Disco

Dance—and more precisely disco—became one of the most prominent manifestations of gay liberation when crowds of hundreds and even thousands of men collectively moved together. Though at times perceived as a turn away from leftist militancy, the rewards of such political and ideological work were perhaps nowhere more *felt* and *lived* than on the dance floor. At gay discos, dancing could carry on all night, all morning, into the next day, and even beyond. Disco culture effectively began to coalesce in New York circa 1970 via multiple sites: Gay Liberation Front's and Gay Activists' Alliance's respective dances, David Mancuso's parties at the Loft, Seymour and Shelly's gay takeover of the Sanctuary, the opening of the Ice Palace (Cherry Grove) and Sandpiper (the Pines) on Fire Island, and the incorporation of a dance floor into the Continental Baths.[80] These formative venues ranged from racially and sexually mixed (the Loft) to predominantly white and exclusively male (the baths). Disco historian Alice Echols points out that although many historians take a utopian view of the Loft and other influential clubs as egalitarian, the fact that they operated as invitation-only or membership clubs made them exclusive in their subcultural cool.[81]

Leading dance-music historian Tim Lawrence has argued that disco was inherently queer in multiple ways, reflecting and extending beyond its emergence in tandem with gay liberation. At early venues, the mix of gay and straight dancers across racial lines meant that men danced next to both men and women in a blur of sexualities and a flow of momentary juxtapositions. Solo dancing was still safer than partnered contact dancing for gay men in the event of early 1970s raids, and dancing on one's own allowed men to cruise the crowd.[82] Esther Newton observed the irony that "just when police harassment had ended and men could dance with men and women with women, disco almost dissolved the couple as a dancing unit."[83] As Lawrence writes, "The idea of dancing with a partner did not so much implode as expand."[84]

Perhaps most importantly, at discos people *danced with a crowd* in a way that manifested a kind of pansexuality. Indeed, disco music was understood as the music of sex, and the dance floor fostered an experience of communal erotics. The dance floor reflected the kinds of casual intimacies that sustained gay male life in the 1970s. In Holleran's *Dancer from the Dance*, the narrator attests that "now of all the bonds between homosexual friends, none was greater than that between the friends who danced together. The friend you danced with, when you had no lover, was the most important person in our life."[85] Reflecting on new relationships such as the disco buddy, Crimp concurred: "The innovations of disco mirrored the ethos of gay liberation regarding the expansion of affectional possibility."[86]

Accounts of gay discos repeatedly stress the dance floor's transformative effect in producing a kind of collective body—one in which the eroticism of the crowd would be rechanneled back into dancing to the point of transcending singular consciousness or physical exhaustion. The thousands of men who danced at the Ice Palace—as at Paradise Garage and the Saint later—took a submissive role in their relationship with the DJ: "They said, '*Do it to us!*'"[87] The Ice Palace in Fire Island was the 1970s' leading trendsetting disco, gay or straight; owner Michael Fesco (who also owned the Flamingo in Manhattan) introduced popular Sunday afternoon tea dances, riffing on tea service he had seen at a London gay bar.[88] A denizen of the Ice Palace scene recalled that "there were two thousand writhing, drugged, beautiful bodies dancing on this dancefloor. By 6 a.m., we were outside around the pool, and we were dancing under the stars as the sun was coming up. And I believed at that moment in time that we were having more fun than anybody in the *history* of civilization had ever had." Soon, the same men would be dancing under simulated stars at the Saint.[89]

Gay disco would achieve a critical mass of press coverage in 1975.[90] Straight disco's popularity and backlash followed between 1976 and 1979.[91] *Saturday Night Fever* and its soundtrack were released in late 1977 and pushed a whitened version of the phenomenon to the point of pop-culture saturation.[92] Earlier that same year, Studio 54 opened in a former television studio in Times Square at the peak of the neighborhood's connotative sleaze; it purportedly introduced a velvet rope to keep sex workers out.[93] The club was famous for its obsession with status and exclusivity, which created a door policy that made people even more desperate to get in. No other dance club before or since has elicited such public fascination and fame. The venue capitalized on the mixing of gay men, celebrities, and eccentric libertines and sought to cultivate a space of affirming energy inside. The venue's innovation was producing a kind of theatricality; the dance floor was set on the stage. Offstage, men engaged in sex and drugs, further contributing to the club's reputation for decadence. For some purists, Studio betrayed disco's core element; Lawrence claims that "the primary activity at Studio was not dancing but looking," although Studio 54's DJ Richie Kaczor did launch Gloria Gaynor's B-side "I Will Survive" into the disco canon.[94] Studio's rise was famously matched by a precipitous fall, fueled by cocaine, skimming, tax evasion, and public schadenfreude.[95] Gay men were always part of its scene, and the club had gay nights, but it was never the most important disco venue for gay men. Studio 54 suggested the influence of gay male culture on the mainstream rather than Studio itself shaping gay male culture.

It must also be said that gay liberation did not alter men's consciousness alone; drugs played a key role in changing minds and moods as well. As others have observed, disco advanced a shift from alcohol as the social lubricant for gay men toward various chemical combinations of drugs to orchestrate a peak experience.[96] Angel dust, LSD, mescaline, and pot altered perception; MDA and cocaine boosted energy; and Quaaludes blocked inhibitions. Poppers topped off the experience by giving a head rush and relaxing muscles (see chapter 1). In contrast, alcohol's sedative effects risked fatiguing dancers, and its diuretic effects could interrupt the dancing with the need for bathroom breaks.[97] The more serious a venue was about music and dancing, the less likely it was to have a licensed bar serving alcohol—although most dance venues in and beyond New York *did* serve liquor. For instance, the leading disco entrepreneur in Texas designed his venues to have bars surround the dance floor on three sides to ensure a steady flow of traffic, liquor, and profits.[98]

Gay discos carried on into the 1980s and reached their climax only then. Paradise Garage and the Saint operated in different orbits despite their geographic proximity. Each one vied for the title of the greatest gay disco of all time. Both were private downtown clubs with curated memberships where men danced for seemingly impossible durations in a state of tribal, even transcendent bliss. The Paradise Garage felt more democratic, whereas the Saint's patrons felt like the chosen people. The music mixing was more radically playful, the sound system more meticulously calibrated, and the dancing more intense at the Paradise Garage, whereas the musical flow was more controlled and seamless, the balcony more sexually active, and the built environment a total aesthetic experience at the Saint. The Paradise Garage was seen as underground, whereas the Saint aspired to the celestial. To put it simply, the music, the DJs, the men, and the culture at the Paradise Garage were majority Black; at the Saint they were majority white.[99] Both defined their overlapping era for their respective memberships, which by and large did not overlap.

Work That Body: Paradise Garage

Paradise Garage, sometimes called the G*ay*rage by members, has been heralded as "the most iconic nightclub in dance music's history; mythologised, idealised, lovingly eulogised for its sense of musical freedom and adventurousness."[100] It opened at the beginning of 1977 in a former parking garage (thus the name) that had also briefly housed the Chameleon disco. Because of delays with the arrival of the sound system during a blizzard, the opening-night party was disastrous, and the white gay men the club initially courted never really came back.[101] Although Paradise Garage was primarily identified with DJ Larry Levan—around whose skills the venue was oriented from the start—it was owned by white gay man Michael Brody, and most of the money to open it came from loans from white friends, including West End Records founder Mel Cheren and writer and future AIDS activist Larry Kramer. Nonetheless, the club hosted theme parties celebrating African heritage, events sponsored by the National Coalition of Black Gays, and meetings, consciousness-raising sessions, and fund-raisers for Black and White Men Together (later renamed Men of All Colors Together).[102] Inadvertently or not, Paradise Garage would become the most important queer-of-color dance venue for a decade. It also hosted the Gay Men's Health Crisis's first major AIDS-related benefit in 1982.

As a private club, Paradise Garage carried on the legacy of the early disco venue the Loft. At its zenith, a crowd of two thousand would dance for ten, twelve hours at a stretch. The crowd was predominantly Black and Latinx (including Afro-Latinx), with a minority of white dancers. The club was open from midnight until noon; when it hosted performances, the talent would take the stage at 4 or 5 a.m. On Friday nights (technically Saturday mornings) the club opened to straight dancers, and Saturdays (technically Sundays) were exclusively gay. The club had two tiers of membership: Friday-only and Core-Mechanic, which permitted entry either night but specified that these members must be "GAY." Core-Mechanic members complained when the club allowed the Friday members to mix with the Saturday crowd during a holiday party. Members could bring up to four guests on Saturdays, but only one person per party could be female; this kept the club mostly male but made it more gender mixed than many gay venues.[103] Although it opened in the 1970s, the Garage hit its stride around 1980 and sustained momentum for the next several years.[104] The venue was less connotative of sex than other gay venues of its time, and it wasn't particularly social; it was for sweaty, all-in, all-night-into-the-next-day dancing. A mid-1980s guide to queer-of-color venues advised the uninitiated to "bring a few changes of clothes. You probably won't leave until sometime Sunday afternoon and you'll want to look presentable for the ride home."[105] Few of its regulars lived anywhere near the venue. Paradise was a destination, an island unto itself.

The entrance was up a long driveway ramp to the second story, which created a transitional zone that was lit like a runway; the music from inside the club throbbed and built anticipation. At the top of the ramp, a neon sign replicated the club's logo of a racially ambiguous, curly-haired man wielding a tambourine overhead with a whistle and an amyl-nitrate inhaler hanging from his neck; the club's name appears as a tattoo on his beefy bicep. The sensorium of heat, smell, and sound pounded members upon entering. "The sound went right into your mouth, and you swallowed it whole," as one regular told me.[106] The front room was known as the Grey Room; this was the first space opened for dancing during preopening construction parties and mostly functioned as the warm-up and cool-down space. The space was later redone with art-deco-glass brick walls as a location for Woody Allen's film *Radio Days*; the Parade Garage kept it, added blue neon, and rechristened it the Crystal Room.[107] The private club did not serve liquor but offered fruit, juice, and baked goods to keep the crowd's blood sugar up. The main dance floor was essentially a massive black box (later featuring a perimeter mural by club regular Keith Haring) that featured a knee-high stage for performances (see figure 5.7).[108] Located in a former garage, the club did not have central heating or air-conditioning.[109] A rooftop deck allowed patrons to cool off.

More importantly than the visual design, the club had the most fine-tuned sound anywhere. Crowds would often have to wait, even in the cold, for Levan to finish tweaking the audio setup each night to get the effect he

FIGURE 5.7 Panoramic photo of the crowd during the Paradise Garage's closing party on September 26, 1987. The club's logo is visible at center, flanked by a mural that Garage devotee Keith Haring painted on the dance floor's perimeter. © Tina Paul. Courtesy of Tina Paul.

desired: "bass so *penetratingly loud* it pulsed through your veins, combined with a crystal-clear top-end."[110] Levan wanted his crowd to feel the bass in their asses, not to hear it with their heads—and he arranged the speakers accordingly.[111] (Levan dated and collaborated with sound designer Richard Long, who developed some of the club's audio technology. Levan used German electronic music composer Manuel Göttsching's *E2–E4* to calibrate the soundscape.)[112] With thousands of dancers and no air-conditioning, the speakers would get hot and change the sound during peak hours of Saturday-night parties; Levan would continue adjusting them during sets.[113] He would even at times stop the music mid-set to pull out a ladder and polish the disco ball if it didn't glint perfectly. At other times, Levan would turn out the lights "when a song speaks of giving one's body over to the music. The result is that bodies are actually lost in blackness."[114]

Levan, often rated as the greatest DJ of the era, "showed that dance music could be made of a multitude of sources, that . . . there was a whole world of possibilities"[115] (see figure 5.8). He queered musical forms by introducing promiscuous mixing and remixing. In segueing among otherwise distinct songs, genres, and sounds, DJs exploded the form of individual

FIGURE 5.8 Photo of Larry Levan in the Paradise Garage DJ booth on May 16, 1986. © Tina Paul. Courtesy of Tina Paul.

tracks in a polyphonic ebb and flow.[116] Levan was often unconcerned with smoothing his transitions between tracks, emphasizing instead a radical array of genres and even playing some tracks repeatedly the same night. He reportedly also played Diana Ross's "Love Hangover" every Sunday morning at 9 a.m.[117] Taana Gardner and Loleatta Holloway ranked among Levan's favored divas, although the more prominent Grace Jones, Chaka Khan, Thelma Houston, and even early-career Madonna and Whitney Houston also graced the stage with live appearances. The crowd would bark and woof in approval; Madonna reputedly flopped, although her video for "Everybody" was shot there anyway.[118] Compilation CDs and streaming playlists of Levan's remixes and DJ sets abound, and they still sound fresh. Change's "Paradise," Sparkle's "Handsome Man," and Levan's mix of Loose Joints' "Tell You (Today)" stand out as favorite tracks I've come to know through such listening, and their disco-funk bass lines and vocal refrains perhaps approximate the Paradise Garage's dance-floor vibe. (Although it postdates the Paradise Garage by decades, Roland Clark's "I Get Deep" may be the greatest ode to the joy of dancing to a DJ's house-music mix.)[119]

Levan had an unparalleled communion with his crowd by the sheer force of his sensibility. As a retrospective profile suggests, "It was an expression of a collective joy that went beyond mere pleasure.... Garage patrons were on a quest for transcendence through music and partying, a journey that involved an excessive stimulation of the senses that promised spiritual enlightenment." The account continues: "Essential to the Levan experience was the life-affirming lyrical narrative—one that spoke of love, hope, freedom, and universal brotherhood."[120] One white club member described to me that if he was standing alone, someone in the crowd would take him by the hand to bring him into their group on the dance floor. He also described the "heavenly torture" when Levan would work a song the crowd loved for an hour, interweaving it in and out of other songs, and effectively keeping the crowd captive on the dance floor; the crowd would cry and beg Levan to be released, but he kept them dancing. Levan's music and the mass of people on the dance floor created a magnetic field.[121] Paradise Garage was reportedly one of the first venues where ecstasy became a popular club drug in the 1980s because the drug promoted the affects of shared joy and musical fascination.[122] As a retrospective tribute reflected, "The Garage had velocity and glamour and ghetto all in one!... The Paradise Garage was where you lived your life for all it was worth. It was where everyone felt if they danced together, not just African Americans but everyone as a family, perhaps they would save tomorrow."[123]

After a high-end apartment building was constructed next to the Paradise Garage, the tenants didn't want the dance club's lease renewed, and the venue closed in 1987. (See also chapter 3.) Brody, the owner, was living with AIDS and was too ill to reopen elsewhere.[124] Levan died of heart failure in November 1992. Demonstrating both Levan's stature and the enormity of queer losses at the time, his obituary ran alongside those for Marsha P. Johnson, Audre Lorde, Melvin Dixon, and Melvin G. Ross Jr. in the same issue of *BLK*.[125] Although the epidemic undoubtedly decimated the club's membership, retrospective accounts of it focus primarily on the life that Levan's music gave the crowd.

Rapture: The Saint

No other venue was seen to epitomize 1980s white gay male culture in New York City as much as the Saint. Almost immediately it was understood both as part of a genealogy and as its telos. A series of venues had refined the white gay male disco scene during the 1970s: the Tenth Floor, 12 West, and the Flamingo. The Tenth Floor and the Flamingo were minimally designed spaces that were virtually all dance floor; the *men* were the decoration, especially when they stripped off their shirts to reveal their Nautilus-sculpted "disco tits."[126] The Flamingo purposely didn't have air-conditioning to ensure that the men would sweat, and it was designed so that men *had* to touch each other's bodies as they danced or made their way through the space; this meant the men dissolved into each other.[127] As membership clubs, these discos could both stay open for extended hours and also exclude women, men of color, and poor gay men to maintain an homogenous crowd. The Saint, the heir apparent to this disco genealogy, opened in 1980, combining the theatricality of Studio 54, the skyward orientation of the Ice Palace, and the men of the Flamingo. It quickly ran its Manhattan competitors out of business.

The Saint was loved and hated for many of the same qualities: its ostentatiousness and its white gay macho clone clientele. Here, the cultures of disco and of sex came together most spectacularly, and the club would be seen as ground zero for the AIDS crisis. As one commentator asserted, "The Saint created the context by which gay men in New York lived—even for those who never went there. It shaped our understanding of what being gay was or was not." Years after it closed, *Out* magazine maintained that "disagreement over whether the Saint was the pinnacle or the nadir of gay male culture still polarizes the community today."[128] No other disco inspired as many think pieces and tributes in the gay press.

The Saint was the Sistine Chapel of dance. The club was the vision of Bruce Mailman, who owned the phenomenally successful New St. Marks Baths nearby. It opened in fall 1980 to mark a new decade, although in effect it embodied the cresting of the 1970s. Mailman commissioned architect Charles Terrell to design a disco under a planetarium dome in the former Commodore Theater movie palace, which had more recently been the rock venue Fillmore East (1968–71). Construction cost $4.6 million ($14.7 million in 2021 dollars), with another half-million in upgrades each summer.[129] Emphasizing the built environment, *After Dark* magazine ran six pages of color photos and architectural sketches of the venue (see plate 7); as its text remarked, "The Saint may seem frozen in time (Fire Island, 1977) or freed into infinity, but its theatrical innovations are unlike any before it." Another critic remarked that the club was "considered by some the eighth wonder of the world."[130]

The facility was three stories, each with distinct spaces. The first-floor entry maintained the elegant monumentality of the building's heritage architecture.[131] The membership check-in and coat-check systems were hailed for their computerized efficiency. The first floor also featured a snack bar with complementary juices, fruit, popcorn, seltzer, and beer; in 1985 Mailman belatedly secured a license to serve hard liquor in order to increase revenues. However, the Saint's defining features were its second-story dance floor and third-story balcony. The dance floor was a massive circular space capped by a perforated aluminum planetarium dome; the dome acted as a scrim, which could be opaque or translucent, depending on how it was illuminated. At the center of the dance floor was a star-projection system on a hydraulic lift that was ten times brighter than those used in traditional planetariums (see figure 5.9); the lighting design could simulate the outer cosmos, the dawn, or atmospheric conditions such as lightning storms. The speakers were installed behind the dome to produce the illusion of pure sound by masking its source.[132] A twenty-foot section of the dome could lift to reveal a stage for performances. Among the Saint's size-queen boasts:

Dance floor: 4,800 square feet

Dome: 38 feet high by 76 feet diameter

Lighting: 1,500 lights in addition to the star projector

Sound system: 500 speakers and 32 amplifiers

The dance floor was designed without pillars or any other obstructions to limit the sense of an expanse. The Saint claimed that it "transcends the physical, creating the illusion of infinite space. At such a place, anything is possible."[133] Paradise Garage backer and West End Records founder Cheren recalled that on the opening night of the Saint, "you could actually hear the gasps of astonishment above the pounding music. The invitation had depicted the floor plan of Rome's Pantheon, and everyone assumed that this was a gross exaggeration, but it wasn't."[134]

As opening night peaked, the DJ put on Donna Summer's "Could It Be Magic," and the lighting designer cut the lights and displayed the star projection system for the first time: "Everyone gasped . . . [and] was frozen and in awe" during the song's breathy opening. "As the song took off, the galaxies began to rotate. . . . There was nothing to do but scream, throw up your hands, and keep screaming."[135] Even though the song was already four years old, I can think of no better track than "Could It Be Magic" to reveal the lighting system's virtuosity, between its dramatic musical shifts and its lyrical incantations: "I want you to come, come, come" and "Spirits move

FIGURE 5.9 The dome, star projection system, and men on the dance floor at the Saint. Courtesy of The Saint Foundation Archives.

me." The dance floor was initially painted black, but with thousands of men under both the influence of drugs and a starscape dome, the dancers could not see anything under their feet and lost all sense of horizon. Some embraced dancing in space's zero gravity, and others toppled over in disorientation. The management immediately stripped the floor to modify the effect. Lawrence concludes his account of opening night: "When asked, 'Will you go back?' another dancer replied, 'I'll go back every Saturday night until I die.'"[136]

Testimonies from the Saint routinely avow its spiritual resonance. Kantrowitz mused that "the ultimate letting go is raising my arms up to the sky. I forget the Dionysian scene that surrounds me, and I am transported to the stars where I can commune with God. So what if the sky is made of laser light and scrim? What church doesn't use a few props?"[137] A later reflection recalled that "those nights and mornings into Sunday afternoons were rituals of ecstasy, glorious pagan liturgies of maddened spirits. We lost our minds in melody and rhythm and the sweat of bodies on the dance floor, pulsing silhouettes beyond all life." Advised a gay guide from the time, "The dance floor is sacrosanct."[138]

The third floor, constructed of concrete and steel, was a balcony where men could look down at the dancers; from this vantage point, the glowing scrim dome over the dance floor "reminded people of the extraterrestrial mothership from *Close Encounters of the Third Kind*."[139] However, the balcony was best known for its bacchanalian sexual congregations amid its tiers of banquets. The late-1970s straight white "disco sucks" rhetoric was not simply a matter of expressing distaste for the music but a blatantly homophobic reference to cocksucking.[140] The Saint carried the torch for both—disco and sucking. One account recalled an exchange between a member and visiting friend who asked, "It seems a little cliquish.... How do you meet any of these gorgeous guys?" The member responded, "On your knees in the balcony, if you're lucky."[141] Studio 54 had been mildly scandalous for allowing public sex in its shadowy areas, but the Saint upped the ante as the true confluence of disco with elements of the sex clubs and bathhouses. During its early years, much of the Saint staff came from the Mineshaft, and the prevailing aesthetic was leather macho before transitioning toward monied preppy as the AIDS crisis escalated.[142] Mailman would contend that it was never his intention for the balcony to be used for orgies, and in periodic mailings he urged members to refrain.[143] But because he was the proprietor of the New St. Marks Baths, where men commonly took sexual siestas between Saturday and Sunday parties, his protestations rang disingenuous to many. Meanwhile, a cleaning crew used a wet vac and baby powder to dry up the condensed sweat between Saturday and Sunday hours.[144]

Mailman didn't want the DJs to become more famous than his club, so the Saint had a rotation of primary and secondary DJs.[145] Nonetheless, the members were well aware of the specific DJs who spun ten-hour sets guiding their all-night musical journeys. The music played at the Saint tended toward crowd favorites and Hi-NRG with minimal lyrical content. The evening became a finely orchestrated arc, beginning with classical music as members arrived and then building to high-tempo tracks at 132 beats per minute and above, which DJs sustained from 2 a.m. until 6 a.m. The crowd would applaud the DJ and the lighting designer as they wrapped their set at dawn. The morning "sleaze" session after 6 a.m. was when the DJs could be looser and more experimental in their down-tempo grooves; as the crowds thinned, hard-core dancers hit their stride, and their pretenses loosened.[146] In the histories of dance music, the Saint has been positioned as influential in developing a narrowed and whitened dance music sound, one that is often contrasted with Levan's musical opening-out at Paradise Garage; by the mid-1980s, the two clubs' set lists rarely overlapped.[147] Effectively canonizing its halcyon days and reviving a disappearing culture, during the 1986–87 season the Saint also hosted a series of parties that played tapes "from the Saint Archives" of DJ sets from specific nights between 1981 and 1984; flyers for the series include a poignant new tagline: "Where the Spirit of Dancing Lives On" (see figure 5.10).[148]

Every account of the Saint that I've encountered suggests that the built environment, light show, and control of the music made it the most extraordinarily produced immersive dance experience ever fabricated but that the social scene of clones and yuppies might have also been the most alienating.[149] The Tenth Floor's membership had been known as "the 500" elite and the Flamingo's as "the A-list" thousand or so gays. Describing the Flamingo membership's "appetite for success," White wrote that "one must have the drive of a tycoon, the allure of a kept boy, the stamina of an athlete, the bonhomie of a man of the world"—a virtuosity that is unattainable for most, unsustainable for all.[150] The Saint courted the same men who had been members at its precursors. Its initial membership was set at between 2,000 and 2,500 to ensure a crowd but closed with a waiting list even before opening night. One employee described the members as "artists, lawyers, doctors, city planners, people who ran the world."[151] The members were an insular social network: "One had to be recommended by two members just to be eligible for membership; many were turned down."[152] Membership and admission were almost exclusively male to support what Mailman believed was "the gay male dance ritual."[153] As many remarked, in this self-mythologizing temple the gym-sculpted men—a still-new aesthetic in gay male culture—were like gods. Other New York gay and lesbian venues were protested against for discrimination at the time, but apparently not the Saint, despite its exclusionary practices (see also chapter 4).

Because the core membership was assumed to summer in Fire Island, the Saint operated in seasons, from fall to spring, like the Flamingo before it. The venue was known for its decadence and ambition, and it hosted

> **FROM THE SAINT ARCHIVES...**
> **MUSICAL MEMORIES**
> JOIN YOUR FELLOW SAINT DISCOPHILS
> BEGINNING SUNDAY, DECEMBER 28, 1986
> A MONTH OF TAPED-T'S
> DOORS OPEN AT 5 PM
>
> SUNDAY, DECEMBER 28, 1986
> RE-LIVE ROY THODE'S
> "SECOND SEASON OPENING PARTY"
> (SEPTEMBER 19, 1981)
>
> SUNDAY, JANUARY 4, 1987
> RECALL GEORGE CADENAS'
> "WRECKED PARTY"
> (NOVEMBER 28, 1981)
>
> SUNDAY, JANUARY 11, 1987
> REMEMBER SHAUN BUCHANAN'S
> "LAND OF MAKE BELIEVE PARTY"
> (APRIL 12, 1984)
>
> SUNDAY, JANUARY 25, 1987
> RECOLLECT "ROY'S PARTY"
> FEATURING SHARON WHITE,
> HOWARD MERRITT,
> ROBBIE LESLIE,
> WAYNE SCOTT
> (JUNE 2, 1982)
>
> THE SAINT'S TAPED-T'S ARE FREE FOR EVERYONE
> COMPLIMENTARY ADMISSION FROM 5 TO 10 PM
> THE SAINT—WHERE THE SPIRIT OF DANCING LIVES ON
>
> THE SAINT
> 233 EAST 6TH STREET, NYC
> 212.674.8541

FIGURE 5.10 During the 1986–87 season, the Saint hosted "musical memories" parties that played tapes "from the Saint Archives" of DJ sets from golden-age nights between 1981 and 1984. Courtesy of The Saint Foundation Archives.

frequent theme parties evocative of Fire Island events and announced with elaborately designed invitations. This was gay high society. The most legendary Saint events were its annual White Party (inherited from the Flamingo) and the S&M-themed Black Party. At the 1981 Black Party, a performer did a live sex show involving a boa constrictor (although, as Mailman recalled, the snake didn't seem very interested), and in 1982 the invitation featured a step-by-step illustrated guide to circumcision and promised "strange live acts," although no live circumcision was performed (see figure 5.11). By the 1987 installment, the invitation cautiously stated, "Return of the Black party ... but safer" and had a condom attached to the mailer.[154]

CHAPTER 5

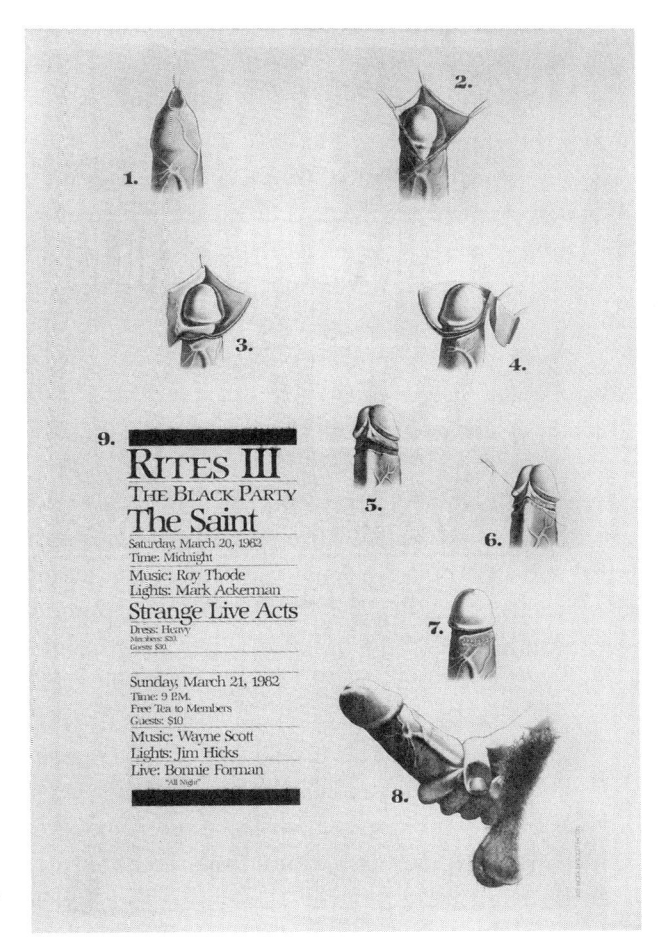

FIGURE 5.11 The infamous invitation for Rites III: The Black Party featured illustrated circumcision instructions and promised "Strange Live Acts." Courtesy of The Saint Foundation Archives.

So many of the Saint's members were among the prominent early casualties of AIDS that, according to Randy Shilts, the syndrome was colloquially referred to as "Saint's disease."[155] By 1983, journalists already began observing a palpable shift in the tenor of the Saint as the crisis ravaged its community. One member recounted an exchange with two strangers who had likewise started to avoid the club:

"I can't face it . . . I think too much of the men who have"—he hesitates—"died."

"Once in a while," the first says, "if I close my eyes and listen to the music and pretend with all my might that it's three years ago, for a little while, maybe a couple of minutes, I feel a wonderful elation as if it really *is* three years ago."[156]

When the angelic-voiced Irish tenor Colm Wilkinson performed his number "Bring Him Home" from *Les Misérables* at the Saint in 1987, the song would have been heartrendingly recontextualized as a hymn for all the young men who had become sick or died from AIDS.[157]

The club struggled by the mid-1980s. In addition to the losses and connotations of AIDS, few could sustain the energy for dancing every weekend past dawn; many members would burn out after a couple of years. The closing of the St. Marks Baths in 1985 meant that it couldn't underwrite the Saint, which had been so expensive to maintain that it was never very profitable even at its prime.[158] The venue began serving alcohol to increase its income in 1985 and began opening to straight crowds on Fridays year-round.[159] In 1986 the club hosted its first women's party, featuring female bodybuilders; women's parties continued as recurring events organized by Our Parties, Ourselves. These nights were open to women only for the first few hours, then opened to men for co-gender dancing at peak times.[160] The Saint finally closed, despite a rebound in attendance, in 1988 because a developer made Mailman an eight-figure offer on the building that more than doubled his investment.[161] The rampant gentrification of the East Village from the 1980s onward has made launching another club on that scale prohibitively expensive. The widely advertised closing gala, simply titled the Last Party, featured forty hours of continuous music from Saturday, April 30, to Monday, May 2 (see plate 8).[162]

At the Last Party, a spray of flowers next to the cashier subtly paid tribute to the staff and members who had been lost to AIDS.[163] Mailman himself reflected that as the AIDS crisis developed, gay men "blamed their institutions, rightly or wrongly. . . . [The Saint] was just a barometer of what was happening in the community."[164] Looking back on the Saint and what it meant, a novelist urged, "Be gentle to The Saint. We all loved it. We shouldn't regret it now. It was a wonderful part of my life. There's such a tendency to tie The Saint scene in with AIDS, and that's all bullshit. It's just an end of an era."[165] As always, some of the most incisive commentary came from the scene's most storied chronicler, Holleran: "Some writer said that a movement, an epoch, always builds its most magnificent headquarters, its monument, when the movement itself is already on the wane. . . . The Saint opened in 1980, at what seemed to be the high point of disco, when in reality that was already past."[166] Holleran contended that "the Saint represented everything I regretted about the development of disco—huge scale, ridiculous hours, hordes of strangers, special effects, and an atmosphere as conformist as a country club in Scarsdale." Perhaps most cuttingly, he professed that "the Saint thought of everything but the Plague."[167]

Although there were always other bathhouses, back rooms, sex clubs, and dance floors, the venues in this chapter were the defining institutions of their moments and in cultural memory of gay nightlife. In subsequent years, parties would attempt to re-create the Anvil, the Paradise Garage, and the Saint for their survivors and for those too young to have experienced them in their original glory. But these could be, at best, only performances of the past. The Continental Baths, the Mineshaft, the Paradise Garage, and the Saint remain apex expressions of gay male pleasure palaces, ideals of another era.

INTERLUDE 5

The Saloon in Minneapolis

In fall 1998 the Saloon in Minneapolis began running a series of ads with the tagline "Your body will betray you." These appeared on the back cover of the local bar rag *Lavender* shortly after it went glossy. Each ad featured a man's body in close-up, seen through a tinted filter as though he was under the colored lights of the dance floor. Text appeared in a small white font, demanding a closer look. The various iterations stated

> subtle signs of your sexual attraction are apparent in tender muscle fluctuations of the iris. your body will betray you. the saloon.[1] (See figure 15.1.)
>
> waves of desire are expressed by a firmness in particular tissues. your body will betray you. the saloon.
>
> a sudden erection of cells produces a tactile surface on your skin. your body will betray you. the saloon. (See plate 9.)
>
> tiny beads of sweat are excreted through the epidermis during sexual arousal. your body will betray you. the saloon.

FIGURE 15.1 The Saloon's "your body will betray you" advertisements ran on the back cover of *Lavender* magazine from 1998 to 2000. This version includes the text "subtle signs of your sexual attraction are apparent in tender muscle fluctuations of the iris. your body will betray you." Collection of the author.

> when aroused, a sudden rush of chemicals is involuntarily released into your bloodstream. your body will betray you. the saloon.

One final version dispensed with the prologue and simply stated, "your body will betray you. the saloon." That one was set against the only photo in the series that cropped the model's body down to his crotch. The ads, which appeared well into the year 2000, did not include the bar's address. This ad spoke to those already in the know. As the Twin Cities' most popular gay bar and dance club, the venue was more concerned with creating an image and an atmosphere than with conveying information, anatomy lessons aside. These millennial ads titillated and threatened in their play with arousal, optics, knowledge, and surrender. And like so much dance music, they implored potential patrons to submit to carnal pleasures.[2] What they marketed was desire itself.

THE SALOON IN MINNEAPOLIS

Minneapolis was my coming-out city, and the Saloon was my primary bar in my early twenties. The Twin Cities act as magnet and gateway for queer transplants from the surrounding midwestern region; according to an improbable 1983 statistic, 17 percent of Minneapolis's population was estimated to be LGBTQ+.[3] My first gay bar outing in the Cities had been to the Gay 90's super-bar complex with straight coworkers on its 18+ night; at the time, I usually went dancing at First Avenue, the city's legendary live music venue prominently featured in *Purple Rain*.[4] I later alternated between the Saloon and the more gender-mixed Club Metro in St. Paul with queer friends. In our early days of coming out by going out, young queers often try on different venues until we find the one that fits or, more likely, adapt ourselves in an attempt to belong somewhere. Some LGBTQ+ people never feel similitude or eventually tire of nightlife pretenses and disappointments, then declare themselves "not into the bar scene."

I turned twenty-one in 1996, the first year that AIDS-related deaths dropped since the beginning of the epidemic because of new "cocktail" treatments (as they were called at the time). This means that I grew up and came of age when HIV/AIDS and gayness were culturally conflated but also that I was spared the waves of loss that older queer people experienced. Many of the important people in my life are HIV+, but their health has affirmed the medications' effectiveness. My peak dancing years meant moving to Madonna's "Ray of Light," Cher's "Believe," and Whitney Houston's "It's Not Right but It's Okay" on a weekly rotation.[5]

The Saloon had changed its image—even its owners and its name—before I entered it. The bar opened in 1977 as the Y'all Come Back Saloon, named after an Oak Ridge Boys song.[6] Its owners were a straight family, and its environment was reportedly sleazy (in a bad way). Two of the gay bartenders, Jim "Andy" Anderson and John Moore, walked out on the job one night after smashing all the liquor bottles; then they bought the business in 1981.[7] By mid-decade, the duo began a concerted effort to market the bar to the collegiate crowd with ads in the *Minnesota Daily*, the University of Minnesota's student newspaper. Their new marketing taglines included the suggestive "The kind of place mother warned you about" and "Turn night into play."[8] Little did I know that I would be part of the bar's target market, engineered a decade before my arrival at the U of M. The bar announced itself as gay owned and operated (in contrast to the Gay 90's), and it soon presented itself as a responsible community supporter by offering a designated-driver program and hosting a Hot, Horny & Healthy safe-sex workshop in collaboration with the Minnesota AIDS Project.[9] After

New and Improved. Bigger and Better. The City has expanded our sidewalks to meet your shopping needs.
Nightly. At the Saloon.

The Y'all Come Back Saloon
830 Hennepin Avenue
Minneapolis, Minnesota

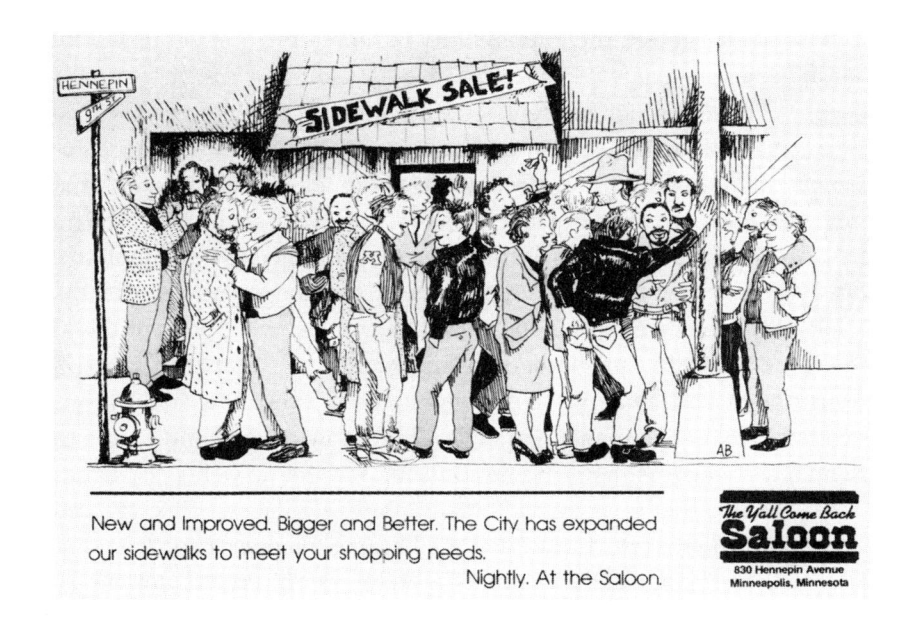

FIGURE 15.2 Still operating under the name the Y'all Come Back Saloon, the bar ran this advertisement to promote its expanded sidewalks for cruising after last call, which was known as the nightly "sidewalk sale" at gay bars. Reflecting its collegiate market, one of the men in the center wears a University of Minnesota letterman jacket. *Equal Time*, March 4, 1987. Courtesy of ONE Archives at the USC Libraries.

the city expanded the sidewalks out front, one ad visualized the nightly "sidewalk sale" as men loitered and cruised for hookups after last call (see figure 15.2). In August 1988 the bar dropped the "Y'all Come Back" from its name.[10] I was surprised to learn it had ever been called that because I had never detected a hint of twang about the place. A 1990 survey of area gay bars affirmed that the Saloon was Twin City's primary boy bar, and that position has stuck.[11]

I was already going to the Saloon when the "your body will betray you" campaign started, but it ran contemporaneously with my frequent returns. I remember that many people thought these ads were creepy, but for me the campaign was fascinating in its insinuations of inevitability, lust, tactility, and ultimately the necessity of accepting one's sexuality. The ad intuitively understood that gay bars are sites of queer exposure: entering the space marks the person who enters, and those inside will tend to make assumptions about the sexuality and identity of the others they see. Even one's eyes, the debut ad alleged, could reveal as much as they saw.

The slogan suggested the impossibility of repressing one's urges—with the dialectic of anxiety and liberation that this implies.

The campaign's high concept, striking graphics, and minimal text also signaled a new era in sleek gay bar aesthetics just before other, more upscaled bars such as Boom and Jet Set were about to open in town. But what intrigued me more, then and now, about the campaign's timing was that in the late 1990s the idea of disclosure and risk continued to be connotative of HIV status. Therefore, this campaign could only have appeared *after* the availability of new treatments effectively changed the public perceptions of the epidemic from a plague to a chronic condition—that is, after AIDS transitioned from *epidemic* to *endemic* status.[12] These new medications saved and extended many men's lives. But knowledge of and access to them have been unequal, and the continued epidemic yields disparities in life chances that track along demographic differences. (This was also about the time that the local gay press became filled with ads from Big Pharma.) The Saloon's ad campaign curiously rescripted recent memory when the bodies of men with AIDS *did* visibly betray them via such stigmatized symptoms as Kaposi sarcoma lesions and wasting. These ads reclaim gay men's bodies as desirable again and reframe their anxieties via dichotomies of enticement and diagnosis, visibility and vulnerability. These ads feel unresolved, reflective of a moment when gay public life was figuring out its next act with both excitement and unease. As I write in interlude 7 on Somerset County, PA, this was a contradictory moment when gay life approached a tipping point toward assimilation yet also when hate crimes were more visible than ever.

Years later, older and maybe queerer, when I returned to Minneapolis during the holidays and for extended summer stays, my routine changed because I had. The Saloon had added showers for go-go boys and renovated its back patio, but it began to seem so predictably mainstream to me. Instead, I began to frequent the long-standing 19 Bar, a tavern that drew an older crowd and served pitchers of beer with baggies of ice floating in them. It warmed my heart to see the 19 packed, even when the temperature outside was twenty degrees below zero. And then, for a heady moment during summer 2007, the new bar Pi struck me as utopian for its community of people across the gender spectrum; when its lease was up the following year, however, this bastion became impossible to sustain.

For many of us, which bars we go to likely changes over time as do we, whether we are trying out different clubs while we are figuring out who we are, or we must find a new place when a favorite venue closes, or we age out of one scene and settle into another. More likely, we are nonmonogamous and go to more than one bar during any given period in our lives. Yet we may have fond memories of formative venues and identifications with a home bar. The Saloon was neither my first nor ever my only gay bar, but it epitomized my developing understanding of what a gay bar was.

6

Proud Mary's

An Institution in Houston

"If there is a gay utopia, Mary's is it." So claimed the leather magazine *Drummer* after a reporter's visit to Houston. "While it was the first bar in Houston in which the words 'leather' and 'SM' were ever spoken aloud, it is, at the same time, the hangout of every possible sexual preference on earth. That night the bar was hosting its own Mr. & Ms. Mary's Contest in the patio, a scene somewhere between Kraft-Ebbing and Hieronymus Bosch."[1] Referencing the author of *Psychopathia Sexualis* and the painter of *The Garden of Earthly Delights*, respectively, this leather tour guide both educates readers in the history of sexual deviance and stakes Mary's place within it. Ever prone to spinning a feverish yarn (see interlude 1 on Denver), *Drummer* nonetheless asserted the veracity of lore surrounding the bar in a follow-up account: "Whatever wild tale or outrageous story you've heard about Mary's—no matter how incredible—it is probably true.... Mary's has crossed over into a world of its own that defies definition or comparison."[2]

Mary's inspired hyperbole for decades, which made it both literally and figuratively legendary. When the regional gay bar magazine *Out in Texas* began a series of profiles on "famous and infamous gay bars in Texas," the magazine started with Mary's. The writer described the venue as "the mother house of all the gay bars in Houston" and as "that insane, bizarre, pungent, often disastrous place on the corner of Westheimer and Waugh."[3] Some of the stories I've found and heard about the bar are alluringly far-fetched, and others seem true enough: plausible with some flourishes. As one missive recounted, "How you respond to Mary's may depend on your mood. I once saw a clone slap a dwarf clear across the courtyard for saying the wrong thing at the wrong time, and I left, disgusted. But the dwarf stayed."[4] Although I intend to document a close-to-accurate account of its history, I also recognize that part of what made Mary's *Mary's* was its powers of fabulation. Thus the place where the anecdotal bends into the tall tale may be where the meanings of the joint exist most poignantly.

I've been punch-drunk in love with Mary's ever since learning of it in the archive, although it closed before I ever visited Houston. The bar exemplifies everything a gay bar can be, good and bad: a freewheeling sanctuary for sexual self-invention and expression, a transformative space for political organizing, and a home for alternative kinships and memorialization. For all its live-and-let-live attitude, the bar's past also includes controversies about its racial politics that complicate its legacy. With a decades-long run, Mary's has been commemorated more than perhaps any other gay bar in America except the Stonewall Inn, and two terms recur in accounts of the place: *raunchy* and *institution*.

I Was Born This Way: Making Mary's

Gay father-and-son entrepreneurs Joe and Michael Anthony moved from Los Angeles to Houston in the late 1960s. They had already established a mail-order business in gay adult media in California when they expanded operations with two bookstores in Houston in 1969. In Texas they advertised their status as "Houston's only gay owned and operated vending company," Coin-O-Matic, which offered coin-operated adult film arcades at their bookstores, as well as pinball machines, jukeboxes, pool tables, and vending machines for candy and cigarettes. They were based in the Montrose, which in the 1960s was emerging as the new center for gay venues if not yet a gay community. Soon they ventured into bars and publishing, purchasing the neighborhood lounge Tommy's Bar, located near one of their bookstores, and giving it the name Mary's in 1971.[5] Legend has it that the name originated when Michael asked his father, "Well, Mary. Now that you own the bar, what are you going to call it?"[6] "Mary" served as a campy, affectionate pronoun used between gay men, sometimes indicating effeminacy. In its early incarnation, Mary's Lounge was marketed as "A touch of California" in Houston's "Homo Heights" and featured "bikini boy dancers & waiters."[7] Happy hour was called "Camp Time."

In 1973 Jim "Fanny" Farmer purchased the bar from the Anthonys and remade the bar into the Mary's that would become a living legend. Almost immediately upon taking ownership, Farmer had the front window painted with an illustration of a rodent resembling Joe Anthony alongside the text "The Rat is Gone." Farmer has been described as a "one-time world champion rodeo performer, owner of the largest collection of fishnet hose in Houston, ... [and an] accomplished classical pianist."[8] He also drove a pink 1959 Cadillac convertible and was an avid biker. Farmer "despised rules and was a notoriously bad bookkeeper," so he was in ongoing trouble with the Texas Alcoholic Beverage Commission. To maintain the bar's license, Cliff Owen became co-owner in 1978.

The bar's golden age appears to have coincided with Andy Mills's tenure as the manager, from 1977 to 1985. Mills was a musician and had previously managed the Ice Palace disco on Fire Island before settling in Houston. Mills, like Farmer, was a leader in the community; although Mary's made him visible, he was also instrumental in developing and leading the Montrose Marching Band (later known as the Pride Band) and the Montrose Singers (later the Gay Men's Chorus).[9] Immediately after leaving Mary's, Mills worked at Charlie's Coffee Shop, an all-night diner across the street where the regulars often went after hours. Before and after Mills's run, the bar reportedly cycled through numerous managers—seventeen by 1990. The staff went by nicknames or feminine alter egos; the all-male cast of characters who worked the bar included Jail Bait, Vivian, Hedda, Toma, Prissy, Helen, Nurse, Geraldine, Torchy, and Mumbles, among others, circa 1978. The bar hosted recurring "ex-employee" parties, and former workers remained regulars, suggesting continuing social bonds.[10]

As one decades-long patron who spent upward of twelve hours a day in the bar recalled, "Mary's tried to be a leather bar in the beginning, but it kinda came out different. Instead of S&M as it's usually known, it stood for sequins and mascara here. ... We had butch guys who were just a bit on the nelly side."[11] The bar's ads explicitly reflect this, as in one promoting an Easter hat beer bust by featuring a genderfuck collage of a man with a mustache and drag makeup, a body stocking, and a collaged

FIGURE 6.1 This genderfuck collage for an Easter hat party and beer bust at Mary's exemplifies the bar's wild and campy sensibility. *TWT*, April 4, 1980. Courtesy of ONE Archives at the USC Libraries.

hat (see figure 6.1). In another image, an angular cartoon leatherman's imposing figure gives way to an affected posture with a cinched waist, a prancing knee, a slightly arched wrist, and an announcement for *Auntie Mame* as the week's screening (see figure 6.2).[12]

Inside the bar, Farmer could not abide underwear and declared it "illegal" on the premises. He offered patrons the option of stripping it off themselves or having it cut off: "Most liked to have it cut off." The briefs were then flung to the rafters, where they accumulated until they became a health or fire hazard.[13] A trapeze swing hung over the bar so that men literally could swing nude from the rafters; this was removed after someone fell off. A motorcycle chained to the ceiling above the pool table (apocryphally alleged to be Janis Joplin's) was a more enduring fixture. The staff mopped

FIGURE 6.2 This Mary's ad puts a nelly twist on leather masculinity: its imposing figure's broad shoulders taper to a cinched waist and prancing knee, and the week's feature film was *Auntie Mame*. *Montrose Voice*, January 8, 1982. Courtesy of ONE Archives at the USC Libraries.

every night, yet a ripe stench permeated the venue, so much so that at least one ad posed the question "What's that smell?"[14] *Torso* magazine advised travelers that Mary's was "considered pretty sleazy by the more hygienically oriented!" Many preferred the outdoor space in back. "Fresh Fruit" is how one Mary's ad promoted the patio bar.[15]

Mary's successively expanded its space by buying up adjoining lots behind the main bar. Mary's opened a back patio bar in 1975; it was destroyed in a fire in 1978 but was soon rebuilt and expanded to include a stage.[16] Further back, there was a passage to another outdoor area called the Out Back. In the rear there was also a two-story building that housed a short-lived leather shop; the side of the building facing the patio had a large Texas Opry House sign that had been liberated from a straight bar. Reflecting Mills's touch and the expanded space, the bar's advertising and programming became more playful in the late 1970s, including various drag and costume parties in 1977 and a series of live performances in 1979. Tuesdays became movie nights, and Sundays were bacchanalian beer busts with orgies in the patio area. The bar developed a full roster of events. For instance, during a single week in 1982 it hosted its weekly leather night, its weekend beer bust, a screening of *Lawrence of Arabia*, a Tupperware party ("Come as your favorite housewife"), the Mr. and Mrs. Mary's Contest, and a benefit for the Kaposi's Sarcoma Committee (which would evolve into the AIDS Foundation Houston and was the first HIV/AIDS organization in Texas) and the Montrose Counseling Center (which would become the LGBT community center).[17] During its heyday, the bar operated from 7 a.m. until 4 a.m. daily. Early-morning customers were required to eat a bite of breakfast with their drinks; sometimes bartenders were paid to come in early to feed the unhoused. Everyday regulars at the bar included Ray Hill and Judy Reeves, who were both sober, and many others who were drunks.[18] Regulars each had their spot and their place in the community.

More than any bar in town, Mary's flaunted a public visibility. It was the first gay bar in Houston with windows.[19] The windows were repainted as often as weekly to celebrate holidays or simply make a scene; the building itself was also periodically repainted, from lavender (circa 1979) to red, white, and blue (circa 1981). The bar's advertisements varied so wildly in aesthetics that they helped construct the free-for-all sensibility the bar promised. Images ranged from surreal illustrations and postmodern photomontages to portraits of the Houston Motorcycle Club, which claimed Mary's as its home bar (see figure 6.3). Across all of these come-ons, however, wit prevailed. As I will discuss later in the chapter, by the 1990s, the bar would also present a series of murals that were plainly visible to passing traffic and that further made the bar iconic (see plate 11). Mary's location facing the busy Westheimer thoroughfare also made it the optimal spot for watching annual gay pride parades. Hundreds of men would scope out the festivities and other men from the roof or in front (see figure 6.4). Despite the bar's liberated ethos, some men would wear masks or even bags on their heads to remain anonymous during pride events; patrons also frequently left their IDs at home because, if arrested, they could lose their jobs or custody of their children.[20]

The bar was also one of the most debaucherous hosts of the annual Let Us Entertain You (LUEY, pronounced "Louie") party each spring; the name references the burlesque number from the musical *Gypsy*.[21] This tradition started in 1971 as a motorcycle run from New Orleans to Houston following Mardi Gras to keep the party going. The event became

FIGURE 6.3 The Houston Motorcycle Club (*pictured*) made Mary's its home bar. Owner and birthday boy Jim "Fanny" Farmer appears in a white T-shirt and sunglasses in the back row; Farmer's dog Sam appears in front. *TWT*, November 4, 1978. Courtesy of ONE Archives at the USC Libraries.

more formalized in 1973 as a gesture of southern hospitality to the service workers from New Orleans by hosting them for a carnival of their own. Texas Pinnings became a rite of passage during LUEY: each motorcycle club member would get his suitor engorged and then mark his jeans with an insignia pin at the tip of his cock. This both documented the size of the men's endowments and kept their heads stimulated; once a guy was pinned, others could slap him on the pin to get his attention.[22]

The Mary's gang played by its own rules, according to *Drummer*'s John Preston: "Mac and his side-kicks and I spent a good hour talking about the finer points of semantics. Seems the fellas in Houston have decided that 'Sir' is no longer an appropriate term for a bottom to use when addressing a top. Too many little Naugahyde fairies have caught onto it and watered down

FIGURE 6.4 Men watching the 1982 pride parade from Mary's roof and front sidewalk. Photo by and courtesy of JD Doyle.

its meaning." Rather, they had decided on "Lord." (Preston was conversing with Mary's fixture Michael "Lord Mac" McAdory.) Preston concluded that "Texans have never been known for their humility. Houston gives them few reasons to learn that lesson in life."[23] In the mid-1980s, the bar began immodestly hailing itself as the National Bar of Texas.[24] Signaling that the bar's reputation preceded itself, Mary's ads featured the tagline "Mary's ... of course" in 1977 and 1978. By 1979, the phrasing shifted slightly to "Mary's ... naturally." This revision stuck—so much so that people often thought that "... naturally" was part of the bar's name.[25]

With all due respect to Fanny, Lord Mac, and all the others, however, two furry creatures were perhaps the *real* masters of the joint. Farmer's German shepherd mutt Sam sat at the bar on a stool and drank Jim Beam. Sam had been a stray who leapt into Farmer's convertible at some point in the 1970s and soon took to riding in front of Farmer on his motorcycle; Farmer estimated they clocked up to eighty thousand miles on his bike together (see figure 6.5). Sam was regularly featured in ads starting in 1978, and in 1982 he was named employee of the month and inspired a Miss Dog Face USA contest.[26] He passed in 1988 at age seventeen. Some years later, Mr. Balls, a cat with low-hanging genitals, dropped out of a tree in

FIGURE 6.5 Mary's owner Jim "Fanny" Farmer and his dog, Sam, rode thousands of miles together on motorcycle. Sam was a regular who had his own seat at the bar. *Upfront America*, August 29, 1980. Courtesy of ONE Archives at the USC Libraries.

the back area and took ownership of the venue. He likewise had his own stool at the bar and was given a studded leather collar.[27]

Anything Goes: The Houston Boom

Mary's was a product of Houston's dynamism. Houston was the fastest-growing major city in the United States during the 1970s, with a boom economy fueled by the oil industry. This made the city a destination for adult transplants, including many gay men, and it exemplified the reimagined urbanities of the New South. In 1977 the *Advocate* would describe Houston as "a city almost without a history." Houston's rapid emergence as a mecca was repeatedly reported in the gay press during the 1970s and early 1980s, signaling that the center of gravity for visible gay life was shifting away from the coasts. But this was still Texas, which meant an embrace of individualism, from a lack of zoning laws to a sense of personal liberty.[28] The same year Farmer took over Mary's, *Texas Monthly* called the Montrose, where the bar was located, "the strangest neighborhood in Texas" for its eclectic mix of old money, academics, artists, hippies, gays, and freaks.[29] Mary's was right at home and would soon be an anchor for the emergent gayborhood. A decade later, a gay porn magazine remarked, "Saying 'I live in the Montrose,' you'll discover, is virtually the same thing as saying, 'I suck cock.'"[30]

In Houston the bars remained the center of public and political life in the gay community throughout the 1970s and 1980s.[31] Houston's Montrose developed into a visible gayborhood with its concentration of bars and gay services in a relatively compact area, often with venues clustered on what would otherwise be residential streets. The juxtaposition of bars and houses—and of restaurants inside former single-family homes—maintained an intimate scale and haphazard feel. Although rents started rising as early as the 1970s, the neighborhood still looks comparatively free from real estate developers' speculation.[32] The city was infamous for its lack of zoning and for its dependence on automobiles. Mary's, by facing the Westheimer thoroughfare, also solicited the attention of all the traffic that cruised or crawled along the gay strip. By 1975, the traffic was so bad that neighborhood residents formed the Montrose Citizens Association and had "No Turns" signs installed to prevent cars from circling back through side streets.[33] (See also chapter 3.) As Reeves told me, traffic would come to such a standstill that people could get out of their cars, go into Mary's to pick up a drink, and return without losing their spot or holding up traffic; alternately, patrons would hand drinks to cruisers through the car window as they drove past. (There were no open-container laws yet.)[34] The congestion also meant that patrons often had to park blocks away from the bars, and street violence targeting gay pedestrians in the neighborhood was common; the Montrose Patrol formed in the early 1980s as a volunteer street-safety group.[35]

Mary's was the leading public sphere for gay civic life in Houston. "There would be no gay rights movement in Houston without Mary's," gay political leader Larry Bagneris Jr. asserted to me.[36] Houston's self-mythologizing Ray Hill—a former teen evangelist turned jewel thief turned gay-rights, antiwar, and ex-con prison activist—likewise found a vibrant public sphere for political discussions at Mary's.[37] Hill recalled that "I found everything an activist could want: creative artists and writers, people with connections all over the advertising industry and GLBT folk aplenty yearning to be equal and free, not to mention a few very good-looking men ready to invest their energy in having a good time." Yet he soon recognized that if he wanted to do organizing work, he needed to arrive early enough "before everyone got so drunk that an intelligent political conversation could no longer be had."[38] Hill told me that Farmer didn't like loud music, so the venue was conducive to conversations and even meetings.[39] Reeves—a decades-long regular at Mary's—captures its sensibility by referring to gay preppies as "riff-raff" and dismissing the lesbian bar Kindred Spirits as "too prissy."[40] Mary's refused such uptight respectability. Nonetheless, Mary's was where organizing started for the AIDS Foundation Houston, the Montrose Clinic (now Legacy Community Health Services), McAdory House (a residence for people with AIDS), and the Montrose Center (the LGBTQ+ community center). Surely not everyone in the Houston gay community went to Mary's or would have wanted to do so, but all of them benefited from its existence and what it made possible.[41]

A groundswell of political fervor followed protests of Anita Bryant's local appearance during the Texas Bar Association convention in 1977. In the wake of these protests, the Town Meeting I at the Astro Arena drew six thousand LGBTQ+ activists in 1978, and the first gay pride parade in Montrose was held belatedly in 1979 as part of a ten-day series of events to commemorate the Stonewall riots' tenth anniversary and to promote the first National March on Washington for Lesbian and Gay Rights that fall.[42] Mary's had the first float in the parade. Two Mary's patrons—Hill and Bagneris—were among the organizers for the first march on Washington. Mary's ran advertisements publicizing the march (see figure 6.6) and funded the Montrose Marching Band's travel to it; the Houston contingent led the march.

Although police raids were a perennial issue dating back decades, a gay pride week raid on Mary's in 1980 stands out as the most politicized. Sixty-one people—including owner Farmer, manager Mills, six employees, dozens of patrons, and a couple of bystanders on the street—were arrested and hauled away in inhumanely crowded paddy wagons amid a media spectacle. Farmer had been selected as the honorary grand marshal for the pride parade that year but spent the evening leading up to the event in jail. The raid became a cause célèbre, and community members began wearing "Mary's Fairies Out of Jail" T-shirts in support of the arrestees. The arresting officers failed to appear in court, and only three people were convicted of charges; appeals exonerated them.[43] The same week as the raid, an off-duty officer shot and killed Houston Gay Political Caucus

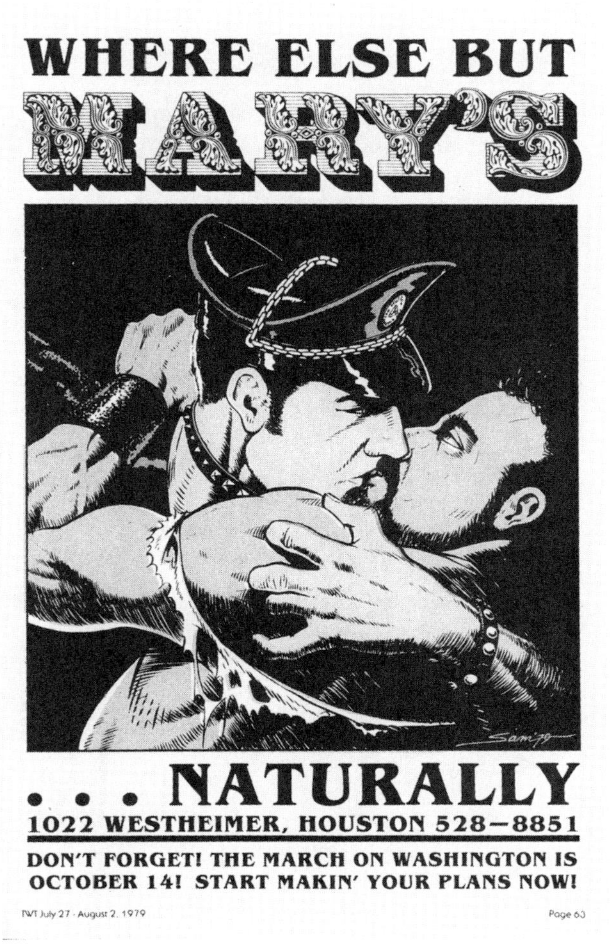

FIGURE 6.6 Mary's promoted the 1979 National March on Washington for Lesbian and Gay Rights (*bottom of ad*) and paid for the Montrose Marching Band to travel to it. The Houston contingent led the March. *TWT*, July 27, 1979. Courtesy of ONE Archives at the USC Libraries.

(HGPC) secretary Fred Paez, which further escalated tensions between the gay community and the police.

By the early 1980s, the HGPC proved to have an extraordinary impact on election outcomes. It boasted the largest membership of any local gay organization in the country and was "rivaled only by... the National Gay Task Force."[44] In part, the HGPC's success was a product of the fact that many men in the gay community were recent transplants, so they did not have ties to long-standing local traditions, conservative institutions, or the residual good-old-boy network. Four lesbian and gay activists—Pokey Anderson, Bill Buie, Hugh Crell, and Keith McGee—formed HGPC in 1975. They held the first gay voter rally in the region, drawing more than five hundred

FIGURE 6.7 Mary's satirized newly inaugurated Ronald Reagan with this publicity still from his film *Bedtime for Bonzo* (1951). Insinuating forbidden love, the text says, "We met at Mary's." *Montrose Voice*, February 27, 1981.

people. In its first year, HGPC distributed ten thousand election-guide pamphlets through the gay bars and was credited with influencing three thousand votes.⁴⁵ Mary's was one of the caucus's most visible early supporters and was a good venue for community outreach. One of the myths about Mary's is that HGPC started there, but none of its founders were regulars.⁴⁶ In 1979 HGPC effectively swayed its first municipal race with an upset victory for city councilwoman Eleanor Tinsley over a two-decade incumbent. In fall 1980, nine out of ten precincts where HGPC campaigned voted for Jimmy Carter over Ronald Reagan, contrasting with Reagan's sweep in the rest of Houston and nationally.⁴⁷ After Reagan's inauguration, Mary's began a series of ads that subversively appropriated vintage images of the new president; my favorite features a publicity still from *Bedtime for Bonzo* to insinuate a touch of interspecies romance as Reagan embraces a chimpanzee behind the text "We met at Mary's" (see figure 6.7).⁴⁸

The HGPC garnered national news attention for endorsing Democrat Kathy Whitmire, a Montrose resident, for mayor. During the primary she was uncertain to even make a runoff against her better-financed opposition. Yet the HGPC contributed to securing Whitmire's victory as the city's first female mayor in 1981 and again in 1983; she would be reelected in 1985, 1987, and 1989 as well. By 1982, HGPC had compiled a 15,000-name "computerized" mailing list and by 1983 had registered 45,000 people to vote.[49] In 1983, eighteen candidates sought HGPC endorsements and "vied for the right to have their names printed on the 50,000 wallet-sized endorsement cards the GPC distributed at gay bars and discos."[50] The organizing efforts of the HGPC helped sway the majority of city council races.[51]

Foregrounding the bars' role in city politics, Mayor Whitmire and a trio of city council members went on a well-publicized tour of nine gay bars during their 1983 campaign and on a subsequent victory lap after the election to thank the gay community for its support. They started at Mary's.[52] At a subsequent city council meeting, a group of conservative citizens protested the mayor, and a fundamentalist spokeswoman claimed that Whitmire was "slipping and slithering over semen-soaked floors" at the gay bars. When asked if she would visit the gay bars again, Whitmore responded, "I probably will."[53] Houston police went on their own bar tour in retribution for the mayor's support for the gay community, carrying out at least ten raids on gay venues in the following weeks and arresting more than fifty people.[54] In press reporting on the raids, it was discovered that "vice squad officers admit the existence of a 'faggot list' where names, photos and license plates of homosexuals and many nongays have been recorded" as part of an active surveillance program to monitor and harass gay men.[55]

For the 1984 election cycle, the HGPC officially identified as bipartisan and took the tactic of endorsing both Republican and Democratic candidates for the presidential primary "so as not to be taken for granted by either liberals or conservatives."[56] As then-HGPC president Bagneris told the *Advocate* the same year, "We've been successful in Houston in gaining political strength because we will no longer try to explain or justify our private lives in public. We deal with the issue of our basic rights and then move on to other areas of concern."[57] Those basic rights soon came under siege.

Didn't We Almost Have It All: The End of an Era

Both the general rightward turn in US politics during the Reagan era and homophobia stoked by the developing AIDS epidemic influenced a reactionary pivot by mid-decade. In 1984 the HPGC-friendly city council passed an ordinance prohibiting discrimination on the basis of sexual orientation; the following January a referendum vote repealed the protections by a devastating *82 percent*. The political enfranchisement that gay organizers had worked toward suddenly seemed to evaporate. In fall 1985 none of the major candidates in local races sought HGPC's endorsement. The popular Whitmire still handily won reelection in 1985 with 64 percent of the vote, but her support for gay rights was considered "her strongest negative in polling."[58] Her opponent was quoted on a hot mic saying that his solution to the developing AIDS crisis would be to "shoot the queers."[59] Although Whitmire's opponent lost the race, he vocalized an emboldened homophobia.

As with political clout, business at gay bars across Houston began declining by 1985.[60] In addition, during the early months of 1986, fifty armed robberies were reported at Montrose-area businesses, including four separate hits on the bar Outlaws, the stabbing of a bartender at Brazos River Bottom, and the shooting death of local lesbian bar owner Marion Pantzer.[61] In the middle of the year, bar owners convened to discuss financial troubles, and that fall, the longest-running gay bar in Texas, the Exile, closed its doors downtown.[62] By 1987, a local "severe economic depression" was reported alongside gay venue closures and a "bar war."[63]

Though now largely forgotten, the mid-1980s gay bar crisis was not only a consequence of the casualties, anxieties, and behavioral changes caused by the AIDS epidemic but also of new policies and expenses for bars that had dire financial impacts. In 1984 the US Congress passed the National Minimum Drinking Age Act, which required states to raise the drinking age to twenty-one or lose federal funding for highways. This law was motivated by significant lobbying by Mothers against Drunk Driving (MADD). Prior to this national policy, states determined their own drinking ages. This change has been mostly overlooked, but its impact on both the economics and culture of gay bars (indeed, bars generally) was enormous: ages eighteen to twenty are prime party years for many people as well as formative for dating and sexual exploration. This policy especially affected queer youths' access to community and sexual partners; correspondingly, bars lost a thirsty segment of their market. Some enterprising youths surely procured fake IDs, and some venues introduced 18+ nights, but the impact was severe nonetheless. In September 1986, Texas finally adhered to the national law by raising the legal drinking age from nineteen (the existing age to drink beer and wine) to twenty-one (for all types of alcohol). An immediate "severe business slump" was reported for October 1986.[64] Concurrently, Houston law enforcement and the Texas Highway Patrol increased enforcement of drunk-driving laws, which further changed the long-standing cultures of drinking, particularly binge drinking.[65] As the sprawling city became increasingly suburbanized, patrons became more wary of risking DUIs or DWIs by driving to the Montrose for a night out.[66] Both the new policy and its enforcement limited *who* could patronize gay bars and also shifted the norms of *how much* patrons drank while in them.

Relatedly, insurance rates at least *tripled* for bars within the span of a year as insurers became newly concerned about liability. In the event of an alcohol-related accident or death, the last place a person drank could become liable for damages, even if the incident took place beyond the business's property. Some insurance companies began refusing to cover bars at all, shrinking the pool of competitors and further raising premiums. Exacerbating the problem, spikes in state liquor taxes, which rose 21.5 percent in 1986, made the profit margins for bars even leaner.[67] The year 1987 began with reports of new local health codes creating challenges for bars to get certification to open.[68] All of these policies, which were ostensibly sexuality neutral, had disproportionate effects on gay men because bars had long been their primary social institutions.

Around this same time, Mary's became not only financially precarious but also politically controversial by promoting racist humor during some of its advertised theme parties. During gay pride weekend in 1987, the bar hosted a Juneteenth holiday costume party with "blackface requested." In addition, the front window featured images of minstrel characters Uncle Remus and Aunt Jemima, and the bar served watermelon cocktails.[69] The event prompted commentary in the gay press, which asserted that it was "time to address racism in the Houston gay community" in the wake of such "cruel parody" at Mary's.[70] I have not been able to find evidence of an apology from Mary's or further fallout from the Juneteenth event.

Mary's egregious humor signaled backsliding in the community. Houston was the site of the earliest campaign I've found to address racism at bars, dating from 1971, when the Gay Liberation Front allied itself with black power and protested the Red Room.[71] Conspicuous racism at some bars continued through the 1970s and into the 1980s, when Black and White Men Together brought attention to discriminatory ID checks in Houston, as did other local chapters in cities across the country.[72] (See chapter 4.) Part of what is so dissonant about the Juneteenth party is that I have never found any account naming Mary's among the discriminatory venues. On the contrary, a Mary's manager had previously commented that "we've always had all sizes, all races, and colors. This is probably a good reason Mary's is still popular today. This is a bar where you can be 'yourself,' having a good time and not be pretentious."[73] Bagneris, who is Creole-Latino, described the scene to me as "diverse," meaning not only along racial lines but across various axes.[74] This is the party line I've found in all accounts of the bar, although the images I've seen of the bar's staff and patrons over the years indicate that the scene was predominantly white and male. The bar had previously satirized the Ku Klux Klan when it marched in Montrose against the gay community in advance of a pride event a few years earlier; the front windows were painted "Send in the Klowns," and speakers blasted "Springtime for Hitler."[75] (See also interlude 7 on Somerset County, PA.) On the roof, Mary's raised the rainbow flag, the American flag, the Texas flag, and—curiously—the Confederate flag together.[76]

Disregarding critiques—or perhaps relishing them—Mary's gained national attention when it ran an ad for a "wet----" costume contest the following year for a Cinco de Mayo party. The event also promised "1 Year Free Swimming & Englich [sic] Lesson [sic] from Maria" and "Green Cards Will Be Made."[77] All Mujeres Interested in Getting Active (AMIGA) organized a protest in collaboration with Tejanos with AIDS, the National Organization of Women, American Gay Atheists, and the Latino Lesbian and Gay Organization. Missing the point of the critiques, assistant manager Mark "Pickles" Casselberry told a reporter that "we have always been notorious and we are not about to stop now."[78] The Houston pride week committee censured both Mary's and the *Montrose Voice*, which printed the ad, although the committee retracted its boycott a week later.[79] Complicating the politics of the situation, the Cinco de Mayo party and ad were conceived by the bar's manager, Adrian Luera, known as "Maria"; he was Latino and had hosted parties for the holiday at the bar every year since 1982. Luera came up with the promotion as a "humorous jab" at the various racists who had called him the slur his entire life.[80] When he died the following year, his obituary in *TWT* remarked that he was often misunderstood."[81] Luera likely thought he was skewering taboos in line with Mary's ethos of transgression, but hate speech qualitatively differs

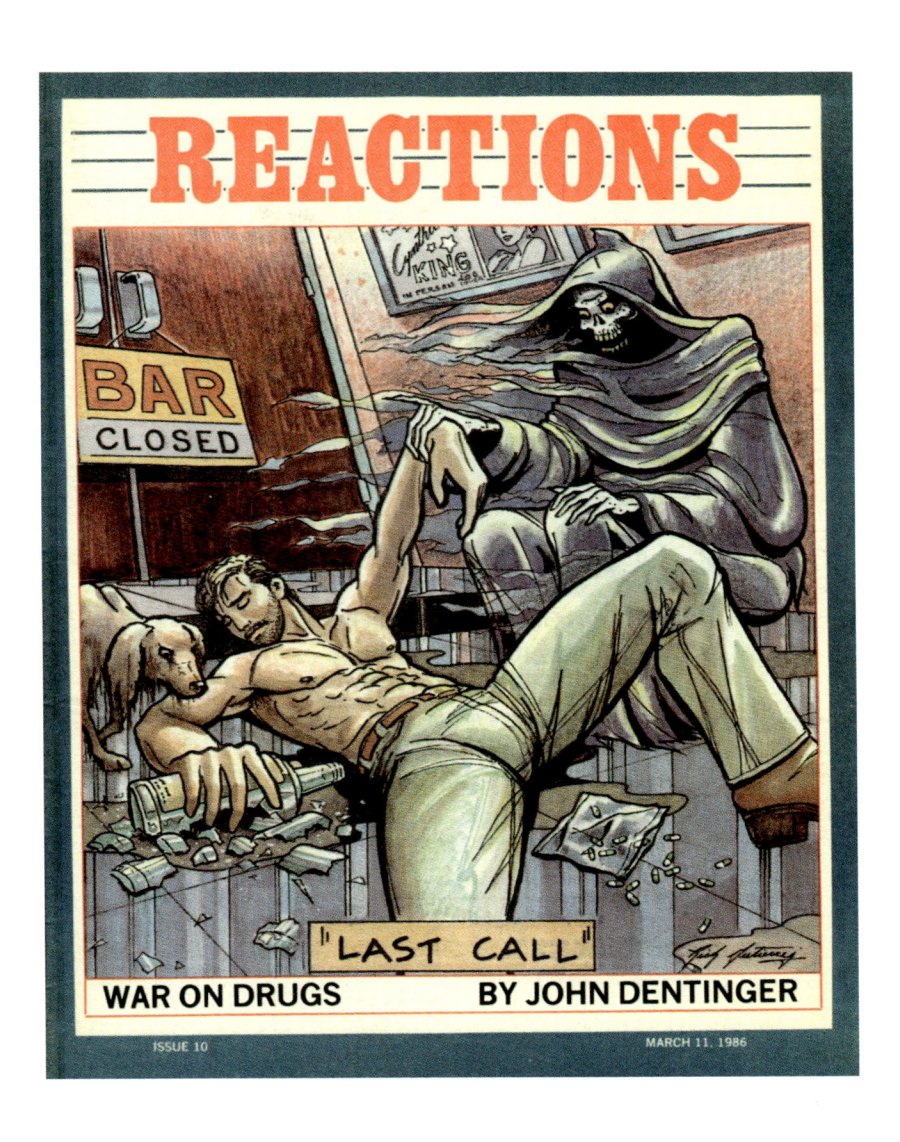

PLATE 1 The death of the gay bar as ominously imagined on the cover of *Reactions*, March 11, 1986. Courtesy of ONE Archives at the USC Libraries.

PLATE 2 (*above*) The most iconic Etienne (Dom Orejudos) mural for the Gold Coast, painted on plywood in 1966. This image was reproduced on souvenir posters. Courtesy of the Leather Archives & Museum.

PLATE 3 (*opposite*) Snowflake (Glenn Zehrbaugh, 1928–1992), *Cocktail Hour*, 1982. This painting of the Ambush in San Francisco is permanently on view in the basement of the Omaha Mining Company bar. Despite the artist's pseudonym and the apparent ethnicity of most of his figures, this painting's politics are not necessarily reducible to exhibiting whiteness; a B ack gay man owns the bar where he proudly displays the painting alongside other works by Snowflake. Photo by Kameron Bayne, by permission of Robert Roberts and bar owner Joseph Al en.

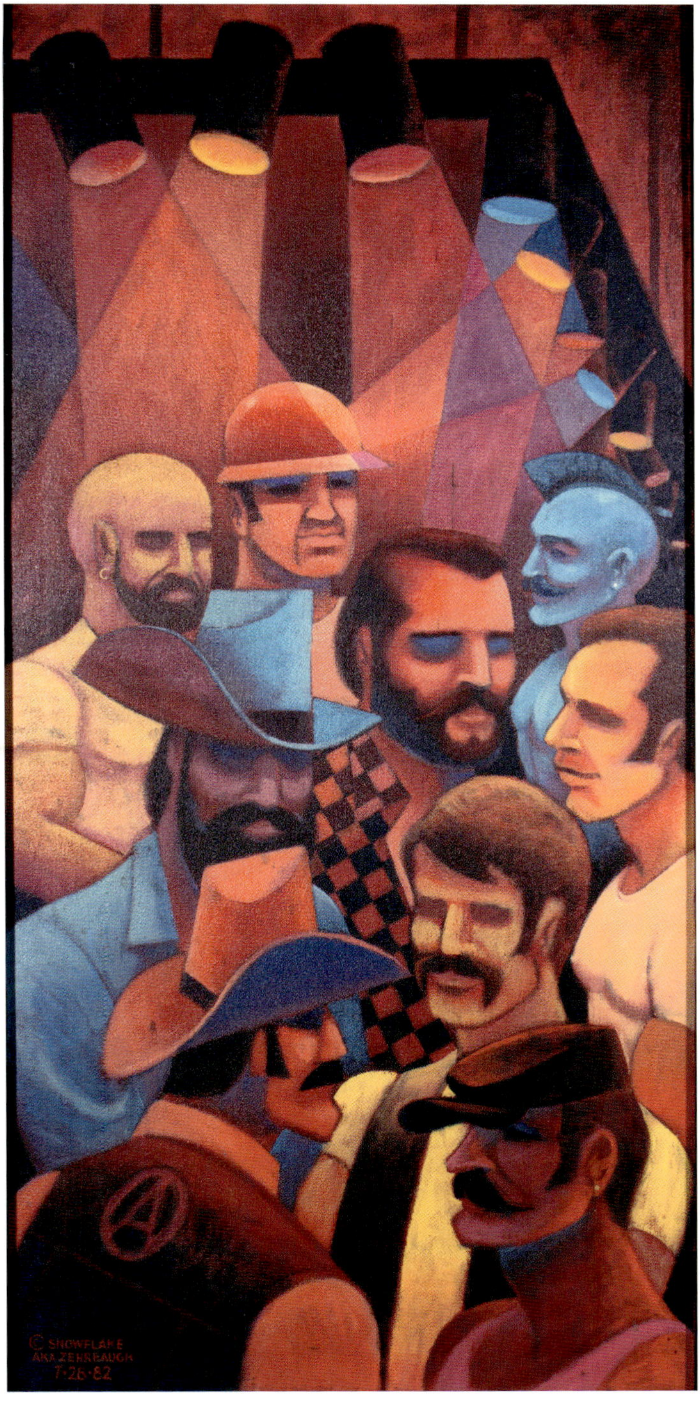
© SNOWFLAKE
AKA ZEHREAUGH
7·26·82

PLATE 4 Crowd inside the Pit, in the basement of the Gold Coast at 501 N. Clark Ave., circa 1980s. Chuck Renslow Collection. Courtesy of Leather Archives & Museum.

PLATE 5 José Sarria performing at the Black Cat in San Francisco, circa the early 1960s. Sarria was the Bay Area's grand dame drag queen and led the audience in singing "God Save Us Nelly Queens" at the end of each show. He was the first openly gay candidate for public office in the US when he ran for the board of supervisors in 1961; he also cofounded the homophile organization Society for Individual Rights. Sarria christened himself Her Royal Majesty, Empress of San Francisco, José I, and the Widow Norton. In addition, he founded the Imperial Court System. Harold L. Call Papers. Courtesy of ONE Archives at the USC Libraries.

PLATE 6 Jewel Box Lounge commemorative expandable postcard fan (front view), circa 1961–65. Chris Collins Collection. Courtesy of the Gay and Lesbian Archive of Mid-America, University of Missouri–Kansas City.

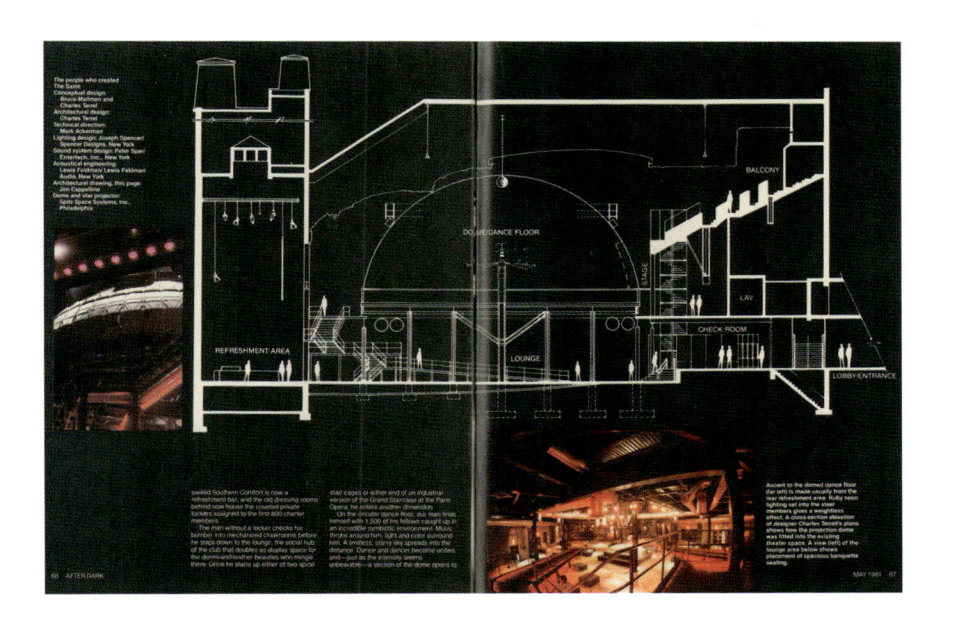

PLATE 7 The marvel of Charles Terrell's design for the Saint was featured across six pages of *After Dark* magazine. The middle spread (shown here) showcased a side-view architectural schematic of the three-story space with silhouetted figures included for scale. *After Dark,* May 1981. Courtesy of the University of California, Irvine Libraries Special Collections.

THE SAINT

THE LAST PARTY

SATURDAY APRIL 30
THROUGH MONDAY MAY 2, 1988

LIVE:
BETTY BUCKLEY
THELMA HOUSTON
FRANCE JOLI
SHARON REDD
MARLENA SHAW
WEATHER GIRLS
VIOLA WILLS
...AND MORE

MUSIC:
JIM BURGESS
MIKE CAVALLONE
MICHAEL FIERMAN
WARREN GLUCK
ROBBIE LESLIE
TONY LUMEN
HOWARD MERRIT
NAO NAKAMURA
CHUCK PARSONS
TERRY SHERMAN
MARK THOMAS

LIGHTS:
MARK ACKERMAN
RICHARD ERSKINE
TONY LUMEN
RICHARD SABALA
RICHARD TUCKER

a sudden erection of cells produces a tactile surface on your skin. your body will betray you. the saloon.

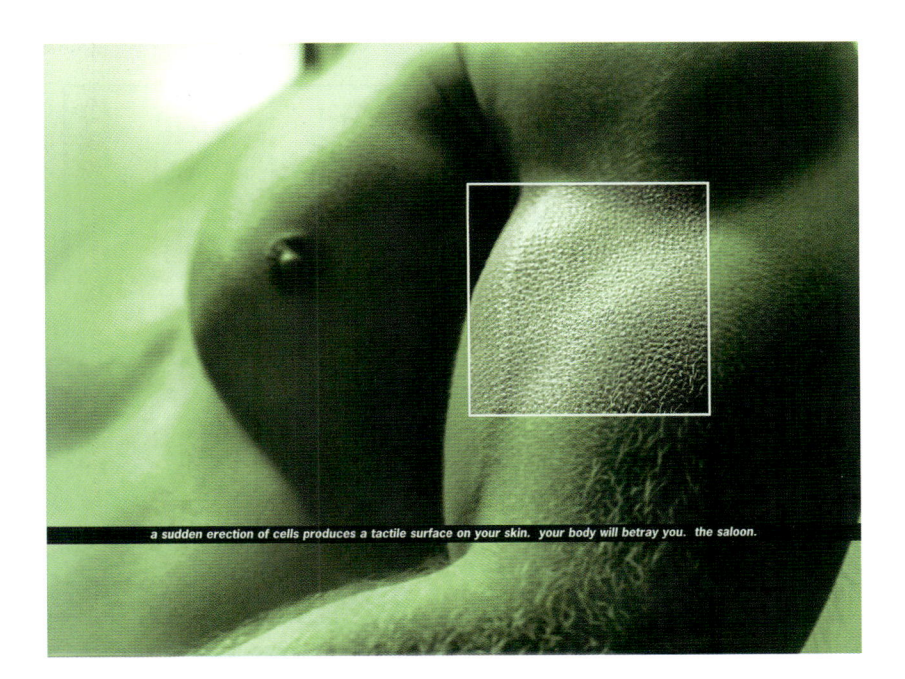

PLATE 8 (*opposite*) This poster for The Last Party at the Saint showcases the scale and effects of the bar's star-projection system for simulating both stars and lightning. The closing party ran for forty continuous hours, April 30–May 2, 1988. Courtesy of The Saint Foundation Archives.

PLATE 9 (*above*) The Saloon's "your body will betray you" advertisements ran on the back cover of *Lavender* magazine from 1998 to 2000. This version includes the text "a sudden erection of cells produces a tactile surface on your skin. your body will betray you." Collection of the author.

PLATE 10 Snapshots of Mary's staff and patrons embedded in the bar's countertops. Photo by author. Courtesy of Gulf Coast Archive and Museum.

PLATE 11 Scott Swoveland's most famous mural for Mary's east exterior wall, originally visible 1997–2006, as digitally re-created in 2016 for the Houston Eagle. Courtesy of Scott Swoveland.

PLATE 12 (*above*) Stick puppets from the Bob Jansen Roast, a benefit to reopen the Main Club after the bar was destroyed by fire. Photo by Lisa Vecoli. Robert Jansen Papers. Courtesy of the Jean-Nickolaus Tretter Collection in GLBT Studies, University of Minnesota Libraries.

PLATE 13 (*opposite*) Club Uranus reveled in kitsch and celebrated weirdness, as demonstrated in this flyer from 1990 printed on neon chartreuse paper stock. LGBT Business Ephemera collection. Courtesy of GLBT Historical Society.

CLUB URANUS

WEIRD FANTASY

SUNDAY NIGHTS 10 - 2am
401 6th & HARRISON DJ's MIKE & LEWIS

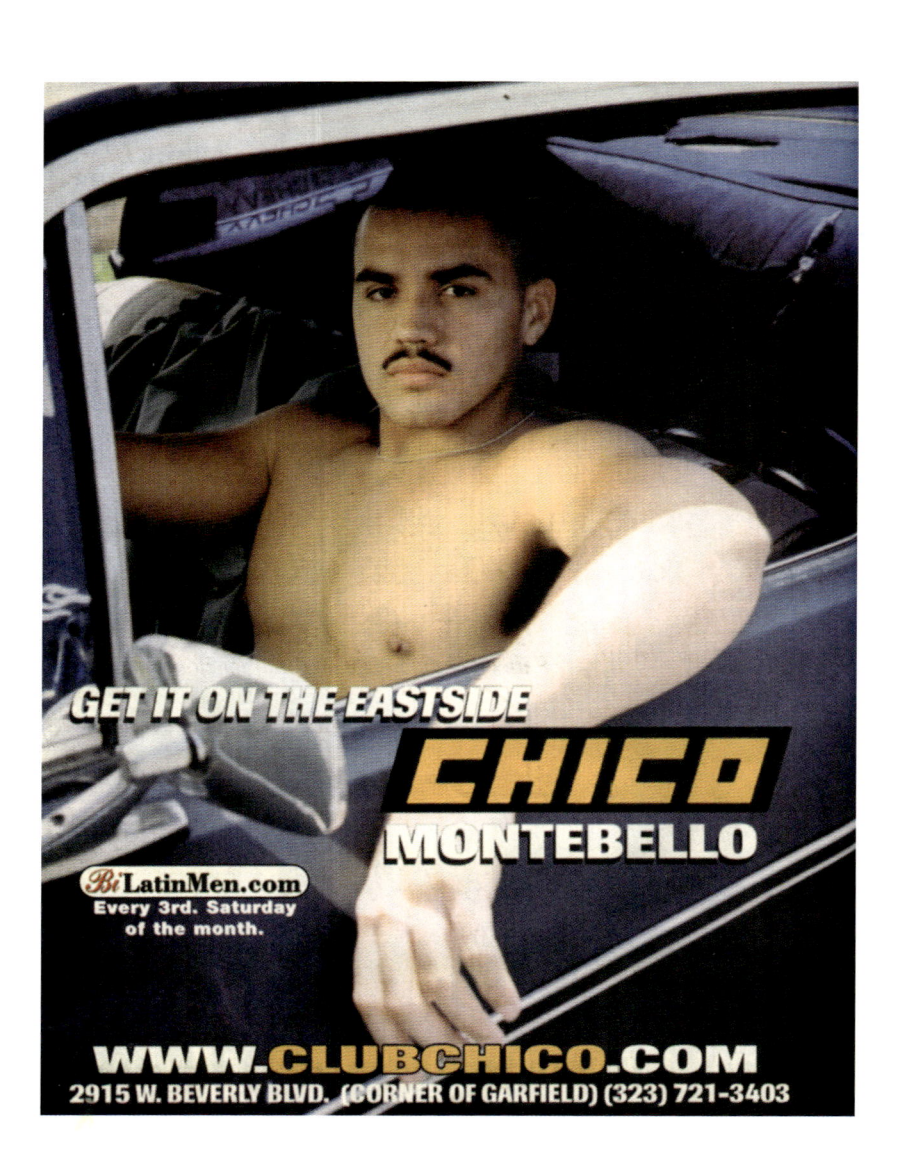

GET IT ON THE EASTSIDE

CHICO
MONTEBELLO

BiLatinMen.com
Every 3rd. Saturday of the month.

WWW.CLUBCHICO.COM
2915 W. BEVERLY BLVD. (CORNER OF GARFIELD) (323) 721-3403

PLATE 14 (*opposite*) Chico advertisement featuring a photo by Dino Dinco that invokes cholo style and low-rider culture: the text urges readers to "Get it on the East Side." The ad also promotes a monthly bi Latino men's party. *Adelante*, June 2003. Collection of the author.

PLATE 15 (*above*) *Nostra Fiesta*, a mural by Rafa Esparza and Gabriela Ruiz, commissioned for the facade of the New Jalisco Bar in 2019. Photo by author, 2022.

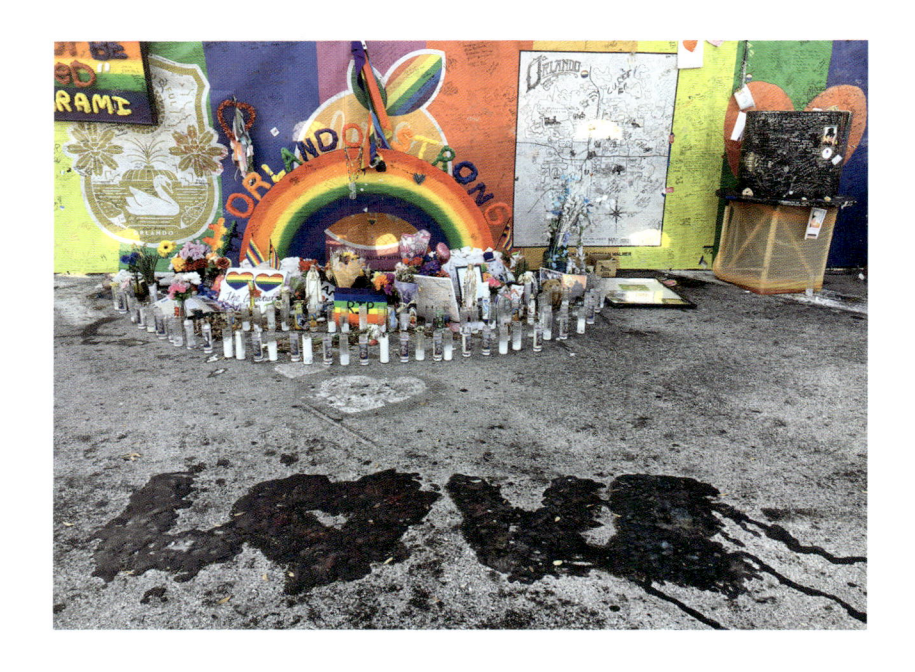

PLATE 16 Grassroots memorial shrine at the Pulse Nightclub site in February 2017. Photo by the author.

from sexual self-invention. The Juneteenth party was an indefensibly racist provocation, but the Cinco de Mayo event purported to play with the queer potential of negative representations, which can sometimes express affects, experiences, social positions, critiques, and subversions that positive representations disallow.[82] The latter party's political critique of bias simply didn't register for many people, who took the joke at face value, which means that it failed as satire.

As with the previous year's Juneteenth party, the event's ad generated significant commentary in the local gay press and weeks of letters to the editor. The controversy productively stimulated discussions of intracommunity racism and reflections on organizing tactics, such as the fact that organizers protested the bar without directly engaging its management in discussion.[83] In her response to a letter from Linda Morales of AMIGA, the lead local reporter wrote, "Linda, you are right that we need to address the problems of racism in this and every other community, but we should try to address those problems in ways that will alleviate them not exacerbate them. If you agree, I'd love to buy you a cocktail (or any other beverage) at Mary's. Let's try to mend this thing, shall we?"[84] Mary's advertised a Boycott Party with "free drinks all day & all night to all boycotters" and doubled down by obstinately billing itself "your local racist bar."[85]

The bar's problematic humor tarnishes its legacy. I do not absolve Mary's of these parties' harm, which indexed the uncomfortable truth that Mary's could be a sanctuary for white queers who felt like social outcasts and also be aggressively hostile or malignantly indifferent to people of color. Many gay bars and clubs—as well as other LGBTQ+ community organizations—were and are. During a challenging period for bars generally, these events compromised Mary's role in the community.

Take Another Little Piece of My Heart: Mary's in the Age of AIDS

The history of Mary's from the mid-1980s onward is far more complex than a narrative of decline. A bartender at Mary's exhibited one of the first known cases of Kaposi sarcoma in Houston, numerous staff and patrons would eventually die from AIDS-related illnesses, and the bar became the symbolic epicenter of AIDS in the city.[86] Bar owner Farmer died in 1991 of AIDS-related illness and left his portion of the bar to employees Gaye Yancy, who started as the first female bartender at Mary's in 1986, and Terry Smith, who died in 1992. One account recalls that "when Fanny became sick, Gaye and Cliff sat on either side of him to ensure he wouldn't fall, allowing him to remain associated with the community he helped to form."[87] Owen and Yancy would run the bar until 2002, when it initially closed. Immediately, Michael Gaetz purchased and reopened the venue, which continued until 2009; despite attempts to maintain its former glory, however, the culture of the place had changed.

The epidemic and gay bars would become inextricable. In 1982 the number of gay venues in Houston peaked at ninety-four.[88] That same year, the first local death related to AIDS was reported in the gay press. By summer 1983, *TWT* introduced a new obituary section rather than reporting individual deaths as news. Bars played a central role in distributing condoms (as of 1984), in training bartenders as AIDS and safer-sex educators (as of 1985), and in hosting the vast majority of community fund-raisers for AIDS services (as of 1985).[89] Bagneris told me he left the city in 1986 because he had lost so many people in the epidemic that it had become unbearable.[90] By the end of 1990, Houston had the fourth-highest incidence of HIV/AIDS in the country, after New York, Los Angeles, and San Francisco.[91] Although exact accounting for AIDS-related deaths is unreliable, tracking obituaries in *TWT* suggests that the peak years for mortality in the gay community spanned 1986–96, with the highest numbers in 1990–94.[92] Mary's became an extraordinary site of commemoration, a monument even, both for its people and for the bar itself. These acts of remembering celebrated the bar's wilder days and honored its community with solemnity.

In 1985, the same year that the bar scene took a demonstrable turn, Mary's ran an advertisement beckoning patrons past and present: "Want to be immortalized at Mary's in our new bartop? If so, bring your photos to Mary's Naturally!"[93] The endeavor was pitched as an alternative family photo album; later, it functioned as a community memorial (see plate 10). Countless snapshots of Mary's staff and patrons covered the entire surface of the bar top, embedded under resin, for more than sixty linear feet. Old friends continued to be seen at the bar, even after they were no longer around.

When the bar finally closed for the last time, Reeves, a longtime regular and leader of the Gulf Coast Archive and Museum, sneaked into the building and saved the bar tops before the building was gutted. I had never heard about the bar tops until Reeves pulled them out during my trip to Houston in 2017. They were yellowed from years of cigarette smoke, and the underside was stuck with dried gum and condoms. Reeves had cleaned

FIGURE 6.8 Snapshots of Mary's staff and patrons were embedded into the bar tops in 1985 as a kind of family album; later, the bar tops served as a community memorial. Seen here after restoration. Photo by Judy Reeves. Courtesy of Gulf Coast Archive and Museum.

away as much grime and age as she could with WD-40 to reveal the men's faces more clearly (see figure 6.8). The photos show groups of men embracing; men in wigs, in drag, and in costumes; men competing in contests; men on motorcycles; naked men; drunk men. Yes, mostly men and mostly white. Men whom I'll never know. Men we've lost, still living and so full of playful joy. Perhaps more than any other object in the archives, the bar tops offer a material trace of gay bar history (see figure 6.9).

The bar tops were one of countless literal memorials at the bar.[94] The outdoor area behind the bar, which was famous for public trysts and all manner of queer sexual exploration, became the site for hundreds—*hundreds*—of celebration-of-life ceremonies for people who were part of the Mary's community. At some of these commemorations, the mourners spread the ashes of the departed or planted bushes or trees, including a sugar maple for Farmer. At other ceremonies, drinks were simply raised. Some Mary's ceremonies were listed in published obituaries, and some were more intimate or informal.[95] These ceremonies continued from the 1980s into the 2000s. Most but not all of those lost died of AIDS-related causes.

An online forum collecting patrons' memories of Mary's identifies dozens of people who were memorialized with ceremonies, buried ashes, and/or plantings, although it estimates that many more were memorialized there.

FIGURE 6.9 This view of Mary's bar tops, installed as part of the *Stonewall 50* exhibition at the Contemporary Arts Museum Houston in 2019, demonstrates their massive scale. Photo by Emily Peacock. Courtesy of Contemporary Arts Museum Houston.

No one has been able to compile a comprehensive list or accurate count. Among the people laid to rest or memorialized there were longtime owner Farmer; co-owner Terry Smith; manager David "Meg" Williamson; drag queens Torchy Lane, Lady Victoria Lust, Eartha Quake, and Rita Charles; former KS/AIDS Foundation president Michael "Lord Mac" McAdory; the bar's "burger lady" Judy Mathis; and seventy-five-year-old bar regular Rita Livingston. The dog Sam's ashes were interred there as well; he and Farmer would never be separated again.[96] All had a profound attachment to the bar.

Raise Your Glass: Memorializing Mary's

Mary's itself has been memorialized repeatedly, both through numerous profiles in the press and by artists.[97] Although Mary's had always been flagrantly visible, its iconic status developed further in the 1990s. The front windows of the bar were Plexiglas and featured a newly painted mural each week, dating back to the venue's early years. The bar's most important artist in residence, Scott Swoveland, came later and worked at the bar throughout the 1990s. He painted more than five hundred scenes on the bar's front windows, but his work as a muralist on the bar's exterior brick wall was what most endured.[98] These murals faced a parking lot and were prominently visible to westbound traffic on Westheimer. His first murals paid tribute to Janis Joplin and the Houston Motorcycle Club. But his most famous mural, visible from 1997 to 2006, portrayed the interior of Mary's, as though the wall was a window (see plate 11). The mural featured co-owners Owen (in red in front of the dartboard) and Yancy (in green next to the Gay St. sign), the ghost of Farmer (center background, in his favorite seat), some of the regulars, and amalgams of others. In the foreground, Mr. Balls sits on his stool, back turned to the viewer with feline indifference. Swoveland intended the image to "pay homage to the past, as well as depict the way the bar was then."[99] The mural stayed up for nearly a decade before it was painted over, and in that time it became both a landmark and a kind of time capsule.

Thanks to this mural, anyone who passed by might feel like they had been to a gay bar, even if they had never crossed one's threshold. Not long after the bar was closed for the last time, the mural was re-created by a straight artist in June 2011 as a public art project; this re-creation was still up on the abandoned building when I visited the city for the first time in early 2012, and it hailed me to write this chapter. I'm not the only one who has been so taken in by it. Eagle Houston owner Mark DeLange commissioned Swoveland to re-create the mural digitally for reinstallation at the upstairs Phoenix Room, a community space commemorating local bar history in collaboration with JD Doyle. When I returned to Houston for research in 2017, DeLange was preparing to open a local franchise of Hamburger Mary's. He refers to it simply as "Mary's."

Gay bars have long functioned as de facto institutions, but Mary's stands out as the closest a bar can come to actually manifesting community in all its messy and generative forms. Mary's fostered sexual free-for-alls and political organizing, out-and-proud visibility, and public mourning. Wild men and domesticated beasts converged at the corner of Westheimer and Waugh to forge what for some was the greatest gay bar of all time.

INTERLUDE 6

The Main Club in Superior, WI

In 2011 I kept hearing about the Main Club in Superior, Wisconsin. I was spending the summer in Minneapolis, staying with my old friend Dean and doing archival research at the Jean-Nickolaus Tretter Collection in GLBT Studies at the University of Minnesota. Friends described the Main Club as a pretty wild bar, but in the archive I encountered comparatively earnest press accounts, event flyers, and personal, handwritten letters. From my research it became clear that the bar's owner, Bob Jansen, had been an important leader in fostering community, providing an inclusive space, and fighting for progressive causes. From my findings it seemed that the Main Club fulfilled all of the political and social potential of gay bars. Few bars can claim this kind of singular importance for their communities.

It's rare to find the personal papers of a gay bar owner in the archive, and I got misty-eyed reading a file of handwritten thank-you notes to him. But my favorite findings of the summer were a pair of cute poster board stick puppets of Jansen with his iconic mustache from a benefit roast to reopen the Main Club after a fire (see plate 12). I can't be sure if it was these cartoonish effigies' charming handmade quality or the fact that I'd never seen anything like this tribute to a bar owner in archives elsewhere. But somehow these funny little objects made me feel like I knew Jansen and had some sense of the Main Club's affective significance for its community.[1]

Of course, there's always a gap between the projections one imagines from encountering documents in the archive and experiencing the original moment. Curious, I made contact with Jansen, booked a room, and drove 150 miles north to Superior, across a bridge from the better-known Duluth, Minnesota. Jansen met with me and generously talked at the bar for three hours, introduced me to all of the regulars who came in, and showed me some of the materials from years past that he had stored in the basement. When we met for lunch the next day, we continued talking for another two hours, and he brought extra clippings, photos, and ephemera to share. He remains as warm as you'd imagine and has kept his trademark daddy mustache, although he seemed a bit more contemplative than feisty during our interactions.

The Main Club opened in its first location in 1983 as the first full-fledged gay bar in the area. (There have typically been one or two other gay venues in town since he opened the Main.) Jansen opened the bar "with a grant from the Catholic church": he was denied tenure in the Theater Department at the College of St. Scholastica, he sued for discrimination on the basis of sexual orientation, and he used his settlement to help open the bar. The bar faced various obstacles early on, from difficulty in securing an initial loan to a police raid on the eve of the bar's opening to delays in securing a liquor license. However, Jansen developed a liaison program between the gay community and the police departments in Duluth and Superior. He has a playful sensibility and a strong sense of social commitment, demonstrated by his range of original projects, protest ideas, and rabble-rouser spirit. "When I disagree with something, I try to find out why I disagree with it and then put myself in the middle of it," he told me. He and his bar have been profiled repeatedly in local and regional press as well as featured in two documentary shorts.[2] One local gay press profile marking the bar's twentieth anniversary ended by remarking, "His favorite color is leather."[3] It's become well accepted that the bar is a community institution. If Harvey Milk was the "mayor of Castro Street," Jansen is the impresario of the Great North.[4]

An article in the Twin Cities' gay press commemorating the bar's second anniversary stated that "the club draws a clientele in a 150-mile radius of Duluth-Superior, including northern Wisconsin, the Iron Range and northern Minnesota. A Range-Night Party last year featured a map to help people meet neighbors closer to home. People stuck pins in their hometowns and that prompted many new acquaintances."[5] According to Jansen, when he opened the Main, there were approximately 120 bars in Superior, compared to about 40 in Duluth; conversely, 20 percent of the region's population lives in Superior, compared to 80 percent in Duluth. Until recently there were no gay bars in greater Minnesota beyond the Twin Cities metro area, whereas every significant town in Wisconsin has at least one. Despite having lived in the same house in Duluth since the 1970s, for Jansen it made economic and cultural sense to open his bar across the bridge, where liquor licenses were a fraction of the cost and where closeted Duluth men would not fear running into associates.

When the Main Club opened, Jansen was committed to the space being both openly gay and inclusive of all constituents of the community. He made a point of hiring staff to reflect and attract different demographics. Jansen has been a leader in creating and sustaining the local pride festivities as well as early grassroots efforts at AIDS education. His older gay brother, based in San Francisco, would send Jansen information about AIDS from the Bay Area to post in the bar because his clients weren't getting information anywhere else.

Just after Christmas 1996 a late-night fire (cause unknown, though likely electrical) destroyed the original Main Club building and killed two men who were in a second-story apartment. The fire received significant attention in the press, which also offered testimonies to the venue's role in fostering community. The Duluth daily newspaper described the bar's typical scene in depth and with affection on the front page the next day:

> Walking into Superior's Main Club was like going to the theater. And, like theater, the Main could change lives.
>
> Bob Jansen, the bar's owner, was typically at center stage. A gregarious, burly character with a moustache from another era, Jansen would stand behind the bar ... dressed in blaze orange for the deer hunting opener. Or in a hard hat and construction uniform while a road crew paved the street outside. Or a Nordic hat with horns for Vikings football Sundays.
>
> For Easter, he wore bunny ears. For Christmas, he made glittery centerpieces fashioned from condoms....
>
> Ask any patron and you'll discover The Main was much more than a watering hole. It was ground zero for activism in causes like AIDS

awareness and fund raising, Toys for Tots campaigns and food collections for area food shelves....

Others talked wistfully of seeing younger people come to the bar for the first time and learn to discover themselves and to thrive....

Customers jockeyed to sit in the "opera seats," a small cluster of bar stools that offered a prime view of anyone walking in the front door.[6]

After the fire, Bob relocated the Main Club from a discreet location to a prominent one on Tower Avenue along the main strip in town. Several members of the community pitched in to help him ready the space.

When I visited, the Main Club was in an old brick building that coincidentally has brown bricks and arched windows reminiscent of the legendary Stonewall in New York. There was a marquee with a rainbow flag and a pink neon sign above the door. A sign on the front door advised: "The MAIN CLUB is Gay owned and operated and supports the community and the culture of this community. If you are uncomfortable with this you are free to choose not to enter this establishment." The space inside was quite large, with a small entryway between the two front doors—typical of bars in cold climates—and a shelf where people could set drinks while they step outside to smoke. The front room was large with high ceilings and holds two pool tables with custom-ordered *pink felt*. After the front room, the bar stretched lengthwise, with stools along the bar and a large bulletin board with events, news clippings, and other announcements posted opposite. Above the bar hung dozens of stuffed bears (and a few moose) in leather kink outfits for sale; Jansen found the stuffed animals at thrift stores and made the outfits himself as a hobby. When I visited, all of the customers were clustered around the bar. Beyond the seating area was a dance floor, a stage, and a back door.

When I ordered a drink, Jansen served it with a denim back pocket, cut from a pair of Levi's, as a coaster. It's this sort of touch that indicated Jansen's sensibility and ingenuity. The jean pocket clearly referenced the historic 1970s macho stylings of Levi-leather bars and gay clones (see interlude 2 about Denver), but Jansen modestly explained that they were environmentally responsible as an alternative to paper coasters. Despite Wisconsin's beer industry, like most gays bars elsewhere the Main sold far more vodka.

In the 2000s, Jansen attempted to maintain the bar's diversity by hosting a range of events such as fund-raisers for the gay rodeo, transfest, *L Word* viewing parties, sex-toy bingo, a monthly leather night, and drag shows and pool tournament fund-raisers for AIDS. I came across a flier for a women's softball body-shots party. Customers were seasonal: in summer, a lot of patrons visited from the Twin Cities on vacation, and the pride event, on Labor Day weekend, was 90 percent out-of-towners with 10 percent "working locals." During fall, winter, and spring, Jansen knew most of the customers; many regulars were working-class white males. When I first visited, he greeted the regulars by name. When George, the bar's longest-running regular, walked in, and people in the bar yelled, "Jorge!" He responded, "Hey, whores!"

Jansen was always more interested in building community than in running a business. The bar had seen its business fall off in the 2000s. Jansen said he'd heard similar struggles from other gay bar owners and event organizers across the country, although he also suggests that there isn't really a communication network for bar owners. By all accounts, there also seemed to be a generation gap, such that local queer youths are not invested in gay bars as community spaces the way that prior generations of gay men and lesbians were. The bar developed a reputation as an older man's bar—and a salacious one at that—despite a political commitment to inclusiveness. According to one of the bartenders, bars were Superior's primary industry, despite being a shipping port, and business seemed to be off all over town. Jansen was preparing for a presentation on the history of the community when we met, and he was clearly concerned about the bar's current relevance as well as its legacy. At the time, the Main Club was patronized primarily by older males, the Flame up the street by women, and a new dance club across the bridge, the Duluth Flame, by the region's younger mixed crowd. Jansen eventually sold the Main Club in 2018, but the bar continues operations under new ownership. Jansen still stops in sometimes.

Part IV

Reinventions

7

Further Tales of the City

Queer Parties in Post-disco San Francisco

In 1988 San Francisco's disco era seemed to come to a definitive end with the passing of local legend Sylvester, best known for his hit "(You Make Me Feel) Mighty Real," and the closing of the famed Trocadero Transfer nightclub.[1] An appraisal of the Troc's last dance suggested that the club had an "aging market," whereas "younger people look at the Trocadero and they resent it because it's an older gay men's club. Any new generation that comes up tends to want to have their own club."[2] That same year, the Bay Area's gay press described an upstart gay boys' scene, a "new lesbianism," and a spate of next-generation parties that signaled tectonic ruptures in LGBTQ+ nightlife and culture.[3] San Francisco became the epicenter of a rift between the baby boomers of the gay-liberation era and what would soon be called Generation X. Both the partiers and the press looked to nightlife to make sense of this generational divide.

The 1970s was the first time that an entire gay lifestyle was conceivable, and San Francisco attained the status of a gay Atlantis for "refugees from Amerika."[4] Baby boomers built the prevailing gay community institutions and nightlife cultures at that time; in doing so, they had often refused the politics and bar cultures of their homophile and sweater-queen elders.[5] Whereas the liberation generation experienced the thrill of inventing new publics, the 1980s generation came of age *after* the AIDS crisis had radically altered gay sex, socializing, and politics.[6] A 1990 overview of the club scene signaled a changed era with the turn of phrase "post-mecca San Francisco."[7] Nonetheless, a second wave of queers migrated to the city: "a whole generation of queers who came to San Francisco to try and cope ... to create something else, something we could live with."[8]

That sense of world making was realized at night. New zeitgeist parties articulated a new generation defined by *youth* at the BOY parties, a queer politics of mixed-gender and multiethnic *inclusion* at the Box, and queer performances of *deviance* at Club Uranus. These three parties figure as my emblematic case studies for this chapter, but each stands in for numerous others at the time, including Boy Club, Young Men's Dance Club, Crew, Fraternity, Hero, and Colossus as extensions of the BOY party scene; Code Blue, Club Q, Club Rapture, Skirts, Female Trouble, G-Spot, Girldome, Snatch, Muff Dive, and Faster Pussycat as lipstick lesbian and queer women's parties that intersected with the Box; and Chaos, Dekadance, Klubstitute, Junk, Baby Judy's, Fusion, and Boing as part of Club Uranus's queer universe. The all-ages and sexually fluid rave scene that emerged concurrently with the parities in this chapter extended some of its key principles: "an inclusive, open-access ethos" of community via shared pleasures that exceeded narrow demographic scenes, "a series of possibilities which people could use to define their own identities."[9]

This surge of new events signaled an epochal paradigm shift *from gay to queer*. This conceptual and self-definitional transformation rejected and reimagined the world that gay men had realized in the liberation era (see chapter 5). Pointedly, none of the new parties took place in the Castro, possibly the most famous gay ghetto in the world and the one that connoted the very *idea* of 1970s gay San Francisco. This moment also reconstituted nightlife as queer *parties* instead of the existing model of every-night gay bars or weekend discos; the new nightlife parties were "one-night-a-week stands" or venue "time shares" that operated as recurring or itinerant events.[10] These dance parties fomented a range of new ways to imagine who constituted the queer community and what forms that collective queer experience might take. In many ways these parties have remained the templates for subsequent queer nightlife.

Thank U, Next: Generations

The term *generation gap* became popular in the 1960s as the baby boomers came of age and rejected the World War II generation's values. By the mid-1980s, a new generation—which would alternately be called Generation X, the thirteenth generation, baby busters, slackers, and the MTV generation—emerged as the next cohort to come of age after the baby boomers. In the gay community this was also recognized as the first one to come of age after a public gay culture had already existed and during the AIDS epidemic. As early as 1982, the New York gay press remarked upon the emergence of "the new gay man" who thought that "the '70s was a bit much."[11] The first rumblings of gay intergenerational tensions emerged in the early 1980s; these were "subsumed" by attention to the developing AIDS crisis and then began to "reassert" themselves by the decade's end.[12]

After benignly reporting on an emergent generation and its new parties, in 1989 the liberation-aligned *Bay Area Reporter* (*BAR*) published a front-page article sounding the alarm about a "clash of generations."[13] This generational dissonance reverberated across the same issue of the *BAR*, which ran two other stories that gushed over an appearance by Connie Francis, best known for her 1961 single "Where the Boys Are," for eight hundred older gay men during an AIDS charity beer bust at the Eagle.[14] The *boys* were not at the Eagle. That same summer, the somewhat hipper *San Francisco Sentinel* likewise reported on "post-Stonewall gays" as "the next generation." Although the *Sentinel* focused less on intergenerational friction, the paper recognized that "young gays are starting out with different advantages, among which are recognition and pre-established political structures." Reductively and somewhat inaccurately, the *Sentinel*'s account suggested that the boomer gays had focused on self-acceptance, whereas the Xers now focused on equal rights.[15] Both newspapers pointed to the new parties as primary evidence of generational difference.

The earliest prominent embrace of the term *queer* that I've found in this context appeared in 1988 on the cover of the pride edition of the *Sentinel*; "queer" operated as an inclusive term there, in an issue featuring an article that questioned whether gay culture would survive the impact of AIDS and generational shifts.[16] That same summer, the word *queer* prominently circulated via the Big Queer Disco Club parties (apparently related to the Boy Club and Fag Club parties); these events proffered a wide range of attractions *across* generational sensibilities and refused nostalgia for the

FIGURE 7.1 Photo of Ggreg Taylor's Halloween costume fusing art, performance, and transgression at Club Uranus in 1990. © Melissa Hawkins. Courtesy of Melissa Hawkins.

recent disco past with the affirming tagline "The Good *New* Days."[17] Five years later, San Francisco's 1993 gay pride festivities were themed Year of the Queer. By then, the power to define gay culture in San Francisco had officially tipped toward the younger generation, as party promoter and artist Ggreg Taylor was elected as the chair of the parade. Taylor was affiliated with raves, Club Uranus, the street art group Boy with Arms Akimbo, and his persona Nambla the Clown—referencing the controversial National Man-Boy Love Association (NAMBLA) (see figure 7.1). These new nightlife scenes importantly intersected with the rise of playfully militant activist groups such as ACT UP, Queer Nation, and the Lesbian Avengers; with publications such as *Out/Look* (1988–92) and a proliferation of countercultural zines; with lipstick lesbian chic, riot grrrl, and homocore/queercore; and with queer theory and New Queer Cinema.[18]

As a concept, *queer* strategically refused the politics and cultures of heteronormativity, subverted assimilationist homonormativity, and questioned *all* identity categories, including gay and lesbian.[19] In their history of LGBTQ+ life in San Francisco, Susan Stryker and Jim Van Buskirk define *queer* as "an ideological and generational shift as profound as the transition from a homophile mentality to gay liberation." As they explain, "Queerness is not about carving out a culturally sanctioned niche for a carefully crafted minority identity. Rather, it involved the perception of sharing space with people quite different from oneself who were nonetheless adversely affected by the same power structures."[20] In explaining the meaning of queer as a new political identity, Jeffrey Escoffier and Allan Bérubé approvingly write that "*queer* is meant to be confrontational—opposed to gay assimilationists and straight oppressors while inclusive of people who have been marginalized by anyone in power. Queer Nationals . . . bring together people who have been made to feel perverse, queer, odd, outcast, different, and deviant, and to affirm sameness by defining a common identity on the fringes."[21] The term was controversial, often along generational lines, as some people felt the slur's history of tormenting LGBTQ+ people made it irredeemable; others accused the term of whitewashing forms of difference within the LGBTQ+ community. Kadji Amin astutely argues that "queer," in refusing to name political, sexual, or academic methodological particularity, articulates "a set of historical emotions" specific to the United States in the early 1990s that haunt us still.[22] Indeed, although we typically define generational cohorts in terms of chronological time, the experience of generational membership manifests in affects, attachments, and refusals.

For queer Generation Xers, there was a pervasive feeling of having missed the ideological and sexual liberation of the 1970s, an investment in redefining public life and community, and a rejection of the gay scene as they inherited it. For the liberation generation, there was a pervasive affect of loss, and the younger generation's refusals and call-outs compounded the sense of woundedness.[23] Younger gay men in the 1980s at times exhibited an alarming indifference toward their elders and the AIDS epidemic. One twenty-one-year-old misguidedly told the *BAR* in 1989 that AIDS "is affecting the older gay community, not the younger community," and a twenty-three-year-old complained that the focus on raising money for AIDS in Castro venues made them "depressing."[24] Not all young men were quite so unaffected, of course; a twenty-two-year-old remarked with flippant honesty that his HIV-positive ex-lover "is the biggest bitch I know, but nobody deserves this disease."[25]

The primary generational difference that Gen X gay men articulated was that they would never experience gay identity or sex without AIDS. Wayne Hoffman argues that for his generation there was a discernible "narrowing of sexual freedoms, a clamping down on sexual expression, a withering of sexual worlds." He continues: "We young gay men *do* know what we're missing as the sexual devolution envelops us."[26] In a deeply moving essay about the dialectic of mourning and activism in the first decade of the AIDS crisis, Douglas Crimp likewise argued that "here, I think, the difference between generations of gay men makes itself felt most sharply. For men in their twenties, our sexual ideal is mostly just that—an ideal, the cum never swallowed."[27] Don Romesburg reflected on arriving in San Francisco in 1993, recalling that "it seemed as if the age of desire had passed, replaced by courageous but troubled older men, young men who dreamed for a time that perhaps never was, and the gulf between them."[28]

In 1992 Dave Ford expressed a succession of community building and loss for young gay men in AIDS-ravaged San Francisco:

> Even in the early plague years, I felt powerful and joyous as I crisscrossed paths with similar rogues and comrades, establishing a cheerfully tangled web of tricks and fuck-buddies and boyfriends and lovers that, without irony, I could call "my family." For as the generation before me buried its best and learned, long before its time, to grieve on a massive scale, I was, without conscious design or a clear road map, building a community around me that would buoy me through times foggy and clear, rainy and wind-whipped.
>
> This, I thought, was what it meant to be living in a city. This, for me, was San Francisco.[29]

Whereas Ford recalls that he lost his best friend in 1987 and "an acquaintance here, a favorite bartender there," by the early 1990s, the "trickle" of losses "turned into a gush." He remarks that "the next generation is taking its turn at bereavement," yet "now there's a sense of [the same] generation dancing while the city burns. True, the energy's high, but so is the incidence of seroconversion among young gay men."[30] Between 1987 and

1991, a quarter of the people who seroconverted with HIV in the United States were under twenty-one. New diagnoses of AIDS peaked in San Francisco in 1992.[31]

By the 1990s, new publications worked to make sense of these emergent epochal turns. In 1991 both Douglas Coupland's novel *Generation X* and a special issue of the feminist journal *differences* titled "Queer Theory" were published, thereby popularizing their respective terms.[32] Also in 1991, William Strauss and Neil Howe's ambitious tome *Generations* offered an expansive theory and taxonomy of generations. Reflecting a turn from understanding generations in familial/genealogical terms to understanding them as sociohistorical cohorts, Strauss and Howe suggest that peer groups, born in the same historical moments, have shared generational experiences of formative historical events that shape their worldviews.[33] Moreover, these generational paradigms conflict with those before and after—so much so that there is often a breakdown between generations in understanding each other's differing values and frames of reference. Gay boomers and queer Xers internalized and reflected many of their peers' experiences and values, and I posit that for queers who often experienced familial rejection and invented their own chosen families, the emphasis on historical cohorts rather than family legacies makes Strauss's and Howe's theory of generations even more germane.

Strauss and Howe suggest that the boomers "remain the twentieth century's most generation-conscious peer group, one that has overwhelmed all thinking about the subject." In contrast, they argue that Generation X had been understood as having no identity at all and grew up comparatively unprotected as latchkey children, which led to a generational fatalism. One female college Xer in their study asserted that "the sexual revolution is over, and everybody lost." Strauss and Howe identify four generational archetypes, taxonomizing the boomer generation as "idealist" and Generation X (which they call the thirteenth generation) as "reactive."[34] In their schema, Millennials would be "civic," and Gen Z would be "adaptive."[35] As they suggest, "Idealist generations... typically come of age attacking elder-built institutions before retreating into self-absorbed remission, but later mature into uncompromising 'Gray Champion' moralists. Reactive generations... bubble over with alienated risk-taking in their twenties, but age into mellow pragmatists."[36] The previous "reactive" cohort had been called "the Lost Generation." Gay novelist David Leavitt dubbed his peers "the new Lost Generation" in 1985. Portraying himself and his colleagues as believing that there would be no future—because of nuclear holocaust, not AIDS—Leavitt writes that "if we are truly a generation without character, as is often claimed, it is because we have seen what has happened to generations with character."[37]

Focusing on generational culture in the gay community, anthropologists Gilbert Herdt and Andrew Boxer conducted a study of queer youths (ages 14–20) in Chicago between 1987 and 1989; this research coincided with the reporting on the new gay generation and parties, although their informants skewed some years younger than the drinking age at the time. Like Strauss and Howe, Herdt and Boxer distinguish four distinct gay generational cohorts: those who came of age after World War I, during/after World War II, after Stonewall/during gay liberation, and in the age of AIDS, respectively. Herdt and Boxer suggest that the latter cohort was the first to grow up in a world where gay institutions and social roles already existed as well as a sense of a gay past.[38]

These cycles continue, such that the Millennial generation came of age after more-effective HIV/AIDS treatments had been widely adopted, as social media afforded new ways of coming out and socializing, and as dating/hookup apps significantly changed the norms of cruising. For the still-young Gen Z, new articulations of gender identity and expression appear to be among the most significant generational innovations. One of the major developments for both the Millennial and Gen Z cohorts has been the rising number of youths who come out or redefine their gender expressions years before drinking age. This may contribute to the decentering of gay bars as an institution for younger people.

To position my own relation to this era, I am an Xer but too young to have gone to the parties in this chapter. (See interlude 5 on Superior, WI) The Box and Club Uranus parties feel to me like a cool older sibling's or friend's world: proximate, aspirational, and what I imagined being a few years older would be like. These parties offer the most immediate reimaginations of queer life that I inherited. Encountering so many references to a generational divide from this period was an "aha" moment for me; I was unaware of these discussions at the time, for I had no access to the gay press then, but suddenly I saw anew these discourses everywhere in queer writings from the time, including in canonical academic essays I'd read years before. This generational debate both complicated my understanding of this period as an era of coalitional AIDS activism *and* immediately made intuitive sense to me. I also recognized my own sense of subsequent cultural gaps between myself and Millennials and Gen Zers.

Everything He Wants: BOY Parties

During the 1980s the emergence of a new generation of gay men was initially articulated in terms of age. The word *boy* named a turn away from the fetishization of manliness and other values in the 1970s gay clone scene (see chapters 1 and 5 and interlude 1 on Denver). In 1983 Boy Bar opened as the It bar in New York's East Village and signaled a fundamentally different set of social mores. As one commentator derided, "You behaved at Boy Bar. There was a strictly post-AIDS preoccupation with decorum.... 'Boys' don't engage in S&M: 'boys' don't use poppers. 'Boys' don't fistfuck. Dancing was totally *verboten*."[39] On the West Coast, there would soon be talk of a "Boy movement" in the Bay Area and in Los Angeles among under-thirty gay men who "want their own identity."[40] The first rumblings I've found of this generational shift in the Bay Area appeared in late 1984, when an 18+ party called Normalville was marketed as "for a new generation of gay people."[41] "Boy" soon named a legion of young gay twerps, what we would now call twinks.

The BOY parties started in 1986, when Ben Dhong began hosting them in his apartment while a student in Berkeley; he was studying business en route to working as a financial adviser and real estate developer. Early on, he and his friends invited "good looking, clean-cut, under-30 gay friends" and asked them to "Bring-Your-Own-Boy." Subsequent press accounts of the events frequently mentioned the partiers' school affiliations, which were virtually always either UC Berkeley or Stanford; Dhong subsequently promoted a party called Fraternity.[42] The by-invitation BOY parties swelled in popularity to the point that Dhong rented out Sutter's Mill and other locations for his events starting in 1987. Dhong told the *San Francisco Examiner* that before his parties, the San Francisco gay scene "was sort of seedy, dark—people didn't dress very nicely. What I wanted was a nice clean-cut alternative, people who took care of their appearance."[43] Dhong referred to his parties as "quality," "wholesome" enterprises that attracted preppy A-gays in the making.[44] The party's admission practices became infamous for "screening" partygoers for their outfits and for their looks. "Bow-wows" were not allowed entry.[45] As a snarky profile of the parties remarked, "Dhong recognizes that guests who are too attractive intimidate even each other, and therefore tries to 'sprinkle in some humans among the gods.'"[46] Commentators complained about the overwhelming whiteness among the attendees as well as the amount of hair mousse and gel they used.

By 1988, the BOY parties figured as the lightning rod for the "brouhaha" of intergenerational conflict in the Bay Area's gay community.[47] The parties were so popular that they also inspired knock-off Boy Club events at the I-Beam that co-opted the term *boy* to compete for its market. Both Dhong and the I-Beam owner filed "doing business as" paperwork with the city in order to claim rights to the word *boy*.[48] Ironically, after appropriating the BOY brand, the Boy Club's publicity took pains to distinguish itself from associations with the homogenous whiteness of Dhong's events (see figure 7.2).[49]

Dhong and fellow party promoter Gus Bean described their generation as "materialistic" and "self-indulgent" rather than community minded. As Bean surmised, "After eight years of Ronald Reagan, kids are more interested in BMWs than in fighting for their rights. I think it's kind of sad but that is the way it is."[50] (Strauss and Rowe found that the Xers were "by far the most Republican-leaning youths in the sixty-year history of age-based polling," with a 52 percent majority by 1985.)[51] Dhong claimed that the BOY parties were "sort-of" a "rebellion against the gays right before us." Yet his politics were antimilitant and pro-assimilationist. In a controversial *Sentinel* profile of the BOY parties, he was quoted as saying that "there's no reason to fight.... I think we've already won.... I think we just want to fit in with the rest of society."[52] As an early missive sneered, "If a Boy were to do anything so vulgar as to place a personal ad, you can be sure he would describe himself as 'straight-acting,' a phrase with all the aphrodisiacal qualities of roadkill."[53]

Dhong's most controversial statement in the press claimed that younger gays "aren't involved at all" in AIDS.[54] In a letter to the *Sentinel* editor, Dhong responded that this was a misquote of his statement "that it is a *shame* that younger gays aren't as involved in the fight against AIDS as they should be."[55] In an editorial, a fellow Gen Xer retorted that "Dhong and the boys no more speak for me and my generation than Reagan speaks for the Sandinistas." He continues: "The power of boy as symbol is fueled by the specter of AIDS." BOY parties promote "a look that says, 'I am young and innocent. I am untainted, immune'—in short, an illusion.... If some boys are not 'involved' with AIDS, it is because, so far, they have had the luxury of choice. What they have chosen is *denial*."[56] In the *BAR*, a gay boomer likewise viewed these parties as reactionary: "If the 'boys' are at all representative of their generation, then I tremble for the future of the gay community."[57] I do not recall encountering *any* positive coverage of the BOY parties in the gay press, which contrasts with the published

FIGURE 7.2 After effectively appropriating the BOY party's name, Boy Club at the I-Beam sought to distance itself from criticisms of the BOY party's exclusionary admission practices with this verbose advertisement. *San Francisco Sentinel*, July 15, 1988. Courtesy of GLBT Historical Society.

celebrations of the Box and Club Uranus. Rather, a BOY flyer for the 1988 Dreaming in Black and White party reveled in the press's disdain by using pull quotes from the *BAR* and *Sentinel*, respectively: "Youth it is said is wasted on the young. If that is true, there was enough waste at the recent BOY Party to have (it) declared a toxic dump" and "a gaggle of drunken post-adolescents celebrating nothing but their own good looks and ferocious sexuality."[58]

Bean became an even more prolific promoter than Dhong, with prominent "Gus Presents" parties called Crew and Colossus, marked as for a "safe new generation," circa 1990 (see figure 7.3), among other events. Bean told the *BAR* that "the word 'Boy' is like paramount. It is like 'stud' or 'queen', it is a really strong word that, I think really defines the whole generation."[59]

GENERATION X QUEER SAN FRANCISCO   237

FIGURE 7.3 Gus Bean's flyer for the Safe New Generation party at Colossus in 1990 featured a photo of buff white twinks in tighty whities, exemplifying the zeitgeist boy aesthetic. The blond holds a condom, and the party theme emphasized both youth and health. This event promoted campaigns for the SF AIDS Foundation and the Haight Ashbury Free Clinics. The information line for Colossus was (415) 431-BOYS. LGBT Business Ephemera collection. Courtesy of GLBT Historical Society.

The promotional flyers for Bean's parties often resemble the era's Calvin Klein underwear ads with photos of gym-sculpted men in tight briefs or retro physique photos of nude men with their genitals teasingly obscured. Such images would become standard for gay dance-club promotions across the country in 1990s and after, but they stand out compared to the imagery before this moment and to contemporaneous alternative parties in the city.[60] Bean promoted his events with a more playful aesthetic, more overt sexual expression (including an embrace of kink), and a more gym-sculpted masculinity than the BOY parties. Nevertheless, the marketing images' frequent emphases on youth and on fitness worked overtime to signify health at a time when AIDS-related wasting and death were hypervisible in the community at large.

These parties were massively successful and indicated a rebirth of a gay male mainstream scene, one that prefigured the aesthetics of circuit parties that exploded a decade later. Since first reading about these parties and their boys, I have tended to view them as exemplifying the most retrograde and shallow elements of gay male culture. Later, in a more generous moment, I started to think that maybe these guys just wanted the chance to be young in the face of a future seemingly foreclosed by AIDS. But mostly I still think of these young men as privileged brats. Whereas the BOY parties and their ilk staked a claim to generational difference but maintained an investment in normative white male gayness, alternative parties such as the Box and Club Uranus exemplified a turn away from homogenous crowds toward diverse and self-consciously demented queer scenes.

Everybody Everybody: The Box

Part of what was significant about the queer parties of the late 1980s and early 1990s was that they sought to integrate the genders and to produce a parallel new scene of women's parties that were every bit as vibrant as the men's. For parties such as the Box, queerness meant a new model of multiculturalism and integration that defied the essentialist separatism and homogenized whiteness that were endemic to the 1970s gay male and lesbian/women's milieus. The *BAR* described the Box's scene: "A certain and critical balance of lesbionic-ethno-pan-racial-sexual future-world reigns here, a for-love-of-funk, non-exclusionary (beyond demonstrating your sincerity to the door person, if need be) camaraderie of 'we're all in this together and in a big way.'"[61] Music writer and DJ Don Baird concurred: "The most extraordinary aspect of the Box is the unprecedented and comfortable mixture of gay men and lesbians under one roof."[62] That co-gender clubbing was reported as so novel, even radical, suggests how gender segregated the previous generation's gay and lesbian nightlife had been. Nationally, the number of queer venues serving both male and female clientele doubled between 1987 and 1992.[63] The newness of the era's women's parties indicates that dancing had *not* previously been as central to women's nightlife as men's; in effect, women created spaces, parties, and attachments to fashion that had previously been associated with gay male nightlife. That both women's and co-gender parties were contemporaneously new indicates the dual logics of the moment: integrating the queer scene and elevating women's parties.

Mixtress Page Hodel provided the beating heart of this movement (see figure 7.4). Hodel was born during the later days of the baby boom but was a bridge figure with the new queer generation. She worked at

FIGURE 7.4 Photo of Mixtress Page Hodel (*at center with microphone*) announcing the winner of a weekly boom-box giveaway at the Box, circa 1990. © Melissa Hawkins. Courtesy of Melissa Hawkins.

the lesbian bar Amelia's, at the Dyke March, at the Folsom Street Fair, at political events, for the soul radio station KSOL, on Olivia Cruises, and at a range of recurring events, including her signature parties at the Box and Club Q. Hodel had unparalleled reach in the venues where she built a following: she spun records at straight clubs, Black clubs, punk clubs, gay male clubs, and women's clubs. Her wide-ranging audiences followed her and converged at the Box, which not only had a diverse crowd but was also more multigenerational than the other parties. On the Box's first night 450 dancers showed up; the following week 1,300 did so.[64]

The Box was initially scheduled on Thursdays at the Kennel Club and within a few months expanded to Saturdays as well. A flyer produced for Hodel's last night DJing the party after eleven years—572 Thursdays, it calculated—recalled:

> On April 7, 1988 I opened a dance club called The Box. I began with a dream of a dance club where gay men and women of all colors and their friends could come together and share a love for deliciously sweet soulful dance music. I began with a dream I that I could start a club where everyone who entered would be treated with respect and dignity

that I feel we so deeply deserve. That I would create a club where we could grow and thrive as a community and learn together what the word community meant. As we removed our clothes and danced into the night our bodies glistening with sweat ... close and connected ... the music and our sweat the conduit that joined us. And it worked![65]

Virtually every published account of the Box mentions *sweat*. In its early months one profile described "long lines and catastrophic temperatures inside" from which the dancers "emerge blithe, drenched and beatific."[66] As Hodel remarked, "The best compliment I ever receive for my work is when someone approaches the booth smiling and drenched in sweat."[67] Acknowledging the club's previously overheated conditions, a recurring summer 1989 ad in the *Sentinel* beckoned, "Come experience the fresh air with our new ventilation system."[68]

For Hodel, the dance floor allows hundreds of people to share a euphoric experience and be transformed by it. "DJing is like making love. It's very intimate and an exchange of energy back and forth," she told me. "You find the sweet spot, and I am a fanatic about giving pleasure to the audience."[69] Hodel observed that gay men and women had divergent musical tastes, which created challenges for her as a DJ.[70] Hodel kept the fog machines off and the lights a bit brighter at her parties so that she could see the dancers' faces. Rather than a dazzling strobe effect, she wanted *people* to be the visual focal point. A dance troupe also performed weekly routines.

Reflecting its community orientation, the Box held recurring photo shoots by Chloe Atkins for its club-goers to be featured in slide shows during the party and in its publicity materials. Party flyers routinely featured gender-mixed and ethnically diverse collectives with limbs suggestively intertwined, like a queer spin on contemporaneous United Colors of Benetton ads (see figure 7.5). Solo shots anticipate the portrait styling of 1990s Gap and Calvin Klein ads (see figure 7.6). Promotional materials alternately proclaimed the party as "A Homosexual Dance Club," "A Club for All Colors," and "Everybody's Dance Club." Occasional parties were presented as benefits for organizations such as ACT UP or Asian Pacific Sisters and Gay Asian Pacific Alliance.[71] The success of the Box inspired other queer-of-color parties, including the mid-1990s Latinx event Pan Dulce.[72] As Hodel told the lesbian press at the time, "I wanted our clubs to reflect the way we want the world to be."[73]

Although her sets adapted to different parties, Hodel played "cutting edge R&B, classic Hip Hop, Funk and Soul in an era where these records

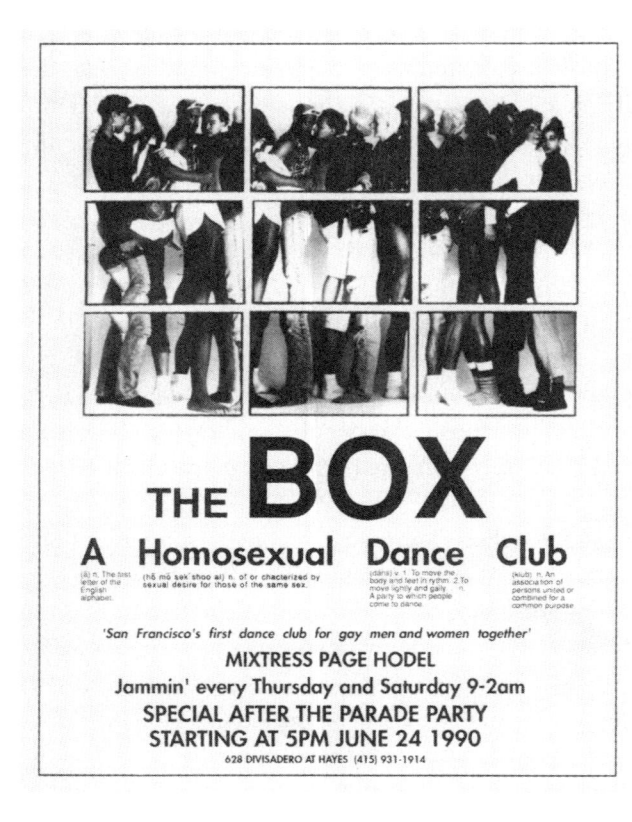

FIGURE 7.5 This advertisement for the Box's 1990 pride party features a photo grid of its co-gender, multiethnic queer crowd in overlapping embraces. LGBT Business Ephemera collection. Courtesy of GLBT Historical Society.

were not on the roster at any [other LGBTQ+] venue."[74] A banner hung during its first anniversary party proclaimed, "San Francisco's first night club of funk and soul for gay men and women." It was also described as "rock 'n' roll free" and "disco-free," which suggests that both connoted "white" by this time.[75] Although she is white, Hodel was known for her love and deep knowledge of Black music. A local music scholar recalled that "in the '80s, if you wanted to hear good hip-hop, you went to where Page and the lesbians were. Straight people and hip-hop people went to her clubs, because she had respect."[76] In the club's early years she primarily played soul and funk, but as music changed, her record collection evolved toward more house and hip-hop. Mr. Lee's "Get Busy" and L'Trimm's "Cars with the Boom" ranked among the most popular tracks at the Box.[77]

In the mid-1990s the Box changed venues following noise complaints from neighbors; the party moved to a larger venue with two dance floors: one for house music and another for hip-hop. This effectively cleaved the

FIGURE 7.6 This advertisement for the Box's 1991 pride party features a mosaic of patron portraits by Chloe Atkins to model the club's inclusiveness. LGBT Business Ephemera collection. Courtesy of GLBT Historical Society.

Box community; white dancers gravitated toward the house room, whereas dancers of color did so toward the hip-hop room. Nonetheless, the party remained the most diverse in the city. On the club's tenth anniversary, the Oakland-based queer-of-color magazine *Whassup!* remarked that "a Box Family spontaneously emerged reflecting ground-breaking ethnic diversity. The mix of people all sweating and dancing together without barriers was divine. People came every week like it was food for their soul, many family members often called it Church."[78] (On the religious connotations of Black queer nightlife, see chapter 4.)

This cultural shift toward coming together—which was never fully achieved or sustained in the community at large—also reflected new realities and priorities during the first decade of the AIDS crisis. The reorientation of gay male nightlife away from cruising or hookups, as well as the perceived necessity of all-male spaces, fundamentally changed the purpose of going out for many men. Some gay men who came of age with AIDS sought out the emergent dyke culture as fun and intriguing, whereas some queer women embraced new opportunities to socialize fluidly with gay men.[79] However, it must be noted that even this cultural shift did not immediately make most male bars welcoming to women.[80] Rather, in many cities it took years of the AIDS crisis to begin moving the needle on gay male misogyny. To put it simply, women (lesbians, bisexuals, and allies) showed up for gay men in ways that men had never shown up for them—as caretakers, as doctors and medical professionals, as civil service and nonprofit organization workers, as volunteers, as coalition activists, and as people doing the work to sustain community.[81] People came to the Box with years of pent-up sexual energy and sweated it out on the dance floor during the AIDS crisis, and the club produced T-shirts proclaiming, "Dancing is safe sex." As Hodel recalled, people would come to the Box after a shift of caretaking for a friend or even after memorial services.[82] Dancing at the Box was nothing short of cathartic. Resonantly, one 1989 ad for the Box in the *Sentinel* appeared embedded in an article on women as caretakers during the AIDS epidemic (see figure 7.7).[83]

The AIDS crisis and its devastation also opened up public spaces and the possibility for queer women to claim them. For women, the queer turn built on a recent embrace of sex positivity as well as gender play that contrasted with much of the prior generation's vision of lesbian feminism. By the late 1980s, a new lesbianism was proclaimed via the flourishing of women's parties, of lipstick-lesbian style, and of new sexual practices.[84] Suggesting a reversal of cultures, a *Sentinel* cover proclaimed, "Gay Men Get Intimate... While Lesbians Learn to Lust."[85] San Francisco, which Annie Sprinkle called "the clitoris of America," became an important center for these new dyke cultures.[86] British promoter Caroline Clone's lipstick-lesbian dance party Code Blue, which featured a dress code, transformed the scene as early as 1986. Clone told the local gay press, "Young gay women absolutely refuse to accept the old stereotype," signaling that young gay men were not alone in articulating a generational rupture or in refusing status-quo bars.[87] Clone's Code Blue parties drew crowds of fashionable women revelers and inspired rival parties such as Club Rapture and Skirts. Skirts was marketed with a seductive image of a dandy butch in a fitted suit touching cigarettes with her bandeau-clad femme (see

FIGURE 7.7 This advertisement for the Box, resembling the artwork for Soul II Soul's contemporaneous releases, appears in the context of an article about women as caregivers to gay men with AIDS. San Francisco Sentinel, August 10, 1989. Courtesy of GLBT Historical Society.

figure 7.8). Its opening-night party—at which Hodel spun records—drew a thousand people, confirming the demand for such events.[88] Savvily, a later version of the ad also reassured its target audience that the venue has "16 bathroom stalls" to serve the massive crowd.[89]

Hodel DJed at some of Clone's parties before starting Club Q as a women's party *without* a dress code.[90] Club Q was poppier, even flirtier, than the Box. As Deborah P. Armory described the scene, "The lesbian identity forged at Club Q revolved around an open celebration of sexuality, expressed through dance and cruising, built around the power of the lesbian gaze."[91] Club Q ads reflected much the same aesthetic and ethic as the Box, including women of different races and ethnicities, gender presentation, and body type who participated in similar photo shoots at

FIGURE 7.8 This seductive flyer for the Skirts opening party in early 1989 signaled a new lesbian chic spin on butch/femme aesthetics and drew a crowd of a thousand. A later version of this advertisement reflected the turn toward co-gender clubbing by specifying that guys "with gusto" are "welcome." It also reassured women that the venue featured "16 bathroom stalls." LGBT Business Ephemera collection. Courtesy of GLBT Historical Society.

both parties (see figure 7.9). Other publicity for Club Q cultivated a lesbian chic aesthetic, featured images of female bodybuilders, and promoted playful events such as bra parties and Twister games.[92] Nonetheless, Hodel did not envision her parties as cruising grounds. As she told *Deneuve* magazine, "I've met wonderful people in the dance clubs, but I don't like the idea of going into a bar with four hundred lesbians all bundled together and these are your choices. I'd like to think I'd find the love of my life in a hardware store behind the counter."[93] In the early 2020s, Hodel founded Page's Carpentry School.

Club Q quickly ascended to be *the* recurring party for Bay Area queer women; it outgrew its first venue and moved to Club Townsend (home of the boy-adjacent parties Fraternity, Pleasuredome, and Club Universe), which was the largest dance hall in the city, with a capacity of three thousand. There were no full-time lesbian-owned women's bars at the time,

FIGURE 7.9 Page Hodel promoted Club Q, her long-running dance party for women, with photos of its diverse patrons. LGBT Business Ephemera collection. Courtesy of GLBT Historical Society.

so weekly or itinerant parties such as Club Q provided Gen X women with a "lifeline" and effectively traded stability for dynamism.[94] Although neither operated as a fixed venue, both the Box and Club Q kept queer San Franciscans dancing for more than a decade.

Cosmic Thing: Club Uranus

Rejecting the BOY parties' yuppie normativity and trading the Box's diversity for a cultivated *deviance*, Club Uranus came to define an emergent alternative culture that celebrated freaks, druggy hedonism, and performance. Uranus, promoted by Lewis Walden and Michael Blue of the Chaos party (which had a "no acid wash" door policy), marked a turn toward queer as in transgressive when it debuted in 1989.[95] By Uranus's second week, "a sub-culture was being defined."[96] The party embraced a sense of extremity, subversion, unpredictability, risk, and militant campy fun in a specific pre-internet moment. One nightlife overview called the crowd "the *avant* of the *avant*," while yet another synopsized "tasty trendoids and effluvia."[97]

At Uranus, generational alienation gave way to a sense of play. There, homocore punks intersected with ravers, radical drag, and Queer Nation activists.[98] Remarked the *BAR* in an overview of the changed nightlife culture of 1990, "Uranus is the *Star Wars* cantina. Neo-new wave transvestite meets punkskins, sex-industry meets beauty pageant, cultural activism blends with frivolity, and a polka can turn into minor slam dancing in a second. The dual DJings of Lewis and Mike balance an excruciatingly sharp industrial beat and hard-edged noise with rock and punk, both classic and kitsch."[99] The DJs spun Coil, Psychic TV, Throbbing Gristle, My Life with the Thrill Kill Cult, and Front 242 on heavy rotation. Uranus parties were promoted through flyers that were photocopied onto color paper stock and then quartered. Their collaged image-and-text aesthetic resembles zines, and these flyers feature appropriated artwork ranging from retro kitsch to popular media references to kink photography; indeed, the scene intersected with the new zine culture exemplified by *Tantrum, Whorezine,* and *Homocore*. Party flyer taglines include "Strange and unworldly go-go things," "Weird Fantasy," and "Come where the pleasure lovers are" (see plate 13).[100] The party would have been underground if not for the fact that so many of its regulars wrote for the gay press and the party consistently drew more than eight hundred revelers.[101]

Club Uranus showcased abject drag performers who refused glamour and go-go boys who defied the conventions of gym-sculpted dancers. Both were exemplified by artist and local legend Jerome Caja, who loved to flirt with, wrestle with, and "terrorize" the crowd.[102] Exemplifying its alternative queer logic, the 1992 Miss Uranus contest publicity proclaimed, "Beauty doesn't have to be pretty."[103] Footage of the Club Uranus contingent during a pride parade—including go-go dancer Drew Macaroni-and-Cheese, clad only in a hollow plastic fish strapped on as a literal codpiece—was even used in the 1992 religious-right scare video *The Gay Agenda* as evidence of homosexuality's corruptive decadence.[104] Party promoter Ggreg Taylor and Diet Popstitute—who chose his name "because he says he is the love child of Princess Di and ET"—would be among the other leading personalities on the scene.[105] In a profile of Taylor, Frank Browning referred to him "and his band of kindred spirits" as "the court jesters of the queer movement."[106] (See figure 7.1.) Surveying the range of parties in the city in 1992, Justin Vivian Bond proclaimed, "It's finally happened—the lunatics have taken over the asylum!"[107]

The clubbers cultivated outrageous personas, ingenious fashion, and a taste for self-incapacitating drugs. (Speed was probably the most popular party drug among the crowd, although LSD and ecstasy were common as well.) The party mixed elements of punk, drag, art, and BDSM and presented San Francisco's answer to New York's club-kid phenomenon and to Los Angeles' Club Fuck and High Karate parties.[108] Expressing its outré sensibility and advancing its own primacy, a 1991 postcard for Club Uranus featured a person in a gimp mask fellating a sheathed penis and the proclamation "Fuck LA Fuck New York" (see figure 7.10). The rise of club-kid culture in New York happened, in part, when the various queer freaks who had moved from their respective hometowns recognized that they constituted a critical mass after moving to the city.[109] A parallel phenomenon happened with the celebutantes and Popstitutes in San Francisco. Whereas the scenes on the East and West coasts may superficially resemble each other, the sensibilities differed: in New York the club kids were more cynical, ultimately pursuing fame or at least infamy; in San Francisco there was a more earnest investment in letting one's freak flag fly.[110] The San Francisco clubbers who dressed in leather or rubber gear were legitimately into kink, and the more outlandish and playful fashions were likewise expressions of self that rejected homonormativity. Then again, outrageous or goofy sex acts were sometimes performed just to keep queerness perverse. Betty, the coauthor of *Betty & Pansy's Severe Queer Review*, includes in his bio that he "reigns as Ms. Uranus 1992 for attempting to 'gerbil' a hamster the size of a guinea pig."[111] Club Uranus also apparently inspired the rave party Bowel, billed as "deeper than Uranus."[112]

Like the Box, Uranus offered "co-gender clubbing" experiences—although the Box skewed more female and ethnically mixed, whereas at Club Uranus gender was more self-consciously performative but predominantly male and white (see figure 7.11). Remarked commentator Lily Braindrop, "It's not unusual to trip into Uranus and see a mingling of buzz-cut, pierced, Doc Marten-clad women, boys in stiletto heels and football jerseys, and queens in sky-high platforms sporting two-foot bouffant wigs (altitude as well as attitude, dontcha know)." Braindrop continued: "If, as the current club scene illustrates, girls will be boys (and vice versa), is there really any logical basis for separation?"[113] Straight men were allowed entrance to the club only if they kissed their same-sex buddies on the lips for the doorman.[114] Rachel Pepper synopsized the scene for a women's party guide: "A haven for activist boys and girls who

FIGURE 7.10 Club Uranus embraced BDSM and espoused a confrontational sensibility, as demonstrated by this flyer from 1991. LGBTQIA Club and Event Flyers Collection (GLC 194), LGBTQIA Center, San Francisco Public Library.

like to network as they party, this is the most truly 'queer' hip club in town, attracting punks, leather wanna-be's, ACT UP and Queer Nation kids, and all manner of outrageous and fabulous drag. Doorman Tom [Maffei] is a sweetie, the bartenders don't ignore you if you're a woman, and I often feel more comfortable at this club than at the more cruisy all-women locales." Pepper captures the familiar textures of misogyny pervasive in the gay male scene as she continues to note that such gendered frictions vexed Uranus, too: "Unfortunately, though, the predominantly male clientele seems to have gotten pushier here recently.... However, there's no doubt that this is one hot, sex-positive spot for girls as well as boys."[115]

Although indicative of a new queer cultural moment, Uranus nonetheless can be understood as part of a local genealogy of gay male genderfuck

FIGURE 7.11 Photo of Rodney O'Neal Austin playing with gender in his baby-doll-head bustier at Club Uranus. © Melissa Hawkins. Courtesy of Melissa Hawkins.

performance that includes the Cockettes, the Angels of Light, and the Sisters of Perpetual Indulgence, and as part of emergent play with gender expression that exploded the possibilities of self-presentation and identity exemplified by Caja, Bond, Miss Kitty, and Kate Bornstein. As film scholar and artist Marc Siegel reflects, Club Uranus was where he "first came to understand a concept of *queer*"—particularly in terms of rethinking gender attribution. He recalls a revelatory moment during a Miss Uranus contest when a judge asked a cis female contestant, "What was the largest thing you've ever had in your ass?" The contestant responded, without missing a beat, "Her name was Daddy."[116]

Suggesting a politics to dancing, Braindrop wrote that "in an era when gays and other sexual minorities are fighting for their lives, as well as for their rights, there is a newfound sense of determination and unity that extends from the political demonstration to the dance floor."[117] As Alvin Orloff—aka Remix von Popstitute or Alvin à Go-Go—recounted in a memoir of the Bay Area queer underground, "The prospect of an early grave left me feeling cheated and miserably depressed, sure, but also a little relieved. There was no need to choose a career or save for a rainy day. No need to grow up and be responsible. The only sensible course of action would be to cram as much merriment as humanly possible into my few remaining years. I might die young, but I'd go out swinging!" Orloff continues: "My friends and I were still in our twenties when we started greeting each other after prolonged absences with a surprised, 'Wow, *you're still alive!*'"[118]

Uranus existed in the same orbit as a plurality of other queer parties that emerged at the end of the 1980s and very early 1990s. Arguably the most significant other party of this milieu, Klubstitute, was the Popstitutes' cabaret-style event with theme nights, spoken-word poetry, original theater productions, live bands, and whatever acts they could find to explode nightlife conventions. One report from 1991 characterized Klubstitute: "This is the place where scenesters are finally given the chance to put on that show they've always wanted to do since junior high, only now . . . they can do it as the sex-workers, junkies, fierce poets, drag queens, anarchists, bitter cynics, bar flies, sexual deviates, Fairies, and frequent wig-wearers that they are today. The results run the gamut from brilliant to painful, with a constant sick-fuck element that admittedly scares away the meek or unenthused."[119] The Popstitutes sought "the total eradication of conformity, complacency, and elitism" in the gay scene.[120] Whereas Uranus was a dance party, Klubstitute showcased performances, including by Tribe 8, Lypsinka, Jennifer Blowdryer, Holly Woodlawn, Elvis Herselvis, and the Sick and Twisted Players. These scenes were often about *making a scene*. Still, there was substance beyond shock value. Klubstitute hosted a benefit for the Prevention Point needle-exchange program that featured death rock and a rumored raffle for "hearse rides" as well as a pride weekend party called "Out of the Closets and into the Ovens: A Night of Gay Shame."[121] This effectively invented a new discourse of dissident queer critique.

Extending Uranus's queer genealogy, Joan Jett Blakk moved to San Francisco from Chicago and hosted an important radical queer drag performance cabaret at Josie's Cabaret and Juice Joint. In 1996 Heklina started T-Shack in the mold of Klubstitute, focusing on drag but skipping the spoken word after a wave of deaths in the Uranus/Popstitutes orbit; this party sustained its predecessors' queer legacy locally.[122] After Caja and Miss Kitty died, Bond moved to New York and hosted events such as Mario Diaz's Foxy party at the Cock—where attendees were induced to do the most outrageous, often sexual things they could think of—as a tribute to this moment in queer San Francisco.[123]

Can We Keep Moving in the After Hours: Queer San Francisco 2.0

Parties are subject to the changing conditions of the city, like the fog that rolls in and out. This period of queer invention and exploration responded to both government and real estate interventions that had constrained gay nightlife in the first half of the 1980s. In 1984 the city shut down bathhouses and sex clubs as a measure to curtail the spread of HIV/AIDS (see also chapter 5). Around the same time, San Francisco witnessed real estate overdevelopment that raised fears of the "Manhattanization" of the city alongside rent gouging that drove many gay businesses to close.[124] Reflecting on closures, the BAR surmised that "gay bars are probably at the epicenter of the 'second epidemic, the epidemic of fear.'"[125] After San Francisco was rocked by the Loma Prieta earthquake in 1989, parts of the city stood in ruins for years. This opened up new possibilities for parties to make space within the city for a brief time. These factors necessitated a creative reinvention of what queer nightlife could be.

Further queering boundaries, during a nationwide recession in the early 1990s, straight venues began hosting both weekly gay nights to underwrite a nightlife slump and parties that embraced freakery, fetish, and alternative sensibilities that undid gay/straight divides.[126] Conversely, Queer Nation chapters organized queer-ins of straight bars called Queer Nights Out, a phenomenon that would be revived under the mantle of Guerilla Queer Bar a decade later.[127] Each of these worked to undo—or at least destabilize—the dominant model of the gay bar that had been so pervasive in the city for decades before.

Economic conditions soon drove "the end of San Francisco" as it existed in this queer moment.[128] The city became more unaffordable in the mid-late 1990s during the Willie Brown mayoral administration and inflation from the first dot-com bubble. Escalating property values motivated evictions starting around 1996, and within a few years venture capital permeated everything. One party promoter even compared competition between clubs to the then-rivalry between Microsoft Explorer and Netscape.[129] In the new millennium, Google and social media companies would invade the city in a second tech wave that further pushed out the socially and economically dissident queer residents and the enclaves that had remained. Bar owners usually rent rather than own their spaces; the move toward recurring and itinerant parties created doubly precarious conditions for queer nightlife as promoters operate at the mercy of both landlords and venue management.

Signaling a tonal shift from a decade before, in 2004 DJ Bus Station John began the long-running Thursday night party Tubesteak Connection at Aunt Charlie's in the Tenderloin, a drag and trans bar in a neighborhood that had been intransigent against gentrification. The party took a "curatorial" relation to the past.[130] Rather than reject the liberation-era gay male culture as its Gen X predecessors did, Tubesteak Connection reclaimed it by paying "glorifying homage... with a revival of an underground gay culture that should have never been lost." Occupying an old-school hole-in-the-wall bar, the party promised retro sleaze and played club kitsch and classic tracks to re-create an imagined queer past for an "insouciant" *younger* younger generation.[131]

Nightlife scenes do not last forever. The Box and Club Q were the most enduring of this chapter's parties: the Box continued until 1999, and Club Q did so until 2003. Ironically, their models of multicultural dancing and of massive women's parties have been the least replicated. The BOY parties and Club Uranus lasted only a few years, but they provided templates for parties that persist. Innumerable dance clubs that privilege youth and conventional standards of male beauty continue to play pop and Hi-NRG music in the model of the BOY parties, and I've seen countless late-night drag-cum-performance art acts during parties at bars. As revolutions in gay nightlife, they exemplify both meanings of the word: radical new starts that continue to spin 'round on repeat.

INTERLUDE 7

The Casa Nova in Somerset County, PA

The Casa Nova gay bar in rural western Pennsylvania exemplified the contradictions of late-1990s gay politics in America. The gay press at the time revealed discordant juxtapositions among breakthroughs, complacency, and violence. The prognosis of the AIDS epidemic began to dramatically shift when new treatments produced the first major decline in deaths, starting in 1996 (and reported in 1997). In spring 1997 Ellen Degeneres and her sitcom double on *Ellen* came out in a media frenzy, signaling new mainstream acceptance followed by a drop in ratings; the manhunt for serial killer Andrew Cunanan developed as the *other* most prominent gay-related news story of the moment.[1] The term *post-gay* began gaining traction in 1998 to indicate that urbane queers found identify politics to be passé because of the perceived "end" of AIDS; that fall, the premiere of the long-running must-see TV sitcom *Will & Grace* (on which characters didn't come out because they were *already* out) seemed to suggest a tipping point toward what would soon be called homonormativity.[2] Twelve days before that sitcom debuted, however, Matthew Shepard was beaten, tied to a fence, and left for dead in Laramie, Wyoming, in what would become the most publicized antigay hate crime of the era. Shepard died in a hospital five days later from head traumas and hypothermia. Rural areas, such as Laramie and Somerset County, emerged as the imagined last frontier for gay activists and as sites appropriated for their cause. They also attested to the existence and conditions of queer lives beyond the city.[3]

The Casa Nova opened in January 1997 along Pennsylvania state route 985 between Johnstown and Jennerstown in Somerset County, approximately sixty-five miles east of Pittsburgh. The owners were a married heterosexual couple who also ran the gay bar Yuppies in Mt. Pleasant. In March a campaign against the Casa Nova began when an unidentified culprit altered flyers for the bar's "Blackout Blowout" party to read "Blackout Blowjobs," stuffed them inside gay male porn magazines, and distributed them to neighboring homes. This prank sparked outrage among local residents and subsequent gunfire at the bar's front door; inside the bar, one man was hit in the jaw, another was hit in the back of the head with nine pieces of buckshot, and a third was hit in the eye by ricocheting glass.[4] For as long as gay bars have been recognized as the primary public venues of gay life, they have also been targets for arson, bombs, shootings, and street violence. (See references to the 1973 Up Stairs Lounge fire in New Orleans in the preface and to the mass shooting at Pulse nightclub in Orlando in the epilogue, "After Hours.") Just a month before the Casa Nova's troubles began, the Other Side lesbian bar in Atlanta was bombed by the Army of God, an extremist Christian group that had previously attacked a local abortion clinic and an Olympics site; that bar reopened and demonstrated its queer wit and resilience by distributing cardboard hand fans with the slogan "Have a blast at the Other Side."[5]

The day after the shooting at the Casa Nova, local "self-proclaimed Anabaptist Bishop" Ron McRae began to organize protests of the bar in the manner of the Westboro Baptist Church's infamous "God Hates Fags" pickets.[6] In standard moral-panic mode, McRae conflated scripture, public health, and homophobia in his claims that AIDS was God's punishment for "sodomites," who would burn in hell. McRae and his ilk believed that the mere presence of homosexuals threatened the community at large with disease and sought to drive them from the area. To do so, they targeted the most visible local manifestation of gay life: the gay bar.

Such protests ignited queer counterprotests and solidarity parties with a renewed spirit of bar activism. The Lesbian Avengers and *CRY OUT!* ACT UP co-opted McRae's rhetoric to organize a "Burn in Hell" counterprotest bus trip from Pittsburgh to visit the Casa Nova in April 1997.[7] Pittsburgh's

Planet Q reported that the bus was escorted by state police vehicles, and additional state police awaited in riot gear along the highway as more than a hundred protesters "and curious neighbors" observed the bus's arrival. On departure, the police escort mysteriously disappeared as someone—likely affiliated with the Ku Klux Klan—threw a brick at the bus while it was winding down slick mountain roads; no one was injured.[8] Groups including PFLAG (Parents and Friends of Lesbians and Gays) and the Metropolitan Community Church (the primary gay Christian denomination) also later visited the bar to support it.

In May the Casa Nova owners brokered a deal with McRae to allow him to deliver Sunday sermons at the bar. Meanwhile, the KKK took over protesting the bar when a nearby farm hosted a rally and a cross burning, after which two dozen robed and hooded Klansmen traveled to the bar for a faceoff (see figure 17.1). McRae initially said he would not participate in the KKK protests "because the Klan promotes hate." However, he resumed his protests hours after his second sermon at the bar.[9] During the ensuing months, three different groups protested the bar—McRae's Anabaptists, the KKK, and locals not publicly affiliated with either—as the pickets expanded from weekends to every day. As protests continued, an unknown assailant smashed the bar's windows with rocks, and local law enforcement illegally provided McRae with information about bar patrons by running their license plates. I've repeatedly found accounts of similar practices of surveillance and intimidation elsewhere (see chapter 6). McRae pursued having the bar shut down by filing complaints about its septic system and by reporting the bar as a "nuisance" to the state Bureau of Liquor Control and Enforcement. A close McRae associate also stalked the owners; although police confiscated his firearm, a local judge threw out the charges against the stalker.[10] As the gay press pointed out, freedoms of speech and of religion protected the rights of the homophobic protesters, but no state or federal law specifically protected the bar and its patrons from harassment.[11]

The year 1997 ended at the Casa Nova with a holiday/solstice party promoting peace and empowerment. *Planet Q* reported that "more than 100 people circled a large Christmas tree in the parking lot and with their backs to the protesters continued to sing. As the protesters screamed, the song became fuller and for several moments the protesters could not be heard."[12] The protests and parties continued in the new year and beyond. *Planet Q* published images of Lesbian Avengers eating fire in the snow during the second annual Burn in Hell party and offered to publicize any

FIGURE 17.1 Starting in 1997, the Casa Nova bar in Somerset County, Pennsylvania, was harassed by ongoing protests by the Anabaptist bishop Ron McRae (*both lower right inset images*) and by members of the Ku Klux Klan. *Planet Q*, June 1997. Courtesy of ONE Archives at the USC Libraries.

future trips to the Casa Nova. As the paper urged its readers, "Here's our solution to the Casa Nova situation. Go there.... The bigots believe that they can shame gays and lesbians into staying away."[13] A third Burn in Hell party was advertised in 1999.[14]

Antigay and other forms of biased-motivated violence have always existed, but during the 1990s they increasingly became recognized and reported as hate crimes.[15] Concurrently, the number of such acts grew as extremist ideologies gained a foothold of acceptance and free-speech protections.[16] The federal Hate Crimes Statistics Act was passed in 1990 "to collect statistics on crimes motivated by hate based on race, religion, sexual orientation, or ethnicity" and marked "the first time a gay-inclusive bill had ever become national law."[17] At the state level across the country, both antihate crime bills and legislation to prohibit gay marriage became staple late-1990s controversies and reflected contradictory politics.

In 1998 the connotations of aggression against the Casa Nova shifted as public discourses on hate crimes burgeoned. That summer one of the

Casa Nova owners testified before the US Congress in hearings on federal hate-crime legislation a few months before the murder of Shepard. Extending the logic that had long understood the gay bar as a stand-in for the gay community, it now seemed that a bar (not just a person) could be understood as the target of hate crimes. Meanwhile, the local KKK organized a White Pride Day for the same date that 150 people attended a Unity Celebration picnic at the Casa Nova.[18] The year ended with a candlelight vigil at the bar, organized by MCC pastors from Hagerstown, Maryland, Harrisburg, and Pittsburgh in memory of hate-crime victims, further forging associations between the Casa Nova and Shepard's death.[19]

Just as gay life was often imagined to exist primarily in urban spaces, the rural then figured in the popular imagination as the location of antigay hate—even though such violence was and remains far more prevalent in cities. As the symbolic face of antigay hate crimes, Shepard's whiteness (as well as his boyishness and class privilege) also occluded the fact that queer and trans people of color are disproportionately targeted in such attacks. The Casa Nova protests remained a local story that gained little national attention, in contrast to the flood of outsiders who came to Wyoming to report on the events with little sense of the place. Likewise, the organized trips from surrounding larger cities to the Casa Nova were intended as acts to support the rural queers rather than opportunities to exploit a specific incident for a national agenda.

Altogether, protests of the Casa Nova carried on for nearly *four years* until the bar closed in 2001. However, gay solidarity found its limitations in business. The region's rival gay bar, Lucille's, ran ads mocking the Casa Nova's travails in 1998. But when the Casa Nova closed, McRae moved his homophobic crusade to Lucille's.[20] The federal Matthew Shepard and James Byrd Jr. Hate Crimes Prevention Act finally passed in 2009, more than a decade after its namesakes' deaths.

8

Donde Todo es Diferente

Queer Latinx Nightlife in Los Angeles

RESEARCHED AND WRITTEN WITH DAN BUSTILLO

The late, glittering Mexican divo Juan Gabriel's hit song "El Noa Noa" paid tribute to the Juárez bar where he got his start: "Este es un lugar de ambiente donde todo es diferente."[1] He sang of a *place* ("lugar") where *everything is different* ("donde todo es diferente"), but the rhyme he made with "diferente"—"de ambiente"—remains alluringly open to different interpretations and translations. Taken literally, "de ambiente" means *environment* or *ambience*, but it has also long functioned euphemistically as code for homosexual men. Gabriel was likewise widely understood as de ambiente, and his music continues to play at gay bars and queer parties.

Gay Latinx bars reflect their de ambiente—both lugar and gente (*people*)—in ways that intersect with many of the issues in previous chapters, including discrimination, gentrification, masculinity, and the centrality of performances.[2] They operate in proximity to and distance from, in similarity and contrast to, white Anglo bar scenes. As Frances

Negrón-Muntaner affirms, queer Latinx people in many cities have had to make choices "split... along ethnoracial and sexual fault lines"—between dancing at predominantly white queer clubs or at straight Latinx ones. As she observes, "That Latinos were not seen dancing [at gay venues] created the impression that there were no Latino gays and lesbians at all or, if they existed, were closeted and hence impossible to mobilize or serve."[3] This chapter intends to redress those optics by centering the multiplicities of queer Latinx venues with a geographic focus on Los Angeles; in these spaces, erotic and romantic contacts become possible, community can be imagined, and forms of exclusion and distinction can be escaped or felt anew.

Queer Latinx bars and clubs provide community sanctuaries that create vibrant alternatives to and exceed white gay male bars in culturally specific yet varied ways. Latinx venues often share common elements, such as Spanish-language music, performances, go-go boys, and dancing, yet they also demonstrate a diversity of queer Latinx sensibilities and scenes that refuse a reductive or homogenized identity.[4] Although individual sites across the city may primarily serve distinct clienteles, including Chicanx/US Latinx patrons (Circus Disco, Chico), immigrants (Club Tempo, Frat House), or a mix (New Jalisco Bar), these are porous scenes, and people circulate fluidly between them—and between Spanish-language venues and Anglo ones. The patrons of these venues likewise range in their identifications of sexuality, gender, nationality, region, histories of migration, race, ethnicity, indigeneity, class, fashion, and language.

The queer vida noctura (*nightlife*) in Los Angeles radiates in all directions—though mostly *east:* in Hollywood, Silverlake, the San Fernando Valley, Westlake, South Central, downtown, Boyle Heights, El Sereno, Montebello, El Monte, Long Beach, Garden Grove, and Pomona.[5] In the mid-2000s recurring alternative queer-of-color parties, including Mustache Mondays, Shits & Giggles, A Club Called Rhonda, and Wildness, also reenergized the Los Angeles queer nightlife scene, often combining dancing with drag, live music, or performance art around midnight in ways that built on a prior generation's events (see chapter 7).[6] This non-exhaustive itinerary signals the plenitude of queer Latinx venues in the Los Angeles metropolitan area. As poet Raquel Gutiérrez has beautifully reflected, queer Latinx venues in Los Angeles "assemble a new folklore."[7]

Latinx queer nightlife in Los Angeles extends geographically and historically, but we narrow the focus here to four exemplary venues that emerged at different moments and produced distinct scenes, although each has a decades-long legacy: the massive Circus Disco in Hollywood, which served generations of young men from the 1970s to the 2010s; the immigrant vaquero (*cowboy*) venue Club Tempo, which opened amid early-1990s anti-immigration politics; the Millennial homie-sexual Chico, which produced a queered image of east-side Chicano masculinity; and the evolving downtown New Jalisco Bar, which responded to gentrification and other shifts in the 2000s. Rather than being reducible to a genre of gay bar, Latinx venues contain multitudes of queerly made worlds. In other words, LGBTQ+ Latinx venues negotiate between multiple forms of latinidad.

In dialogue with these historically reconstructed accounts, we intersperse scenes from visits to Latinx venues. Although the work in this chapter has been informed by reading ethnographic studies (of Mexican American migration, of queer Latinx lives, of Los Angeles), ethnography is neither our training nor our primary method here.[8] Nonetheless, this chapter includes interludes with scenes from various local bars reflecting the ways that Lucas's collaboration with coresearcher Dan Bustillo and social relationships with Lucas's friends have mediated our understandings of these spaces. Researching and writing about these bars as different kinds of outsiders (Lucas as a white gay man originally from the Midwest and Dan as a queer, transmasculine Cuban American from Miami), we at once felt it imperative that Latinx venues be represented in this broad history of gay bars and have also been concerned about how to respect the integrity of these venues as safe spaces and how to avoid exoticizing them or exposing them to unwanted attention.

A note on terminology: in this chapter, what may appear to resemble the Anglo-American concepts *drag queens* and *drag shows* function in different and culturally specific ways. Many of the artists in this chapter live and/or perform as travesti or transformistas, not as drag queens.[9] These performers operate within distinct Latinx and Latin American paradigms with their own popular references and transcendent affects. Transformistas can be "vessels between the audience and the artist" when they perform dolidos (heartbreaking Spanish-language numbers, comparable to torch songs): "songs you grew up listening to while your mom cleaned the house but that you couldn't experience as a child because you were supposed to be macho. In a queer space, you can finally feel the emotion of it."[10] Because we often do not know individual artists' preferred terms, throughout this chapter we simply refer to *performers* and *performances*.

Bidi Bidi Bom Bom: Contexts and Rhythms of Queer Latinx Venues

Although Mexican and/or Chicano men may predominate in Los Angeles venues, these spaces are typically pan-Latinx (particularly including Central American patrons) and reflect what Ramón H. Rivera-Servera has described as the "crossings of various inter-Latina/o ethnic-racial and intra-Latina/o class categories."[11] Despite all the ways that the people who converge in these spaces may exceed reductive binary identity categories, patrons nonetheless generally understand these venues as *gay bars*.[12] Thus, Latinx venues reveal the affordances of gay bars in articulating the diversity of unique communities and scenes they make possible. This chapter positions immigration, performance, cultural geography, and lived experience as necessary frameworks for its analysis, arguing that Latinx venues exemplify the necessity and possibilities of queer nightlife.

A cover of the Los Angeles–based Spanish-language queer magazine *De Ambiente* posed the question, "¿Quién Eres?" (*Who are you?*) atop a grid of multicultural figures labeled joto, hueco, marimacha, cochon, mariposa, loca, puto, tortillera, quebrado, and del otro lado—various slang terms for *faggot, dyke, whore,* and *people who play for the other team*.[13] Bar patrons may recognize themselves as one of these terms or as vaquero, travesti, cholo, chulo, punk, or something yet to be named. Bar patrons willingly participate in identity roleplay and erotic fetishization of available cultural archetypes and may well understand that such social positions are performative. But they also likely experience their identities as innate and their social positions as no less real for being ideologically constructed. They often simultaneously resist hegemonic Latinx and gay male identities *and* seek social intelligibility. Here we are bringing into dialogue strains of queer/gay Latinx theory by José Esteban Muñoz and Ernesto Javier Martínez, respectively, that have been conceived as incompatible; we argue that understanding both drives in tension productively speaks to the complexity of what happens in these venues.[14] People can and do experience themselves both as *being* LGBTQ+ (or men who have sex with men, or men who have sex with transwomen) Latinxs and as *performing* their queer latinidad in ways that are alternately liberating, strategic, self-exploiting, and oppressive.

Muñoz's later theorization of *brown* as an affectively performed identity of latinidad further speaks to such life conditions for patrons of these bars:

"brown" as in brown people in a very immediate way, in this sense, people who are rendered brown by their personal and familial participations in South-to-North migration patterns.... brown by way of accents and linguistic orientations that convey a certain difference.... a brownness that is conferred by the ways in which one's spatial coordinates are contested, and the ways in which one's right to residency is challenged by those who make false claims to nativity.... brownness in relation to everyday customs and everyday styles of living that connote a sense of illegitimacy. Brown indexes a certain vulnerability to the violence of property, finance, and to capital's overarching mechanisms of domination.[15]

Queer bars and nightclubs become vital spaces for imagining and making queer Brown—and Black—Latinx lives. But Brownness is also relational; people may be seen or see themselves as Brown in some contexts and communities but not in others. One could argue that Brown names a Latinx immigrant structure of feeling; regardless of an individual's personal history of migration or lack thereof, Latinx people are often *perceived* as immigrants.

As the most common structural bias facing Latinx people in the contemporary United States, immigration xenophobia produces a condition of "alien citizenship"; Latinx people are perceived as foreign and thus entitled to fewer rights, regardless of their immigration or citizenship status.[16] For much of the later part of the twentieth century, immigration policy explicitly prohibited homosexual and trans people from entry into the US, even as the nation witnessed significant growth in Mexican and Latin American immigration. Instead, official policy privileged heteronormative family reunification. *Denial* of LGBTQ+ identity was, in fact, a condition for admissibility or continued residency throughout the 1980s and into the early 1990s.[17] During the same period as the legally enforced queer exclusions, the demographics of Los Angeles changed radically and sparked xenophobic backlash from the historically dominant white population. Whereas white/Anglo residents constituted 86.3 percent of the city's population in 1940, a 1978 *Los Angeles Times* article warned readers that they were expected to become a statistical minority by 1980, with a continuing downward trend thereafter.[18] In contrast, the city's Latinx population increased from 7.1 percent in 1940 to 39.9 percent by 1990, exceeding the non-Hispanic white census numbers for the first time.[19]

Economics as well as immigration policy probably stymied the development of more widespread queer venues for immigrant men. Historian

Ana Raquel Minian found that gay-identified men were less likely to cross the border than straight men with financial obligations to their wives and children. (This poses a reversal of John D'Emilio's theory that such financial structures were the precondition for gay identities and communities to develop; see the introduction.) In addition, Mexican men often found it easier to find sexual contacts with other men in Mexico, both because they understood their local social and cruising customs and because they could move freely without having to evade police or INS agents.[20] Furthermore, in his research sociologist Lionel Cantú Jr. met a number of Mexican men who preferred to stay in Mexico rather than emigrate to the United States because of intolerance north of the border. The men Cantú interviewed who did migrate reported that they were marked as ethnically marginalized in the US, in contrast to their experiences in Mexico.[21] Nonetheless, Cantú and others have found that gay clubs—whether Latin nights at Anglo bars or, more commonly, Latinx bars—are the primary sites for men to find other gay Latinos with whom to forge social bonds and community.[22]

These bars may be understood as borderland spaces, as Gloria Anzaldúa has theorized, where people negotiate disparate Latinx LGBTQ+ cultures.[23] Here US-born and immigrant Latinx people come into contact. These cultures are often distinct, but they also converge, especially within individual families when younger generations born in Los Angeles or brought to the US as children navigate dual cultures at home and often literally translate languages and cultures for their parents in public. Immigrant experiences are also remarkably diverse, ranging from cosmopolitan artists and academics who arrive with relative economic privilege and visas to laborers who come to the United States in search of work and political refugees with comparatively few resources and often without protected legal status. Social positions and differences shift in their significance in Latinx gay bars: sometimes different natal nationalities matter, but more often there's solidarity in pan-Latin American heritage; sometimes Spanish is the default language, but often patrons code switch; some patrons may modulate their regional or national accents depending on the context, or they may emphasize them; some male patrons identify as gay, but many have wives and children; and sometimes patrons perform machismo, yet trans women are more integrated into the social and erotic communities in Latinx venues than in Anglo ones.[24]

As some scholars have argued, the integration of family members into the social scene at some Latinx venues—and the fact that many are run by families—likewise suggests a culturally specific model of who constitutes a gay bar's community. Such a community can also incorporate multiple generations without traditional kinship ties.[25] Powerfully conveying conflicted feelings of discovery, familiarity, and frustration upon his foray into queer Latinx nightlife, the late Chicano AIDS activist and video maker Ray Navarro wrote, "When I was nineteen I remember walking into a Latino drag bar in Los Angeles. There I saw many lesbian and gay people. Each one looked like they could've been my aunt or uncle. It shocked and thrilled me to see so many Latinas and Latinos expressing their sexuality openly, defiantly—but it dissatisfied me that the only safe place to do this was in a dark bar off of Santa Monica Boulevard."[26] Navarro's reflection upon the early 1980s indicates that queer Latinx people had already created bustling spaces of their own but that such spaces acted as refuges in a world that was still unsafe. We must also remember as well that whereas going out opens up the possibility of an everyday gay life for some people, for others queerness can exist only within the confines of the bar.[27]

Publicity for venues indicates that Spanish-language music operates as a primary element in constructing a sense of latinidad, yet listings reveal important regional, taste, and class distinctions in genres of music between different sites, different nights, or even different rooms in the same venue, such as at Club Tempo.[28] Latinx gay bar listings often enumerate specific musical genres for different venues and weekly parties.[29] Such musical genres—including banda, cumbia, norteño, salsa, reggaetón, trap, and rock en español—reflect histories of migration and fusions of various cultures, such that the songs circulate across borders, mark yet transgress distinct regional cultures, connote class differences, and are nonetheless open to remixing. Rivera-Servera has developed this line of thought, remarking that "in these spaces, music that may be recognizable to a mainstream gay audience—a house bass or techno bass musical palette—can very quickly switch to a merengue or a salsa in the Caribbean social-dance tradition. It can very quickly turn into a cumbia or a quebradita in the Mexican-Colombian social dance tradition. And it can just as quickly go into reggaetón, and Jamaican dancehall-, Caribbean-, Central American-inflected choreography and music arise.... Some Latinos gain the expertise of being able to move fluidly across all those genres," whereas when others dance, "you'll see the movement hiccups that occur when trying to fit in."[30]

Songs in queer Latinx spaces contain complex cultural histories that operate as anthems or tales of heartbreak that are at once shared and personally felt. Patrons' shared love of particular tracks—demonstrated by how often they sing along—positions music as that which forges community across difference. Whether in a performance or on the dance floor, Selena's music continues to elicit the strongest reactions. Nonetheless, Gloria Trevi's 2012 cover of "Gloria" became this chapter's unofficial theme song.[31] Trevi, known as the Supreme Diva of Mexican pop, has already been theorized for producing queer anthems.[32] That this track reworks Laura Branigan's hit (itself already a cover of an Italian pop song) made it more immediately intelligible to Lucas across eras and languages. The song travels not only across borders but also in its rotation across venues; we heard it at Club Tempo, the Frat House, and the New Jalisco.

Babe We're Gonna Love Tonight: Circus and Arena

The most legendary venues for queer Latinx nightlife, Circus Disco (later just called Circus) and its belated twin, Arena, did not explicitly identify as Latinx bars. Nonetheless, they were *recognized* as such by their patrons, who converged by the thousands to show off their personal fashions, build social networks, and dance. Circus opened in central Hollywood in 1975, and its world-making role continued for decades. Circus's origin story was one of both social justice and entrepreneurism. Owners Gene La Pietra and his partner Ermilio Lemos opened Circus after Latino friends were systemically asked for multiple forms of ID and denied entry at the homogenously white Studio One gay disco in West Hollywood—at the time the chicest spot in town.[33] This form of discriminatory door policy was well documented from the 1970s onward at white Anglo gay venues across the country and became a vehicle for addressing racism within the gay community (see chapter 4). Activists organized a boycott against Studio One's discriminatory carding policy and produced bilingual handbills with Spanish text on one side and English on the reverse (see figure 8.1).[34] Significantly, the Black lesbian–owned Jewel's Catch One not only provided another queer-of-color alternative to Studio One; Catch One also *preceded* it. The Catch's story has been told elsewhere.[35]

Circus's door policy was, from the start, inclusive, but the clientele was predominantly Latinx. As La Pietra reflected on Circus, "The novelty of Circus Disco was 'allowing everyone to come in.... That just was not heard of in 1975.'"[36] Adding to the venue's accessibility, its Hollywood location placed it along major bus lines and more proximate to the 101 freeway than West Hollywood.[37] Patrons entered Circus, a spectacularly

FIGURE 8.1 The Spanish side of a bilingual handbill for a boycott against West Hollywood disco Studio One's discriminatory admissions practices, circa 1975. Courtesy of ONE Archives at the USC Libraries.

converted former ice factory, through a giant clown's mouth, flanked by elephant statues and funhouse mirrors; a tiger sculpture stood on its hind legs on the roof. La Pietra was a larger-than-life businessman, the unofficial mayor of Hollywood, and something of a self-mythologizer who claimed to have coined the term *disco*.[38] Perhaps this showmanship motivated the venue's theme (see figure 8.2). Inside, the expansive bar featured three dance floors playing disco in its early days and Latin, house, and hip-hop music, respectively, in its later years (see figure 8.3). Circus had a ring of pink neon elephants that the DJ could make move in a stop-motion effect over the main dance floor.[39]

Although Circus surely played its share of such canonical gay divas as Donna Summer and Madonna, its DJ sets privileged songs more embedded in Latinx community life. A twenty-fifth anniversary Circus Disco compilation CD self-mythologizes: "It was the absolute mecca of hi en-

FIGURE 8.2 Invitation to a 1980 ACLU benefit featuring a Circus Disco logo with a leather Latino clone and lion. Courtesy of ONE Archives at the USC Libraries.

ergy music and has become a testament to the staying power of the disco scene."[40] This and follow-up releases offer insights into tracks that spun in heavy rotation. We can imagine the charge on the steamy Circus dance floor when Miquel Brown sang "So Many Men, So Little Time" or Cinema proclaimed "Be they black, white, or tan / I love men."[41] The compilation CDs span pan-Latinx dance musics, including cha cha cha, samba, and freestyle; the majority of the lyrics (largely simple and repetitive dance pop refrains) are in English and reference love affairs, the thrill of transgression, jet-set aspirations, and dancing.[42] Lucas was unfamiliar with most of these tracks, but his boyfriend, Ernesto, immediately identified the genre as "chola disco" as he boogied and sang along to song after song. Ernesto was never a regular at Circus or Arena, but he knew the tunes from school dances, family gatherings, and the swap meet in El Monte. Indeed, Lucas

FIGURE 8.3 Panoramic view of Circus Disco's dance floor during a 1979 Halloween party. Photo by Pat Rocco. Courtesy of ONE Archives at the USC Libraries.

later heard several of these same tracks at Ernesto's niece's quinceañera, despite the fact that they predated the young woman's birth by decades. The sounds of queer nightlife reverberate in the everyday.

Circus has been remembered for its fashions.[43] In its heyday the club was frequented by young crowds who had grown up in Los Angeles or moved there for college. Patrons cultivated a particular aspirational Hollywood Latinx style of self-presentation distinct from the white West Hollywood look as well as from the localized Latinx sensibilities of the Bay Area or San Diego. James Rojas recalled the look of the mid-late 1970s: "The disco clubs' informal dress codes stressed not the physique but the silhouette. Unlike the predominantly male West Hollywood clubs, where buff men wore tight-fitting jeans and t-shirts, here diverse youth used fashion to explore their fantasies and bodies. Glitter babies or Hollywood Swingers, youth with their big hair, scarfs, baggie pants, shoulder pads, and glitter make-up created an avant-garde fashion palette that ranged from Joan Crawford to David Bowie."[44] In its later days, Circus still validated its clientele by making them feel like celebrities. "You spent your week planning your outfit for Circus night.... You ironed your clothes,

FIGURE 8.4 Revelers dance in costumes that effectively perform ethnic drag, including sheik, caveman, Martian, and Native American alongside gender drag at Circus Disco's 1983 Halloween party. What was likely perceived as playful masquerade at the time—observable in the dancers' facial expressions and the outfits' flirtatious skimpiness—is now more widely recognized as problematic appropriation. This image reflects the pervasive contradictions in queer and Latinx pasts, wherein moments of joyful release intersect with uncomfortable histories of oppression and exploitation. Photo by Kent Garvey. Courtesy of ONE Archives at the USC Libraries.

wore your best shirt, your best shoes, and you put on extra cologne," our student Agustín Garcia Meza recalled. It was a scene where people ran into familiar faces, although "the music was too loud and there were too many good-looking people to pay attention to your friends." He continued: "Your retail job didn't matter because you were a star on the weekends. It's where the real you came out." At Circus, "either you're The One or you're going to meet The One."[45]

In a poem paying tribute to Circus, Luis Alfaro captures the ways the club empowered the crowd and made them feel seen:

Two thousand people exactly like me.
Well, maybe a little darker ...
Two thousand square feet
of my men.

Boys like me.
Who speak the languages,
who speak the languages
of the border
and of the other.[46]

Alfaro's poem understands this venue as defined by its scale ("two thousand people," "two thousand square feet"), racialization ("maybe a little darker"), and languages—the effect of which is to experience himself as newly reflected in a larger sensation of community. Writing of his memories of going to Circus in the late 1990s, Anthony Haro asserted that "every Friday night it became the center of the universe if you're gay, Latino, and live in Los Angeles."[47] By all accounts, attendees had never experienced a scene like this anywhere else, and it came to serve as a rite of passage or weekly ritual for generations.

Arena, the adjacent dance club, opened in 1990 and was introduced with a slicker MTV nightclub aesthetic, including a wall of TV consoles.[48] In a short story about going to Arena, poet Ramón García describes the allure of the scene inside the venue as an escape from the outside world: "I wanted to be taken in by the spectacle, the assault of fake smoke, music, disco balls that threw swirling glitter patches of illuminated squares like a confetti of stars upon the crowd." García's account expresses the allure of the space: "On the Arena dance floor everything was cancelled: poverty, the uncertain future, problems at home, the difficulties of work, and surviving. We believed those moments of strobe-lighted rapture were a sort of salvation, that the ecstasy worked up in the frenzy of the music was all that we needed, all that life could possibly offer. But we had doubts—that we never spoke of, that we did not know how to articulate and misunderstood, that we feared would infringe on the restless search for something that would take us out of ourselves." This fantasy could exist only in relation to an outside reality, but even inside there were limitations on this utopia: an "expiration date" of thirty years old for men and the omnipresence of drugs that fostered dysfunctional friendships and inhibited intimacy.[49]

By the 2000s, Arena attracted a younger crowd than Circus, particularly through its all-ages Wednesday-night parties that were more welcoming than those of the rival 18+ party TigerHeat. These nights were open to all ages and allowed teenagers from across the region to explore "the people they would become" and to build connections with other queer youths. Minors would often drink in their cars before entering and later converge at "the gay burrito" (El Gran Burrito) after closing. "It was Disneyland for gay kids," Garcia Meza explained. But "as soon as you turned 18, you graduated from Arena and were ready for the world" of other clubs. Guys under 21 couldn't yet get inside Circus, but they "*could* meet a cute boyfriend in the parking lot."[50]

Patrons who went to both venues often seem to retrospectively refer to them interchangeably or in tandem. Both clubs inspired creative memoir pieces that offer insight into their personal significance. (Regrettably, neither of us experienced Circus or Arena firsthand.) Such retrospective accounts work to write ephemeral experiences into history and reclaim the importance of marginalized spaces. Inevitably, these works romanticize the past, but such reflections nonetheless communicate what meanings endure for their authors and why these spaces were felt as formative.

Performance scholar Rivera-Servera theorizes the transformative potential of queer Latinx dance floors, articulating parallels to Alfaro's and García's experiences at Circus and Arena. Indeed, Circus and Arena are not exceptional but prototypical. Rivera-Servera proposes that "dancing in the club becomes a practice of what I term 'choreographies of resistance,' embodied practices through which minoritarian subjects claim their space in social and cultural realms." These clubs provide manifestations of a community free from homophobia and "sometimes from racism" that are sustaining: "My experience in the club not only allows me to feel desire, love, and community, but gives me the confidence and the knowledge to step proudly into other more dangerous venues and seek, even demand, similar experiences from the world outside it." He continues: "Yet the utopian realm of the club (i.e., community and pleasure) must always be negotiated, sometimes even fought for, in its live material context. In the space of the dance floor, pleasurable exchanges are complicated by social hierarchies inside and outside the club."[51]

Circus was, of course, a business and a very successful one at that. The venue was not primarily a political site, but La Pietra's nightclub earned cachet as a community space through events ranging from a benefit for El Monte Citizens for Fair Housing to an appearance by Cesar Chavez to numerous fund-raisers for AIDS services and the LGBTQ+ community center.[52] The space also hosted numerous events for organizations such as Gay Latinos Unidos from its start in 1981, and La Pietra was named as award recipient, sponsor, and benefactor of Gay and Lesbian Latinos Unidos in 1985.[53]

For many, the opening of Circus Disco in 1975 marked a new era for queer Latinx nightlife, but Circus was not the only venue or the only history. Surely the people and the cultural politics changed over the decades, but the thrill of Circus Disco in 1975 sounds like it continued in the 1980s, 1990s, and 2000s for subsequent generations. Circus operated for forty years until it and Arena both closed in 2016 to be razed for a six-acre mixed-use real estate megadevelopment as gentrification in Hollywood accelerated (see also chapter 3).

SCENES FROM THE FRAT HOUSE, 2007–2019

Lucas's friends Lauren and Kelly took him to the Frat House as a welcome when he moved to Orange County to start work at UC Irvine. He hadn't yet imagined researching gay bars. The Frat House is the last gay bar remaining in Garden Grove, where there used to be a cluster of fifteen bars in the 1980s. Defying his preconceived notions of the OC and the whiteness of "the suburbs," the bar's crowd was primarily Latinx and largely comprised trans femme and masculine male couples.[54] In recent decades it has primarily attracted a working-class Latinx immigrant patronage and catered to the locals in Orange County, separate from Los Angeles County venues. More accurately, the scene changes a bit depending on the time: an older and whiter crowd frequents the bar during happy hour, and the venue becomes predominantly Latinx around 10 p.m. and later. Because Garden Grove has a large Vietnamese immigrant population, there is also a Southeast Asian contingent in the crowd. Whereas Santa Ana's downtown has gentrified and Laguna Beach has become less gay, the Frat House in Garden Grove (sometimes called "Garbage Grove") serves as a very particular queer refuge in Orange County.[55] The bar is situated on a busy thoroughfare next door to a Korean Baptist Church and near a hotel where some of its regular patrons live.[56]

When Lucas ventured back to the Frat House with Dan on a foggy fall night in 2019, the space had been unrecognizably redecorated. The main attraction of the night remained a performance, but the crowd now was predominantly male. Like a number of other venues, Frat House also featured dancing and go-go boys; Dan recognized one of the go-go boys from our previous outing to the Club Papi party at Micky's in West Hollywood. The music was all Latin pop, with some cumbia and some trap. A flat-screen TV mounted above the entrance was playing an A&E Network docuseries about the US Border Patrol doing a raid; meanwhile, a security guard in a bulletproof vest circulated throughout the venue. We were unsettled by these details, but the patrons seemed to be unbothered: they were socializing or watching the go-go boys instead. Dan observed that the venue had the cruisiest vibe of any of the bars we had visited.

The crowd cleared the dance floor when the music subtly changed, cuing patrons that a performance was about to begin there. The announcer didn't have to say anything; the regulars knew the drill. The security guard made himself useful during the performance by deploying his tactical flashlight as a spotlight for the performers' entrances and then collecting their tips off the ground. Each of the performers impersonated old-school Spanish-language divas such as Lola Beltrán and Amanda Miguel, and each performance channeled the gravitas and grandeur of age. (Likewise, we had seen a performance of the great Rocío Dúrcal at La Plaza in Hollywood a couple months before.) One wore a beehive hairdo with flowers, another an aquamarine muumuu. A third queen came out cloaked in a hot-pink shag fur coat on top of a sequined gown to perform Laura León's "El Baile del Tesoro (El Pimpollo)."[57] Midway through the show, the MC, speaking in Spanish, called up all the people in the audiences celebrating birthdays or "sex changes." Then she asked them where they were from and how they identified ("hombre-hombre" [man's man], joto [fag], transexual, lesbiana). Each person who came up identified which state in Mexico they were from—Jalisco, Sonora, Guanajuato—except for a trans femme performer with the night off. She quipped that she was "from Jupiter."[58]

¡Upa yupa yu! Club Tempo

Queer Latinx bars and nightclubs have flourished in Los Angeles in opposition to anti-Latinx and anti-immigrant policies and rhetoric. True to its name, Club Tempo was a product of its time and has maintained a steady rhythm since. It opened in 1993 as banda music was exploding in popularity in Los Angeles and just prior to the 1994 passage of California Proposition 187, which prevented undocumented immigrants from using public services.[59] Scholars have recognized the coincidence of these two events but overlooked their queer confluence at Tempo.

Although banda dates from the 1940s in Mexico, it surged in popularity in the early 1990s among immigrants in the US. As Victor Hugo Viesca writes of banda,

FIGURE 8.5 Tempo promotes its vaquero (*cowboy*) party and its popular show hosted by performer Maritza. *Adelante*, October 2012. Collection of the author.

Nightclubs, radio stations, and swap meets that catered to the emerging ethnic Mexican majority in Los Angeles produced a thriving dance and music scene based on the sound of the *tambura* (bass drum) and the dance of the *quebradita* (little break). Many of the immigrants in the initial market audience had come from rural areas that had not previously sent many migrants to Los Angeles. This audience responded enthusiastically to *banda*'s rural immigrant identity. *Banda* artists presented themselves in the *vaquero* (cowboy) style of dress, wearing hats, boots, and jeans, and sang of life on the ranch and the experiences of crossing the border in the *ranchera* voice of the region.[60]

From the start, Tempo's combination of live banda music and its self-styled vaqueros were its signature elements (see figure 8.5). An article in the first issue of *De Ambiente* heralded that the venue featured the best bands from Mexico and also promised "puedes conocer unos vaqueros guapísimos, tan varoniles que dan ganas de tirarse los pelos de punta" (*you can meet some handsome cowboys so virile they will make your hair stand on end*).[61] Some of the regulars immigrated from rural pueblos in Mexico, and others perform the look of vaqueros in order to attract the same. We were told, somewhat wistfully, that "the real cowboys are usually already taken."[62]

The publicity for the venue suggests that it has always been a primarily Spanish-language scene where men could find other immigrant men, meet up with groups of friends, or dance in couples. Word of mouth was probably its primary mode of publicity, which contributed to an intra-community feel. Yet Tempo also advertised in bilingual publications such as the gay magazine *Adelante* and its own newsletter, *Ritmo de la Noche* (Rhythm of the Night). Although its newsletter effuses with pride about Mexican heritage, Tempo's owner is a white Anglo man (a widower of a Latino partner), and the managers of the venue have likewise been white Anglos.[63] That the publicity for the venue is bilingual or at least partially translated indicates the management's desire and choice to make the venue accessible to non-Spanish speakers. However, the only times we've heard English spoken at the venue beyond our own conversations have been when a bartender conspicuously defaulted to English upon Lucas's approach; this act recognizes him as an outsider (which he is) and reproduces a deferential power dynamic.[64]

Sundays have typically been the most popular days at the venue, especially so on holiday weekends; on such days it opens early for a mid-afternoon performance and drink specials upstairs, followed by live banda, Sinaloense and/or Norteño music downstairs, and live mariachi karaoke followed by a second performance upstairs. A scaled-down version of Mariachi Arcoiris de Los Angeles, founded by Carlos Samaniego as the first all-queer mariachi group, appeared as the regular house band for Sunday karaoke, hosted by performer Maritza. The band plays songs on request, demonstrating an encyclopedic knowledge of the genre's standards and popular hits. Band members also take the opportunity to serenade audience members with the occasional Juan Gabriel song.

Samaniego perceives that whereas the majority of clientele used to be immigrant Mexican, the ratio has become increasingly Central American over the years (see figure 8.6). For the clientele, it's a refuge.[65] There's a pervasive, tacit presumption that many of the men at the club may be bisexual or closeted, so rather than call it a gay bar, it is perhaps more accurately described as a venue where *"men could dance with men."*[66]

FIGURE 8.6 Reflecting its clientele's histories of immigration, Tempo presents pageants for Miss Mexico, Miss Guatemala, and Miss El Salvador, hosted by Chica Swapmeet. *Adelante*, August 2011. Collection of the author.

Cindy García's analysis of straight salsa clubs in the city illuminates the dancing at Tempo as well: "A couple dancing... does not dance alone. Even an intimate partnership cannot evade becoming embedded within the continually changing social body of practitioners that often determines a person's identity by how and with whom that person moves. Who you desire to be and how you desire to move do not always coincide with how others interpellate you. For many Latinas and Latinos, dancing... becomes a way to claim a presence, both globally and in Los Angeles." Yet as García also observes, reflecting the diversity of latinidad, each club has its own culture with different social norms and forms of etiquette, including topics of conversation, seating arrangements, and how much space couples occupy on the dance floor.[67] Varied life histories and social positions coexist at Tempo, which operates as a safe space, a liberatory dance venue, and a site of public intimacies. Descriptions of Club Tempo from 1993 sound remarkably similar to the same venue in the present. This venue could not have been static, but the need it filled and the communities it produced persisted.

SCENES FROM CLUB TEMPO, 2016–2019

Before Lucas moved to Los Angeles, his ex Agustin told him about a gay bar with Mexican men in cowboy hats where he liked to go while he was in grad school. He even took the bus from the west side to get there. Years later, when Lucas's friend Enrique met up with him and some friends at the Sunday beer bust at the Faultline, Enrique suggested going to Club Tempo to see live queer mariachi. Lucas realized this must have been the place he had heard about. It was the same and so much more. They danced in the crowd upstairs, and soon Mariachi Arcoiris de Los Angeles performed. Afterward, they went downstairs, and Enrique taught Lucas how to dance to banda. He admittedly had trouble picking up the rhythm. Lucas was introduced to Club Tempo through word of mouth and queer social bonds, and his first visit was one of those nights out that felt special, even perfect—that exemplified why we go out at all. He felt uneasy about being a tourist in this space, but he loved that it existed. His return visits for research have perhaps been less heady, but his gratitude has not diminished. This is the bar that made Lucas want to write this chapter.

Tempo is tucked in the corner of an unassuming L-shaped strip mall on Santa Monica Boulevard near Western Avenue in East Hollywood. The most pervasive style at Tempo is impeccable western wear: elegant vaqueros in fitted embroidered western shirts, embossed leather belts with decorative buckles, black jeans, cowboy hats, and well-groomed beards. Men appear to go as couples or as part of groups rather than solo, and many couples dress in coordinated outfits. At peak times the surrounding area transforms as vaqueros can be seen converging at the venue from surrounding intersections, and as the hour grows later, Central American women set up carts to sell tamales, papusas, plantains, yucca, tacos, and bacon-wrapped hot dogs.

Out front there is one line to pay the cover fee and another to enter; upon entry, patrons immediately face a staircase to the second floor, which is flanked by separate dance floors with different genres of music on either side. The first room to the right inside the entrance is the darkest, with fine swirling lights. The optics are disorienting and dizzying. This is the room where vaqueros dance in tight embrace to live banda music. We suspect the twilight is intentional, to facilitate intimacies. The room to the left, which opens later in the evening, features cumbia and draws a younger, more animated crowd lighted by the video projections.

Upstairs in the main dance room, most of the patrons seem to be in groups with reserved seats and buckets of beers or pitchers of drinks. The area is set up with tables while the DJ plays Latin pop and rock en español with corresponding videos projected over the dance floor. While we were standing to the side of the dance floor, an older gentleman walking by in a Panama hat and guayabera very gently squeezed Dan's arm and smiled, like an elder welcoming a fellow Caribbean to the space. Dan remarked that every song we heard in this room felt like a queer anthem (such as Fey's "Muévelo") or a staple of a family parties (such as Los Tucanes de Tijuana's "La Chona").[68] Both the live mariachi and the performances take place on a low stage here, which is effectively a raised platform of the dance floor. As Dan pointed out, the assemblage of people dancing on the stage at one point reflected a perfect cross section of the scene as a whole: partnered vaqueros, trans women, lesbian couples, twinks, a seemingly straight couple, and a solo man singing along and fanning his arms in dramatic gestures. A rooftop patio and taco stand are adjacent through a door at the top of the stairs; this outdoor space is where it's easiest to make conversation and meet new people. We repeatedly saw men embrace when they ran into old friends here. The bar feels like a queer family picnic.

Fulfill My Fantasies: Chico

Chico (*boy*) came out of a different context: providing a homegrown space on the east side to serve Chicano men attracted to masculine men at the turn of the millennium. The Chico scene refused the homonormative version of gay and lesbian life gaining mainstream acceptance at the time and offered an alternative that read as more authentic to its patrons—though one that was just as open to fantasy. Here the "boy" connotations differ significantly from those in San Francisco a decade and a half earlier (see chapter 7). Chico eroticized and reproduced a performative image of Latino masculinity—the cholo, homothug, homiesexual—as an alternative to the whiteness of West Hollywood, the twinks at Circus/Arena, and the vaqueros of Tempo.[69] The club also exuded a defiant edge that was missing from pop acts such as Ricky Martin, Enrique Iglesias, Marc Anthony, Christina Aguilera, Shakira, and Jennifer Lopez, who were collectively ballyhooed as constituting a crossover Latin pop explosion at the time.

Significantly, Chico opened *after* a circuit of east-side Latina women's bars, such as Redz, the Plush Pony, and the Sugar Shack, had operated for decades; these bars overlapped for a time. Men were often tolerated in these prior spaces as long as they respected the women; queer communities also coalesced in otherwise straight venues.[70] Despite its avowed masculinity (and perhaps the unacknowledged influence of butch lesbian styling), Chico's culture as a neighborhood venue perhaps more closely resembled these Chicana women's bars than the venues in Hollywood.

Chico opened in 1999 after bartender Julio Licon introduced Marty Sokol, a Jewish TV producer from the East Coast, to an existing dive bar in Montebello and suggested remaking it as a new kind of gay bar. They bought it and did so. Chico's debut ad featured a male cartoon character with a mohawk, white T-shirt, wide-legged pants, and a mischievous grin (see figure 8.7). The text above the figure states, "*Lo que todos esperabamos*" (What we've all been waiting for), and the tagline proffers, "The new spot for *mi gente*" (my people) in Spanglish. The bottom text states, "*Nuevo dueño. Nuevo Aventura. Nuevo lugar*." (New owner. New Adventure. New place.) Information about open days and location appears in English. The ad, featuring text in both Spanish and English but nowhere translating, specifically targeted a fluidly bilingual audience able to code switch between languages; this contrasts with the dual address of publicity materials for venues that do translate.[71] Soon, the bar's imagery transitioned to photos by Dino Dinco featuring men with shaved heads, often shirtless and in cars evocative of low riders (see plate 14).[72]

From the start, Chico cultivated what Richard T. Rodríguez has aptly termed a queer homeboy aesthetic.[73] The venue at once recognized a specific southern California Latino cultural formation and situated it away from the existing gay venues. A fascinated *Los Angeles Times* reporter explained the scene to those uninitiated: "The clientele [is] a mix of homeboys, ex-gangbangers, cops and guys who trek out from West Hollywood, the desert and the San Fernando Valley in search of something edgier, more urban. 'Tough, masculine-looking guys. Rough, bald guys. That's Chico,' says Licon. 'Straight people come in and they still don't know it is a gay bar.' And, even when they do, some stay for the party." Signaling that the bar's image is largely that—an image—or possibly to quell reader anxiety, the reporter then discloses that a tattooed go-go dancer "has never been in a gang."[74] Chico's parties were so successful in creating a new scene that in the early 2000s, Tempo hosted a rival party called Club Ghetto to capitalize on the cholo homeboy aesthetic.

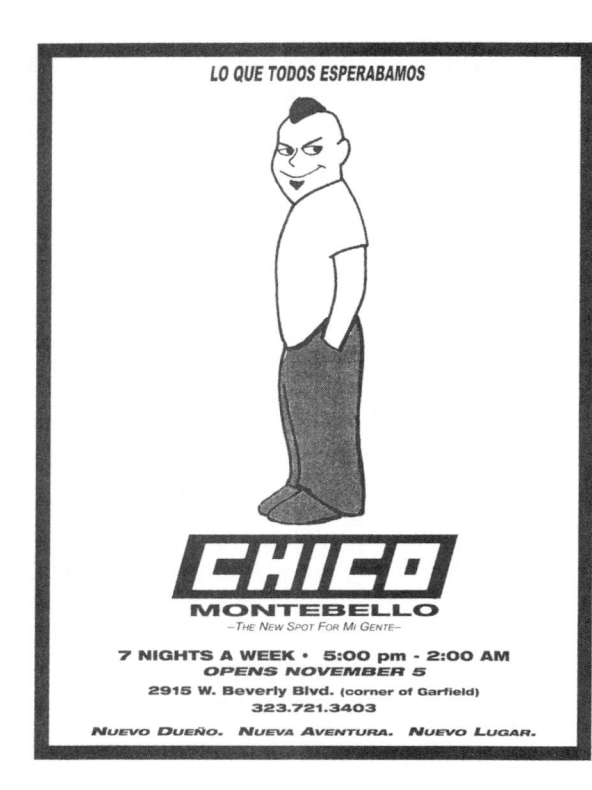

FIGURE 8.7 Chico's inaugural advertisement states, "Lo que todo esperabamos" (*What we've all been waiting for*). The ad features text in both English and Spanish but bilingually code-switches rather than translates. *Adelante,* November 1999. Courtesy of ONE Archives at the USC Libraries.

Offering a concurring, insider's viewpoint, Joël Barraquiel Tan recalled that "sure enough, there were Homothugs everywhere. Black and brown, varying ages, pressed khakis and drooping jeans, drinking Alizé and Cuba Libres, smoking Newports, and affecting ghetto fabulous."[75] Dinco, who helped construct the bar's image, told us that early on, 90 percent of the bar's crowd had shaved heads and baggy pants—reflecting the cholo aesthetic, which had a strong erotic charge. But the look eventually shifted, both because personal style changed but also, he suspects, when "posers" likely got sick of harassment from the police.[76] Chico endured hostility from both bigots and police in its early years, though both subsequently diminished as LGBTQ+ life became more normalized in the culture at large.[77] Later marketing invoked the term *chulo* (*pimp* and/or *handsome*) rather than *cholo*.

Chico continued to evolve—for instance, by hosting the monthly queer Latinx punk party Club sCUM, dating from 2016. This party was

FIGURE 8.8 An early flyer for the queer Latinx punk party Club sCUM at Chico, drawn by Martin Sorrondeguy, in 2016. "Noche de Jotiar" translates as *"Night of faggotry."* Courtesy of Martin Sorrondeguy.

promoted by Rudy Bleu and Hex-ray Sanchez (as Noche de Jotiar—*Night of Faggotry*) rather than by the bar (see figure 8.8); they wanted to make their queer Latinx party more geographically accessible to its constituents than existing parties. This strategy of manifesting alternative queer formations via recurring parties dates back at least three decades (see chapter 7). Bleu and Sanchez initially pitched the night as featuring Morrissey and British new-wave music because the sound seemed more bankable; when they packed the house, they felt emboldened to make the set lists more punk.[78] The popular event also traveled to San Francisco (at El Rio and the Stud), New York City, and Mexico City, connecting with a queer Latinx punk diaspora.

In 2006 Chico's owners also bought the gay bar Rawhide in the San Fernando Valley and renamed it Club Cobra, where they reproduced the Chico scene and often shared the same staff and performers. During the COVID-19 pandemic shutdowns, Club Cobra launched an OnlyFans page to promote its dancers. Chico closed its physical venue in 2020 and briefly resurfaced as a recurring party in West Hollywood while Club Cobra resumed operations in its own space. Chico reopened in its original location in summer 2022.

SCENES FROM CHICO, 2019

Chico in Montebello is in a small strip mall across a busy thoroughfare from a Super A grocery store. The bar is relatively small: a one-room venue with flocked red velvet wallpaper and a large tavern-style bar to the left of the entrance. It's a neighborhood bar cum nightclub. We carpooled to Chico with friends Josh and Albert for Cockfight, a weekly boxing-themed night that culminates in a title match between two go-go boys in boxing shorts. The social media posts for the night play up the long-standing connotation of hypersexualized Latin lovers. The crowd was small, chill, and more gender- and age-mixed than we expected; the marketing had been suggestive of a raunchy party. The music was a mix of Latin pop and reggaetón, but the mounted TV screens showed videos for Anglo pop that didn't match what the DJ was playing. Whereas the music was in Spanish, the marketing and the competition commentary addressed the audience in English.

The Cockfight competitors were introduced as hailing from Honduras and Tijuana, respectively. Alex, the beefy dancer from Honduras, seemed like he was probably straight; he danced looking at himself in the mirror rather than at the crowd. Kike, the more lithe dancer from Tijuana, was more ambiguous in his sexuality; he was friendlier with the crowd, although he repeatedly stopped dancing to look at his phone while on the podium. When the competition was underway, one patron made it rain by tossing single after single onto Kike as he danced. Kike won the match based on crowd cheers; it was unclear if nationalist pride played a role in the crowd's favor or if it was primarily his endowment.

After the show, as the manager was disassembling the miniature boxing ring, Josh asked if one of the dancers was a returning champion defending his title. The manager matter-of-factly explained that both dancers were new because the previous week's winner had been deported.[79]

Estoy Aquí: New Jalisco Bar

Downtown Los Angeles has a long history of gay bars, from the men's bar at the Biltmore Hotel to the dives and hustler bars described in John Rechy's *City of Night*. However, the 1960s redevelopment of Bunker Hill pushed the bars west.[80] Police harassment of gay venues in the city likewise drove gay bar owners to set up shop in an unincorporated parcel in the center of the county but outside the LAPD's jurisdiction: what became West Hollywood. Already a gay mecca, West Hollywood incorporated as its own municipality in 1984 and continues to loom large in the cultural imagination of gay Los Angeles. It functions as shorthand for a homogenized idea of consumerist gay lifestyles and public spaces, even if today it is more diverse than its reputation. Importantly, though, it has always only been one of many places for local queer nightlife, but one against which much of the rest of the gay scene self-defines.[81]

Nonetheless, queerness has persisted downtown. The long-running gay bar Score, known for its keyhole-shaped doorway, served a largely Latinx, often working-class to down-and-out clientele. Though considered by some a dive bar, it also hosted exhibitions curated by famed artist and ASCO alumnus Gronk in the 1980s. When Score closed in 2006 amid a wave of gentrification, its patrons migrated a block and a half to the Jalisco Inn #2. (It's unclear where or when #1 was.[82]) The Jalisco had opened in 1982 as a billiards bar with an immigrant clientele that often did not identify as gay and had a reputation for attracting trans femme sex workers and their johns.[83] There was also a contingent of unhoused clientele and street cruising on the block. Longtime bartender and manager Maria Rosa Garcia effectively ran the bar from the 1990s onward, and she inherited the bar formally when its original owner passed away in 2005. With the influx of people from the Score, 80 percent of its clientele were LGBTQ+.

Recognizing that the bar had effectively transitioned into a gay bar, Garcia and her husband, Sergio Hernandez, who works as the bar's bouncer, decided to make it official by hanging a rainbow flag outside and rechristening the venue the New Jalisco Bar in 2006.[84] They began to advertise in *Adelante* (although now they rely on social media for publicity), expanded from weekly to nightly shows at 11 p.m. and 1 a.m., and built a community of regulars. The New Jalisco demonstrates two common histories for gay bars: first, they are often heterosexual family businesses; second, it's often clientele who claim space and *make* the bars gay rather than bars being born that way. For several years, the New Jalisco was the only gay bar in downtown. Although Hernandez told us that it draws patrons from all over, including about 10 percent tourists, its identity and its fortunes feel rooted in downtown.[85]

The New Jalisco has operated and evolved amid the up-and-down fortunes of downtown and of gay bars generally in the twenty-first century. In the 2010s, numerous bars serving marginalized queer populations closed in quick succession: the old-timer Hollywood bar Spotlight and the Latinx Silverlake bar Le Barcito in 2011, the vintage Silverlake piano bar the Other Side in 2012, and the ethnically mixed Silverlake nightclub MJ's in 2014. Then in 2015, end-of-an-era closures included landmark queer-of-color venues Circus and Arena, Jewel's Catch One, and Redz. Almost simultaneously in 2015, three new gay bars opened in downtown: the Precinct leather bar, Bar Mattachine (named after the early, locally founded homophile group—it closed in 2018), and Redline, which features the youngest and most diverse crowd among the three. This gay reterritorialization downtown was built upon developer gentrification and the neighborhood's rebranding as DTLA. The New Jalisco now collaborates with other, predominantly white DTLA gay venues, whereas it competes with other Latinx venues—both for business and for talent to perform.

In fall 2019 the New Jalisco owners commissioned a mural by artists Rafa Esparza and Gabriela Ruiz, two regulars at the bar and friends of the owners (see plate 15). Cladding the building's facade in pink, the painting was inspired by an illustration of "Los 41 Maricones," a mass arrest during a 1901 drag ball in Mexico City; the central figures in the mural reference the source image. In addition, the mural includes Juan Gabriel, queen of salsa Celia Cruz, a vaquero couple (including a trans male figure), two dancing lesbians, and the recently deceased queer Latinx nightclub promoter Nacho Nava (of Mustache Mondays) as an angel. The lettering for the bar incorporates the rainbow flag, the trans pride flag, and the Mexican flag. During an artists' talk in front of the building, Ruiz recounted that Hernandez approached her about the project by asking if she had ever done a mural. She responded, "Yeah, I'm a Chicana artist." Despite the frequent conflation of Chicanx art and muralism, neither she nor Esparza had ever actually painted a mural. As Esparza added, "It's a classic immigrant story: getting hired to do something you didn't know how to do and doing it well." During the artists' talk, Lucas heard Trevi's "Gloria" blasting from the performance inside.[86] When he went in for a beer, the emcee was styled to look like Jennifer Lopez. But almost immediately he noticed that there was also a large flat-screen TV mounted above her so that patrons could watch the live performances *and* soccer games at the same time.

SCENES FROM THE NEW JALISCO BAR, 2016–19

During one of Lucas's first visits to the New Jalisco Bar, his friend Enrique ordered an Indio (an imported Mexican beer, the name translating as *Indian*) in Spanish, and the bartender (probably owner Garcia) promptly served his beer. When she turned to Lucas, he said in feeble Spanish that he would have an Indio, too. This time, she gestured toward the indigenous Mexican men sitting on stools at the bar and said, in Spanish, "Choose one." Although she and Enrique laughed at her joke, it signaled the racialized erotics when white Anglo men enter the venue.

The bar is one deep room, with a dimly lit long bar and tables and chairs in the front half. Deeper inside, a dance floor/performance area is situated under high ceilings and brighter lighting. On a visit in 2019, Dan was impressed that the bartender decked out their agua mineral with a salted rim, tajín, and lime like a michelada. Noting all the chandeliers and lacy curtains over the dance floor, they observed warmly, "If I could turn my grandmother's house into a disco, this is what I would imagine it to look like." They continued: "It seems to proudly flaunt extravagance over elegance, which is kind of everything I would want a queer Latinx bar to do."[87]

El Último Trago: Latinx Gay Bars as Essential Institutions

After surviving cycles of gentrification, the New Jalisco, like all other bars, had to close for more than a year because of government-mandated COVID restrictions from spring 2020 until summer 2021. The bar survived only because of a GoFundMe campaign organized by Ruiz to cover the rent and other continuing expenses during the shutdown. Hernandez said they even had to throw out and replace their stock of beer, which expired in the interim. The bar's landlord, who owns multiple parking lots in the area, also recently bought out every unit on the block for redevelopment; the landlord agreed to a five-year reprieve for the bar as a culturally significant site, but many other neighboring businesses have already closed. Although the bar survived the first waves of the COVID pandemic, as of summer 2022 the owners have felt the effects of subsequent inflation; they have held out against raising prices, but their own expenses have increased so much that staying open remains a struggle. They appear to be relying more on go-go boy shows and amateur strip contests than before to draw patrons. When Dan mentioned that they had noticed a statue of San Judas Tadea (the patron saint of lost causes) behind the bar on a previous visit, Hernandez remarked matter-of-factly, "We're Catholic." He went on to explain that they occasionally light candles and burn sage to protect the business.[88]

Each of the bars in this chapter reflects its contexts and has catered to distinct Latinx clienteles as it produced unique queer worlds. Circus opened as an antidote to gay racism during the disco era, and Tempo emerged as a refuge from an anti-immigrant public sphere; both continued to serve their communities as the need for them endured. Chico differentiated itself from the increasingly mainstream white gay male culture with the emergent cultural legibility of gay homeboys, whereas the New Jalisco evolved in an old downtown location facing constant change. In effect, each has reimagined the gay bar as an essential institution that reflects different ways to be LGBTQ+ and Latinx.

INTERLUDE 8

Mable Peabody's Beauty Parlor
and Chainsaw Repair in Denton, TX

In January 2017 I embarked on a three-month research road trip for this project, starting from Los Angeles and driving through Texas, New Orleans, dipping down to Florida, up through Atlanta and the mid-Atlantic coast, then looping back through the rust belt and across the plains, the Rockies, and the Southwest. I covered thousands of miles and visited gay bars and archives in dozens of cities. My trip, scheduled to align with a sabbatical, also took me through a newly charged political map; I started driving the week that Trump was inaugurated, and most of my route took me through red states. In those places and in that moment, I not only found that queer people were indeed everywhere but also that we *needed* the sanctuary of gay bars more than ever.

Five days into the trip, I had the most sublime gay bar night of my journey at Mable Peabody's Beauty Parlor and Chainsaw in Denton, Texas. By that time, it felt like I had experienced a lot on the road. My then-already-ex-boyfriend Mazdak joined me for the first few days' drive. We started on a Saturday, which was the day that Trump's Muslim ban went into effect; Mazdak's brother-in-law was flying home from Tehran that day, and we were uncertain if he would be detained. (He made it home, but his family waited for excruciating hours to find out.) Our first stop was Phoenix, and we serendipitously caught rides with a series of queer Lyft drivers who made recommendations on where to go next, recalling the days when a cab driver might be the only way a gay person could find a sympathetic watering hole. We ended the night at Charlie's, a massive bar where a truly diverse crowd converged across ages, genders, and ethnicities.[1] I initially felt old because I found myself judging the young people lined up outside for not dressing warmer on a chilly night. Inside, I quickly unclenched as I sensed how much people, myself included, needed to be together in this precarious political moment. On the massive back patio, fire dancers were performing for a Lunar New Year party sponsored by Fireball whisky, and patrons were lined up to order from a taco truck ingeniously accessible through a window. We bought a commemorative T-shirt out of a vending machine, using dimes and quarters, while a couple of guys laughed at us fumbling with the coins; it turned out that we had bought spandex go-go boy underwear by mistake. The next night in El Paso, we went downtown to a cluster of bars. At Chiquita's the bartender informed us that what looked like a hot tub in the middle of the bar used to be a fountain, but it had to be covered after one patron tried to drown another in it during a fight. The bartender also told us to "be careful" on our next day's drive to Abilene. When I opened Grindr back at our hotel, a promo popped up, proclaiming "Grindr has no borders" against an image of a chain-link fence and a solicitation for users' immigration and refugee stories; it was, in fact, ambiguous if the men in my feed were in the US or Mexico. A couple days later, I dropped Mazdak off at Love Field airport in Dallas and started research in the special collections at the University of North Texas in Denton.[2]

Mable Peabody's Beauty Parlor and Chainsaw Repair was the only gay bar in Denton, home of both UNT and Texas Women's University. (The bar closed in September 2017 after thirty-eight years.) It was located in a 1960s-style strip mall, and a sign announced its name in large block letters; the front windows featured murals of Divine in *Pink Flamingos* and Tim Curry in *The Rocky Horror Picture Show*, as well as a smaller but more elaborate logo for the bar (see figure 18.1).[3] The joint had me before I even walked in the door. Inside to the right, a sign announced a room flanked with red fringe as the Rouge Parlour; to the left, a chainsaw hung over the pool table and near a pair of disco balls. Mid-century hospital signage identified the dance floor/stage area as Gynecology & Obstetrics. Both

FIGURE 18.1 Mable Peabody's Beauty Parlor and Chainsaw Repair logo mural on one of its front windows. Photo by the author, 2017.

restrooms were gender neutral. It was quiet when I stopped in during my first night in town, but I noticed a flyer for an event called Glitterbomb two nights later and decided to check it out. That may have been the best decision of my life.

On Thursday the bar was much busier, and before the show it was difficult to distinguish performers from audience members. The clientele was gender mixed and gender fluid. A table near the entrance collected tampons and sanitary pads for the local food bank. One patron presented—in archaic terms—as a bearded lady as they circulated with glowing Christmas lights draped around their neck and shoulders. The crowd cheered for a birthday girl when she arrived. It felt more like a community than any bar

I'd ever visited. The line for the bar—just one bartender was working—was long but single file and very orderly. I had arranged to meet up with a nice guy I had chatted with on the apps and his fun gal pal, and we settled at a back corner table to watch the show.

Glitterbomb unveiled itself to be a variety show featuring genderqueer burlesque and drag. The theme for each act in that week's installment was junk food, and it was *amazing*. If I used Twitter, I would have live-tweeted it; instead, I posted a series of tipsy Facebook updates to document the proceedings. The boi emcee went by Milo Cox, and most of the performers appeared to present as female, although most also toyed with gender. The stage manager performed the opening number: a lesbian Oompa Loompa burlesque routine in which she stripped down to golden-ticket pasties. Next, first-time audience members were ritually devirginized as at midnight screenings of *The Rocky Horror Picture Show* and then baptized in glitter. To counteract the terror and depression of Trump's new presidency, the emcee made a practice of announcing *good news* between acts; these dispatches ranged from global progress (like a species making it off the endangered species list) to very local breakthroughs (Lucy finally got her ex off the lease; someone heard from his parents for the first time in twenty years; another person got a new job). The crowd was here to witness and support people getting through life.

Performers with such pop-culture double-entendre stage names as Justin Beaver and Strawberry Squirtcake took their turns on the stage, as did drag king Oliver Clothesoff, who offered an Oreo-themed act to "Weird Al" Yankovic's "The White Stuff."[4] A genderqueer performer with a beard and amazing dance moves pulled Twinkies out of their underwear, crammed one whole in their maw, and then deep-kissed it into the mouth of someone standing in the front row. A femme dancer displayed her body strength and control, and a chaotic duo drizzled each other with Easy Cheese followed by bowls of queso. A woman in Ronald McDonald drag—a long red wig and terrifying clown makeup—pulled off her pants while eating French fries. Like the processed foods that inspired it, the show was delicious. I have seen my share of questionable queer performance art and after-midnight nightclub genderfuck drag acts on the coasts, but this show managed to feel cathartic yet be in on its own joke. Queerness has been famously difficult for theorists to pin down and define, but *here it was* in its fabulous, playful, transgressive, messy, and world-making essence.

After the last act, the emcee announced that the following week's show would be themed for Galentine's Day—referencing the alternative holiday celebrating female friendships invented by the sitcom *Parks and Recreation*—and said, "Come see some Leslie Knope action you never thought you'd see."[5] As soon as the show was over, the audience spontaneously rushed the stage to line dance for two songs. Everyone seemed to know every gesture and step. This was still Texas, after all. But seemingly the queer heart of it.

Epilogue: After Hours
Pulse in Orlando

We cannot understand or even imagine American gay male cultures and histories without considering the ways that bars and nightclubs have been instrumental in both. As I have argued already, virtually every aspect of gay male public life has been expressed through or against the gay bar as its medium. Although my orientation in this book has been toward refracting gay bars' many forms, politics, and knowledges rather than narrowing my focus to a singular thesis, here I offer a brief historical summation before turning to this epilogue that attests to queer nightlife's ongoing resonances.

US gay bars and nightclubs as we know them effectively emerged after Prohibition and solidified as the primary institution of gay life in the postwar era. They provided a private business response to a social need, and new sexual subcultures (chapters 1 and 5, and interlude 1 on Denver) and queer cultural forms (chapters 1, 2, 5, 7, and 8, and interlude 8 on Denton, TX) flourished in these spaces. Gay bars have functioned as safe spaces for queer people who had nowhere else to congregate, but their role as sanctuaries has always exposed that they exist in relation to contexts of political and physical violence (see also interludes 2, 7, and 8 on Detroit, Somerset County, PA, and Denton, TX, respectively, as well as After Hours). In many jurisdictions, gay bars operated outside the law for decades, surviving through police payoffs and mafia exploitation, yet these bars and their patrons remained always at risk of closing or arrest by vice cops. Early gay political organizing and spontaneous protests responded to these conditions; the riots at Stonewall erupted because the belief in queer people's right to come together in community already existed (introduction). Bars became bastions of their local communities (chapter 6 and interlude 6 on Superior, WI). Not all gay people went to bars, but their existence telegraphed that a gay public world was possible.

In the 1970s a gay-liberation consciousness prompted resistance not only to oppressive external structures but also to problems among gay people themselves, including substance abuse, social alienation, sexism, classism (chapter 3), and racism (chapter 4). The gay bar presented the medium through which intracommunity biases could be made visible, documented, and redressed. Gay bars also spurred symbiotic community outlets, such as the gay press (which relied on bar advertising), and inspired the development of hotlines (interlude 4 on Philadelphia) and community centers as alternative resources. Many sexual minorities resisted the new liberation politics because they felt happy enough carrying on as they had before (interlude 3 on Seattle). Others sought to reinvent gay nightlife in creative ways that integrated previously segregated scenes (chapters 4 and 7) and sustained marginalized ones (chapters 4 and 8). Although by the 1970s and 1980s bars and nightclubs were no longer the only institutions for gay public life, they remained its centers.

In the 1980s and 1990s the AIDS epidemic transformed gay life and politics, so much so that it affected virtually every aspect of gay bar and club culture. This book does not have an "AIDS chapter" because the crisis touches each chapter (and interlude 5 on Minneapolis) in some way. After the millennial turn, gay bars have carried on in much the same fashion that they have for decades, though perhaps with less sex and almost assuredly less of a sense that they provide the only venues to express and explore one's sexuality. They continue to provide a space to dance to the latest pop divas and to make social connections tangible, not just virtual. They remain sites of potential, even in the age of their reported obsolescence (interludes 2 and 8 on Detroit and Denton, TX). No other moment has produced as many testaments to how queer bars and clubs are still essential as the response to the violence at Pulse Nightclub. Amid the mourning, recognition and reclamation.

Around 2 a.m. on Sunday, June 12, 2016, a man armed with a semiautomatic assault rifle and a handgun opened fire at the Orlando gay nightclub Pulse during its popular Saturday-night Latin party. He killed forty-nine people, injured fifty-three more, and held dozens of others hostage during a three-hour siege before SWAT police killed him. The press immediately described these horrific events as the largest mass shooting in US history, positioning this instance as part of an ongoing crisis of violence.[1] Politicians and the press likewise called the attack terrorism, pointing to the shooter Omar Mateen's professed allegiance to ISIS; such rhetoric erroneously positioned homophobic violence as foreign while it also restoked decades of Islamophobia.[2] The shooting was also understood as a hate crime: the gunman had targeted this club to kill LGBTQ+ people, and the victims were 90 percent Latinx, many Puerto Rican. Predictably, politicians and journalists framed the shooting in broader terms as an American tragedy—some to rhetorically legitimate queer Latinx people *as* Americans, others to elide their identities. (Remember, this all happened during the toxic 2016 presidential election campaign, when the Right was becoming more emboldened in its xenophobia but polling still alleged it was implausible that Donald Trump would be installed in office.) Nonetheless, the victims' names and faces circulated widely in the press and online, their lives were repeatedly memorialized in person and on social media, and efforts to commemorate and archive these events are ongoing.[3] At no moment in US history have queer Latinx lives and deaths been more visible.

This tragedy rendered Pulse the most publicized gay bar in the world. The massacre there also inspired an outpouring of reflections on why gay bars matter and celebrations of Latin nights specifically. Much like the case studies in this book, these think pieces often negotiated between local specificity and generalizable tendencies; between the promise of liberation and the ongoing practices of violence and exclusion; between documentable facts, personal experiences, and queer speculation; between the peculiar details and the big picture; between ephemera and built environments; and between past, present, and the persistent beat of the dance floor. Gay bars—in real life and in our imaginations—continue to mediate how we define ourselves, where we find our people, and how we make sense of queer cultures and politics in their full complexities and ambivalences.

Although elements of gay bar cultures from throughout this book reappear here, this is not a conclusion or an ending. Rather, this epilogue operates as an after-hours venue where the meanings of queer nightlife perpetuate.

Pulse was located south of downtown Orlando on S. Orange Avenue, a north-south commercial thoroughfare; the side streets there immediately become residential, lined with modest middle-class homes. When I walked around the neighborhood in February 2017, what most struck me was that location looked so *ordinary*. The building and its signage resembled a chain restaurant. An all-night Dunkin' Donuts stood across the side street, and a Wendy's faced it across Orange. I imagined tipsy clubbers boisterously running across the street nightly to offset liquor with grease. Taco Bell and McDonald's are a few blocks farther for those with cars. As with so many gay bars, it was situated in a neighborhood undergoing redevelopment; a new shopping complex with a massive Target was two blocks away. Pulse was neither downtown nor in a gayborhood nor tucked away discreetly as so many gay bars are.[4] Instead, it was unusually visible and located in the routes of everyday life.

Orlando may be synonymous with Walt Disney World and tourism, but 2.5 million people actually live in the area. Pulse primarily served locals, and the bartenders remembered their regulars' drink orders. Many of these locals and regulars were originally from somewhere else. The city has become the primary destination of refugees from the economic strife in Puerto Rico; numerous commentators insisted upon the particularity of the rampage as a Puerto Rican tragedy.[5] (Twenty-three of those who died were Puerto Rican.) As José Quiroga writes, "That we mourn the fact that they were killed because of their sexuality does not exclude the fact that we also mourn because they had no choice but to restart their lives as defined by diaspora, exile, and bureaucracy."[6] Pulse was a place that generations of queers sought out as they were looking for a better life; it was a place they might have found that better life, or at least felt its possibility.

Pulse was an institution of the local community. The night after the shooting, *All Things Considered* host Ari Shapiro spoke to people at another Orlando gay bar. One exchange conveyed the social connections the club sustained and the complex emotions of the moment:

ARI SHAPIRO: Why did you decide to come out tonight?

EDGAR GOMEZ: I didn't want to be alone.

ARTURO YUGALDI: Yeah, we spent most of the day terrified that everybody we loved had died.

SHAPIRO (*narrating*): Yugaldi says a drag queen whispered a bit of wisdom into his ear earlier in the evening.

YUGALDI: She said happiness is the ultimate rebellion.[7]

For Yugaldi, the people who went to Pulse regularly were not an anonymous crowd but constituted "everyone we loved." Another account emphasized that Pulse was *known* in local communities of color as way to name and locate queerness. "Growing up in a black and brown community where hyper-masculinity was acted out as a form of survival, I actually grew up hating on Pulse," Daniel Leon-Davis reflects. Later, he continues, "Pulse was where I learned to love my community."[8] These social and affective bonds were constituted not only by a sense of shared identity but also by the intoxicating experiences of its nightly drag shows and dancing.[9]

The attack and its public mourning were mediated by the mobile phones that structure contemporary sociality. So many of the accounts of that night and the immediate aftermath tell of the people at the club making calls and texting in terror, people waking up to panicked messages and news alerts on their phones, people messaging friends the next day to check if they were safe, and people sending unreturned texts to those who were lost. I'm also struck that so many of the images of the victims that later circulated in the news, on social media, and in memorials were *selfies*, queer self-representations rather than studio portraits or family photos that tried to force them into normativity. Looking at the images, you can sense that they had made the effort to look sharp with their contoured eyebrows and dressy outfits and that they felt cute as they worked their angles. This was how they wanted to be seen and how they solicited attention; these self-styled close-ups taken in the spaces where they lived offer a sense of intimacy and vitality. Writing in the wake of Pulse, Loma titles a heartbreaking poem "All the Dead Boys Look Like Me."[10]

Many people had visceral reactions to the violence and loss at Pulse because they saw themselves in the crowd and knew the draw of the dance floor on Latin Night. So many expressed the sense that they might have been there, too, because they've been to so many *theres* like it.[11] Deborah R. Vargas recognized El Gran Combo de Puerto Rico's 1979 song "Brujería" playing in a smartphone video that one of the victims took that night.[12] That the song—alleging witchcraft—remained in rotation over the decades might speak to the reverberating, history-repeating, perpetual now of the queer dance floor's enchantments. Referencing a Madonna lyric, Alfred Soto titled his ode to queer nightlife "Only When I'm Dancing Can I Feel This Free."[13] Writing for *MTV News*, Soto argued that Latinx queers "find on crowded dance floors a sense of fellowship that is no less deep for being ephemeral."[14] Likewise, Louie A. Ortiz-Fonseca reflected that "our Latin nights are usually in borrowed spaces that we magically transform into community."[15] Performance-studies scholar Juana María Rodríguez acknowledged that gay clubs have long been spaces of "bravery" rather than safety and that Latin nights exist "because many gay clubs have a history of racial profiling, excluding not just Latin rhythms and beats, but the black and brown bodies that carry them."[16] Scholars and critics continue to argue that gay bars have never been truly safe spaces; the shooting and the media attention that followed violated this sanctuary by exposing it to the pubic beyond its community.[17] Nonetheless, Rodríguez reflected, "Let this be a moment to affirm queer latinidad in all its glittery fabulousness and political complexity, to mourn, to party, to agitate, to act in the hope of another world of possibilities. Let that moment be now."[18]

Perhaps the most celebrated piece written in immediate response to Pulse is Justin Torres's "In Praise of Latin Night at the Queer Club." Torres interpellates his reader as a club-goer with his use of *you* while speculating on the varied conditions of a night out. Torres creatively fleshes out the lived-in textures of Latin night at the gay bar in relation to economics, domestic arrangements, and *la familia*:

> Maybe your Ma blessed you on the way out the door. Maybe she wrapped a plate for you in the fridge so you don't come home and mess up her kitchen with your hunger. Maybe your Tia dropped you off, gave you cab money home. Maybe you had to get a sitter. Maybe you've yet to come out to your family at all, or maybe your family kicked you out years ago. Forget it, you survived.... Maybe you're flush, maybe you're broke as nothing, and angling your pretty face barside, hoping someone might buy you a drink. Maybe your half-Latin-ass doesn't even speak Spanish; maybe you barely speak English. Maybe you're undocumented....
>
> You are queer and you are brown and you have known violence. You have known a masculinity, a machismo, stupid with its own fragility. You learned basic queer safety, you have learned to scan, casually, quickly, before any public displays of affection.

Torres continues inside the club, "The only imperative is to be transformed, transfigured in the disco light. To lighten, loosen, see yourself reflected in the beauty of others."[19]

Beyond Torres's essay, family relations also structured much of the reporting on Pulse and worked to make many of the most reiterated accounts relatable and grievable.[20] Barbara Poma, a straight woman, opened Pulse in 2004 in memory of her brother who had died of AIDS in the early 1990s. Among the victims, Brenda Lee Marquez-McCool, a forty-nine-year-old mother of eleven, shielded her son Isiah from the gunfire and saved his life by giving hers; she was fighting leukemia at the time but loved dancing and sported a fierce cropped platinum hairstyle. Juan Ramon Guerrero, twenty-two, and Christopher Andrew "Drew" Leinonen, thirty-two, had been planning their wedding; their families held a joint funeral instead. Eddie Jamoldroy Justice, thirty, texted his mom from the bathroom; addressing her as Mommy, he wrote from the restroom, "He's coming.... I'm gonna die."[21] Akyra Murray, the youngest victim at eighteen, initially escaped the club but returned when she realized that her cousin was still inside. Numerous commentaries speculated about how many of the deceased were outed to their families by the shootings, and one father reportedly refused to take custody of his gay son's body. Some families set up GoFundMes to underwrite funeral expenses; some families could not afford the costs of having their kin's remains shipped to their homelands.

Part of the sadness of Pulse was also that, despite the public performance of mourning, nothing seemed to change. The nation's polarized and intransigent governmental system once again failed to take any substantive action on gun control, just like after every other mass shooting. Five years later, a mass shooting at Club Q in Colorado Springs killed five patrons and injured numerous more.[22] Cynically, we can expect that such homophobic attacks will continue to happen. That such violence symbolically targets gay bars demonstrates both the continued need for them as sanctuaries and their condition as always at risk.

In the wake of the shooting at Pulse, queer pride events and venues hired armed guards in the name of security; queer and trans people color—who were the targets of this attack—countered that increased policing does not make them safer. Numerous reports remarked that men who have sex with men are still banned from donating blood in the US—a policy that dates from an earlier time in the AIDS epidemic—even when their own people need it. White queers claimed solidarity, but too often it seemed more like co-optation; predictably, many such claims to sharing in loss retained the myopia of seeing themselves as constituting the queer "community."

Working to express terror, grief, and critique in other language modes, writer after writer turned to poetry. Poet Amal Rana brilliantly conveys the limits of queer solidarity:

> Orlando 49
> emblazoned on the back of a t-shirt
> worn by a white queer
> who looked through and past
> our table of Latinx, Indigenous, Black, Muslim queers
> right in front of her
> as if we never existed
> as if we were not sitting there
> laughing and thriving
> radiating life[23]

In a different register, Maya Chinchilla acknowledges exhaustion in the penultimate line of her poem: "We're tired of being so resilient."[24]

Mourning is a complex and contradictory affective state, marked by shock, sadness, and the memories of joy that make the loss hurt; it's both personal and political. In numerous accounts of Pulse's clientele the then-still-new gender-neutral term *Latinx* appeared and was explained, but the most debated pronoun was *we*. Slogans, hashtags, and statements proclaimed We Are Orlando, Somos Orlando, and We Are Not All Orlando. This raised the question "Who are 'we' after Orlando?"[25] There are multiple *we*'s with different stakes and congregations. We must not overlook the particular constituency that Pulse served, nor can we deny that these events reverberated to affect queer people far and wide. Maintaining the collective first-person plural, Jason Alley introduces a *GLQ* dossier on Pulse with the statement "We must continue to hold each other in desire and political accountability alike if the affects we have in and effects we have on the world are still worth fighting for."[26] If this book has focused on the *bars* of its title, let this epilogue emphasize the *ours*: the bars are *ours*.

When I visited the Pulse site, the building was surrounded by fencing and a vinyl wrap printed with works by local artists. A tree reached up and over the fencing, decorated with multicolored wood stars inscribed for each victim. Tribute flyers and objects adorned the site; some had already been bleached by the sun, but others appeared fresh. Everywhere there were messages—some in Spanish, most in English—handwritten in Sharpie by mourners who had made the pilgrimage to the site. A formal pedestal engraved with the victims' names and featuring small framed images of each was stationed front and center. To its left, a more makeshift shrine shone more vibrantly and emotively with numerous candles, a Virgin Mary, a teddy bear, and a rainbow sculpture supporting the words *Orlando Strong*. Several feet in front of this shrine, the word LOVE appeared in the blackened residue of melted candle wax (see plate 16). A steady stream of visitors, many of whom had probably never danced there, came to pay their respects. Pulse was no longer a nightclub but was a symbol of collective pasts and political aspirations.

Appendix 1

Selected Bars and Clubs

Atlanta

The Armory, 836 Juniper St., 1981–2005

Backstreet, 845 Peachtree St., 1975–2004

Bulldogs, 893 Peachtree St., 1978–present

The Cove, 586 Worchester Dr., 1968–90

Foster's on Peachtree, 980 Peachtree St. NE, 1984–87

Illusions, 1021 Peachtree St., 1982–85

Jocks, 887 Peachtree St., early 1980s; location previously The Difference and The In-Between

Loretta's, 708 Spring St., 1987–1990s

The Marquette, 809 Martin Luther King Jr. Dr., mid-1960s–2000; 868 Joseph E. Boone Blvd., 2000–present

The Other Side, 1924 Piedmont Rd., 1990–99

Sweet Gum Head, 2284 Cheshire Bridge Rd. NE, 1971–81

Traxx, 306 Luckie St. NW, 1989–2009; Warehouse entrance (straight), 339 Marietta St. NW; Legendary Traxx parties moved to other venues, including 1287 Columbia Drive, Decatur, until 2012

Baltimore

The Drinkery, 205 W. Read St., 1972–present

Boston

Jacque's, 79 Broadway, 1946–present

The Napoleon Club, 52 Piedmont St., 1929–98

The Other Side, 78 Broadway, 1965–76

Playland, 21 Essex St., 1937–98

The Punch Bowl, 230 Stuart St., 1946–69

Sporters, 228 Cambridge St., 1957–95

Chicago

Bistro Too, 5015 N. Clark St., 1987–92

The Bushes, 3320 N. Halsted, 1976–96

Chicago Eagle, 5015 N. Clark St., 1992–2006

Dugan's Bistro, 420 N. Dearborn Ave., 1973–82

Gold Coast, 1130 N. Clark, 1110 N. Clark, 2265 N. Lincoln, 501 N. Clark, and 5025 N. Clark, 1960–88

Granville Anvil, 1137 W. Granville Ave., 1988–present; location previously the Terrace Lounge, gay from 1975

Little Jim's, 3501 N. Halsted, 1975–2020

Man's Country (bathhouse), 5015 N. Clark, 1974–2017

Manhandler Saloon, 1948 N. Halsted St., 1980–2020

Touché, 2825 N. Lincoln Ave., 1976–90 (closed by fire); 6412 N. Clark St., 1990–present

The Warehouse, 206 S. Jefferson St., 1977–82

Dallas

The Round Up Saloon, 3912 Cedar Springs Rd., 1980–present; location previously Magnolia's Thunderpussy

Sue Ellen's, 3903 Cedar Springs Rd., later 3014 Throckmorton St., 1989–present

Denton, TX

Mable Peabody's Beauty Parlor and Chainsaw Repair, 1979–2007 (fire), 2008–17

Denver

Charlie's, 900 E. Colfax Ave., 1981–present
Don's Alley, 1512 Broadway, 1972
Triangle Lounge, 2036 Broadway, 1973–2007

Detroit

Gigi's, 16920 W. Warren Ave., 1973–present
Menjo's, 950 W. McNichols Rd., 1973–present
The Woodward Bar, 6426 Woodward Ave., 1954–2022

Fire Island, NY

The Ice Palace, 1 Ocean Walk, Cherry Grove, 1950s–present
The Sandpiper, 37 Fire Island Blvd., The Pines, 1970–79

Fort Lauderdale, FL

The Copa Disco, 624 SE 28th St., 1975–2005

Houston

Eagle Houston, 611 Hyde Park Blvd., 2014–present; location previously the 611 Club, 1973–2013
The Exile, 1011 Bell St., 1954–86
The Farmhouse, 2710 Albany, 1971–76
Hamburger Mary's, 2409 Grant St., 2017–present
Mary's, 1022 Westheimer, 1971–73, 1973–2002, 2002–09
Pink Elephant, 1218 Leeland, 1936–84

Kansas City

Bar Natasha (lesbian), 1911 Main St., 2003–08

The Colony Bar, 3325 Troost Ave., 1959–72

Dante's Inferno, 1104 Independence Ave., 1933

Hamburger Mary's, 3700 Broadway Blvd., 2009–present

Ivanhoe Lounge/Ivanhoe Cabaret/Pegasus/The Cabaret, 1014 Oak St., 1971–79; 5024 Main St., 1982–early 2002

Jewel Box Lounge, 3219 Troost Ave., 1960–71; 3110 Main St., 1971–82

Missie B's, 805 W. 39th St., 1994–present

Los Angeles Metro Area

Akbar, 4356 Sunset Blvd., 1996–present

Arena, 6655 Santa Monica Blvd., 1990–2015

Bar Mattachine, 221 W. 7th St., 2015–18

Black Cat, 3909 W. Sunset, 1966–69; later the Bushwacker, Tabasco's, Basgo's Disco, and Le Barcito (Latinx), 1960s–2011

Chico, 2915 W. Beverly Blvd., Montebello, 1999–2020, 2022–present

Circus Disco, 6648 Lexington Ave., 1975–2015

Club Cobra, 10937 Burbank Blvd., 2006–present; the space was previously Rawhide, which hosted a weekly Latin night: Olé Olé

Club Tempo, 5520 Santa Monica Blvd., 1993–present; location previously Faces (Asian)

Eagle LA, 4219 Santa Monica Blvd., 2006–present; location previously The Shed, The Outcast, and Gauntlet II since 1968

Frat House, 8112 W. Garden Grove Blvd., Garden Grove, 1985–present

Jewel's Catch One, 4067 W. Pico Blvd., 1973–2015

Manhandler Saloon, 2692 S. La Cienaga Blvd., 1976–86

New Jalisco Bar, 245 S. Main, 2006–present; location previously the Jalisco Inn #2, 1982–2005

Plaza, 739 N. La Brea Blvd., 1975–present

The Plush Pony (lesbian), 5261 Alhambra Ave., 1960s–2008

Precinct, 357 S. Broadway, 2015–present

The Redline, 131 E. 6th St., 2015–present

Redz (lesbian), 2218 E. First St.; the name of the venue changed over the years, including to the Redhead, Red's, and Redz Angelz, late 1950s–2015; reopened (date unconfirmed)–present

The Score, 107 W. 4th St., 1983–2005

Silver Platter, 2700 W. 7th St., 1963–present

Studio One, 661 North Robertson Blvd., West Hollywood, 1974–88; the venue later operated as the Factory, 1993–2013

Sugar Shack (lesbian), 4101 Arden Dr., El Monte, 1987–2006; previously Eddie's, late 1970s–1987

Miami Beach, FL

Twist, 1057 Washington Ave., 1993–present

Minneapolis/St. Paul

Club Metro, 733 Pierce Butler Route, St. Paul, 1992–2001

Gay 90's, 408 Hennepin Ave., Minneapolis, 1956–present

The 19 Bar, 19 W. 15th St., Minneapolis, 1956–present

Pi, 2532 25th Ave. S., Minneapolis, 2007–08

The Y'all Come Back Saloon/The Saloon, 830 Hennepin Ave., Minneapolis, 1977–present

New York

The Anvil, 500 W. 14th St., 1974–85

Better Days, 316 W. 49th St., 1972–88

The Club Baths, 24 1st Ave., 1971–83

The Continental Baths, 230 W. 74th St., 1968–75

Danceteria, 252 W. 37th St. and later 30 W. 21st St., 1979–86

Eagle's Nest, 142 11th Ave., 1970–2000

Eagle NYC, 554 W. 28th St., 2001–present

The 82 Club, 82 E. 4th St., 1953–73

La Escuelita, 806 8th Ave., 1967–2016

Everard Baths, 28 W. 28th St., 1888–1986

Flamingo, 599 Broadway (second floor), 1974–81

GAA Firehouse, 99 Wooster St., 1971–74

Julius', 159 W. 10th St., 1950s–present

The Loft, 654 Broadway, 1970–75; 99 Prince St., 1975–84; and subsequent locations

The Mineshaft, 835 Washington St., 1976–85

The New St. Marks Baths, 6 St. Marks Place, 1979–1985

Paradise Garage, 84 King St., 1977–87

The Saint, 105 2nd Ave., 1980–88

Sound Factory, 530 W. 27th St., 1989–95

Stonewall Inn, 51–53 Christopher St., 1967–69; 51 Christopher St., 1987–89; 53 Christopher St., 1991–present

Studio 54, 254 W. 54th St., 1977–80

Tenth Floor, 151 W. 25th St., 10th floor, 1972–74

Tracks NYC, 531 W. 19th St., 1986–91

12 West, 491 West St., 1975–80

Oakland

White Horse Inn, 6547 Telegraph Ave., 1933–present

Omaha

The Max, 1417 Jackson St., 1984–present

Omaha Mining Company, 1715 Leavenworth St., 1991–present; previously The Run, mid-1970s–1991

Orlando

Parliament House, 410 N. Orange Blossom Trail, 1975–2020

Pulse, 1912 S. Orange Ave., 2004–16

Philadelphia

The Bikestop, 206 S. Quince St., 1982–present

El Bravo/Bravo's Lounge, 3600 N. 5th St., 1980–83; location later Two Faces

Cell Block, 204 S. Camac St., 1975–83

DCA, 204 S. Camac St., 1975–88; previously the Land of Oz, 1973–75; later the 2–4 Club

iCandy, 254 S. 12th St., 2011–18

JP's, 1511 Spruce St., 1978–86

Odyssey II, 1526 Delancey St., 1981–84; previously Steps, 1973–80; later Parks Place

The Post, 1705 Chancellor St., 1976–82

Smart Place, 922 Arch St., 1978–86

The Tavern on Camac, 243 S. Camac St., 1998–present; previously Maxine's, 1936–82, and Raffles, 1982–98

Too Much/The Much, 5727 N. Broad St., 1980s; previously The Swan, 5727 N. Broad St., 1941–80s

Venture Inn, 255 S. Camac St., 1973–2016

Phoenix

Charlie's, 727 W. Camelback Rd., 1984–present

Portland, OR

Embers Avenue, 110 NW Broadway, 1969–2017

San Francisco

Ambush, 1351 Harrison, 1973–86

Amelia's (lesbian), 647 Valencia St., 1978–91

Black Cat, 710 Montgomery St., 1933–63

The Box (dance party) at Kennel Club, 628 Divisidero, 1988–94 and 1998–99; 715 Harrison, 1994–98

Club Q (lesbian dance party) at Kennel Club, 628 Divisidero, 1988–90; at Club Townsend, 177 Townsend, 1990–2003

Club Uranus (party), Sundays at the EndUp, 401 6th St., 1989–92

Code Blue (lesbian party), various locations, 1987

Colossus, 1015 Folsom, 1990–2000

Dreamland, 715 Harrison, 1987–90

The EndUp, 401 6th St., 1966–2011; ambiguously gay 2012–present

Esta Noche, 3079 16th St., 1979–2014

Fe-Be's, 1501 Folsom St., 1966–86

Finocchio's, 506 Broadway, 1936–99

I-Beam, 1748 Haight, 1977–94

Josie's Cabaret and Juice Joint, 3583 16th St., 1990–98

Klubstitute (party) at Crystal Pistol, 842 Valencia St., 1990–91; at EndUp, 401 6th St., 1991–95

Lexington Club (lesbian), 3464 19th St., 1996–2014

Maud's (lesbian), 937 Cole St., 1966–89

Pleasuredome, 177 Townsend St., 1991–2001

El Rio, 3158 Mission St., 1978–present

The Tool Box, 399 4th St., 1962–71

T-shack (party) at the Stud, 399 9th St., 1996–2008, at other venues, 2010–20; renamed Mother, 2015–20

Trocadero Transfer, 520 4th St., 1977–88

Tubesteak Connection (party) at Aunt Charlie's Lounge, 133 Turk St., 2004–present

Twin Peaks Tavern, 401 Castro St., 1971–present

Seattle

Columbus Tavern, 167 S. Washington St., 1949–date unconfirmed

The Double Header, 407 Second Ave. S., 1934–2015

Garden of Allah, 1213 First Ave., 1946–56

Golden Horseshoe, 207 Second Ave. S., 1961–76

Shelly's Leg, 77 S. Main St., 1973–77

The 611, 611 Second Ave., 1962–2003

Spags Tavern, 924 Pine St., date unconfirmed–1987; 1118 E. Pike St., 1988–date unconfirmed

Somerset County, PA

Casa Nova, Rte. 985 Old Somerset Pike, 1997–2001

Superior, WI

The Main Club, 1983–96; 1217 Tower Ave., 1997–present

Washington, DC

The Clubhouse, 1296 Upshur St., NW, 1975–90; location previously Metropolitan Capitalites, the 4011 Club, the Zodiac Den, and the Third World

DC Eagle, 904 9th St. NW, 1971–79; 908 7th St. NW, 1979–87

Lost and Found, 56 L St. SE, 1971–91

Nob Hill, 1101 Kenyon St. NW, 1957–2004

Plus One, 829 8th St., 1968–date unconfirmed

Tracks, 1111 First St. SE, 1984–99

Appendix 2
LGBTQ+ Periodical Sources

Adelante (Los Angeles, bilingual in Spanish and English)
The Advocate (initially Los Angeles, then national)
After Dark (New York/national, discreetly gay)
Alternate News (Kansas City)
The Alternative (Kansas City)
The Barb (Atlanta)
Bay Area Reporter (San Francisco)
Blacklight (Washington, DC/national, Black)
BLK (Los Angeles/national, Black)
Body Politic (Toronto)
Camp (Kansas City)
Christopher Street (New York, literary magazine)
Ciao! (national, travel)
Citizen News (San Francisco)
Cleveland Gay News
Clikque (Atlanta, Black)
Come Out! (New York, liberation)
Cruise (Atlanta)

Cruise Weekly (Detroit)

David (Jacksonville/southern regional)

De Ambiente (Los Angeles, in Spanish)

Deneuve/Curve (national, lesbian)

Drummer (national, leather)

DungeonMaster (national, leather)

Dykespeak (San Francisco, lesbian)

Entertainment West (Los Angeles)

Equal Time (Twin Cities)

Erie Gay Community News

Erie Gay News

Esplanade (Boston)

Fag Rag (Boston, liberation/radical)

Folsom (national, leather)

Friends (Atlanta, Black)

Frontiers (Los Angeles)

Frontiers (San Francisco)

Gay (New York, liberation)

Gay Chicago Magazine

Gay Community News (Boston)

Gay Community News (Kansas City)

Gay Dealer (Philadelphia)

Gay Flames (New York, liberation/radical)

Gay Life (Chicago)

Gay News (Ohio East edition)

Gay Power (New York, liberation)

Gay Sunshine (San Francisco, liberation)

Gay Times (London)

Gayboy (Houston)

Gaysweek (New York, newsmagazine)

Gaze/Twin Cities Gaze/TC Gaze (Twin Cities)

Gazette (Atlanta)

GLC Voice (Twin Cities)

High Gear (Cleveland)

Honcho (national, pornography and lifestyle)

Houston Voice

Impact (New Orleans)

Knight Life (Miami)

Lavender Lifestyles/Lavender (Twin Cities)

Metra (Detroit)

Michael's Thing (New York)

Montrose GEM (Houston)

Montrose Star (Houston)

Montrose Voice (Houston)

New Gay Life (Philadelphia)

New Way (Denver)

New York Native

Nite Scene (Atlanta)

Numbers (national, pornography and lifestyle)

Nuntius (Houston)

One (Los Angeles/national, homophile)

Out (national, lifestyle)

Out (Pittsburgh)

Out Front (Denver)

Out in Texas (Texas regional)

Out Post (Detroit)

Outlines (Chicago)

Out/Look (San Francisco/national, queer cultural commentary magazine)

OutSmart (Houston)

Outweek (New York, queer newsmagazine)

Philadelphia Gay News

Phoenix/Phoenix News (Kansas City)

Pittsburgh Gay News

Pittsburgh Gay Times

Planet Q (Pittsburgh)

QQ/Queen's Quarterly (national, lifestyle)

QV/Quo Vadis (Los Angeles, Latino)

Radical Queen (Philadelphia, liberation/radical)

Reactions (Studio City, CA)

Rhinoceros (Denver)

San Francisco Bay Times

San Francisco Sentinel

Seattle Gay News

Southern Voice (Atlanta)

Stallion (national, pornography and lifestyle)

Texas Triangle (regional)

Torso (national, pornography and lifestyle)

TWT (This Week in Texas, regional)

Update (San Diego)

Upfront/Upfront America (Houston)

Vector (San Francisco, homophile)

Venus (Atlanta, Black lesbian)

Washington Blade (Washington, DC)

Whazzup! Magazine (Oakland, Black/queer of color)

Windy City Times (Chicago)

Womanews (New York, lesbian)

Notes

Preface

The title of this preface references *Drunk History* (created by Derek Waters and Jeremy Konner, Comedy Central, 2013–19); and Deee-Lite, "Good Beat" (Dmitry Brill/Herbie Hancock/Kier Kirby/Towa Tei, Elektra, 1990).

1. Allen, *There's a Disco Ball*, 1.
2. Thank you to Joshua Javier Guzmán for helping me articulate this.
3. See, for instance, Delgado and Muñoz, *Everynight Life*; Rivera-Servera, *Performing Queer Latinidad*; Vogel, *Scene of the Harlem Cabaret*; Moore, *Fabulous*; Chambers-Letson, *After the Ball*; Khubchandani, *Ishtyle*; Adeyemi, Khubchandani, and Rivera-Servera, *Queer Nightlife*; and Adeyemi, *Feels Right*. See also Yuzna, *Fun*; and Colucci and Yereban, *Party Out of Bounds*.
4. See my book *Inherent Vice*, 34–35.
5. Fawaz, *Queer Forms*, 10, 6, 36.
6. A kitschy earlier ad for the Forthsooth the Dragon bar beckoned patrons to "spend a Knight inside a warm mouth." Advertisement, *Advocate*, December 8, 1971, 12.
7. On Rihanna, Britney Spears, and other gay bar music, see my piece, "I Wanna Go, or Finding Love in a Hopeless Place."
8. I have fleshed out my archival research with numerous personal conversations to understand local contexts, but these have not been as formalized as oral history interviews.
9. The queer archive is also evidence of lives lived and lost; many collections comprise the personal effects of men who died of AIDS that were some-

10 *Beaches* (dir. Garry Marshall, 1988). Phil Johnson papers, AR0838, box 38, now the Resource Center LGBT Collection of the University of North Texas Libraries. Lollie Johnson Papers, MS 117, box 4, University of Texas at San Antonio Libraries Special Collections.

11 Ad, *David*, May 24, 1983. On evoking the past on the dance floor, see Bredbeck, "Troping the Light Fantastic."

12 Speculative historiography has become a major new model for understanding otherwise underrepresented or undocumented pasts, as exemplified by Saidiya Hartman's work. Hartman poses the question, "How can narrative embody life in words and at the same time respect what we cannot know?" She developed the practice of "critical fabulation" to narrate such lives and histories where the archive fails to offer evidence or insight. (See Hartman, "Venus in Two Acts," 3, 11.) Hartman's book *Lose Your Mother* stands as one of the most powerful reckonings with the past and what one can understand of it that I have ever encountered; Hartman's subsequent *Wayward Lives, Beautiful Experiments* is more overtly speculative.

13 Larry Blagg gay club matchbook covers and ephemera, 7738, Human Sexuality Collection, Cornell University Library.

14 Lin, *Gay Bar*, 112, 247.

15 Muñoz, "Ephemera as Evidence." Ann Cvetkovich has coined the alluring phrase "an archive of feelings" to expand the forms that queer archives might take. Cvetkovich, *Archive of Feelings*. My thinking about the "evidentiary paradox" of queer archives—that queer lives and expressions existed even when and where they were not supposed to—has been most shaped by Anjali Arondekar's "Without a Trace." On queer archives, see also Frantz and Locks, *Cruising the Archive*; Stone and Cantrell, *Out of the Closet*; Arondekar et al., "Queering Archives"; McKinney, *Information Activism*; Cifor, *Viral Cultures*; Marshall and Tortorici, *Turning Archival*; and my essay "Historical Fantasies."

16 Tongson, *Relocations*; Mattson, "Small-City Gay Bars"; Brown-Saracino, "How Places Shape Identity." On gay suburbanite identity, see also Brekhus, *Peacocks, Chameleons, Centaurs*.

17 Mattson, *Who Needs Gay Bars?*, 7, 106–13.

18 *Small Town Gay Bar* (dir. Malcolm Ingram, 2006).

19 On queer rural life, see also Loffreda, *Losing Matt Shepard*; Gray, *Out in the Country*; and Allen, *Real Queer America*. Jack Halberstam and Scott Herring have critiqued urban centrism in queer studies, employing the term *metronormativity*. Halberstam, *In a Queer Time*, 36–38; Herring, *Another Country*. On the geographies of where LGBTQ+ people live, see Hasenbush et al., "LGBT Divide."

20 Roland Barthes describes the punctum as the detail that transfixes or even wounds the viewer. Barthes, *Camera Lucida*, 25–27.

21 So-called wrinkle rooms attract an older clientele. *Chicken* was the 1970s term for pubescent boys; *chicken hawk* was the term for their pederast admirers. The Horny Bull in Tampa and the Other Side in Los Angeles advertised themselves as chicken bars. In the wake of late 1970s right-wing moral panics that conflated homosexuals with pedophiles, a paradigm shift turned away from chicken bars toward LGBTQ+ youth centers to specifically protect younger queer people from predatory elders.

22 "Part of Your World" from *The Little Mermaid* (Howard Ashman/Alan Menken, 1989).

23 Gene Elder, conversation with the author, January 11, 2012.

24 For early reporting, see George Schwandt, "Holocaust in New Orleans," *Advocate*, July 18, 1973, 2; and multiple articles in *Advocate*, August 1, 1973, 1–7. For historical accounts, see Townsend, *Let the Faggots Burn*; Delery-Edwards, *Up Stairs Lounge Arson*; and Fieseler, *Tinderbox*. A trove of primary documents is gathered in the Skylar Fein Upstairs Fire Collection at the Historic New Orleans Collection.

25 Baldor, "No Girls Allowed?" See also Doan and Higgins, "Demise of Queer Space?"; Ghaziani, *There Goes the Gayborhood?*; Orne, *Boystown*; Hartless, "Questionably Queer"; and Jason Farber, "How 'Gay' Should a Gay Bar Be?," *New York Times*, June 25, 2017, ST10.

26 See Tongson, "Karaoke, Queer Theory."

Acknowledgments

The title of the acknowledgments references Donna Summer, "I Feel Love" (Summer/Giorgio Moroder/Pete Bellotte, Casablanca, 1977), and Kylie Minogue, "Can't Get You Out of My Head" (Cathy Dennis/Rob Davis, Parlophone, 2001).

The first phrase of each paragraph in this section references a song or songs, in the following order: Bonnie Tyler, "Total Eclipse of the Heart" (Jim Steinman, CBS, 1983); Indigo Girls, "Closer to Fine" (Emily Saliers, Epic, 1989); The Staple Sisters, "I'll Take You There" (Al Bell, Stax, 1972); Edith Piaf, "La Vie en Rose" (Piaf/Louiguy, Columbia, 1947), and Grace Jones, "La Vie en Rose" (Piaf/Louiguy/Mack David, Island, 1977); Janet Jackson, "When I Think of You" (James Harris III/Terry Lewis, A&M, 1986); Missy Elliott, "Work It" (Melissa Elliott/Timbaland, Elektra, 2002); RuPaul, "Supermodel (You Better Work)" (RuPaul/Jimmy Harry/Larry Tee, Tommy Boy, 1992), and Britney Spears, "Work Bitch" (William Adams/Otto Jettman/Sebastian Ingrosso/Anthony Preston/Ruth-Anne Cunningham/Spears, RCA, 2013); Garth Brooks, "Friends in Low Places" (Dewayne Blackwell/Earl Bud Lee, Capitol Nashville, 1990); and The Postal Service,

"Brand New Colony" (Benjamin Gibbard/Jimmy Tamborello, Sub Pop, 2003).

Introduction: "We Were Never Being Boring"

The chapter title references Pet Shop Boys, "Being Boring" (Chris Lowe/Neil Tennant, Parlophone/EMI, 1990).

The subheads in this chapter reference the following songs: Peggy Lee, "Is That All There Is?" (Jerry Leiber/Mike Stoller, Capitol, 1969); Rihanna featuring Calvin Harris, "We Found Love" (Harris, Def Jam, 2011) ; Erasure, "A Little Respect" (Vince Clarke/Andy Bell, Mute/Sire Records, 1988); Gloria Gaynor, "I Will Survive" (Freddie Perren/Dino Fekaris, Polydor, 1978); and Bizarre Inc, "I'm Gonna Get You" (Andy Meecham/Dean Meredith/Carl Turner/Toni Collandreo, Sony, 1992).

The following abbreviations for periodical titles and the names of archival sites are used in the notes to this introduction: BAR (*Bay Area Reporter*); GCN (*Gay Community News*); NYN (*New York Native*); NYT (*New York Times*, daily newspaper); ONE (ONE National Gay & Lesbian Archives at University of Southern California Libraries, Los Angeles); VV (*Village Voice*, New York City downtown alternative weekly newspaper); WB (*Washington Blade*); and WP (*Washington Post*, Washington, DC, daily newspaper).

1 Muñoz, *Disidentifications*; *Sense of Brown*, 11.
2 On queer world making, see Berlant and Warner, "Sex in Public"; Muñoz, *Disidentifications*. Buckland further develops this concept in *Impossible Dance*.
3 Male-centric spaces historically have operated with the assumption that their patrons were cisgender males.
4 My thinking on the role of gay bars is informed by Ryan Powell's articulation of the "elaboration of gay male life" via cinema. Powell, *Coming Together*. The emergence of gay men as "sexual subjects" is a political formation that has been critiqued in much of queer theory. See, for instance, Eng and Puar, "Introduction."
5 Oldenburg, *Great Good Place*, 14. Straight bar and drinking cultures in the US have also been studied, historically and sociologically. See, for instance, Barrows and Room, *Drinking*; Cavan, *Liquor License*; Palmer, *Cultures of Darkness*; Grazian, *On the Make*; Hunter, "Nightly Round"; and Sismondo, *America Walks into a Bar*.
6 Habermas, *Structural Transformation*; Calhoun, *Habermas and the Public Sphere*; Clarke, *Virtuous Vice*; Warner, *Publics and Counterpublics*.
7 For an early history, see Chauncey, *Gay New York*, 163–76.
8 See, for instance, accounts of the Compton's Cafeteria riot in Stryker, *Transgender History*, 63–66. On queer spaces, see Knopp, "Sexuality and the Spatial Dynamics"; Bell and Valentine, *Mapping Desire*; Betsky,

Queer Space; Ingram, Bouthillette, and Retter, *Queers in Space*; Valentine and Skelton, "Finding Oneself, Losing Oneself"; and referenced work by Brown-Saracino, Doan, Ghaziani, and Greene.

9   My thinking here is indebted to Jane Jacobs's analysis of the social structures of urban spaces. Jacobs, *Death and Life*. On urban social contact, see also Delany, *Times Square Red*.

10 Cartier, *Baby, You Are My Religion*, xii.

11 My thinking here is influenced by Hall, "New Ethnicities" and "Cultural Identity and Cinematic Representation"; and by Gilroy, *Black Atlantic*, 101–2.

12 My (re)thinking about media and mediation is influenced by Jue, *Wild Blue Media*; and Liu, "Queer Theory and the Specter." On communal sweat, see Sarkar, "Industrial Strength Queer."

13 Luna, "Jock Straps and Crop Tops."

14 Although I do not dwell on drugs in this book, I would be remiss not to acknowledge that marijuana, LSD, poppers (amyl nitrate), Quaaludes, cocaine, Special K, ecstasy, GHB, and crystal meth have all been favored substances in queer bars and clubs. Most of these enhance sensations, reduce inhibitions, or act as uppers.

15 Patrick Hernandez, "Born to Be Alive" (Patrick Hernandez, Columbia/CBS, 1979); Crystal Waters, "100% Pure Love" (Waters/Teddy Douglas/Thomas Davis/Jay Steinhour, Mercury, 1994); The Magnetic Fields, "You and Me and the Moon" (Stephin Merritt, Merge Records, 1995); Anita O'Day, "The Ballad of the Sad Young Men" (Fran Landesman/Tommy Wolf, Verve, 1962); Book of Love, "Boy" (Theodore Ottaviano, Sire Records, 1985); Robyn, "Dancing on My Own" (Robyn/Patrik Berger, Konichiwa, 2010); Lauren Bacall, "But Alive" (Lee Adams/Charles Strouse, 1970); *All about Eve* (dir. Joseph L. Mankiewicz, 1950).

16 Historians have identified such precursors as Paresis Hall and the Slide in downtown New York, which date back to the 1890s. T. R. Witomski, "1300 Years of Gay Bars," *Stallion,* July 1982, 48; Chauncey, *Gay New York*, 37–40.

17 Ad in *Advocate*, November 5, 1975, 16.

18 Altman, *Homosexualization of America*, 20–21, 85; Warner, "Introduction," xvi–xvii; Binnie, "Trading Places"; Gluckman and Reed, *Homo Economics*; Chasin, *Selling Out*; Sender, *Business, Not Politics*; Johnson, *Buying Gay*. For a parallel history of sex-toy stores and the development of a sex-positive feminist culture, see Comella, *Vibrator Nation*.

19 Bronski, *Pleasure Principle*, 146. See also my essay "A Suitcase Full of Vaseline, or Travels in the 1970s Gay World."

20 D'Emilio, "Capitalism and Gay Identity."

21 McGarry and Wasserman, *Becoming Visible*; Chauncey, *Gay New York*; Beemyn, *Creating a Place for Ourselves*; Mumford, *Interzones*; Vogel,

Scene of the Harlem Cabaret; Heap, *Slumming*; Ryan, *When Brooklyn Was Queer*; Kaiser, *Gay Metropolis*; Stein, *City of Sisterly and Brotherly Loves;* The History Project, *Improper Bostonians*; Boyd, *Wide Open Town*; Atkins, *Gay Seattle*; Hurewitz, *Bohemian Los Angeles;* Faderman and Timmons, *Gay L.A.*; de la Croix, *Chicago Whispers*; Howard, *Men Like That*; Van Cleve, *Land of 10,000 Loves*; Kelsey, "Cleveland Bar Scene in the Forties." On specific bars, see Branson, *Gay Bar*; Paulson and Simpson, *Evening at the Garden of Allah*; Brown, *Evening Crowd at Kirmser's*; and Perez and Palmquist, *In Exile*.

22 Chauncey, *Gay New York*, 9, 28, 305–6, 347, 348.

23 Bérubé, *Coming Out under Fire*, 113.

24 Weston, "Get Thee to a Big City." See also Bronski Beat, "Smalltown Boy" (Steve Bronski/Jimmy Somerville/Larry Steinbachek, London, 1984).

25 D'Emilio, *Sexual Politics, Sexual Communities*, 32.

26 Leonard, "Gay Bar and the Right to Hang Out," 190.

27 Chauncey, *Gay New York*, 335–51, 25.

28 Branson, *Gay Bar*.

29 Agee, "Gayola," 474.

30 Thomas Heath, "Law Banning Gay Bars Challenged in Virginia," *WP*, August 28, 1991, A6.

31 These cases were *Stoumen v. Reilly* (1951) and *Stoumen v. Munro* (1959). See Will Snyder, "Sol Stoumen," *BAR*, February 24, 1987, 16; Agee, "Gayola," 473–75; Siegel, "Right to Boogie Queerly." On the policing of gay spaces generally, see Lvovsky, *Vice Patrol*.

32 Campbell, *Queer × Design*, 26–27.

33 Cory, *Homosexual in America*, 120–21; Cory and LeRoy, *Homosexual and His Society*, 108, 120.

34 For historical accuracy, here and throughout the book I maintain the original language that gay men used to refer to other gay men, even if certain terms now appear offensive; however, I have removed dated racial terms and slurs that refer to communities of which I am not a part.

35 Robert Gregory, "The Gay Bar," *One*, February 1958, 5–8.

36 Hotel bars that drew queer clienteles included the Astor Hotel Bar in New York City, Top of the Mark in San Francisco, the Biltmore Hotel Men's Bar in Los Angeles, and the Mayflower and Statler hotels in Washington, DC. *Sweater queen* is vintage gay slang for an effeminate, class-aspirational gay man who wears fluffy sweaters; this type contrasted with butch gay men and straight trade (who have sex with men for money). On piano bars, see Miller, *Place for Us*, 28–64.

37 See Achilles, "Homosexual Bar" and "Development of the Homosexual Bar"; Hoffman, *Gay World*; Hooker, "Homosexual Community" and "Male Homosexuals and Their 'Worlds'"; Harris and Crocker, "Fish Tales";

Humphreys, "New Styles in Homosexual Manliness"; Harry, "Urbanization and the Gay Life"; Harry and DeVall, *Social Organization of Gay Males*; Lee, "Gay Connection"; Levine, *Gay Men*; Leznoff and Westely, "Homosexual Community"; Masters, *Homosexual Revolution*; Milinski and Black, "Social Organization of Homosexuality"; Read, *Other Voices*; Reiss, "Social Integration of Queers"; Reitzes and Diver, "Gay Bars as Deviant Community"; Sage, "Inside the Colossal Closet"; Stearn, *Sixth Man*; Taub and Leger, "Social Identities"; Warren, *Identity and Community*; Weightman, "Gay Bars as Private Places" and "Towards a Geography of the Gay"; Weinberg, "Male Homosexual"; Weinberg and Williams, *Male Homosexuals*; and Weltge, *Same Sex*. See also Love, *Underdogs*.

38 Meeker, *Contacts Desired*, 214.

39 See Knopp and Brown, "Travel Guides, Urban Spatial Imaginaries and LGBTQ+ Activism." Underground gay guides date from at least 1949. Hugh Hagius produced a compilation of facsimiles in *Swasarnt Nerf's Gay Guides for 1949*. See also Meeker, *Contacts Desired*.

40 "Tavern Charges Police Brutality," [Los Angeles] *County Courier*, January 19, 1967, 1 and 3; "The Case of the Black Cat Raid," *One*, April 1967, 6; Jim Highland, "Raid!," *Tangents*, January 1967, 7; John Bryan, "Monster of a Protest Set for Saturday," *Los Angeles Free Press*, February 10, 1967, 1; "Pride Demonstration," PRIDE *Newsletter*, February 1967, 1; "3,000 Swarm Strip for 4th Big Protest," *Los Angeles Free Press*, February 17, 1967, 1; Faderman and Timmons, *Gay L.A.*, 155; Goldberg, "Riot at the Black Cat." After the protests, the gay-rights group PRIDE (Personal Rights in Defense and Education) launched the *Advocate*, a local newspaper that later became the leading national gay magazine. A raid on the Patch in Los Angeles in August 1968 prompted another declaration of gay rights and flower-power protest before Stonewall. See also Kuda, "Chicago's Stonewall."

41 Armstrong and Crage, "Movements and Memory." See also D'Emilio, "Stonewall: Myth and Meaning"; Manalansan, "In the Shadows of Stonewall"; McGarry and Wasserman, *Becoming Visible*; Duberman, *Stonewall*; Stein, *Stonewall Riots*; New York Public Library/Jason Baumann, *Stonewall Reader*; and Riemer and Brown, *We Are Everywhere*.

42 Thomas Johnson, "3 Deviates Invite Exclusion by Bars," NYT, April 22, 1966, 43. See also Leonard, "Gay Bar and the Right to Hang Out." Julius's is still serving and now distributes cards about its role in gay history; it has also hosted a twenty-first-century party called Mattachine. Signaling reclamation across genders and generations, artist Ginger Brooks Takahashi re-created a line drawing of men gathered at Julius that still hangs on the bar's walls; Brooks Takahashi's revision, however, tags the image with stickers announcing presence: "an enby was here" and "a lesbian was here." The original image is signed "Lowry, 1978." Ginger Brooks Takahashi made her

first facsimile in 2000 and created the version described here, titled *Julius Bar, 1978/2022*, in 2022.

43   Charles Grutzner, "Mafia Buys Clubs for Homosexuals," NYT, November 30, 1967, 1, 50. See also Randolf Wicker, "Gay Power Challenges Syndicate Bars," *Gay*, June 21, 1971, 1, 13; Howard Blum, "The Gay Bar Business: Systems of Exploitation," VV, February 22, 1973, 1, 76, and "The Mafia & Gay Bars: A Percentage of Every Drink," VV, March 22, 1973; and Carter, *Stonewall*, 91–100, 262–66.

44   Duberman, *Stonewall*, 182.

45   Leitsch, "Stonewall Riots: The Gay View," 176–77.

46   Lanigan-Schmidt, "1969 Mother Stonewall," 106.

47   Vito Russo, quoted in Carter, *Stonewall*, 74. Angelo d'Arcangelo is dismissive of the Stonewall in his tour of West Village watering holes. D'Arcangelo, *Homosexual Handbook*, 127–40.

48   Leitsch, "Stonewall Riots: The Gay View," 177. Even though the Mattachine Society, which Leitsch represented and was addressing, was viewed as outmoded compared to the new gay militancy, Leitsch's early accounts recognize the stakes of the actions and who spurred them.

49   Leitsch, "Stonewall Riots: The Police Story," 173; Leitsch, "Stonewall Riots: The Gay View," 175.

50   A biracial butch woman, DeLaverié hosted, sang, and stage-managed the Jewel Box Revue from January 1955 until September 1969 (see chapter 2). DeLaverié is the subject of Michelle Parkerson's documentary short *Stormé: The Lady of the Jewel Box* (1991), of Parkerson's article "Beyond Chiffon," and of Elizabeth Drorbaugh's "Sliding Scales." Black trans activist Marsha P. Johnson is also often mentioned, but she said that the bar was already on fire when she arrived that night. See the Johnson and Wicker interview with Eric Marcus in New York Public Library/Jason Baumann, *Stonewall Reader*, 135.

51   Leitsch, "Gay Riots in Village," 169.

52   Carter, *Stonewall*, 11.

53   Segal, "From *And Then I Danced*," 123; Leitsch, "Gay Riots in Village," 170.

54   Leitsch, "Stonewall Riots: The Gay View," 175.

55   Di Brienza, "Stonewall Incident," 155.

56   Correspondingly, the liberation publications *Come Out!* (published by the GLF), *Gay Power*, and *Gay* began out of this foment. Numerous books likewise documented the emergent politics and cultures of gay liberation, including Teal, *Gay Militants*; Altman, *Homosexual*; Humphreys, *Out of the Closets*; and Jay and Young, *Out of the Closets* and *Lavender Culture*. See also the collected political writings in Blasius and Phelan, *We Are Everywhere*.

57 See Guy Nassberg, "Revolutionary Love: An Introduction to Gay Liberation," *Gay Flames* 11 (1971); and Kissack, "Freaking Fag Revolutionaries."

58 Miller, *Out of the Past*, 349.

59 Haden-Guest, *Last Party*, xxvii; Ralph Hall, "Gay Liberation Front," *Gay Power*, no. 5 (1969), 18; Kathy Braun, "The Dance," *Come Out!* 3 (April/May 1970): 3.

60 Crawford, *Mafia and the Gays*. I have not sought to verify the specifics of mafia involvement or to determine the mafia's reach in other cities.

61 Bell, *Dancing the Gay Lib Blues*, 40–41. See also John Francis Hunter, "The Iron Spikes," *Gay*, April 13, 1970, 16.

62 "Largest Bar Raids in N.Y. History," *Gay*, August 16, 1971, 1, 16.

63 Bell, "Black Tie and Blood," *VV*, October 12, 1982, 1, 11; Andy Humm, "Midtown Cops Go Berserk in Gay Bar," *NYN*, October 11, 1982, 1, 7; Eric Lerner, "Police Enter Blue's Again: Investigations Opened," *NYN*, October 25, 1982, 8, and "Militant Blue's Rally Draws 1,100," *NYN*, November 8, 1982, 8; Peg Byron, "Blue's in the Night," *NYN*, September 10, 1984, 9–11; Hanhardt, "Broken Windows at Blue's."

64 Carter, *Stonewall*, 252. Thank you to my anonymous reader for clarifying this chronology.

65 Harry, "Urbanization and the Gay Life"; Harry and DeVall, *Social Organization of Gay Males*, 140–43.

66 "Gay Bars," *Gay Dealer* 1 (1970): 3.

67 Leo E. Laurence, "Shit on a White Horse," *Berkeley Barb*, September 24, 1970.

68 "The Bars Are Ours," *Gay Sunshine* 1, no. 2 (October 1970): 1.

69 GLF poster, collection of ONE.

70 "Is 'Gay Lib' Hurting 'Gay Life?'" *Pittsburgh Gay News*, April 13, 1974, 4.

71 Gay Alcoholics Anonymous groups existed at least as early as 1971, as referenced in Donald Robertson, "Something for Everyone in San Diego," *QQ*, November–December 1971, 21. See also Ron Skinner and Kevin McGirr, "Gay Bars and the Use of Alcohol," *GCN*, May 11, 1974, 8, and "Alcoholism: Conflict and Alcohol," *GCN*, May 25, 1974, 8; Frank W. Scott, "Through a Glass, Darkly," *Pittsburgh Gay News*, February 1, 1975, 15; Randy Shilts, "Alcoholism," *Advocate*, February 25, 1976, 16–19, 22–25; Thomas O. Ziebold, "Alcoholism and the Gay Community," *The Blade* (Washington, DC), April 1978, 14–15; Margie Cohen, "Alcoholism in Our Community," *GCN*, February 21, 1981, 8–9 (and related stories on same spread); the special issue of *Journal of Homosexuality* on gay alcoholism, edited by Ziebold and Mongeon, especially Nardi, "Alcoholism and Homosexuality"; Weinberg, *Gay Men, Drinking, and Alcoholism*; and McKirnan and Peterson, "Alcohol and Drug Use." In 1986 the Pride Institute opened as a residential recovery center for LGBTQ+ patients.

72 Evans, "Gay Business vs. Gay Liberation," *NYN*, March 1, 1982, 10, 31; Read, *Other Voices*.

73 *Some of My Best Friends Are...* (dir. Mervyn Nelson, 1971). For a visceral account of mid-century gay binge drinking, see also Barrows, *Whores, Queers and Others*, 39–40.

74 Ad, *BAR*, April 3, 1974; Whitman-Radclyffe Foundation ad, *BAR*, May 29, 1974. One bartender fondly recalled that his patrons' sustained imbibing demonstrated admirable rigor; Abramson, *For My Brothers*, 94–95.

75 Embers (Portland) owner Steve Suss, conversation, September 16, 2012.

76 Randy Shilts, "Big Business: Gay Bars and Baths Come Out of the Bush Leagues," *Advocate*, June 2, 1976; Sage, "Inside the Colossal Closet," 17; Terry McWaters, "Gay 'Goes Public': The Super Forums," *QQ*, February 1976, 36–37. Theo Greene terms latter-day versions of this phenomenon "nightlife complexes." Greene, "'You're Dancing on My Seat!'"

77 Ads, *Advocate*, September 13, 1975, 48; and *Knight Life*, November 23, 1978, n.p. See also Tim Barrus, "Barhopping with *Stallion*: The Copa," *Stallion*, September 1985, 64.

78 On working-class bars, see Chauncey, *Gay New York*, 41; Kennedy and Davis, *Boots of Leather*; Fienberg, *Stone Butch Blues*; Kahn and Gozemba, "In and Around the Lighthouse"; Harris and Crocker, "Fish Tales"; and Cartier, *Baby, You Are My Religion*.

79 Newman, "Why I'm Not Dancing," 140.

80 Fawaz, *Queer Forms*, 203. Nonetheless, Fawaz cautions against wholesale dismissal of white gay male cultural texts. "We rail against rigid conceptions of racial, gender, and sexual identity, but then deploy the most unshakeable identitarian logics to everything we set our gaze upon.... The desire to demolish every work of queer culture that comes our way for its perceived representational failures seems to me wildly ungrateful." Fawaz, "Bros Before 'Nos,'" *Los Angeles Review of Books*, November 4, 2022, www.avidly.lareviewofbooks.org/2022/11/04/bros-before-nos/.

81 Mike Hippler, "Dancing in Jockstraps," *BAR*, May 2, 1985, 14–15. Ann Miller, for my uninitiated readers, was a star of classical Hollywood musicals.

82 Thank you to Kristen Hatch for helping me articulate this.

83 On consent, see also Mattson, *Who Needs Gay Bars?*, 52, 208.

84 See, for instance, Arthur Evans, "Gay Bars Can Liberate; They Need Not Oppress," *Advocate*, August 15, 1973, 37–38.

85 Bouthillette, "Queer and Gendered Housing." See also Wolf, *Lesbian Community*, especially 43–48. On lesbian bars, see Kennedy and Davis, *Boots of Leather*; Wolfe, "Invisible Women in Invisible Places"; Enke, *Finding the Movement*; Faderman, *Odd Girls and Twilight Lovers*; Kahn and Gozemba, "In and Around the Lighthouse"; Harris and Crocker, "Fish Tales"; Hankin, *Girls in the Back Room*; Cartier, *Baby, You Are My Religion*; Nestle,

Restricted Country; King, "Audre Lorde's Lacquered Layerings"; Morris, *Disappearing L*; Tolentino et al., "Sum of All Questions"; Bess and Lynch, *Our Happy Hours*; Gieseking, *Queer New York*; Adeyemi, *Feels Right*; and Mattson, *Who Needs Gay Bars?*, 157–200. In 1987, US lesbian bars peaked in number at 206. Mattson, *Who Needs Gay Bars?*, 161. Gieseking's book-length project titled "Dyke Bars*" is in progress. See also Kaucyila Brooke's lesbian bar–mapping project, *The Boy Mechanic*, which covers 1996 to the present, www.theboymechanic.com; and the virtual lesbian-bar–archive project the Last Butch, www.lastbutch.com.

86 There have been comparatively fewer queer Asian and Asian-American bars and parities. See Wat, *Making of a Gay Asian Community*; Manalansan, *Global Divas*; and Khubchandani, *Ishtyle*.

87 Bill Alexander, "Gay Bar Wars," *WP*, February 5, 1981, DC5; Holmes, *Chocolate to Rainbow City*, 116–17, and "Beyond the Flames," 314–18; Bost, "At the Club" and *Evidence of Being*; Beemyn, *Queer Capital*, 206, 208, and 219.

88 For thinking beyond the centrality of (white) gay bars, see Johnson, *Sweet Tea*; and Greene, "Whiteness of Queer Urban Placemaking." Churches and the house ballroom scene provide important structures within black gay communities. See McCune, "Transformation"; Allen, "For 'the Children' Dancing the Beloved Community"; Bailey, *Butch Queens Up in Pumps*; and Jackson, "Social World of Voguing."

89 Ads, *WB*, April 23, 1993, 110–14.

90 See Mattson, *Who Needs Gay Bars?*

91 Charles Reich and James Roediger, "Beneath the Bar Facades: A Look at Why We Don't 'Connect,'" *Advocate*, May 4, 1977, 37–41; Michael Musto, "Every Night Fever," *Christopher Street*, May 1978.

92 See Joseph Arsenault, "Video on the Barroom Wall," *NYN*, November 22, 1982, 24; Glenn Person, "Dancing with the Video Jockeys," *NYN*, August 15, 1983, 36; Scott P. Anderson, "Video Bars," *Advocate*, August 18, 1983, 50–52; Allen White, "Dynasty Fever Sweeping SF Gay Bars," *BAR*, November 23, 1983, 1, 14; Tracy Baim, "Making Video Tracks at Sidetrack," *Gay Life*, May 16, 1985, 9; and Cante, "Pouring on the Past."

93 This conversation responded to Michael Hobbes, "Together Alone: The Epidemic of Gay Loneliness," *Huffington Post*, March 2, 2017, https://highline.huffingtonpost.com/articles/en/gay-loneliness.

94 Bee Gees, "How Deep Is Your Love?" (Barry Gibb/Robin Gibb/Maurice Gibb, RSO, 1977).

95 June Thomas, "The Gay Bar: Part I–VI," *Slate.com*, June 27–30, 2011, https://slate.com/human-interest/the-gay-bar.

96 Lin, *Gay Bar*.

97 Mattson, *Who Needs Gay Bars?*, 9.

98 Oldenburg, *Great Good Place*, 9.

99 Putnam, *Bowling Alone*, 101–2.

100 Bar impresario Frank Caven estimated that, circa 1979, only 10 percent of gay men went to gay venues. David Bauer, "Lords of an Underground Empire," *D Magazine*, June 1, 1979, accessed online at www.dmagazine.com/publications/d-magazine/1979/june/lords-of-an-underground-empire/.

101 Mattson, *Who Needs Gay Bars?*, 4, 280, 319

102 Putnam, *Bowling Alone*, first published in 2000 and revised and updated in a 2020 edition.

103 The most visible early losses to AIDS were white gay men in the coastal gay meccas; many of them were prominent on the scene at exclusive discos or other influential venues. Attention to these white gay men skewed perceptions of the epidemic, which prompted homicidal xenophobia from conservative politicians and myopia from medical researchers, health-care providers, and white gay men themselves as they overlooked the transmission and impacts of HIV/AIDS among women and communities of color. With the belated development of more effective treatments in the mid-1990s, the disease transitioned from epidemic to endemic status, which has yielded even more stark demographic disparities for treatment access and life chances. The lives, losses, and traumas of white gay men still need to be commemorated, grieved, and processed, but we must also recognize the epidemic's wider and continuing impact on people of color in the US and on people globally. The disease was and is political as much as medical. For recent work that revisits and reframes the AIDS crisis, see Bell et al., "Interchange: HIV/AIDS and U.S. History"; and Cheng, Juhuasz, and Shahani, *AIDS and the Distribution of Crises*.

104 Mattson, *Who Needs Gay Bars?*, 25–26.

105 See Lee, "Staying In"; and Vider, *Queerness of Home*.

106 Mattson, *Who Needs Gay Bars?*, 204.

107 Mattson, *Who Needs Gay Bars?*, 5.

108 Michael Doughman, conversation with the author, February 4, 2017. See also Whittemore, "Dallas Way"; and Smart and Whittemore, "There Goes the Gayborhood?" Caven Industries, which owns Sue Ellen's and multiple other legacy venues on this strip, later participated in a high-rise development deal. Mattson, *Who Needs Gay Bars?*, 277.

109 Excellent performance studies theorizations of the queer dance floor include Bollen, "Queer Kinesthesia"; Buckland, *Impossible Dance*; Rivera-Servera, "Choreographies of Resistance"; Román, "Dance Liberation"; and Rodríguez, *Queer Latinidad*, 154–55, and *Sexual Futures, Queer Gestures*, 99–138. For a new ethnographic study, see Garcia-Mispireta, *Together, Somehow*.

110 Restrooms can feel like spaces of violation because of voyeurism in the men's room and guys crashing the women's room. Bar lavatories can also be

disgusting in their disrepair or the mess of careless customers; one 1973 ad for the Norreh Social Club in Pittsburgh even boasted of "working restrooms." Ad, *Pittsburgh Gay Times*, December 1, 1973, back cover.

111 Liza Minnelli, "Cabaret," from the film musical *Cabaret* (John Kander/Fred Ebb, Probe, 1972).

112 Dua Lipa, *Future Nostalgia* (Warner, 2020); Agnes, *Magic Still Exists* (Universal Music Sweden, 2021); Beyoncé, *Renaissance* (Parkwood, 2022).

113 Button, Rienzo, and Wald, *Private Lives, Public Conflicts*, 64; Ghaziani, *Dividends of Dissent*, 48.

114 There are now multiple digital mapping projects to pinpoint bygone venues and reveal densities of past queer spaces. Examples include the Philadelphia LGBT Mapping Project Google Map, https://thegayborhoodguru.wordpress.com/2016/08/31/the-philadelphia-lgbt-mapping-project-google-map/; Lost Gay Bars of San Francisco, www.google.com/maps/d/u/0/viewer?ll=37.75885902236967%2C-122.42642&spn=0.094288%2C0.052295&hl=en&t=h&msa=0&source=embed&ie=UTF8&mid=1AYGvzYQJgwzr3V32LiZF_2RcAzI&z=12; Queer Terrains, https://one.usc.edu/qt; and Queer Maps, https://queermaps.org.

Chapter 1. Nights in Black Leather

The chapter title references *Nights in Black Leather* (dir. Richard Abel, 1973); and Bette Midler, "My Knight in Black Leather" (Jerry Ragovoy, Atlantic, 1979).

The subheadings in this chapter reference the following: *The Wild One* (dir. László Benedek, 1953); The Shangri-Las, "Leader of the Pack" (George "Shadow" Morton, Jeff Barry, and Ellie Greenwich, Red Bird, 1964); The Rolling Stones, "Paint It Black" (Mick Jagger/Keith Richards, London, 1966); Madonna, "Vogue" (Madonna/Shep Pettibone, Sire, 1990); "Pits and Perverts" (this was the name of a 1984 benefit concert organized by Lesbians and Gays Support the Miners during the UK miners' strike, as dramatized in the film *Pride* [dir. Matthew Marchus, 2014]); and Soft Cell, "Fun City" (David Bell/Marc Almond, Some Bizarre, 1982).

The following abbreviations for periodical titles and the names of archival sites are used in the notes to this chapter: Gale (Gale Primary Sources Database: Archives of Sexuality and Gender) and LA&M (Leather Archives & Museum, Chicago).

1 Located in Burbank. Ad, *Entertainment West*, December 23, 1970, 23.

2 Playing off this tribal connotation, Geoff Mains later termed people who engage in "leathersexuality" "urban aboriginals." Mains, *Urban Aboriginals*.

3 Paul Welch, with photographs by Bill Eppridge, "Homosexuality in America," *Life*, June 26, 1964, 66–67. See also Meeker, *Contacts Desired*, 151–96; Meyer,

"At Home in Marginal Domains"; Campbell, *Bound Together*, 150–69; and the cover of *Drummer*, December 1980.

4 *Police Academy* (dir. Hugh Wilson, 1984).
5 Baldwin, "Second Coming Out," 170–71.
6 Bronski, "Dream Is a Wish," 60. Emphasis added.
7 Jon Lorrimer, "Stud City USA: A Chicago Update," *Ciao!*, November 1979, 12.
8 Rubin, *Valley of the Kings*, 106–7. See also Magister, "One among Many," 96–97.
9 Rubin, *Valley of the Kings*, 110–11.
10 Magister, *Biker Bar*, 6.
11 *The Wild One* (dir. Lásló Benedek, 1953). Reflecting on this norm, Douglas Crimp's memoir recalls a scene from the Eagle's Nest in New York: "On one summer Sunday in 1973, a customer turned up dressed in *white* leather, which would have been heresy at night, but was perhaps a fittingly camp commentary on brunch at a leather bar." Crimp, *Before Pictures*, 236.
12 Magister, *Biker Bar*, 20.
13 Carney, *Real Thing*, 37, 12.
14 Townsend, *Leatherman's Handbook*, 105–6.
15 Magister, *Biker Bar*, 26.
16 Magister, "One among Many," 96, 102.
17 Magister, "One among Many," 98.
18 Rubin, *Valley of the Kings*, 120–22.
19 Brown, *Familiar Faces, Hidden Lives*, 56–57.
20 Rubin, *Valley of the Kings*, 127.
21 Rubin, *Valley of the Kings*, 123, 127–28.
22 "DC Eagle," *Drummer* 1, no. 5 (1976): 59.
23 Preston, "What Happened?," 212–13, 217. Film scholar Juan A. Suarez makes a parallel argument in *Bike Boys, Drag Queens, and Superstars*, 158–59.
24 Rubin, *Valley of the Kings*, 104–5. In 1976 the Los Angeles police raided a bathhouse hosting a charity "slave auction" benefit for the Gay Community Services Center and arrested forty participants under an involuntary-servitude law. The arrests prompted a major protest against the LAPD, and two subsequent slave auctions were held to raise money for the arrestees' legal fees. Judy Willmore, "The Great Slave-Market Bust: A Story Only Los Angeles Could Produce," *Advocate*, May 5, 1976, 13–14. On the ways that BDSM indexes race and histories of chattel slavery, see Cruz, *Color of Kink*.
25 Rubin, *Valley of the Kings*, 104–5, 128–29.
26 George Busse interview with Chuck Renslow, June 14, 1994, transcript courtesy of the LA&M. For prehistories of Chicago gay nightlife, see Heap, *Slumming*; and de la Croix, *Chicago Whispers*. For histories of LGBTQ+ Chicago

contemporaneous with this chapter, see Baim, *Out and Proud in Chicago*, and Stewart-Winter, *Queer Clout*.

27 Spring, *Secret Historian*, 274.
28 Baim and Keehnen, *Leatherman*, 74.
29 This history is based on Baim and Keehnen, *Leatherman*, 87–90, and Busse interview with Renslow, undated. Renslow was frequently fuzzy on dates and details.
30 Baim and Keehnen, *Leatherman*, 87–90; Busse interview with Renslow.
31 Randy Shilts, "Big Business: Gay Bars and Baths Come Out of the Bush Leagues," *Advocate*, June 2, 1976, 37.
32 Police cases include "7 Gay Bars Cited in Payoffs," *Advocate*, October 10, 1973, 18; and Albert Williams, "5 Indicted for Alleged Gay Bar Shakedowns," *Gay Life*, December 15, 1983, 1, 6. The following year, four organized-crime affiliates faced charges, and one was convicted of extortion. William B. Crawford Jr., "3 Freed, 1 Found Guilty in Gay Bar Shakedown," *Chicago Tribune*, September 28, 1984, A4. For a broader history, see also Kuda, "Chicago's Stonewall," 79–83; and de la Croix, *Chicago after Stonewall*, 1–13.
33 Jack Rinella, interview with Renslow, December 29, 1994. Transcript courtesy of LA&M.
34 Quoted in Baim and Keehnen, *Leatherman*, 268.
35 Shilts, "Gay Rights in Chicago in the Year 1 AD," *Advocate*, March 22, 1978, 15.
36 Joe Parisi, "Chicago's Renslow & Co.," *Advocate*, June 2, 1976, 41. The Gold Coast locations, chronologically, were 1130 N. Clark, 1110 N. Clark, 2265 N. Lincoln, 501 N. Clark, and 5025 N. Clark. I have found conflicting dates for the move to 501 N. Clark, ranging from 1967 to 1972.
37 Robert W. Bosely, "Interview with Chuck Renslow," *Cruise*, June 1980, 18.
38 Thompson, "Introduction," xvi.
39 Renslow also began the annual White Party at his residence, the historic Dewes mansion, in 1974.
40 Gold Coast Collection in Chuck Renslow papers (unprocessed), box 10/5/96, LA&M.
41 This imagery has been excavated in much queer contemporary art. See Campbell, *Bound Together*.
42 Renslow and Orejudos closed the Kris studio after full frontal nudes became legal and the market was flooded with competition. Bill Christy, interview with Etienne (Orejudos) for National Gay Art Archives, March 1, 1983. Transcript courtesy of LA&M.
43 Orejudos later also used the name Stephen (his middle name) to signal a style distinct from his work as Etienne.

44 Christy, interview with Etienne.

45 Bill Lumen, "Real-Life Artist Draws Fantasies," *Gay Life*, October 28, 1977, 33.

46 Baim and Keehnen, *Leatherman*, 89–90.

47 Baim and Keehnen, *Leatherman*, 89, 107.

48 Tom Lehrer, "The Masochism Tango" (Tom Lehrer, Reprise, 1959); Baim and Keehnen, *Leatherman*, 122.

49 Orejudos remarked that "I don't assume either viewpoint while I'm drawing a domination/subjugation drawing; I just see it as a scene, rather like looking at a movie." Christy, interview with Etienne.

50 Rubin, *Valley of the Kings*, 143.

51 Fritscher, "Artist Chuck Arnett."

52 When the artist who created the Studz game died, his estate reclaimed the machine for probate.

53 In the 1970s some of their most popular selections included *The Rocky Horror Picture Show* (dir. Jim Sharman, 1975) and the Craig Russell drag queen comedy *Outrageous!* (dir. Richard Benner, 1977). Undated bound flyers for Sunday Movie Night, Gold Coast Collection, in Chuck Renslow papers (unprocessed), box 10/5/96, LA&M.

54 Quoted in Baim and Keehnen, *Leatherman*, 120.

55 Powell, *Coming Together*, 47.

56 Both celebrating and satirizing the code, the Pleasure Chest adult store expanded it into a playful, astonishingly specific, and impossible-to-remember taxonomy of fetishes, although the classic colors were standard references.

57 Parisi, "Chicago's Renslow & Co," 41–43.

58 See Russo, "Camp," 206.

59 On Callas and gay fandom, see Koestenbaum, *Queen's Throat*, 134–53.

60 Baim and Keehnen, *Leatherman*, 104–5.

61 Fierstein, *I Was Better Last Night*, 104. The film adaptation of Fierstein's *Torch Song Trilogy* (dir. Paul Bogart, 1988) was my first exposure to back rooms.

62 Allan Bérubé, "The History of the Baths," *Coming Up!* (San Francisco), December 1984, quoted in Donna J. Graves and Shayne E. Watson, "San Francisco," 17, www.nps.gov/subjects/tellingallamericansstories/lgbtqthemestudy.htm.

63 For an account of one such space in contemporary Chicago, see Gamboa, "Pedagogies of the Dark." I recognize the anonymized venue but maintain Gamboa's discretion here.

64 Orne, *Boystown*, 43.

65 Baim and Keehnen, *Leatherman*, 120.

66 De la Croix, *Chicago after Stonewall*, 292; Baim and Keehnen, *Leatherman*, 105; "The Gold Coast Party," *Drummer* 1, no. 9 (1976): 51.

67 Rinella, interview with Renslow.
68 Quoted in Baim and Keehnen, *Leatherman*, 112.
69 "Bartender, 7 Men Nabbed in North Side Vice Raid," *Chicago Tribune*, September 29, 1983, A8; "'Lurid' Coverage of Bar Raid Criticized," *Gay Life*, October 6, 1983, 6; William B Kelley, "Gold Coast Bar Open Pending License Appeal," *Gay Life*, February 23, 1984, 6.
70 Rubin, *Valley of the Kings*, 174.
71 Mattson, *Who Needs Gay Bars?*, 203.
72 Baim and Keehnen, *Leatherman*, 102.
73 The Bistro, as it was commonly called, was razed in 1982 for a North Loop redevelopment project. "Bistro Closing after 9 Years," *Gay Life*, May 7, 1982, 10.
74 Rick Karlin, "Rhythm of the Street: Halsted Street and Market Days," *Gay Chicago*, August 10–20, 1995.
75 Karlin, "Rhythm of the Street." The clustering of gay venues on the North Side has consistently reinforced a conflation of gayness and whiteness in the city. In the 1970s and early 1980s, multiple gay venues were protested for their discriminatory door policies or other issues, including Dugan's Bistro, the Broadway Limited, Carol's Speakeasy, Den One, Augie's, CK's, Coconuts, and Alfie's. The local gay press reported on these claims and protests at least as early as 1975, and in 1978 the Gay and Lesbian Coalition of Metropolitan Chicago formed a committee to study discrimination. The committee published a report in 1980. David Boyer papers, 94–8, box 1, Gerber/Hart Library. See also Stephen Kulieke, "Picketers Protest Alleged Discrimination at Bistro," *Gay Life*, September 12, 1980, 1, 6. (See also chapter 4.) Racial tensions escalated in Boystown decades later between affluent white home owners and queer and trans youths of color who congregated on the streets. See Blair, "Boystown," 287–303; and Orne, *Boystown*. (See also chapter 3.)
76 Rich Pier, "Good Times Lurk among the Bushes," *Gay Life*, February 18, 1977.
77 *Drummer*, December 1980, 73.
78 Baim and Keehnen, *Leatherman*, 130.
79 Chuck Renslow, letter to the editor, *Outlines*, February 11, 1988, n.p., Atlanta Lesbian Feminist Alliance Archives, accessed via Gale.
80 Baim and Keehnen, *Leatherman*, 152, 248. Visual descriptions based on photographs among Renslow papers, LA&M.
81 Baim and Keehnen, *Leatherman*, 10; Stewart-Winter, *Queer Clout*, 111.
82 Sample parties date from 1982 to 1983. Flyers in Touché vertical file, LA&M.
83 Hank Trout, "The Second City: Second to None!," *Drummer* 5, no. 38 (1980): 48.
84 "About," Onyx Midwest, accessed March 22, 2021, www.onyxmidwest.com/about-onyx-2; Touché manager David Boyer, personal communication, April 13, 2021.

Interlude 1. Triangle Lounge in Denver

1. Initial brand preference may also have been tied to the fact that Levi Strauss & Co. was based in San Francisco.
2. Artist Hal Fischer's 1977 annotated photo series *Gay Semiotics* repeatedly identifies his models' denim by brand name as Levi's rather than generically as jeans.
3. *New Way*, 1972, back cover. Collection of Stephen H. Hart Library & Research Center at the History Colorado Center.
4. Jim Rudolph, "Queen City of the Fruited Plains: A Study of the Gay Population of Denver, Colorado," unpublished paper for Anthropology 431 course, summer 1974, and "The Butch Camp: A Study of Communication in Two Gay Bars of Denver," unpublished paper for Anthropology 481 course, fall 1974, both at University of Colorado-Denver, Denver Public Library Western History and Genealogy collections. See also the hyperbolic description of men's "peacock-like" behavior in Noel, "Gay Bars and the Emergence of the Denver Homosexual Community."
5. Keith L. Moore, "Queen City of the Plains? Denver's Gay History, 1940–1975," master's thesis, University of Colorado, 2014, 103, https://lgbtqcolorado.org/programs/colorado-lgbtq-history-project/research-resources.
6. Copy of municipal code, MSS 1151: Gay Coalition of Denver Collection, carton 1, folder 10, Stephen H. Hart Library & Research Center.
7. "Dilemma in Denver," *Advocate*, March 28, 1973, 15.
8. "Dilemma in Denver"; "Gay Coalition News," *New Way*, July 1, 1973, 1; Andy Rogers, "Homosexuals Protest Criminal-Code Draft," *Denver Post*, October 24, 1973, 3.
9. Officials included William McNicols, mayor; William L. Koch, manager of safety of the city; Arthur Dill, chief of police; and Max P. Zall, city attorney. Letter to membership, undated, 1973, MSS 1151: Gay Coalition of Denver Collection, carton 1, folder 10, carton 1, folder 8, Stephen H. Hart Library & Research Center. Joan White, "Judge Rules Homosexual Act Not Lewd if Done Privately," *Denver Post*, March 23, 1973, 16; "Feature," *Rhinoceros*, December 1, 1974, 8.
10. Lee Anderson, "Denver Free," *Advocate*, November 6, 1974, 3.
11. Effectively, the agreement put an end to double standards: if an act was illegal for heterosexuals, it was illegal for homosexuals, and vice versa. MSS 1151, Gay Coalition of Denver Collection, carton 1, folder 10, Stephen H. Hart Library & Research Center.
12. "Men's Bar Scene: Denver," *Drummer* 4, no. 32 (1979): 74–75. Likely inspired by the ad or by *Drummer*, *Honcho* featured a similar erotic story set in a Denver bar where the narrator cruises masculine cowboys in tight faded jeans. Jason Pierce, "Crotch Watch," *Honcho*, October 1979, 20–22, 34.

13 Jerome Perlinksi, "Colorado: The Gay Life," *Gaysweek*, March 26, 1979, 10.
14 "Commission to Hear Progress Report on Gay Grievances," *Out Front* (Denver), November 23, 1979, 34–37. Denver Public Library.
15 Listing for Triangle Lounge in Noel, *Colorado*, 111. See also Noel's essay "Gay Bars and the Emergence of the Denver Homosexual Community."
16 Triangle, accessed March 7, 2018, https://thetriangledenver.com/about-us.

Chapter 2. Show Me Love

The chapter title references Robin S., "Show Me Love" (Allen George/Fred McFarlane, Big Beat, 1990–93).

The subheadings in this chapter reference the following: Dolly Parton, "False Eyelashes" (Parton, RCA Victor, 1968); Lou Reed, "Walk on the Wild Side" (Reed, RCA, 1972); Barbra Streisand, "People," from the musical *Funny Girl* (Jule Styne/Bob Merrill, 1964); David Bowie, "Queen Bitch" (Bowie, RCA, 1971); and Marlene Dietrich, "Falling in Love Again (Can't Help It)" (Friedrich Hollaender/Sammy Lerner, Victor, 1930).

The following abbreviations for periodical titles and the names of archival sites are used in the notes to this chapter: AHC (Atlanta History Center); BAR (*Bay Area Reporter*); Gale (Gale Primary Sources Database: Archives of Sexuality and Gender); GLAMA (Gay and Lesbian Archives of Mid-America, University of Missouri–Kansas City Libraries, Kansas City); IGIC (International Gay Information Center collection at New York Public Library); LAT (*Los Angeles Times*, Los Angeles daily newspaper); NYN (*New York Native*); and ONE (ONE National Gay & Lesbian Archives at University of Southern California Libraries, Los Angeles).

1 Both were owned by John Tuccillo and Joe Lombardo. One source insinuates mafia connections by describing Tuccillo's operations as "Italian 'family' bars." Mickey Ray, "Phoenix Rises after 45 Years: Drew Shafer and Phoenix Society for Individual Rights," in Jackson, *Changing Times*, 111.
2 There are exceptions in both directions, such as the sketch comedians Milton Berle and Benny Hill for straight audiences and celebrations of realness in the drag scene.
3 *P.S. Burn This Letter Please* (dir. Michael Seligman and Jennifer Teixeira, 2020).
4 For instance, Melinda Ryder has performed in Kansas City gay clubs for more than forty years and earned multiple titles, including Miss Midwest, Miss Kansas, Miss Missouri, and Miss Show-Me State. Bruce Winter (Melinda Ryder), conversation, May 10, 2021.
5 Newton, *My Butch Career*, 112.
6 Khubchandani, *Ishtyle*, 123.

7   On feminist critiques of gay male drag, see Tyler, "Boys Will Be Girls"; Lin, *Gay Bar*, 265.

8   Martin Padgett indicates that drag emerged in the late 1960s in Atlanta; showplaces such as Sweet Gum Head exploded in popularity from 1971 onward—after the Jewel Box Lounge moved and approximately when the Colony Bar closed. Padgett, *Night at the Sweet Gum*.

9   "Drag, which once occupied a central place in the life of gay men, has now been shunted to the side as a quaint and slightly freakish reminder of a less liberated time." Thom Willenbecher, "The Queens Are King No More," *Real Paper* (Cambridge, MA), January 14, 1978, 18. On the late-1970s ebbs and flows of gay discourse on drag, see also Mark Thompson, "The Politics of Drag," *Advocate*, June 15, 1977, 33–36; and Fierstein, *Torch Song Trilogy*, 25, first performed 1978.

10 Countering drag's popular nadir, new-wave proto-club kid drag became a movement in the 1980s, most notably at the Pyramid Cocktail Lounge and Wigstock in New York City. See, for instance, Richard Breath, "What Makes a Starbooty?," *NYN*, February 5, 1987, 29; and Mark M. Leger, "The Drag Queen in the Age of Mechanical Reproduction," *Out/Look*, Fall 1989, 28–33. For 1990s responses to a drag resurgence, see Jeffrey Essmann, "Big Wigs in the Mainstream," *Theater Week*, April 23, 1990, 19–22; Jeffrey Hillbert, "The Politics of Drag," *Advocate*, April 23, 1991, 42–47; Chermayeff, David, and Richardson, *Drag Diaries*; and Fleisher, *Drag Queens of New York*.

11 Bolze, "Female Impersonation," 420–21. Bolze found that the earliest written usage of the term *drag queen* dates from 1956.

12 These histories build upon one another and include, chronologically, Baker, *Drag* (1968) and *Drag* (1994); Willard, *Female Impersonation*; Slide, *Great Pretenders*; Garber, *Vested Interests*; Ferris, *Crossing the Stage*; Bullough and Bullough, *Cross Dressing, Sex, and Gender*; Bolze, "Female Impersonation;" Senelick, *Changing Room*; and Schacht and Underwood, "Absolutely Fabulous but Flawlessly Customary."

13 Frederick Howe, "An Exploration of the History of Female Impersonators, Part II," *Advocate*, October 5, 1977, 28. See also "Part I," *Advocate*, September 21, 1977, 26–29.

14 Rare exceptions included the proto-drag queen Bert Savoy (popular in the early 1920s, died 1923) and the unabashed pansy with a cutting wit Jean Malin (popular in the early 1930s). Eltinge would pose for portraits that emphasized his masculinity offstage. Despite his performance of masculinity *and* heterosexuality, evidence suggests that he had a series of male companions. See also Hurewitz, *Bohemian Los Angeles*, 34–38.

15 McCracken, *Real Men Don't Sing*.

16 Some cities alternatively outlawed masquerading—costumes intended to obscure a citizen's identity—a move that could similarly be weaponized against queer and trans people.

17 Sears, *Arresting Dress*, 3–6, 97–120.
18 Hurewitz, *Bohemian Los Angeles*, 147.
19 This is evident in the souvenir programs for venues such as Finocchio's, Club My-Oh-My, and the Jewel Box Lounge, as well as in journalistic profiles such as Raymond Jacobs, "The Jewel Box Revue," *Eros*, Winter 1962, 14–23.
20 Bullough and Bullough, *Cross Dressing, Sex, and Gender*, 244.
21 Newton, *Mother Camp*, 17, 14. See also Stryker on "street queens" in *Transgender History*, 60–61, 66–67.
22 County, *Man Enough to Be*, 147.
23 Jessica Dressler (Dirty Dorothy), conversation, May 12, 2021.
24 Newton, *Mother Camp*, 4–5.
25 Chauncey, *Gay New York*, 310, 314, 316–17.
26 Howe, "Exploration, Part II," 29.
27 Bolze, "Female Impersonation," 368; Jacobs, "Jewel Box Revue," 15.
28 Boyd, *Wide Open Town*, 53. See also popular press coverage, including Leah Garchik, "Finocchio's: 45 Years of Guys Dolled Up as Women," *San Francisco Chronicle Datebook* (Sunday magazine), July 12, 1981, 19; and Sam Bruchey, "Drag Club Finocchio's Set for Last Curtain Call," *LAT*, November 26, 1999, A50.
29 "Joseph Finocchio Dies; S.F. Transvestite Show," *LAT*, January 20, 1986, n.p. Grey Line figure appears in the 1982 souvenir program, collection of ONE Archives.
30 A troupe called the Gay Boy Revue was already touring by 1937, prior to the Jewel Box's road show. There is also limited evidence of an African American troupe called the Booty Greens that comprised railroad workers who performed by night in the rust belt during the 1940s–50s. Bolze, "Female Impersonation," 334–37.
31 "'Jewel Box Revue' Gets L.A. Police Greenlight on Rules Technicality," *Variety*, November 1, 1961, 69; Coleman, "Jewel Box Revue," 88.
32 Jewel Box Revue full-page ad, *Variety*, January 6, 1960, 257. The Apollo Theater in Harlem and the Town and Country Theater in Brooklyn were the revue's primary venues in the city starting in 1959. Each venue is listed in a Jewel Box Revue program, undated but circa 1960s, in the ONE Archives Programs Collection.
33 Newton, *Mother Camp*, 43.
34 Coleman, "Jewel Box Revue," 85.
35 Parkerson, "Beyond Chiffon," 375. Nonetheless, the show's residency at the Apollo Theater was picketed to "Keep homosexuals out of Harlem" starting in 1961. Kali, "Picketing Do[e]sn't Mar Apollo's OK 'Jewel Box Revue,'" *Variety*, July 12, 1961, 55.
36 Pearl Box Revue, *Call Me MISSter* (Snake Eyes, 1972).

NOTES TO CHAPTER 2

37 This practice of hustling drinks is described at length in Bolze, "Female Impersonation," and in Marlowe, *Mr. Madam*, 73–109.

38 "Minneapolis Cracks Down on Femme Impersonator Spots," *Variety*, December 14, 1949, 51; "Mpls. Censors Blow Whistle—On an Oldie," *Variety*, December 31, 1949, 32.

39 "Mpls. Lifts Ban on Switch Shows," *Variety*, February 2, 1955, 61; "Too Many Switch Artists in Town So Mpls. Judge Orders Revue Checkup," *Variety*, February 23, 1955, 51; "Mpls. Cops Padlock Switch Show after 2 Parade in 'Drag,'" *Variety*, March 2, 1955, 57, 59. See also Tyson, "Skirting Boundaries."

40 Jose., "Lads-in-Drag & 1 Mustachioed Girl, Or Limp-Wrist Time on Broadway," *Variety*, December 10, 1958, 67. *Variety* regularly abbreviated writers' names.

41 Jose., "Jewel Box Revue," *Variety*, December 9, 1959, 65; Jose., "Apollo, N.Y.," *Variety*, March 9, 1960, 67; Jose., "Apollo, N.Y.," *Variety*, January 24, 1968, 59. Bolze recounts an earlier, similar recognition of the gay audiences at Francis Renault's performances. Bolze, "Female Impersonation," 427–29.

42 Jacobs, "Jewel Box Revue," 15; Coleman, "Jewel Box Revue," 88.

43 Paulson and Simpson, *Evening at the Garden*, 1–2.

44 Boyd, *Wide Open Town*, 58.

45 An announcement for Michelle's twentieth-anniversary gala appears in the January 9, 1975, issue of the *Bay Area Reporter*. See also Allen White, "Out of the Closets and into High Heels," BAR, May 9, 1985, 14. Bar ads in *Vector* frequently reference Michelle, indicating her as a known personality on the scene by 1965.

46 Rupp and Taylor, *Drag Queens at the 801*, 190.

47 Cantwell, Hinds, and Carpenter, "Over the Rainbow," 245.

48 Stuart Hinds, "From Blackface to Max Factor: The Evolution of Female Impersonation in Kansas City." Presentation, Kansas City Museum, 2012.

49 Hinds, "From Proscenium to Inferno."

50 Hinds, "From Blackface to Max Factor"; J. J. Maloney, "Off Stage into Kitchen," *Kansas City Star*, April 7, 1974, 4A; Brian Burnes, "The Gays among Us," *Kansas City Star Magazine*, August 5, 1979, 12.

51 This conference founded the North American Conference of Homophile Organizations, NACHO (pronounced "nay-cho"). The Colony ran a full-page ad in the same issue that extended "Best Wishes for a Successful Meeting in Washington D.C." in reference to NACHO's subsequent national conference. Ad, *Phoenix* 2, no. 7 (August 1967): 11. Later, Kansas City's Phoenix Society "was selected as the home and operator of the 'Homophile Clearinghouse'" of national gay and lesbian publications. NACHO met again in Kansas City in 1969. The Phoenix Society disbanded in 1970. Jackson, *Changing Times*, 16, 23, and 25. See also D'Emilio, *Sexual Politics, Sexual Communities*, 197–99, 227–29.

52 Cantwell, Hinds, and Carpenter, "Over the Rainbow," 256.

53 Quoted in "The Phoenix Interview: Steve Ginsberg," *Phoenix*, August 1967, 5. The local daily newspaper presented a comparatively bleak exposé of the gay bar scene in 1973. See David Zeeck and Diane Stafford, "Secret Lives Merge in Gay Bars amid Aura of Fear," *Kansas City Star*, April 3, 1973, 1.

54 MS228 Chris Collins Collection and Vertical file: Bars—Jewel Box, both GLAMA.

55 Donny O'Bryan, "Remembering When," *Alternative*, May 2, 1996, 12.

56 R. S. Lindemann, "Purple Fades to Lavender," *Alternate News*, February 27, 1987, 23.

57 "Skip Arnold Wows Kansas City Audiences," *San Francisco Mattachine Newsletter*, June 1959, 6, Allan Bérubé papers, box 126, folder 19, accessed via Gale.

58 Burnes, "Gays among Us," 12.

59 See Romesburg, "Longevity and Limits."

60 Rhyne, "Racializing White Drag." In addition, drag can perform ethnicity, nationality, and diaspora; see chapter 8 and Khubchandani, *Ishtyle*.

61 Newton, *Mother Camp*, 28.

62 Newton, *Mother Camp*, 81, 124; Mr. Gerri of Hollywood, letter to Olene Crowley, January 21, 1972, MS 229 Olene Crowley Papers, GLAMA. Tom Leathers, "The Boys with the Bulges," *Town Squire*, March 1976, cover story. Photos by Marilyn Spencer.

63 Stuart Hinds, conversation with the author, May 12, 2021.

64 Ad in *L.C.E.* [League for Civil Education] *News*, January 7, 1963, 8. Wide Open Town History Project Records, box 4, folder 10, accessed via Gale.

65 "Kansas City's Top Four," *Citizen News* 4, no. 13 (1965): n.p., accessed via Gale.

66 Ephemera in the GLAMA collection.

67 Hinds, May 12, 2021. See also Arthur S. Brisbane, "Club Has Last Chance to Shine," *Kansas City Times*, March 8, 1982, B1–B2.

68 The Pink Garter claimed to feature "Leggs Diamond's famous bubble bath." Drink menu, 1970s, MS229 Olene Crowley Collection, folder 3, GLAMA.

69 Leathers, "Boys with the Bulges," 46.

70 Clipping, MS228 Chris Collins Collection, GLAMA. E. A. Torriero, "Lack of Interest Closes Lid on the Once-Popular Jewel Box," [probably *Kansas City Star*], n.d., B1. Other late coverage includes Michael Bauer, "Who's the Man behind the Female Impersonator?," *Kansas City Star*, May 20, 1980, B1–B2.

71 Newton, *Mother Camp*, 113. Bob Damron address books, 1965–74 editions, collection of ONE Archives.

72 Gene Tod, "Gay Scene in K.C.," *Phoenix* 1, no. 4 (August 1966): 5; Eric Damon, "Around Town out of Town," *Phoenix*, August 1967, 15.

73 Scharlau, "Navigating Change," 237.
74 Hinds, May 12, 2021.
75 Stuart Hinds, oral history interview with Charla Blankenship et al., May 16, 2013, audio courtesy of GLAMA.
76 Donny O'Bryan, "Remembering When," *Alternative*, May 2, 1996, 12.
77 *Mother Camp* has likewise been instrumental in queer theory, with citations in Judith Butler's *Gender Trouble* among other texts.
78 Newton, *Mother Camp*, 3.
79 Newton, *Mother Camp*, 66, 68.
80 Hinds, May 12, 2021.
81 Newton, *Mother Camp*, 106, 105, 118.
82 John McFie, "Kansas City," *Ciao!*, September 1975, 20.
83 Newton, *Mother Camp*, 59. Newton surmises that disparities of straight/gay social norms were most stark among middle-class venues but that the social mixing occurred "at the two [classed] ends of the social spectrum," 60.
84 Newton, *Mother Camp*, 59n1, 60.
85 Newton, *Mother Camp*, 115, 61, 116–19, 63–64.
86 Camp plays a key role in Newton's analysis of the drag queen milieu, and her fieldwork took place shortly after the publication of Susan Sontag's 1964 essay "Notes on 'Camp'" introduced the concept to a straighter, more mainstream audience. Despite its influence, I have never found Sontag's essay to quite get camp right. Sontag, "Notes on 'Camp.'"
87 Emphasis added. Babuscio, "Camp and the Gay Sensibility," 20.
88 Cohan, *Incongruous Entertainment*, 1. See also Sedgwick, *Epistemology of the Closet*, 156, and "Paranoid Reading and Reparative Reading," 149–50.
89 Dyer, "It's Being So Camp," 49.
90 Dango, "Camp's Distribution," 39.
91 My pantheon of camp songs includes the Angela Lansbury and Bea Arthur duet "Bosom Buddies" from the musical *Mame* (Jerry Herman, 1966), for its tête-à-tête of shade between theatrical women, and both Nancy Wilson's "The Greatest Performance of My Life" (R. E. Allen/S. Anderle, Capitol, 1971) and Charlene's "I've Never Been to Me" (Ron Miller/Kenneth Hirsch, Prodigal 1977, rereleased Motown 1982) for their overwrought qualities that make them dialectically heartbreaking and laughable. More recently, Jennifer Coolidge's performance as Tanya in *The White Lotus* (created by Mike White, HBO, 2021–22) and her own star image have solicited camp-tinged gay male fandom.
92 Bette Davis, *Miss Bette Davis* (EMI, 1976).
93 Román, *Performance in America*, 137–78.
94 *Mommie Dearest* (dir. Frank Perry, 1981). Ad for party at the Underground in New York, September 18, 1981. Ephemera collection, IGIC.

95 Harris, *Rise and Fall of Gay Culture*, 15–16. Harris's account suggests that gay men's camp eventually soured into "gay mockery" (28) and "necrophilic depredations" (32) when female stars continued to perform past their prime—for instance, with the fandom for *Whatever Happened to Baby Jane?* (dir. Robert Aldrich, 1962).

96 Dyer was not specifically discussing camp with this phrase, but I nonetheless find it a rich, concise explanation. Dyer, *Heavenly Bodies*, 155.

97 The painting was made by Darren Cathcart for the bar but was stolen during renovations in the mid-2010s.

98 Ad in *Gay Community News* (Kansas City), March 1977. Black and White Men Together established a national action fund and awarded its first monies to the Kansas City chapter "for challenging the Cabaret Disco's racist admission policy." "BWMT, a History," IA/BWMT Convention 1984 booklet. MSS 903 BWMT, box 1, folder 13, AHC.

99 Winter, May 10, 2021. An annual drag ball called Steppin' Out started in the mid-1970s beyond the club context and continued for at least four years; it drew crowds of eight hundred people and was hosted by Wanda Lust. Shifra Stein, "'Steppin' Out' Opens Doors to Other Worlds, Other Lives," *Kansas City Star*, November 9, 1978, 24.

100 Winter, May 10, 2021.

101 Hinds, May 12, 2021.

102 The Flo shows were preceded by AIDS benefit shows by the Kinsey Trollops starting in 1986. The AmFAR benefits began in April 1995. "Club Cabaret to Raise a Quarter of a Million Dollars for AmFAR AIDS Research Programs," *Alternative*, June 12, 1997, 4. The show continued at Tootsie's and then Missie B's following the closing of the Cabaret, but I have not found the end date for these benefits.

103 Mary Sanchez, "Just Call Him 'Flo,'" *Kansas City Star Magazine*, March 26, 2000, 10–15.

104 Winter, May 10, 2021.

105 She began performing as part of the live-singing ensemble Girlie Show at the lesbian Bar Natasha and then as part of the Madness Show hosted by Daisy Buckët (pronounced "bouquet") at Sidekicks. Dressler handed the reins over to drag magician Kiki Uchawi (Victor Leon) in 2020.

106 *The Wizard of Oz* (dir. Victor Fleming, 1939).

107 Dressler, May 12, 2021.

108 Katy Perry, "Last Friday Night (T.G.I.F.)" (Perry/Lukasz Gottwald/Max Martin/Bonnie McKee, Capitol, 2011).

109 J. Geils Band, "Love Stinks" (Peter Wolf/Seth Justman, EMI, 1980).

110 See Bauer, "Who's the Man behind the Female Impersonator?" I have found press coverage with alternate spellings: Kay and Kaye.

111 Dressler, May 12, 2021.

112 Judy Garland, "Over the Rainbow," from *The Wizard of Oz* (Harold Arlen/E. Y. Harburg, 1939).

113 Winter, May 10, 2021.

Interlude 2. Safe Spaces in Detroit

1 In my travels, I've learned that Yelp provides an unreliable guide to local gay bars because many reviews express complaints from people who are not part of the LGBTQ+ community; general web searches likewise present unreliable and often outdated information.

2 Brown et al., "Gay Bar as a Place."

Chapter 3. Somewhere There's a Place for Us

The chapter title references "Somewhere," from the musical *West Side Story* (Leonard Bernstein/Stephen Sondheim, 1957).

The subheadings in this chapter reference the following: ABBA, "The Winner Takes It All" (Benny Andersson/Björn Ulvaeus, Polar, 1980); Diana Ross, "Theme from *Mahogany* (Do You Know Where You're Going To)" (Michael Messer/Gerald Goffin, Motown, 1975); Elton John, "Saturday Night's Alright for Fighting" (John/Bernie Taupin, MCA, 1973); and "I'm Still Here," from the musical *Follies* (Stephen Sondheim, 1971).

The following abbreviations for periodical titles and the names of archival sites are used in the notes to this chapter: BG (*Boston Globe*, daily newspaper); GCN (*Gay Community News*); SV (*Southern Voice,*); and WB (*Washington Blade*).

1 Thom Willenbecher, "Gentrification," *Advocate*, August 7, 1980, 17. John Francis Hunter's *The Gay Insider USA* previously referenced gay gentrification in Boston in 1972 (391).

2 Allen Young, "Gentrification," *Fag Rag* 26 (1979): 14.

3 See Levine, "Gay Ghetto"; Weightman, "Gay Bars as Private Places" and "Towards a Geography"; and Bronski, *Pleasure Principle*, 183–225.

4 See Nero, "Why Are the Gay Ghettos White?"; Blair, "Boystown"; and Gieseking, *Queer New York*.

5 See Ghaziani, *There Goes the Gayborhood*; Brodyn and Ghaziani, "Performative Progressiveness"; and Doan and Higgins, "Demise of Queer Space?"

6 Schulman, *Gentrification of the Mind*.

7 Richard Florida's *The Rise of the Creative Class* was particularly influential in promoting gay contributions to innovating urban neighborhoods and economies.

8 Kennedy and Davis, *Boots of Leather*, 93.

9 For example, the Washington, DC, Eagle was razed in 1979 to build a convention center, and a second location was sold in 1985 for a proposed devel-

opment called Techworld; decades later, a number of Black gay clubs were razed to build a stadium. In Chicago, Dugan's Bistro, the first major disco in the Midwest, was razed in 1982 for redevelopment in Chicago's North Loop. In San Francisco, a number of South of Market bars were razed in the 1970s to build the Moscone Center. More recent examples include the Marquette and Backstreet in Atlanta and Circus Disco in Los Angeles. Tom Huhn, "Eagle Owner Speaks Out," *WB*, February 1, 1979, 15, 18; Lou Chibbaro Jr., "The Eagle Is ... Sold!," *WB*, August 23, 1985, 1; Greene, "Aberrations of 'Home,'" 200; "Bistro Closing after 9 Years," *Windy City Times*, May 7, 1982, 10; Lisa Henderson, "Requiem for the Marquette," *SV*, September 21, 2000, 77; Ryan Lee, "Backstreet Faces Demolition for Condo Towers," *SV*, July 8, 2005, 5.

10 Stein, *Capital City*. See also Moskowitz, *How to Kill a City*.

11 Hae, *Gentrification of Nightlife*, 65. Hae argues that in New York, discos acted as "catalysts for the gentrification of the very neighborhoods" where residents soon complained about noise, traffic, loitering, litter, and xenophobia (2). Hanhardt, *Safe Space*, 84; see also Osman, "Decade of the Neighborhood."

12 San Francisco's Castro neighborhood developed as an iconic gay mecca concurrently with the events in this chapter and similarly exposed conflicting, classed sectors of the gay community. The Castro's emergence operated in contradistinction to the Tenderloin: "The ideas of deviance and criminality that were ascribed to the deep poverty of so-called red light districts and skid rows of the city were not assumed to have a relationship to the new gay culture that was taking form." Hanhardt, *Safe Space*, 78. This phenomenon also appeared in the early 1980s in Chicago and Washington, DC, where neighborhood associations and condominium owners battled against the gay bars and nightclubs that had, in part, attracted new residents. Stephen Kulieke, "La Salle Drive Association, Carol's Speakeasy Owner to Meet Tonight," *Gay Life*, September 11, 1981, 1, 5, 19; Lou Chibarro Jr., "Neighbors Upset by Frat House Patrons," *WB*, July 23, 1982, 1, 24.

13 Berlant and Warner, "Sex in Public"; Greene, "Gay Neighborhood."

14 Bronski, *Pleasure Principle*, 211, 209.

15 Greene, "Whiteness of Urban Placemaking," 144, and "Aberrations of 'Home.'"

16 Bronski told me that this became one of Charley Shively's refrains in these debates. Zoom conversation, May 7, 2021.

17 See a photo of the building, dated 1992, in Goldin, *Other Side*, 144.

18 For a social study of the period, see Lukas, *Common Ground*.

19 See Mitzel, *Boston Sex Scandal*; and Tsang, *Age Taboo*. During this period the Boston-based Combahee River Collective also formed and authored its foundational Black feminist coalitional political treatise.

NOTES TO CHAPTER 3   343

20 Schaefer and Johnson, "Quarantined!," 432.
21 Von Hoffman, *House by House*, 9.
22 Gans, *Urban Villagers*, 329, xiv, 387.
23 Schaefer and Johnson, "Quarantined!," 434.
24 Stephen A. Trinward, "Boston's Gay Bars—A History," *Esplanade*, November 26, 1976, 14; Rose Flower, "Playland: The Friendliest Place in Town," *GCN*, February 7, 1976, 17.
25 Description based on snapshots in the Boston History Projects Playland collections.
26 Giorlandino, "Origin, Development, and Decline," 22.
27 Hunter, *Gay Insider USA*, 394. See also my article, "Suitcase Full of Vaseline."
28 Schaefer and Johnson, "Quarantined!," 440–41.
29 Schaefer and Johnson, "Quarantined!," 432.
30 Berson, *Naked Result*, 118.
31 Teaford, *Metropolitan Revolution*, 182.
32 Pattison, "Stages of Gentrification," 89.
33 The neighborhood was also home to Napoleon's, an elegant, tweedy piano bar that endured until 1997; its class connotations appear to have shielded it from complaints from neighbors; it is rarely mentioned in reporting. Chris Mahoney, "Life in the Punch Bowl," *Boston Spirit*, January 15, 2010, http://bostonspiritmagazine.com/home/2010/1/15/life-in-the-punch-bowl.html. See also Trinward, "Boston's Gay Bars," 14.
34 Trinward, "Boston's Gay Bars," 14. This account has a notably positive spin on Vara's contributions to the scene. Frank Cashman, letter to the editor, "View from the Other Side," *GCN*, January 25, 1975, 4–5.
35 Flower, "Playland," 17. Samuel R. Delany celebrates such cross-class "contact" in his critique of gentrification, *Times Square Red, Times Square Blue*.
36 Thank you to Bronski for this insight.
37 Hunter, *Gay Insider USA*, 392.
38 "Guide: Bars, Baths, Books," *Fag Rag* 4 (January 1973): 2.
39 Goldin, *Other Side*, 5.
40 *All the Beauty and the Bloodshed* (dir. Laura Poitras, 2022).
41 Bobby Bausnach, "About," The Other Side Facebook page, accessed June 10, 2022, www.facebook.com/The-Other-Side-244190555594714. See also the compilation video *The Other Side 1965–1976: We Were the People Our Parents Warned Us Against—Remix*, YouTube, posted June 28, 2014: www.youtube.com/watch?v=31OVBZ0ADA4.
42 Michael Blanding, "The Bay Village Drag Bar War," *Boston*, May 15, 2006, www.bostonmagazine.com/2006/05/15/the-bay-village-drag-bar-war.

43 "Editorial," *GCN*, April 26, 1975. For similar commentary, see also Kevin J. McGirr, "News Commentary: Amen ... Bar Hearings Concluded," *GCN*, May 31, 1975, 3; and Joe Beckman, "The Vara Bars—What Solution?" *GCN*, December 20, 1975, 3. A contemporaneous *Boston Globe* commentary offered a more scathing view of the bars and their owners' business practices. "Bars in Bay Village," *BG*, May 16, 1975, 18.

44 John Kyper, "Bar Decision Near," *GCN*, October 18, 1975, 1.

45 "Editorial," *GCN*, April 26, 1975. "Vivisected" appears in Trinward, "Boston's Gay Bars," 14.

46 Thanks to Bronski for these observations. The bar was also accessible by transit from the Arlington Green Line T stop. See also David P. Brill, "The Block: Complaints Spur Police," *GCN*, June 1, 1974, 3.

47 Tissot, *Good Neighbors*, 100–107, 201–11.

48 "Preliminary Report of Findings: A Profile of Boston's Gay & Lesbian Community," prepared for the Boston Project, office of the mayor's liaison to the gay and lesbian community, 1983. Located in Boston (General File), Canadian Lesbian and Gay Archives vertical files collection.

49 For an account of the ways in which educational migration is classed, raced, and gendered, see Bérubé, "Intellectual Desire."

50 Smith, *New Urban Frontier*.

51 Caulfield, "'Gentrification' and Desire," 161–70.

52 Castells, *City and the Grassroots*, 151.

53 Black et al., "Why Do Gay Men Live?"; Lauria and Knopp, "Toward an Analysis," 152. See also Knopp, "Sexuality and the Spatial Dynamics"; Collins, "Sexual Dissidence, Enterprise and Assimilation"; and Ruting, "Economic Transformations."

54 Freeman, *There Goes the 'Hood*, 4. See Stein's overview of criticism of this claim in *Capital City*, 72–73.

55 Zukin, "Gentrification as Market and Place," 37, and "Gentrification," 135.

56 Auger, "Politics of Revitalization," 516.

57 Hanhardt, "Broken Windows at Blue's," 50–51.

58 See Osman, *Invention of Brownstone Brooklyn*; and Freeman, *There Goes the 'Hood*.

59 Hoffman, *Army of Ex-lovers*, 118. According to Bronski, the *GCN* team frequented Playland on layout nights because it was friendly to women, whereas the *Fag Rag* group would go to the Other Side after every meeting. Bronski, personal communication, April 28, 2021.

60 "Other Side vs. Back Bay Civic Ass. [sic]," *GCN*, November 3, 1973, 1. Hearings to revoke the bars' licenses in response to claims of violence would escalate the following spring. "Bay Village Bars," *GCN*, April 6, 1974, 2.

61 Cashman initially owned the Other Side and sold it to the Vara brothers because of financial problems. "Bar Aide Questioned on Finances," *BG*, May 14, 1975, 4.

62 The Vara brothers had investments in nightclubs, real estate, hotels, and the Rocky Point Amusement Park. Altogether, they owned twenty-six bars—most of them straight—with the Kenmore Club as their most prized venue. Henry Vara filed a half-million-dollar libel suit against the BVNA president for alleging organized-crime connections in a public statement. See "Other Side vs. Back Bay Civic Ass. [sic]," *GCN*, November 3, 1973, 1; "Neighbors Seek Ouster of Gay Bars," *Advocate*, July 3, 1974, A–5; David Farrell, "Hearing on Vara Bars Set to Begin Tomorrow," *BG*, April 22, 1975, 23; Mary Thornton, "Supt. Jordan Urges Closing of Gay Bars," *BG*, May 2, 1975, 3; Thornton, "Kiley Accused of Trying to Extort Funds," *BG*, May 9, 1975, 1, 6; Shelley Murphy, "Vara Pleads Innocent in Heist," *BG*, January 27, 1980, 59.

63 Bronski, personal communication with the author, April 28, 2021.

64 "Bars in Bay Village," *BG*, May 16, 1975, 18.

65 Betsy, "Let's Change Bars and Stop Being a Side Show" (letters), *Focus*, December 1971, 6.

66 R. S. Kindleberger, "State Overturns City's Closing Order on Two Bay Village Bars," *BG*, October 17, 1975, 46.

67 Charley Shively, "Jacque's and The Other Side: Pro," *GCN*, January 18, 1975, 6.

68 David Brill, "Jacque's and The Other Side: Con," *GCN*, January 18, 1975, 7. See also the author's later commentary: David P. Brill, "Talking Points: Jacque's, The Other Side," *GCN*, April 26, 1975, 12.

69 "View from the Other Side" *GCN*, January 25, 1975, 4–5.

70 Vanessa R. Panfil examines gayborhoods as "criminogenic" spaces: areas where police target queer street and bar life for harassment and where homophobes travel to commit hate crimes. Panil, "Gayborhoods as Criminogenic Space."

71 Thornton, "Supt. Jordan Urges Closing," 3.

72 David Farrell, "Varas' Gay Bars Again under Fire," *BG*, December 22, 1974, A5.

73 Farrell, "Bay Villagers Win Fight for Probe of Problem Bars," *BG*, February 10, 1974, A5. Farrell's first column on the bars was "Bay Villagers Complain," *BG*, April 5, 1973, 27. Farrell, "Slaying Spurs Drive to Close Two Bars," *BG*, April 3, 1975, 23. This murder preceded the highly publicized stabbing death of a Harvard football player leaving a strip club in the Combat Zone in 1976; that incident effectively turned public opinion against the zoning experiment. Schaefer and Johnson, "Quarantined!," 430.

74 "Bay Village Bars Blasted," *GCN*, April 19, 1975, 3.

75 McGirr, "Hearings on Jacque's and The Other Side," *GCN*, May 10, 1975, 1.

76 Hanhardt, *Safe Space*, 115.

77 Hae, *Gentrification of Nightlife*, 111. Emphasis added.

78 "Bay Village Bars: Round Fifteen," *GCN*, May 3, 1975, 1, 7; McGirr, "Hearings on Jacque's and The Other Side"; McGirr, "Jacque's and The Other Side," *GCN*, May 24, 1975, 6; "Jacque's Bar in Bay Village Damaged by Fire," *BG*, May 4, 1975, 40; Thornton, "Kiley Accused of Trying to Extort Funds," 1, 6; McGirr, "Deputy Mayor Accused" *GCN*, May 17, 1975, 1; McGirr, "News Commentary: Amen . . . Bar Hearings Concluded," *GCN*, May 31, 1975, 3; Farrell, "The Fear of Smear," *BG*, March 11, 1976, 31; "Vara Bars Claim to Be Insolvent," *BG*, March 16, 1976, 4; Dean McLaughlin, "Varas Call on Creditors to Help Pressure ABCC," *GCN*, March 27, 1976, 1; David Rogers, "ABCC Suspends Vara Bar Licenses," *BG*, May 25, 1976, 3; Farrell, "Vara Tax Case to Be Heard Today," *BG*, May 25, 1976, 16; "Several Vara Bars on Late Tax Lists," *BG*, December 19, 1977, 3.

79 Paul Langner, "Attorney for 2 Bay Village Bars Sees Prejudice in License Case," *BG*, April 26, 1975, 25; Thornton, "Kiley Accused of Trying to Extort Funds."

80 Charles Claffley, "ABCC Lets Gay Bars Run until 2," *BG*, March 27, 1976, 28; Richard Martin, "Bars Raided, Vara, Staff Face Court," *BG*, March 29, 1976, 5; McLaughlin, "ABCC Delays Again on Bay Village Hours," *GCN*, April 3, 1976, 7; McLaughlin, "Vara, Employees Arrested in 'After Hours' Raid," *GCN*, April 10, 1976, 3; "Vara Fined for Operating after Hours," *BG*, April 27, 1976, 10; "Liquor Fine Appeal," *BG*, April 29, 1976, 5; Rogers, "ABCC Suspends Vara Bar Licenses," 3; Mike Callen, "Bar Scenario Moves Back to Licensing Board," *GCN*, May 29, 1976, 6; "Close Call for Bay Village Bars," *GCN*, June 5, 1976, 1; "Two Bay Village Bars Ordered by Court to Stay Closed 60 Days," *BG*, July 22, 1976, 3; McGirr, "Bars Ordered Out," *GCN*, August 2, 1975, 1; McLaughlin, "ABCC Delays Again on Bay Village Hours," *GCN*, April 3, 1976, 7.

81 Joe Beckman, "Battle of the Bars Goes On," *GCN*, November 1, 1975, 1. See also "ABCC Rejects Cashman Bar Bid," *GCN*, January 31, 1976, 1.

82 Doan, *Planning and LGBT Communities*, 19.

83 See Ghaziani, "Cultural Archipelagos"; Greene, "Queer Cultural Archipelagos Are New"; Doan, "Cultural Archipelagos or Planetary Systems"; Brown-Saracino, "Aligning Our Maps"; Carrillo, "Cultural Archipelagos and Immigrants' Experiences"; and Gieseking, *Queer New York*.

84 Joe Beckman, "The Vara Bars—What Solution?," *GCN*, December 20, 1975, 3.

85 Rubin, "Thinking Sex."

86 Schulman, *Gentrification of the Mind*.

87 Tom Hurley, "The Evolution of Sporters," *GCN*, December 17, 1977, 12. Importantly, Sporters was accessible by transit and on a major street with proximate parking lots, in contrast to the tight streets where Jacque's was situated.

88 Brill, "Boston," *Advocate*, February 25, 1976, 27.

89 Hurley, "Evolution of Sporters," 8.

90 Hunter, *Gay Insider USA*, 395.

91 Bronski, "Boston: Sporters," *Stallion*, June 1985, 46–49. See also Bronski, "20 Years of Dwindling Gay Male Sex in Boston," *GCN*, June 10, 1990, 21. Sporters also figures in Reid, *Best Little Boy in the World*.

92 Betsy, "Let's Change Bars and Stop Being a Side Show," 6. A. Finn Enke documents a similar misogynist tactic at the Townhouse in St. Paul, where women staged a sit-in on the dance floor in protest. Enke, *Finding the Movement*, 47.

93 Peter Tenney, "Fort Hill Faggots, in Drag, Invade Sporters," *GCN*, August 21, 1976; Neil Miller, "Fort Hill Faggots Picket at Sporters," *GCN*, September 4, 1976, 3.

94 "Sylvia Sidney Claims Firing," *GCN*, May 4, 1974, 1; The History Project, *Improper Bostonians*, 172.

95 Farrell, "Vara, Like Lola, Seems to Get What He Wants," *BG*, June 13, 1976, A5.

96 *GCN* reported that "residents complained about a dramatic increase in noise, litter, male and female prostitution, auto traffic, vandalism, and general harassment since the establishment re-opened. One resident described finding human feces on his front stairs one morning, while one woman, eight months pregnant, told of how she was awakened one night by a man standing in her bedroom who threatened to shoot her if she did not hand over her jewelry.... One of the most serious incidents occurred early in the morning of July 8, when a 28-year-old Charlestown man was arrested for assaulting a police officer with intent to murder, assault with a dangerous weapon, and unlawful possession of a firearm." "Boston Neighborhood Battles against Bay Village Bar," *GCN*, July 22, 1978, 8.

97 See Laura Briggs, "Drag Bar under Attack," *GCN*, March 4, 1990, 6; Susanna Baird, "Jacque's Keeps License," *Bay Windows* (Boston), March 6, 2003; and Michael Blanding, "The Bay Village Drag Bar War," *Boston*, May 15, 2006, www.bostonmagazine.com/2006/05/15/the-bay-village-drag-bar-war.

98 Larry Goldsmith, "Bay Village Residents Halt Jacque's Dancers," *GCN*, November 3, 1984, 3.

99 "Boston Neighborhood Battles against Bay Village Bar," 8; Goldsmith, "Request for Bar License Draws Strong Opposition," *GCN*, September 19, 1981, 1, and "Bay Village Residents Halt Jacque's Dancers," *GCN*, November 3, 1984, 3; Susan Hutchinson, "Jacque's Shocks," *Boston Ledger*, October 14, 1984, n.p.

100 Shelley Murphy, "Vara 'Getting Out of Booze Business,'" *Boston Herald*, February 2, 1989, 24.

101 Peter Gelzinis, "In Hub, It Takes a Village to Stop Cabaret's Owner," *Boston Herald*, July 2, 2010, www.bostonherald.com/2010/07/02/in-hub-it-takes-a

-village-to-stop-cabarets-owner. Russ Lopez affirms the venue's transition to a destination for bachelorette parties in *The Hub of the Gay Universe*, 260, 303.

102 Briggs, "Drag Bar under Attack," 6.
103 Donna Turley, "Black/White Men Release Boston Bar Study," GCN, October 20, 1984, 3. The Boston gay bars flagged for racist practices included Buddies, Campus, Chaps, the Loft, and 1270.
104 Quoted in Blanding, "Bay Village Drag Bar War."
105 Kevin Cullen, "Cocoanut Grove Plaque Shoved Down the Street," BG, July 9, 2016, www.bostonglobe.com/news/nation/2016/07/09/cocoanut-grove-tragedy-pushed-aside-name-privacy/DEKsnSwRUDK3fF5YvPWHJK/story.html.

Interlude 3. Seattle Counseling Service

1 The SCS originated in 1969 as a program of the Dorian Society gay-rights organization; by 1970, it would become independent but was affiliated with the University of Washington. Atkins, *Gay Seattle*, 120–21, 158–61. For a study of the regulation of Seattle's gay bars between Prohibition and the early 1970s, see Brown and Knopp. "Sex, Drink, and State Anxieties."
2 The Golden Horseshoe and the 611 (as well as the 614) opened in the area contemporaneously with the 1962 World's Fair. Atkins, *Gay Seattle*, 81–84.
3 Seattle Counseling Service's gay bar survey materials are held in the Charna Klein papers, box 4, folders 1–3, University of Washington Libraries Special Collections. Accessed by permission of Charna Klein.
4 Kenneth E. Read initiated a fascinating ethnographic study of the gay Columbus Tavern in Pioneer Square two years after the SCS survey. The Columbus was frequented by a mix of outsiders who felt themselves displaced by change in the area and who looked upon more "respectable" middle-class gay bars with disdain as attracting "sissies" or "phonies." Many of the regulars Read befriended wore makeup and female clothing to the bar but did not identify as women or as transgender in their daytime or domestic lives; most of the regulars had feminine nicknames. Read remarks that gay men who frequented "more decorous" bars were often "appalled" that he was studying the Columbus. Read, *Other Voices*, 15.
5 Most responded 0–5, although one person said 40, perhaps to fuck with the surveyor.
6 Most reported between 0 and 2; the highest number was 16.
7 Ad for the Body Shop, *Out Post*, February 7, 1996, 18.
8 Atkins, *Gay Seattle*, 189.
9 Mattson, *Who Needs Gay Bars?*, 46.

Chapter 4. Midtown Goddam

The chapter title references Nina Simone, "Mississippi Goddam" (Simone, Philips, 1964).

The subheadings in this chapter reference the following: Mary J. Blige, "Family Affair" (Blige/Andre Young/Bruce Miller/Camara Kambon/Michael A. Elizondo, MCA, 2001); Queen Latifah, "U.N.I.T.Y." (Latifah/Kier "Kay Gee" Gist, Motown, 1993); Thelma Houston, "Don't Leave Me This Way" (Kenneth Gamble/Leon Huff/Cary Gilbert, Motown, 1976); and Janet Jackson, "Alright" (James Harris/Jackson/Terry Lewis, A&M, 1989).

The following abbreviations for periodical titles and the names of archival sites are used in the notes to this chapter: AHC (Atlanta History Center); BAR (*Bay Area Reporter*); Gale (Gale Primary Sources Database: Archives of Sexuality and Gender); GCN (*Gay Community News*); GSU (Georgia State University Libraries Special Collections, Atlanta); KRL (Kiplinger Research Library at DC History Center, Washington, DC); LAT (*Los Angeles Times*, Los Angeles daily newspaper); LF (Lorraine Fontana papers, Q110, at GSU); NYN (*New York Native*); SFS (*San Francisco Sentinel*); SV (*Southern Voice*); VV (*Village Voice*, New York City downtown alternative weekly newspaper); and WP (*Washington Post*, Washington, DC, daily newspaper).

1 Thom Beame, "From a Black Perspective: Racism," *Advocate*, April 1, 1982, 23–25. Previous *Advocate* coverage of this issue includes "Bar Controversies Lead to New Group," August 28, 1974, 5; John Victor Soares, "Black and Gay: Problems and Possibilities," November 17, 1976, 13; David Aiken, "Discrimination Exists in the Gay Community," March 23, 1977, 7–8 (Aiken was a founding member of GLF and GAA in Washington, DC); Lenny Giteck, "Gays from Other Ghettos," April 19, 1979, 12–13, 15; Louie Crew, "Coalitions and Admonitions," April 19, 1979, 13, 21; Scott Anderson, "Discrimination," February 19, 1981, 14–16; and Matthew Daniels, "Breaking the Color Barrier," November 26, 1981, 17–20. See also Frank Raffa, "Discrimination: The Gay Way," *Radical Queen* 4 (1974): 15–17; Jon Clayborne, "Barred at the Bars," *New Gay Life*, June 1977, 17–18, 23–24, and "Poll Tax Mentality in a Gay Bar," GCN, July 30, 1977, 8–11; and Stanley Crouch, "Gay Pride, Gay Prejudice," VV, April 27, 1982, 1, 13–19. For an early critique of homophobia within leftist Black and Latinx movements, see Third World Gay Revolution, "Oppressed Shall Not Become."

2 This chapter aims to expand our understanding of the complex histories of what Jacqueline Dowd Hall has termed "the long civil rights movement." Hall, "Long Civil Rights Movement." I have found extensive documentation of activism to expose and address racism at white gay bars, including in the organizational papers for multiple Black and White Men Together chapters in respective local archives in Atlanta, Washington, Philadelphia, and elsewhere. Conversely, I have encountered comparatively little archival material pertaining to Black gay bars and clubs.

3   Racialized dress codes include prohibiting sneakers, jerseys, logo apparel, hats and caps, and/or do-rags; sexist dress codes include banning open-toed shoes and/or high heels.
4   In some cases, inclusion in listings is contingent on whether the bar pays for advertising in the publication.
5   See Baldwin, "White Man's Guilt"; Bérubé, "How Gay Stays White"; and Dyer, "White" and *White*.
6   Quoted in DeMarco, "Gay Racism."
7   For critiques of "community," see Joseph, *Against the Romance of Community*.
8   Ghaziani, *Dividends of Dissent*.
9   Despite foundational work by women-of-color feminists, intersectionality was not yet an articulated concept or a prevalent strategy. White lesbian bars likewise discriminated against women of color and transgender patrons.
10 See, for instance, Vaid, *Virtual Equality*, especially 274–306. In addition to the references cited below, see Harris, "'Where We Could Be Ourselves.'"
11 Washington, DC, offers precursors and parallels to this chapter's history. The DC Gay Liberation Front protested the gay dance clubs the Plus One and the Lost and Found for discrimination in 1971. In November 1973 the DC city council passed the Title 34 Human Rights Ordinance, forbidding discrimination on the basis of sex, race, or sexual orientation in areas of employment, housing, lending, and service at bars and restaurants. Subsequent protests of the Lost and Found and other venues accordingly shifted from grassroots boycotts to pressing for bureaucratic enforcement of local regulations. These remedies proved inefficient and insufficient. The Lost and Found would repeatedly be the site of discrimination complaints throughout the decade, in 1973–1974, 1976, and 1979, as extensively reported in the *Advocate* and the *Washington Blade* at the time. Kwame Holmes and Darius Bost offer important recovery work documenting the histories of Washington's Black gay social clubs, which had provided thriving spaces for men since mid-century. See Bost, *Evidence of Being*, 5, and "At the Club"; and Holmes, *Chocolate to Rainbow City*, 116–17, and "Beyond the Flames," 314–18. See also Beemyn, *Queer Capital*, 206, 208, 219.
12 When I visited, I was told that it was Coca-Cola that effectively pushed the city to desegregate for the sake of liberal corporate optics.
13 Stone, *Regime Politics*; Bayor, *Race and the Shaping*; Kruse, *White Flight*. See also Rutheiser, *Imagineering Atlanta*; and Brown-Nagin, *Courage to Dissent*.
14 Keating, *Atlanta*, 38–39, 42–44, 62.

NOTES TO CHAPTER 4   351

15 "Atlanta Chapter Completes Bar Study," NA/BWMT Newsletter, Fall 1991, 6. Rainbow History Project MS 0764, Series VII, BWMT, box 6, folder 111, KRL.

16 Reverend Duncan Teague, Zoom conversation, June 10, 2021.

17 Padgett, *Night at the Sweet Gum*, 215, 30–31. Oleen's in Charlotte, NC, advertised itself as the "Oldest Show Bar in the South." Ad, *Cruise*, April 1978, 29.

18 Dave Bryant, "Sexism in the Gay Bars," *Great Speckled Bird*, June 26, 1972, 14.

19 In the following paragraph, the reporter describes Powell's "pink Izod shirt" and remarks that in his piano bar, "there's a photo of him hobnobbing with the late comedian Paul Lynde ('a dear man') and another of him dressed to the nines as actress Bette Davis ('I look pretty good, huh?')." Jim Auchmutey, "Gays Find City an Oasis, Exert Subtle Impact" (part five in series "The Shaping of Atlanta"), *Atlanta Journal-Constitution*, August 13, 1987, clipping. Gay History Thing MSS 773, box 37, folder 13, AHC.

20 Bryant, "Sexism in the Gay Bars," 14.

21 Gay businesses also clustered in and around Ansley Mall, Cheshire Bridge Road, and Little Five Points; nearby Virginia Highland became a popular gay residential neighborhood. The drag club Illusions was the first to have its marquee and entrance face Peachtree in 1982. Ken Bond, "Southern Exposure: Atlanta and Its Blossoming Gay Community," *Advocate*, December 9, 1982, 17. Local activists responded that this profile of the city featured neither images of men of color nor attention to their experiences. For parallel histories of white gay gentrification in New Orleans and Chicago, see Nero, "Why Are the Gay Ghettos White?," and Blair, "Boystown."

22 *The Birds* (dir. Alfred Hitchcock, 1963). Diamond Lil Oral History, conducted by Dave Hayward, January 2011. Touching Up Our Roots collection, GSU.

23 "Backstreet: An Oral History of Atlanta's Most Fabled 24-Hour Nightclub," *Eminetra*, October 9, 2020, https://eminetra.com/backstreet-an-oral-history-of-atlantas-most-fabled-24-hour-nightclub-atlanta-georgia/122537; Gregg Dougherty, oral history interview, May 1, 2018, for the Georgia State University Gender and Sexuality Oral History Project, www.youtube.com/watch?v=ZZgG7RDv8_Y.

24 Howard, "Library, the Park, and the Pervert," 108.

25 Jacobs, *Death and Life*; Midtown Neighborhood Association, Inc., "Midtown Land Use Policy Plan," Atlanta, August 1980, Lesbian and Gay History Thing collection, box 46, folder 5 (GAMA), AHC; John Carter, "Midtown Gays Charge Bias in Zoning Cases," *Intown Extra*, October 2, 1980, 4D, Lesbian and Gay History Thing collection, box 36, folder 2, AHC. See also David Goldman, "Can Midtown Stay Gay?," *SV*, April 16, 1998, 1, 19, and "Can Midtown Stay Gay?," *SV*, April 23, 1998, 21. For an excellent academic analysis of this history, see Doan and Higgins, "Demise of Queer Space?"

26 Padgett, *Night at the Sweet Gum*, 211–48; Worthy, quoted in Sears, *Rebels, Rubyfruit, and Rhinestones*, 297. Anita Bryant's 1977 "Save Our Children" campaign became a national cause for gay activists to protest, but it was particularly impactful in mobilizing gays and lesbians in the major southern cities.

27 GAMA appears to have disbanded in 1982; NCBG appears not to have been involved.

28 D. Teague and C. Jones, "The Lack of Organization among Black Gays in Atlanta," *Journal of AID Atlanta*, May 1986, 3. BWMT, box 3, folder 12, AHC.

29 Beame, "Interview: BWMT Founder—Mike Smith," 187–95. Smith published the first national directory to Black gay venues as *Colorful People and Places* and edited the semi-erotic anthology *Black Men/White Men*, which importantly publicized writings by gay men of color but problematically featured nude images of Black men but none of white men. Smith moved from the Bay Area to Atlanta shortly before his AIDS-related death in 1989.

30 BWMT/NY, "Open Letter to Mike Smith," September 29, 1980, signed by ten steering committee members. BWMT/NY vertical file, Canadian Lesbian and Gay Archives.

31 Mumford, *Not Straight, Not White*, 175; Bost, *Evidence of Being*, 111. See also Mumford, *Interzones*, xi.

32 Notably, the most diverse and successfully integrated venue in Atlanta—for both staff and patrons—was the full-nude male strip club Swinging Richard's; the eroticization of racial performance appears to have been a driving force in its popularity. As Adam Isaiah Green has argued, men of color are differentially eroticized and rejected not purely along racial and ethnic lines but often *also* according to different "tiers of desirability organized around specific physical and affective characteristics." Thus, although racism—including racial fetishism that *increases* desirability—undeniably pervades gay male culture, it does so according to logics of beauty, body type, masculinity, and class, as well as other factors that intersect with race and ethnicity in ways that produce "a racialized currency of erotic capital that stratifies particular *kinds* of black men." Green, "Social Organization of Desire," 35.

33 Joseph Beam, "Caring for Each Other," *Black/Out*, Summer 1986, 9; Han, *Racial Erotics*.

34 See Marlon Riggs's first-person documentary *Tongues Untied* (1989). Jafari S. Allen grapples with the seeming contradictions of Black gay leaders at this time who advocated Black love yet dated white men. Allen, *There's a Disco Ball*, especially 97–102.

35 L. Lloyd Jordan, "Black Gay vs. Gay Black," *BLK*, June 1990, 29.

36 Teague, June 10, 2021.

37 The Boston bar study is referenced in Donna Turley, "Black/White Men Release Boston Bar Study," *GCN*, October 20, 1984, 3. See also interlude 4.

38 Jim Marks, "Black and White Men Together: Fighting Racism and the Forces of Separatism," *Advocate*, September 16, 1986, 30.

39 Padgett, *Night at the Sweet Gum*, 305. Even with the generous research support of public librarians in Atlanta/Fulton County, I have been unable to determine an accurate genealogy of local Black gay bars during this period.

40 "We Have a Dream," BWMT/A newsletter, December 1982, 1. BWMT, box 1, folder 2, AHC.

41 Eric S. Caplan, letter to editor, dated August 5, 1982, BWMT/A newsletter, September 1982. BWMT, box 1, folder 2, AHC.

42 "Fighting Bar Discrimination in Atlanta," IABWMT Convention booklet, 1984, 17. Lorraine Fontana papers (hereafter LF), box 18, folder 14, GSU.

43 "Can We Dance at the Armory?," BWMT/A newsletter, December 1982, 1–2. BWMT, box 1, folder 2, AHC.

44 Press release: August 10, 1982. Reprint of article from *Metropolitan Gazette* 3, no. 34 (1982): "BWMT Confers with the Armory on Racism." Continued coverage of the Armory appears in October and December 1982 BWMT/A newsletters. BWMT, box 1, folder 2, AHC.

45 "Fighting Bar Discrimination in Atlanta," IABWMT convention booklet, 1984, 17. LF, box 18, folder 14, GSU.

46 Teague told me he had "a lot of good times" at the Armory, although his favorite bar was the majority-Black In-Between, located between Backstreet and Bulldogs on Peachtree. Teague, June 10, 2021. For a different history of the Armory, see Bennett and West, "United We Stand."

47 *Atalanta*, December 1983, 12, ALFA, box 6, folder 11; and *Atalanta*, April 1984, 11, ALFA, box 6, folder 12, both Duke University Library, accessed via Gale.

48 Minority-access questionnaire for bar owners/managers, Lesbian/Gay Rights Chapter of the ACLU of Georgia, November 1981. LF, box 18, folder 14, GSU.

49 Memo from T. to Smokey, November 17, 1981. LF, box 18, folder 14, GSU.

50 Draft 1, unaddressed and unsigned memo, November 23, 1981. LF, box 18, folder 14, GSU.

51 Draft 2, unaddressed and unsigned memo, November 23, 1981. LF, box 18, folder 14, GSU.

52 Minority-access questionnaire for bar owners/managers, FLGO, September 1982. LF, box 18, folder 14, GSU.

53 "IABWMT Position Paper on Bar Discrimination," in Mallon, *Resisting Racism*, 58.

54 Community survey, FLGO, September 1982. LF, box 18, folder 14, GSU.

55 Letter from Lorraine Fontana to Sisters, undated (1984). LF, box 18, folder 14, GSU.
56 Copy of poster in BWMT, box 1, folder 13. Ellipses appear on poster.
57 Report of the Employment Discrimination Project, BWMT/SF, February 1983, 1. LF, box 18, folder 14, GSU. Cleve Jones, "Gay Bars Encourage Institutional Racism," *California Voice*, March 25, 1983, clipping. However, the local press raised questions about the validity of the data and analysis. Allen White, "Gay Racism Charged," *BAR*, March 25, 1982, 9; George Mendenhall, "Do Gay Bar Owners Discriminate?," *BAR*, March 10, 1983, 5; Dan Boren, "BWMT Discrimination Report Is Dubbed 'Naïve,'" *SFS*, March 17, 1983, 1.
58 Dion B. Sanders, "BWMT Mounts Nationwide Assault on Gay Racism," *BAR*, November 17, 1983, 14.
59 News release: International Association of BWMT, August 24, 1983. National Gay and Lesbian Task Force records, collection 7301, box 164, folder 64, Human Sexuality Archives, Cornell University.
60 Also in fall 1983, discrimination at New York gay and lesbian venues likewise received significant publicity and redress. David France, "Reports of Discrimination Persisting," *NYN*, October 10, 1983, 9–12; "Union Club Said to Apologize," *NYN*, October 24, 1983, 6; David France, "Union Club Signs Agreement with BWMT," *NYN*, October 24, 1983, 11–12.
61 The ALFA newsletter credits attorney Judd Hernon, who was a member of both the ACLU and BWMT, with coordinating the effort to get the antidiscrimination ordinances through the city council. *Atalanta*, December 1983, 12, ALFA, box 6, folder 11; and *Atalanta*, April 1984, 11, ALFA, box 6, folder 12, both Duke University Library, accessed via Gale.
62 Contemporaneously, Atlanta-based Michael Bowers became a test case to challenge the Georgia state sodomy law after an arrest in 1982; the US Supreme Court would uphold the sodomy law in 1986 and not reverse its decision until 2003. Bowers v. Hardwick, 478 U.S. 186 (1986); Lawrence v. Texas, 539 U.S. 558 (2003).
63 Fleischmann and Hardman, "Hitting below the Bible Belt," 422.
64 "An Ordinance." LF, box 18, folder 14, GSU. "Discrimination Ordinance Introduced in City Council," *Cruise News*, September 30–October 6, 1983, 1; "Atlanta City Council Members Unanimously Pass Ordinances," *Cruise News*, November 25–December 1, 1983, 1; *ALFA Newsletter* 7, no. 4 (1984): 11. ALFA, box 6, folder 12, Duke University Library, accessed via Gale.
65 "Fighting Bar Discrimination in Atlanta," IA/BWMT 1984 convention booklet, 17. LF, box 18, folder 14, GSU.
66 Proposal for an Atlanta DRS, undated, 1983. LF, box 18, folder 14; BWMT, box 2, folder 6, GSU.

67. Minutes, AADP meeting, January 15, 1984. LF, box 18, folder 14, GSU; discrimination report form, AADP. LF, box 18, folder 14, GSU. According to meeting minutes for ALFA, Lorraine Fontana reported that the antidiscrimination committee was "stalled" by April 1984. ALFA meeting minutes, April 1, 1984. ALFA, box 7, folder 13, Duke University Library, accessed via Gale.
68. Spade, *Normal Life*, 29, 86, 90–91. See also Adler, *Gay Priori*.
69. Andrea L. Berry, "Fighting against Gay Racism," *SV*, February 17, 1994, 6, 16.
70. In 1984 the International Association would produce *Resisting Racism: An Action Guide*, edited by Gerald L. Mallon, as well as the IABWMT "Position Paper on Bar Discrimination" and the IABWMT education committee's report "Racial Discrimination in the Gay Community: An Analysis" (the latter two included in the former, as well as available separately).
71. Kevin Orr, "Being Different but Staying Together," *Body Politic*, November 1984, 20–21.
72. Teague, June 19, 2021.
73. Charles Michael Smith, "Discrimination and Its Discontents," *NYN*, September 26, 1983, 17.
74. See Ellingson and Schroeder, "Race and the Construction"; and Greene, "Aberrations of 'Home.'"
75. Lorde, *Sister Outsider*, 110–14; Cohen, "Punks, Bulldaggers, and Welfare Queens."
76. "Atlanta Chapter Completes Bar Study," 6.
77. Playing off the nonidentitarian term *men who have sex with men*, one club in Atlanta has marketed to "men who dance with men." Ad for the Wonderland party at the Velvet Room; the ad also includes the phrase "women who dance with women." *Clikque*, March 2001, n.p. Issues of *Friends*, *Venus*, and *Clikque* in African American Lesbian and Gay Print Culture Collection, AARL 98–008, Auburn Avenue Research Library on African-American Culture and History.
78. Young Hughley, Zoom conversation with the author, June 28, 2022.
79. The two most enduring were the middle-class Nob Hill in Columbia Heights, which became the oldest gay bar in the city before it closed in 2004, and the Clubhouse, which opened in 1975. Bost has concurred that "for many black gay Washingtonians, racial discrimination in white gay-owned establishments was not an issue, because the majority of black gay social life existed outside these clubs and bars." Bost, "At the Club."
80. Bill Alexander, "Gay Bar Wars," *WP*, February 5, 1981, DC5.

81 Where bars play a more prominent role, they are narrated as part of life during military service or incidentally as the venues for drag shows. Johnson, *Sweet Tea*.

82 Washington, "Fall Down on Me," 85–86.

83 The first year's festivities occurred amid renewed attention to bias at white gay venues. See the series of articles "Racism under the Rainbow" in *Venus*: Charlene Cothran, June 1995, 12–13; Douglas E. Jones, July 1995, 12–13; and Beryl Jackson, August/September 1995, 15–17.

84 Laura Brown, "Race Relations in Gay Atlanta," *SV*, January 14, 1999, 1. See also Brown, "Race Relations in Gay Atlanta, Part 2: Where Can We Go from Here," *SV*, January 21, 1999, 5, 26.

85 Ryan Lee and Dyana Bagby, "Gay Atlanta in Black and White," *SV*, March 24, 2006, 1, 11.

86 Washington, "Fall Down on Me," 86.

87 Hughley told me that the Marquette's social diversity contrasted with white gay bars, such as the Piccolo piano bar and the long-running Mrs. P's, that segmented the gay scene into types and that, selectively, admitted some Black gay men. Dots, a straight Black neighborhood bar, also permitted congregations of gay men but was not a gay bar per se and necessitated a bit more discretion. Hughley, June 28, 2022.

88 Freddie Styles, personal communication, July 18, 2022.

89 KC Wildmoon, "Bar Closings Spark Racism Charges," *SV*, May 5, 1994, 11, 3.

90 Charles Stephens, Zoom conversation, June 17, 2022.

91 Teague, June 10, 2021.

92 Jerry Boles, "Around Atlanta," *Clikque*, May–June 2001, 58–59.

93 Sidney Brinkley, "Atlanta," *Blacklight*, July–August 1981, 8.

94 *BLK*, February 1989, 24; April 1989, 26; June 1989, n.p.; Green, "Into the Darkness," 252–54, 284–86.

95 Black lesbian Jewel Thais Williams opened what may have been the most cherished black queer club in the country, Jewel's Catch One, in Los Angeles in 1973; it served as a community anchor until it closed in 2015. See Green, "Into the Darkness," 255–79. The venue and its owner have been the subject of numerous profiles, including the documentary *Jewel's Catch One* (dir. C. Fitz, 2016); Ayofemi Stowe Folayan, "The Many Faces of Jewel," *BLK*, November 1989; Tre'vell Anderson, "Jewel's Catch One Disco's Demise Marks Era's End for L.A.'s Gay Blacks," *LAT*, March 16, 2015, www.latimes.com/entertainment/great-reads/la-et-c1-black-gay-clubs-20150316-story.html; Gwynedd Stuart, "Remembering Legendary L.A. Gay Bar Jewel's Catch One," *Los Angeles*, April 27, 2018, www.lamag.com/culturefiles/jewels-catch-one; and August Brown, "The Story of L.A. Club Jewel's Catch One and Its Pioneering Owner Finds Its Way to Netflix," *LAT*, May 2, 2018, www

96 Lisa Henderson, "Requiem for the Marquette," *SV*, September 21, 2000, 77. The Marquette closed and reopened soon thereafter in a new location. Henderson, "Findin' the Kids," *SV*, December 14, 2000, 70.

97 "The 411," *Venus*, January 1995. The white-owned Other Side, which hosted a popular hip-hop Wednesday night, likewise attracted a 50–50 gender-mixed crowd; other nights it was primarily white and lesbian. In an excellent early 2000s participant-observer study of a lesbian-owned gay male bar in Atlanta, the authors observed that racial diversity typically increased on lesbian nights, whereas the bar was otherwise predominantly white and male. Johnson and Samdahl, "Night *They* Took Over," 339–40.

98 Instagram post, July 9, 2021, www.instagram.com/p/CRIMB4fjrv3. Full disclosure: I have never been to the Marquette.

99 Allen, *There's a Disco Ball*.

100 Gay A.F., https://gayatlflashback.com/fosters.

101 Teague, June 10, 2021.

102 *SoVo Guide to Atlanta*, 1996, 21.

103 Phillip Boone, personal conversation, January 27, 2023. "Spotlight on Traxx," *Friends*, April 1992, 8. Boone took over the venue and reopened it as the Legendary Traxx in 1993. Hampton was murdered in 1998; Boone's subsequent business partner, Durand Robinson, was killed in 2010. "Pride on Our Side," *Clikque*, August 2004, 36–37; Patrick Saunders, "Catching up with . . . Phillip Boone, Owner and Founder of Traxx," *Georgia Voice*, August 15, 2014, https://thegavoice.com/news/atlanta/catching-phillip-boone-owner-founder-traxx. Tracks in Washington, DC, hosted a popular weekly party for Black men in the 1990s. (See figure I.10.) Keith Boykin has written on Tracks in both critique and celebration. Boykin, *One More River to Cross*, 27–28, 215–16. E. Patrick Johnson likewise offers a similar account in "Remember the Time," 227.

104 Boone, January 27, 2023.

105 Johnson, "Remember the Time," 230.

106 Johnson, "Feeling the Spirit," 408.

107 Allen, "For 'the Children' Dancing," 317, 322.

108 Ryan Lee, "Trying to Keep Up with the Atlanta Party Scene Is Like Playing Musical Chairs!" *Clikque*, June 2005, 55–56.

109 *Clikque*, August 2004, n.p.

110 Ad, *Clikque*, August 2005, n.p.

111 In addition to those mentioned, other venues included Fusion, the Palace, and Club Colours.

Interlude 4. Gay Switchboard in Philadelphia

1. Quotations from 1976 Switchboard staff manual, as recorded in the archive finding aid, Gay and Lesbian Switchboard of Philadelphia Records, MS-Coll 47, John J. Wilcox Archives, https://wilcoxarchives.org/repositories/2/resources/51. See also Marc Stein's excellent history of Philadelphia, *City of Sisterly and Brotherly Loves*.

2. Joseph Benjamin offers an account of volunteering for the New York switchboard; he says that about a quarter of callers asked for advice on finding gay bars. Benjamin, "Gay Switchboards."

3. Cait McKinney's excellent analysis of the Lesbian Switchboard of New York draws on call-log notebooks that give a rich accounting of the range of calls. I have seen only the cards detailing information offered, not logs of caller questions for the Philadelphia switchboard. See McKinney, *Information Activism*, 67–104.

4. Among the information the switchboard offered was the phone number for other hotlines, including the Hustler Hotline: "to help people who have been blackmailed, abused or ripped off by hustlers."

5. *Before Stonewall* (dir. Greta Schiller and Robert Rosenberg, 1984).

6. Archivist Bob Skiba has also produced the Philadelphia Gayborhood Guru blog and the Philadelphia LGBT Mapping Project: https://thegayborhoodguru.wordpress.com.

7. The local bar racism study was initiated by Black and White Men Together/Philadelphia and credited to a coalition of additional groups, including Beth Ahavah, Dignity/Philadelphia, Gay Fathers of Greater Philadelphia, Integrity, Mayor's Commission on Sexual Minorities, Metropolitan Community Church, Philadelphia Lesbian and Gay Task Force, and Sisterspace of Philadelphia. All of the materials from the Philadelphia study, including planning notes, self-reported survey results from bar owners, and observation worksheets, are in the Coalition on Lesbian-Gay Bar Policies records, John J. Wilcox Archives.

8. Attention to racism in Philadelphia gay bars renewed in 2016 when the owner of iCandy was recorded using the N-word. The local chapter of Black Lives Matter responded, and the Philadelphia Commission on Human Relations "issued a subpoena to all Gayborhood bar owners to attend a public hearing on racism and discrimination." Jen Colletta, "Community, City Leaders Meet to Address Racism," *Philadelphia Gay News*, October 21, 2016, 17. See also Ernest Owens, "Gayborhood's Diversity Problem, *Metro*, October 18, 2015, 8; Alexis Sachdev, "Protesters Are Demanding Resignation of the Mayor's LGBT Community Liaison," *Metro*, October 11, 2016; and Sam Newhouse, "Philly's Queer Community of Color Demands Change," *Metro*, October 27, 2016.

Chapter 5. Welcome to the Pleasuredome

The chapter title references Frankie Goes to Hollywood, *Welcome to the Pleasuredome* (ZTT Records, 1984).

The subheadings in this chapter reference the following: The Weather Girls, "It's Raining Men" (Paul Jabara/Paul Shaffer, CBS, 1982); Peaches, "Fuck the Pain Away" (Merrill Nisker, XL, 2000); Andrea True Connection, "More, More, More" (Gregg Diamond, Buddah, 1976); Taana Gardner, "Work That Body" (Kenton Nix, West End, 1979); and Blondie, "Rapture" (Debbie Harry/Chris Stein, Chrysalis, 1981).

The following abbreviations for periodical titles and the names of archival sites are used in the notes to this chapter: BAR (*Bay Area Reporter*); Gale (Gale Primary Sources Database: Archives of Sexuality and Gender); GCN (*Gay Community News*); IGIC (International Gay Information Center collection at New York Public Library); LA&M (Leather Archives & Museum, Chicago); LAT (*Los Angeles Times*, Los Angeles daily newspaper); NYN (*New York Native*); NYT (*New York Times*, daily newspaper); ONE (ONE National Gay & Lesbian Archives at University of Southern California Libraries, Los Angeles); RBMA (*Red Bull Music Academy*, dance-club history journal); SFS (*San Francisco Sentinel*); and VV (*Village Voice*, New York City downtown alternative weekly newspaper).

1 George Stambolian, "Requiem for a Great Pink Bird," NYN, March 9, 1981, 14. The *Native* was an important source of early reporting on AIDS, but the publication and its publisher, Charles Ortleb, later fell into disrepute for denying that HIV was the cause of AIDS.

2 Moore, *Beyond Shame*, 16.

3 To be clear, I intend no moralizing judgment in referencing drug use and sexual promiscuity in this chapter or elsewhere in this book.

4 Jan Carl Park, "The Season of the Saint," NYN, July 4, 1983, 32.

5 Bill Bahlman, telephone conversation, August 4, 2021.

6 David Rothenberg, "Gay Bars as Gay Lib—The Future of an Illusion," VV, March 14, 1977, 21.

7 Treichler, "AIDS, Homophobia, and Biomedical."

8 Signaling that gay men could not have known the crisis ahead, in 1981 the Handball Express sex club in San Francisco hosted a party marketed with the come-on "Are You Sick Enough for HOSPITAL." The event featured medical role-playing kink, including "surgical preps" and "catheterizations." Hospital flyer, "San Francisco Bars" subject file, ONE Archives.

9 Village People, "Y.M.C.A." (Jacques Morali/Victor Willis, Casablanca, 1978). Bérubé, "History of Gay Bathhouses," 190. For 1970s social-science studies of gay bathhouses, see Weinberg and Williams, "Gay Baths and the Social Organization of Impersonal Sex"; and Styles, "Outsider/Insider." For a critique of bathhouses, see Altman, "Gay Oppression in the

Baths." See also later studies, including Bolton, Vincke, and Mak, "Gay Baths Revisited," and the special issue of *Journal of Homosexuality*, "Gay Bathhouses and Public Health Policy," edited by William Woods and Diane Binson.

10 Lee Solomon, "Are We Getting Burned?," *Advocate*, October 5, 1977, 6.

11 See Tattleman, "Speaking to the Gay Bathhouse." The predominantly Black Mount Morris Baths in Harlem was uniquely social and remained open after the city closed prominent white gay venues. See Craig G. Harris, "Coming Together at the Baths," *Outweek*, July 3, 1989, 26–27.

12 Ad, *Advocate*, July 30, 1975, 11. On the development of house music in Chicago queer-of-color clubs, see Thomas, "House the Kids Built"; and Salkind, *Do You Remember House?* Although house music has been identified with the Warehouse (as the source of the term), Knuckles also credits the Clubhouse in Washington, DC, along with the Paradise Garage, as among its founding venues. Ronda Mundhenk, "Spinning into the Hall of Fame," *Outlines*, November 1996, 28.

13 Perry Deane Young, "So You're Planning to Spend a Night at the Tubs?," *Rolling Stone*, February 15, 1973, 50.

14 Arthur Bell, "The Continental Hadassah," *Gay Power* 1, no. 20 (1970): 6. See also Peter Ogren, "Doin' the Continental," *Gay*, July 6, 1970, 11.

15 Brewster and Broughton, *Last Night a DJ*, 156–58.

16 Collin, *Rave On*, 4.

17 Young, "So You're Planning," 50.

18 Dennis Rubini, "Continental Baths Revisited," *Gay News* (Ohio East edition), September 1976, X5–X7. Much of the history in this section is drawn from Winkler, "Stars of the Tubs!"

19 Woods, Tracy, and Binson, "Number and Distribution," 62.

20 Bérubé, "History of Gay Bathhouses," 200. For accounts of the New York Club Baths, see Vito Russo, "The Dressed-Up Look of the Club Baths New York," *Advocate*, June 2, 1976, 39; Arthur Bell, "The Bath Life Gets Respectability," *VV*, September 27, 1976, 19–20; and Brown, "Queen for a Day."

21 In effect, it picked up the mantle from the Everard Baths (called the "Everhard"), which had been a popular and functional but derelict bathhouse; a fire killed nine patrons there in 1977, but it continued in diminished capacity for years.

22 Brooks Peters, "The Sexual Revolution Mailman Delivered," *Out*, July/August 1994, 79–82.

23 Ralph Blumenthal, "At Homosexual Establishments, a New Climate of Caution," *NYT*, November 8, 1985, 34.

24 Susan Tomkin in the documentary *Gay Sex in the Seventies* (dir. Joseph F. Lovett, 2005).

25 Tim Gay, "150 Near-Naked Men Attend Private Party," *NYN*, May 23, 1983, 35.

26 White, *States of Desire*, 284.
27 Halperin, *Saint Foucault*, 92.
28 Steven C. Arvanette, "Anvil Targeted for Shutdown," *NYN*, December 17, 1984, 12.
29 Maurice Carroll, "Bar Shut Down for High-Risk Sex Was Given a Not-for-Profit Status," *NYT*, November 9, 1985, 34.
30 White, *States of Desire*, 275.
31 Fledermaus (Tony DeBlase), "The Mineshaft," *DungeonMaster* 30 (n.d.): 14.
32 Flyer, Anvil vertical file, CANADIAN LESBIAN AND GAY ARCHIVES, TORONTO.
33 Brodsky, "Mineshaft," 240.
34 Fledermaus, "Mineshaft," 14.
35 Seymour Kleinberg, "Where Have All the Sissies Gone?" *Christopher Street*, March 1978, 4.
36 Jan Carl Park, "The Anvil Legend," *NYN*, November 19, 1984, 27–28; "Night on the Town," *NYN*, February 11, 1985, 40.
37 The *Native* published a dossier of articles on the emergent East Village scene in its September 10, 1984, issue.
38 Bahlman, August 4, 2021. See also David C. Morrison, "The Gay Face of the 'No Wave' Scene," *Advocate*, December 23, 1982, 61. Visage, "Anvil (Night Club School)" (Billy Currie/Rusty Egan/Dave Formula/Steve Strange/Midge Urge, Polydor, 1982).
39 Fritscher, *Gay San Francisco*, 469.
40 John Preston, "The Theatre of Sexual Initiation," *Masquerade Erotic Book Society*, January/February 1993, 7; Michael Bronski, Zoom conversation, May 7, 2021.
41 Preston, "Theatre of Sexual Initiation," 6.
42 Moore, *Beyond Shame*, 23.
43 Fritscher, *Profiles in Gay Courage*, 60, 68.
44 Preston, "Theatre of Sexual Initiation," 6.
45 Mineshaft newsletter, summer 1977. Wally Wallace papers, LA&M.
46 Gerald Hannon, "The Heart of the Mineshaft," *Body Politic*, July/August 1981, 43.
47 Fritscher, *Profiles in Gay Courage*, 68.
48 Moore, *Beyond Shame*, 23.
49 Craig Rowland, "Barhopping with *Stallion*: Mineshaft," *Stallion*, August 1985, 35.
50 Fritscher, *Profiles in Gay Courage*, 62.
51 Cardini, *Mineshaft Nights*, 7; Preston, "Theatre of Sexual Initiation," 7; Fritscher, "Men's Bar Scene: Mineshaft," *Drummer*, December 1977, 82.

52 Moore, *Beyond Shame*, 20; Cardini, *Mineshaft Nights*, 7. See Laurie Anderson, "O Superman" (Anderson, Warner Bros., 1981). "Introducing the gay community to foot fetishes, fisting, electronic synthesizer music, golden showers, slings, bondage, body shaves, dress code humiliation—these are only some of the Mineshaft's achievements." Gay, "150 Near-Naked Men," 35.

53 Moore, *Beyond Shame*, 21.

54 White, *States of Desire*, 284.

55 Hannon, "Heart of the Mineshaft," 43.

56 Original 1978 Mineshaft dress code sign, on exhibit at LA&M.

57 Two women were famous at different moments as the "only" women to be allowed to be members: Camille O'Grady and Gail Wilcox.

58 Fritscher, *Gay San Francisco*, 484–85.

59 Rowland, "Barhopping with Stallion," 35.

60 Quoted in Fritscher, *Gay San Francisco*, 475–76.

61 Mineshaft newsletter, October 18–25, 1981. Wally Wallace papers, LA&M.

62 Califia, "San Francisco," 193.

63 Preston, "Theatre of Sexual Initiation," 7.

64 Fledermaus, "Mineshaft," 14.

65 Alan Bowne, "Mine Shaft," *Pittsburgh Gay News*, March 1977, 13.

66 *Cruising* (dir. William Friedkin, 1980).

67 Wilson, "Friedkin's *Cruising*."

68 Wallace collaborated with Internal Affairs to counter-survey the police he accused of raiding the Mineshaft. Wallace letter to editor of *BAR*, in response to July 24, 1997, article on the film, in Wally Wallace papers at the Leather Archives and Museum; Fritscher, *Gay San Francisco*, 483. See also Miller, "*Cruising*."

69 Darrell Yates Rist, "Policing the Libido," *VV*, December 3, 1983, 1, 17; Barry Adkins, "Judge Orders Mine Shaft Closed," *NYN*, November 18, 1985, 10; verified complaint, *City of New York v. Mine Shaft, et al.*, November 6, 1985, 4. Allan Bérubé papers, accessed via Gale.

70 Warner, *Trouble with Normal*, 211. For a survey of policies, see Woods and Binson, "Gay Bathhouses and Public Health Policy," 12–13.

71 Crimp, "How to Have Promiscuity," 253. This essay builds from the seminal work by Richard Berkowitz and Michael Callen in their 1983 pamphlet "How to Have Sex in an Epidemic" (New York: News from the Front Publications, 1983).

72 See, for instance, Marcos Batiscas-Cocoves, "New York Locks Up the 'Mineshaft': 'First the Baths . . . Then Your Bedroom,'" *GCN*, November 23, 1985, 1–2; Bruce Mailman letter to Mayor Koch, printed in *NYN*, December 2, 1985, 7.

73 Arnie Kantrowitz, "Romance New/Old," *Advocate*, August 30, 1981, 16, 18.

74 Rist, "Policing the Libido," *VV*, December 3, 1983, 17. See also Stephen Greco, "Some Things Never Change: Future Sex," *Advocate*, January 10, 1984, 24–25; and Fritscher, *Gay San Francisco*, 481.

75 Rowland, "Barhopping with *Stallion*," 36.

76 Letter from Deep Throat to Wally Wallace, October 27, 1985. Wally Wallace papers, LA&M.

77 John A. Fall, "St. Marks Baths Closed," *NYN*, December 23, 1985, 12; Barry Adkins, "Bad News for St. Marks," *NYN*, January 20, 1986, 15; open letter signed by Marj Conn et al., n.d. Bars subject file, folder 01760, Lesbian Herstory Archives, accessed via Gale.

78 Peter Freiberg, "Gay Anti-Defamation League Forms in N.Y.," *Advocate*, December 24, 1985, 14–15.

79 Kenneth Sedilla, "Sleaze, Mister, Sleaze," *Outweek*, July 3, 1989, 38; Sidney Morris, "Cruising in the Age of the Mine Shaft," *NYN*, December 2, 1985, 30.

80 Richard Umans, "The New—Improved?—Ice Place," *NYN*, June 15, 1981, 14.

81 Echols, *Hot Stuff*, 68–70.

82 Lawrence, "Disco and the Queering." See also his "Beyond the Hustle," *Love Will Save the Day*, and *Life and Death*.

83 Newton, *Cherry Grove, Fire Island*, 244.

84 Lawrence, "Beyond the Hustle," 202–3.

85 Holleran, *Dancer from the Dance*, 111. This was a formative novel for me and in many ways structured my fantasy of gay male life in the 1970s. Revisiting it for this chapter, I was struck by its characters—and by extension the book's—persistent casual racism, which appears to me an accurate if troubling reflection of the milieu it represents.

86 Crimp, "*Disss-Co*," 15.

87 Albert Goldman, quoted in Brewster and Broughton, *Last Night a DJ*, 169, emphasis added. For the classic theorization of disco and submission, see Hughes, "In the Empire of the Beat."

88 Miezitis, *Night Dancing*, 61; and Parlett, *Fire Island*, 141.

89 Quoted in Brewster and Broughton, *Last Night a DJ*, 170. 12 West had a skylight that allowed people to literally dance until the morning light. Crimp, "*Disss-Co*," 14.

90 The August 13, 1975, issue of the *Advocate* includes a dossier of articles on disco and numerous ads for discos across the country. See also Richard Szathmary and Lucian K. Truscott IV, "Inside the Disco Boom," *VV*, July 21, 1975, 6–9; and Sage, "Inside the Colossal Closet."

91 See Jack Slater, "Discotheques Dance to Another Tune," *LAT*, August 11, 1976, G1, for one example of the straight uptake of the new phenomenon.

92 *Saturday Night Fever* (dir. John Badham, 1977; soundtrack RSO, 1977).

93 *Studio 54* (dir. Matt Tynauer, 2018).

94　Lawrence, "Disco and the Queering," 241; Brewster and Broughton, *Last Night a DJ*, 188.

95　The club also applied for nightly catering permits to bypass liquor licensing. *Studio 54* (dir. Matt Tynauer, 2018).

96　Levine, *Gay Macho*, 75; Newton, *Cherry Grove, Fire Island*, 244; Crimp, "Disss-Co," 13; Lawrence, *Love Will Save the Day* and *Life and Death*.

97　Lawrence, "Beyond the Hustle," 205.

98　David Bauer, "Lords of an Underground Empire," *D Magazine*, June 1, 1979, www.dmagazine.com/publications/d-magazine/1979/june/lords-of-an-underground-empire/ (accessed March 22, 2023).

99　Richard Dyer began thinking through his seminal interrogation of whiteness, *White*, by dancing at New York clubs including the Paradise Garage (but not the Saint) in 1981. Personal correspondence, June 27, 2021. Better Days was the other leading Black gay disco of the era. See Lawrence, "Forging of a White Gay."

100　Collin, *Rave On*, 342.

101　Brandon Judell, "There and Back," *Gaysweek*, February 13, 1978, 18.

102　Cheren, *Keep on Dancin'*, 180. The club embraced African identifications early on, as when it hosted a King Tut–themed party in 1978, contemporaneous with King Tut fever in the US. Paradise Garage ephemera, IGIC. *Gaysweek* published images of men done up in gold body paint, djellabahs, and pith helmets. Rex Narrido-Gardner, "Page 5," *Gaysweek*, October 16, 1978, 5. See also numerous mentions in BWMT/NY–MACT/NY information bulletins, 1981–87.

103　1982 season membership renewal letter and undated letter to members. Dance Club Collection, 23, box 1, folder 10, National History Archives at the LGBT Community Center. Cheren, *Keep on Dancin'*, 200–201.

104　Frank Owen, "Paradise Lost," *Vibe*, November 1993, 64.

105　Craig G. Harris, "Uptown Boys," *NYN*, September 9, 1985, 39. Jafari S. Allen suggests that for queer men of color from the outer boroughs, going into Manhattan connoted that they were "sus": "(suspected) to be gay." Allen, *There's a Disco Ball*, 127.

106　Brian Howard, telephone conversation with the author, July 22, 2021.

107　*Radio Days* (dir. Woody Allen, 1987).

108　Cathay Che, "Avant Garage," *Advocate*, February 13, 2001, 54–56; see also Haring, *Journals*.

109　Jon Pareles, "Paradise Garage, a Gay Club That Forever Changed Night Life," *NYT*, June 18, 2000, www.nytimes.com/2000/06/18/style/paradise-garage-a-gay-club-that-forever-changed-night-life.html.

110　Owen, "Paradise Lost," 64.

111　Fikentscher, *"You Better Work!,"* 85–86.

112 Sheryl Garratt, "Going Back to Our Roots," *Gay Times*, September 1999, 33. Howard, July 22, 2021. Manuel Göttsching, *E2–E4* (Inteam GmbH, 1984).

113 Peter Shapiro, "Saturday Mass: Larry Levan and the Paradise Garage," *RBMA*, April 22, 2014, https://daily.redbullmusicacademy.com/2014/04/larry-levan-feature.

114 Miezitis, *Night Dancing*, 68.

115 Brewster and Broughton, *Last Night a DJ*, 281.

116 Lawrence, "Disco and the Queering." See also Dyer, "In Defence of Disco."

117 Diana Ross, "Love Hangover" (Marilyn McLeod/Pamela Sawyer, Motown, 1976). C. Gianni Tindall-Gomes, "Speaking of 'The Garage Experience,'" *GCN*, March 8, 1992, 9.

118 Madonna, "Everybody" (Madonna, Sire, 1982).

119 Change, "Paradise" (David Romani/Mauro Malavasi/Tanyayette Willoughby, Atlantic, 1981); Sparkle, "Handsome Man" (Bernard Torelli/Jean-Pierre Massiera/Marco Attali/Tony Bonfils, Vitman, 1979); Loose Joints, "Tell You (Today)" (Arthur Russell, Island, 1983); Roland Clark, "I Get Deep" (Clark, Shelter, 2000), remixed in Fatboy Slim, "Song for Shelter" (Clark/Norman Cook, Astralwerks, 2000).

120 Owen, "Paradise Lost," 62.

121 Howard, July 22, 2021.

122 Collin, *Altered State*.

123 Tindall-Gomes, "Speaking of 'The Garage Experience,'" 7–11.

124 *Maestro* (dir. Josell Ramos, 2003).

125 "BLK Veil," *BLK*, December 1993, 30.

126 Crimp, "*Disss*-Co."

127 White, *States of Desire*, 270–71.

128 R. J. Markson, "Second Avenue and Sixth Street Blues," *NYN*, May 2, 1988, 22; Brooks Peters, "The Sexual Revolution Mailman Delivered," *Out*, July/August 1994, 141.

129 Barry Walters, "Nightclubbing: New York City's The Saint," *RBMA*, July 22, 2015, http://daily.redbullmusicacademy.com/2015/07/nightclubbing-the-saint; Darrell Yates Rist, "A Scaffold to the Sky and No Regrets," *NYN*, May 2, 1988, 17.

130 William Alvis, "The Saint: The Vatican of Clubs," *After Dark*, May 1981, 69; James M. Saslow, "The New York Syndrome," *Advocate*, November 11, 1982, 21.

131 Buckland, *Impossible Dance*, 52.

132 The I-Beam disco in San Francisco was actually owned by an astronomer, Dr. Sanford Kellman. Previous discos had embraced space themes, most overtly the gimmicky Starship: Discovery 1 in Times Square, circa 1977, billed as "the Entertainment Starship Discotheque in the cosmos!" Starship: Discovery 1, bar ephemera, IGIC. One of the innovations at the Saint was to

dispense with the pretense of a vessel and to allow men to dance unprotected in space.

133 Scrapbook. Dance Club Collection, 23, box 1, folder 7, National History Archives.

134 Cheren, *Keep on Dancin'*, 277.

135 Lawrence, *Life and Death*, 117. Donna Summer, "Could It Be Magic" (Barry Manilow, Casablanca, 1976).

136 Moore, *Beyond Shame*, 40; Lawrence, *Life and Death*, 428, 117.

137 Kantrowitz, "The Synagogue, the Saint, and the Mine Shaft," *Advocate*, April 15, 1982, 33.

138 Rist, "Scaffold to the Sky," 18; "Night on the Town," 40.

139 Cheren, *Keep on Dancin'*, 278.

140 Luis-Manuel Garcia, "An Alternative History of Sexuality in Club Culture," *Resident Advisor*, January 28, 2014, www.residentadvisor.net/feature.aspx?1927.

141 Richard Umans, "New Year's at the Saint," *NYN*, January 18, 1982, 15.

142 Moore, *Beyond Shame*, 38–43.

143 Rist, "Scaffold to the Sky," 18. See also fifth-anniversary party invitation, 1985. Dance Club Collection, 23, box 1, folder 6, National History Archives.

144 Moore, *Beyond Shame*, 41.

145 Lawrence, *Life and Death*, 222.

146 Umans, "New Year's at the Saint," 15.

147 Lawrence suggests that the Sound Factory is where the musical aesthetics of the Paradise Garage and the Saint would finally meet, particularly when Junior Vasquez spun. "The Forging of a White Gay Aesthetic at the Saint." Tracks NYC would also develop as a post–Paradise Garage venue and intersect with the house ballroom scene. See Andy Thomas, "Nightclubbing: Tracks," *RBMA*, April 27, 2016, https://daily.redbullmusicacademy.com/2016/04/nightclubbing-tracks.

148 Flyers for events in December 1986–February 1987. Saint ephemera, IGIC. In San Francisco in 1988, an ad for the Dreamland proclaimed that "Dreamland presents a night to DANCE THROUGH TIME! [Steve] Fabus plays New York cult and San Francisco classics. Club anthems from: Anvil, 12 West, Flamingo, The Saint, Paradise Garage, Palladium, Dreamland I, Trocadero [Transfer], I-Beam 1974 to Present. Count up the years starting with 1974... and going up to 1988." Ad, *BAR*, November 3, 1988, 5.

149 Neil Alan Marks, "The Saint Reopens," *NYN*, October 5, 1981, 16; Saslow, "New York Syndrome," 21.

150 White, *States of Desire*, 272.

151 Richard Peters, quoted in Moore, *Beyond Shame*, 42.

152 Walters, "Nightclubbing."

153 Lawrence, "Forging of a White Gay."
154 Rites III: The Black Party, March, 20, 1982. Saint ephemera, IGIC. See also Glenn Person, "Pre-black Party at the Saint," *NYN*, March 29, 1982, 5; Rites VIII: March 31, 1987. Ephemera collection of IGIC.
155 Shilts, *And the Band Played On*, 149. Shilts says that the Saint later became "invaluable" as a venue for AIDS fundraisers (307).
156 Glenn Person, "New York: Partying in the Age of AIDS," *Christopher Street West (Los Angeles Pride) Program*, 1983, 57.
157 Colm Wilkinson, "Bring Him Home," from the musical *Les Misérables* (Claude-Michel Schönberg/Alain Boubil/Jean-Marc Natel, 1987); Wilkinson appearance, May 24, 1987. Flyer in Bars subject file, Lesbian Herstory Archives, accessed via Gale.
158 Peters, "Sexual Revolution Mailman Delivered," 141.
159 Rist, "Scaffold to the Sky," 17.
160 Ad in *Womanews*, September 1986, 17; member newsletter, November 1986 and January 17, 1987; party flyer in IGIC. Party flyers in Bars subject file, Lesbian Herstory Archives, accessed via Gale.
161 Lawrence, "Big Business," 298.
162 National full-page ads for the Saint's The Last Party appeared in the *Advocate*, April 12, 1988, 53, and April 26, 1988, 8.
163 Leslie Gevirtz, "Gay Landmark Goes Out in Style," *SFS*, May 6, 1988, 6.
164 Brandon Judell, "The Saint Says Good-Bye," *Advocate*, July 5, 1988, 41.
165 Christopher Davis, quoted in Judell, 40.
166 Holleran, "Adios, Sebastian," *NYN*, May 2, 1988, 19. Holleran had also reviewed the club's opening in "Another Opening, Another Laser Beam," *Christopher Street*, December 1980, 14–16.
167 Holleran, "Adios, Sebastian," 19, 20.

Interlude 5. The Saloon in Minneapolis

1 This specific version of the ad debuted on the back cover of *Lavender*'s October 23, 1998, issue and reappeared at least four times through the June 30, 2000, issue. Others likewise alternated and repeated.
2 See Hughes, "In the Empire."
3 Tim Campbell, "Nontraditional Households Taking over Minneapolis," *GLC Voice*, July 18, 1983.
4 *Purple Rain* (dir. Albert Magnoli, 1984).
5 Madonna, "Ray of Light" (Madonna/William Orbit/Clive Maldoon/Dave Curtiss/Christine Leach, Maverick, 1998); Cher, "Believe" (Brian Higgins/Stuart McLennen/Paul Barry/Steven Torch/Matthew Gray/Timothy Powell/Cher, Warner Bros, 1998); Whitney Houston, "It's Not Right but It's

Okay" (Thunderpuss remix) (LaShawn Daniels/Rodney Jerkins/Fred Jerkins III/Isaac Phillips/Toni Estes, Arista, 1999).

6. The Oak Ridge Boys, "Y'all Come Back Saloon" (Sharon Vaughn, Dot, 1977).
7. J. C. Ritter, "Saloon's Roots Dated to 1972 Gay Murder in Loring Park," *Equal Time*, April 3, 1986, 8–9.
8. J. C. Ritter, "New Saloon Marketing Campaign," *Equal Time*, May 15, 1985, 12.
9. Ad, *Equal Time*, May 28, 1986, back page; ad, *Equal Time*, February 4, 1987, back page.
10. Ad, *Equal Time*, March 4, 1987, back page. The first ad without the Y'all Come Back name appeared in the *Twin Cities Gaze*, August 17, 1988.
11. Mark Swanson, "An Odyssey through Minneapolis–St. Paul Gay Bars," *Equal Time*, November 9, 1990, 10–11.
12. Gill-Peterson, "Haunting the Queer Spaces."

Chapter 6. Proud Mary's

The chapter title references Creedence Clearwater Revival, "Proud Mary" (John Fogerty, Fantasy, 1969); and Ike and Tina Turner, "Proud Mary" (cover, Liberty, 1971).

The subheadings in this chapter reference the following: Carl Bean, "I Was Born This Way" (Chris Spierer and Bunny Jones, Motown, 1977), and Lady Gaga, "Born This Way" (Stefani Germanotta/Jeppe Laursen, Interscope, 2011); "Anything Goes" (Cole Porter, 1934), covered by Harper's Bizarre (Warner Bros, 1967); Whitney Houston, "Didn't We Almost Have It All" (Michael Masser/Will Jennings, Arista, 1987); Janis Joplin, "Piece of My Heart" (Jerry Ragovoy/Bert Berns, Columbia, 1968); and P!nk, "Raise Your Glass" (Max Martin/P!nk/Shellback, Jive, 2010).

The following abbreviations for periodical titles and the names of archival sites are used in the notes to this chapter: GCN (*Gay Community News*); MV (*Montrose Voice*); and NYT (*New York Times*, daily newspaper).

1. "Houston Picks Mr. Leather," *Drummer*, November 1982, 23.
2. Jim Moss, "Leatherman's Guide to Texas," *Drummer*, March 1987, 58.
3. Ed Martinez, "Mary's: A Houston Institution," *Out in Texas*, March 31, 1983, 11–13.
4. Scott Heumann, "Deep in the Heart of Texas: Gay Houston," *Numbers*, April 1983, 12–13. See also Ralph W. Davis, "Houston," *Ciao!*, December 1974, 10–12; and Bob Zygarlicki, "Houston: Men Playing for Real," *Folsom* (no month), 1981, 61.
5. Sears, *Rebels, Rubyfruit, and Rhinestones*, 48–58. By 1973, two-thirds of Houston's gay bars were reportedly in the Montrose. Thorne Dreyer and Al Reinert, "Montrose Lives!," *Texas Monthly*, April 1973, 58. The Anthonys

also opened the private club Gayboy and published the lifestyle magazine *Gayboy*; they envisioned a gay male equivalent of the Playboy empire. See Freibert, "Distribution, Bars, and Arcade Stars."

6 Henry McClurg, "So Long from the House That Fanny Built," *Montrose GEM*, November 9, 2009, 4.

7 Ad, *David*, April 1972, 29; ads, *Gayboy*, 1972, JD Doyle Archives.

8 McClurg, "So Long from the House"; Gay Pride Week 1980 Guide (Houston), 22. Larry Bagneris papers, Amistad Research Center, Tulane University, folder 5.

9 Mills passed away in 2017 at age eighty. See his obituary, www.texasobituaryproject.org/010517mills.html.

10 Sheri Cohen Darbonne, "Mary's Celebrates 20th Anniversary (... Naturally)," *MV*, May 18, 1990, n.p.; ad, *TWT*, late 1978. JD Doyle Archives.

11 Quoted in Kay Days, "Montrose Landmark Celebrates 30 Years," *Houston Voice*, May 19, 2000, n.p.

12 *Auntie Mame* (dir. Morton DaCosta, 1958).

13 Gaye Yancy, quoted in Days, "Montrose Landmark Celebrates 30 Years." One account indicates they were removed in 1978 as a fire hazard, and another suggests they were removed by order of the health department in the late 1980s. It's plausible they were cleared out, reaccumulated, and cleared again. See Darbonne, "Mary's Celebrates 20th Anniversary"; and Days, "Montrose Landmark Celebrates 30 Years."

14 Judy Reeves, conversation, February 6, 2017; ad, *TWT*, May 21, 1982, 100.

15 Robert Ralph, "Houston: Something for Everyone," *Torso*, September 1983, 96; ad, *Upfront*, May 30, 1979, 23.

16 The Mary's fire was one of five fires in a single night, four of which targeted gay businesses or homes.

17 *Lawrence of Arabia* (dir. David Lean, 1962). Ad, *TWT*, August 20, 1982, 57.

18 Reeves, February 6, 2017.

19 Literalizing new gay visibility, the Twin Peaks bar in San Francisco is credited as the first to have plate-glass windows that allowed the patrons inside to be seen from the street; however, the bar had a strict no-touching policy to maintain respectability and an image of decorum. Romesburg, "The Glass Coffin."

20 Reeves, February 6, 2017.

21 "Let Me Entertain You," from the musical *Gypsy* (Jule Styne/Stephen Sondheim, 1959).

22 John Broadhurst, conversation, January 4, 2012.

23 Jon Preston, "S/M in the New West," *Drummer*, December 1980, 11–12.

24 The earliest use of this slogan that I've found appears in the *Advocate*, November 24, 1983, 37.

25 Ads in JD Doyle archive, www.houstonlgbthistory.org/houston-marys-history.html.
26 Billie Duncan, "The Story of 'Sam,' Life of a Dog," *MV*, July 6, 1988, 9; ad, *TWT*, March 5, 1982, 72.
27 Days, "Montrose Landmark Celebrates 30 Years."
28 Bill Whiting, "Haven in Houston," *Advocate*, March 23, 1977, 4; George DeWoody, "Getting off to Houston," *Advocate*, November 5, 1975, 36–37; Scott Anderson, "Houston," *Advocate*, May 3, 1979, 10–12, and "Houston," *Advocate*, September 17, 1981, 18–22; Craig Rowland, "The Houston Attitude," *Advocate*, July 22, 1982, 28–31, 55–56. See also Michael Ennis, "What Do These Rugged Texas He-Men Have in Common?," *Texas Monthly*, June 1980, 107–13, 209–22, 226.
29 Dreyer and Reinert, "Montrose Lives!," 56.
30 Heumann, "Deep in the Heart," 12.
31 Remington, "Twelve Fighting Years," 11, 13.
32 In comparison, Oak Lawn in Dallas reflects "the Dallas way," with an orderly row of big bars, strong neighborhood planning, and a proliferation of private nonprofit organizations. Eric Celeste, "Gay, Inc," *D: The Magazine of Dallas*, June 1992, 62–63, 73–79; Whittemore, "Dallas Way."
33 Riedel, "Cruising Grounds."
34 Reeves, February 6, 2017.
35 Rowland, "Houston Attitude," 56. Similar gay street patrols existed in other cities; see Hanhardt, *Safe Space*, 81–116.
36 Larry Bagneris, telephone conversation, May 7, 2021. Bagneris joined the Houston Gay Political Caucus in 1976, eventually ascending to its leadership in 1982–83; he also served on the boards of the National Gay Task Force and the 1979, 1986, and 1993 marches on Washington. He was at the Stonewall during a raid in May 1969 but not there during the riots a month later, as claimed in some sources.
37 Ray Hill, conversation, February 8, 2017. When I met Hill at Barnaby's Café in 2017, he handed me his business card, which identified him as "Ray Hill, Citizen Provocateur" and listed "raconteur" among his professions. Hill started going to bars in 1957 and came out the following year. He spent the first half of the 1970s in jail. After his release in 1975, he went to Mary's every day. Hill passed away in 2018. See Sears, *Rebels, Rubyfruit, and Rhinestones*; and Ben McGrath, "The Improbable Life of Ray Hill," *New Yorker*, December 1, 2018, www.newyorker.com/culture/postscript/the-improbable-life-of-ray-hill.
38 Quoted in Jone Devlin, "Mary's Tradition Continues under New Ownership," *Texas Triangle*, January 3, 2003, clipping.
39 Hill, February 8, 2017.
40 Reeves, February 6, 2017.

41 My thinking here is influenced by Berlant and Warner, "Sex in Public."

42 Remington, "Twelve Fighting Years"; David Lee, "6,000 Gays Gather for Town Meeting 1 at Astroarena," *Houston Chronicle*, June 25, 1978, sec. 4–1; Bagneris, May 7, 2021. The 1979 parade is frequently referenced as the first, but an earlier march in downtown Houston in 1976 predates it. See the JD Doyle Archives page dedicated to the early march here: http://houstonlgbthistory.org/misc-1976pride.html.

43 "61 Arrested at Mary's," *TWT*, June 27, 1980, 5–12; Paul J. Theall, "Proud to Be . . . in Jail," *TWT*, June 27, 1980, 23–24; "Last Two 'Mary's Fairies' Win Their Court Appeals," *MV*, February 26, 1982, 3.

44 Anderson, "Houston," 1981, 18. The Diana Foundation, named for the goddess, was the "oldest social organization in Houston," starting in 1953. The Promethean Society, the first political homophile organization in Houston, met in 1967–68; the more radical Gay Liberation Front was active in 1970–72; and the Houston Gay Political Coalition (not to be confused with the Caucus), was organized in 1973. The Houston Gay Political Caucus was renamed the Gay & Lesbian Political Caucus in 1987 and the GLBT Political Caucus in 2005.

45 DeWoody, "Getting off to Houston," 36; Roger Ricklefs, "A New Constituency: Political Candidates Seek Out Gay Votes," *Wall Street Journal*, October 20, 1976, 35.

46 JD Doyle, Zoom conversation, May 6, 2021.

47 Anderson, "Houston," 1981, 18.

48 *Bedtime for Bonzo* (dir. Frederick De Cordova, 1951).

49 William Marberry, "The GPC Mailing List: Probably Bigger Than You Thought," *MV*, February 26, 1982, 15.

50 Daniel Pedersen, "Morality and Mayorality," *Newsweek*, September 30, 1985, 34.

51 Melinda Beck with Stryker McGuire, "Gay Power in Macho Houston," *Newsweek*, August 10, 1981, clipping; Jim Simmons, "Gay Political Caucus Endorses Mayor Whitmire," *Houston Post*, September 1, 1981, A25; William K. Stevens, "Houston Accepts New Political Force," *NYT*, November 2, 1981, A16. In contrast, the Dallas Gay Political Caucus operated through "discretion" and worked "behind the scenes" rather than publicly endorsing candidates: 60 percent of its membership voted Republican. Arnold Hamilton, "Gay Clout in Dallas," *Dallas Times Herald*, May 17, 1982, 1.

52 Robert Hyde, "Whitmore and Group Make Surprise Gay Bar Tour," *MV*, January 13, 1984, 1.

53 Robert Hyde, "Whitmore Denounced for 'Barhopping through Community,'" *MV*, January 20, 1984, 7.

54 "Houston Police Also Go on 'Bar Tour,'" *MV*, January 6, 1984, 7; Robert Hyde, "Bartenders, Customers Arrested by HPD at J.R.'s," *MV*, January 6, 1984, 8, and Hyde, "Bartenders Charged with Serving Alcohol to Publicly Intoxicated Persons," *MV*, January 20, 1984, 10; Robert Hyde, Hollis Hood, and

Billie Duncan, "HPD Vice Stages Numerous Raids in Montrose," *MV*, January 20, 1984, 1–2.

55 Robert Hyde, "Brown and Vice Squad Confronted over Numerous Arrests," *MV*, January 27, 1984, 1, 5. See also Robert Hyde and Billie Duncan, "Activist Ray Hill Claims HPD's Vice Maintain 'Faggot File,'" *MV*, January 27, 1984, 1, 6.

56 HGPC press release, 1983. Houston Vertical File, Canadian Lesbian and Gay Archives; "EPHA SPEECH." Larry Bagneris papers, folder 3, Amistad Research Center.

57 Quoted in Joe Baker, "In Search of the Average Gay Texan," *Advocate*, November 24, 1983, 29.

58 Pedersen, "Morality and Mayorality," 34.

59 Button, Rienzo, and Wald, *Private Lives, Public Conflicts*, 70.

60 Jerel Shaw, "An Interview with HOBO's Alan Pierce," *MV*, August 16, 1985, 8; Darbonne, "Mary's Celebrates 20th Anniversary."

61 Connie Woods, "String of Nightclub Robberies Continue in Montrose," *MV*, April 4, 1986, 1, 6, and "Nightclub Robberies Continue in Montrose," *MV*, April 11, 1986, 4. Pantzer co-owned Just Marion and Lynn's.

62 "Finances Was Main Topic at HOBO Meeting," *MV*, June 20, 1986, 13; Darbonne, "Texas' Oldest Gay Bar Is Over 32 Years Old," *MV*, September 26, 1986, 3. The Pink Elephant had previously been the city's oldest gay bar.

63 Jim Moss, "Leatherman's Guide to Texas," *Drummer*, March 1987, 59.

64 Linda Wyche, "Higher Drinking Age a Few Days Away," *MV*, August 22, 1986, 3; Darbonne, "Bar Owners Irked by City's Health Codes," *MV*, January 16, 1987, 3.

65 Woods, "Some Club Owners Cool to Taxi Programs," *MV*, February 21, 1986, 6.

66 Broadhurst, January 4, 2011.

67 Woods, "Local Club Owners Feel Economic Crunch," *MV*, March 7, 1986, 9, and "Bar Owners to Fight Rising Liquor Taxes," *MV*, July 18, 1986, 3.

68 Darbonne, "Bar Owners Irked by City's Health Codes"; "Health Codes Delay Opening of New Montrose Bar Roosters," *MV*, February 6, 1987, 3.

69 Ad, *MV*, June 19, 1987, 27.

70 Gene Harrington, "Time to Address Racism in the Houston Gay Community," *MV*, July 3, 1987, 7.

71 "GLF Pickets Gay Bar," *Nuntius*, January 1971, 1.

72 Jerel Shaw, "An Interview with Larry Bagneris," *MV*, August 30, 1985, 15.

73 Quoted in Jerel Shaw, "A Lasting Entity," *MV*, August 23, 1985, 8.

74 Bagneris was originally from New Orleans and was understood as Creole there; when he moved to Houston, he was perceived as "Mexican." His grandparents were French and Haitian on one side, Guatemalan and Honduran on the other. He was president of the Chicano Caucus of the HGPC before leading the organization as a whole.

75 "Send in the Clowns," from the musical *A Little Night Music* (Stephen Sondheim, 1973); "Springtime for Hitler," from the movie *The Producers* (Mel Brooks, RCA Victor, 1967).

76 The Klan marched on June 9, 1984. Press coverage and photo documentation in the JD Doyle Archives, http://houstonlgbthistory.org/misc-kkk.html.

77 Ad, *MV*, April 29, 1988.

78 Quoted in Chris Bull, "Houston Gay Bar's 'Wet----' Contest Sparks Protests," *GCN*, June 12, 1988, 1, 9.

79 Duncan, "Pride Week Withdraws Boycott Request, Bar Owners Back Mary's," *MV*, May 27, 1988, 3.

80 Duncan, "Pride Week Committee Censures Mary's and Voice for 'Wet----' Ad," *MV*, May 20, 1988, 8. See also the editorial, Duncan, "Would a Wet---- by Any Other Name Smell as Sweet?," *MV*, May 20, 1988, 13.

81 See obituary at Texas Obituary Project, www.texasobituaryproject.org/020089luera.html.

82 Gates, *Double Negative*, 20. Gates theorizes Black media representations.

83 Letters appear in the *Montrose Voice* issues of May 13, 20, and 27, 1988.

84 "Morales Responds to Duncan Editorial," *MV*, May 27, 1988, 3.

85 Ad, *MV*, May 27, 1988.

86 Hill, February 8, 2017; Brandon Wolf, "Mary's Infamous Mural," *OutSmart*, December 2011, 48.

87 Mark DeLange, "Scott Swoveland Murals," www.houstonlgbthistory.org/eagle-murals.html.

88 Riedel, "Cruising Grounds."

89 Michael Helquist, "Now in the Bars: Rubber Machines," *MV*, November 30, 1984, 3; "San Antonio Hosts Bartenders AIDS Education Seminar," *MV*, December 6, 1985, 3; Shaw, "A Lasting Entity," 8.

90 Bagneris, May 7, 2021. He moved back to New Orleans, where he grew up.

91 Doug Sadownick, "Cities in Crisis," *Advocate*, January 15, 1991, 35.

92 Data courtesy of JD Doyle's Texas Obituary Project, www.texasobituaryproject.org/comments.html.

93 Ad, *TWT*, November 8, 1985.

94 In addition, at least one full square of the NAMES Project AIDS Memorial Quilt featured panels with the Mary's logo and names of people from its community.

95 See JD Doyle's Texas Obituary Project, www.texasobituaryproject.org/comments.html.

96 "Memorials Held in Mary's Patio & Outback," Mary's Naturally Bar, http://houstonlgbthistory.org/houston-marys-memorials.html.

97 Cathy Matusow, "Zipping up Mary's," *Houston Press*, December 26, 2002, 11–12; Alex Wukman, "Remembering Mary's," *Houston Free Press*, July 6,

2011, www.freepresshouston.com/remembering-marys-naturally-or-is-montrose-still-a-gayberhood; Wolf, "Mary's Infamous Mural," 49.

98 Wolf, "Mary's Infamous Mural," 47.

99 DeLange, "Scott Swoveland Murals"; Wolf, "Mary's Infamous Mural," 49.

Interlude 6. The Main Club in Superior, WI

An earlier version of this interlude appeared online in *Recaps Magazine* (Summer 2013).

1 Robert (Bob) Jansen papers, Jean-Nickolaus Tretter Collection in GLBT Studies, University of Minnesota Libraries.

2 In addition to the articles cited, see "Bar Lets Gay People Know They're Not Alone," *Duluth Tribune & Herald*, March 24, 1985, 5C; Elise Matheson, "Pride Grand Marshal Profile: Bob Jansen," *Lavender Lifestyles*, May 24, 1996, 34–35; Noam Levey, "Bar Owner Back, Pink Walls and All," *Duluth News Tribune*, May 29, 1997, 2B; and Chris Homan, "Bob Jansen's Gay Activism Predated Northland Pride," *Lavender*, August 13–26, 2010, 16–18. Documentaries include *Treading Water* and *The Main*. The bar is also mentioned in Van Cleve, *Land of 10,000 Loves*, 152–54.

3 Angela C. Nicols, "The Main Club Celebrates Its 20th Anniversary," *Lavender*, February 7–10, 2003, 40.

4 Among his community involvements are cofounding Gays of Duluth–Superior (GODS) and being on the board of the Minnesota Committee for Gay and Lesbian Rights—both before opening the bar—and cofounding the Duluth–Superior Pride Committee, the Greater North AIDS Project, the North Star Gay Rodeo, and a GLBT community–police liaison program. He's served on the Duluth Community Health Center board, the city's human rights task force, and the Superior Business Improvement District committee. He has also supported women's causes, such as the Women's Legal Defense Fund, Take Back the Night, Aurora, the Women's Health Center, and the Women's Coffeehouse.

5 "Main Club Has Become Mainstay in Superior," *Equal Time*, February 2, 1986, 7.

6 Jason Skog and Naom Levey, "Main Served as Harbor, Home for Gays, Others," *Duluth News-Tribune*, December 28, 1996, 1.

Chapter 7. Further Tales of the City

The chapter title references Armistead Maupin, *Further Tales of the City*. The subheadings in this chapter reference the following: Ariana Grande, "Thank U, Next" (Grande/Charles Anderson/Kimberly Krysiuk/Michael Foster/Njomza Vitia/Tayla Parx/Tommy Brown/Victoria Monét, Republic, 2018); Wham!, "Everything She Wants" (George Michael, Epic, 1984); Black

Box, "Everybody Everybody" (Daniele Davoli/Mirko Limoni/Valerio Semplici, RCA, 1990); The B-52s, *Cosmic Thing* (Reprise, 1989); and Jessie Ware, "Remember Where You Are" (Danny Parker/James Ford/Jessica Ware/Shungudzo Kuyimba, PMR, 2020).

The following abbreviations for periodical titles and the names of archival sites are used in the notes to this chapter: BAR (*Bay Area Reporter*); GLBT (San Francisco LGBT Business Ephemera Collection at the Gay and Lesbian Historical Society, San Francisco); NYN (*New York Native*); RBMA (*Red Bull Music Academy*, dance-club history journal); SFPL (M43 GLC VF: club flyers box at San Francisco Public Library); SFS (*San Francisco Sentinel*); and SFBT (*San Francisco Bay Times*).

1 Sylvester, "You Make Me Feel (Mighty Real)" (James Mirrick/Sylvester James, Fantasy, 1978). See also Sandra Bernard, "You Make Me Feel (Mighty Real)" (Epic, 1994).

See Diebold, *Tribal Rites*; and Niebur, *Menergy*. For a retrospective account of the club, see Andy Thomas, "Nightclubbing: San Francisco's Trocadero Transfer," RBMA, September 1, 2014, http://daily.redbullmusicacademy.com/2014/09/nightclubbing-trocadero-transfer.

2 Allen White, "Disco Era to End When Troc Closes," BAR, February 18, 1988, 3. See also White, "Sex, Drugs, and Disco: The 'Gold Old Days' Are Relived in 'Tribal Rites,'" BAR, June 23, 1988, 50, and "Ten Years After: Polk Had Glitter; Castro Had Clones; and Everybody Had a Good Time," BAR, June 23, 1988, 30, 39.

3 Dave Ford, "Boy, Oh Boy," SFS, February 6, 1988, 27; Marc Breindel, "Boys Will Be Boys: Scenes from the Gilded Closet," SFS, April 22, 1988, 18–19; Chris Whitney, "Boy: The Marketing of a Counter-Clone," SFS, May 6, 1988, 11; Mike Hippler, "Learn from Our Mistakes," BAR, July 21, 1988, 11. See also Wendell Ricketts, "Ah, Youth! The Bundeswehr Were Doffed, the Hair Was Moussed and the Attractive Boys 'Yupped Til They Dropped,'" BAR, October 15, 1987, 26, 44.

Arlene Stein, "The New Lesbianism," SFS, August 18, 1988, 20–21. See also Camille Roy, "Speaking in Tongues: Lesbian Sex in the '80s," SFS, June 24, 1988, 26–27; and Karen Everett, "Lipstick Lesbians Love the Night Life," SFS, October 29, 1988. *On Our Backs* magazine exemplified the new lesbian sexuality.

Allen White, "New Generation Brings New Vision to Gay Life," BAR, June 2, 1988, 1, 12, and "New Party Places: Young Gays Find Out There Are Plenty of Places to Dance," BAR, July 14, 1988, 26.

4 Wittman, "Refugees from Amerika."
5 Humphreys, *Out of the Closets*, 115–20; Hippler, "Learn from Our Mistakes," 11.
6 Marika Cifor likewise acknowledges this queer generational relationship to AIDS in *Viral Cultures*, 15.

7 Stan Maletic, "Hip Hoppin,'" *BAR*, February 22, 1990, 25.
8 Sycamore, *End of San Francisco*, 82–83. See also Sycamore, *Between Certain Death*.
9 Collin, *Altered State*, vii.
10 White, "New Generation Brings New Vision," and "New Party Places"; Maletic, "Hip Hoppin.'"
11 Neil Alan Marks, "The New Gay Man," *NYN*, April 12, 1982, 18.
12 Blake, "Curating *In a Different Light*," 25.
13 Allen White, "Clash of Generations," *BAR*, June 8, 1989, 1, 14–15.
14 Mr. Marcus, "Where the Boys Were," *BAR*, June 8, 1989, 38–41; Allen White, "Connie-Mania Sweeps Eagle," *BAR*, June 8, 1989, 40–41; Connie Francis, "Where the Boys Are" (Neil Sedaka/Howard Greenfield, MGM, 1961).
15 Penny Anderson with Michele DeRanleau, "Post-Stonewall Gays: The Next Generation," *SFS*, August 17, 1989, 1, 9.
16 "Queer Folk," *SFS*, June 24, 1988, 1, and Steve Abbott, "Will We Survive? The Challenge of Gay Culture Today," *SFS*, June 24, 1988, 25 and 43.
17 Ad, *BAR*, July 28, 1988, 5.
18 The AIDS Coalition to Unleash Power (ACT UP) started in 1987; Queer Nation, an ACT UP offshoot focusing on LGBTQ+ issues, started in 1990; and Lesbian Avengers, a direct-action feminist group that splintered from ACT UP, started in 1992. Riot Grrrl represented a playful punk-rock third-wave feminism. Major films included *Tongues Untied* (dir. Marlon Riggs, 1989); *Looking for Langston* (dir. Isaac Julien, 1989); *Paris Is Burning* (dir. Jennie Livingston, 1991); *Poison* (dir. Todd Haynes, 1991); *Edward II* (dir. Derek Jarman, 1991); *My Own Private Idaho* (dir. Gus Van Sant, 1991); *The Living End* (dir. Gregg Araki, 1992); *Swoon* (dir. Tom Kalin, 1992); and *Go Fish* (dir. Rose Troche, 1994).
19 See Warner, "Introduction"; Butler, "Critically Queer"; Duggan, "Making It Perfectly Queer" and *Twilight of Equality?*; and Gamson, "Must Identity Movements Self-Destruct?"
20 Stryker and Van Buskirk, *Gay by the Bay*, 118, 121.
21 Bérubé and Escoffier, "Queer/Nation," 12.
22 Amin, "Haunted by the 1990s," 289.
23 Tim Vollmer, "Young Gays Long on Style, Short on Substance," *SFS*, May 10, 1990, 7.
24 Allen White, "The Next Generation," *BAR*, June 22, 1989, 62, and "New Generation Brings New Vision," 1.
25 White, "New Generation Brings New Vision," 12.
26 Hoffman, "Skipping the Life Fantastic," 340.
27 Crimp, "Mourning and Militancy," 238–39. Beyond nightlife, Eric E. Rofes recognized a "civil war" between gay-rights activists and AIDS service

organizations over the latter's strategic erasure of the impact of AIDS on gay men in publicity and fund-raising campaigns from the mid-1980s onward; this rift predates and complicates the gay-versus-queer binary that I pose here. Rofes, "Gay Lib vs. AIDS."

28 Romesburg, "Glass Coffin," 166. On the East Coast, liberation activist Arnie Kantrowitz penned a "Letter to the Queer Generation" in which he recognized a cyclical "oedipal rebellion" in which a younger generation seeks to "redefine and rename itself" in contradistinction to their gay elders; he calls for members of the younger generation to learn their history and for his generation to "put away their cozy bitterness . . . long enough to pass on what they know." Kantrowitz, "Letter to the Queer Generation."

29 Dave Ford, "San Francisco Chronicles: The Evolution of a Gay Mecca," *Frontiers*, July 3, 1992, 50.

30 Ford, "San Francisco Chronicles," 52.

31 Armstrong, *Forging Gay Identities*, 155.

32 Special issue editor Teresa de Lauretis had organized a conference under this title at UC Santa Cruz in 1990. De Lauretis, "Queer Theory."

33 A prior sociological survey of generational collective memory—conducted in 1985 and published in 1989—affirmed expectations that cohorts tend to consider events and changes from their late adolescence and early adulthood to be the most historically significant and influential in shaping their worldviews. Schuman and Scott, "Generations and Collective Memories."

34 Strauss and Howe, *Generations*, 13, 322, 453. The authors also released a follow-up aimed at Xers titled *13th Gen*.

35 They later revised the terminology such that boomers are prophets, Gen X are nomads, Millennials are heroes, and Gen Z are artists. Strauss and Howe, *Fourth Turning*.

36 Strauss and Howe, *Generations*, 39. Challenging these findings and claims to rupture, Robert D. Putman's study of broad shifts in social and political participation finds that the baby-boomer generation demonstrated a steady decline in civic engagement, which Generation X effectively continued. Putman, *Bowling Alone*, 247–76.

37 David Leavitt, "The New Lost Generation," *Esquire*, May 1985, 94.

38 Herdt and Boxer, *Children of Horizons*, 9. See also Herdt, "Intergenerational Relations and AIDS in the Formation of Gay Culture in the United States," 266–70.

39 E. Brooks Peters, "Wünder Bars," *NYN*, Sept 10, 1984, 31, 47.

40 Gorman, "Pursuit of a Wish," 100.

41 Ad, *BAR*, November 15, 1984, 21.

42 White, "New Party Places," 26.

43 Quoted in Lily Eng and Michael O'Laughlin, "The Next Generation," *San Francisco Examiner*, June 24, 1989, 58.

44 Quoted in Breindel, "Boys Will Be Boys," 18–19.
45 Hippler, "Learn from Our Mistakes," 11; Ricketts, "Ah, Youth!"
46 Breindel, "Boys Will Be Boys," 18–19.
47 Eng and O'Laughlin, "Next Generation," 58; Hippler, "Learn from Our Mistakes," 11.
48 Ford, "Boy, Oh Boy," 27.
49 Ad, *SFS*, July 15, 1988, 2.
50 White, "Clash of Generations," 14.
51 Strauss and Howe, *Generations*, 326.
52 Quoted in Breindel, "Boys Will Be Boys," 18–19.
53 Ricketts, "Ah, Youth!"
54 Quoted in Breindel, "Boys Will Be Boys," 18–19.
55 Ben Dhong, letter to editor, *SFS*, April 29, 1988, 10. Multiple other scathing letters responded to the boy phenomenon itself.
56 Whitney, "Boy," 11.
57 Hippler, "Learn from Our Mistakes," 11.
58 BOY flyer, November 1988, GLBT.
59 Quoted in White, "Clash of Generations," 15.
60 Flyers, SFPL.
61 Maletic, "Hip Hoppin'."
62 Don Baird, "Magic Spinner," *SFS*, June 24, 1988, 11.
63 Mattson, "Are Gay Bars Closing?," 1.
64 Page Hodel, telephone conversation, August 23, 2021.
65 The Box flyer, April 1999, GLBT. Ellipses in the original.
66 Adam Block, "Arresting Aromas," *SFS*, June 24, 1988, 39.
67 Quoted in Baird, "Magic Spinner," 11.
68 This ad appears in every *Sentinel* issue in July and early August 1989.
69 Hodel, August 23, 2021.
70 Andrew Lewis, "Vinyl Junkie," *Atmosphere*, November 1991, 19–20.
71 Flyers, SFPL. A slightly later version proclaimed "The Box dance club proudly celebrates our human rainbow." The Box flyer, undated, GLBT.
72 Ramírez, "'¡Mira, Yo Soy Boricua y Estoy Aquí!,'" 284. More-enduring Latinx venues included Esta Noche and La India Bonita in the Mission and El Rio in Bernal Heights.
73 Quoted in Rebecca Alber, "Ms. Page Hodel Is Spinning Magic," *Deneuve*, March/April 1995, 24.
74 "Legendary Dance Club Celebrates Move with Ten-Year Anniversary," *Whazzup!*, October 1998, 33.
75 Dennis McMillan, "The Box Booms into 2nd Disco-Free Year," *BAR*, April 27, 1989, 30.

76 Dave "Davey D" Cook, quoted in Meredith May, "Pioneer Female DJ Page Hodel Has Marched to Her Own Beat," *San Francisco Chronicle*, March 22, 2014, n.p.
77 Mr. Lee, "Get Busy" (Lee Ricky Haggard, Jive, 1989); L'Trimm, "Cars with the Boom" (Rachel Patricia De Rougemont, Atlantic, 1988).
78 "Legendary Dance Club Celebrates Move with Ten-Year Anniversary," 33.
79 S. Topiary Landberg, telephone conversation, August 3, 2021.
80 Laura Cottingham, "Buddies, Can We Share a Bar?," *NYN*, September 10, 1984, 30.
81 See Stoller, "Lesbian Involvement"; and Cvetkovich, *Archive of Feelings*, 156–204. Sarah Schulman's history of ACT UP adamantly states that, contrary to the popular imagination, care work was not gendered; men did it, too. Nonetheless, the crisis was transformative for bringing gay men and women together. *Let the Record Show*, 22–23.
82 Hodel, August 23, 2021.
83 Ad, *SFS*, August 10, 1989, 9.
84 Stein, "New Lesbianism."
85 *SFS*, February 9, 1989, 1. Interior story by Karen Everett, "Trading Places," 3.
86 Quoted in Preciado, *Apartment on Uranus*, 213. See also *Gendernauts* (dir. Monica Treut, 1999).
87 Quoted in Everett, "Lipstick Lesbians Love the Night," 11.
88 Quoted in Everett, "Skirts Opening Draws Record Crowd," *SFS*, January 26, 1989, 9. The subheadline observes, "'Lesbian Heaven' Welcomes Gay Men."
89 Ad, *SFS*, January 19, 1989, 8.
90 Everett, "Lipstick Lesbians Love the Night," 11.
91 Amory, "Club Q," 149.
92 Ad, *Dykespeak*, 1994, n.p.; Club Q flyers, GLBT; flyers, SFPL.
93 Quoted in Alber, "Ms. Page Hodel Is Spinning," 24.
94 Maud's closed in 1989, and Amelia's closed in 1991. The Lexington Club opened in the Mission in 1996. See also Rachel Pepper, "Pussy, Pussy Everywhere...," *BAR*, April 23, 1992, 11.
95 Daniel Nicoletta, *LGBT San Francisco*, 224.
96 Baird, "Beat This," *SFBT*, January 1990, 29.
97 David Taylor-Wilson, "Going to a Go-Go," *BAR*, June 21, 1990, 55; "La Vie en Club," *BAR*, September 3, 1992, 39. This write-up also added, "PC warning: Those supporting the workers recently canned for trying to unionize should boycott the EndUp."
98 Daniel, August 11, 2021; Robert Barrett, Zoom conversation, August 10, 2021.
99 Maletic, "Hip Hoppin,'" 34.
100 Club Uranus flyers, GLBT.

101 Ggreg Deborah Taylor, "Don't Believe a Word," SFBT, May 1991, 49.

102 Drew Daniel, Zoom conversation, August 11, 2021; Marc Siegel, Zoom conversation, August 20, 2021. See also Blake and Bond, *Jerome Caja*, 28. Quotation from Oral history interview with Caja, August 23 and September 29, 1995. Archives of American Art, Smithsonian Institution.

103 Club Uranus flyer, 1992, GLBT.

104 *The Gay Agenda* (produced by The Report, 1992). The dancer (Daniels) also appears in a Daniel Nicoletta photo from the same day in *LGBT San Francisco*, 145. Steve Abbott's novel *The Lizard Club* positions denizens of Club Uranus and intersecting parties as part of the heritage of the Borborites, a "sect described as 'hated by God' in the canonical *Book of Revelation*," 34.

105 John Blanco, "Diet Popstitute: Endearing Degenerate," BAR, February 9, 1995, 33.

106 Browning, *Culture of Desire*, 56.

107 Justin Vivian Bond, "Up Uranus," BAR, March 26, 1992, 26.

108 On Club Fuck, see Sarkar, "Industrial Strength Queer."

109 Owen, *Clubland*, 103.

110 M. Apparition, telephone conversation, July 22, 2021; Landberg, August 3, 2021.

111 *Betty & Pansy's Severe Queer Review*, 5. This references a popular urban legend that actor Richard Gere, sometimes believed to be closeted, was anally penetrated by a gerbil during sex play.

112 Ford, "San Francisco Chronicles," 56.

113 Lily Braindrop, "Dressing Up and Acting Out," BAR, October 11, 1990, 34, 46.

114 Michael Flanagan, "BARchive: Fond Memories of Uranus," BAR, June 28, 2015, www.ebar.com/entertainment/culture/179890.

115 Pepper, "Where the Girls Go," *Deneuve*, May-June 1991, 13. *Valencia*, Michelle Tea's essential chronicle of 1990s queer dyke San Francisco, likewise opens with a scene on the Stud dance floor, where the guys are pushy—but the women fight back (4).

116 Siegel, August 20, 2021.

117 Braindrop, "Dressing Up and Acting Out," 46.

118 Orloff, *Disasterama!*, 68, 115.

119 Baird, "Beat This: Klubstitute," SFBT, June 1991, 55.

120 Remix Von Popstitute (Orloff), "The Popstitutes," *Homocore* 7 (Winter/Spring 1991): 54.

121 Ggreg Deborah Taylor, "Now Boarding: Obscure Tour #2," SFBT, June 1991, 64. For the 1990 pride parade, Club Uranus and Klubstitute jointly entered a Stonewall-inspired smashed-up police cruiser with revelers dancing and kissing on top of it. Daniel, August 11, 2021. It was captioned as the "Hell

on Wheels" contingent for the Daniel Nicoletta photograph, *LGBT San Francisco*, 12–13, 302. For a later account of Gay Shame, see Stanley, "Affective Commons."

122 Nell Jehu, oral history interview with Heklina, December 8, 2008. T-shack Collection, folder 12, SFPL. Tony Bravo, "T-----shack Updates Name to T-Shack as Terms, Times Change," *San Francisco Gate*, May 22, 2014, www.sfgate.com/performance/article/Trannyshack-updates-name-to-T-Shack-as-terms-5499509.php. Slur redacted. Heklina died in 2023.

123 Blake and Bond, *Jerome Caja*, 28.

124 In SoMa, the Folsom Street Fair (begun 1984) and Up Your Alley (begun 1985) started as efforts to revive the area; the Eagle thrived by shifting from overt public sex to beer busts and embracing its clientele via leather-daddy contests. Ray O'Loughlin, "Downtown Plan," *BAR*, May 30, 1985, 1, 16; Charles Linebarger, "Singing the Swan Song for South of Market," *BAR*, May 23, 1985, 1, 14; Wayne Friday, "Rent Gouging Drives Out Gay Businesses," *BAR*, March 20, 1986, 9.

125 Quoting Laurie McBride of the Golden Gate Business Association, Charles Linebarger, "Castro St. Squeeze," *BAR*, September 19, 1985, 3.

126 Richard Laermer, "Straight Clubs Go Gay," *Advocate*, January 29, 1991, 49. For example, the Cave nightclub in Las Vegas opened as a straight venue in 1992, turned gay in 1993, and quickly embraced an "alternative" scene before closing in 1994. Cave Nightclub collection at UNLV Library.

127 Joyce Slaton, "Guerilla Queer Bar," *San Francisco Bay Guardian*, December 13, 2000, 6–9; Don Romesburg, "Guerrilla Queer Bar," *Advocate*, August 14, 2001, 45–50.

128 Sycamore, *End of San Francisco*.

129 Mark Mardon, "Latin Dance-Club Rivalry Erupts over Who Takes Stage at Pride," *BAR*, June 4, 1998, 19.

130 Daniel, August 11, 2021. The Crisco Disco parties at the Crow Bar in New York had done much the same in the 1990s. See Bredbeck, "Troping the Light Fantastic."

131 Tubesteak Connection flyer, GLBT.

Interlude 7. The Casa Nova in Somerset County, PA

The following abbreviations for periodical titles and the names of archival sites are used in the notes to this interlude: GSU (Georgia State University Libraries Special Collections, Atlanta); NYT (*New York Times*, daily newspaper); and PQ (*Planet Q*).

1 *Ellen* (created by Carol Black, Neal Marlens, David S. Rosenthal, ABC, 1994–98).

2 "Sexual Politics: A New Way of Being," NYT, June 21, 1998, SM13; *Will & Grace* (created by David Kohan and Max Mutchnick, NBC, 1998–2006).

3   See Loffreda, *Losing Matt Shepard*. Shepard met his murderers at a straight bar; there was no gay bar or any other public gay venue in Laramie.
4   "Pennsylvania Gay Bus Trip Met by Religious Hate Group and KKK," *PQ*, May 1997, 3; "Johnstown Hate Campaign," *Erie Gay Community News*, May 1997, 9.
5   Mike Weiss and Craig Schneider, "Explosion Injures 2 at Nightclub," *Atlanta Journal-Constitution*, February 22, 1997, n.p. (clipping); Lillian Lee Kim, "Gays React with Alarm, Outrage," *Atlanta Journal-Constitution*, February 23, 1997, A8. Fan in Maria Helena Dolan Papers, W134, box 20, folder 25, GSU.
6   Billy Hileman, "Casa Nova Bar Owner Testifies before Senate Committee on Hate Crimes," *PQ*, August 1998, 2.
7   *Planet Q* publisher Billy Hileman was the newspaper's primary reporter and a member of the Pittsburgh CRY OUT! ACT UP group; coverage of the Casa Nova became a major cause for Hileman.
8   "Pennsylvania Gay Bus Trip," 3–5.
9   "McRae Breaks Truce; KKK Threatens Casa Nova, Holds Cross Burning," *PQ*, June 1997, 3.
10 "Casa Nova Attacked; Owner Threatened; KKK Planning July 12 Rally at Neighbor's Farm," *PQ*, July 1997, 4–6; "Religious Bigots and Neighbors Plan Daily Protests at Casa Nova," *PQ*, August 1997, 5; ad, *PQ*, October 1997, 10; Hileman, "Casa Nova Bar Owner Testifies before Senate Committee on Hate Crimes," 2–5; Hileman, "FBI Gives Report to Federal Civil Rights Division," *PQ*, November 1998, 7–10; "Police Chief Accused of Running License Plates of Casa Nova Patrons," *PQ*, April 1999, 5. State Attorney General Mike Fisher likewise failed to take action on the harassment of the Casa Nova. Deb Spilko, "Pennsylvania Elections," *Erie Gay News*, December 2002, 11.
11 Hileman, "Casa Nova Bar Owner Testifies before Senate Committee on Hate Crimes," 2.
12 "Christmas Carols Drown Out Protesters at Casa Nova," *PQ*, January 1998, 2.
13 "Casa Nova Calendar," *PQ*, May 1998, 19.
14 Ad, *PQ*, April 1999, n.p.
15 Jenness and Grattet, *Making Hate a Crime*.
16 Petrosino, "Connecting the Past," 19–20.
17 Dufour, "Mobilizing Gay Activists," 67–68.
18 Hileman, "Casa Nova Bar Owner Testifies," 2–5.
19 "Candlelight Vigil Held at Casa Nova," *PQ*, January 1999, 4.
20 Hileman, "FBI Gives Report," 7; Marty Levine, "New Target, Old Methods for Street Preachers," *Pittsburgh City Paper*, August 31, 2006, www

.pghcitypaper.com/pittsburgh/new-target-old-methods-for-street-preachers
/Content?oid=1337404.

Chapter 8. Donde Todo es Diferente

The subheadings in this chapter reference the following: Selena, "Bidi Bidi Bom Bom" (Selena Quintanilla-Pérez/Pete Astudillo, EMI Latin, 1994); Lime, "Babe, We're Gonna Love Tonight" (Denis Lepage, Unidisc, 1982); Linda Ronstadt, "La Charreada" (Felipe Bermejo, Elektra, 1987); Sean Paul featuring Beyoncé/Beyoncé featuring Sean Paul, "Baby Boy" (Beyoncé Knowles/Scott Scortch/Robert Waller/Sean Paul Henriques/Shawn Carter, 2002/2003, Atlantic/Columbia); Shakira, "Estoy Acuí" (*I'm Here*) (Shakira/ Luis Fernando Ochoa, Sony, 1995); and Chavela Vargas, "En el Último Trago" (*The Last Drink*) (José Alfredo Jiménez, Orfeo, 1979).

The following abbreviations for periodical titles and the names of archival sites are used in the notes to this chapter: LAT (*Los Angeles Times*, Los Angeles daily newspaper); ONE (ONE National Gay & Lesbian Archives at University of Southern California Libraries, Los Angeles); and RBMA (*Red Bull Music Academy*, dance-club history journal).

1 Juan Gabriel, "El Noa Noa" (Gabriel, RCA, 1980); see also the film *El Noa Noa* (dir. Gonzalo Martinez Ortega, 1980). A queer Boyle Heights venue called Noa Noa Place, after the Gabriel song, opened in December 2020.

2 *Latinx* is a pan-ethnic category that refers to people of Latin American origin across a wide range of geographic, cultural, linguistic, racial, class, and gendered experiences. Whereas the *x* aims to make space for gender nonconformity, it also points to the many exclusions this term is predicated on—namely its linguistic and cultural investment in a gender binary and its often-assumed distance from Indigeneity and Blackness, despite their centrality and prevalence throughout Latin America. See Alan Pelaez Lopez, "The X in Latinx Is a Wound Not a Trend," *ColorBloq*, 2018, www.colorbloq.org/the-x-in-latinx-is-a-wound-not-a-trend; and Milian, *LatinX*.

3 Negrón-Muntaner, "Dance with Me," 313, 314. She is responding to David Román's moving account of his formative experiences along these fault lines in "Dance Liberation."

4 Esta Noche in San Francisco and La Escuelita in New York stand among the most canonized queer Latinx bars in the United States, but there are also vibrant scenes in Phoenix, in various Texas cities, and in Chicago, as well as an increasing dispersion of queer Latinx lives throughout the rural US. See Quiroga and Frank, "Cultural Production of Knowledge," 141; Guzmán, "'Pa' La Escuelita'"; Rivera-Servera, "History in Drag"; Ramos, "Dirt That Haunts"; and Rodríguez, "Public Notice." See also Ramírez, "'¡Mira, Yo

Soy Boricua!'"; and Rodriguez, "Beyond Boystown," unpublished article manuscript.

5   In Central Hollywood: Circus Disco and Arena and Gino's II, the Latinx performance lounge Plaza, and the corner dive bar Spotlight. East Hollywood: Club Tempo, the Study, the Blacklite, and the Asian drag lounge Mugy's. (Reynaldo Rivera evocatively photographed the talent at a range of queer-of-color performance venues, including Plaza, Mugy's, and Silverlake Lounge. See El Kholti and Mackler, *Reynaldo Rivera*.) Silverlake: Ken's River Club (Asian and Latino), Butch Gardens, Le Bar, Le Barcito (site of the Black Cat—see introduction), Woody's Hyperion/MJ's, and two formerly gay bars that became straight in the 2000s: Silver Lake Lounge and Little Joy. In the Valley: Club Cobra. Westlake: Silver Platter. South Central: Coco Bongo. Downtown: The Score and the New Jalisco Bar. Boyle Heights: Redz, previously the Redhead, and Red's, primarily lesbian. El Sereno: The Plush Pony, primarily lesbian. (Photographer Laura Aguilar's portraits shot at this venue have become some of the most canonical documentation of early-1990s queer Latinx life in Los Angeles; see Epstein, *Laura Aguilar*; and Chavoya and Frantz, *Axis Mundo*.) Montebello: Chico. El Monte: Sugar Shack (previously Eddie's), primarily lesbian. Long Beach: Executive Suite. Garden Grove: Frat House. Pomona: Alibi and Robbie's.

6   Mustache Mondays at La Cita, created by Nacho Nava, Danny Gonzales, Josh Peace, and Dino Dinco. See Marke B., "Celebrating Ten Years of Mustache Mondays, LA's Iconoclast Party," *RBMA*, October 20, 2017, https://daily.redbullmusicacademy.com/2017/10/mustache-mondays. Shits and Giggles at various venues, created by Chris Bowen and Victor Rodriguez. A Club Called Rhonda at various venues, created by Gregory Alexander and Loren Granich. Wildness at Silver Platter, created by Wu Tsang, Asma Maroof, Daniel Pineda, and Ashland Mines. Wildness was an early influence on Lucas's desire to work on nightlife because he found the event to be world making. Yet it also became a site for interrogating the politics of exposing a community to invasion by outsiders. This queer-of-color art and performance party occupied Tuesday nights in an otherwise predominantly trans feminine Central American immigrant bar near MacArthur Park and arguably demonstrated the (im)possibility of actually integrating and reconciling the worlds that it brought together. For a thoughtful reflection on the party and its politics, see Wu Tsang's *Wildness* artist statement in the 2012 Whitney Biennial exhibition catalogue, as well as Muñoz, *The Sense of Brown*, 128–40. Promoter Mario Diaz also organized popular long-running parties such as Big Fat Dick and Full Frontal Disco, although these scenes were not predominantly Latinx or queer of color.

7   Gutiérrez, "Concatenation of Sprawls."

8   See Carrier, "Miguel" and *De los Otros*; Sanchez-Crispin and Lopez-Lopez, "Gay Male Places"; Prieuer, *Mema's House, Mexico City*; Carrillo, *Night Is*

Young and *Pathways of Desire*; Philen, "Social Geography of Sex"; Cantú, *Sexuality of Migration*; and Thing, "Gay, Mexican and Immigrant," 820–22. For community-based oral histories, see Lopera, *¡Cuéntamelo!* The classic study of immigrant gay bars is Manalansan, *Global Divas*; see also his follow-up essay, "That Magical Touch."

9 Agustín Garcia Meza, personal communication, June 21, 2022. See also Ochoa, *Queen for a Day*, 3–6; and La Fountain-Stokes, *Translocas*, 28–44.

10 Garcia Meza, Zoom conversation, July 11, 2022.

11 Rivera-Servera, "Dancing Reggaetón with Cowboy Boots," 377.

12 Cáceres and Cortiñas parse the demographics of a Latino gay bar in the Bay Area and identify six types of patrons: drag queens (*travestis/transformistas*), non–gay-identified macho Latino men, gay-identified Latino men, gay-identified Anglo men, Latina lesbians, and heterosexual Latino couples. "Fantasy Island," 251–52.

13 *De Ambiente*, February-March 1994.

14 Muñoz, *Disidentifications*; Martínez, *On Making Sense*.

15 Muñoz, *Sense of Brown*, 3.

16 See Ngai, *Impossible Subjects*, and Chavez, *Borders of AIDS*.

17 The Immigration Reform Act of 1990 (effective 1991) finally removed the homosexual exclusion, but a separate 1986 law required testing for HIV and made those positive inadmissible until 2010. Lucas learned much of this history via subject file clippings and documents in the ONE Archives, which affirm that immigration and sexuality are interdependent. Although the ban against immigrants who tested positive for HIV/AIDS extended to all migrants, the motivation for this policy appears rooted in antiblack xenophobia against Haitians and Africans. Chavez, *Borders of AIDS*. See also Peña, "Latina/o Sexualities in Motion," and Luibhéid and Chávez, *Queer and Trans Migrations*.

18 Ray Herbert, "Vast Shift Noted in L.A. Ethnic Makeup," LAT, February 27, 1978.

19 Campbell Gibson and Kay Jung, "Historical Census Statistics on Population Totals by Race, 1790 to 1990, and by Hispanic Origin, 1970 to 1990, for Large Cities and Other Urban Places in the United States" (Working Paper No. 76, Population Division, U.S. Census Bureau, Washington, DC, February 2005), https://www.census.gov/content/dam/Census/library/working-papers/2005/demo/POP-twps0076.pdf (accessed March 23, 2023).

20 Minian, *Undocumented Lives*, 1–13 and 77–103.

21 Cantú, *Sexuality of Migration*, 92, 135. In contrast, Carrillo's research found that moving to the United States presented an easier alibi for many men to leave home because of familial histories of transborder migration and

because of networks of kin already in California. Carrillo, *Pathways of Desire*, 74.

22 Cantú, *Sexuality of Migration*, 143–44; Carrillo, *Pathways of Desire*, 141–49. See also Thing, "Gay, Mexican and Immigrant," 820–22.

23 Anzaldúa, *Borderlands/La Frontera*.

24 For more attention to trans Latinx and travesti studies, see Rizki, "Latin/x American Trans Studies"; and Rose, "Guiseppe Campuzano's Afterlife."

25 See Rodríguez, *Next of Kin*; and Macías, "Gay Bar, Some *Familia*."

26 Navarro, "Eso, Me Esta Pasando," 38.

27 For an alternative formation, see Delgado and Muñoz, *Everynight Life*.

28 Because latinidad is a heterogeneous and contested collective identity that is not defined solely by geographic location, race, national identity, or even language, it holds possibilities for fluid and generative exchanges as well as limitations that perpetuate exclusions and inequalities. It is a sense of belonging that is inherently pan-ethnic, imagined, and felt. See Rodríguez, *Queer Latinidad*.

29 Various publications have served the local LGBTQ+ Latinx market, including *De Ambiente* (in Spanish, 1993–95), *QV* (in English, 1997–2003), and *Adelante* (bilingual, 1999–present). These publications routinely feature bar listings and nightlife photos.

30 Spencer Kornhaber interview with Rivera-Servera, "The Singular Experience of the Queer Latin Nightclub," *Atlantic*, June 17, 2016, www.theatlantic.com/entertainment/archive/2016/06/orlando-shooting-pulse-latin-queer-gay-nightclub-ramon-rivera-servera-intrreview/487442/.

31 Gloria Trevi, "Gloria," on *Gloria En Vivo* (Umberto Tozzi/Giancarlo Bigazzi, Universal, 2012); Laura Branigan, "Gloria" (Tozzi/Bigazzi/Trevor Veitch, Atlantic, 1982); Umberto Tozzi, "Gloria" (Tozzi/Bigazzi, CGD, 1979).

32 Alvarez, "Finding Sequins in the Rubble," 620.

33 They had previously owned a small coffee shop, an adult bookstore, and the first black (heterosexual) disco in Los Angeles. Lemos died in 1990. J. Victor Abalos, "The Man Who Would Be King," *LA Weekly*, October 9, 2002, www.laweekly.com/the-man-who-would-be-king/.

34 Dave Johnson, "Studio One Hit with Charges of Racism, Sexist Discrimination," *Los Angeles Free Press*, June 13, 1975; handbills for boycott in Studio One subject files, ONE.

35 The venue and its owner, Jewel Thais Williams, have been the subject of numerous profiles, including the documentary *Jewel's Catch One* (dir. C. Fitz, 2016); Ayofemi Stowe Folayan, "The Many Faces of Jewel," BLK, November 1989; Gwynedd Stuart, "Remembering Legendary L.A. Gay Bar Jewel's Catch One," *Los Angeles*, April 27, 2018, www.lamag.com/culturefiles/jewels-catch-one; and August Brown, "The Story of L.A. Club Jewel's Catch One and Its Pioneering Owner Finds Its Way to Netflix," *LAT*, May 2,

2018, www.latimes.com/entertainment/music/la-et-ms-jewels-catch-one-documentary-20180502-story.html. See also Green, "Into the Darkness," 255–79.

36 Quoted in Emily Alpert Reyes, "Gay Nightclub Nears Its End, at Crossroads," *LAT*, December 4, 2015, B10.

37 Faderman and Timmons, *Gay L.A.*, 284–85.

38 Abalos, "Man Who Would Be King."

39 Ad, *Update*, August 8, 1980, n.p.; "In Los Angeles," *After Dark*, May 1981, n.p.

40 *Circus Disco Twenty Fifth Anniversary* (Thump Records, 1999). See also *Latin Disco* (Thump Records, 2001); *Circus Disco Non Stop Mixed* (Thump Records, 2002); and *Circus Disco Mixed Volume 2* (Thump Records, 2007). A *Latin Disco* compilation (Thump Records, 2001) was produced by the same team and cross-promoted but is not branded as a Circus Disco compilation; the latter two mixes are credited to Circus DJ Martin Rodríguez, 1978–86.

41 Miquel Brown, "So Many Men, So Little Time" (Ian Levine/Fiachra Trench, Polydor, 1983). This song title and lyric was reportedly inspired by seeing a man at Circus wearing a T-shirt with this saying emblazoned on it. See Niebur, *Menergy*, 203. Cinema, "I Love Men" (Warren Schatz, Trebol, 1984).

42 Desire, "Crazy over You" (Rae Flores/Sabby Rayas/Steve Galindo, Sheik, 1986); J. D. Hall, "#1 Lover" (Hall/Sebastian Rayas, JDC, 1985); La Flavour, "Mandolay" (Mark Avsec, Sweet City, 1979); Lisa Smith, "Sweet Fantasy" (Sebastian Rayas, TSR, 1986); and Stop, "Wake Up" (Bijan, Damabi, 1985) recur across compilations.

43 Ramón García, conversation with the author, September 13, 2019.

44 James Rojas, "From the Eastside to Hollywood: Chicano Queer Trailblazers in 1970s L.A.," KCET, September 2, 2016, www.kcet.org/shows/lost-la/from-the-eastside-to-hollywood-chicano-queer-trailblazers-in-1970s-l-a.

45 Garcia Meza, July 11, 2022.

46 Alfaro, "Heroes and Saints."

47 Haro, "Antología," 148.

48 Dino Dinco, telephone conversation, October 25, 2019.

49 García, "Dreamings of the Dead," 60–61. García also contributed texts on historical east-side gay Latinx venues to De la Loza, *Pocho Research Society Field Guide*, 72, 76.

50 Garcia Meza, July 11, 2022.

51 Rivera-Servera, "Choreographies of Resistance," 282, 269, 270. On Circus, see also Ocampo, *Brown and Gay in LA*, 102–3.

52 Event flyer, May 20, 1978 or 1979, Circus Disco subject file, ONE Archives; Dennis Romero, "The Founder of One of L.A.'s Earliest Gay Discos Isn't Crying Over Its Destruction," *LA Weekly*, December 4, 2015, www.laweekly.com/the-founder-of-one-of-l-a-s-earliest-gay-discos-isnt-crying-over-its-destruction; Abalos, "Man Who Would Be King."

53 GLLU subject files, ONE Archives. The group formed in 1981, and Lesbianas Unidas formed as a committee to do outreach to encourage Latina lesbian participation before the group consolidated and renamed itself GLLU.

54 For a queer-of-color analysis of Southern California suburbs, see Tongson, *Relocations*.

55 Thank you to Ricky Rodríguez for these insights.

56 The venue was run by white gay man Ted Heier; when he died in 2013, his daughter Shelly continued running it. See the documentary *Frat House* (dir. Nancy Nguyen, 2019) and Lilly Nguyen, "The Frat House Is the Last Gay Bar in Garden Grove," *LAT*, June 13, 2019, www.latimes.com/socal/daily-pilot/entertainment/tn-wknd-et-frat-house-garden-grove-oc-lgbt-bars-20190613-story.html.

57 Laura León, "El Baile del Tesoro (El Pimpollo)" (CBS, 2002).

58 Site visit, November 16, 2019.

59 The local Spanish-language radio station KLAX, which played banda, shot to number one in the local ratings in 1992 with more than a million listeners at any given time, according to Lipsitz, *Footsteps in the Dark*, 55–56.

60 Viesca, "Battle of Los Angeles," 727.

61 Luís Fernando Gutiérrez, "Bandas, Bandas y Mas Bandas," *De Ambiente*, October 1993, 8. For a study of parallel straight dance cultures, see Hutchinson, *From Quebradita to Duranguense*.

62 Garcia Meza, July 11, 2022.

63 *Ritmo de la Noche*, November 1994. Like this newsletter, Tempo's website is bilingual, but different parts appear in English and Spanish, respectively, rather than appearing fully translated.

64 In contrast, Manalansan suggests that "refus[ing] to translate" operates as "an act of resistance to assimilation." Manalansan, *Global Divas*, 47.

65 Carlos Samaniego, telephone conversation, October 3, 2019.

66 Guzmán, "'Pa' La Escuelita,'" 212.

67 García, *Salsa Crossings*, 148, 79–83. See also Rodríguez, *Queer Latinidad*, 155, and *Sexual Futures*, 116.

68 Fey, "Muévelo" (Mario Ablanedo, Sony, 1996); Los Tucanes de Tijuana, "La Chona" (Mario Quintero Lara, Master Q, 1995).

69 Crew-organized T Parties—effectively itinerant house parties—have also provided an accessible alternative to bars for queer Latinx youth. See Ocampo, *Brown and Gay in LA*, 104–9.

70 See Macías, "Gay Bar"; and Tan, "Homothugdragsterism."

71 Ad, *Adelante*, November 1999, 7. My analysis here is influenced by Rodríguez, *Queer Latinidad*, 54.

72 The first ads for Chico with photographs appear in January 2001.

73 Rodríguez, "Queering the Homeboy Aesthetic," 128, 131.

74 Hilary E. MacGregor, "Into the Night: In Montebello, Producer Puts Down Roots at New Breed of Gay Bar," *LAT*, May 23, 2001, E-1.

75 Tan, "Homothugdragsterism," 211.

76 Dinco, October 25, 2019.

77 Mattson, *Who Needs Gay Bars?*, 90.

78 Hugo Cervantes, "East LA's Club sCUM Hosts the Spanish-Language Queer Punk Party of Your Dreams," *Remezcla*, July 2, 2019, https://remezcla.com/features/music/la-club-scum-latin-queer-punk-party. See also Stephanie Mendez, "Club Scum Celebrates Three Years of Championing the LGBTQ Latinx Community," *LAT*, March 30, 2019.

79 Site visit, August 22, 2019.

80 Rechy, *City of Night*; Kenney, *Mapping Gay L.A.*, 23, 84–85.

81 See Forest, "West Hollywood as Symbol"; and Kenney, *Mapping Gay L.A.*, 23, 39, 84–85.

82 Sergio Hernandez, conversation, July 27, 2022.

83 Dinco, October 25, 2019; Ramón García's poem about the original venue, "El Jalisco." See also Bolivar, "I Came Here to Work."

84 Andrea Castillo, "A Lifeline for LGBTQ Latinos on the Brink of Closure," *LAT*, February 15, 2021, https://www.latimes.com/california/story/2021-02-15/a-lifeline-for-lgbtq-latinos-on-the-brink-of-closure.

85 Hernandez, July 27, 2022.

86 The artists' talk was sponsored by the ONE Archives in association with the exhibition *Liberate the Bar! Queer Nightlife, Activism, and Spacemaking*, curated by Paulina Lara and Joseph Valencia, October 13, 2019.

87 Site visit, October 13, 2019.

88 Hernandez, July 27, 2022.

Interlude 8. Mable Peabody's Beauty Parlor and Chainsaw Repair in Denton, TX

1 I had first been to the Charlie's in Denver during a conference in 2002, and it has become a sentimental favorite that I visit whenever I am in town. A mirrored disco ball in the shape of cowboy boots spins above the main dance floor.

2 The Phil Johnson Collection, effectively the community archive for gay Dallas, is now housed in special collections at the UNT Library.

3 *Pink Flamingos* (dir. John Waters, 1972); *The Rocky Horror Show* (dir. Jim Sharman, 1975).

4 "Weird Al" Yankovic, "The White Stuff" (Maurice Starr/Yankovic, Rock'n'Roll Records, 1992), parody of New Kids on the Block, "You Got It (The Right Stuff)."

5   Leslie Knope is Amy Poehler's character on *Parks and Recreation* (created by Greg Daniels and Michael Schur, NBC, 2009–15) and one of my favorite people of all time, real or fictional. The episode "Pawnee Zoo" (season 2, episode 1, 2009) takes Knope to the local gay bar, the Bulge, where she has the time of her life.

Epilogue: After Hours: Pulse in Orlando

1   Omar Mateen worked in private security, had purchased his weapons legally, and was licensed to carry them. The trial "revealed that there was no evidence" that Mateen "knew that Pulse was a gay bar," and "the FBI refused to classify the Pulse shooting as a hate crime." Mattson, *Who Needs Gay Bars?*, 305. Marcia Ochoa corrects the public record that the massacres of Sioux people at Wounded Knee in 1890 and of African Americans in Tulsa in 1921 had higher casualties. Ochoa, "Toxic Masculinity."
2   Ferguson, "Pulse Nightclub and the State." See also Spencer Kornhaber interview with Ramón Rivera-Servera, "The Singular Experience of the Queer Latin Nightclub," *Atlantic*, June 17, 2016, www.theatlantic.com/entertainment/archive/2016/06/orlando-shooting-pulse-latin-queer-gay-nightclub-ramon-rivera-servera-intrerview/487442; Young, "Imagining Queer Life after Death"; Beauchamp, "In Security"; Meyer, "Omar Mateen as US Citizen"; Randell-Moon, "Mediations of Security"; and Stanley, *Atmospheres of Violence*, 41–51.
3   The site was designated a national memorial in 2021; plans for a museum are in process. Writings on Pulse have been collected via Eng-Beng Lim, "The #Orlando Syllabus," and the 2016 Pulse Nightclub Shooting Web Archive, Internet Archive, https://archive-it.org/collections/7570. Dossiers have also been published in *QED* 3, no. 3 (2016), and in *GLQ* 24, no. 1 (2018).
4   In contrast, the sprawling Parliament House gay resort and bar compound was relatively far flung west of downtown.
5   Julio Capó Jr., "Gay Bars Were Supposed to Be Safe Spaces. But They Often Weren't," *Washington Post*, June 14, 2016, www.washingtonpost.com/posteverything/wp/2016/06/14/gay-bars-were-supposed-to-be-safe-spaces-but-they-often-werent; La Fountain-Stokes, "Queer Puerto"; Díaz-Sánchez, "Bailando." See also Salvador Vidal-Ortiz, "Queer-Orlando-América," *Society Pages*, June 17, 2016, https://thesocietypages.org/feminist/2016/06/17/queer-orlando-america.
6   Quiroga, "Straw Dogs."
7   Ari Shapiro, "At Another Orlando Gay Club, LGBT Community Mourns Shooting Victims," *All Things Considered*, June 13, 2016, www.npr.org/2016/06/13/481914346/at-another-orlando-gay-club-lgbt-community-mourns-shooting-victims.

8   Daniel Leon-Davis, "The Site of the Orlando Shooting Wasn't Just a Gay Nightclub. It Was My Safe Haven," *Fusion*, June 12, 2016, http://fusion.net/story/312960/pulse-orlando-safe-haven.

9   Angelica Sanchez seems to be the club's most beloved drag mother, although others who came up there went on to greater fame via *RuPaul's Drag Race*, including Tyra Sanchez, Trinity "the Tuck" Taylor, and Kennedy Davenport.

10 Loma, "All the Dead Boys Look Like Me," *Literary Hub*, June 15, 2016, https://lithub.com/all-the-dead-boys-look-like-me.

11 Díaz-Sánchez, "Bailando."

12 El Gran Combo de Puerto Rico, "Brujería" (Sara Sclange, Combo, 1979); Vargas, "Playlist for Pulse," 49.

13 Madonna, "Into the Groove" (Madonna/Stephen Bray, Sire, 1985).

14 Alfred Soto, "Only When I'm Dancing Can I Feel This Free," *MTV News*, June 12, 2016, www.mtv.com/news/2891842/only-when-im-dancing-can-i-feel-this-free.

15 Louie A. Ortiz-Fonseca, "Queer Latinx: Tired of Being Targets," *Advocate*, June 15, 2016, www.advocate.com/commentary/2016/6/15/queer-latinx-tired-being-targets.

16 Juana María Rodríguez, "Voices: LGBT Clubs Let Us Embrace Queer Latinidad, Let's Affirm This," *NBC News*, June 16, 2016, www.nbcnews.com/storyline/orlando-nightclub-massacre/voices-lgbt-clubs-let-us-embrace-queer-latinidad-let-s-n593191.

17 Capó, "Gay Bars Were Supposed to Be"; Veronica Bayetti Flores, "The Pulse Nightclub Shooting Robbed the Queer Latinx Community of a Sanctuary," *Remezcla*, June 13, 2016, http://remezcla.com/features/music/pulse-nightclub-sanctuary; Hanhardt, "Safe Space Out of Place."

18 Rodríguez, "Voices."

19 Justin Torres, "In Praise of Latin Night at the Queer Club," *Washington Post*, June 13, 2016, www.washingtonpost.com/opinions/in-praise-of-latin-night-at-the-queer-club/2016/06/13/e841867e-317b-11e6-95c0-2a6873031302_story.html.

20 For a study of *la familia* in Latinx cultures (Chicana/o culture specifically), see Rodríguez, *Next of Kin*; on grievable lives, see Butler, "Beside Oneself."

21 Quoted in Michael E. Miller, "'He's Coming . . . I'm Gonna Die,'" *Washington Post*, June 13, 2016, www.washingtonpost.com/news/morning-mix/wp/2016/06/13/hes-coming-im-gonna-die-heartbreaking-final-texts-from-orlando-victim-to-his-mom.

22 The shooter was stopped by a veteran named Richard M. Fierro, who was at the bar to watch a drag show with his wife, daughter, and friends. He said he went into "combat mode" to intervene. A detail from reporting on these events went viral on queer social media: "A drag performer stomped on the

gunman with high heels." Dave Philipps, "Army Veteran Says He Went Into 'Combat Mode' to Disarm Colorado Gunman," *New York Times*, November 21, 2022.
23 Rana, "Night Poetry Danced with Us," 16.
24 Chinchilla, "Church at Night for Orlando," 8.
25 Halberstam, "Who Are 'We' after Orlando?"
26 Alley, "Introduction," 2.

Bibliography

Newspaper, magazine, archival, interview, and online sources are referenced in full in the notes.

Abbott, Steve. *The Lizard Club*. Brooklyn: Autonomedia, 1992.
Abramson, Mark. *For My Brothers*. San Francisco: Minnesota Boy, 2017.
Achilles, Nancy. "The Development of the Homosexual Bar as an Institution." In *Sexual Deviance*, edited by John H. Gagnon and William Simon, 228–44. New York: Harper and Row, 1967.
Achilles, Nancy. "The Homosexual Bar." Master's thesis, University of Chicago, 1964.
Adeyemi, Kemi. *Feels Right: Black Queer Women and the Politics of Partying in Chicago*. Durham, NC: Duke University Press, 2022.
Adeyemi, Kemi, Kareen Khubchandani, and Ramón H. Rivera-Servera, eds. *Queer Nightlife*. Ann Arbor: University of Michigan Press, 2021.
Adler, Libby. *Gay Priori: A Queer Critical Legal Studies Approach to Law Reform*. Durham, NC: Duke University Press, 2018.
Agee, Christopher. "Gayola: Police Professionalization and the Politics of San Francisco's Gay Bars, 1950–1968." *Journal of the History of Sexuality* 15, no. 3 (July 2006): 462–89.
Alfaro, Luis. "Heroes and Saints." In *The Tide Was Always High: The Music of Latin America in Los Angeles*, edited by Josh Kun, 244–50. Oakland: University of California Press, 2017.
Allen, Jafari Sinclaire. "For 'the Children' Dancing the Beloved Community." *Souls* 11, no. 3 (2009): 311–26.
Allen, Jafari S. *There's a Disco Ball between Us*. Durham, NC: Duke University Press, 2021.

Allen, Samantha. *Real Queer America: LGBT Stories from Red States.* New York: Little, Brown, 2019.

Alley, Jason. "Introduction: GLQ Forum/Aftereffects: The Pulse Nightclub Shootings." *GLQ* 24, no. 1 (2018): 1–2.

Altman, Dennis. "Gay Oppression in the Baths." In *Coming Out in the Seventies*, 42–45. Sydney: Wild & Woolley, 1979.

Altman, Dennis. *Homosexual: Oppression and Liberation.* New York: Outerbridge and Lazard, 1971.

Altman, Dennis. *The Homosexualization of America, the Americanization of the Homosexual.* New York: St. Martin's, 1982.

Alvarez, Eddy Francisco, Jr. "Finding Sequins in the Rubble: Stitching Together an Archive of Trans Latina Los Angeles." *TSQ* 4, nos. 2–4 (November 2016): 618–27.

Amin, Kadji. "Haunted by the 1990s: Queer Theory's Affective Histories." In *Imagining Queer Methods*, edited by Amin Ghaziani and Matt Brim, 277–93. New York: NYU Press, 2019.

Amory, Deborah P. "Club Q: Dancing with (a) Difference." In *Inventing Lesbian Cultures in America*, edited by Ellen Lewin, 145–60. Boston: Beacon, 1996.

Anzaldúa, Gloria. *Borderlands/La Frontera: The New Mestiza.* San Francisco: Aunt Lute, 1987.

Armstrong, Elizabeth A. *Forging Gay Identities: Organizing Sexuality in San Francisco, 1950–1994.* Chicago: University of Chicago Press, 2002.

Armstrong, Elizabeth A., and Suzanna M. Crage. "Movements and Memory: The Making of the Stonewall Myth." *American Sociological Review* 71, no. 5 (October 2006): 724–51.

Arondekar, Anjali. "Without a Trace: Sexuality and the Colonial Archive." *Journal of the History of Sexuality* 14, nos. 1/2 (January 2005): 10–27.

Arondekar, Anjali, Ann Cvetkovich, Christina B. Hanhardt, Regina Kunzel, Tavia Nyong'o, Juana María Rodríguez, Susan Stryker, Daniel Marshall, Kevin P. Murphy, and Zeb Tortorici. "Queering Archives: A Roundtable Discussion." *Radical History Review* 122 (2015): 211–31.

Atkins, Gary L. *Gay Seattle: Stories of Exile and Belonging.* Seattle: University of Washington Press, 2003.

Auger, Deborah A. "The Politics of Revitalization in Gentrifying Neighborhoods: The Case of Boston's South End." *Journal of the American Planning Association* 45, no. 4 (1979): 515–22.

Babuscio, Jack. "Camp and the Gay Sensibility." In *Camp Grounds: Style and Homosexuality*, edited by David Bergman, 19–38. Amherst: University of Massachusetts Press, 1993.

Bailey, Marlon M. *Butch Queens Up In Pumps: Gender, Performance, and Ballroom Culture in Detroit.* Ann Arbor: University of Michigan Press, 2013.

Baim, Tracy, ed. *Out and Proud in Chicago: An Overview of the City's Gay Community.* Chicago: Surrey, 2008.

Baim, Tracy, and Owen Keehnen. *Leatherman: The Legend of Chuck Renslow.* Chicago: Prairie Avenue, 2011.

Baker, Roger. *Drag: A History of Female Impersonation on the Stage.* London: Triton, 1968.

Baker, Roger. *Drag: A History of Female Impersonation in the Performing Arts.* London: Cassell, 1994.

Baldor, Tyler. "No Girls Allowed? Fluctuating Boundaries between Gay Men and Straight Women in Gay Public Space." *Ethnography* 20, no. 4 (2019): 419–42.

Baldwin, Guy. "A Second Coming Out." In *Leatherfolk: Radical Sex, People, Politics, and Practice*, edited by Mark Thompson, 169–78. Boston: Alyson, 1991.

Baldwin, James. "The White Man's Guilt." In *James Baldwin: Collected Essays*, edited by Toni Morrison, 722–27. New York: Library of America, 1998.

Barrows, Philip. *Whores, Queers, and Others*, vol. 2. New York: Traveler's Companion, 1967.

Barrows, Susanna, and Robin Room, eds. *Drinking: Behavior and Belief in Modern History.* Berkeley: University of California Press, 1991.

Barthes, Roland. *Camera Lucida: Reflections on Photography.* Translated by Richard Howard. New York: Hill and Wang, 1981.

Bayor, Ronald H. *Race and the Shaping of Twentieth-Century Atlanta.* Chapel Hill: University of North Carolina Press, 1996.

Beame, Thom. "Interview: BWMT Founder—Mike Smith." In *Black Men/White Men*, edited by Michael J. Smith, 187–95. San Francisco: Gay Sunshine, 1983.

Beauchamp, Toby. "In Security." *GLQ* 24, no. 1 (2018): 13–17.

Beemyn, Genny, ed. *Creating a Place for Ourselves: Lesbian, Gay, and Bisexual Community Histories.* New York: Routledge, 1997.

Beemyn, Genny. *A Queer Capital: A History of Gay Life in Washington, D.C.* New York: Routledge, 2015.

Bell, Arthur. *Dancing the Gay Lib Blues: A Year in the Homosexual Liberation Movement.* New York: Simon and Schuster, 1971.

Bell, David, and Gill Valentine, eds. *Mapping Desire: Geographies of Sexualities.* New York: Routledge, 1995.

Bell, Jonathan, Darius Bost, Jennifer Brier, Julio Capó Jr, Jih-Fei Cheng, Daniel M. Fox, Christina Hanhardt, Emily K. Hobson, and Dan Royles. "Interchange: HIV/AIDS and U.S. History." *Journal of American History* 104, no. 2 (2017): 431–60.

Benjamin, Joseph. "Gay Switchboards." In *Gay Life*, edited by Eric Rofes, 273–78. Garden City, NY: Doubleday, 1986.

Bennett, Jeffrey, and Isaac West. "'United We Stand, Divided We Fall: AIDS, Armorettes, and the Tactical Repertoires of Drag." *Southern Communication Journal* 73, no. 3 (2009): 300–13.

Berlant, Lauren, and Michael Warner. "Sex in Public." *Critical Inquiry* 24, no. 2 (Winter 1998): 547–66.

Bernstein, Robin, and Seth Clark Silberman, eds. *Generation Q.* Los Angeles: Alyson, 1996.

Berson, Jessica. *The Naked Result: How Exotic Dance Became Big Business.* New York: Oxford University Press, 2016.

Bérubé, Allan. *Coming Out under Fire: The History of Gay Men and Women in World War Two.* New York: Free Press, 1990.

Bérubé, Allan. "The History of Gay Bathhouses." In *Policing Public Sex*, edited by Dangerous Bedfellows, 187–220. Boston: South End, 1996.

Bérubé, Allan. "How Gay Stays White and What Kind of White It Stays." In *My Desire for History: Essays in Gay, Community, and Labor History*, edited by John D'Emilio and Estelle B. Freedman, 202–30. Chapel Hill: University of North Carolina Press, 2011.

Bérubé, Allan. "Intellectual Desire." GLQ 3, no. 1 (February 1996): 139–57.

Bérubé, Allan, and Jeffrey Escoffier. "Queer/Nation." *Out/Look* 11 (Winter 1991): 12–14.

Bess, S. Renée, and Lee Lynch, eds. *Our Happy Hours: LGBT Voices from the Gay Bars.* Sardinia, OH: Flashpoint, 2017.

Betsky, Aaron. *Queer Space: Architecture and Same-Sex Desire.* New York: Morrow, 1997.

Betty and Pansy's Severe Queer Review of San Francisco, no. 3. San Francisco: Bedpan, 1993.

Binnie, Jon. "Trading Places: Consumption, Sexuality and the Production of Queer Space." In *Mapping Desire: Geographies of Sexualities*, edited by David Bell and Gill Valentine, 182–99. New York: Routledge, 1995.

Black, D., G. Gates, S. Sanders, and L. Taylor. "Why Do Gay Men Live in San Francisco?" *Journal of Urban Economics* 51 (2002): 54–76.

Blair, Zachary. "Boystown: Gay Neighborhoods, Social Media, and the (Re)production of Racism." In *No Tea, No Shade: New Writings in Black Queer Studies*, edited by E. Patrick Johnson, 287–303. Durham, NC: Duke University Press, 2016.

Blake, Nayland. "Curating *In a Different Light*." In *In a Different Light: Visual Culture, Sexual Identity, Queer Practice*, edited by Nayland Blake, Lawrence Rinder, and Amy Scholder, 9–44. San Francisco: City Lights, 1995.

Blake, Nayland, and Justin Vivian Bond. *Jerome Caja.* New York: Visual AIDS, 2018.

Blasius, Mark, and Shane Phelan, eds. *We Are Everywhere: A Historical Sourcebook of Gay and Lesbian Politics.* New York: Routledge, 1997.

Bolivar, Andrea. "I Came Here to Work: Transgender Latinas' Labors in the Club." In *Queer Nightlife*, edited by Kemi Adeyemi, Kareen Khubchandani, and Ramón H. Rivera-Servera, 113–19. Ann Arbor: University of Michigan Press, 2021.

Bollen, Jonathan. "Queer Kinesthesia: Performativity on the Dance Floor." In *Dancing Desires: Choreographing Sexualities On and Off the Stage*, edited by Jane Desmond, 285–314. Madison: University of Wisconsin Press, 2001.

Bolton, Ralph, John Vincke, and Rudolf Mak. "Gay Baths Revisited: An Empirical Analysis." GLQ 1, no. 3 (1994): 255–73.

Bolze, Thomas. "Female Impersonation in the United States, 1900–1970." PhD diss., SUNY Buffalo, 1994.

Bost, Darius. "At the Club: Locating Early Black Gay AIDS Activism in Washington, D.C." *Occasion* 8 (Fall 2015): https://arcade.stanford.edu/occasion/club-locating-early-black-gay-aids-activism-washington-dc.

Bost, Darius. *Evidence of Being: The Black Gay Cultural Renaissance and the Politics of Violence*. Chicago: University of Chicago Press, 2019.

Bost, Darius. "Evidence of Being: Urban Black Gay Men's Literature and Culture, 1978–1995." PhD diss., University of Maryland, 2014.

Bouthillette, Anne-Marie. "Queer and Gendered Housing: A Tale of Two Neighborhoods in Vancouver." In *Queers in Space: Communities, Public Places, Sites of Resistance*, edited by Gorden Brent Ingram, Anne-Marie Bouthillette, and Yolanda Retter, 213–32. Seattle: Bay, 1997.

Boyd, Nan Alamilla. *Wide Open Town: A History of Queer San Francisco to 1965*. Berkeley: University of California Press, 2003.

Boykin, Keith. *One More River to Cross: Black & Gay in America*. New York: Anchor, 1996.

Branson, Helen P. *Gay Bar*. San Francisco: Pan-Graphic, 1957.

Branson, Helen P. *Gay Bar*. Madison: University of Wisconsin Press, 2010.

Bredbeck, Gregory W. "Troping the Light Fantastic: Representing Disco Then and Now." *GLQ* 3, no. 1 (1996): 71–107.

Brekhus, Wayne H. *Peacocks, Chameleons, Centaurs: Gay Suburbia and the Grammar of Social Identity*. Chicago: University of Chicago Press, 2003.

Brewster, Bill, and Frank Broughton. *Last Night a DJ Saved My Life: The History of the Disc Jockey*. New York: Grove, 2000.

Brodsky, Joel. "The Mineshaft: A Retrospective Ethnography." *Journal of Homosexuality* 24, nos. 3–4 (1993): 233–51.

Brodyn, Adriana, and Amin Ghaziani. "Performative Progressiveness: Accounting for New Forms of Inequality in the Gayborhood." *City & Community* 17, no. 2 (2018): 307–29.

Bronski, Michael. "A Dream Is a Wish Your Heart Makes: Notes on the Materialization of Sexual Fantasy." In *Leatherfolk*, edited by Mark Thompson, 56–64. Boston: Alyson, 1991.

Bronski, Michael. *The Pleasure Principle*. New York: St. Martin's, 1998.

Brown, Howard. *Familiar Faces, Hidden Lives: The Story of Homosexual Men in America Today*. New York: Harcourt Brace Jovanovich, 1976.

Brown, Michael, Stefano Bettani, Larry Knopp, and Andrew Childs. "The Gay Bar as a Place of Men's Caring." In *Masculinities and Place*, edited by Andrew Gorman-Murray and Peter Hopkins, 299–315. Burlington, UK: Ashgate, 2014.

Brown, Michael, and Larry Knopp. "Sex, Drink, and State Anxieties: Governance through the Gay Bar." *Social & Cultural Geography* 17, no. 3 (2016): 335–58.

Brown, Ricardo. *The Evening Crowd at Kirmser's: A Gay Life in the 1940s*. Minneapolis: University of Minnesota Press, 2001.

Brown, Rita Mae. "Queen for a Day: A Stranger in Paradise." In *Lavender Culture*, edited by Karla Jay and Allen Young, 69–76. New York: Jove, 1978.

Browning, Frank. *The Culture of Desire: Paradox and Perversity in Gay Lives Today.* New York: Vintage, 1994.

Brown-Nagin, Tomiko. *Courage to Dissent: Atlanta and the Long History of the Civil Rights Movement.* New York: Oxford University Press, 2012.

Brown-Saracino, Japonica. "Aligning Our Maps: A Call to Reconcile Distinct Visions of Literatures on Sexualities, Space, and Place." *City & Community* 18, no. 1 (March 2019): 1–7.

Brown-Saracino, Japonica. "How Places Shape Identity: The Origins of Distinctive LGQ Identities in Four Small U.S. Cities." *American Journal of Sociology* 121, no. 1 (July 2015): 1–63.

Buckland, Fiona. *Impossible Dance: Club Culture and Queer World-Making.* Middletown, CT: Wesleyan University Press, 2001.

Bullough, Vern L., and Bonnie Bullough. *Cross Dressing, Sex, and Gender.* Philadelphia: University of Pennsylvania Press, 1993.

Butler, Judith. "Beside Oneself: On the Limits of Sexual Autonomy." In *Undoing Gender*, 18–39. New York: Routledge, 2004.

Butler, Judith. "Critically Queer." *GLQ* 1, no. 1 (1993): 17–32.

Butler, Judith. *Gender Trouble: Feminism and the Subversion of Identity.* New York: Routledge, 1990.

Button, James W., Barbra A. Rienzo, and Kenneth D. Wald. *Private Lives, Public Conflicts: Battles over Gay Rights in American Communities.* Washington, DC: Congressional Quarterly Press, 1997.

Cáceres, F., and Jorge I. Cortiñas. "Fantasy Island: An Ethnography of Alcohol and Gender Roles in a Latino Gay Bar." *Journal of Drug Issues* 26, no. 1 (1996): 245–60.

Calhoun, Craig, ed. *Habermas and the Public Sphere.* Cambridge, MA: MIT Press, 1992.

Califia, Pat. "San Francisco: Revisiting 'The City of Desire.'" In *Queers in Space: Communities, Public Places, Sites of Resistance*, edited by Gordon Brent Ingram, Anne-Marie Bouthillette, and Yolanda Retter, 177–96. Seattle: Bay, 1997.

Campbell, Andy. *Bound Together: Leather, Sex, Archives, and Contemporary Art.* Manchester, UK: Manchester University Press, 2020.

Campbell, Andy. *Queer × Design.* New York: Black Dog, 2019.

Cante, Richard C. "Pouring on the Past: Video Bars and the Emplacement of Gay Male Desire." In *Queer Frontiers: Millennial Geographies, Genders, and Generations*, edited by Joseph A. Boone et al., 135–65. Madison: University of Wisconsin Press, 2000.

Cantú, Jr., Lionel. *The Sexuality of Migration: Border Crossings and Mexican Immigrant Men.* Edited by Nancy A. Naples and Salvador Vidal-Ortiz. New York: NYU Press, 2009.

Cantwell, Christopher D., Stuart Hinds, and Kathryn B. Carpenter. "Over the Rainbow: Public History as Allyship in Documenting Kansas City's LGBTQ Past." *Public Historian* 41, no. 2 (May 2019): 245–68.

Cardini, Leo. *Mineshaft Nights.* Herndon, VA: STARbooks, 2007.

Carney, William. *The Real Thing.* New York: Masquerade, 1995. First published 1968.

Carrier, Joseph. *De los Otros: Intimacy and Homosexuality among Mexican Men.* New York: Columbia University Press, 1995.

Carrier, Joseph. "Miguel: Sexual Life History of a Gay Mexican American." In *Gay Culture in America: Essays from the Field*, edited by Gilbert Herdt, 202–24. Boston: Beacon, 1992.

Carrillo, Héctor. "Cultural Archipelagos and Immigrants' Experiences." *City & Community* 18, no. 1 (March 2019): 1–5.

Carrillo, Héctor. *The Night Is Young: Sexuality in Mexico in the Time of AIDS.* Chicago: University of Chicago Press, 2002.

Carrillo, Héctor. *Pathways of Desire: The Sexual Migration of Mexican Gay Men.* Chicago: University of Chicago Press, 2017.

Carter, David. *Stonewall: The Riots That Sparked the Gay Revolution.* New York: St. Martin's, 2004.

Cartier, Marie. *Baby, You Are My Religion: Women, Gay Bars, and Theology before Stonewall.* New York: Routledge, 2014.

Castells, Manuel. *The City and the Grassroots: A Cross-Cultural Theory of Urban Social Movements.* Berkeley: University of California Press, 1983.

Caulfield, Jon. "'Gentrification' and Desire." In *The Gentrification Reader*, edited by Loretta Lees, Tom Slater, and Elvin Wyly, 161–70. New York: Routledge, 2010.

Cavan, Sherri. *Liquor License: An Ethnography of Bar Behavior.* Chicago: Aldine, 1966.

Chambers-Letson, Joshua. *After the Ball: A Manifesto for Queer of Color Life.* New York: NYU Press, 2018.

Chasin, Alexandra. *Selling Out: The Gay and Lesbian Movement Goes to Market.* New York: Palgrave, 2000.

Chauncey, George. *Gay New York: Gender, Urban Culture, and the Making of the Gay Male World, 1890–1940.* New York: Basic Books, 1994.

Chavez, Karma R. *The Borders of AIDS: Race, Quarantine and Resistance.* Seattle: University of Washington Press, 2021.

Chavoya, C. Ondine, and David Evans Frantz, eds. *Axis Mundo: Queer Networks in Chicano L.A.* Los Angeles: ONE Archives, 2017.

Cheng, Jih-Fei, Alexandra Juhuasz, and Nishant Shahani, eds. *AIDS and the Distribution of Crises.* Durham, NC: Duke University Press, 2020.

Cheren, Mel, as told to Gabriel Rotello. *Keep on Dancin': My Life and the Paradise Garage.* New York: 24 Hours for Life, 2000.

Chermayeff, Catherine, Jonathan David, and Nan Richardson. *Drag Diaries.* San Francisco: Chronicle, 1995.

Chinchilla, Maya. "Church at Night for Orlando." *GLQ* 24, no. 1 (2018): 3–8.

Cifor, Marika. *Viral Cultures: Activist Archiving in the Age of AIDS.* Minneapolis: University of Minnesota Press, 2022.

Clarke, Eric O. *Virtuous Vice: Homoeroticism and the Public Sphere.* Durham, NC: Duke University Press, 2000.

Cohan, Steven. *Incongruous Entertainment: Camp, Cultural Taste, and the MGM Musical.* Durham, NC: Duke University Press, 2005.

Cohen, Cathy J. "Punks, Bulldaggers, and Welfare Queens: The Radical Potential of Queer Politics." *GLQ* 3, no. 4 (1997): 437–65.

Coleman, Bud. "The Jewel Box Revue: America's Longest Running Touring Drag Show." *Theatre History Studies* 17 (June 1997): 79–92.

Collin, Matthew. *Altered State: The Story of Ecstasy Culture and Acid House.* London: Serpent's Tail, 2009.

Collin, Matthew. *Rave On: Global Adventures in Electronic Dance Music.* Chicago: University of Chicago Press, 2018.

Collins, Alan. "Sexual Dissidence, Enterprise and Assimilation: Bedfellows in Urban Regeneration." *Urban Studies* 41, no. 9 (August 2004): 1769–1806.

Colucci, Emily, and Osman Can Yereban, eds. *Party Out of Bounds: Nightlife as Activism since 1980.* New York: Visual AIDS, 2015.

Combahee River Collective. "Combahee River Collective Statement." In *This Bridge Called My Back: Writings by Radical Women of Color*, 4th ed., edited by Cherríe Moraga and Gloria Anzaldúa, 210–18. Albany: SUNY Press, 2015.

Comella, Lynn. *Vibrator Nation: How Feminist Sex-Toy Stores Changed the Business of Pleasure.* Durham, NC: Duke University Press, 2017.

Cory, Donald Webster. *The Homosexual in America: A Subjective Approach.* New York: Greenberg, 1951.

Cory, Donald Webster, and John P. LeRoy. *The Homosexual and His Society.* New York: Citadel, 1963.

County, Jayne. *Man Enough to Be a Woman.* New York: Serpent's Tail, 1995.

Coupland, Douglas. *Generation X: Tales for an Accelerated Culture.* New York: St. Martin's, 1991.

Crawford, Phillip. *The Mafia and the Gays.* Self-published, 2015.

Crimp, Douglas. *Before Pictures.* Chicago: University of Chicago Press, 2016.

Crimp, Douglas. "*Disss*-Co (A Fragment)." *Criticism* 50, no. 1 (2008): 1–18.

Crimp, Douglas. "How to Have Promiscuity in an Epidemic." *October* 43 (Winter 1987): 237–71.

Crimp, Douglas. "Mourning and Militancy." In *Out There: Marginalization and Contemporary Culture*, edited by Russell Ferguson, Martha Gever, Trinh T. Minh-ha, and Cornel West, 233–45. Cambridge: MIT Press, 1990.

Cruz, Ariane. *The Color of Kink: Black Women, BDSM, and Pornography.* New York: NYU Press, 2016.

Cvetkovich, Ann. *An Archive of Feelings: Trauma, Sexuality, and Lesbian Public Cultures.* Durham, NC: Duke University Press, 2003.

Dango, Michael. "Camp's Distribution: 'Our' Aesthetic Category." *Social Text* 131 (June 2017): 39–67.

D'Arcangelo, Angelo. *The Homosexual Handbook.* New York: Ophelia, 1969.

De la Croix, St. Sukie. *Chicago after Stonewall: A History of LGBTQ Chicago from Gay Lib to Gay Life.* Cathedral City, CA: Rattling Good Yarns, 2021.

De la Croix, St. Sukie. *Chicago Whispers: A History of LGBT Chicago before Stonewall.* Madison: University of Wisconsin Press, 2012.

De la Loza, Sandra. *The Pocho Research Society Field Guide to L.A.: Monuments and Murals of Erased and Invisible Histories.* Los Angeles: UCLA Chicano Studies Research Center Press, 2011.

De Lauretis, Teresa, ed. "Queer Theory: Gay and Lesbian Sexualities." Special issue, *differences* 3, no. 2 (1991).

Delany, Samuel R. *Times Square Red, Times Square Blue.* New York: NYU Press, 1999.

Delery-Edwards, Clayton. *The Up Stairs Lounge Arson.* Jefferson, NC: McFarland, 2014.

Delgado, Celeste Fraser, and José Esteban Muñoz, eds. *Everynight Life: Culture and Dance in Latino/a America.* Durham, NC: Duke University Press, 1997.

DeMarco, Joe. "Gay Racism." In *Black Men/White Men,* edited by Michael J. Smith, 109–18. San Francisco: Gay Sunshine, 1983.

D'Emilio, John. "Capitalism and Gay Identity." In *Making Trouble: Essays on Gay History, Politics, and the University,* 3–16. New York: Routledge, 1992.

D'Emilio, John. *Sexual Politics, Sexual Communities: The Making of a Homosexual Minority in the United States, 1940–1970.* Chicago: University of Chicago Press, 1983.

D'Emilio, John. "Stonewall: Myth and Meaning." In *The World Turned: Essays on Gay History, Politics, and Culture,* 146–53. Durham, NC: Duke University Press, 2002.

Di Brienza, Ronnie. "Stonewall Incident." In *The Stonewall Riots: A Documentary History,* edited by Marc Stein, 153–56. New York; NYU Press, 2019.

Díaz-Sánchez, Micaela J. "Bailando: 'We Would Have Been There.'" *QED* 3, no. 3 (2016): 154–56.

Diebold, David. *Tribal Rites: The San Francisco Dance Music Phenomenon, 1978–88.* San Francisco, Time Warp, 1988.

Doan, Petra L. "Cultural Archipelagos or Planetary Systems." *City & Community* 18, no. 1 (March 2019): 30–36.

Doan, Petra L., ed. *Planning and LGBT Communities: The Need for Inclusive Queer Spaces.* New York: Routledge, 2015.

Doan, Petra L., and Harrison Higgins. "The Demise of Queer Space? Resurgent Gentrification and the Assimilation of LGBT Neighborhoods." *Journal of Planning Education and Research* 31, no. 1 (2011): 6–25.

Drorbaugh, Elizabeth. "Sliding Scales: Notes on Stormé DeLaverié and the Jewel Box Revue." In *Crossing the Stage: Controversies in Cross-Dressing,* edited by Lesley Ferris, 120–43. New York: Routledge, 1993.

Duberman, Martin. *Stonewall.* New York: Dutton, 1993.

Dufour, Claude. "Mobilizing Gay Activists." In *Social Movements and American Political Institutions,* edited by Anne N. Costain and Andrew S. McFarland, 59–72. Lanham, MD: Rowman & Littlefield, 1998.

Duggan, Lisa. "Making It Perfectly Queer." *Socialist Review* 22, no. 1 (1992): 11–31.

Duggan, Lisa. *The Twilight of Equality? Neoliberalism, Cultural Politics, and the Attack on Democracy.* Boston: Beacon, 2003.

Dyer, Richard. *Heavenly Bodies: Film Stars and Society.* New York: St. Martin's, 1986.

Dyer, Richard. "In Defence of Disco." *Gay Left* 8 (Summer 1979): 20–23.

Dyer, Richard. "It's Being So Camp as Keeps Us Going." In *The Culture of Queers,* 49–62. New York: Routledge, 2001.

Dyer, Richard. "White." *Screen* 29, no. 4 (Autumn 1988): 44–65.

Dyer, Richard. *White: Essays on Race and Culture.* New York: Routledge, 1997.

Echols, Alice. *Hot Stuff: Disco and the Remaking of American Culture.* New York: Norton, 2010.

El Kholti, Hedi, and Lauren Mackler, eds. *Reynaldo Rivera.* South Pasadena, CA: Semiotext(e), 2020.

Ellingson, Stephen, and Kirby Schroeder. "Race and the Construction of Same-Sex Markets in Four Chicago Neighborhoods." In *The Sexual Organization of the City,* edited by Edward O. Laumann, Stephen Ellingson, Jenna Mahay, Anthony Paik, and Yoosik Youm, 69–92. Chicago: University of Chicago Press, 2004.

Eng, David L., and Jasbir K. Puar, "Introduction: Left of Queer." *Social Text* 145 (December 2020): 1–24.

Enke, A. Finn. *Finding the Movement: Sexuality, Contested Space, and Feminist Activism.* Durham, NC: Duke University Press, 2007.

Epstein, Rebecca, ed. *Laura Aguilar: Show and Tell.* Los Angeles: UCLA Chicano Studies Research Center Press, 2017.

Faderman, Lillian. *Odd Girls and Twilight Lovers: A History of Lesbian Life in Twentieth Century America.* New York: Columbia University Press, 1991.

Faderman, Lillian, and Stuart Timmons. *Gay L.A.: A History of Sexual Outlaws, Power Politics, and Lipstick Lesbians.* New York: Basic Books, 2006.

Fawaz, Ramzi. *Queer Forms.* New York: NYU Press, 2022.

Ferguson, Roderick A. "The Pulse Nightclub and the State of Our World." *GLQ* 24, no. 1 (2018): 36–37.

Ferris, Lesley, ed. *Crossing the Stage: Controversies in Cross-Dressing.* New York: Routledge, 1993.

Fienberg, Leslie. *Stone Butch Blues.* Ithaca, NY: Firebrand, 1993.

Fierstein, Harvey. *I Was Better Last Night: A Memoir.* New York: Knopf, 2022.

Fierstein, Harvey. *Torch Song Trilogy.* New York: Signet, 1988.

Fieseler, Robert W. *Tinderbox: The Untold Story of the Up Stairs Lounge Fire and the Rise of Gay Liberation.* New York: Liveright, 2018.

Fikentscher, Kai. *"You Better Work!" Underground Dance Music in New York City.* Hanover, NH: Wesleyan University Press, 2000.

Fleischmann, Arnold, and Jason Hardman. "Hitting below the Bible Belt: The Development of the Gay Rights Movement in Atlanta." *Journal of Urban Affairs* 26, no. 4 (2004): 407–26.

Fleisher, Julian. *The Drag Queens of New York: An Illustrated Field Guide.* New York: Riverhead, 1996.

Florida, Richard. *The Rise of the Creative Class: How It's Transforming Work, Leisure, Community, and Everyday Life.* New York: Basic Books, 2002.

Forest, Benjamin. "West Hollywood as Symbol: The Significance of Place in the Construction of a Gay Identity." *Environment and Planning D: Society and Space* 13, no. 2 (1995): 133–57.

Frantz, David Evans, and Mia Locks, eds. *Cruising the Archive: Queer Art and Culture in Los Angeles, 1945–1980.* Los Angeles: ONE Archives, 2011.

Freeman, Lance. *There Goes the 'Hood: Views of Gentrification from the Ground Up.* Philadelphia: Temple University Press, 2006.

Freibert, Finley. "Distribution, Bars, and Arcade Stars: Joe Anthony's Entrepreneurial Expansion in Houston's Gay Media Industries." *Synoptique* 9, no. 2 (2021): 33–54.

Fritscher, Jack. "Artist Chuck Arnett: His Life/Our Times." In *Leatherfolk: Radical Sex, People, Politics, and Practice*, edited by Mark Thompson, 106–18. Boston: Alyson, 1991.

Fritscher, Jack. *Gay San Francisco: Eyewitness Drummer.* San Francisco: Palm Drive, 2008.

Fritscher, Jack. *Profiles in Gay Courage: Leatherfolk, Arts, and Ideas.* San Francisco: Palm Drive, 2022.

Gamboa, Eddie. "Pedagogies of the Dark: Making Sense of Queer Nightlife." In *Queer Nightlife*, edited by Kemi Adeyemi, Kareen Khubchandani, and Ramón H. Rivera-Servera, 91–100. Ann Arbor: University of Michigan Press, 2021.

Gamson, Joshua. "Must Identity Movements Self-Destruct? A Queer Dilemma." *Social Problems* 42, no. 3 (August 1995): 390–407.

Gans, Herbert J. *The Urban Villagers: Group and Class in the Life of Italian-Americans*, rev. ed. New York: Free Press, 1982.

Garber, Marjorie. *Vested Interests: Cross Dressing and Cultural Anxiety.* New York: Routledge, 1992.

García, Cindy. *Salsa Crossings: Dancing Latinidad in Los Angeles.* Durham, NC: Duke University Press, 2013.

García, Ramón. "Dreamings of the Dead." In *Geographies of Rage: Remembering the Los Angeles Riots of 1992*, edited by Jervey Tervalon, 59–63. Los Angeles: Really Great, 2002.

García, Ramón. "El Jalisco." In *Other Countries*, 78–79. Los Angeles: What Books, 2010.

Garcia-Mispireta, Luis Manuel. *Together, Somehow: Music, Affect, and Intimacy on the Dancefloor.* Durham, NC: Duke University Press, 2023.

Gates, Racquel J. *Double Negative: The Black Image and Popular Culture.* Durham, NC: Duke University Press, 2018.

Ghaziani, Amin. "Cultural Archipelagos: New Directions in the Study of Sexuality and Space." *City & Community* 18, no. 1 (March 2019): 1–19.

Ghaziani, Amin. *The Dividends of Dissent: How Conflict and Culture Work in Lesbian and Gay Marches on Washington.* Chicago: University of Chicago Press, 2008.

Ghaziani, Amin. *Long Live Queer Nightlife: How the Closing of Gay Bars Sparked a Revolution.* Princeton, NJ: Princeton University Press, 2024.

Ghaziani, Amin. *There Goes the Gayborhood?* Princeton, NJ: Princeton University Press, 2014.

Gieseking, Jen Jack. *A Queer New York: Geographies of Lesbians, Dykes, and Queers.* New York: NYU Press, 2021.

Gilroy, Paul. *The Black Atlantic: Modernity and Double Consciousness.* Cambridge, MA: Harvard University Press, 1995.

Gill-Peterson, Jules. "Haunting the Queer Spaces of AIDS: Remembering ACT UP/New York and an Ethics for an Endemic." *GLQ* 19, no. 3 (2013): 279–300.

Giorlandino, Salvatore M. "The Origin, Development, and Decline of Boston's Adult Entertainment District: The Combat Zone." Master's thesis, MIT, 1986.

Gluckman, Amy, and Betsy Reed, eds. *Homo Economics: Capitalism, Community, and Lesbian and Gay Life.* New York: Routledge, 1997.

Goldberg, Eve. "Riot at the Black Cat." *Gay & Lesbian Review* (May/June 2012): 10–12.

Goldin, Nan. *The Other Side.* New York: Scalo, 1993.

Gorman, E. Michael. "The Pursuit of a Wish: An Anthropological Perspective on Gay Male Subculture in Los Angeles." In *Gay Culture in America: Essays from the Field*, edited by Gilbert Herdt, 87–106. Boston: Beacon, 1992.

Gray, Mary L. *Out in the Country: Youth, Media, and Queer Visibility in Rural America.* New York: NYU, 2009.

Grazian, David. *On the Make: The Hustle of Urban Nightlife.* Chicago: University of Chicago Press, 2008.

Green, Adam Isaiah. "The Social Organization of Desire: The Sexual Fields Approach." *Sociological Theory* 26, no. 1 (March 2008): 25–50.

Green, Marshall. "Into the Darkness: A Quare (Re)Membering of Los Angeles in a Time of Crises, 1981–Present." PhD diss., University of Southern California, 2014.

Greene, Theodore. "Aberrations of 'Home': Gay Neighborhoods and the Experiences of Community among GBQ Men of Color." In *The Handbook of Research on Black Males*, edited by Theodore S. Ransaw, C. P. Gause, and Richard Majors, 189–209. East Lansing: Michigan State University Press, 2019.

Greene, Theodore. "Gay Neighborhood and the Rights of the Vicarious Citizen." *City & Community*, 13, no. 2 (June 2014): 99–118.

Greene, Theodore. "Queer Cultural Archipelagos Are New to US." *City & Community* 18, no. 1 (March 2019): 1–7.

Greene, Theodore. "The Whiteness of Queer Urban Placemaking." In *The Gayborhood: From Sexual Liberation to Cosmopolitan Spectacle*, edited by Christopher T. Conner and Daniel Okamura, 143–60. Lanham, MD: Rowman & Littlefield, 2021.

Greene, Theodore. "'You're Dancing on My Seat!': Queer Subcultures and the Production of Places in Contemporary Gay Bars." *Subcultures* 54 (2022): 137–65.

Gutiérrez, Raquel. "A Concatenation of Sprawls." *Places*, September 2021. https://placesjournal.org/article/queer-latinx-nightlife-and-urbanist-aesthetics-los-angeles.

Guzmán, Manuel. "'Pa' La Escuelita con Mucho Cuida'o y por Orillita': A Journey through the Contested Terrains of the Nation and Sexual Orientation." In *Puerto Rican Jam: Rethinking Colonialism and Nationalism*, edited by Frances Negrón-Muntaner and Ramón Grosfoguel, 209–28. Minneapolis: University of Minnesota Press, 1997.

Habermas, Jürgen. *The Structural Transformation of the Public Sphere: An Inquiry into a Category of Bourgeois Society*. Translated by Thomas Burger. Cambridge, MA: MIT Press, 1991.

Haden-Guest, Anthony. *The Last Party: Studio 54, Disco, and the Culture of the Night*. New York: William Morrow, 1997.

Hae, Laam. *The Gentrification of Nightlife and the Right to the City: Regulating Spaces of Social Dancing in New York*. New York: Routledge, 2012.

Hagius, Hugh, ed. *Swasarnt Nerf's Gay Guides for 1949*. New York: Bibliogay, 2010.

Halberstam, Jack. *In a Queer Time and Place: Transgender Bodies, Subcultural Lives*. New York: NYU Press, 2005.

Halberstam, Jack. "Who Are 'We' after Orlando?" *Bully Bloggers*, June 22, 2016. https://bullybloggers.wordpress.com/2016/06/22/who-are-we-after-orlando-by-jack-halberstam.

Hall, Jacqueline Dowd. "The Long Civil Rights Movement and the Political Uses of the Past." *Journal of American History* 91, no. 4 (March 2005): 1233–63.

Hall, Stuart. "Cultural Identity and Cinematic Representation," *Framework* 36 (1989): 68–81.

Hall, Stuart. "New Ethnicities." In *Selected Writings on Race and Difference*, edited by Paul Gilroy and Ruth Wilson Gilmore, 246–56. Durham, NC: Duke University Press, 2021.

Halperin, David. *Saint Foucault: Towards a Gay Hagiography*. New York: Oxford University Press, 1995.

Han, C. Winter. *Racial Erotics: Gay Men of Color, Sexual Racism, and the Politics of Desire*. Seattle: University of Washington Press, 2021.

Hanhardt, Christina B. "Broken Windows at Blue's: A Queer History of Gentrification and Policing." In *Policing the Planet: Why the Policing Crisis Led to Black Lives Matter*, edited by Jordan T. Camp and Christina Heatheron, 41–61. New York: Verso, 2016.

Hanhardt, Christina B. *Safe Space: Gay Neighborhood History and the Politics of Violence*. Durham, NC: Duke University Press, 2013.

Hanhardt, Christina B. "Safe Space Out of Place." *QED* 3, no. 3 (2016): 121–25.

Hankin, Kelly. *The Girls in the Back Room: Looking at the Lesbian Bar*. Minneapolis: University of Minnesota Press, 2002.

Haring, Keith. *Journals*. New York: Viking, 1996.

Haro, Anthony. "Antología." In *From Macho to Mariposa: New Gay Latino Fiction*, edited by Charles Rice-González and Charlie Vásquez, 147–54. Maple Shade, NJ: Tinture, 2011.

Harris, Daniel. *The Rise and Fall of Gay Culture*. New York: Hyperion, 1997.

Harris, Jeffrey A. "'Where We Could Be Ourselves': African American LGBTQ Historic Places and Why They Matter." In *LGBTQ America*, edited by Megan E. Springate. Washington, DC: National Park Foundation, 2016, www.nps.gov/subjects/tellingallamericansstories/lgbtqthemestudy.htm.

Harris, Laura, and Liz Crocker. "Fish Tales: Revisiting 'A Study of a Public Lesbian Community.'" In *Femme: Feminists, Lesbians, and Bad Girls*, edited by Harris and Crocker, 40–51. New York: Routledge, 1997.

Harry, Joseph. "Urbanization and the Gay Life." *Journal of Sex Research* 10, no. 3 (1974): 238–47.

Harry, Joseph, and William B. DeVall. *The Social Organization of Gay Males*. New York: Praeger, 1978.

Hartless, Jaime. "Questionably Queer: Understanding Straight Presence in the Post-Gay Bar." *Journal of Homosexuality* 66, no. 8 (2019): 1035–57.

Hartman, Saidiya. *Lose Your Mother: A Journey along the Atlantic Slave Route*. New York: Farrar, Straus and Giroux, 2007.

Hartman, Saidiya. "Venus in Two Acts." *Small Axe* 26 (June 2008): 1–14.

Hartman, Saidiya. *Wayward Lives, Beautiful Experiments: Intimate Histories of Riotous Black Girls, Troublesome Women, and Queer Radicals*. New York: W. W. Norton, 2019.

Hasenbush, Amira, Andrew R. Flores, Angeliki Kastanis, Brad Sears, and Gary J. Gates. "The LGBT Divide: A Data Portrait of LGBT People in the Midwestern, Mountain, & Southern States." Los Angeles: Williams Institute, December 2014. https://williamsinstitute.law.ucla.edu/wp-content/uploads/LGBT-Divide-Dec-2014.pdf.

Heap, Chad. *Slumming: Sexual and Racial Encounters in American Nightlife, 1885–1940*. Chicago: University of Chicago Press, 2009.

Herdt, Gilbert. "Intergenerational Relations and AIDS in the Formation of Gay Culture in the United States." In *Changing Times: Gay Men and Lesbians Encounter HIV/AIDS*, edited by Martin P. Levine, Peter M. Nardi, and John H. Gagnon, 245–82. Chicago: University of Chicago Press, 1997.

Herdt, Gilbert, and Andrew Boxer. *Children of Horizons: How Gay and Lesbian Teens Are Leading a New Way out of the Closet*. Boston: Beacon, 1993.

Herring, Scott. *Another Country: Queer Anti-Urbanism*. New York: NYU Press, 2010.

Hilderbrand, Lucas. "Historical Fantasies: Gay Pornography in the Archives." In *Porno Chic and the Sex Wars: American Sexual Representation in the 1970s*, edited by Carolyn Bronstein and Whitney Strub, 326–48. Amherst: University of Massachusetts Press, 2016.

Hilderbrand, Lucas. *Inherent Vice: Bootleg Histories of Videotape and Copyright*. Durham, NC: Duke University Press, 2009.

Hilderbrand, Lucas. "I Wanna Go, or Finding Love in a Hopeless Place." *Media Fields* 7 (December 2013). http://mediafieldsjournal.squarespace.com/i-wanna-go.

Hilderbrand, Lucas. "A Suitcase Full of Vaseline, or Travels in the 1970s Gay World." *Journal of the History of Sexuality* 22, no. 3 (September 2013): 373–402.

Hinds, Stuart. "From Proscenium to Inferno: The Interwar Transformation of Female Impersonation in Kansas City." In *Wide-Open Town: Kansas City in the Pendergast Era*, edited by Diane Mutti Burke, Jason Roe, and John Herron, 291–306. Lawrence: University Press of Kansas, 2018.

The History Project. *Improper Bostonians: Lesbian and Gay History from the Puritans to Playland.* Boston: Beacon, 1998.

Hoffman, Amy. *An Army of Ex-lovers: My Life at the* Gay Community News. Amherst: University of Massachusetts Press, 2007.

Hoffman, Martin. *The Gay World: Male Homosexuality and the Social Creation of Evil.* New York: Basic Books, 1968.

Hoffman, Wayne. "Skipping the Life Fantastic: Coming of Age in the Sexual Devolution." In *Policing Public Sex*, edited by Dangerous Bedfellows, 337–54. Boston: South End, 1996.

Holleran, Andrew. *Dancer from the Dance.* New York: William Morrow, 1978.

Holmes, Kwame A. "Beyond the Flames: Queering the History of the 1968 D.C. Riots." In *No Tea, No Shade: New Writings in Black Queer Studies*, edited by E. Patrick Johnson, 304–22. Durham, NC: Duke University Press, 2016.

Holmes, Kwame A. "Chocolate to Rainbow City: The Dialectics of Black and Gay Community Formation in Postwar Washington, D.C., 1946–1978." PhD diss., University of Illinois, 2011.

Hooker, Evelyn. "The Homosexual Community." In *Sexual Deviance*, edited by John H. Gagnon and William Simon, 167–83. New York: Harper and Row, 1967.

Hooker, Evelyn. "Male Homosexuals and Their 'Worlds.'" In *Sexual Inversion*, edited by Judd Marmor, 83–107. New York: Basic Books, 1965.

Howard, John. "The Library, the Park, and the Pervert: Public Space and Homosexual Encounter in Post–World War II Atlanta." In *Carryin' on in the Lesbian and Gay South*, edited by Howard, 107–31. New York: NYU Press, 1997.

Howard, John. *Men Like That: A Southern Queer History.* Chicago: University of Chicago Press, 1999.

Hughes, Walter. "In the Empire of the Beat: Discipline and Disco." In *Microphone Fiends: Youth Music and Youth Culture*, edited by Tricia Rose and Andrew Ross, 147–57. New York: Routledge, 1994.

Humphreys, Laud. "New Styles in Homosexual Manliness." In *The Homosexual Dialectic*, edited by Joseph A. McCaffrey, 65–83. Englewood Cliffs, NJ: Prentice-Hall, 1972.

Humphreys, Laud. *Out of the Closets: The Sociology of Homosexual Liberation.* Englewood Cliffs, NJ: Prentice-Hall, 1972.

Hunter, John Francis. *The Gay Insider USA.* New York: Stonehill, 1972.

Hunter, Marcus Anthony. "The Nightly Round: Space, Social Capital, and Urban Black Nightlife." *City & Community* 9, no. 2 (June 2010): 165–86.

Hurewitz, Daniel. *Bohemian Los Angeles and the Making of Modern Politics.* Berkeley: University of California Press, 2007.

Hutchinson, Sydney. *From Quebradita to Duranguense: Dance in Mexican American Youth Culture.* Tucson: University of Arizona Press, 2007.

Ingram, Gordon Brent, Anne-Marie Bouthillette, and Yolanda Retter, eds. *Queers in Space: Communities, Public Places, Sites of Resistance*. Seattle: Bay, 1997.

Jackson, David W. *Changing Times: Almanac and Digest of Kansas City's Gay and Lesbian History*. Kansas City, MO: Orderly Pack Rat, 2011.

Jackson, Jonathan David. "The Social World of Voguing." *Journal for the Anthropological Study of Human Movement* 12, no. 2 (2002): 26–42.

Jacobs, Jane. *The Death and Life of Great American Cities*. New York: Vintage, 1961.

Jay, Karla, and Allen Young, eds. *Lavender Culture*. New York: Jove, 1978.

Jay, Karla, and Allen Young, eds. *Out of the Closets: Voices of Gay Liberation*. New York: Jove, 1977. Originally published 1972.

Jenness, Valerie, and Ryken Grattet. *Making Hate a Crime: From Social Movement to Law Enforcement*. New York: Russell Sage Foundation, 2001.

Johnson, Corey W., and Diane M. Samdahl. "'The Night They Took Over: Misogyny in a Country-Western Gay Bar." *Leisure Sciences* 27, no. 4 (2005): 331–48.

Johnson, David K. *Buying Gay: How Physique Pioneers Sparked a Movement*. New York: Columbia University Press, 2019.

Johnson, E. Patrick. "Feeling the Spirit in the Dark." *Callaloo* 21, no. 2 (Spring 1998): 399–416.

Johnson, E. Patrick. "Remember the Time: Black Queer Nightlife in the South." In *Queer Nightlife*, edited by Kemi Adeyemi, Kareen Khubchandani, and Ramón H. Rivera-Servera, 222–34. Ann Arbor: University of Michigan Press, 2021.

Johnson, E. Patrick. *Sweet Tea: Black Gay Men of the South*. Chapel Hill: University of North Carolina Press, 2008.

Joseph, Miranda. *Against the Romance of Community*. Minneapolis: University of Minnesota Press, 2002.

Jue, Melody. *Wild Blue Media: Thinking through Seawater*. Durham, NC: Duke University Press, 2020.

Kahn, Janet, and Patricia A. Gozemba. "In and Around the Lighthouse: Working-Class Lesbian Bar Culture in the 1950s and 1960s." In *Gendered Domains: Rethinking Public and Private in Women's Histories*, edited by Dorothy O. Hell and Susan M. Reverby, 90–106. Ithaca, NY: Cornell University Press, 1992.

Kaiser, Charles. *The Gay Metropolis, 1940–1996*. New York: Houghton Mifflin, 1997.

Kantrowitz, Arnie. "Letter to the Queer Generation." In *We Are Everywhere: A Historical Sourcebook of Gay and Lesbian Politics*, edited by Mark Blasius and Shane Phelan, 812–17. New York: Routledge, 1997.

Keating, Larry. *Atlanta: Race, Class, and Urban Expansion*. Philadelphia: Temple University Press, 2001.

Kelsey, John. "The Cleveland Bar Scene in the Forties." In *Lavender Culture*, edited by Karla Jay and Allen Young, 146–49. New York: Jove, 1978.

Kennedy, Elizabeth Lapovsky, and Madeline D. Davis. *Boots of Leather, Slippers of Gold: The History of a Lesbian Community*. New York: Routledge, 1993.

Kenney, Moira Rachel. *Mapping Gay L.A.: The Intersections of Place and Politics*. Philadelphia: Temple University Press, 2001.

Khubchandani, Kareem. *Ishtyle: Accenting Gay Indian Nightlife.* Ann Arbor: University of Michigan Press, 2020.

King, Katie. "Audre Lorde's Lacquered Layerings: The Lesbian Bar as a Site of Literary Production." *Cultural Studies* 2, no. 3 (1988): 321–42.

Kissack, Terence. "Freaking Fag Revolutionaries: New York's Gay Liberation Front, 1969–71." *Radical History Review* 62 (1995): 104–34.

Knopp, Larry, and Michael Brown. "Travel Guides, Urban Spatial Imaginaries and LGBTQ+ Activism: The Case of Damron Guides." *Urban Studies* 58, no. 7 (2021): 1380–96.

Knopp, Lawrence. "Sexuality and the Spatial Dynamics of Capitalism." *Environment and Planning D: Society and Space* 10, no. 6 (1992): 152–69.

Koestenbaum, Wayne. *The Queen's Throat: Opera, Homosexuality, and the Mystery of Desire.* New York: Poseidon, 1993.

Kramer, Larry. *Faggots.* New York: Random House, 1978.

Kruse, Kevin M. *White Flight: Atlanta and the Making of Modern Conservatism.* Princeton, NJ: Princeton University Press, 2005.

Kuda, Marie J. "Chicago's Stonewall: The Trip Raid in 1968" and "Cops, Bars and Bagmen." In *Out and Proud in Chicago: An Overview of the City's Gay Community,* edited by Tracy Baim, 79–83. Chicago: Surrey, 2008.

La Fountain-Stokes, Lawrence. "Queer Puerto Ricans and the Burden of Violence." *QED* 3, no. 3 (2016): 99–102.

La Fountain-Stokes, Lawrence. *Translocas: The Politics of Puerto Rican Drag and Trans Performance.* Ann Arbor: University of Michigan Press, 2021.

Lanigan-Schmidt, Thomas. "1969 Mother Stonewall and the Golden Rats." In *The Stonewall Reader,* edited by New York Public Library/Jason Baumann, 105–8. New York: Penguin, 2019.

Lauria, Mickey, and Lawrence Knopp. "Toward an Analysis of the Role of Gay Communities in the Urban Renaissance." *Urban Geography* 6, no. 2 (1985): 152–69.

Lawrence, Tim. "Beyond the Hustle: 1970s Social Dancing, Discotheque Culture, and the Emergence of the Contemporary Club Dancer." In *Ballroom, Boogie, Shimmy Sham, Shake: A Social and Popular Dance Reader,* edited by Julie Malnig, 199–214. Urbana: University of Illinois Press, 2009.

Lawrence, Tim. "Big Business, Real Estate Determinism, and Dance Culture in New York, 1980–88." *Journal of Popular Music Studies* 23, no. 3 (2011): 288–306.

Lawrence, Tim. "Disco and the Queering of the Dance Floor." *Cultural Studies* 25, no. 1 (2011): 230–43.

Lawrence, Tim. "The Forging of a White Gay Aesthetic at the Saint, 1980–84." *Dancecult* 3, no. 1 (2011): 1–24.

Lawrence, Tim. *Life and Death on the New York Dance Floor, 1980–1983.* Durham, NC: Duke University Press, 2016.

Lawrence, Tim. *Love Will Save the Day: A History of American Dance Music Culture, 1970–79.* Durham, NC: Duke University Press, 2003.

Lee, John Alan. "The Gay Connection." *Urban Life* 8, no. 2 (July 1979): 175–98.

Lee, Summer Kim. "Staying In: Mitski, Ocean Vuong, and Asian American Asociality." *Social Text* 138 (March 2019): 27–50.
Leitsch, Dick. "Gay Riots in Village." In *The Stonewall Riots: A Documentary History*, edited by Marc Stein, 169–72. New York; NYU Press, 2019.
Leitsch, Dick. "The Stonewall Riots: The Gay View." In *The Stonewall Riots: A Documentary History*, edited by Marc Stein, 175–77. New York; NYU Press, 2019.
Leitsch, Dick. "The Stonewall Riots: The Police Story." In *The Stonewall Riots: A Documentary History*, edited by Marc Stein, 172–74. New York; NYU Press, 2019.
Leonard, Arthur S. "The Gay Bar and the Right to Hang out Together." In *Sexuality and the Law*, 190–96. New York: Garland, 1993.
Levine, Martin P. "Gay Ghetto." *Journal of Homosexuality* 4, no. 4 (1979): 363–77.
Levine, Martin P. *Gay Macho: The Life and Death of the Homosexual Clone*, edited by Michael S. Kimmel. New York: NYU Press, 1998.
Levine, Martin P., ed. *Gay Men: The Sociology of Male Homosexuality*. New York: Harper and Row, 1979.
Leznoff, Maurice, and William A. Westely. "The Homosexual Community." In *Sexual Deviance*, edited by John H. Gagnon and William Simon, 184–96. New York: Harper and Row, 1967.
Lim, Eng-Beng. "The #Orlando Syllabus." *Bully Bloggers*, June 24, 2018. https://bullybloggers.wordpress.com/2016/06/24/the-orlando-syllabus.
Lin, Jeremy Atherton. *Gay Bar: Why We Went Out.* New York: Little, Brown, 2021.
Lipsitz, George. *Footsteps in the Dark: The Hidden Histories of Popular Music*. Minneapolis: University of Minnesota Press, 2007.
Liu, Petrus. "Queer Theory and the Specter of Materialism." *Social Text* 145 (December 2020): 25–47.
Loffreda, Beth. *Losing Matt Shepard: Life and Politics in the Aftermath of Anti-gay Murder.* New York: Columbia University Press, 2000.
Lopera, Juliana Delgado. ¡*Cuéntamelo! Oral Histories by LGBT Latino Immigrants.* San Francisco: Aunt Lute, 2014.
Lopez, Russ. *The Hub of the Gay Universe: An LGBTQ History of Boston, Provincetown, and Beyond.* Boston: Shawmut Peninsula, 2019.
Lorde, Audre. *Sister Outsider: Essays and Speeches.* Berkeley: Crossing Press, 2007.
Love, Heather. *Underdogs: Social Deviance and Queer Theory.* Chicago: University of Chicago Press, 2021.
Luibhéid, Eithne, and Karma R. Chávez, eds. *Queer and Trans Migrations: Dynamics of Illegalization, Detention, and Deportation.* Urbana: University of Illinois Press, 2020.
Lukas, J. Anthony. *Common Ground.* New York: Vintage, 1985.
Luna, Caleb. "Jock Straps and Crop Tops: Fat Queer Femmes Dressing for the Night." In *Queer Nightlife,* edited by Kemi Adeyemi, Kareen Khubchandani, and Ramón H. Rivera-Servera, 31–41. Ann Arbor: University of Michigan Press, 2021.
Lvovsky, Anna. *Vice Patrol: Cops, Courts, and the Struggle over Urban Gay Life before Stonewall.* Chicago: University of Chicago Press, 2021.

Macías, Stacy I. "A Gay Bar, Some *Familia*, and Latina Butch-Femme: Rounding out the Eastside Circle at El Monte's Sugar Shack." In *East of East: The Making of Greater El Monte*, edited by Romeo Guzmán, Caribean Fragoza, Alex Sayf Cummings, and Ryan Reft, 250–60. New Brunswick, NJ: Rutgers University Press, 2020.

Magister, Thom. *Biker Bar: Bikes, Beer & Boys*. New York: Perfectbound, 2013.

Magister, Thom. "One among Many: The Seduction and Training of a Leatherman." In *Leatherfolk: Radical Sex, People, Politics, and Practice*, edited by Mark Thompson, 91–105. Boston: Alyson, 1991.

Mains, Geoff. *Urban Aboriginals: A Celebration of Leathersexuality*, 20th anniversary ed. Los Angeles: Daedalus, 2002.

Mallon, Gerald L., ed. *Resisting Racism: An Action Guide*. Lafayette Hill, PA: IAB-WMT, 1984.

Manalansan, Martin F., IV. *Global Divas: Filipino Gay Men in the Diaspora*. Durham, NC: Duke University Press, 2003.

Manalansan, Martin F., IV. "In the Shadows of Stonewall: Examining Gay Transnational Politics and the Diasporic Dilemma." *GLQ* 2, no. 4 (October 1995): 425–38.

Manalansan, Martin F., IV. "That Magical Touch: Migrant Nocturnal Stories in Queer Jackson Heights." In *Queer Nightlife*, edited by Kemi Adeyemi, Kareen Khubchandani, and Ramón H. Rivera-Servera, 19–30. Ann Arbor: University of Michigan Press, 2021.

Marlowe, Kenneth. *Mr. Madam*. New York: Paperback Library, 1965.

Marshall, Daniel, and Zeb Tortorici, eds. *Turning Archival: The Life of the Historical in Queer Studies*. Durham, NC: Duke University Press, 2022.

Martínez, Ernesto Javier. *On Making Sense: Queer Race Narratives of Intelligibility*. Stanford, CA: Stanford University Press, 2013.

Masters, R. E. L. *The Homosexual Revolution*. New York: Julian, 1962.

Mattson, Greggor. "Are Gay Bars Closing? Using Business Listings to Infer Rates of Gay Bar Closure in the United States, 1977–2019." *Socius* 5, nos. 1–2 (2019): 1–2.

Mattson, Greggor. "Small-City Gay Bars, Big-City Urbanism." *City & Community* 19, no. 1 (March 2020): 76–97.

Mattson, Greggor. *Who Needs Gay Bars? Bar Hopping through America's Iconic LGBTQ+ Places*. Stanford, CA: Stanford University Press, 2023.

Maupin, Armistead. *Further Tales of the City*. New York: Harper & Row, 1982.

McCracken, Allison. *Real Men Don't Sing: Crooning in American Culture*. Durham, NC: Duke University Press, 2015.

McCune, Jeffrey Q., Jr. "Transformance: Reading the Gospel in Drag." *Journal of Homosexuality* 46, nos. 3–4 (2004): 151–67.

McGarry, Molly, and Fred Wasserman. *Becoming Visible: An Illustrated History of Lesbian and Gay Life in Twentieth-Century America*. New York: Penguin, 1998.

McKinney, Cait. *Information Activism: A Queer History of Lesbian Media Technologies*. Durham, NC: Duke University Press, 2020.

McKirnan, David J., and Peggy L. Peterson. "Alcohol and Drug Use among Homosexual Men and Women." *Addictive Behaviors* 14, no. 5 (1989): 545–53.

Meeker, Martin. *Contacts Desired: Gay and Lesbian Communications and Community, 1940s–1970s.* Chicago: University of Chicago Press, 2006.

Meyer, Doug. "Omar Mateen as US Citizen, Not Foreign Threat: Homonationalism and LGBTQ Online Representations of the Pulse Nightclub Shooting." *Sexualities*, February 27, 2019. https://journals.sagepub.com/doi/10.1177/1363460719826361.

Meyer, Richard. "At Home in Marginal Domains." *Documents* 18 (Summer 2000): 19–32.

Miezitis, Vera. *Night Dancing.* New York: Ballantine, 1980.

Milian, Claudia. *LatinX.* Minneapolis: University of Minnesota Press, 2019.

Milinski, Maureen, and Donald J. Black. "The Social Organization of Homosexuality." *Urban Life and Culture* 1, no. 2 (July 1972): 187–202.

Miller, D. A. "Cruising." *Film Quarterly* 61, no. 2 (Winter 2007): 70–73.

Miller, D. A. *Place for Us: Essay on the Broadway Musical.* Cambridge, MA: Harvard University Press, 1998.

Miller, Neil. *Out of the Past: Gay and Lesbian History from 1869 to the Present.* New York: Alyson, 2006.

Minian, Ana Raquel. *Undocumented Lives: The Untold Story of Mexican Migration.* Cambridge, MA: Harvard University Press, 2018.

Mitzel, John. *The Boston Sex Scandal.* Boston: Glad Day, 1980.

Moore, Madison. *Fabulous: The Rise of the Beautiful Eccentric.* New Haven, CT: Yale University Press, 2018.

Moore, Patrick. *Beyond Shame: Reclaiming the Abandoned History of Radical Sexuality.* Boston: Beacon, 2004.

Morris, Bonnie J. *The Disappearing L: Erasure of Lesbian Spaces and Culture.* Albany: SUNY Press, 2016.

Moskowitz, Peter. *How to Kill a City: Gentrification, Inequality, and the Fight for the Neighborhood.* New York: Nation Books, 2017.

Mumford, Kevin. *Interzones: Black/White Sex Districts in Chicago and New York in the Early Twentieth Century.* New York: Columbia University Press, 1997.

Mumford, Kevin. *Not Straight, Not White: Black Gay Men from the March on Washington to the AIDS Crisis.* Chapel Hill: University of North Carolina Press, 2016.

Muñoz, José Esteban. *Cruising Utopia: The Then and There of Queer Futurity.* New York: NYU Press, 2009.

Muñoz, José Esteban. *Disidentifications: Queers of Color and the Performance of Politics.* Minneapolis: University of Minnesota Press, 1999.

Muñoz, José Esteban. "Ephemera as Evidence: Introductory Notes to Queer Acts." *Women & Performance* 8, no. 2 (1996): 5–15.

Muñoz, José Esteban. *The Sense of Brown.* Edited by Joshua Chambers-Letson and Tavia Nyong'o. Durham, NC: Duke University Press, 2020.

Nardi, Peter. "Alcoholism and Homosexuality: A Theoretical Perspective." *Journal of Homosexuality* 7, no. 4 (1982): 9–25.

Navarro, Ray. "Eso, Me Esta Pasando." In *Queer Looks: Perspectives on Lesbian and Gay Film and Video,* edited by Martha Gever, John Greyson, and Pratibha Parmar, 38–40. New York: Routledge, 1993.

Negrón-Muntaner, Frances. "Dance with Me." In *Gay Latino Studies: A Critical Reader*, edited by Michael Hames-García and Ernesto Javier Martínez, 311–20. Durham, NC: Duke University Press, 2011.

Nero, Charles. "Why Are the Gay Ghettos White?" In *Black Queer Studies*, edited by E. Patrick Johnson and Mae G. Henderson, 228–45. Durham, NC: Duke University Press, 2005.

Nestle, Joan. *A Restricted Country*. Ithaca, NY: Firebrand, 1987.

New York Public Library/Jason Baumann, eds. *The Stonewall Reader*. New York: Penguin, 2019.

Newman, Felice. "Why I'm Not Dancing." In *Lavender Culture*, edited by Karla Jay and Allen Young, 140–45. New York: Jove, 1978.

Newton, Esther. *Cherry Grove, Fire Island*. Boston: Beacon, 1993.

Newton, Esther. *Mother Camp: Female Impersonators in America*. Chicago: University of Chicago Press, 1979.

Newton, Esther. *My Butch Career: A Memoir*. Durham, NC: Duke University Press, 2018.

Ngai, Mae M. *Impossible Subjects: Illegal Aliens and the Making of Modern America*. Princeton, NJ: Princeton University Press, 2004.

Nicoletta, Daniel. *LGBT San Francisco*. London: Reel Art, 2017.

Niebur, Louis. *Menergy: San Francisco's Gay Disco Sound*. New York: Oxford University Press, 2022.

Noel, Thomas J. *Colorado: A Liquid History and Tavern Guide to the Highest State*. Golden, CO: Fulcrum, 1999.

Noel, Thomas J. "Gay Bars and the Emergence of the Denver Homosexual Community." *Social Science Journal* 15 (1978): 59–74.

Ocampo, Anthony Christian. *Brown and Gay in LA: The Lives of Immigrant Sons*. New York: NYU Press, 2022.

Ochoa, Marcia. *Queen for a Day: Transformistas, Beauty Queens, and the Performance of Femininity in Venezuela*. Durham, NC: Duke University Press, 2014.

Ochoa, Marcia. "Toxic Masculinity and the Orlando Pulse Shooting." *Mujeres Talk*, June 28, 2016. https://mujerestalk.org/2016/06/28/countering-hate-with-love-latinao-scholars-respond-to-orlando-massacre.

Oldenberg, Ray. *The Great Good Place*. New York: Marlowe, 1999.

Orloff, Alvin. *Disasterama! Adventures in the Queer Underground 1977–1997*. New York: Three Rooms, 2019.

Orne, Jason. *Boystown: Sex and Community in Chicago*. Chicago: University of Chicago Press, 2017.

Osman, Suleiman. "The Decade of the Neighborhood." In *Rightward Bound: Making America Conservative in the 1970s*, edited by Bruce J. Schulman and Julian E. Zelizer, 106–27. Cambridge, MA: Harvard University Press, 2008.

Osman, Suleiman. *The Invention of Brownstone Brooklyn: Gentrification and the Search for Authenticity in Postwar New York*. New York: Oxford University Press, 2011.

Owen, Frank. *Clubland: The Fabulous Rise and Murderous Fall of Club Culture*. New York: Broadway, 2003.

Padgett, Martin. *A Night at the Sweet Gum Head: Drag, Drugs, Disco, and Atlanta's Gay Revolution*. New York: Norton, 2021.

Palmer, Bryan D. *Cultures of Darkness: Night Travels in the Histories of Transgression*. New York: Monthly Review Press, 2000.

Panfil, Vanessa R. "Gayborhoods as Criminogenic Space." In *The Gayborhoood: From Sexual Liberation to Cosmopolitan* Spectacle, edited by Christopher T. Conner and Daniel Okamura, 67–84. Lanham, MD: Lexington, 2021.

Parkerson, Michelle. "Beyond Chiffon: The Making of Storme." In *Blasted Allegories*, edited by Brian Wallis, 375–79. Cambridge, MA: MIT Press, 1987.

Parlett, Jack. *Fire Island: A Century in the Life of an American Paradise*. Toronto: Hanover Square, 2022.

Pattison, Timothy. "The Stages of Gentrification: The Case of Bay Village." In *Neighborhood Policy and Planning*, edited by Phillip L. Clay and Robert M. Hollister, 77–92. Lexington: MA: Lexington, 1983.

Paulson, Don, and Roger Simpson. *An Evening at the Garden of Allah: A Gay Cabaret in Seattle*. New York: Columbia University Press, 1996.

Peña, Susana. "Latina/o Sexualities in Motion: Latina/o Sexualities Research Agenda Project." In *Latina/o Sexualities: Probing Powers, Passions, Passions, and Policies*, edited by Marysol Asencio, 188–206. New Brunswick, NJ: Rutgers University Press, 2010.

Perez, Frank, and Jeffrey Palmquist. *In Exile: The History and Lore Surrounding New Orleans Gay Culture and Its Oldest Gay Bar*. Hurlford, Scotland: LL, 2012.

Petrosino, Carolyn. "Connecting the Past to the Future: Hate Crime in America." In *Hate and Bias Crime: A Reader*, edited by Barbara Perry, 9–26. New York: Routledge, 2003.

Philen, Robert C. "A Social Geography of Sex: Men Who Have Sex with Men (MSMs) and Gay Bars on the U.S./Mexican Border." *Journal of Homosexuality* 50, no. 4 (2006): 31–48.

Powell, Ryan. *Coming Together: The Cinematic Elaboration of Gay Male Life, 1945–1979*. Chicago: University of Chicago Press, 2019.

Preciado, Paul B. *An Apartment on Uranus: Chronicles of the Crossing*. Translated by Charlotte Mandell. South Pasadena, CA: Semiotext(e), 2020.

Preston, John. "What Happened?" In *Leatherfolk: Radical Sex, People, Politics, and Practice*, edited by Mark Thompson, 210–20. Boston: Alyson, 1991.

Prieuer, Annick. *Mema's House, Mexico City: On Transvestites, Queens, and Machos*. Chicago: University of Chicago Press, 1998.

Putnam, Robert. *Bowling Alone: The Collapse and Revival of American Community*, rev. and updated ed. New York: Simon and Schuster, 2020.

Quiroga, José. "Straw Dogs: On the Massacre at Club Pulse." *Bully Bloggers*, June 27, 2016. https://bullybloggers.wordpress.com/2016/06/27/straw-dogs.

Quiroga, José, and Melanie López Frank. "Cultural Production of Knowledge on Latina/o Sexualities." In *Latina/o Sexualities: Probing Powers, Passions, Pas-

sions, and Policies, edited by Marysol Asencio, 137–49. New Brunswick, NJ: Rutgers University Press, 2010.

Ramírez, Horacio N. Roque. "'¡Mira, Yo Soy Boricua y Estoy Aqui!' Rafa Negrón's *Pan Dulce* and the Queer Sonic *Latinaje* of San Francisco." CENTRO: *Journal for the Center of Puerto Rican Studies* 19, no. 1 (2007): 274–313.

Ramos, Iván A. "The Dirt That Haunts: Looking at Esta Noche." *Studies in Gender and Sexuality* 16, no. 2 (2015): 195–210.

Rana, Amal. "The Night Poetry Danced with Us." In *Pulse/Pulso: In Remembrance of Orlando*, edited by Roy G. Guzmán and Miguel M. Morales, 16. Richmond, VA: Damaged Goods, 2018.

Randell-Moon, Holly. "Mediations of Security, Race, and Violence in the Pulse Nightclub Shooting: Homonationalism and Anti-immigrant Times." *GLQ* 28, no. 1 (2022): 1–28.

Read, Kenneth E. *Other Voices: The Style of a Male Homosexual Tavern*. Novato, CA: Chandler and Sharp, 1980.

Rechy, John. *City of Night*. New York: Grove, 1963.

Reid, John. *The Best Little Boy in the World*. New York: Ballantine, 1977.

Reiss, Albert J., Jr. "The Social Integration of Queers and Peers." In *Sexual Deviance*, edited by John H. Gagnon and William Simon, 197–27. New York: Harper and Row, 1967.

Reitzes, Donald C., and Juliette K. Diver. "Gay Bars as Deviant Community Organizations: The Management of Interactions with Outsiders." *Deviant Behavior* 4 (1982): 1–18.

Remington, Bruce. "Twelve Fighting Years: Homosexuals in Houston, 1969–1981." Master's thesis, University of Houston, 1983.

Rhyne, Ragan. "Racializing White Drag." *Journal of Homosexuality* 46, nos. 3–4 (2004): 181–94.

Riedel, Brian. "Cruising Grounds: Seeking Sex and Claiming Place in Houston, 1960–1980." *Southern Spaces*, December 18, 2020. https://southernspaces.org/2020/cruising-grounds-seeking-sex-and-claiming-place-houston-1960-1980.

Riemer, Matthew, and Leighton Brown. *We Are Everywhere: Protest, Power, and Pride in the History of Queer Liberation*. New York: Ten Speed, 2019.

Rivera-Servera, Ramón H. "Choreographies of Resistance: Latina/o Queer Dance and the Utopian Performative." *Modern Drama* 47, no. 2 (Summer 2004): 269–89.

Rivera-Servera, Ramón H. "Dancing Reggaetón with Cowboy Boots." In *Transnational Encounters: Music and Performance at the U.S.–Mexico Border*, edited by Alejandro L. Madrid, 373–92. New York: Oxford University Press, 2011.

Rivera-Servera, Ramón H. "History in Drag: Latina/o Queer Affective Circuits in Chicago." In *The Latina/o Midwest Reader*, edited by Omar Valerio-Jimenez, Santiago Vaquera-Vasquez, and Claire F. Fox, 184–96. Urbana: University of Illinois Press, 2017.

Rivera-Servera, Ramón H. *Performing Queer Latinidad: Dance, Sexuality, Politics*. Ann Arbor: University of Michigan Press, 2012.

Rizki, Cole. "Latin/x American Trans Studies: Toward a *Travesti*-Trans Analytic." *TSQ* 6, no. 2 (May 2019): 145–55.

Rodríguez, Juana Maria. "Public Notice from the Fucked Peepo: Xandra Ibarra's 'The Hookup/Displacement/Barhopping/Drama Tour.'" In *Queer Nightlife*, edited by Kemi Adeyemi, Kareen Khubchandani, and Ramón H. Rivera-Servera, 211–21. Ann Arbor: University of Michigan Press, 2021.

Rodríguez, Juana Maria. *Queer Latinidad: Identity Practices, Discursive Spaces*. New York: NYU Press, 2003.

Rodríguez, Juana Maria. *Sexual Futures, Queer Gestures, and Other Latina Longings*. New York: NYU Press, 2014.

Rodríguez, Richard T. *Next of Kin: The Family in Chicano/a Cultural Politics*. Durham, NC: Duke University Press, 2009.

Rodríguez, Richard T. "Queering the Homeboy Aesthetic." *Aztlán* 13, no. 2 (2006): 127–37.

Rofes, Eric E. "Gay Lib vs. AIDS: Averting Civil War in the 1990s." In *We Are Everywhere: A Historical Sourcebook of Gay and Lesbian Politics*, edited by Mark Blasius and Shane Phelan, 652–58. New York: Routledge, 1997.

Román, David. "Dance Liberation." In *Gay Latino Studies: A Critical Reader*, edited by Michael Hames-García and Ernesto Javier Martínez, 286–310. Durham, NC: Duke University Press, 2011.

Román, David. *Performance in America: Contemporary U.S. Culture and the Performing Arts*. Durham, NC: Duke University Press, 2005.

Romesburg, Don. "The Glass Coffin." *Studies in Gender and Sexuality* 14 (2013): 163–74.

Romesburg, Don. "Longevity and Limits in Rae Bourbon's Life in Motion." In *The Transgender Studies Reader 2*, edited by Susan Stryker and Aren Z. Aizura, 483–95. New York: Routledge, 2013.

Rose, Malú Machuca. "Giuseppe Campuzano's Afterlife: Toward a Travesti Methodology for Critique, Care, and Radical Resistance." *TSQ* 6, no. 2 (May 2019): 239–53.

Rubin, Gayle. "The Catacombs: A Temple of the Butthole." In *Leatherfolk: Radical Sex, People, Politics, and Practice*, edited by Mark Thompson, 119–41. Boston: Alyson, 1991.

Rubin, Gayle. "The Miracle Mile: South of Market and Gay Male Leather, 1962–1997." In *Reclaiming San Francisco: History, Politics, Culture*, edited by James Brook et al., 247–72. San Francisco: City Lights, 1998.

Rubin, Gayle S. "Thinking Sex: Notes for a Radical Theory of the Politics of Sexuality." In *The Lesbian and Gay Studies Reader*, edited by Henry Abelove, Michèle Aina Barale, and David M. Halperin, 1–44. New York: Routledge, 1993.

Rubin, Gayle S., "The Valley of the Kings: Leathermen in San Francisco, 1960–1990 Volume I." PhD diss., University of Michigan, 1994.

Rupp, Leila J., and Verta Taylor. *Drag Queens at the 801 Cabaret*. Chicago: University of Chicago Press, 2003.

Russo, Vito. "Camp." In *Gay Men: The Sociology of Male Homosexuality*, edited by Martin P. Levine, 205–10. New York: Harper and Row, 1979.

Rutheiser, Charles. *Imagineering Atlanta: The Politics of Place in the City of Dreams.* New York: Verso, 1996.

Ruting, Brad. "Economic Transformations of Gay Urban Spaces: Revisiting Collins' Evolutionary Gay District Model." *Australian Geographer* 39, no. 3 (2008): 259–69.

Ryan, Hugh. *When Brooklyn Was Queer.* New York: St. Martin's, 2019.

Sage, Wayne. "Inside the Colossal Closet." *Human Behavior*, August 1975, 16–23.

Salkind, Micah E. *Do You Remember House? Chicago's Queer of Color Underground.* New York: Oxford University Press, 2019.

Sanchez-Crispin, Alvaro, and Alvaro Lopez-Lopez. "Gay Male Places in Mexico City." In *Queers in Space: Communities, Public Places, Sites of Resistance*, edited by Gordon Brent Ingram, Anne-Marie Bouthillette, and Yolanda Retter, 197–212. Seattle: Bay, 1997.

Sarkar, Bhaskar. "Industrial Strength Queer: Club Fuck! and the Reorientation of Desire." *Media Fields Journal* 7 (December 2013). http://mediafieldsjournal.squarespace.com/industrial-strength-queer/2013/12/5/industrial-strength-queer-club-fuck-and-the-reorientation-of.html.

Schacht, Steven P., and Lisa Underwood. "The Absolutely Fabulous but Flawlessly Customary World of Female Impersonators." *Journal of Homosexuality* 46, nos. 3–4 (2004): 1–17.

Schaefer, Eric, and Eithne Johnson. "Quarantined! A Case Study of Boston's Combat Zone." In *Hop on Pop: The Politics and Pleasures of Popular Culture*, edited by Henry Jenkins, Tara McPherson, and Jane Shattuc, 430–54. Durham, NC: Duke University Press, 2002.

Scharlau, Kevin. "Navigating Change in the Homophile Heartland: Kansas City's Phoenix Society and the Early Gay Rights Movement, 1966–71." *Missouri Historical Review* 109, no. 4 (July 2015): 234–53.

Schulman, Sarah. *Gentrification of the Mind: Witness to a Lost Imagination.* Berkeley: University of California Press, 2012.

Schulman, Sarah. *Let the Record Show: A Political History of ACT UP New York, 1987–1993.* New York: Farrar, Straus and Giroux, 2021.

Schuman, Howard, and Jacqueline Scott. "Generations and Collective Memories." *American Sociological Review* 54 no. 3 (June 1989): 359–81.

Sears, Clare. *Arresting Dress: Cross-Dressing, Law, and Fascination in Nineteenth-Century San Francisco.* Durham, NC: Duke University Press, 2015.

Sears, James T. *Rebels, Rubyfruit, and Rhinestones: Queering Space in the Stonewall South.* New Brunswick, NJ: Rutgers University Press, 2001.

Sedgwick, Eve Kosofsky. *Epistemology of the Closet.* Berkeley: University of California Press, 1990.

Sedgwick, Eve Kosofsky. "Paranoid Reading and Reparative Reading, or You're So Paranoid, You Probably Think This Essay Is about You." In *Touching Feeling: Affect, Pedagogy, Performativity*, 123–52. Durham, NC: Duke University Press, 2003.

Segal, Mark. "From *And Then I Danced*." In *The Stonewall Reader*, edited by New York Public Library/Jason Baumann, 119–27. New York: Penguin, 2019.

Sender, Katherine. *Business, Not Politics: The Making of the Gay Market.* New York: Columbia University Press, 2004.

Senelick, Laurence. *The Changing Room: Sex, Drag and Theater.* New York: Routledge, 2000.

Shilts, Randy. *And the Band Played On.* New York: Penguin, 1988.

Siegel, Paul. "A Right to Boogie Queerly: The First Amendment on the Dance Floor." In *Dancing Desires: Choreographing Sexualities On and Off the Stage,* edited by Jane Desmond, 267–84. Madison: University of Wisconsin Press, 2001.

Sismondo, Christine. *America Walks into a Bar.* New York: Oxford University Press, 2011.

Slide, Anthony. *The Great Pretenders: A History of Female and Male Impersonation in the Performing Arts.* Lombard, IL: Wallace-Homestead, 1986.

Smart, Michael J., and Andrew H. Whittemore. "There Goes the Gayborhood? Dispersion and Clustering in a Gay and Lesbian Real Estate Market in Dallas, TX, 1986–2012." *Urban Studies* 54, no. 3 (2017): 600–615.

Smith, Michael J. *Black Men/White Men: A Gay Anthology.* San Francisco: Gay Sunshine, 1983.

Smith, Michael J. *Colorful People and Places.* San Francisco: Quarterly, 1983.

Smith, Neil. *The New Urban Frontier: Gentrification and the Revanchist City.* New York: Routledge, 1996.

Smith, Neil. "Toward a Theory of Gentrification: A Back to the City Movement by Capital, Not People." In *The Gentrification Debates,* edited by Japonica Brown-Saracino, 71–85. New York: Routledge, 2010.

Sontag, Susan. "Notes on 'Camp.'" In *Against Interpretation,* 275–92. New York: Delta, 1966.

Spade, Dean. *Normal Life: Administrative Violence, Critical Trans Politics, and the Limits of Law.* Boston: South End, 2011.

Spring, Justin. *Secret Historian: The Life and Times of Samuel Steward, Professor, Tattoo Artist, and Sexual Renegade.* New York: Farrar, Straus and Giroux, 2010.

Stanley, Eric. "The Affective Commons: Gay Shame, Queer Hate, and Other Collective Feelings." *GLQ* 24, no. 4 (October 2018): 489–508.

Stanley, Eric. *Atmospheres of Violence: Structuring Antagonism and the Trans/Queer Ungovernable.* Durham, NC: Duke University Press, 2021.

Stearn, Jess. *The Sixth Man.* New York: Doubleday, 1961.

Stein, Marc. *City of Sisterly and Brotherly Loves: Lesbian and Gay Philadelphia, 1945–1972.* Philadelphia: Temple University Press, 2004.

Stein, Marc, ed. *The Stonewall Riots: A Documentary History.* New York: NYU Press, 2019.

Stein, Samuel. *Capital City: Gentrification and the Real Estate State.* New York: Verso, 2019.

Stewart-Winter, Timothy. *Queer Clout: Chicago and the Rise of Gay Politics.* Philadelphia: University of Pennsylvania Press, 2016.

Stoller, Nancy E. "Lesbian Involvement in the AIDS Epidemic: Changing Roles and Generational Differences." In *Women Resisting AIDS: Feminist Strategies of*

Empowerment, edited by Beth E. Schneider and Stoller, 270–85. Philadelphia: Temple University Press, 1995.

Stone, Amy L., and Jaime Cantrell, eds. *Out of the Closet, into the Archives: Researching Sexual Histories.* Albany: SUNY Press, 2015.

Stone, Clarence N. *Regime Politics: Governing Atlanta, 1946–1988.* Lawrence: University Press of Kansas, 1989.

Strauss, William, and Neil Howe. *The Fourth Turning: What the Cycles of History Tell Us about America's Next Rendezvous with Destiny.* New York: Broadway, 1997.

Strauss, William, and Neil Howe. *Generations: The History of America's Future, 1584 to 2069.* New York: William Morrow, 1991.

Strauss, William, and Neil Howe. *13th Gen: Abort, Retry, Ignore, Fail?* New York: Vintage, 1993.

Stryker, Susan. *Transgender History.* Berkeley: Seal, 2008.

Stryker, Susan, and Jim Van Buskirk. *Gay by the Bay.* San Francisco: Chronicle, 1996.

Styles, Joseph. "Outsider/Insider: Researching Gay Baths." *Urban Life* 8, no. 2 (July 1979): 135–52.

Suarez, Juan A. *Bike Boys, Drag Queens, and Superstars: Avant-Garde, Mass Culture, and Gay Identities in the 1960s Underground Cinema.* Bloomington: Indiana University Press, 1996.

Sycamore, Mattilda Bernstein, ed. *Between Certain Death and a Possible Future.* Vancouver: Arsenal Pulp, 2021.

Sycamore, Mattilda Bernstein. *The End of San Francisco.* San Francisco: City Lights, 2003.

Tan, Joël Barraquiel. "Homothugdragsterism." In *Total Chaos: The Art and Aesthetics of Hip-Hop*, edited by Jeff Chang, 209–18. New York: Basic Books, 2006.

Tattleman, Ira. "Speaking to the Gay Bathhouse: Communicating in Sexually Charged Spaces." In *Public Sex/Gay Space*, edited by William L. Leap, 71–94. New York: Columbia University Press, 1999.

Taub, Diane E., and Robert G. Leger. "Social Identities in a Young Gay Community." *Sociological Forum* 3 (Fall 1980): 47–61.

Tea, Michelle. *Valencia.* Seattle: Seal, 2000.

Teaford, Jon C. *The Metropolitan Revolution: The Rise of Post-urban America.* New York: Columbia University Press, 2006.

Teal, Don. *The Gay Militants.* New York: Stein and Day, 1971.

Thing, James. "Gay, Mexican and Immigrant: Intersecting Identities among Gay Men in Los Angeles." *Social Identities*, 16, no. 6 (November 2010): 809–31.

Third World Gay Revolution. "The Oppressed Shall Not Become the Oppressor." In *We Are Everywhere: A Historical Sourcebook of Gay and Lesbian Politics,* edited by Mark Blasius and Shane Phelan, 400–401. New York: Routledge, 1997.

Thomas, Anthony. "The House the Kids Built: The Gay Black Imprint on American Dance Music." In *Out in Culture: Gay, Lesbian and Queer Essays on Popular Culture,* edited by Corey K. Creekmur and Alexander Doty, 437–45. Durham, NC: Duke University Press, 1995.

Thompson, Mark. "Introduction." In *Leatherfolk: Radical Sex, People, Politics, and Practice*, edited by Thompson, xi–xx. Boston: Alyson, 1991.

Tissot, Sylvie. *Good Neighbors: Gentrifying Diversity in Boston's South End*. New York: Verso, 2015.

Tolentino, Julie, et al. "The Sum of All Questions: Returning to the Clit Club." *GLQ* 24, no. 4 (2018): 467–88.

Tongson, Karen. "Karaoke, Queer Theory, Queer Performance." In *Oxford Handbook on Music and Queerness*, edited by Fred Everett Maus and Sheila Whiteley, 211–26. New York: Oxford University Press, 2022.

Tongson, Karen. *Relocations: Queer Suburban Imaginaries*. New York: NYU Press, 2011.

Townsend, Johnny. *Let the Faggots Burn: The Upstairs Lounge Fire*. Self-published, 2011.

Townsend, Larry. *The Leatherman's Handbook*. New York: Olympia, 1972.

Townsend, Larry. *The Leatherman's Handbook II*. New York: Modernismo, 1983.

Treichler, Paula A. "AIDS, Homophobia, and Biomedical Discourse: An Epidemic of Signification." *October* 43 (Winter 1987): 31–70.

Tsang, Daniel. *The Age Taboo: Gay Male Sexuality, Power, and Consent*. Boston: Alyson, 1981.

Tyler, Carole-Anne. "Boys Will Be Girls: The Politics of Gay Drag." In *Inside Out: Lesbian Theories, Gay Theories*, edited by Diana Fuss, 32–70. New York: Routledge, 1991.

Tyson, Amy M. "Skirting Boundaries: Queer Bar Cultures in the Postwar Twin Cities." In *Queer Twin Cities*, edited by Twin Cities GLBT Oral History Project, 171–202. Minneapolis: University of Minnesota Press, 2010.

Urry, John. *Consuming Places*. New York: Routledge, 1995.

Vaid, Urvashi. *Virtual Equality: The Mainstreaming of Gay & Lesbian Liberation*. New York: Anchor, 1995.

Valentine, Gill, and Tracey Skelton. "Finding Oneself, Losing Oneself: The Lesbian and Gay 'Scene' as a Paradoxical Space." *International Journal of Urban and Regional Research* 27, no. 4 (December 2003): 849–66.

Van Cleve, Stewart. *Land of 10,000 Loves: A History of Queer Minnesota*. Minneapolis: University of Minnesota Press, 2012.

Vargas, Deborah R. "A Playlist for Pulse." *GLQ* 24, no. 1 (2018): 49–51.

Vider, Stephen. *The Queerness of Home: Gender, Sexuality, and the Politics of Domesticity after World War II*. Chicago: University of Chicago Press, 2022.

Viesca, Victor Hugo. "The Battle of Los Angeles: The Cultural Politics of Chicana/o Music in the Greater Eastside." *American Quarterly* 56, no. 3 (September 2004): 719–39.

Vogel, Shane. *The Scene of the Harlem Cabaret: Race, Sexuality, Performance*. Chicago: University of Chicago Press, 2009.

Von Hoffman, Alexander. *House by House, Block by Block: The Rebirth of America's Urban Neighborhoods*. New York: Oxford, 2003.

Warner, Michael. "Introduction." In *Fear of a Queer Planet*, edited by Warner, vii–xxx. Minneapolis: University of Minnesota Press, 1993.

Warner, Michael. *Publics and Counterpublics*. New York: Zone, 2002.

Warner, Michael. *The Trouble with Normal: Sex, Politics, and the Ethics of Queer Life.* Cambridge, MA: Harvard University Press, 1999.

Warren, Carol A. B. *Identity and Community in the Gay World*. New York: Wiley, 1974.

Washington, Craig. "Fall Down on Me: Stories of the Club from Black Gay Men in the South." In *Queer South Rising: Voices of a Contested Place*, edited by Reta Ugena Whitlock, 73–89. Charlotte, NC: Information Age, 2013.

Wat, Eric C. *The Making of a Gay Asian Community: An Oral History of Pre-AIDS Los Angeles*. Lanham, MD: Rowman & Littlefield, 2002.

Weightman, Barbara. "Gay Bars as Private Places." *Landscape* 23 (1980): 9–16.

Weightman, Barbara. "Towards a Geography of the Gay Community." *Journal of Cultural Geography* 1, no. 2 (1981): 106–12.

Weinberg, Martin S. "The Male Homosexual: Age-Related Variations in Social and Psychological Characteristics." *Social Problems* 17, no. 4 (Spring 1970): 527–37.

Weinberg, Martin S., and Colin J. Williams. "Gay Baths and the Social Organization of Impersonal Sex." *Social Problems* 32, no. 2 (1975): 124–36.

Weinberg, Martin S., and Colin J. Williams. *Male Homosexuals: Their Problems and Adaptations*. New York: Oxford University Press, 1974.

Weinberg, Thomas S. *Gay Men, Drinking, and Alcoholism*. Carbondale: Southern Illinois University Press, 1994.

Weltge, Ralph W., ed. *The Same Sex: An Appraisal of Male Homosexuality*. Philadelphia: United Church Press, 1969.

Weston, Kath. "Get Thee to a Big City: Sexual Imaginary and the Great Gay Migration." *GLQ* 2, no. 3 (1995): 253–77.

White, Edmund. *States of Desire: Travels in Gay America*. New York: Dutton, 1980.

Whittemore, Andrew H. "The Dallas Way: Property, Politics, and Assimilation." In *Planning and LGBT Communities: The Need for Inclusive Queer Spaces*, edited by Petra L. Doan, 39–55. New York: Routledge, 2015.

Willard, Avery. *Female Impersonation*. New York: Regiment, 1971.

Wilson, Alexander. "Friedkin's *Cruising*, Ghetto Politics, and Gay Sensibility." *Social Text* 4 (Autumn 1981): 98–109.

Winkler, Kevin. "Stars of the Tubs! A History of Performance at the Continental Baths, 1970–1976." *Theatre History Studies* 20 (2000): 47–65.

Witomski, T. R. "Gay Bars, Gay Identities." In *Gay Life*, edited by Eric Rofes, 201–9. Garden City, NY: Doubleday, 1986.

Wittman, Carl. "Refugees from Amerika: A Gay Manifesto." In *The Homosexual Dialectic*, edited by Joseph A. McCaffrey, 157–71. Englewood Cliffs, NJ: Prentice-Hall, 1972.

Wolf, Deborah G. *The Lesbian Community*. Berkeley: University of California Press, 1979.

Wolfe, Maxine. "Invisible Women in Invisible Places: The Production of Social Space in Lesbian Bars." In *Queers in Space: Communities, Public Places, Sites of Resistance*, edited by Gordon Brent Ingram, Anne-Marie Bouthillette, and Yolanda Retter, 301–24. Seattle, Bay, 1997.

Woods, William J., and Diane Binson, eds. "Gay Bathhouses and Public Health Policy." Special issue, *Journal of Homosexuality* 44, nos. 3–4 (2003).

Woods, William J., and Diane Binson. "Public Health Policy and Gay Bathhouses." *Journal of Homosexuality* 44, nos. 3–4 (2003): 1–21.

Woods, William J., Daniel Tracy, and Diane Binson. "Number and Distribution of Gay Bathhouses in the United States and Canada." *Journal of Homosexuality* 44, nos. 3–4 (2003): 1–21.

Young, Thelatahia "Nikki". "Imagining Queer Life after Death." *GLQ* 24, no. 1 (2018): 9–12.

Yuzna, Jake, ed. *The Fun: The Social Practice of Nightlife in NYC*. New York: Museum of Arts and Design, 2013.

Ziebold, Thomas O., and John E. Mongeon, eds. "Alcoholism and the Gay Community." Special issue, *Journal of Homosexuality* 7, no. 2 (1982).

Zukin, Sharon. "Gentrification as Market and Place." In *The Gentrification Debates*, edited by Japonica Brown-Saracino, 37–44. New York: Routledge, 2010.

Zukin, Sharon. "Gentrification: Culture and Capital in the Urban Core." *Annual Review of Sociology* 13 (1987): 129–47.

Index

12 West (New York), 182, 364n89, 367n148
19 Bar (Minneapolis), 196
82 Club (New York), 74
806 Cabaret (Key West), 77

ACT UP, 230, 241, 250, 256, 377n18, 380n81
activism, 17–21, 24, 30, 127–50, 154, 214, 256–59, 267–68, 351n11. *See also* ACT UP; feminism and feminists; Gay Liberation Front; gay liberation; homophile; Houston Gay Political Caucus; Lesbian Avengers; Mattachine Society; Queer Nation; Stonewall riots
Adelante, 277, 285
Address Book, The (Damron), 11
advertising, xv–xvi, 5–7, 33, 192–96. *See also* social media
Advocate, The, xv, 45–46, 65, 101, 121, 127–28, 134, 206, 211
African American Lesbian/Gay Alliance, 136
Agnes, 32
Aguilar, Laura, 385n5
AIDS, xx, 22, 29–30, 58, 71, 90, 130, 136, 147, 157–60, 162–74, 183, 189–203, 212–18, 228–29, 231–45, 255, 295, 328n103
AIDS Foundation Houston, 203. *See also* Houston, TX

Alaska (drag queen), 89
Alcoholic Beverage Antidiscrimination Act (1983), 140–41
alcoholism, 19–20, 325–26n71
alcohol regulation, xx, 6–9, 12, 17–19, 78, 113, 119–20, 122, 159–60, 166, 177, 200, 213, 221–22, 257.
Alfaro, Luis, 271–73
All About Eve, 4, 52. *See also* Davis, Bette
Allen, Jafari S., 148
Alley, Jason, 301
All Mujeres Interested in Getting Active (AMIGA), 214
All the Beauty and the Bloodshed, 111
Amin, Kadji, 231
amyl nitrate. *See* poppers.
Angels of Light, 251
Anthony, Joe, 199. *See also* Mary's
Anthony, Michael, 199. *See also* Mary's
Anvil, The (New York), 158, 164–68, 191
Anzaldúa, Gloria, 265
Applause, 4
Archive of Feelings (Cvetkovich), 318n15
archives, xvii–xx, 84, 127, 130, 317n9, 318n15
Arena (Los Angeles), 267–74
Armory, The (Atlanta), 136–38
Arnett, Chuck, 38, 50–51
Arnold, Skip, 70, 79–80, 85

Atlanta, GA, 127–50, 343n9, 353n32
Atlanta Anti-Discrimination Project (AADP), 134, 141–42. *See also* discrimination
Atlanta Friends of Lesbian/Gay Organizations (AFLGO), 134, 138–39
Atlanta Lesbian Feminist Alliance (ALFA), 133, 137, 141–42
Aunt Charlie's (San Francisco), 254
Auntie Mame, 201–2

baby boomers, 227–29, 233, 378n36
bachelorette parties, xx, 78, 92, 122
Backstreet (Atlanta), 132, 342–43n9
Bagneris, Larry, Jr., 207–8, 211, 214, 216, 371n36, 373n74
Bahlman, Bill, 168
Baim, Tracy, 60
Baird, Don, 239
Baldwin, Guy, 38
banda (music), 275–76
bar closures, xiv, 29–32, 174–75, 212, 253, 286, plate 1
Barthes, Roland, 319n20. *See also* punctum
bar tops (as archives), 216–18, plate 10
bathhouses, 2, 5, 53, 54–55, 160–64, 330n24
Bay Area Reporter (*BAR*), xv–xvi, 229
Bay Village (Boston neighborhood), 105, 109, 115–23, 346n73
BDSM, 38–39, 43–44, 47, 54, 56, 58–61, 164–75, 188–89, 200, 235, 249–50.
Beam, Joseph, 135
Bean, Gus, 236–39
Bee Gees, 28
Beltrán, Lola, 275
Benner, Doc, 75. *See also* Jewel Box Lounge
Bérubé, Allan, 54, 160, 231
Beyoncé, 32
Bike Stop (Philadelphia), 57
Black and White Men Together (BWMT), 122, 133–44, 178, 214, 341n98, 350n2, 359n7. *See also* Men of All Colors Together (MACT)
Black Cat (Los Angeles), 12–13, 323n40
Black Cat (San Francisco), 77, plate 5
Black gay bars, 24–25, 130–31, 136, 144–50, 154, 207, 351n11

Bleu, Rudy, 283
BLK, 135–36, 146, 182
Blue, Michael, 247–48
Blue's (New York), 16
Bob the Drag Queen, 89
Bond, Justin Vivian, 248, 251, 252
Book of Love, 4
Boone, Philip, 147–48, 358n103
Bornstein, Kate, 251
Bosch, Hieronymus, 198
Boston, MA, 101–23
Boston Globe, 116–17
Boston Redevelopment Agency (BRA), 106, 112
Bourbon, Rae, 80–81
Bowie, David, 270
Box, The (San Francisco), 228, 234, 239–47, 254. *See also* Hodel, Page
Boxer, Andrew, 234
boy (aesthetic), 235–37. *See also* twinks
Boy Bar (New York), 235
Boy Club (San Francisco), 236–37
BOY parties (San Francisco), 228, 235–38. *See also* Dhong, Ben
Boystown (Chicago neighborhood), 58–59
Brando, Marlon, 40–42
Branigan, Laura, 267
Brill, David, 118
Brody, Michael, 178, 182
Bronski, Michael, 39, 121–22
brown (term), 263–64
Brown, Danny, 75. *See also* Jewel Box Lounge
Brown, Miquel, 269
Bryant, Anita, 133, 208. *See also* "Save Our Children" campaign; Southern Baptist Convention Pastor's Conference
Burrage, Frank, 55
Bushes, The (Chicago), 58–59
Busnach, Bobby, 111–12
Bus Station John, 254

Cabaret, The (Kansas City), 89–90
Café Lafitte in Exile (New Orleans), 5
Caffee, Mike, 51
Caja, Jerome, 248, 251, 252
Califia, Pat, 171

426 INDEX

Callas, Maria, 53
camp (gay male sensibility), 52, 69–71, 87–89, 200–201, 340n91
Cantú, Lionel Jr., 265
Capitol Hill (Seattle neighborhood), 126
Carter, Lynn, 76. *See also* Jewel Box Revue
Casa Nova, The (Somerset County, PA), 255–59
Cashman, Frank, 116, 119. *See also* Jacque's; The Other Side
Castro (San Francisco neighborhood), 228, 232, 343n12
Change, 181
Charlie's (Phoenix), 290
Chauncey, George, 6
Cher, 194
Cheren, Mel, 178, 184
Chicago, IL, 37–61, 333n75
Chicago Eagle (Chicago), 60
Chicago Hellfire Club, 46
Chico (Los Angeles), 261–62, 280–84, plate 14
Chinchilla, Maya, 301
Chiquita's (El Paso), 290
cholo (aesthetic), 280–82
Circus Disco (Los Angeles), 261–62, 267–74, 343n9. *See also* Arena; La Pietra, Gene; Lemos, Ermilio
City of Night (Rechy), 11, 285
civil rights, 18, 128, 130, 134, 140–44, 350n2
Clark, Roland, 181
classism, 101–5, 340n83
Clone, Caroline, 244–45
Club Baths (New York and national), 165
Club Cobra (Los Angeles), 283–84
Clubhouse, The (Washington, DC), 144, 356n79
club kids, 249
Club Metro (St Paul), 194
Club Papi (Los Angeles), 274
Club Q (Colorado Springs), 300
Club Q (San Francisco), 245–47, 254
Club sCUM (Los Angeles), 282–83
Club Tempo (Los Angeles), 261–62, 266, 275–80
Club Uranus (San Francisco), 228, 234, 247–54, plate 13

Cock, The (New York), 252–53
Cockettes, 251
Code Blue (San Francisco), 244
Cohen, Cathy J., 144
Colony Bar (Kansas City), 68–69, 78–86, 89–93
Colossus (San Francisco), 237–39
Columbus Tavern (Seattle), 349n4
Combat Zone (Boston neighborhood), 106–8, 113
Coming Together (Powell), 320n4
Continental Baths (New York), 158, 161–63, 191. *See also* Ostrow, Steve
Copa, The (Fort Lauderdale), xvii, 20–21. *See also* super-bars
Corey, Dorian, 76
Cory, Donald Webster (Edward Sagarin), 9
Coupland, Douglas, 233
Cove, The (Atlanta), 132
COVID-19 pandemic, 30, 32, 90, 174–75, 284, 287
Crawford, Joan, 52–53, 88, 270
criminalization (of gayness), 65
Crimp, Douglas, 173, 176, 232, 330n11
cross-dressing (laws against), 72–73
Crowley, Olene, 82–84
Cruising, 171–72
cruising, 2, 21–24, 37, 47, 65, 103, 113, 118, 123, 160–61, 167, 195, 234, 244, 245–46, 265
Cruz, Celia, 286
Cvetkovich, Ann, 318n15

Dallas, TX, 371n32, 372n51
Dame Edna, 88
Damron, Bob, 11
Dancer from the Dance (Holleran), 159, 176, 364n85
dating apps. *See* hook-up apps
Davis, Bette, 52–53, 54, 88. *See also* All About Eve
Davis, Madeline D., 102
DC Eagle (Washington, DC), 42–43, 343n9
De Ambiente, 263, 276–77
DeBlase, Tony, 167, 171
Degeneres, Ellen, 255
deindustrialization, 103

DeLange, Mark, 219
DeLaverie, Stormé, 15, 75, 324n50
D'Emilio, John, 6–8, 265
Denton, TX, 289–93
Denver, CO, 62–67. *See also* Gay Coalition of Denver (GCOD)
Detroit, MI, 94–97
Dhong, Ben, 235–37. *See also* BOY parties
Diamond Lil, 132
Diaz, Mario, 252, 385n6
Dinco, Dino, 281–82, plate 14
Dirty Dorothy Show (Kansas City), 90–92. *See also* Dressler, Jessica
disco, 157–59, 175–91, 227
discrimination, xviii, 17, 20–21, 24–25, 65, 122–23, 127–50, 154, 212, 214, 267, 333n75, 351n11, 355nn60–61, 356n70, 359n8. *See also* Atlanta Anti-Discrimination Project (AADP)
Discrimination Response System (DRS), 141
Divine, xvii, 290
Doyle, JD, 219
drag, 68–93, 262, 336nn8–10
drag balls, 74
drag queen. *See* drag
Dressler, Jessica, 90–92. *See also* Dirty Dorothy Show
Drinkery, The (Baltimore), 27
drugs, 21, 159, 177, 249, 321n14
Drummer magazine, 58–59, 60, 65–67, 170, 198, 204–5
drunk driving, 212–13
Dugan's Bistro, 58, 60, 333n75, 343n9
Dúrcal, Rocío, 275
Dyer, Richard, 88
Dynasty, 26, 327n92

Eagle (San Francisco), 229, 382n124
Eagle Houston (Houston), 219
Eagle's Nest (New York), 42–43, 167, 330n11, 343n9. *See also* Modica, Jock
Echols, Alice, 175
Ehemann, Ron, 45
Ellen, 256
Eltinge, Julian, 72–73
EndUp, The (San Francisco), 20, 22, 390n97

Escoffier, Jeffrey, 231
Esparza, Rafa, 236, plate 11
Etienne. *See* Orejudos, Dom

Faggots (Kramer), 159
Fag Rag, 71, 110
Farmer, Jim "Fanny," 200–208, 215–18. *See also* Mary's
Farmhouse (Houston), 20
fashion, 270–71
Fautline (Los Angeles), 51, 279
Fawaz, Ramzi, xv, 20, 326n80. *See also* queer forms
female impersonation, 68–93
feminism and feminists, 20, 24, 133, 137, 321n17, 377n18
Fesco, Michael, 176. *See also* Ice Palace (Fire Island)
fetishism, 135, 353n32
Fey, 280
Finocchio's (San Francisco), 75
fisting, 165–67
Flamingo (New York), 157, 182–83, 188, 367n148
Flo & Friends show (Kansas City), 90
Ford, Dave, 232
Francis, Connie, 229
Frat House (Garden Grove), 274–75, 389n56
Fun Hog Ranch (Las Vegas), 51

Gabriel, Juan, 260, 277, 286
García, Cindy, 278
Garcia, Maria Rosa, 285
García, Ramón, 272–73
Garcia-Mispireta, Luis Manuel, xiv
Garden of Allah (Seattle), 77
Gardner, Taana, 181
Garland, Judy, 14, 88–89, 106
Gay Activists' Alliance (GAA), 16, 151
Gay Agenda, The, 248
Gay Alcoholics Anonymous, 325n71
Gay and Lesbian Latinos Unidos (GLLU), 273
Gay Atlanta Minorities Association (GAMA), 133
Gay Bar (Lin), xiv, 8, 29

428   INDEX

gay bars: Black, 24–25, 130–31, 136, 144–50, 154, 207, 351n11; and coming out, 1, 5–6; and culture, xiii, xv, xix, 15, 212, 294–96; drag in, 68-72, 85-87; finances of, 17, 22, 212; gender–integrated, 24–25, 57, 239–42, 244–46, 249; histories of, xiii–xiv, xviii, xix, 5–11, 29–33, 294; and identity formation, 1, 5–6, 296; as institutions, xiii, 3, 143; Latinx, 24–25, 260–89, 294–302; leather, 37–61; legality of, xx, 8–9, 16, 119, 212–13, 295; and the mafia, xx, 7, 12, 15–17, 29, 45–46, 113, 116, 166, 295; as a medium xiv–xv, 1, 9, 24, 33, 127, 294–95; and politics, xiii, 17, 121, 296, 385n6; and public life, 4–8, 15, 256, 294–95; and racism, xviii, 6–21, 81–82, 120, 127–50, 154, 213–15, 267, 353n32, 359nn7–8; raids on, xx, 8, 12–16, 18, 44–46, 55, 64, 87, 161, 171, 208–9, 211, 221, 331n32; rural, xix, 20, 130, 255–59, 318n19; as safe spaces, 94–97, 294, 299; and sexism, xviii, 20–25, 56–57, 64, 127–29, 132, 244, 250; social dynamics of, 2–3, 11, 26–29, 84–87, 95, 124–26, 143; and violence, 256, 300; and whiteness, xvii, 6, 16, 20–21, 24–26, 81, 129–33, 139–40, 142–43, 178, 182–83, 187, 214–15, 235–38, 259, 260–61, 267, 280, 300–301, 333n75
GayCLU (Atlanta ACLU chapter), 133, 137–38
Gay Coalition of Denver (GCOD), 65. See also Denver, CO
Gay Community News (GCN), 112, 116–20
gay ghetto. See *gay neighborhoods*
Gay Health Consortium (Philadelphia), 151. See also gay switchboard
gay liberation, 6, 16–29, 64, 69, 157–60, 175–77, 227–28, 295, 324n56, 351n11
Gay Liberation Front (GLF), 16–19, 131–32, 175, 213, 372n44
Gay Men's Health Crisis (GMHC), 164, 174
gay neighborhoods, xix, 31, 58, 101–5, 109–16, 120, 132–33, 159, 167, 199, 206–7, 285, 319n25, 333n75, 352n21, 371n32. See also gentrification
Gay 90's (Minneapolis), 77, 194

Gaynor, Gloria, 177
gay press, xv, xviii–ix, 11, 33, 127, 129, 196, 255, 295
gay switchboard, 151–55
genderfuck, 200–201, 250–51, 292
Generations (Strauss & Howe), 233
Generation X, 227–33, 236, 378n36
Generation X (Coupland), 233
Generation Z, 233–34
gentrification, 30–31, 101–23, 126, 190, 253–54, 262, 274, 285, 287, 343n12
Ghaziani, Amin, xiv
Gigi's (Detroit), 96–97
GLAMA (Gay and Lesbian Archives of Mid-America), 84, 133
Gold Coast, The (Chicago), 39, 43–47, 50–55, 58–60, plate 4. See also Renslow, Chuck
Golden Girls, The, 26–27
Goldin, Nan, 110–11
Gran Combo de Puerto Rico, El, 298
Granville Anvil (Chicago), 27–28
Green, Adam Isaiah, 353n32
Greene, Theodore, 104
Green Lantern (Washington, DC), 26–27
Gregory, Edye, 82–83
Grindr. See hook-up apps
Gronk, 285
Guerrero, Juan Ramon, 300
Gutiérrez, Raquel, 261

Hae, Laam, 119
Hamburger Mary's (Houston), 219
Hamburger Mary's (Kansas City), 92–93
Hampton, David, 147
Hanhardt, Christina B., 115, 119
hanky code, 52–54
Haring, Keith, 179–80
Hartman, Saidiya, 318n12
Hassett, Agnes, 44
hate crimes, 256–59, 296
Heklina, 252
Herdt, Gilbert, 234
Hernandez, Patrick, 4
Hernandez, Sergio, 285–88
Hi-Ho (Chicago), 44–45
Hileman, Billy, 383n7

Hill, Ray, 207–8, 371n37
HIV. *See* AIDS
Hodel, Page, 239–47. *See also* The Box
Hoffman, Amy, 116
Hoffman, Wayne, 232
Holleran, Andrew, 159, 176, 191, 364n85
Holloway, Loleatta, 181
Hollywood Spa (Los Angeles), 163–64
Homocore, 248
homonormativity, 255
homophile, 9–10, 12, 78, 228, 231, 338n51, 372n44. *See also* Mattachine Society
homophobia, 296
hook-up apps, 30–32, 64, 234, 290
hotel bars, 322n36
Houston, TX, 198–219, 371n36. *See also* AIDS Foundation Houston
Houston Gay Political Caucus (HGPC), 208–11, 371n36
Houston Motorcycle Club, 203–4
Houston, Thelma, 181
Houston, Whitney, 181, 194
Howe, Neil, 233
Hula's (Honolulu), xvii

I-Beam (San Francisco), 236–37, 366n132
Ice Palace (Fire Island), 175–76, 200. *See also* Fesco, Michael; Mills, Andy
immigration, 262, 264–65, 276–78, 386n17
Immigration Reform Act (1990), 386n17
Ingram, Cliff, 44
"In Praise of Latin Nights at the Queer Club" (Torres), 299
intergenerational conflict, 229, 233–36
International Mr. Leather (IML), 47
Islamophobia, 296
Ivanhoe Cabaret, The (Kansas City), 89–90

Jacobs, Jane, 133, 321n9
Jacque's (Boston), 105, 109–23. *See also* Cashman, Frank; Vara, Carmine; Vara, Henry
Jansen, Bob, 220–24, plate 12. *See also* Main Club
Jett Blakk, Joan, 252
Jewel Box Lounge (Kansas City), 68–69, 73–74, 78–87, plate 6.

Jewel Box Revue (touring act), 74–77, 81, 324n50. *See also* Benner, Doc; Brown, Danny
Jewel's Catch One, 267, 286, 357n95, 387n35
Johnson, E. Patrick, 148
Johnson, Marsha P., 324n50
Jones, Grace, 181
Jordon, L. Lloyd, 135–36
Josie's Cabaret and Juice Joint (San Francisco), 252
Jujubee, 89
Julius' (New York), 12, 323–24n42
Justice, Eddie Jamoldroy, 300

Kansas City, MO, 68–93
Kantrowitz, Arnie, 171, 185, 378n28
Kaye, Sandy, 92
Keehnen, Owen, 60
Kellas, Frank, 55, 59–60
Kennedy, Elizabeth Lapovsky, 102
Khan, Chaka, 181
Khubchandani, Kareem, 70
Kindred Spirits (Houston), 208
King, Martin Luther, Jr., 82
Kitt, Eartha, 89
Klubstitute (San Francisco), 252
Knuckles, Frankie, 162, 361n12
Kramer, Larry, 159, 178
Kris physique studio, 44, 47–48
Ku Klux Klan (KKK), 214, 257–59

La Pietra, Gene, 267–68, 273. *See also* Circus Disco
Latinx (term), 301, 384n2
Latinx gay bars and parties, 24–25, 260–89, 294–302
Lavender Baedeker, The (Strait), 11
Lawrence, Tim, 175–77, 185
Leather Archives and Museum, 50
leather culture, 37–61
Leatherman's Handbook, The (Townsend), 40
Leather Stallion (Cleveland), 47
Leavitt, David, 233–34
Leinonen, Christoher Andrew "Drew", 300
Leitsch, Dick, 13–15, 324n48
Lemos, Ermilio, 267. *See also* Circus Disco

Léon, Laura, 275
Leon-Davis, Daniel, 298
Lesbian Avengers, 230–31, 256–57, 377n18
Lesbian bars and parties, 24–25, 239–40, 244–47, 326n85
lesbian chic, 231, 244–47
lesbian feminism, 24, 133, 244, 326n85
Les Misérables, 190
Let Us Entertain You (LUEY, Houston), 203–4
Levan, Larry, 162, 178–82, 187
Levi's 501 jeans, 46, 62–64, 223
Lewis, John, 140
Liberace, xvi
Licon, Julio, 281
Life magazine, 38
Lin, Jeremy Atherton, xiv, xviii, 29, 70
Lion Pub (San Francisco), xv–xvi
Lipa, Dua, 32
liquor licensing. *See* alcohol regulation
Loma, 298
Long Live Queer Nightlife (Ghaziani), xiv
Long, Richard, 180
Loose Joints, 181
Lopez, Jennifer, 286
Lorde, Audre, 144
Loretta's (Atlanta), 147
Los Angeles, CA, 260–88
Luera, Adrian, 214–15

Mable Peabody's Beauty Parlor and Chainsaw Repair (Denton, TX), 289–93
Madonna, xvii, 96, 181, 194, 299
mafia, xx, 7, 12, 15–17, 29, 45–46, 113, 116, 166, 295
Magister, Thom, 40–42
Magnetic Fields, The, 4
Mailman, Bruce, 163, 166, 183, 186, 190. *See also* New St. Marks Baths; Saint, The (New York)
Main Club (Superior, WI), 220–24, plate 12. *See also* Jansen, Bob
Malin, Jean, 74
Manhandler Saloon (Los Angeles), 23
Manilow, Barry, 161–62
Man's Country (Chicago), 44, 52–53, 58–60, 163

March on Washington for Lesbian, Gay, and Bi Equal Rights and Liberation (1993), 25
Mariachi Arcoiris de Los Angeles, 277–79
Marquette, The (Atlanta), 145–47, 343n9, 357n87
Marquez-McCool, Brenda Lee, 300
Marquis de Sade, 167
Martínez, Ernesto Javier, 263
Mary's (Houston), 198–219, plate 10, plate 11. *See also* Anthony, Joe; Anthony, Michael; Farmer, Jim "Fanny"; Mills, Andy
masculinity, 23–25, 39, 56, 63–64, 165, 280
Mateen, Omar, 296, 391n1
Mattachine Society, 12, 13, 78, 324n48. *See also* homophile
Mattson, Greggor, xiv, 25, 29–30, 57
Max (Omaha), xvii
McRae, Ron, 256–58
Menjo's (Detroit), 96
Men of All Colors Together (MACT), 134. *See also* Black and White Men Together (BWMT)
Metro Council of Lesbian and Gay Organizations (MACGLO, Atlanta), 134
Meza, Agustin Garcia, 270–71, 273
Midler, Bette, 161–62
Midtown (Atlanta neighborhood), 132–33
Miguel, Amanda, 275
millennials, 233–34
Mills, Andy, 200–202. *See also* Mary's
Mineshaft (New York), 47, 51, 158–60, 164–75, 191
Minian, Ana Raquel, 265
Minneapolis, MN, 76, 192–97
Minnelli, Liza, 32, 88, 163
misogyny. *See* sexism
Miss Kitty, 251, 252
Missie B's (Kansas City). *See* Dirty Dorothy Show
Modica, Jock, 42. *See also* Eagle's Nest
Mommie Dearest, 88
Monsoon, Jinkx, 89
Montrose (Houston neighborhood), 199, 206–7
Mother Camp (Newton), 68, 79

INDEX   431

Mothers Against Drunk Driving (MADD), 212
motorcycle clubs, 39–40, 43, 46, 203–4
Muñoz, José Esteban, 263–64
murals, 38, 47, 49–51, 60, 179–80, 203, 218–19, 286, 290–91, plate 2, plate 11, plate 15
Murray, Akyra, 300
My-O-My (New Orleans), 74

National Coalition of Black Gays, 133, 178
National March on Washington for Lesbian and Gay Rights (1979), 209
National Minimum Drinking Age Act, 212
Nava, Nacho, 286
Navarro, Ray, 266
Negrón-Muntaner, Frances, 260–61
New Jalisco Bar (Los Angeles), 261–62, 285–88
New Queer Cinema, 231, 377n18
Newman, Felice, 20, 70, 75
New St. Marks Baths (New York), 163, 166, 174. *See also* Mailman, Bruce
Newton, Esther, 68, 78–87, 175
New York, NY, 157–91
Nob Hill (Washington, DC), 144, 356n79
North Loop (Chicago neighborhood), 58

O'Day, Anita, 4
O'Neal Austin, Rodney, 251
Oak Ridge Boys, 194
One magazine, 9–10
Orejudos, Dom (Etienne), 44, 47–52, 331n42, plate 2
Orloff, Alvin (Remix von Popstitute), 251–52
Orne, Jason, 55
Ortiz-Fonseca, Louie A., 299
Ostrow, Steve, 161–63. *See also* Continental Baths
Other Side, The (Atlanta), 256
Other Side, The (Boston), 105, 109–22, 358n97. *See also* Cashman, Frank; Vara, Carmine; Vara, Henry
Outlaw, The (Detroit), 5
Out/Look, 231
Owen, Cliff, 200, 216, 219

pansy craze, 74
Pantzer, Marion, 212
Paradise Garage (New York), 158, 177–82, 191, 367n147
Parks and Recreation, 292–93
Pearl Box Revue, 76
Pegasus (Kansas City), 89–90
performance studies, xiv, 328n109
Pet Shop Boys, 4
Phoenix Society for Individual Freedom, 78
Pi (Minneapolis), 196
Pierce, Charles, 74
Pioneer Square (Seattle neighborhood), 124–26, 349n4
Planet Q, 257–58
Playland (Boston), 106–7
Plaza, La (Los Angeles), 275
Plush Pony, The (Los Angeles), 281, 385n5
Police Academy, 38
Poma, Barbara, 300
poppers, 56–57, 177
Popstitute, Diet, 248
Popstitutes, 249
post-gay (term), 255
Powell, Frank, 131–32
Powell, Ryan, 320n4
Preston, John, 42
pride parades and festivals, 12, 16–17, 132, 145, 147, 148–49, 203, 205, 208, 213, 222, 229–30, 248, 252, 300
Prohibition, 5–7
Proposition 187 (California), 275
public sex, 17–19, 21–23, 53–61, 64–67, 157–75
Pulse (Orlando), 294–302, 391n3, plate 16
Punch Bowl, The (Boston), 109
punctum, 319n20. *See also* Barthes, Roland
Putman, Robert D., 378n36

queer forms, xv. *See also* Fawaz, Ramzi
queer homeboy (aesthetic), 281
queer Latinx, 260–88, 296
Queer Nation, 230, 231, 248, 250, 253, 377n18
queerness, 1, 6, 228–31, 241, 251, 292, 301, 320n2

432 INDEX

queer nightlife, xiv, 2–6, 102–4, 227–28, 244, 260–88, 299
Queer Nightlife (Lin), xiv
queer theory, xviii, 231, 233, 318n19
queer urban migration, 8, 104
Quiroga, José, 297

racism, xviii, 6–21, 81–82, 120, 127–50, 154, 213–15, 267, 353n32, 359nn7–8. *See also* discrimination
raids, xx, 8, 12–16, 18, 44–46, 55, 64, 87, 161, 171, 208–9, 211, 221, 330n24, 331n32
Rana, Amal, 301
Reagan, Ronald, 210, 236
Rechy, John, 11, 285
Redz (Los Angeles), 281, 286
Reeves, Judy, 203, 207, 208, 216–17
Renslow, Chuck, 39, 43–50, 54–55, 58–60, 331n42. *See also* The Gold Coast
Rex, 51, 168–69
Rihanna, xvii
riot grrrl, 231, 377n18
Rivera, Reynaldo, 385n5
Rivera, Sylvia, 15
Rivera-Servera, Ramón H., 263, 266, 273
Robyn, 4
Rodríguez, Juana María, 299
Rodríguez, Richard T., 281
Rojas, James, 270
Romesburg, Don, 232
Rose, Felipe, 167
Rose Room (Dallas), 77
Ross, Diana, 181
Round Up Saloon (Dallas), 31
Rubin, Gayle, 56–57, 121
Ruiz, Gabriela, 286, plate 11
RuPaul's Drag Race, 27–28, 89
rural bars, xix, 20, 130–31, 255–59, 318n19
Russo, Vito, 52
Ryder, Melinda, 90, 93, 335n14. *See also* Winter, Bruce

Saint, The (Atlanta), 139–40
Saint, The (New York), 158–60, 177–78, 182–91, 367n147, plate 7, plate 8
Saloon, The (Minneapolis), 192–97, plate 9
Samaniego, Carlos, 277–78
Sanchez, Hex–ray, 283
San Francisco, CA, 227–54
San Francisco Sentinel, 229, 236–37, 244–45
Sarria, José, 77, plate 5
Saturday Night Fever, 176
"Save Our Children" campaign, 133. *See also* Bryant, Anita; Southern Baptist Convention Pastor's Conference
Schulman, Sarah, 121, 380n81
Scollay Square (Boston neighborhood), 106
Score (Los Angeles), 285
Scruff. *See* hook-up apps
Seattle, WA, 124–26
Seattle Counseling Service, 124–26, 349n1
second-wave feminism, 24
Selena (Quintanilla), 267
sexism, xviii, 20–25, 56–57, 64, 127–29, 132, 244, 250
sexual consent, 21–23, 64–65
sexual liberation, 23, 174
sexual revolution, 21–24, 158–59
Shapiro, Ari, 297
Shaw's (New York), 42
Shelly's Leg (Seattle), 126
Shepard, Mathew, 255–56, 259
Shilts, Randy, 189
Shively, Charley, 117
Siegel, Marc, 251
Sisters of Perpetual Indulgence, 251
Skirts (San Francisco), 244–46
S&M. *See* BDSM
Small Town Gay Bar, xix
Smith, Michael J., 134, 139
smoking, 28–29, 56
Snake Pit, The (New York), 16
Snowflake (Glenn Zehrbaugh), 51, plate 3
social media, 31, 33, 115, 147, 234, 253, 284, 285, 296
Society for Individual Rights, 9. *See also* homophile
Sokol, Marty, 281
Some of My Best Friends Are . . ., 20
Somerset County, PA, 255–59
Soto, Alfred, 299
Sound Factory (New York), 367n147

INDEX   433

South End (Boston neighborhood), 101, 104, 107–8, 113–15, 121, 123
Southern Baptist Convention Pastor's Conference, 133. *See also* Bryant, Anita; "Save Our Children" campaign
Southern Voice, 145–46
South of Market (SoMa, San Francisco neighborhood), 38, 51, 343n9, 382n124
Spade, Dean, 142
Sparkle, 181
Speakeasy, The (Charlotte), 7
Spears, Britney, xvii
speculative historiography, 318n12
Sporters (Boston), 121–22
States of Desire (White), 11
Stevens, Hal, 44
Steward, Samuel, 44
Stewart-Winter, Timothy, 60
Stonewall Inn (New York), 12–16, 158
Stonewall Riots, 12–17, 295
Strait, Guy, 11
Strauss, William, 233, 236
Streisand, Barbra, 28
Stryker, Susan, 231
Stud, The (Los Angeles), 37
Studio 54 (New York), 158, 176–77, 183
Studio One (Los Angeles), 267–68
Sue Ellen's (Dallas), 31
Sugar Shack (Los Angeles), 281
Summer, Donna, 184–85
super-bars, 20–21, 71, 89, 103, 132, 194. *See also* The Copa
Superior, WI, 220–24
Sweet Gum Head (Atlanta), 131–32, 336n8
Swoveland, Scott, 218–19, plate 11
Sylvester, 227
Symone, 89

Tan, Joël Barraquiel, 282
Tantrum, 248
Tavern Guild (San Francisco organization), 9
Tavern on Camac (Philadelphia), 10
Taylor, Ggreg, 230, 248
Teague, Duncan, 136, 143
Tenth Floor (New York), 182–83, 188
Thomas, June, 29

Tiffany's (Detroit), xvii
TigerHeat (Los Angeles), 272
Title 34 Human Rights ordinance (Washington DC), 351n11
Together, Somehow (Garcia-Mispireta), xiv
Tom of Finland, 49–50
Tom's Bar (Berlin), 55
Tom's Leather Bar (Mexico City), 53
Tool Box (San Francisco), 38, 50
Torres, Justin, 299–300
T-Shack, 252
Touché (Chicago), 60
Touchez (Sioux Falls), 22
Townhouse of New York (New York), xix
Townsend, Larry, 40
Tracks (Washington, DC), 25–26, 148, 358n103
Traxx (Atlanta), 147–49
Trevi, Gloria, 267, 286
Triangle Lounge (Denver), 62–67
Trick Ain't Always a Treat, A (Bourbon), 80
Trocadero Transfer (San Francisco), 227
Trump, Donald, 289, 292, 296
Tubesteak Connection (San Francisco), 254
Tucanes de Tijuana, Los, 280
Turner, Lana, 52–53
twinks, 235. *See also* boy (aesthetic); Boy movement
Twist (Miami Beach), xvii

Up Stairs Lounge (New Orleans), xx, 319n24
urban renewal, 101–5, 321n9

Van Buskirk, Jim, 231
vaquero (cowboy), 276–77
Vara, Carmine, 116, 346n62. *See also* Jacque's; The Other Side
Vara, Henry, 116–17, 120–22, 346n62. *See also* Jacque's; The Other Side
Vargas, Deborah R., 298
vaudeville, 69, 72–73
vice raids. *See* raids
Viesca, Victor Hugo, 275
Villa Fontana (Dallas), 5
Village People, 63, 167

Viñales, Diego, 16
voyeurism, 21–22, 329n110

Waldern, Lewis, 247–48
Wallace, Wally, 171–74, 363n68
Washington, Craig, 145
Washington, DC, 42–43, 144–45, 351n11, 356n79, 358n103
Waters, Crystal, 4
West, Mae, xvi, 80, 89
West End (Boston neighborhood), 106
West Hollywood, 285
White, Edmund, 11, 165
whiteness, xvii, 6, 16, 20–21, 24–26, 81, 101–2, 104, 115, 120, 129–33, 135, 139–40, 142–43, 176, 178, 182–83, 187, 214–15, 235–38, 259, 260–61, 264, 267, 280, 300–301, 326n80, 333n75, plate 3

White Horse Inn (Oakland), 5, 17–18
Whitmire, Kathy, 211–12
Who Needs Gay Bars? (Mattson), xiv
Whorezine, 248
Wild One, The, 40–42
Wilkinson, Colm, 190
Will & Grace, 255
Winter, Bruce, 90. *See also* Ryder, Melinda
Wonderbar (New York), 28
Woodward, The (Detroit), 95
World War II, 7
Worthy, Greg, 133

Yancy, Gaye, 215–16, 219
YMCA, 160

zoning, xx, 55, 94, 103, 105–8, 113, 123, 207